advantage

Dear Valued Customer,

We realize you're a busy professional with deadlines to hit. Whether your goal is to learn a new technology or solve a critical problem, we want to be there to lend you a hand. Our primary objective is to provide you with the insight and knowledge you need to stay atop the highly competitive and ever-changing technology industry.

Wiley Publishing, Inc., offers books on a wide variety of technical categories, including security, data warehousing, software development tools, and networking — everything you need to reach your peak. Regardless of your level of expertise, the Wiley family of books has you covered.

- For Dummies® – The *fun* and *easy* way® to learn
- The Weekend Crash Course® –The *fastest* way to learn a new tool or technology
- Visual – For those who prefer to learn a new topic *visually*
- The Bible – The *100% comprehensive* tutorial and reference
- The Wiley Professional list – *Practical* and *reliable* resources for IT professionals

The book you now hold, *IBM® Data Warehousing: With IBM® Business Intelligence Tools,* is the first comprehensive guide to the complete suite of IBM tools for data warehousing. Written by a leading expert, with contributions from key members of the IBM development teams that built these tools, the book is filled with detailed examples, as well as tips, tricks and workarounds for ensuring maximum performance. You can be assured that this is the most complete and authoritative guide to IBM data warehousing.

Our commitment to you does not end at the last page of this book. We'd want to open a dialog with you to see what other solutions we can provide. Please be sure to visit us at www.wiley.com/compbooks to review our complete title list and explore the other resources we offer. If you have a comment, suggestion, or any other inquiry, please locate the "contact us" link at www.wiley.com.

Finally, we encourage you to review the following page for a list of Wiley titles on related topics. Thank you for your support and we look forward to hearing from you and serving your needs again in the future.

Sincerely,

Richard K. Swadley

Richard K. Swadley
Vice President & Executive Group Publisher
Wiley Technology Publishing

15 HOUR WEEKEND CRASH COURSE

Visual

Bible

DUMMIES

WILEY
Wiley Publishing, Inc.

*more information
on related titles*

The Next Step in Data Warehousing
Available from Wiley Publishing

0471384291

Create more powerful, flexible data sharing applications using a new XML-based standard

0471202436

The official guide, written by the authors of the Common Warehouse Metamodel

0471200522

An introduction to the standard for data warehouse integration

0471219711

The comprehensive guide to implementing SAP BW

WILEY

Wiley Publishing, Inc.

Available at your favorite bookseller or visit
www.wiley.com/compbooks

Advance Praise for *IBM Data Warehousing*

"This book delivers both depth and breadth, a highly unusual combination in the business intelligence field. It not only describes the intricacies of various IBM products, such as IBM DB2, IBM Intelligent Miner, and IBM DB2 OLAP, but it also sets the context for these products by providing a comprehensive overview of data warehousing architecture, analytics, and data management."

Wayne Eckerson
Director of Research, The Data Warehousing Institute

"Organizations today are faced with a 'data deluge' about customers, suppliers, partners, employees and competitors. To survive and to prosper requires an increasing commitment to information management solutions. Michael Gonzales' book provides an outstanding look at business intelligence software from IBM that can help companies excel through quicker, better-informed business decisions. In addition to a comprehensive exploration of IBM's data warehouse, OLAP, data mining and spatial analysis capabilities, Michael clearly explains the organizational and data architecture underpinnings necessary for success in this information-intensive age."

Jeff Jones
Senior Program Manager, IBM Data Management Solutions

"IBM leads the way in delivering integrated, easy-to-use data warehousing, analysis and data management technology. This book delivers what every data warehousing professional needs most: a thorough overview of business intelligence fundamentals followed by solid practical advice on using IBM's rich product suite to build, maintain and mine data warehouses."

Thomas W. Rosamilia
Vice President, IBM Data Management (DB2) Worldwide Development

IBM® Data Warehousing

with IBM Business Intelligence Tools

Michael L. Gonzales

Wiley Publishing, Inc.

Publisher: Joe Wikert
Executive Editor: Robert M. Elliott
Assistant Developmental Editor: Emilie Herman
Managing Editor: Micheline Frederick
Media Development Specialist: Travis Silvers
Text Design & Composition: Wiley Composition Services

Designations used by companies to distinguish their products are often claimed as trademarks. In all instances where Wiley Publishing, Inc., is aware of a claim, the product names appear in initial capital or ALL CAPITAL LETTERS. Readers, however, should contact the appropriate companies for more complete information regarding trademarks and registration.

This book is printed on acid-free paper. ∞

For general information on our other products and services please contact our Customer Care Department within the United States at (800) 762-2974, outside the United States at (317) 572-3993 or fax (317) 572-4002.

Wiley also publishes its books in a variety of electronic formats. Some content that appears in print may not be available in electronic books.

Library of Congress Cataloging-in-Publication Data:

ISBN: 0-471-13305-1

Printed in the United States of America

10 9 8 7 6 5 4 3 2 1

To AMG[2].

Contents

Acknowledgments

I would like to give special thanks to Gary Robinson for all his effort, guidance, and assistance. Without his help we never would have been able to identify and secure the resources necessary to put this book together.

About the Contributors

Nagraj Alur is a Project Leader with the IBM International Technical Support Organization in San Jose. He has more than 28 years of experience in DBMSs, and has been a programmer, systems analyst, project leader, consultant, and researcher. His areas of expertise include DBMSs, data warehousing, distributed systems management, and database performance, as well as client/server and Internet computing.

Steve Benner is currently Director of Strategic Accounts for ESRI, Inc. He has been involved in the geographic information systems (GIS) industry for 13 years in a variety of positions. Steve has led classes on GIS and data warehousing at TDWI and authored an article on GIS integration with SAP for the *SAP Technical Journal.*

Ron Fryer is with IBM Data Management. He has over 20 years experience in the design and construction of decision support environments as a data modeler and database administrator, including over 10 with data warehouses. He has worked on some of the largest data warehouses in the world. Ron's publications include numerous articles on database design and DBMS architecture. He was a contributing author to *Understanding Database Management Systems, Second Edition* (Rob Mattison, McGraw-Hill, 1998).

Jacques Labrie has been a team lead and key developer of multiple IBM products since 1984. He was also the architect for the IBM DB2 Data Warehouse Center and Warehouse Manager. Jacques has over 15 years of experience leading and managing the development of data management products including large mainframe ETL tools like IBM's Data Extract product, workstation-based meta data management like IBM's Data Guide and Information Catalog Manager, and warehouse management tools like IBM Visual Warehouse and DB2 Warehouse Center. He received his Bachelor of Arts in Mathematics from California State University, San Jose.

Gregor Meyer has worked for IBM since 1997, when he joined the product development team for DB2 Intelligent Miner in Germany. He is currently at IBM at the Silicon Valley Laboratory in San Jose, where he is responsible for the integration of data mining and other BI technologies with DB2. Gregor studied Computer Science in Brunswick and Stuttgart, Germany. He received his doctorate from the University of Hagen, Germany.

Wendell B. Mitchell is currently working as a Senior Data Architect for The Focus Group, Ltd. He has provided lab instruction on data mining, extraction transformation and loading (ETL), business intelligence, and OLAP at numerous TDWI conferences. Wendell received his bachelor's degree in math and computer science from Western Michigan University in Kalamazoo, Michigan.

Roger D. Roles is the current architect for the Information Catalog meta-data management application. He is a veteran software developer with 27 years development experience, from computer aided design and manufacturing applications in Fortran to UNIX kernel development in C and assembly language. He has been with IBM since 1993, working in various organizations on micro-kernel, file system, and application development. For the last 6 years he has been a team lead and a key developer in developing business intelligence applications in Java.

Richard Sawa has worked for Hyperion Solutions since 1998. He is currently working out of Columbus, Ohio as Hyperion Solutions' Technology Development Manager to IBM Data Management. He was a key contributor to the IBM Redbook *DB2 OLAP Server Theory and Practice* (April 2001). Formerly an independent consultant, Mr. Sawa has 10 years experience in relational decision support and OLAP technologies.

William Sterling has worked with OLAP since 1992, when he started with Arbor Software, the inventor of ESSBASE. He specializes in tuning OLAP databases, and emphasizes business systems modeling, quantitative analysis, and design. He joined IBM in 1999 as a technical member of the worldwide BI Analytics team.

Phong Truong is a key warehouse server developer in the IBM DB2 Data Warehouse Center and Warehouse Manager and is the team lead for Trillium, MQ Series and OLE DB integration. He has over 13 years of extensive development and customer service experience in various DB2 UDB components. He received his Bachelor of Science degree from the University of Calgary, Alberta Canada.

Paul Wilms has worked at IBM on distributed databases and business intelligence for over 20 years. He authored and co-authored several research papers related to IBM's R* and Starburst research projects. For the last ten years, he has provided technical support and consulting to IBM customers on business intelligence and ETL tools. Paul has also been giving many lectures at international conferences both in the US and overseas. He earned his doctorate in Computer Science from the National Polytechnic Institute of Grenoble, France.

Cheung-Yuk Wu is the current architect for the IBM DB2 Data Warehouse Center and Warehouse Manager. She has over 15 years of relational database tools development experience on DB2, Oracle, Sybase, Microsoft SQL Server and Informix on Windows and UNIX platforms. She also developed products including Tivoli for DB2, IBM Data Hub for UNIX, and QMF, and she was also a DBA for DB2, CICS and IMS at the IBM San Jose Manufacturing Data Center. She received her Bachelor of Science degree in Computer Science from the California Polytechnic State University, San Luis Obispo.

Chi Yeung is a key GUI developer in the IBM DB2 Data Warehouse Center and Warehouse Manager, and is the current team lead for multiple Warehouse GUI components including warehouse sources, targets, import/export/publish, User Groups, Agent Sites, and Replication steps. He has over 13 years of extensive GUI and object oriented design and development experience on various IBM products including Intelligent Miner, Content Management, QMF integration with Lotus Approach, and Visualizer. He received his Bachelor of Science degree from Cornell University, Master of Science degree from Stanford University, and Master of Business Administration degree from University of California Berkeley.

Calisto Zuzarte is a senior technical manager of the DB2 Query Rewrite development group at the IBM Toronto Lab. His expertise is in the key query rewrite and cost-based optimization components that affect complex query performance in databases.

Vijay Bommireddipal is a developer with the IBM DB2 Data Warehouse Center and Warehouse Manager development team and has been working in the warehouse import/export utilities for both tag and CWM formats, warehouse sample, ISV toolkits for warehouse metadata exchange. He joined IBM in July of 2000 with a Masters degree in Electrical and Computer Engineering from the University of Massachusetts, Dartmouth.

Introduction

Architects, project planners, and sponsors are always dealing with multiple technologies, conflicting techniques, and competing business agendas. This combination of issues gives rise to many challenges facing business intelligence (BI) and data warehouse (DW) initiatives. The question you need to ask yourself is this: "Do I have the information needed to make the right decisions about what technology and technique to use in order to address a business requirement at hand?"

We can certainly label the technologies into big classes like data acquisition software, data management software, data access software, and even hardware. But these classes often mislead the decision maker into thinking the choices are simple, when in fact the technology offered under any one of the classes can be overwhelming, with a confusing array of product features and functionality. The myriad of choices is only exacerbated when you add the notion of technique to the decision-making process.

The numerous choices created by the combination of technologies and techniques leave many decision makers looking like a deer caught in the headlights. They are stymied by such questions as:

- Do I build dependent data marts or allow independent data marts?
  - Why build either?
  - What's the difference?
- Should my warehouse environment be centralized or distributed?
  - What type of hardware technology would be required in either case?

- What is SMP, MPP, and clustering; and why does the technology matter to my warehouse efforts?
- How would this architecture affect the atomic layer of the warehouse and any data marts being considered?

- How should I serve up dimensional data to user communities across my enterprise?
  - Do I build stars or cubes?
  - What's the difference?
  - Why would I choose one over the other—or are they even mutually exclusive?
  - What is MOLAP, ROLAP, and HOLAP? How does it affect my architecture? How does it affect my user communities?
- How do I enhance, complement, and supplement the data being poured into my warehouse to support BI?
  - How do I blend data from third party suppliers like Dunn & Bradstreet with my data using techniques like geocoding?
  - What is spatial analysis, and how does it build informational content for the organization?
  - What is data mining, and how can my user communities benefit from its use?

This book helps you answer these types of questions within the domain of IBM technology, which in itself is considerable. IBM offers a broad array of mature technologies designed to support enterprise-level BI environments and warehouse initiatives. From SMP and MPP technical architectures to DB2 Universal Database and DB2 OLAP Server data management technology to Intelligent Miner and Spatial Extender, IBM's suite of products are the pylons necessary on which to build your BI environments and establish your enterprise warehousing needs.

This book focuses only on business intelligence and data warehousing issues and how those issues are addressed using IBM technology. Data architectures, technical architectures, OLAP, data mining, spatial analysis and, extraction, transformation, and loading (ETL) represent some of the core topics covered in this book.

It is our perspective that when the topic is warehousing, the content covered should only be related to warehousing. To that end, you will not find exhaustive coverage of SQL syntax in this book. DB2 SQL books are plentiful and readily available for anyone interested. Only SQL specifically addressing issues related to BI or warehousing is examined in this book.

Moreover, the technologies studied in this book will not be covered in their entirety, either. For example, we do not discuss all the features and functionality of DB2 V8. You can find scores of books that cover all the generic functionality of the database engine. Instead, this book emphasizes only those aspects of the technology that are relevant to BI and data warehouse initiatives.

So, what you will find in this book is coverage of IBM products, where each of these technologies impacts BI and warehousing only. For instance, Part 5 of this book is entitled "OLAP and IBM." Here you will find three chapters: Chapter 11 focuses on DB2 OLAP Server, Chapter 12 defines those aspects of Data Warehouse Center supporting DB2 OLAP Server, and Chapter 13 defines OLAP functions of DB2 V8.

The reason for such a focused approach is simple: It cuts out the noise and provides solid content that pertains only to the issues critical to BI and warehousing efforts. That's it. The goal is to make your reading time a productive experience.

How the Book Is Organized

This books contains 16 chapters organized into six parts as follows:

Part One: Fundamentals of Business Intelligence and the Data Warehouse.   This part focuses on building a common language and understanding of the fundamental concepts of BI and warehouse initiatives. If you are new to this area, you should make sure to read through these first chapters. On the other hand, if you are a seasoned "warehouser," you can simply move on to the next part. The chapters covered here are as follows:

- Chapter 1: Overview of the BI Organization
- Chapter 2: Business Intelligence Fundamentals
- Chapter 3: Planning Data Warehouse Iterations

Part Two: Business Intelligence Architecture.   This is a critical section, since it covers the two architectural areas of warehousing: data architecture and technical architecture. This is must-reading for someone just starting to work with warehouses and should be even reviewed by seasoned individuals to ensure their understanding of IBM's latest technology on these core architectures. There are only two chapters to this section:

- Chapter 4: Designing the Data Architecture
- Chapter 5: Technical Architecture and Data Management Foundations

Part Three: Data Management.   Although the features and functionality of DB2 V8 are broad, we only want to present to the reader those aspects of DB2 V8 that are pertinent to BI and warehouse efforts. There are two chapters in this section, both regarding DB2.

- Chapter 6: DB2 BI Fundamentals
- Chapter 7: Materialized Query Tables

Part Four: Warehouse Management.   Here we examine technology from IBM that facilitates the management of your warehouse. There are three chapters included in this section, covering mainly the IBM DB2 Data Warehouse Center:

- Chapter 8: Warehouse Management with IBM DB2 Data Warehouse Center
- Chapter 9: Data Transformation with IBM DB2 Data Warehouse Center
- Chapter 10: Meta Data and the IBM DB2 Warehouse Manager

Part Five: OLAP and IBM.   This section focuses solely on the topic of OLAP with regard to IBM technology. There are three chapters to this section, each covering a different technology, including DB2 OLAP Server, DB2 V8 and IBM DB2 Data Warehouse Center:

- Chapter 11: Multidimensional Data With DB2 OLAP Server
- Chapter 12: OLAP with IBM DB2 Data Warehouse Center
- Chapter 13: DB2 OLAP Functions

Part Six: Enhanced Analytics.   Finally, the book addresses IBM technology that truly enriches your warehoused data, transforming it into informational content. Here we examine technology and techniques for data mining and spatial analysis. There are three chapters:

- Chapter 14: Data Mining with Intelligent Miner
- Chapter 15: DB2 Enhanced BI Features and Functions
- Chapter 16: Blending Spatial Data into the Warehouse

All of the sections can be independently read, as long as you have a perspective of where and how the technology or technique being covered fits into the overall architecture of the BI organization.

Who Should Read This Book

Two audiences will gain value from the content in this book: decision makers and implementers. If you are the decision maker regarding tools and techniques to be applied in your company's warehouse or BI initiatives and you are adopting (or considering to include) IBM technology, then you should read this book to have a clear understanding of the salient issues addressed by this technology. Also, if you influence the decision-making process because of your role as a data architect, project planner, or sponsor, you also should study the content of this book. It will arm you with pertinent information regarding IBM technology and how to apply specific features and functionality of that technology to meet the needs of your BI or warehouse efforts.

Additionally, if you are in charge of implementing IBM technology into your environment, this book is for you. It cuts out all the fluff and takes you right to only those features and functionality that support your BI and warehouse projects. You will not be spending time reviewing irrelevant syntax or features that do little to advance your BI projects.

What's on the Web Site?

The companion Web site (www.wiley.com/compbooks/gonzales) provides links to the latest technical information, reference material, and software updates available for the products mentioned in the book, as well as other BI-related technology. We plan to include not only IBM products but also an array of partner solutions that complement an IBM BI environment.

Summary

Business intelligence and data warehouse environments require constant monitoring and tuning to ensure you are meeting the needs of your enterprise. The technologies change quickly. From one day to the next, there is always some feature improvement, some software advancement that one vendor has over another, or a new product version or release. This means that, when you are the person responsible for selecting or implementing the right technology for your shop, the pressure to keep up with the change can be considerable. It is our hope that this book provides you with specific, pertinent information you need to keep up with the evolution of BI.

Fundamentals of
Business Intelligence
and the Data Warehouse

Overview of the BI Organization

Key Issues:

- Information silos run contrary to the goal of the business intelligence (BI) organization architecture: to ensure enterprisewide informational content to the broadest audience.

- Corporate culture and IT may limit the success in building BI organizations.

- Technology is no longer the limiting factor to the BI organizations. The question for architects and project planners is not whether the technology exists, but whether they can effectively implement the technology available.

For many organizations, a data warehouse is little more than a passive repository dutifully doling out data to the ever-needy user communities. Data is predictably extracted from source systems and populated into target warehouse structures. The data may even be cleansed with any luck. However, no additional value, no informational content is added to or gleaned from the data during this process. Essentially, the passive warehouse, at best, only provides clean, operational data to user communities. The creation of information and analytical insight is entirely dependent on the users.

Judging whether the warehouse is a success is a subjective business. If we judge success on the ability to efficiently collect, integrate, and cleanse corporate data on a predictable basis, then yes, this warehouse is a success. On the other hand, if we look at the cultivation, nurturing, and exploitation of the information the organization as a whole enjoys, then the warehouse is a failure. A data warehouse that acts only as a passive repository provides little or no information value. Consequently, user communities are forced to fend for themselves, causing the creation of information silos.

This chapter presents a complete vision for rolling out an enterprisewide BI architecture. We start with an overview of BI and then move to discussions on planning and designing for information content, as opposed to simply providing data to user communities. Discussions are then focused on calculating the value of your BI efforts. We end with defining how IBM addresses the architectural requirements of BI for your organization.

Overview of the BI Organization Architecture

Powerful transaction-oriented information systems are now commonplace in every major industry, effectively leveling the playing field for corporations around the world. To remain competitive, however, now requires analytically oriented systems that can revolutionize a company's ability to rediscover and utilize information they already own. These analytical systems derive insight from the wealth of data available, delivering information that's conclusive, fact-based, and actionable.

Business intelligence can improve corporate performance in any information-intensive industry. Companies can enhance customer and supplier relationships, improve the profitability of products and services, create worthwhile new offerings, better manage risk, and pare expenses dramatically, among many other gains. Through business intelligence your company can finally begin using customer information as a competitive asset with applications such as target marketing, customer profiling, and product or service usage analysis. Having the right intelligence means having definitive answers to such key questions as:

- Which of our customers are most profitable, and how can we expand relationships with them?
- Which of our customers provide us profit, or cost us money?
- Where do our best customers live in relation to the stores/branches they frequent?

- Which products and services can be cross-sold most effectively, and to whom?
- Which marketing campaigns have been most successful and why?
- Which sales channels are most effective for which products?
- How can we improve our customers' overall experience?

Most companies have the raw data to answer these questions. Operational systems generate vast quantities of product, customer, and market data from point-of-sale, reservations, customer service, and technical support systems. The challenge is to extract and exploit this information. Many companies take advantage of only a small fraction of their data for strategic analysis. The remaining untapped data, often combined with data from external sources like government reports, trade associations, analysts, the Internet, and purchased information, is a gold mine waiting to be explored, refined, and shaped into informational content for your organization. This knowledge can be applied in a number of ways, ranging from charting overall corporate strategy to communicating personally with vendors, suppliers, and customers through call centers, kiosks, billing statements, the Internet, and other touch points that facilitate genuine, one-to-one marketing on an unprecedented scale.

Today's business environment dictates that the data warehouse (DW) and related BI solutions evolve beyond the implementation of traditional data structures such as normalized atomic-level data and star/cube farms. What is now needed to remain competitive is a fusion of traditional and advanced technologies in an effort to support a broad analytical landscape, naturally serving up a rich blend of real-time and historical analytics. Finally, the overall environment must improve the knowledge of the enterprise as a whole, ensuring that actions taken as a result of analysis conducted are fed back into the environment for all to benefit.

For example, let's say you classify your customers into categories of high to low risk. Whether this information is generated by a mining model or other means, it must be put into the warehouse and be made accessible to anyone, using any access tool, such as static reports, spreadsheet pivot tables, or online analytical processing (OLAP). However, currently, much of this type of information remains in the data silos of the individuals or departments who generate the analysis and act upon it, essentially creating information silos. The organization, as a whole, has little or no visibility to the insight. Only by blending this type of informational content into your enterprise warehouse can you eliminate information silos and elevate your warehouse environment and BI effort to a level called the business intelligence organization.

There are two major barriers to building a BI organization. First, we have the problem of the organization itself, its corporate culture, its discipline (or lack thereof) to rein in rogue executives, and its dedication to IT as a facilitator of the information asset. Although we cannot help with the political challenges of an organization, we can help you understand the components of a BI organization, its architecture, and how IBM technology facilitates its development. The second barrier to overcome is the lack of integrated technology and a conscious approach that addresses the entire BI space as opposed to just a small component. IBM is meeting the challenge of integrating technology. It is your responsibility to provide the conscious planning.

This architecture must be built with technology chosen for seamless integration, or at the very least, with technology that adheres to open standards. Moreover, your company management must ensure that enterprise business intelligence is implemented according to plan and that you do not allow the development of information silos that result from self-serving agendas, or objectives. That is not to say that the BI environment is not responsive to the individual needs and requirements of user communities; instead, it means that the implementation of those individual needs and requirements is done to the benefit of the entire BI organization.

An overview of the BI organization's architecture can be found on page 9 in Figure 1.1. The architecture demonstrates a rich blend of technologies and techniques. From the traditional view, the architecture includes the following warehouse components:

Atomic layer.   This is the foundation, the cornerstone to the entire data warehouse and therefore strategic reporting. Data stored here will preserve historical integrity, data relationships, and include derived metrics, as well as be cleansed, integrated, static, geocoded, and scored using mining models. All subsequent usage of this data and related information is derived from this structure. It is an excellent source for data mining and advanced structured query language (SQL) reporting, and it is the wellspring for data to be used in OLAP applications.

Operational data store (ODS) or reporting database.   These are data structures specifically designed for tactical reporting. The data stored and reported on from these structures may ultimately be propagated into the warehouse via the staging area, where it could be used for strategic reporting.

Staging area. The first stop for most data destined for the warehouse environment is the staging area. Here data is integrated, cleansed, and transformed into useful content that will be populated in target data warehouse structures, specifically the atomic layer of the warehouse.

Data marts. This part of the architecture represents data structures used specifically for OLAP. The presence of data marts, whether the data is stored in star schemas that superimpose multidimensional data in a relational environment or in proprietary data files used by specific OLAP technology, such as DB2 OLAP Server, is not relevant. The only constraint is that the architecture facilitates the use of multi-dimensional data.

The architecture also incorporates critical technologies and techniques that are distinctively BI-centric, such as:

Spatial analysis. Space is an information windfall for the analyst and is critical to thorough decision making. Space can represent information about the people who live at a location, as well as information about where that location physically is in relation to the rest of the world. To perform this analysis, you must start by binding your address information to longitude and latitude coordinates. This is referred to as geocoding and must be part of the extraction, transformation, and loading (ETL) process at the atomic layer of your warehouse.

Data mining. Data mining permits our companies to profile customers, predict sales trends, and enable customer relationship management (CRM), among other BI initiatives. Mining must therefore be integrated with the warehouse data structures and supported by warehouse processes to ensure both effective and efficient use of the technology and related techniques. As shown in the BI architecture, the atomic layer of the warehouse as well as data marts are excellent data sources for mining. Those same structures must also be recipients of mining results to ensure availability to the broadest audience.

Agents. There are various "agents" for examining customer touch points, the company's operational systems, and the data warehouse itself. These agents may be advanced neural nets trained to spot trends, such as future product demand based on sales promotions, rules-based engines to react to a given set of circumstances, or even simple agents that report exceptions to top executives. These agent processes generally occur in real time and, therefore, they must be tightly coupled with the movement of the data itself.

All these data structures, technologies, and techniques guarantee that you will *not* create a BI organization overnight. This endeavor will be built incrementally—in small steps. Each step is an independent project effort and is referred to as an *iteration* in your overall warehouse or BI initiative. Iterations can include implementing new technologies, initiating new techniques, adding new data structures, loading additional data, or expanding the analysis to your environment. This topic is discussed in greater depth in Chapter 3.

In addition to the traditional warehouse structures and BI-centric tools, there are other aspects of your BI organization for which you must plan, such as:

Customer touch points.   As with any modern organization there exist a number of customer touch points in which to influence a positive experience for your customers. There are the traditional channels such as dealers, telephone operators, direct mail, multimedia, and print advertisement, as well as more contemporary channels such as email, and the Web. Data produced at any touch point must be acquired, transported, cleansed, transformed, and then populated to target BI data structures.

Operational databases and user communities.   At the opposite end of the customer touch points lies a firm's application databases and user communities. Existing here are traditional data that must be gathered and blended with data flowing in from the customer touch points in order to create the necessary informational content.

Analysts.   The principal beneficiary of the BI environment is the analyst. It is this person who benefits from the timely extraction of operational data, integrated with disparate data sources, enhanced with features such as spatial analysis (geocoding), and presented in BI technology that affords mining, OLAP, advanced SQL reporting, and spatial analysis. The primary interface for the analyst to the reporting environment is the BI portal. However, the analyst is not the only one to benefit from the BI architecture. Executives, broad user communities, and even partners, suppliers, and customers can and should share in the benefits of enterprise BI.

Back-feed loop.   By design, the BI architecture is a learning environment. A principle characteristic of the design is to afford the persistent data structures to be updated by the BI technology used and the user actions taken. An example is customer scoring. If the marketing department implements a mining model that scores customers as likely to use a new service, then the marketing department should not be the only group that benefits from that knowledge. Instead, the mining model should be implemented as a natural part of the data flow within the enterprise, and the customer scores should become an integrated part of the warehouse informational content, visible to all users.

IBM's suite of BI-centric products—including DB2 UDB, DB2 OLAP Server, Intelligent Miner, and the Spatial Extender—encompasses the vast majority of important technology components, defined in Figure 1.1. We use the architecture shown in this figure throughout the book to give us a level of continuity and to demonstrate where each IBM product fits in the overall BI scheme.

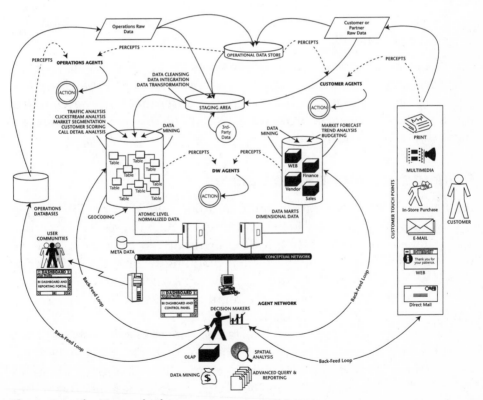

Figure 1.1 The BI organization.

Providing Information Content

Planning, designing, and implementing your BI environment is an arduous task. Planning must embrace as many current and future business requirements as possible. The design of the architecture must be equally comprehensive in order to include all conclusions found during the planning phase. The implementation must remain committed to a single purpose: building the BI architecture as formally presented in the design and founded on the business requirements.

It is particularly difficult to maintain the discipline and political will to ensure its success. This is simply because building a BI environment is not done all at once, but by implementing small components of the environment iteratively over time. Nevertheless, being able to identify BI components of your architecture is critical for two reasons:

- It will drive all subsequent technical architecture decisions.
- You will be able to consciously plan a particular use of a technology even though you may not get to an iteration needing the technology for several months.

Sufficiently understanding your business requirements will, in turn, affect the type of products you purchase for your technical architecture. Planning and designing your architecture ensures that your warehouse is not a haphazard event, but rather a well-thought-out, carefully crafted mosaic of blended technology.

Planning for Information Content

All initial planning must focus on identifying critical or core BI components that will be necessary to the overall environment, present and future. The rationale for even starting a BI effort is driven by known business requirements. Even before any formal planning begins, the architect or project planner is often able to identify one or two components right away. The balance of the components that might be necessary for your architecture, however, may not be as easily identified.

During the planning phase, architects lead joint application design (JAD) sessions on a quest to identify business requirements. Sometimes these requirements can be addressed with little more than querying and reporting tools. For example, users state they want to automate a report they currently have to create manually by integrating two existing reports and adding derived calculations of the combined data. Although this requirement is straightforward, it does define some feature functionality that you must include when purchasing the reporting tool for the organization. The project planner or architect must also pursue additional requirements to gain a complete picture. Do the users want to subscribe to this report? Are subsets of the report to be created and emailed to various users? Do they want to see this report over the corporate portal? All of these requirements are part of the simple need to replace a manual report as requested by users. The benefit of these types of requirements is that everyone, users and project planners, is familiar with the concept of reports. And the architects are well versed on the type of technology that exists to support these efforts.

There are other types of business requirements, however, that we must plan for. When business requirements are stated in the form of strategic business questions, it is easy for the experienced architect to discern dimensional and measure/fact requirements. Figure 1.2 illustrates the dimensional and measure components of a business question. If JAD participants don't know how to state their requirements in the form of a business question, architects will often give examples to jump-start the requirements-gathering session. The experienced architect is able to help user communities to not only understand what strategic business questions look like but also how to form them. Requirement-gathering approaches are discussed in Chapter 3; for now we merely want to point out the need to plan for all types of requirements as early in your BI effort as possible.

Dimensional Business Question

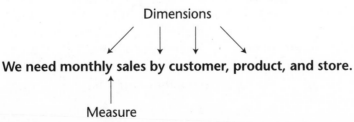

Figure 1.2 Dimensional business question.

A strategic business question is not only a business requirement but also an architectural clue. If you need to answer a multidimensional question, then you need to store and present data dimensionally. And if you need to store multidimensional data, you need to decide what type of technology or technique you are going to employ. Do you implement a Star schema, a proprietary cube, or both?

As you can see, even a simple business question can drive considerable planning. But these types of business requirements are commonplace and well understood, at least by experienced architects and project planners. There has been sufficient debate on OLAP technologies and support, and a wide range of solutions are available.

So far we have mentioned the need to gather simple reporting and dimensional business requirements and how these requirements drive technical architecture decisions. But what about requirements that are not readily understood by either the user communities or warehouse team members?

Will you ever need spatial analysis? Will data mining models be a necessary part of your future? Who knows? It is important to note that these types of technologies are less widely known to general user communities and warehouse team members. In part, this may be because they are typically left to a few in-house technical geeks or outside third parties. It is the limited exposure of these types of technologies that creates the problems. Consider the impact. If users cannot describe the business requirement or frame it in such a way as to provide clues to planners, it may go unnoticed or, worse, simply ignored. More troubling is when the architects and project planners themselves cannot recognize the application of one of these advanced but critical technologies. How often have we heard project planners say, "Well, why don't we put that off until we get this other stuff done?" Are they really concerned about priorities, or are they simply avoiding requirements that they do not understand? Most likely it is the latter.

Let's say your marketing group has communicated a business requirement as stated in Figure 1.3. As you can see, the requirement is framed in the form of a business question. The difference between this question and typical dimensional questions is distance. In this case, the marketing group wants to know, on a monthly basis, the total sales by products, stores, and customers who live within 5 miles of the store they shop. It's a great question and business requirement.

Multiple Technology Business Question

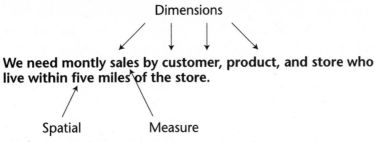

Figure 1.3   Multiple technology business question.

Sadly, uninitiated project planners or architects may simply ignore the spatial component by saying, "We have the customer, product, and store data. Let's hold off on the driving distance until another iteration." Wrong response. This type of business question is what BI is all about. It represents a deeper understanding of our business and a robust analytical landscape for our analysts. BI is beyond simple querying or standard reporting, or even OLAP. That is not to say that these technologies are not important to your overall BI effort. But by themselves, they do not represent the BI environment.

Designing for Information Content

Now that we have identified business requirements that distinguish several core components, we need to include them in an overall architectural design. Some of the BI components are part of our initial efforts, while some will not be implemented for several months. Nevertheless, all known requirements are reflected in the design so that when we need to implement a particular technology, we are prepared to do so.

Some of the design will reflect traditional thinking. For instance, Figure 1.1, earlier in the chapter, shows a data mart farm that maintains dimensional data. This farm is used to support subsequent uses of dimensional data driven by the business questions we identified. As additional documents are created, such as the data architecture design, we will begin formalizing how data is propagated throughout the environment. For instance, we have identified the need for dimensional data and therefore have planned for data marts. The next question to answer is how these data marts will be implemented. Do you build stars to support cubes, or just cubes, or just stars? Do you create the architecture for dependent data marts that require an atomic layer for all source data? Do you allow independent data marts that can source data directly from operational systems? Whose cube technology will you try to standardize on? Do you have massive amounts of data required for dimensional analysis or do you need to email cubes to your national sales force on a weekly basis or both? Do you implement a powerful tool like DB2 OLAP Server for finance or Cognos PowerPlay cubes for your sales organization or both? These are big architectural design decisions that will impact your BI environment going forward. Yes, you have identified a need for OLAP. Now how will you implement that type of technique and technology?

How do some of the more advanced technologies affect your designs? Let's assume you have identified a spatial need in your organization. Now you need to address the architectural design issues even if you do not plan to implement spatial components for several months. The architect must plan for its inclusion today. Anticipating the need for spatial analysis dictates that you create, store, maintain, and provide access to spatial data. This in turn should serve as a constraint regarding the type of software technology and platform specifications you may be currently considering. For example, the relational database management system (RDBMS) you implement for your atomic layer must have a robust spatial extension available. This would ensure maximum performance when you use the geometry and spatial objects in your analytical applications. If your RDBMS cannot handle the spatial-centric data internally, then you will need to establish an external spatial-centric database. This complicates your administration issues and compromises your overall performance, not to mention the additional problems created for your DBAs, since they probably have little understanding of pure spatial databases. On the other hand, if your RDMBS engine handles all the spatial components and its optimizer is aware of the special needs (for example, indexing) of spatial objects, then your DBAs can more readily handle administration issues, and you can maximize performance.

Moreover, you need to scale the staging area and atomic layer environment to include the cleansing of addresses (a key element to spatial analysis), as well as the subsequent geocoding and storage of spatial objects. The cascade of design issues continues now that we have introduced the notion of address cleansing. For one thing, this application will dictate the type of software necessary for your ETL effort. Do you need products such as

Trillium to provide you with a clean address, or will the ETL vendor you select provide that functionality?

Chapters 4 and 5 address architectural design issues in more detail, and spatial data is covered in Chapter 16. For now it is important that you appreciate the level of design that must be completed before you begin implementing your warehouse environment. The preceding examples should demonstrate the cascade of design decisions that must follow the identification of any particular business requirement. If done correctly, these design decisions promote interdependency among the physical structures of your environment, the selection of technology used, and the propagation flow of information content. Without this formal encompassing BI architecture, you will subject your organization to a chaotic mix of detached technologies that are, at best, loosely coupled to provide some semblance of stability.

Implementing Information Content

Bringing information value to your organization is a very difficult task. Without sufficient insight and experience, or proper planning and design, even the most disciplined teams will fail. On the other hand, if you have great insight and detailed planning but no discipline for the implementation, you have just wasted your money and time because your effort is sure to fail. The message should be clear: If you are missing any of these core competencies, insight/experience or planning/design or implementation discipline, it can cripple or crater the building of a BI organization.

Does your team have sufficient insight? Is there someone on your BI team who understands the broad analytical landscape available in BI environments and the techniques and technologies necessary to implement that landscape? Is there someone on your team who can recognize the application difference between advanced, static reporting and OLAP, or the difference between ROLAP and OLAP? Does one of your team members clearly recognize the application of mining and how it might impact the warehouse or how the warehouse can support the mining efforts? Does a team member understand the value of spatial data or agent-based technology? Do you have someone who appreciates the unique application of ETL tools versus message broker technology? If not, get someone. BI is much bigger than a normalized atomic layer, OLAP, star schemas, and an ODS.

Having the insight and experience to recognize BI requirements and their solutions is critical to your ability to correctly formalize user requirements and plan and implement their solutions. If your user communities have a difficult time describing requirements, then it is up to the warehouse team to provide that insight. But if the warehouse team cannot even recognize specific BI applications—for example, data mining—then it is no wonder that BI environments often limit themselves to being passive repositories. However, ignoring these technologies does not diminish their importance and impact on both the business intelligence capability of your organization, as well as the informational asset you plan to foster.

Planning must encompass the notion of design, and planning and design both require an individual with insight. Additionally, planning requires a warehouse team philosophy with respect for standards. For example, if your company has established a platform standard or identified a particular RDBMS it wishes to standardize throughout the enterprise, it is incumbent on the warehouse team to adhere to those standards. Too often a warehouse team espouses the need for standardization to user communities, but the team itself is unwilling to adhere to established standards of other areas in the company or perhaps the parent company. Not only is this hypocritical, but it ensures the enterprise will not be able to leverage existing resources and investments. That is not to say that there do not exist situations that warrant a nonstandardized platform or technology; nevertheless, warehouse efforts should jealously protect standards of the enterprise until business requirements dictate otherwise.

The third core component necessary to building a BI organization is discipline. It is equally dependent on individuals and the enterprise as a whole. Project planners, sponsors, architects, and users must all appreciate the discipline necessary to build the corporate informational asset. Planners must steer their project efforts so as to complement other necessary efforts in the company. For example, suppose your company is implementing an ERP application that has a warehouse component. Then it is the responsibility of the ERP planners to work with the enterprise warehouse team so as not to compete with or duplicate the work already underway. It serves little purpose for the enterprise to have two competing warehouses. If possible, one should feed the other and each should play specific roles supporting the enterprise warehouse requirements.

Discipline is also an issue that must be dealt with by the entire organization, and it is typically established and mandated at the executive level. Are executives willing to adhere to an engineered approach? An approach that promises to create information content that will eventually bring value to all areas of the enterprise, but perhaps compromises current individual or departmental agendas? Remember the saying, "The whole is more important than the one." That saying is true for BI organizations. Unfortunately, many warehouse efforts focus on addressing and bringing value to a particular department or even specific users, with little regard to the overall organization. The rogue executive who has his or her own agenda, business objectives, and budget is a perfect example of this problem. Suppose the executive requests assistance from the warehouse team. The team responds with a 90-day effort that includes not only delivering the reporting requirements defined by the executive but ensures that all sourced data is blended into the atomic layer before being fed into the proposed cube technology. This added engineering ensures that the enterprise warehouse will grow and benefit from the data necessary for this executive. However, the executive has been talking with outside consulting firms who have proposed accomplishing a similar reporting application delivered in less than 4 weeks. Assuming that the internal warehouse team is a competent group, the executive has a choice. He or she can either support the extra engineering discipline necessary to grow the enterprise informational asset or can choose to implement his or her own solution quickly. The latter seems to be chosen far too often and only serves to create information silos benefiting the few or the one.

LONG- AND SHORT-TERM GOALS

Architects and project planners must formalize a long-term vision of the overall architecture and plans for growing into a BI organization. And yet the warehouse itself is evolved an iteration at a time. This combination of short-term gain and long-term planning represent the two faces of BI efforts.

Short-term gain is the facet of BI that is associated with iterations of your warehouse. It is here where planners, architects, and sponsors focus on addressing specific business requirements. It is at this level where physical structures are built, technology is purchased, and techniques are implemented. All are done in order to tackle specific requirements as defined by particular user communities.

Long-term planning, however, is the other facet of BI. It is here where plans and designs have ensured that any physical structures built, technologies selected, and techniques implemented are done so with an eye toward the enterprise. It is the long-term planning that provides the cohesion necessary to ensure that the enterprise benefits from all the subsequent short-term gains found.

Near-term gain and long-term planning is discussed more in Chapter 3.

Justifying Your BI Effort

A data warehouse alone has no inherent value. In other words, there is no inherent value to the warehouse technologies and techniques implemented. The value of any warehouse effort is found in the actions taken as a result of the warehouse environment and the informational content grown over time.

This is a critical point to understand before you ever attempt to estimate the value of any warehouse initiative. Too often, architects and project planners attempt to apply value to the physical, technical warehouse components when in fact the value lies with the business processes that are positively impacted by the warehouse and the information asset acquired.

And there lies the challenge for funding BI-centric initiatives: How do you justify the investment? If the warehouse itself has no intrinsic value, project planners must investigate, define, and formalize the benefits gained by those individuals who will use the warehouse to improve specific business processes or the value of the information asset secured or both.

To complicate matters, any business processes affected by warehouse efforts might provide "hard" or "soft" benefits. Hard benefits provide tangible metrics for measuring return on investment (ROI)—for example, turning the inventory one additional time during a specific period or decreasing freight costs per shipment. Soft benefits, such as improved access to information via a customer facing portal, are more difficult to define in terms of tangible value.

Linking Your Project to Known Business Requirements

Too often, project planners attempt to link the value of a warehouse to amorphous goals of the enterprise. Stating that the "value of the warehouse is found in our ability to address strategic requirements" is a nice opening statement. But in itself it is not sufficient for determining whether an investment in the warehouse makes sense. It is best to link warehouse iterations to specific, known business requirements.

Measuring ROI

Calculating ROI in a warehouse setting can be particularly difficult. It is especially difficult if the primary benefit of a particular iteration happens to be something that is not tangible or easy to measure. One study[1] found that users perceive the top two benefits of BI initiatives to be:

---

[1] "Vendors and Users Agree: Business Intelligence Needed for Better Decisions," Gartner, April 2, 2002.

- Improved ability to make informed decisions

- Improved access to information

These benefits are soft benefits. It is easy to see how we can calculate ROI based on a hard benefit like reduced freight cost, but how do we measure the ability to make better decisions?

This is definitely a challenge for project planners when attempting to convince the company to invest in a particular warehouse effort. Increasing sales or decreasing costs are no longer the central themes driving the BI environment. Instead, we find ourselves addressing business requirements such as better access to information so that a particular department can make faster decisions. These are strategic drivers that happen to be equally important to the enterprise but are more ambiguous and more challenging to characterize into tangible metrics. In this case, calculating ROI can be misleading, if not irrelevant.

Project planners must be able to demonstrate tangible value for executives to decide whether the investment in a particular iteration is worth it. However, we will not propose a new method for calculating ROI, nor will we make any argument for or against it being done. Plenty of articles and books are available that discuss the fundamentals of calculating ROI. There are even special value propositions such as value on investment (VOI), offered by groups like Gartner, that you can research. Instead, we will concentrate on core aspects of any ROI, or other value propositions that you must consider.

Applying ROI

Aside from the issue of soft versus hard benefits associated with BI efforts, there are other problems to consider when applying ROI. For example:

Attributing too much savings to DW efforts that would come anyway.
Let's say your company was moving from a mainframe architecture to a distributed UNIX environment. Then any savings that may (or may not) be realized by that effort should not be attributed solely, if at all, to the warehouse.

Not accounting for all costs.   And there are many. Consider the following list:

- Cost of startup, including feasibility.

- Cost of dedicated hardware with related storage and communications requirements.

- Cost of software, including data management and client/server extensions, ETL software, DSS technologies, visualization tools, scheduling and workflow applications, and monitoring software, just to name a few.

- Cost of data structure design, including implementation, aggregate definition, and query optimization.

- Cost of software development directly associated with the BI effort.

- Cost of ongoing support, including performance optimization, software version control, and help desk operations.

Applying "Big-Bang" ROI.   Just as the implementation of the warehouse as a single, gigantic effort is destined to fail, so too is calculating the ROI for an enterprisewide initiative. What is amazing is that planners continue making feeble attempts at estimating the value of the entire effort. Why would planners attempt to put a dollar value on the enterprise initiative if it is widely known and accepted that estimating specific iterations is difficult? How is that possible? With few exceptions, it isn't. Don't do it.

Now that we have established what not to do when calculating ROI, here are some pointers that will help in establishing a reliable process for estimating the value of your BI efforts:

Getting consensus of ROI.   Whatever your choice of technique for estimating the value of your BI efforts, it must be agreed to by all relevant parties, including project planners, sponsors, and company executives.

Reduce ROI into identifiable parts.   A necessary step to calculating a reasonable ROI is to focus that calculation on a specific project. This lets you then estimate value based on specific business requirements being addressed.

Define costs.   As mentioned, numerous costs must be considered. Moreover, the costs must not only include those associated with the individual iteration but also the costs of ensuring the adherence to the enterprise standards.

Define benefits.   By clearly binding the ROI to specific business requirements, we should be able to identify the benefits that addressing the requirements will bring.

Reduce costs and benefits into today's dollars.   It is best to make your estimates based on net present value (NPV) as opposed to attempting to predict future value in future dollars.

Keep the time frame of your ROI to a minimum. It is well documented that the longer the time period used in your ROI, the more difficult it is to prove.

Use more than one ROI formula. There are several methods for estimating ROI, and you should plan to use one or more of them, including net present value, internal rate of return (IRR), and payback.

Define repeatable process. This is central to any long-term value calculation. There should be a single, documented, repeatable process for all subsequent projects to follow.

The problems listed are the most common ones experienced in the warehouse arena. The insistence by some management that we provide a "Big-Bang" ROI is most mystifying. If you start all your ROI calculations by reducing them into identifiable, tangible parts, you have a good chance at providing an accurate ROI estimate.

Questions for ROI Benefits

Whether your benefits are soft or hard, you can use some fundamental questions to determine their value. Using a simple scale system, for example, 1 to 10, you can survey the impact of any effort using the following questions:

- How would you rate your company's understanding of the data as a result of this project?
- How would you estimate process improvements as a result of this project?
- How would you measure the impact of new insights and inferences now made available from this iteration?
- What has been the impact of newer and more effective computer environments as a result of what was learned?

If answers to these questions are low, the undertaking may not be worth the investment made. Questions with a high score point to significant value gains and should serve as guides for further investigation. For example, a high score for process improvements should lead planners to examine how the processes were improved. You may find that some or all of the improvement gains are tangible and therefore a dollar value can readily be applied.

TIP These questions are used after the project. If you need to calculate expected ROI, you could rephrase some of the questions and have user communities provide estimations.

Making the Most of the First Iteration of the Warehouse

The greatest return of your enterprise effort is often found in the first few iterations. These first efforts traditionally establish the most useful informational content for the broadest audience and help establish a technology foundation for subsequent BI applications. Each subsequent data warehouse project will typically bring less and less additional value to the enterprise as a whole. This is especially true if the iteration does not add new subject areas, or address the needs of new user communities. This characteristic of warehousing also applies to the growing piles of historical data. As subsequent efforts call for more data and as more data is poured into the warehouse over time, more of the data becomes less relevant to the analysis at hand. This data is often referred to as *dormant* data, and it is always expensive to keep since it is almost never used.

What does this mean to project sponsors? Essentially, the first sponsors carry more than their fair share of investment costs. This is primarily because they are the impetus for laying foundational, enterprisewide technology and warehouse resources, including staffing. But these first steps bring the highest value, and therefore project planners can often justify the investment. Comparatively, projects done later in your BI initiative may have lower, direct costs, but they bring less overall value to the enterprise. And the enterprisewide patrons must start considering how to clear out the accumulation of less relevant data and technologies.

IBM and The BI Organization

IBM has dedicated significant resources and sustained the needed discipline to mature several products that cover a wide spectrum of BI technology. These products include DB2 UDB V8, Data Warehouse Center, DB2 OLAP Server, Intelligent Miner, and Spatial Extender. These represent many of IBM's enterprise analytic solutions that allow executives, managers, and business analysts to react rapidly to trends and changes in the marketplace.

IBM focuses on three core BI objectives:

Creating seamless integration between DB2 and BI analytics. DB2 UDB forms the center of IBM's BI strategy. Along with its scalable, parallel database technology, you get extensions for data mining, OLAP, and portal and geospatial technologies. *Seamless integration* means that your database engine is aware of, and optimized for, multiple BI objects and technologies. For example, instead of maintaining a separate database for spatial objects, DB2 UDB V8 Spatial Extender expands the UDB engine to readily import, store, maintain, and serve up spatial data. There is no need for separate database technologies and administration. Another example of seamless integration is the ability in UDB V8 to execute mining models from anywhere you can execute SQL. Integration points such as these give architects and project planners significantly more implementation and architecture options. Moreover, they afford a broader range of BI solutions to address business requirements.

Simplifying the BI analytics delivery system through integrated technology.   A simplified data delivery system requires two elements: the ability to address different data types and the efficient propagation of the different data from its source to your target BI structure. Through DB2's XML support, heterogeneous distributed query capabilities, integrated data replication services, DB2 Extenders for spatial, text, or multimedia data, and MQSeries technology, a company can efficiently move virtually any data type from source to target. But we should not confuse simplified BI analytics and data delivery with extraction, transformation, and loading. Where ETL is excellent for large, batch processing of data into the warehouse, data delivery is concerned with nimble data propagation within your entire organization, including your warehouse. This book provides discussions on how IBM is addressing both ETL and data delivery.

Providing zero-latency analytics.   Real-time (or zero-latency) analytics is a prerequisite for enterprise BI efforts. Building a zero-latent BI environment requires seamless integration between the database engine and your choice of analytic tools, as well as an efficient data delivery system. In other words, to build in zero-latency requires that you address the two previous objectives. IBM has consciously blended their technology to afford user communities the opportunity to offer zero-latency analytics.

Seamless integration, simplified data delivery, and zero-latency are tactical approaches for building your BI architecture. Let's look at each goal in detail.

Seamless Integration

There are numerous integration links between DB2 UDB V8 and your BI environment. Let's isolate specific technologies in the BI architecture to show how BI functions are being integrated in DB2.

Data Mining

Several architectural components require variations of data mining technologies and techniques—for example, the various "agents" for examining customer touch points, the company's operational systems, and the data warehouse itself. These agents may be advanced neural nets trained to spot trends, such as future product demand based on sales promotions; rules-based engines to react to a given set of circumstances, for example, medical diagnosis and treatment recommendations; or even simple agents that report exceptions to top executives. These data mining processes generally occur in real time; therefore, they must be tightly coupled with the movement of the data itself.

DB2 Intelligent Miner Scoring Services provides database engine mining extensions that allow mining models to be database-resident. This translates to the dynamic scoring of mining models in DB2 and allows the models to be implemented on any UDB environment and executed using simple SQL. Also, the mining model supports the industry-standard XML-based Predictive Model Markup Language (PMML), which translates to broader compatibility and your ability to support your environment.

Mining products currently offered by IBM include:

- DB2 Intelligent Miner for Data
- DB2 Intelligent Miner for Text
- DB2 OLAP Server Analyzer
- DB2 Intelligent Miner

More information on these products is provided in Chapters 14 and 15.

Online Analytic Processing

The ability to slice, dice, roll up, drill-down, and perform what-if analysis is well within the scope of the IBM technology suite. For example, online analytical processing (OLAP) functions exist for DB2 that bring dimensional analysis into the database engine itself (refer to Chapter 13). The functions add dimensional utility to SQL while exploiting all the benefits of being a natural part of DB2. Another example of OLAP integration is the mining tool, DB2 OLAP Server Analyzer. This technology lets DB2 OLAP Server cubes be quickly and automatically analyzed to spot and report on unusual or unexpected data values throughout the cube to the business analyst. And, finally, the Data Warehouse Center functions provide a means for architects to control, among other things, the outline of a DB2 OLAP Server cube as a natural part of ETL processes.

Spatial Analysis

Space represents half of the analytical anchors needed for a broad analytical landscape (time represents the other). The atomic-level warehouse depicted in Figure 1.1 includes the fundamentals for both time and space. Timestamps anchor analysis by time, and address information anchors analysis by space. The diagram shows geocoding—the process of converting addresses to points on a map or points in space so concepts like distance and inside/outside can be used in analysis—conducted at the atomic level and spatial analysis being made available to the analyst. IBM provides spatial extensions, developed with the Environmental Systems Research Institute (ESRI), to the DB2 database so that spatial objects may be stored as a normal part of the relational database. DB2 Spatial Extenders also provide all the SQL extensions to exploit spatial analysis. For example, SQL extensions to query on distance between addresses or whether a point is inside or outside a defined polygonal area are standard analytics with the Spatial Extender. Refer to chapter 16 for more information.

Database-Resident Tools

DB2 has many BI-resident SQL features that assist in the analysis effort. These include:

- Recursion functions to perform analysis, such as "find all the possible flight paths from San Francisco to New York."
- Analytical functions for ranking, cumulative functions, cube, and rollup to facilitate tasks that normally occur only with OLAP technology are now a natural part of the database engine.
- The ability to create tables that contain precomputed results.

Leading database vendors are blending more of the BI functionality into the database itself. This provides better performance and more implementation options for BI solutions. DB2 V8 features and functions are discussed in detail in the following chapters:

- Technical Architecture and Data Management Foundations (Chapter 5)
- DB2 BI Fundamentals (Chapter 6)
- DB2 Materialized Query Tables (Chapter 7)
- DB2 OLAP Functions (Chapter 13)
- DB2-Enhanced BI Features and Functions (Chapter 15)

Simplified Data Delivery System

The architecture depicted in Figure 1.1 includes several physical data structures. One is the operational data store. Generally, an ODS is subject-oriented, integrated, and current. You would build an ODS to support, for example, the sales department. The sales ODS would integrate data from several disparate systems but only maintain, for example, today's transactions. The ODS may even be updated several times a day. At the same time, processes push the integrated data into other applications. This structure is designed specifically to integrate current, dynamic data and would be a likely candidate to support real-time analysis, like providing customer service agents with the current sales information of a customer (from the ODS) while extracting sales trend information from the warehouse itself.

Another structure shown in Figure 1.1 is a formal staging area for the data warehouse. Not only is this the place for performing the necessary integration, data quality, and transformation of incoming warehouse data, but it is also a reliable, temporary storage area for replicated data that could be used in real-time analysis.

Whether you decide to use an ODS or a staging area, one of the best tools for populating these data structures using disparate operational sources is DB2's heterogeneous distributed query. This capability is delivered by the optional DB2 feature called DB2 Relational Connect (query only) and through DB2 DataJoiner (a separate product that delivers query, insert, update, and delete capability to heterogeneous distributed RDBMSs).

This technology allows data architects to bind production data with analytical processes. Not only can the technology adapt to virtually any of the replication requirements that might arise with real-time analysis, but it can also connect to a wide variety of the most popular databases, including DB2, Oracle, Sybase, SQL Server, Informix, and others. DB2 DataJoiner can be used to populate a formal data structure like an ODS or even a permanent table staged in the warehouse designed for snapshot updates or rapid wholesale refresh. Of course, these same data structures can be populated using another important technology designed for data replication, IBM DataPropagator Relational. (DataPropagator is a separate product for mainframes. DB2 UNIX, Linux, Windows, and OS/2 include data replication services as a standard feature.)

Another method for moving operational data around the enterprise is an enterprise application integrator otherwise known as a *message broker*. This unique technology affords unparalleled control for targeting and moving data around the enterprise. IBM has the most widely used message broker, MQSeries, or a variation of the product that incorporates e-commerce requirements, IBM WebSphere MQ.

For more discussion on how to exploit MQ to support a warehouse and BI environment, visit this book's companion Web site. For now, suffice it to say that this technology is an excellent means for seizing and transforming (using MQSeries Integrator) targeted operational data recruited for BI solutions. The MQ technology has been integrated and bundled in UDB V8, which means that message queues can now be managed as if they are DB2 tables. The notion of welding message queuing and the relational database universe makes for a powerful data delivery environment.

Zero-Latency

The final strategic objective for IBM is zero-latency analysis. As defined by Gartner, a BI system must be able to gather, assimilate, and provide information for analysts on demand. The challenge, of course, is how to blend current, real-time data with necessary historical information, such as relevant trend/pattern data, or mined insight, such as customer profiling. Such information includes, for example, identifying high- or low-risk customers or which products customers will most likely purchase if they already have cheese in their shopping carts.

Achieving zero-latency is really dependent on two fundamental mechanisms:

- Tightly coupling the data being analyzed with the BI techniques established and tools being implemented

- An efficient data delivery system to ensure that the data needed for the real-time analysis is actually available

These prerequisites for zero-latency are not unlike the two objectives established by IBM and outlined previously. The tight coupling of data is part of the seamless integration agenda set forth by IBM. And creating an efficient data delivery system is completely dependent on technology being available that simplifies the data delivery process. Consequently, two of the three IBM objectives are fundamental to achieving the third. IBM is consciously evolving its technology to ensure that zero-latency is a reality for warehouse efforts.

Summary

The BI organization provides a road map to implement your environment iteratively. It must be tuned to reflect the needs of your business, both present and future. Without a broad architectural vision, warehouse iterations are little more than haphazard warehouse-centric implementations that do little to create an enterprisewide, informational asset.

The first hurdle project managers face is how to justify the investments necessary for building a BI organization. Although calculating ROI has remained a mainstay for warehouse implementations, it is becoming more difficult to accurately predict. This has led to other methods for determining whether you are getting your money's worth. Value on investment[2] (VOI), for example, is being touted as one solution.

It is incumbent on data architects and project planners to deliberately create and provide information content to user communities and not simply serve up data. There is a huge difference between the two. Information is anything that makes a difference in decision-making processes and effectiveness; comparatively, data is building blocks to derive that information. Albeit critical to source data to address business requirements, the BI environment should serve a greater role in creating information content. We must take the extra steps to cleanse, integrate, transform, or otherwise create information content that users act upon, and then we must make sure that those actions and decisions, where reasonable, are fed back into the BI environment. If we relegate the warehouse to merely serving up data, rest assured that user communities will create the necessary information content to act upon. This ensures their community will be able to make better decisions, but the enterprise suffers from the lack of knowledge they used.

As architects and project planners initiate specific projects in the BI environment, they remain responsible to the enterprise as a whole. A simple example of this two-faced characteristic of BI iterations is found in sourcing data. All data sourced for specific business requirements must be populated into the atomic layer first. This guarantees the evolution of the corporate information asset, as well as addresses the specific user requirements defined in the iteration.

[2] Gartner.

Business Intelligence Fundamentals

Key Issues:

- Understanding traditional warehouse-centric technologies and techniques is no longer sufficient. Data architects and project planners must arm themselves with a broader understanding of lesser-known BI tools that add incredible information content to the warehouse, as well as broaden the analytical landscape.

- The architecture of the business intelligence (BI) organization supports a natural flow of data as it propagates from source to target usage, with net actions fed back into the source and warehouse-centric data stores.

A BI organization fully exploits data at every phase of the BI architecture as it progresses through various levels of informational metamorphosis. The raw data is born in operational environments, where transactional data pours in from every source and every corner of the enterprise. While some operational data is staged for warehouse-centric application, other data is propagated into integrated pools of operational content for tactical use called *operational data stores* (ODSs). During the warehouse staging process, raw operational data is cleansed, integrated, and transformed into warehouse-centric content, prepped for assimilation into the atomic level of the warehouse. It is this structure that serves as the foundation of your BI environment.

The atomic layer is an ocean of informational content, at the natural grain of your business, encompassing the breadth of the enterprise. It evolves into a deep, wide body of content unlike any found elsewhere in the organization. And, like all oceans, it is not for the faint of heart or the weekend adventurer. Advanced BI applications are found filtering, sifting, and probing the content for enterprisewide insight. From this ocean, all other BI applications are fed.

It is by design that data marts represent the principal consumer of atomic-level data. This engineered approach ensures information integrity and audit ability. Irrelevant of who extracts information from which BI structure, atomic layer, star schema, or online analytical processing (OLAP) cube utilizing any number of tools including batch reports, spreadsheets, or BI dashboards, the basis of that insight is founded from a single, controlled source: the atomic layer.

Finally, any actions taken, or analytical fodder generated, based on the informational insight gleaned from the natural flow of data, is formally blended back into the relevant areas of the BI organization. This ensures continuity, a natural evolution to the raw data, and it accentuates the information asset.

So, that is the business intelligent organization vision: A natural flow of data, from genesis to action. And at each step in the flow, the data is fully exploited to ensure the increase of information value for the enterprise. The challenge, of course, is to build your vision.

Several chapters in this book will help you build your vision by detailing the specific elements of data warehousing and business intelligence. The main challenge for this chapter is to lay out the fundamentals of the warehouse and BI environment without being redundant with in-depth coverage of each topic in subsequent chapters.

We start this chapter by examining the general components of business intelligence and of the warehouse architecture itself. The chapter continues by defining specific roles of BI technology, techniques, and structures. The different user types are then presented to readers, as well as the types of analytic technology from which user requirements are addressed. The latter part of this chapter provides detailed discussions regarding dimensional data and related analysis. The chapter ends with discussions regarding critical concepts such as user touch points, zero-latency, closed-loop learning, and historical integrity.

BI Components and Technologies

Business intelligence encompasses the process of transforming data from your various data sources into meaningful information content. There are two objectives. The first is to provide you and your company with insights into where your business has been, is today, and is likely to be tomorrow. The second is to help you put that information content into action by making it accessible when and where you need it most.

BI allows you to improve your decision making at all levels by giving you a consistent, valid, and in-depth view of your business by consolidating data from different systems into a single accessible source of information—a data warehouse. Depending on user requirements, there are different types of tools to be used to analyze and visualize the data from the warehouse. These tools range from query and reporting to advanced analysis by data mining or spatial analysis.

Several components comprise BI, from technologies to techniques, from the movement of data to the analysis of information content. This section describes BI and its relevant components.

Business Intelligence Components

Traditionally, information systems have been designed to process discrete transactions in order to automate tasks such as order entry or account transactions. These systems are not designed to support users who wish to extract data at different aggregation levels and utilize advanced methods for enterprisewide data analysis. These systems tend to be isolated to support a single business system, function, or process such as Human Resources or Accounting. All of this results in a great challenge when you require a consolidated view of the state of your business.

Data Warehouse

The data warehouse is only one component of business intelligence, albeit a significant one. Too often, architects and project planners assume that if they implement a data mart, for instance, they have achieved BI. Not even close. That does not mean that the data structures of the warehouse do not support BI. By themselves, however, they are only a part of the BI environment.

The data warehouse supports the physical propagation of data as it moves from source to target to access tool. Typical processes include:

- Extraction
- Transformation/cleansing

- Transportation
- Loading
- Data refinement

The tasks performed on the data warehouse typically require batch performance to handle the numerous records for integration, cleansing, aggregation, pre calculation, and query tasks.

Data Sources

Data sources can be operational databases, historical data (usually archived on tape), external data (for example, from market research companies or from the Internet), or information from the already existing data warehouse environment. The data sources can be relational databases or any other data structure that supports the line of business applications. They also can reside on many different platforms and can contain structured information, such as tables or spreadsheets, or unstructured information, such as plaintext files or pictures and other multimedia information.

Data Targets

Under the umbrella of warehousing, there are three distinct data structures: atomic layer, star schema, and multidimensional cube. Moreover, there is another data structure often considered a part of an overall warehouse solution: the operational data store. We defined these data structures generally in Chapter 1. In this section we outline some of the traditional characteristics of each structure.

Staging Area

The *staging area* can be considered your "whiteboard" for raw source data that is to be transformed into the information content destined for the warehouse. There are no special data structure requirements for your staging area, since it must be flexible to accommodate all types of source data. Nor are there any real guidelines to follow for setting up your staging area, except to make sure that it has sufficient capacity to handle any data preparation processing for your largest data set or your most complex transformations. Most of the requirements to set up your staging area will be dictated by your extraction, transformation, and loading (ETL) tool of choice.

Another important point about staging areas is that there is no rule that says you can only have one. It is not unusual to have a permanent staging area on a specific platform for most of the raw source data for the warehouse. But what if, for example, you have some source data residing on a mainframe, and the mainframe folks are willing to give you resource time to perform some of your staging transformation on the mainframe itself? You should definitely take advantage of the situation. It is always best to perform as much transformation as possible on the same platform as the source data. The rationale is simple. First, the source system simplifies some of the transformation processes such as changing from EBCIDIC to ASCII. Second, the source system platforms are often larger than the platform of your staging area, and therefore you get better performance for sorting, identifying delta records, and so forth.

Atomic Layer

The *atomic layer* of the warehouse is the foundation of all BI content. It represents the basis for all data necessary for strategic analysis. To do so, the atomic layer generally incorporates the following capabilities and characteristics:

It maintains historical integrity (time-variant data).   This is discussed in detail in the *Historical Integrity* section of this chapter.

It represents the lowest level of detail (granularity) for the warehouse.   This is a critical point. The data stored at the atomic layer is the lowest grain of data available for all subsequent data structures of the warehouse and BI analysis.

It is built in iterations.   As described in Chapter 3, you will build your warehouse one step at a time. With each step, you will often add more source data to the atomic layer. This is in contrast to attempting to build your atomic layer in one big-project effort.

It is the source of enterprisewide data.   Over the course of time, the atomic layer will become the source of enterprisewide data for BI. As you add data iteratively, you grow the scope and breadth of the subject areas covered at the atomic layer. This is unique to this data structure. Conversely, data marts, either star schemas or cubes, are almost always focused on a particular subject area.

It is integrated.   The atomic layer is a data structure that provides an integrated source for your enterprise. That means that the most impactive and useful atomic layers are those that have multiple, disparate operational data sources that require integration for an enterprise view.

It is static.   Although the technology exists to increase the frequency at which a warehouse is updated with new source data, the environment as a whole remains static versus dynamic in nature. The original notion of a *dynamic* environment meant that data is capable of being constantly updated—including users literally changing and adding data directly. By this very definition, a dynamic warehouse is not possible. The idea of having end users update, add, and otherwise change warehoused data directly compromises the integrity of the data. So the idea of a dynamic data warehouse is really only in terms of the frequency with which data elements of the warehouse are refreshed.

Data Mart

A data mart sources its data from the atomic layer of the warehouse and is tailored to support the specific requirements of a given business unit, business function, or application. The main purposes of a data mart are as follows:

- To store pre-aggregated information
- To control end-user access to the information
- To provide fast access to information for specific analytical needs or user groups
- To represent the end user's view and data interface of the data warehouse
- To create the multidimensional/relation view of the data

The most common database format is either multidimensional or relational. Of course, there are other possibilities for data marts including a SAS dataset. However, we will focus our discussion on relational or dimensional technology. When building data marts, keep the following in mind:

- Data marts should always be implemented as an extension of the data warehouse, not as an alternative. This is referred to as a *dependent* data mart as opposed to an *independent* data mart. The dependent environment ensures data integrity throughout the warehouse environment. This is not true for independent data marts, which can go directly to operational systems for source data. The problem with independent data marts is that there is no control of the meta data used to manage how the data mart is built and maintained. Consequently, it is not unusual for executives with two independent data marts of the same subject area to have different reported results.

- Data marts are typically constructed to address the requirements within a single subject area. However, you should be aware of the trade-off between the simplicity of design (and performance benefits) and the cost of administrating and maintaining a large number of data marts.

Data marts are essential for serving up dimensional data for OLAP. For more information refer to the *Dimensional Technology and BI* section later in this chapter.

Operational Data Store

The operational data store can be defined as an updateable set of integrated data used for enterprisewide tactical decision-making of a particular subject area. It contains live data, not snapshots, and retains minimal history. Following are some features of an ODS:

It is subject-oriented.   It is designed and organized around the major data subjects of a corporation, such as "customer" or "product." They are typically not organized around specific applications or functions, such as "order entry" or "accounts receivable."

It is integrated.   It represents a collectively integrated image of subject-oriented data that is pulled in from potentially any operational system. If the "customer" subject is included, then all of the "customer" information in the enterprise is considered as part of the ODS.

It is current-valued.   It reflects the "current" content of its legacy source systems. "Current" may be defined in various ways for different ODSs depending on the requirements of the implementation. An ODS should not contain multiple snapshots of whatever "current" is defined to be. That is, if "current" means one accounting period, then the ODS does not include more than one accounting period's data. The history is either archived or flushed into the data warehouse for analysis.

It is volatile.   Because an ODS is current-valued, it is subject to change on a frequency that supports the definition of "current." That is, it is updated to reflect the systems that feed it in the true OLTP sense. Therefore, identical queries made at different times will likely yield different results because the data has changed.

It is detailed.   The definition of "detailed" also depends on the business problem that is being solved by the ODS. The granularity of data in the ODS may or may not be the same as that of its source operational systems.

An ODS is a viable option for tactical reporting.

Warehouse Components

Project managers, architects, and sponsors face a wide array of issues that complicate the warehouse effort. These issues range from project scope to technology choices and from data quality problems to the ever-present end-user expectation. While it is true that the fundamental choices of data architecture—for example, establishing an atomic layer with dependent data marts—remain constant, you will adapt to new issues and technology with each iteration of the warehouse. For instance, you may have DB2 OLAP Server identified as the "approved" OLAP tool, but an organization within your enterprise may rightfully demand the use of MicroStrategies or Business Objects. Or, while some project iterations might be bogged down in dealing with the scope creep, others might be uncovering more data-quality problems than they anticipated. But no matter how many and what variety of issues you face in warehouse iterations, one thing is certain: you will always have to address the four core components shown in Figure 2.1:

- Extraction, transformation, and loading (ETL)
- Data management
- Data access
- Meta data

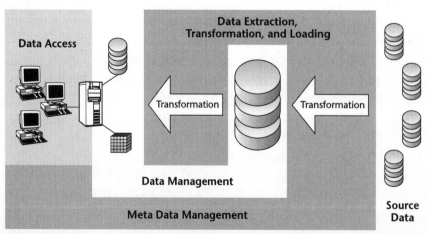

Figure 2.1 Components of a data warehouse.

Whether the source data is in operational systems or already resident in the warehouse, the data must be extracted. If you need to propagate the data to another structure, then transformation and loading also become issues. On the other hand, you might simply need to extract data for an advanced SQL report. In either case, what remains true is that for virtually all warehouse efforts you must plan for and address some source data acquisition, and possibly transformation and loading. Moreover, as the data moves throughout the warehouse landscape, it must be stored, indexed, backed up, and otherwise managed. The data management can be through the use of a relational database management system (RDBMS) or OLAP technology. Of course, once the data has been acquired and stored in target structures, it must be made accessible. Data access can be achieved in a number of ways, from simple spreadsheets to ad hoc reporting to complex mining. And, consistent with all we do in warehouse and BI efforts, there must be some aspect of meta data to be addressed. Whether we need to collect and formalize business rules or gather process and usage statistics, meta data must be considered an anticipated component of every iteration.

Extraction, Transformation, and Loading

A traditional part of warehouse iterations is the need for data acquisition. This typically entails the following steps:

- Identification of the source data relevant to the subject area being examined
- Development of an extraction strategy
- Transformation of the source data to target specifications
- Loading the sourced data into the predefined target

This acquisition process is referred to as extraction, transformation, and loading. As shown in Figure 2.1, a warehouse environment has multiple ETL opportunities. The most common ETL layer is between the actual raw source data from operational systems and the warehouse atomic level. However, there are other ETL layers to bear in mind when you consider your acquisition strategy. There are ETL requirements between the atomic layer and each data mart, whether the data mart is implemented as a star schema or cube. Moreover, ETL exists between the implementation of star schemas and cube technologies.

When building an ETL strategy for a particular subject area, the data architect must consider the following issues:

- When should a business rule be applied?
- How should the chosen business rules be applied?
- What technology will be used to apply the defined rules?

There are two important points to remember about ETL processes. First, you only want to bring into the warehouse data that will lend itself to effective analysis. Second, warehouse builders must ensure the completeness and accuracy of all data brought into the warehouse.

All too often project planners or user communities insist on bringing every column of a record into the warehouse, as opposed to targeting only those columns that provide analytical value and whose data can be effectively transformed and scrubbed into informational content.

As an example, let's suppose the data architect had ETL specifications for sales order number, date, and customer code from a sales order header record. These specs were given to project sponsors for approval. But users insisted in bringing in all the columns of the sales order header, including a column called "Special Instructions." Here is the problem: No one is considering whether the added data lends itself to analysis or whether the data can be made complete and accurate. Addressing these two points can greatly expand your ETL project with potently little benefit.

In our example it may be that contract codes are often entered into the Special Instructions field. However, there are no application screen edits or processes to ensure the contract codes are entered consistently or accurately. This means that your ETL process would have to parse the field looking for potential patterns of contract codes. Moreover, since there are no application requirements to enter contract codes into the sales order, you can be sure that the information is sporadically and inconsistently input by data entry clerks. Now, is it worth the dramatic increase in your ETL development budget to bring in this Special Instructions field? Will you consistently be able to glean out of the free-form text the contract codes you need for analysis?

Some argue that it doesn't matter if the field has consistent codes. This begs the question, then how is it going to be used for strategic analysis? Strategic analysis is primarily based on statistical aggregations, including sum, min, max, mean, variance, average, moving average, and percent of total, just to name a few. If the field on which you plan to perform statistical aggregations (or use as a constraint for that function) is of poor quality, rest assured the results will be dubious at best. And, if the results cannot be relied upon, they why have the data in the warehouse in the first place? These are important questions to answer before you decide to bring anything into the warehouse.

Extraction

Data extraction and data propagation are processes for collecting data from various sources and different platforms and moving it into the data warehouse. Data extraction in a warehouse environment is a selective process to import only relevant information that supports analysis and decision making. This is a critical point often overlooked by acquisition programmers.

Data extraction/data propagation is much more than mirroring or copying data from one database system to another. Architects and ETL programmers must identify the specific data to extract, the trigger that causes the extraction to take place, and the target for the data being extracted. Also, depending on the technique, this process is either referred to as *pulling* (extraction of data) or *pushing* (propagation of data).

Transformation/Cleansing

Transformation of data usually involves code resolution with mapping tables, for example, changing the variable gender to:

- 0 if the value is female
- 1 if the value is male

It involves changing the resolution of hidden business rules in data fields, such as account numbers. Also, the structure and the relationships of the data are adjusted to the analysis domain. Transformations occur throughout the population process, usually in more than one step. In the early stages of the process, the transformations are used more to consolidate the data from different sources; whereas in the later stages, data is transformed to satisfy a specific analysis problem or a tool requirement.

Data warehousing turns data into information; on the other hand, data cleansing ensures that the data warehouse will have valid, useful, and meaningful data from which to create the information. Data cleansing can also be described as *standardization* of data. Through careful review of the data contents, the following criteria are matched:

- Replace missing values.
- Normalize value ranges and units (for example, sales in the euro or dollar).
- Use valid data codes and abbreviations.
- Use consistent and standard representation of the data.
- Use domestic and international addresses.
- Consolidate data (one view), such as house holding.

Data Refining

The data stored at the atomic level of your warehouse represents the lowest level of detail for the entire warehouse environment. This information often must be aggregated, summarized, or otherwise modified to ensure query performance and minimize the amount of data that is transmitted over the network to the end-user query or analysis tool. This data refining process is often associated with data marts that:

- Create a subset of the data in the star schema
- Create calculated or virtual fields
- Summarize the information
- Aggregate the information

Data Management

Data management, the physical handling and control of data, is necessary in each warehouse iteration. Whether you need to store the data in a relational database or a proprietary file management system, the data must be stored somewhere. And, once stored, it must be managed in terms of storage, indexing, backups, and so on. Consequently, data management is a core requirement for any warehouse effort and must be understood and integrated into the overall warehouse strategy.

The important point to understand about data management is that it covers more than just a relational database. If you are implementing OLAP, it will be necessary to address the management needs of multidimensional data stored in cube format as well. Refer to Chapter 5 for more information regarding DB2 data management considerations.

Data Access

All warehouse efforts will implement and maintain one or more methods to access the data being collected, transformed, and stored. These data access applications provide business users at various levels within an organization with an easy-to-use interface for not only accessing the data but also performing analysis in the pursuit of better business decision support.

Simply put, front-end data access tools and technologies allow users to get to the data for analysis. And the variety of data access tools is indicative of the diversity of users and their decision support requirements. Today's access tools target knowledge workers across the organization, including:

Executives.   Often this group requires summarized information and key performance indicator monitoring. However, these same users, when confronted with information that requires further investigation, will expand their requirements to include detailed interrogative technology and even ad hoc analysis.

Business analysts. These users may require detailed analysis and exception reporting, as well as powerful statistical capabilities.

Operational managers. This user group requires trend analysis and forecasting capabilities.

Casual end users. These users may require static reports.

Data access usually provides a graphical interface to the data warehouse, allowing direct access to tables or access through a layer of abstraction. Common access technologies include:

- Query and reporting tools
- Desktop OLAP tools
- Relational OLAP tools
- MDBMS technology with integrated user interface such as DB2 OLAP Server with Excel plug-in
- Data mining tools
- Custom decision support interfaces such as portal dashboards and agent-based technology

Meta Data

Meta data is arguably the only ubiquitous warehouse component covering the entire landscape of core components and issues. Even though it touches virtually everything, it is probably the least understood and most neglected component. Often more difficult to implement then to talk about, meta data is a constant challenge for data architects. Even so, a warehouse is rich with important information on the data being acquired, transformed, stored, accessed, and analyzed.

There are two general categories of meta data:

Technical. If any meta data is captured by your organization, it will likely be this category. This is primarily because technical meta data is generated by the CASE (computer-aided software engineering) tools used in warehouse efforts, as well as the data definition language (DDL) associated with relational databases. Examples of technical meta data include table names, column types and sizes, indexes, and system names.

Business. A layer of meta data that we should gather and keep in repositories has to do with the business-related aspects of the data being stored and processed in the warehouse. Some samples of business meta data include hierarchies, derived data calculations, and business names; for example, p_id may be the technical name of the product key in the product table, but the business name of the same column could be Product ID, which is easier for a user to understand.

Meta data is discussed in detail in Chapter 10. For now, it is important to understand that the warehouse *is* meta data. The BI informational content *is* meta data. What we use and how we use it and when we choose to use it *is* meta data.

Analytical User Requirements

From the end user's perspective, the presentation and analysis layer is the most important component in the BI architecture. Depending on the user's role in the business, his or her requirements for information and analysis capabilities will differ. Typically, the following user types are present in a business:

The "nonfrequent user".   This user group consists of people who are not interested in data warehouse details but need to get access to the information from time to time. These users are usually involved in the day-to-day business and do not have time or any requirements to work extensively with the information in the data warehouse. Their skill in handling reporting and analysis tools is limited.

Users requiring up-to-date information in predefined reports.   This user group has a specific interest in retrieving precisely defined numbers in a given time interval, such as, "I have to get this quality-summary report every Friday at 10:00 A.M as preparation for our weekly meeting and for documentation purposes."

Users requiring dynamic or ad hoc query and analysis capabilities. Typically, this is the business analyst. All the information in the data warehouse may be of importance to these users at some point in time. Their focus is related to availability, performance, and drill-down capabilities to "slice and dice" through the data from different perspectives at any time.

The advanced business analyst—the "power user".   This is a professional business analyst. All the data from the data warehouse is potentially important to these users. They typically require separate specialized data marts for doing specialized analysis on preprocessed data. Examples of these are data mining analysts and advanced OLAP users.

Different user types need different front-end tools, but all can access the same data warehouse architecture. Also, the different skill levels require a different visualization of the results, such as graphics for a high-level presentation or tables for further analysis.

In the remainder of this chapter, we introduce the different types of tools that are typically used to leverage the information in a data warehouse.

Reporting and Querying

Creating reports is a traditional way of distributing information in an organization. Reporting typically involves static figures and tables that are produced and distributed with regular time intervals or for a specific request. Using an automatic reporting tool is an efficient way of distributing the information in your data warehouse through the Web or emails to the large number of users, internal or external to your company, that will benefit from information.

Users that require the ability to create their own reports on the fly or wish to elaborate on the data in existing reports will use a combined querying and reporting tool. By allowing business users to design their own reports and queries, a big workload on IT can be removed while valuable information becomes accessible to a large number of nontechnical employees and customers. In contrast to traditional reporting, this also allows your business users to always have access to up-to-date information about your business.

Because the reports are based on the data in your data warehouse, they supply a 360-degree view of your company's interaction with its customers by combining data from multiple data sources. An example of this is the review of a client's history by combining data from ordering, shipping, invoicing, payment, and support history.

Query and reporting tools are typically based on data in relational databases and are not optimized to deliver the "speed of thought" answers to complex queries on large amounts of data that is required by advanced analysts. An OLAP tool will allow this functionality at the cost of increased load time and management effort.

Online Analytical Processing

During the last 10 years, a significant percentage of corporate data has migrated to relational databases. Relational databases have been used heavily in the areas of operations and control, with a particular emphasis on transaction processing (for example, manufacturing process control and brokerage trading). To be successful in this arena, relational database vendors place a premium on the highly efficient execution of a large number of small transactions and near fault-tolerant availability of data.

It is important to distinguish between the capabilities of a relational database and those of an online analytical processing system. In contrast to relational technology, OLAP uses a multidimensional view of aggregate data to provide quick access to strategic information for further analysis.

OLAP enables analysts, managers, and executives to gain insight into data through fast, consistent, interactive access to a wide variety of possible views of information. OLAP transforms raw data so that it reflects the real dimensionality of the enterprise as understood by the user.

While OLAP systems have the ability to answer the who? and what? questions, it is their ability to answer what if? and why? questions that sets them apart from the other data structures of warehouses. OLAP complements other warehouse structures and expands the analytic offering of your BI environment.

OLAP applications span a variety of organizational functions. Finance departments use OLAP for applications, such as budgeting, activity-based costing (allocations), financial performance analysis, and financial modeling. Sales analysis and forecasting are two of the OLAP applications found in sales departments. Among other applications, marketing departments use OLAP for market research analysis, sales forecasting, promotions analysis, customer analysis, and market/customer segmentation. Typical manufacturing OLAP applications include production planning and defect analysis.

Although OLAP applications are found in widely divergent functional areas, they all require the following key features:

- Multidimensional views of data
- Calculation-intensive capabilities
- Time intelligence

The section *Dimensional Technology and BI* in this chapter provides more information.

Multidimensional Views

Multidimensional views are inherently representative of an actual business model. Rarely is a business model limited to fewer than three dimensions. Managers typically look at financial data by scenario (for example, actual versus budget), organization, line items, and time; and at sales data by product, geography, channel, and time.

A multidimensional view of data provides more than the ability to slice and dice; it provides the foundation for analytical processing through flexible access to information. Database design should not prejudice which operations can be performed on a dimension or how rapidly those operations are performed. Managers must be able to analyze data across any dimension, at any level of aggregation, with equal functionality and ease. OLAP software should support these views of data in a natural and responsive fashion, insulating users from complex query syntax. After all, managers should not have to understand complicated table layouts, elaborate table joins, and summary tables.

Whether a request is for the weekly sales of a product across all geographical areas or the year-to-date sales in a city across all products, an OLAP system must have consistent response times. Managers should not be penalized for the complexity of their queries in either the effort required to form a query or the amount of time required to receive an answer.

Calculation-Intensive Capabilities

The real test of an OLAP database is its ability to perform complex calculations. OLAP databases must be able to do more than simple aggregation. While aggregation along a hierarchy is important, there is more to analysis than simple data rollups. Examples of more complex calculations include share calculations (percentage of total) and allocations (which use hierarchies from a top-down perspective).

Key performance indicators often require involved algebraic equations. Sales forecasting uses trend algorithms, such as moving averages and percentage growth. Analyzing the sales and promotions of a given company and its competitors requires modeling complex relationships among the players. The real world is complicated; the ability to model complex relationships is key in analytical processing applications.

Time Intelligence

Time is an integral component of almost any analytical application. Time is a unique dimension because it is sequential in character (January always comes before February). True OLAP systems understand the sequential nature of time. Business performance is almost always judged over time, for example, this month versus last month, this month versus the same month last year.

The time hierarchy is not always used in the same manner as other hierarchies. For example, a manager may ask to see the sales for May or the sales for the first 5 months of 1995. The same manager may also ask to see the sales for blue shirts but would never ask to see the sales for the first five shirts. Concepts such as year-to-date and period-over-period comparisons must be easily defined in an OLAP system.

In addition, OLAP systems must understand the concept of balances over time. For example, if a company sold 10 shirts in January, 5 shirts in February, and 10 shirts in March, then the total balance sold for the quarter would be 25 shirts. If, on the other hand, a company had a head count of 10 employees in January, only 5 employees in February, and 10 employees again in March, what was the company's employee head count for the quarter? Most companies would use an average balance. In the case of cash, most companies use an ending balance.

Statistics

Statistical tools are typically used to address the business problem of generating an overview of the data in your database. This is done by using techniques that summarize information about the data into statistical measures that can be interpreted without requiring every record in the database to be understood in detail (for example, the application of statistical functions like finding the maximum or minimum, the mean, or the variance). The interpretation of the derived measures requires a certain level of statistical knowledge.

Following are typical business questions addressed by statistics:

- What is a high-level summary of the data that gives me some idea of what is contained in my database?
- Are there apparent dependencies between variables and records in my database?
- What is the probability that an event will occur?
- Which patterns in the data are significant?

To answer these questions, the following statistical methods are typically used:

- Correlation analysis
- Factor analysis
- Regression analysis

These functions are detailed in Chapter 15.

Data Mining

In contrast with statistical analysis, data mining (covered in greater depth in Chapter 14) analyzes all the relevant data in your database and extracts hidden patterns. Data mining is to some extent based on the techniques and disciplines used in statistical analysis. However, the algorithms used in data mining automate many of the tedious procedures that you would need to go through to obtain the same depth of analysis using traditional statistical analysis.

Dimensional Technology and BI

Business intelligence encompasses a variety of techniques and technologies, for instance, techniques for building and using persistent data stores such as normalized structures for atomic-level data and dimensional models for both star schemas and multidimensional cubes. Even operational data is considered a potential target for specific BI efforts. Technologies such as data mining, querying and reporting, OLAP, portals, and agent-based processing all play a role in the range of BI solutions as well. With their distinctive features, each of these technologies and techniques represents a slice of the BI continuum. For this section, our focus is on the role played by dimensional techniques and technologies in BI solutions, specifically OLAP.

OLAP has found a willing audience because it reflects the natural data exploration patterns we employ. It is instinctive for users to consider many dimensions when seeking answers to business questions. This notion of using multiple dimensions in analysis is cornerstone to OLAP. The technology allows users to evaluate business questions based on time, products, vendors, channels, and other factors to gain insight. These dimensions emulate the varied perspectives of a business environment. Moreover, the technology allows users to analyze combinations of these business perspectives, complete with hierarchies and aggregations so that summary information is quickly scanned, while detailed data is readily available for deeper inspection.

OLAP provides a broad landscape of analysis, allowing users to start with simple questions like "What was our revenue?" As the analysis naturally expands, the business questions evolve, spreading across multiple dimensions and different grains of detail. Users travel through the analytical landscape by slicing and dicing the data to learn which products are selling best through which channels and pivoting the data to learn which channels are showing consistent growth.

As the dimensional technology of business intelligence, OLAP continues to be one of the most compelling data delivery technology available. It has quickly spread from the privileged financial analysts, finding its place in the majority of today's data warehouses, delivering reports and ad hoc analysis across the enterprise from the balanced scorecard in the boardroom to the bottom line in the sales office. And, as we change the way we run the modern enterprise, we look toward OLAP servers to meet a more diverse set of requirements. The most striking change in recent years has been the increased focus on customers. Our business questions are no longer focused on the business, but on the business in relation to its customers.

The term *OLAP* is generically used throughout the industry to describe the structure of stored data and the methods we use to access it. The term represents several types of varied technology that tackle the method of access. There are four core adaptations of OLAP:

MOLAP.   Multidimensional OLAP refers to proprietary, multidimensional database OLAP technology. MOLAP is the technology that is built for complex, what-if analysis at the speed-of-thought. One word that best describes this particular technology is *performance*.

ROLAP.   Relational OLAP is a technology that provides sophisticated multidimensional analysis that is performed on open relational databases and other nonproprietary file structures. ROLAP is not bound by the constraints of other OLAP technology. For example, ROLAP can scale to large data sets in the terabyte range, covering a wide array of informational content. The word that best describes ROLAP technology is *scalability*.

HOLAP.   Hybrid OLAP is an attempt to combine some of the features of MOLAP and ROLAP technology. The technology provides solid performance even while analyzing large data sets, which happen to be specific strengths of MOLAP and ROLAP, respectively. However, HOLAP has met with varying degrees of success, since it is not a full implementation of all the strengths indigenous to MOLAP and ROLAP. One word that best describes HOLAP technology is *compromise*.

DOLAP.   Desktop OLAP is a technology that is probably the most common in OLAP user communities. DOLAP represents those OLAP tools that are inexpensive and easy to deploy and use. However, the price and ease of use translate to limited functionality, especially with regard to the entire dimensional spectrum that we will be discussing later in this chapter. A word that best describes this technology is *deployable*.

The OLAP Server

The success of OLAP has resulted in a large number of vendors offering OLAP products and a range of technologies that aim to meet the needs of the growing number of businesses that are deploying OLAP. Despite the diversity of the OLAP marketplace, two architectures are dominant: MOLAP and ROLAP. These architectures are characterized primarily by their approach to OLAP data storage.

MOLAP

MOLAP servers employ dedicated OLAP database engines optimized to manage sparse matrices of data. The OLAP engine generally has a calculation function that supports complex calculations within and across dimensions.

MOLAP storage management maintains the physical storage of OLAP cubes. These cubes are loaded with source data; then a calculation is triggered to aggregate the input data along the hierarchies across each dimension. At the same time, the calculation engine carries out the more complex functions, which might include financial calculations, statistics, and allocations.

Calculating MOLAP cubes is typically a complex and time-consuming operation. All cells at all intersection points across all dimensions are calculated and stored. It is not unusual for a complete cube to require 10 or more times as much storage as the input data, so for every megabyte of data we supply, the MOLAP engine might create 10 MB or more. To combat this problem, most MOLAP servers now offer the administrator some control over how much of the cube is aggregated as part of the calculation operation, and how much of the cube is calculated dynamically in response to queries.

When users query a MOLAP cube, the query operation is usually no more than a simple lookup. When the entire cube is pre-aggregated, no calculations or rollups are required to provide query results. Query processing is simply a matter of determining which data is needed, and whether the data resides in cache or on disk. The required data is retrieved, formatted, and returned to the client. Server-side caching and smart indexing result in consistently fast query response times, which encourage users to continue their analysis and maintain the analytical train of thought.

Pre-aggregation is an expensive operation that usually limits scalability. Unlimited dimensions and aggregation levels is beyond the reach of today's MOLAP servers, and many will struggle to handle 15 to 20 dimensions while maintaining support for other criteria such as consistent query times. More importantly, the time required to build large cubes may exceed the available batch processing time.

MOLAP servers dominate today's OLAP market. Their strength is consistent high-speed data delivery to large populations of users from OLAP cubes that model bounded business processes with suitable dimensionality and levels of detail.

ROLAP

ROLAP technology accesses data stored in a data warehouse to provide OLAP analyses without the requirement to store and calculate data in a multidimensional cube. Relational databases serve as the database layer for data storage, access, and retrieval processes.

ROLAP relies on middle-tier logic to generate structured query language (SQL). End users submit multidimensional analyses to the ROLAP engine that dynamically transforms the request into SQL execution plans. The SQL is submitted to the relational database for processing, the relational query result is cross-tabulated, and a multidimensional result set is returned to the end user. This dynamic SQL transformation allows users access to transaction-level detail data because the source is a relational database, allowing analysis to be performed at any data depth. Moreover, the logical query flow from the user is uninterrupted because analysis can occur over as many dimensions as the data itself provides.

The middle-tier ROLAP engine leverages the database layer for all applicable analytic functionality and processing. For more complex calculations not supported by the database, the necessary data can be manipulated in the ROLAP tool's analytical engine. Advanced analytical functionality is accomplished by accessing stored metrics if available or calculating metrics if necessary.

Performance often presents the largest challenge with ROLAP solutions. Transaction-level calculations are not always necessary and rolling up of data for each query can be time-consuming. To improve performance, you can build summary tables for higher-level data requests.

The ability to depend solely on the relational database itself makes ROLAP well suited to scale to large numbers of dimensions and to support analysis against large atomic data sets. The database, which is leveraged for storage and processing, can accommodate terabytes or more of data.

Defining the Dimensional Spectrum

The application of dimensional technology runs the gamut from MOLAP, best suited for *fast, complex* multidimensional analysis, to ROLAP, for performing multidimensional analysis over *extremely large, constantly changing data volumes.* The solution domain of dimensional BI is as boundless as the permutations of BI requirements themselves; consequently, most BI strategies will embrace OLAP technology. The question that you must ask yourself is this: "Have I sufficiently planned for addressing the range of business requirements of my enterprise?"

Figure 2.2 illustrates the diversity and wide range of OLAP-centric features. Although not all-inclusive, the features identified on the spectrum are specifically selected to draw clear distinctions between the two primary technologies of online analytical processing: ROLAP and MOLAP. As shown, there are two extremes of the spectrum, each representing a specific technology. ROLAP is on the left side, with characteristics that are arguably the technology's most widely acknowledged strengths. On the right side is MOLAP and characteristics indigenous to that technology, equally well known and accepted. That is not to say that ROLAP and MOLAP do not have other strengths. However, those identified afford an excellent means for demonstrating the breadth of the solution domain that these two technologies provide.

The spectrum identifies eight characteristics, outlined in Table 2.1. It should be apparent that to perform all the advanced features of multidimensional analysis, you must plan to implement both MOLAP and ROLAP technology.

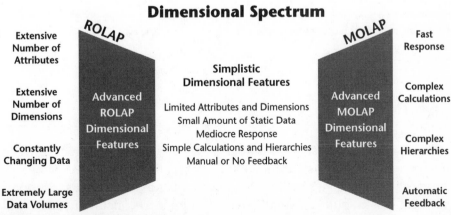

Figure 2.2 Dimensional spectrum.

Table 2.1 Dimensional Spectrum Characteristics

TECHNOLOGY	CHARACTERISTICS	DESCRIPTION
ROLAP	Extensive number of attributes	The use of numerous descriptive attributes during analysis.
	Extensive number of dimensions	Being able to perform analysis against numerous dimensions simultaneously, as well as to add and exchange dimensions on demand.
	Constantly changing data	Analysis that is performed against source data that is constantly changing.
	Extremely large data volumes	The capacity to perform dimensional analysis against data sources in the terabyte range.
MOLAP	Fast response	Being able to maintain "speed-of-thought" performance during analysis.
	Complex calculations[1]	Analysis requiring calculations based on complicated dependencies and derived measures.
	Complex hierarchies	Analysis performed against multiple, asymmetrical hierarchies.
	Automatic feedback[2]	OLAP tools that provide an automated closed-loop feedback to operational systems.

1. The implicit axis nature of OLAP formulas creates unique challenges, because the derived value of any one particular cell is dependent on the combination of dimensions queried. This means that precedence must be established to assign formulas for any given query combination.

2. The business intelligence cycle is not complete until all informational understanding and insight is applied to current business processes for the purpose of improved efficiencies.

Touch Points

For larger organizations, the number of possible touch points between your company and its customers is increasing. Core touch points in today's business climate not only include the traditional advertisements, coupons, stores, and kiosks, but also email, Web, consumer-to-consumer (C2C), and business-to-consumer (B2C) portals.

It has always been a challenge to determine the success of advertising campaigns given media such as direct mailings, print, television, or radio (multimedia). But in addition to those issues, we now have to demonstrate success and decipher trends and market demand from banners and other Web-centric activity. Exacerbated by the Internet is not only the volumes of data being generated that require examination, but also the time span now necessary to adjust to and accommodate for the success or failure of banner or Web store fronts. What used to be a lag between the advertisement getting people into the stores to make their purchase has now shrunk to virtually a real-time cause-and-effect situation. This means that we no longer have the luxury of closing the store and regrouping. Customer touch points have created a situation where real-time analysis must become a natural part of the overall BI effort. The BI environment must be capable of blending real-time and historical analysis for both tactical and strategic purposes.

Zero-Latency and Your Warehouse Environment

Traditional warehouses store integrated, time-variant, static data that is regularly refreshed and used for, among other things, trend analysis, pattern recognition, and forecasting. It was inevitable that the traditional warehouse would ultimately lead to an analytical gap between the data stored in warehouse structures and that contained and maintained in operational systems or that data being created by e-business environments. This is especially true in light of the growing demands for analysis in large organizations.

So, if we agree there is a need for zero-latency analysis, how do we implement the concept? Regarding the data itself, a real-time or zero-latency warehouse does not mean that the entire warehouse is dynamically updated. It simply means that the warehouse environment embraces technologies and techniques necessary to incorporate targeted operational and e-business data to be used and made available in BI, real-time analysis with or without other warehoused data.

Closed-Loop Learning

There is only one objective that is missing from all leading BI vendors, including IBM: *closed-loop learning*. Achieving this objective is fundamental to the information organization. Much of the current information floating about warehouse-centric circles defines a closed-loop environment as requiring an action to be taken as a result of the analysis. Albeit an important step, it is not representative of the entire "loop." A BI organization takes a broader view, one that is representative of the information management cycle. Not only must you act on the analysis, but the enterprise as a whole must grow as a result of the information content, analysis, and subsequent actions taken. Essentially, the BI organization is a closed-loop, learning environment.

Let's use a hotshot marketing person from your firm for illustration. Suppose this person wants to extract data from the warehouse for analysis to make decisions on an advertising campaign or customer relationship management (CRM) effort. A question you need to ask yourself is this: How does the enterprise benefit from the analysis and subsequent decisions of this hotshot? We certainly hope the organization benefits from a better-tuned campaign. But what if the hotshot decided to leave the company? Would we have benefited from his analysis and processes that he took offline? What about all the fancy models and mining stuff the hotshot probably was doing to the data while it was in the marketing information silos? How does the organization benefit from any of that? Simply put, it doesn't.

That is the problem with many warehouse and BI environments. They are designed as passive repositories of data to be doled out on demand of corporate hotshots for further analysis. All this "black-box" stuff happens on concealed systems and runs as clandestine operations. Alternatively, the hotshot should build and test mining models and other statistical processes of discovery with the direct involvement of the warehouse team, on warehouse development platforms. Then, when a mining model or statistical process is ready for production, it should be made a part of the natural flow of data through the warehouse environment. At this point, any great models or processes built by the hotshot are now an established component of the warehouse. The hotshot gets all the kudos for a wonderful model, and the enterprise gains in intellectual and proprietary assets as well.

Historical Integrity

One of the constant mistakes made in warehousing is building history. All too often when asking warehouse builders what is meant by the term *history* in the warehouse, you get a traditional response. History, to many, is reflected by the age of the data stored in the warehouse. Essentially, history means that you have, for example, 5 years' worth of sales transactions or customers or other entities you've chosen to store. Well, certainly if you have 5 years' worth of sales transactions, you have history—or, at least one form of history. Unfortunately, this is not what is considered time-variant history.

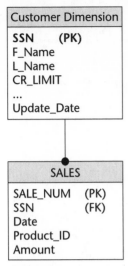

Figure 2.3   Poor design.

The best way to describe time-variant history is by using an example. Figure 2.3 shows a poorly designed dimension and related fact table. The dimension table uses the Social Security number (SSN) of the customer as the primary key. This was probably inherited from operational applications where the use of this type of value for referential integrity is common. So why is this a problem for warehouses?

To answer this question, we have to examine the rows stored. Let's assume that we captured sales transaction information about a particular customer. Table 2.2 shows a couple of sales transactions. We need to focus on the SSN as shown in the dimension and fact tables.

Table 2.2   Sales Transactions

DIMENSION.SSN	CR_LIMIT	FACT.SSN	SALE_NUM	DATE	AMOUNT
123-12-1234	$2,500	123-12-1234	1001	01/01/02	$1,200
123-12-1234	$2,500	123-12-1234	2301	02/25/02	$400

Table 2.3   Credit Limit Increase Impact

DIMENSION.SSN	CR_LIMIT	FACT.SSN	SALE_NUM	DATE	AMOUNT
123-12-1234	$5,000	123-12-1234	1001	01/01/02	$1,200
123-12-1234	$5,000	123-12-1234	2301	02/25/02	$400
123-12-1234	$5,000	123-12-1234	4594	03/13/02	$2,100

From these sales transactions we can calculate a variety of values for customer 123-12-1234. For example, we can sum the total sales ($1,600), we can calculate the average sales ($800), among other statistics. Now let's say we have a business rule that requires us to capture the credit limit value if it changes in the production systems. If the credit limit for customer 123-12-1234 is increased from $2,500 to $5,000, the rows would look like those outlined in Table 2.3.

So, what has happened? Well, simply put, we've restated history. When the credit limit increased to $5,000, the only option available to the warehouse is to update the CR_LIMIT column of the customer dimension. That means all statistical value and trending that might have been available to us is lost. For example, can we answer what the average amount of sales is for each of the credit limits given to the customer? No. The second we updated the customer dimension column CR_LIMIT, we eliminated all previous visibility to previous credit limits. As far as the warehouse knows, there has always been only one credit limit for customer 123-12-1234: $5,000.

Now let's examine how the tables should have been designed to address the business rule of recording credit limit changes while maintaining historical integrity. Figure 2.4 shows a well-designed set of tables.

As illustrated in Figure 2.4, the major design difference between this set of tables and the previous example is the addition of a surrogate key for the customer primary key. The surrogate should adhere to the rules originally established for primary keys: specifically, that they be data-less. That means that the primary key should do nothing more than maintain the referential integrity between the tables. By establishing a surrogate key, we can now implement a process of recording a second row in the customer dimension for the same customer. So now when a credit limit is changed, we can take a complete snapshot of the customer record, with the new credit limit, and insert it into the customer dimension table while maintaining the original customer record. Let's see how that affects our historical integrity as demonstrated in Table 2.4.

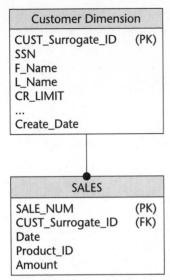

Figure 2.4   Time-variant design.

What should be apparent is that the surrogate key now provides the referential integrity between the tables. Consequently, we now can create a new record for customer 123-12-1234 to capture the new credit limit while keeping the original record. Furthermore, all the sales transactions associated with the original record are still intact and all new sales transactions are associated with the new customer record. Thus, historical integrity is maintained. Now we can answer questions like "What is the trend in average sales for each credit limit increase provided customer 123-12-1234?"

Table 2.4   Historical Integrity

DIMENSION CUST_ SURROGATE_ ID	SSN	CR_LIMIT	FACT CUST_ SURROGATE_ ID	SALE_ NUM	DATE	AMOUNT
91101	123-12-1234	$2,500	91101	1001	01/01/02	$1,200
91101	123-12-1234	$2,500	91101	2301	02/25/02	$400
111211	123-12-1234	$5,000	111211	4594	03/13/02	$2,100

Fundamental to maintaining historical integrity is creating surrogate keys to be used as primary keys in the warehouse and life-stamping the records themselves. By simply adding these two components to warehoused records, you dramatically increase the analytical capability of the environment by ensuring historical integrity of the data as opposed to simply restating history.

Summary

BI is bigger than a star schema, cube, or atomic-level data. It represents the successful culmination of the implementation of techniques, technologies, and, of course, data structures. Business intelligence is the informational content derived from sourced data that is integrated, transformed, and cleansed. This content represents the corporate information asset. But BI is more than just content; it is also the analysis conducted on the content. The ad hoc query capability, advanced SQL reporting, data mining, OLAP, and portal dashboards that present key performance indicators all enable better decision making.

If the typical BI environment fostered better decision making, most people would uncork the champagne and toast to a successful implementation. However, BI must go two steps further. The decision making must lead to actionable steps that improve the organization's performance. And, finally, BI must feed all that knowledge gleaned from the content, analyzed and acted upon, back into the enterprise. This means that your organization learns from its own data and actions taken.

CHAPTER 3

Planning Data
Warehouse Iterations

Key Issues:

- Iterations of your warehouse must focus on addressing the immediate requirements of specific user communities while ensuring adherence to enterprise guidelines and growing your corporate information asset.

- The first iterations are unique because of the investment necessary to establish the fundamental data and because they provide the technical architecture on which most subsequent iterations will be based. You will, of course, continue to invest in technology and implement other data designs over time, but only the first iterations normally carry the brunt of technology investment and implement the core architectural data designs.

- The Dysfunction, Impact, and Feasibility (DIF) Matrix is an excellent tool for defining and prioritizing BI iterations based on statistically valid methods. Prioritizing the competing business requirements across your enterprise can be a daunting task, peppered with political landmines. This approach establishes a statistically valid method for user communities to rank their own business requirements.

- The spiral approach to implementing BI iterations is an excellent means of reducing risk. It is the only project approach that addresses risk, by design. You can use the spiral approach with a simple iteration task list you define, or you can combine the approach with your favorite life cycle development methodology.

Architects and project sponsors frequently relate BI and warehouse efforts to particular technologies. Too often, the notion of implementing an OLAP tool or building a star schema overshadows the rationale and purpose for these tools and techniques. It was a business requirement, hopefully, that drove an architect or project sponsor to recommend the use of OLAP or building a star schema.

Even though we agree that business requirements drive the actual warehouse iterations, the data architect or project planner must recognize when a particular technique or technology will be necessary. Moreover, he must plan the overall BI architecture in advance of any iteration being implemented. This includes considering any data structures required to support the plan, as well as predicting the types of technologies to implement. Project planners thus have a dual role: defining an agenda for virtually any combination of BI applications that might be necessary in their particular enterprise while simultaneously focusing the attention of iterations on the business requirement itself. Iterations are selfish by nature, driven by a self-serving agenda. The project must address the requirements at hand and do so without compromising the enterprise BI objectives.

It is easy to lose sight of the enterprise requirements in favor of the immediate iterations, which results in effective warehouse-centric applications for specific communities at the expense of the enterprise. The reverse is also true. Some architects and project planners have established well-defined enterprise architectures but provide little leeway for user communities to participate. This can severely handicap the warehouse environment, driving the users to become self-sufficient by creating their own variation of a warehouse. In the end, the enterprise suffers as well.

This chapter discusses the elements of a good project plan, as well as how a specific project plan fits within the overall BI framework you establish. Moreover, we examine the differences between the first iterations of a warehouse effort and subsequent iterations. This distinction in critical for project planners, since it provides a sense of project scope that affects investment cost, resources, and time lines. The chapter also details an approach to identify your BI iterations called the DIF Matrix, which represents a proven technique to methodically define, document, and prioritize multiple warehouse iteration opportunities. The goal is to identify those opportunities with the most impact to the organization.

Planning Any Iteration

The project iteration itself is driven by a business requirement to address a specific need. This need is typically for a focused audience, for example, a department. This, of course, means that the iteration is likely to be sponsored by the department for its own use. The notion of enterprise architecture or corporate warehouse standards is not necessarily on the minds of these project sponsors. But it should be on the radar screen of the data architect. This is where the enterprisewide BI vision comes in. It provides a guide for architects to follow and a menu of techniques and technologies from which to select in order to deliver the BI applications being sponsored by disparate user communities.

Implementing the warehouse as a big-bang effort has long since been deemed a formula for disaster. Instead, warehouses and BI initiatives are grown iteratively, addressing business requirements one at a time (see Figure 3.1). On the other hand, iterations of the warehouse must be assimilated into the long-term vision of the enterprise BI initiative. You can interpret iterations as being schizophrenic because they are driven by specific requirements but guided by the broader, enterprisewide road map. The conceptual model of the business-intelligent organization shown in Figure 1.1 serves as the basis for such a road map.

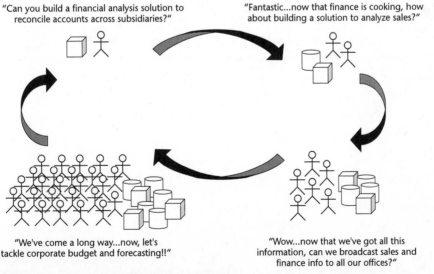

"Can you build a financial analysis solution to reconcile accounts across subsidiaries?"

"Fantastic...now that finance is cooking, how about building a solution to analyze sales?"

"We've come a long way...now, let's tackle corporate budget and forecasting!!"

"Wow...now that we've got all this information, can we broadcast sales and finance info to all our offices?"

Figure 3.1   Business intelligence is iterative.

Architects and project planners therefore must target for near-term gains with each iteration but establish long-term plans to guarantee the overall information asset of the enterprise. Architects and planners are often not in control of the order or even the selection of BI iterations, as the iterations themselves must be organically grown from user communities to ensure that the warehouse is useful.

If planners do not control the order of iterations being implemented, how can they guarantee cohesiveness among them? How can planners deliver what users want and yet use the iterations themselves as building blocks to the larger goal of creating an enterprisewide asset?

In a nutshell, a successful iteration requires careful planning. When building an "architected" data warehouse, the idea is to source all raw data into an atomic-level data structure. From this structure, all subsequent warehouse-centric data is sourced, including data for star schemas and OLAP cubes. How can we guarantee that rogue departments will not use their own checkbooks to fund their own warehouse agendas and not wait for IT to blend the data into the atomic layer? Technically, nothing can stop them from building data silos and compromising the enterprise asset. However, adhering to the concept of an architected data warehouse starts at the top level of the organization. The same holds true for protecting the overall BI vision from maverick executives or divisions. Irrelevant of which iteration is done first, or how many times the strategic direction of your company changes, there must be a high-level plan for how BI will be rolled out in your enterprise.

Building Your BI Plan

There is often confusion regarding the content required in a BI project plan. Several competing methodologies are used for building data warehouses and supporting BI initiatives. Numerous industry leaders and vendors offer some approach that has proven successful. But all of these approaches and methodologies agree that the following building blocks should be included in your BI plan:

- Strategy
- Data architecture
- Technical architecture
- Implementation and maintenance

The BI organization diagram in Figure 1.1 provided a road map of your enterprise initiative and an opportunity for architects and project planners to define and described, in some detail, the individual components. Let's say your BI conceptual diagram includes the use of data marts. In your BI plan you will want to define and describe these data marts. Are they going to be implemented as star schemas, with each distributed on an NT platform dedicated to a specific department? Or, are the data marts DB2 OLAP cubes, centrally implemented on a UNIX server configured for serving up dimensional data to a broad audience of users? As you can see, there is plenty of detail to explain in a BI plan even if we do not know any specifics about the first iteration of a data mart.

Since your BI plan is a "living" document, you will be able to continuously refine your enterprise road map with subsequent iterations of your warehouse. You should update your enterprise plan after each iteration. For example, let's assume that we know data mining will be needed at some time in the future. We need to emphasize that fact and establish the standard for its use. But we probably do not have any other detail about the mining tool or technology necessary. Consequently, we will wait to document the exact software to be implemented until we have a specific iteration that would trigger such a decision.

The following sections further detail each component of your BI plan.

Enterprise Strategy

When defining your enterprise strategy, you should address at least five subjects:

Architecture goals and constraints.   This provides a means for architects and planners to set overall goals and objectives for the BI initiative. Constraints that impact the BI effort must be defined as well. For example, the BI initiative may not be able to start until the new data center is complete or the overall BI effort needs to begin with finance, or it needs to start with offices in the Pacific Rim.

Conceptual view.   The information organization conceptual diagram is the type of view expected in this section, along with a brief discussion of each component illustrated.

Use case view.   A use case can be developed to formalize the intention of the BI initiative. As with all use cases, you can start with a high-level perspective, like those shown in Figures 3.2 to 3.4.

Architecturally significant design components. There may be any number of significant components that are part of your overall architecture design. Perhaps you are planning for extensive spatial data and analysis. That is the level of design significance that should be mentioned here. Or, your enterprise may need an ODS for tactical reporting, or you may be planning to implement a message broker or XML server as a data delivery mechanism for the warehouse. These are all examples of significantly important design components.

Standards. This applies to any standards that warehouse participants must adhere to. For instance, a standard may be to use a BI committee to give final approval to any particular iteration sought.

Each of these subjects builds upon another, starting from overall architectural goals and ending with the establishment of formal standards. This provides project planners and sponsors with a strategic vision of the BI environment and a formal definition of its use and direction.

Designing the Technical Architecture

When you first lay out your technical architecture, it may be limited. You may know that you want to implement star schemas in a relational database. What you may not know by the time the first draft of your BI plan is published is whose RDBMS you are going to use or on what platform it will be implemented. That's okay. What's important is to start designing your architecture, including detail where possible, and leaving placeholders where subsequent decisions will provide more information. The BI plan is a living document. You will revisit the technical architecture many times and publish updated versions as necessary to ensure communication to your audience of project sponsors and user communities.

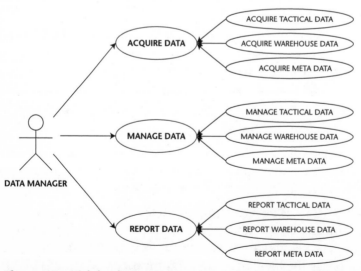

Figure 3.2   High-level use case.

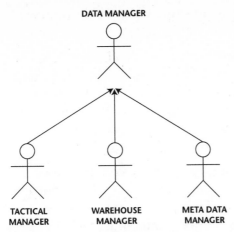

Figure 3.3 Generalization use case.

An example of this situation is shown in Figure 3.5. We've identified workstations and warehouse-centric servers for the atomic layer, data marts, and staging area. Because it is an initial draft of the technical architecture components, we've left placeholders for vendors, models, operating systems, and even locations. Figure 3.5 provides a general sense of the architecture as it is currently known and yet ensures a place for additional information as it becomes available.

High-Level Realization of the User

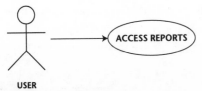

Figure 3.4 Realization use case.

As with the overall strategy, the technical architecture should address certain issues, including:

Technical architecture goals and constraints.   The technical architecture focuses on hardware, software, and communication components of the warehouse effort. Therefore, the goals, objectives, and constraints outlined in this section should be specific to those topics. An example might be the implementation of a specific relational database management system over the entire BI initiative.

Technical architecture.   Figure 3.5 illustrates how technical components of a warehouse are represented in diagram form. It specifically identifies the hardware, software, and network/communication components. Components in the BI conceptual model must be found somewhere in a technical architecture diagram, and as more detail becomes available, the technical architecture diagrams can become more specific. For example, if you have a large effort with regard to data marts, you may have a diagram that focuses only on that component of your architecture.

Architecturally significant design component.   Any significant technical component of your architecture must be identified in this section. For example, you may require a 24x7 implementation and therefore must establish mirroring across two distinct data centers.

It should be noted that each diagram is associated with sufficient narrative to describe the components identified. This often means that your technical architecture documentation includes several technical diagrams and many pages of related narrative.

Designing the Data Architecture

The data architecture provides designers a venue to convey what data structures will be implemented, how that data is stored in each, and how the data will propagate throughout the warehouse environment. It is obviously a critical section for any warehouse-centric initiative. Just like the technical architecture, you will often start at a high level and grow the details of data architecture as successive iterations of the warehouse are undertaken. Following are core topics to consider for a data architecture design document:

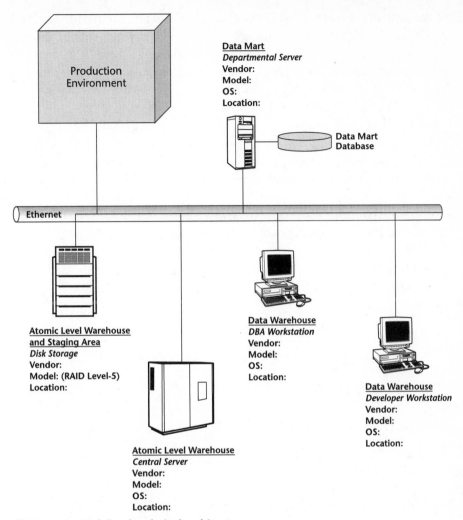

Figure 3.5   High-level technical architecture.

Data architecture goals and constraints.   All the goals, objectives, and constraints to your strategy should be documented in this section. For example, the goal might be data integrity in the sense of creating an architecture that maintains a single version of the truth. As one of the objectives to achieve such a goal, planners might identify the following: All warehouse-centric data must be incorporated into the atomic layer first. All subsequent use of that data will be sourced from this data structure. This objective may even serve as a constraint. Other constraints might include three-party data or technologies.

Logical data architecture.   This is your opportunity to provide logical models that support your data architecture goals. Remember that initially you will be limited in the models that you can provide, since you are not addressing a specific warehouse iteration yet. Therefore, you could provide a subject area model of your enterprise or a series of subject area models that describe core subjects within your enterprise (see Figure 3.6). You can include rules for mutating raw source data into atomic-level data and even guidelines defining how and when to use star schemas and OLAP cubes. You will want to update this document as subsequent iterations of your warehouse rollout.

Architecturally significant design components.   The establishment of an atomic layer is a significant architect component, along with an ODS and an enterprise cube farm. These are traditional design components; however, there are others, such as geo-spatial data structures, specialized data staging, and living warehouse databases, just to name a few.

Product Subject Area High-Level Model

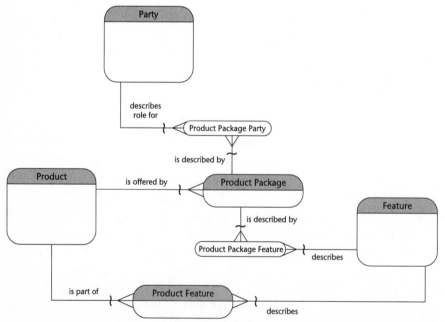

Figure 3.6   Specific subject area used as part of a series.

Test plans.   A component of the overall road map that is often over-looked is how iterations will be tested before rollout. This section provides planners an opportunity to establish a standard to follow for all subsequent warehouse iterations with regard to testing and acceptance. Topics should include test templates to be completed by future project sponsors and planners, criteria for enterprise adherence and approval, criteria for test data selection, and performance testing (including unit, suite, and stress testing), to name just a few.

Chapter 4 discusses in greater detail the data architecture and related models.

Implementing and Maintaining the Warehouse

Here designers and project planners establish the guidelines necessary for building and maintaining the purposed warehouse structures and related technologies. The implementation of core processes and sequence of establishing data structures are detailed in this section. As with the previous sections, the implementation view can start from a high-level perspective, with details added as they become known. Generally the implementation view contains three distinct perspectives:

Strategy.   The implementation view might cover a time span or discuss when resources will be available for warehouse-centric projects. Here is also the place to define how iterations will be selected. Describing, for instance, the use of the DIF Matrix defined later in this chapter is excellent content for this perspective. Finally, this section should outline how funding will be addressed. For example, funding might be the responsibility of the requesting department, or there may be some form of shared funding between corporate and individual departments.

Architecture.   This perspective includes topics such as size and performance requirements, data quality issues, meta data control, and retention policies. Decisions made on retention, for instance, will impact data architecture issues such as partitioning of the data, as well as technical architecture considerations regarding disk storage.

Process.   Here the architect must outline, at a high level, process issues such as refresh rates, backup/recovery, archive, workflow, and security. Again, you will address as many of these topics as possible even though no particular iteration of the warehouse is being discussed.

Your BI plan should start with high-level diagrams, broad policy statements, and general definitions. As your warehouse matures, so, too, will the formal documentation and depth of detail identified in your BI plan.

Planning the First Iteration

When warehouse participants speak of 90-day iteration cycles, you can bet that they are talking about subsequent iterations, because the first iteration of a warehouse effort invariably takes longer than 90 days. The reason is simple: During your first iteration you will go through the process of identifying and defining your BI and warehouse strategies, your data and technical architecture, meta data strategy, and data access method. You will identify the tools of choice for extraction, transformation, and loading (ETL), data management, meta data, and data access, and you will have to work through what can become a lengthy procurement process. Finally, you will be training your internal people on the new tools. For all of these reasons, it is very difficult for most companies to implement their first data warehouse effort within a 90-day window.

Project planners and sponsors must be aware of the significant difference between the first iteration and subsequent cycles. The first iteration is where you will make and implement virtually all the strategic decisions about your warehouse. The time frame is obviously based on scope and budget, but it is safe to say that the first iteration can take 6 or more months.

Often your first warehouse iteration is actually two warehouse iterations in one. The first part of the effort is spent on identifying and defining warehouse strategies, selecting and purchasing tools of choice, and training internal staff. The second half of the first iteration is usually represented by the impetus for the warehouse effort getting started. This puts a great deal of strain on the initial project team, the first sponsor, and every other sponsor in the organization paying for the warehouse infrastructure. As the project starts, the planners begin to understand the size and scope of issues that must be considered and addressed. This can sometimes translate into budget overruns and time delays. The sponsors only want a business requirement to be met and never expect that it will require a slew of strategic decisions to be made and potentially expensive technical foundations to be obtained—including tools to be selected and implemented—before they can even get started toward addressing their business requirement. Therefore, it is critical that warehouse planners understand the unique characteristics of the first iteration and set sponsor expectations accordingly.

Aligning the Warehouse with Corporate Strategy

A data warehouse is designed primarily to address strategic business questions and planning. That does not mean a data warehouse cannot answer tactical questions, but if that is the rationale for the warehouse effort, there are less expensive and less challenging ways to deal with that type of reporting.

There are four principles on which to focus your warehouse efforts:

Identify executive sponsorship.   The best individuals to target for warehouse iterations are company executives. The rationale is simple: Executives are responsible for planning the business as opposed to doing the business. Since the warehouse should primarily focus on strategic analysis, it is logical for executives to define the iterations. By doing so, you guarantee that the warehouse will be aligned with the corporate strategy.

Focus on strategic requirements.   Build the data warehouse primarily to address strategic requirements and not to address tactical issues.

Business requirements drive warehouse iterations.   This is a critical point that is discussed in more detail in the following section. For now it is important to understand that business requirements will afford your greatest chance of a widely accepted warehouse. To use anything else to scope, define, and determine your warehouse iterations is to invite unnecessary risk.

Consider the data warehouse as an evolving asset.   The actual information content collected, derived, and maintained in the warehouse evolves into an important corporate asset. And, like all assets, it is vital to recognize its value and protect it as successive iterations are layered into the BI environment.

When project planners perform the tasks outlined they guarantee that the warehouse and BI environment is designed and implemented as a corporate asset, addressing relevant business requirements of strategic importance to the organization.

Conducting a Readiness Assessment

Readiness assessment serves as a formal method for project planners to profile the corporation and help identify potential problem areas. Planners are then able to determine the company's chance for success in a warehouse effort. A readiness assessment should:

- Identify historical successes and failures of warehouse projects
- Highlight problem areas for the organization and identify deficiencies that need to be addressed
- Understand the company's technical capabilities
- Examine the corporate culture
- Pinpoint areas of organizational or resource deficiencies

Formal readiness assessments will vary to accommodate individual organizational, technical, and practical characteristics of a company with regard to the warehouse effort. The net outcome of an assessment can even help planners with budget estimates. For instance, if the assessment finds the organization is lacking in its ability to implement a warehouse, then planners can determine the necessary investment to shore up the areas of weakness. Although no survey tool can guarantee your success or failure for a particular effort, the readiness assessment improves your chance for success. Table 3.1 shows sample questions that have been used to survey technical and organizational aspects of a firm.

Table 3.1   Readiness Assessment

CATEGORY	TOPIC	LEAST DESIRABLE	AVERAGE	MOST DESIRABLE
Organizational	Do you have a strong, well-positioned executive sponsor?	No.	Sponsor has limited say in corporate affairs.	Yes. Well-respected and active in corporate strategy.
	Has the warehouse project scope been defined and success factors identified?	Only a general idea of what they see the warehouse doing is known at this time.	They are actively debating and drafting the scope and success factors.	Yes. The project scope and success factors are defined.
	Is funding available?	Funding is a problem.	Some funds are available.	Cost is not an issue.
	Is the sponsor actively involved?	Not at all.	Limited involvement.	Sponsor actively participates with the team.

Table 3.1   (Continued)

CATEGORY	TOPIC	LEAST DESIRABLE	AVERAGE	MOST DESIRABLE
	What are the expectations?	Completely unreasonable. The sponsor wants everything, now.	Expectations are unreasonable but sponsor is willing to listen and adjust.	Realistic expectations are set. Sponsor wants a planned, methodical rollout.
Technical	Do the source systems have current, accurate meta data?	Little or no meta data exists.	Meta data exists for most of the systems.	Comprehensive and current meta data exists for all relevant source systems.
	What portion of the source data suffers from inaccuracy or incompleteness?	Most of the source data is inaccurate or incomplete.	Some of the source data is inaccurate or incomplete.	Most source data is clean and complete.
	Is the warehouse viewed as a place to clean up source data?	Yes.	For only a few of the data problems.	No.
	Do the target users have any experience with warehouse-centric tools?	None.	A few users have experience.	Most users have some experience or exposure.
	Does there exist a warehouse-centric infrastructure?	No. The project would require purchasing all new technology.	Some system components exist, while others will need to be purchased.	A robust, warehouse-centric environment exists.

The bibliography of this book lists sources for more information on readiness assessment.

Resource Planning

For small data warehouse efforts and small IT shops, a team of two or three may need to play multiple roles and yet be quite successful. For larger project efforts, however, more team members with specialized skills are needed. Table 3.2 lists roles common to warehouse efforts.

Table 3.2   Data Warehouse Roles

ROLE	DESCRIPTION
Executive sponsor	This individual is responsible for ensuring the project has the necessary resources, as well as for eliminating potential barriers that might be encountered by team members as they source data and build warehouse content.
Project manager (PM)	The project manager is responsible for planning as well as managing the entire warehouse iteration. Any warehouse iteration, small or large, for any size of IT department should maintain a full-time, dedicated PM.
Business requirements analyst	This role is focused on translating the business requirements for the technical team. They often serve as the communication link between the end users and IT.
Subject matter expert (SME)	An SME is typically from the end-user community and provides the DW project team with a wealth of information regarding the business requirement side of the project effort.
Data architect	To a large extent, the success or failure of a warehouse iteration is on the shoulders of the data architect. It is this individual who must understand the business requirements and design the warehouse to address the requirements, while at the same time maintaining the long-term viability and integrity for the overall warehouse. For small or large shops it is recommended that you invest in an experienced data architect.
Technical architect	The evaluation and selection of software, hardware, operating system(s), networking, and so on, will involve the technical architect. This role is responsible for ensuring a warehouse environment/platform accomplishes the strategic direction of the warehouse.

Table 3.2 *(Continued)*

ROLE	DESCRIPTION
Technical architect *(continued)*	Very large shops may have an individual who is referred to as the technical architect. However, for smaller IT departments, the architect may be an experienced networking or systems engineer.
Meta data administrator	An administrator of the meta data requirements, processes, and tools might be necessary. However, this role is typically only found in large IT shops.
Database administrator (DBA)	Since performance and extremely large database size is a real concern in warehouse environments, DBAs are required.
Data warehouse administrator	For enterprise warehouse initiatives, it is not unusual to have someone dedicated to the loading, archiving, and general administration of warehouse activity. This role differs from a DBA in the sense that a DW administrator is concerned with the overall operation of the warehouse, as opposed to the designing and tuning of, say, table indexes.
Data extract developer	The process of identifying required source data, its extraction and transformation to be loaded into target data structures is assigned to the extraction developer. This role is best filled by individuals with knowledge of the source systems.
Data access developer	Access developers are focused on the design and development of the established data access strategies, using the tools identified.

A typical warehouse team would have at least four full-time individuals and two or three part-time participants. Table 3.3 shows the makeup of a typical project team. Part-time members such as DBAs would not be necessary until there exist content or physical structures to implement and manage. Even then, for small shops, their role may remain part-time. BAs or SMEs are also potential part-time team members. Although they are not absolutely required during development, they do play a critical role in requirements gathering, design, and testing. Larger projects will require their expertise. It is common for large warehouse environments to have someone dedicated to the management of the warehouse, as well as an individual focused on meta data.

Table 3.3 A Typical Project Team

FULL-TIME	PART-TIME
Project manager	DBA
Data architect	Business analyst
Extract developer	Subject matter expert
Access developer	

When planning your team, it is important to remember that a single DW iteration will probably not require a team of more than four to six full-time members. If your project has many members on a single team for a single iteration, then perhaps you have too large a scope and should consider redefining the effort into smaller, incremental steps. Additionally, keep in mind that the value of your team increases as they work together and become a seasoned, cohesive group. If you find yourself constantly working with new team members, you may compromise the effort and negatively impact the time it takes to complete subsequent iterations.

Figure 3.7 illustrates how to grow your data warehouse teams as you expand your project iterations. As shown, you will probably start your warehouse effort with a team of inexperienced members. To compensate for this lack of experience, it is recommended that you hire consultants to temporarily fill that gap and provide your group with the necessary mentoring. Make sure that there is a knowledge transfer clause and a knowledge transfer plan in your agreement with the consulting firm. Once the first iteration is complete, you will have four members with warehouse experience. To handle subsequent iterations, divide the experienced crew in half, with each pair providing the experienced leadership for two new teams. You should assign new, inexperienced members with each experienced pair and give each team a new project assignment. The goal is to methodically grow your warehouse team members as you take on more warehouse iterations. By doing so, you ensure that your group has the sufficient controls and management experience in place to take on multiple, simultaneous projects.

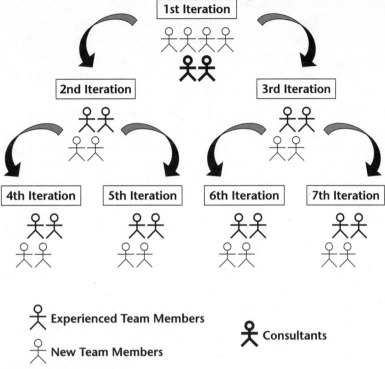

Figure 3.7 Team building.

Identifying Opportunities with the DIF Matrix[1]

All senior IT professionals have found themselves in situations where the conduct of executives, from within IT or the surrounding user communities, compromised the success of a project. Personally, I recall once vigorously trying to persuade the executive sponsor (from IT) that building a data warehouse without involving end users was not the best approach. My argument was that we should get feedback from the user community to identify potential warehouse iterations; consequently, the warehouse would be built based on relevant business requirements instead of assuming that IT knows what is best for the users. After several minutes of banter, the executive sponsor simply turned to me and said: ". . . it may not be the best way, but don't we have the right to be wrong . . . ?" Well, you can't argue with *that* logic! Yes, you are the client and ultimately, I suppose, you do have the *right* to be *wrong*.

[1] This material was taken with permission from "Fear and Loathing in Project Management," Michael L. Gonzales, *Intelligent Enterprise,* June 2001. Copyright CMP Media LLC. All rights reserved.

In these cases it is important to remove—or at the very least insulate—the project team from the potentially devastating decision making that often accompanies misguided or inexperienced executives. To that end, the Dysfunction, Impact, and Feasibility (DIF) Matrix[1] was implemented to provide a statistically valid method for quantifying and prioritizing the project's iterations, thus eliminating emotion or political intrigue. The technique was originally developed to deal with process redesign efforts whose projects may contain numerous potential starting points and iteration opportunities. However, data warehouse efforts exhibit similar project characteristics and therefore can also benefit from the methodological approach. The original approach was modified to accommodate the nuances of BI efforts.

It is best to use the DIF Matrix when you are charged with the task of recommending where to begin a project and in what order the subsequent project iterations should be implemented. It allows decision makers to set the project direction based on empirical evidence, removing emotion from the decision-making process and empowering executives to debate amongst themselves if they choose to follow the recommendations or set a different direction. Of course, a quantifiable recommendation often has the affect of neutralizing even a heated political climate.

Determining the Right Approach

The first question you need to ask is whether or not the project you are leading has multiple starting points and iterations. For instance, in data warehousing there may be many projects queued and waiting to get started. And, once you "open the doors" for business, the warehouse team may be besieged by user community requests. Marketing might be explaining that their project is more important than sales, while sales may be arguing that theirs takes priority over manufacturing. The DIF Matrix will help you deal with environments having multiple starting points. Projects that are less suitable for the approach are those with essentially a single iteration. For example, writing a report or adding a feature to an application are essentially single iteration projects with obvious starting points.

Applying the DIF Matrix

As mentioned earlier, it is important to establish a conscious method to identify and prioritize the iterations necessary to achieve the overall goal. To that end, there are 10 steps necessary to identify, define, quantify, and rank the project iteration opportunities:

1. Identify and gather antecedent documentation and known problems.

2. Set up JAD (joint application development) sessions for IT subject matter experts.

3. Select candidate iteration opportunities.

4. Have IT SMEs score candidate opportunities.

5. Create a DIF Matrix with IT candidates.

6. Set up JAD session for User Community (UC) SMEs.

7. Have UC SMEs score opportunities.

8. Average the scores from IT and UC.

9. Prioritize scores based on highest score to lowest.

10. Submit to management.

These steps are illustrated in Figure 3.8 and are detailed in the following sections.

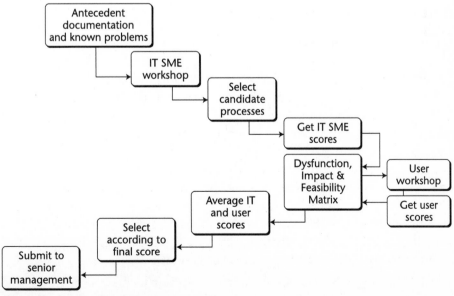

Figure 3.8 Ten steps of the DIF Matrix.

Antecedent Documentation and Known Problems

Generally speaking, much of what IT needs to do for users is already well known and documented. Too often, new consultants or IT personnel charge ahead assuming nothing has been done. Consequently, users often become frustrated because they are continually explaining to different IT people the problem at hand. To avoid adding unnecessary aggravation to any situation, we first fully investigate existing documentation and interview IT subject matter experts.

IT JAD Sessions

We always begin with the IT perspective. IT SMEs often have the advantage of knowing what is happening "under the hood." In other words, users may see one area as being of significant concern, but the real issues may be the result of other, less obvious components to the process not visible to the user. So, we conduct a joint application development session with IT SMEs to get their perspective on what iteration opportunities exist. Participants are invited by the facilitator to nominate candidate processes, giving a very brief explanation for the reasons they are nominating a particular iteration opportunity. You may even allow IT SMEs to propose tentative solutions. A limited amount of brainstorming should be allowed to motivate the nomination process. However, at no time are participants allowed to shut down or attempt to discredit any candidate nominated.

Select Candidate Iteration Opportunities

All the candidate opportunities are formally documented in the JAD sessions. One method for documenting the opportunities identified is to write them on flip chart paper that can be taped around the room for everyone to see. Figure 3.9 is an example of what you can include. If the session generates too many candidate processes, you have the option to add a filter in order to reduce the number. For example: Can this candidate opportunity be completed within 90 days? Using this type of filter is a means to focus the candidate list to only those project iterations consistent with your immediate, achievable needs. It is important to remember that although candidates may be filtered out for this cycle, they may be resurrected in future planning cycles. For each candidate process, it is recommended that you gather additional information, such as the most significant features (i.e., a reporting cycle or data quality assessment).

#1 Candidate:
Weekly sales trend report. The sales
dept. currently must put this report
together manually using weekly sales
data and performing trending in
spreadsheets.

Proposed Solution:
**Expand sales data mart reports to
calculate trends.**

Figure 3.9   Candidate nomination sample.

Get IT Scores

Once a candidate list has been formalized, IT SMEs are invited to complete
the set of three surveys described in the next sections of this chapter. The
level of dysfunction (how ineffective and inefficient the process is), impact
(how many other processes/applications/user groups are affected by the
candidate), and feasibility (how likely we are to succeed in implementing
the process) of a particular candidate are the three topics covered in the
survey set. Participants are asked to complete the survey. Answers to
the survey require the application of a simple scale from 0 to 5, with 5 being
the most dysfunctional, having the greatest impact, or being the most
feasible.

Create DIF Matrix

The core to the model is the matrix, which accounts for the survey results
of candidate processes from each participant. The scores are summed per
participant and averaged based on the number of respondents. Those candidate processes that have the highest overall DIF score are considered to
be potential starting points for the executive committee to review.

User JAD Session and Scoring

After the IT SMEs have made and scored their candidates, the User Community SMEs are invited to a JAD session. The session begins with the

candidates suggested by IT SMEs. The users are asked to add their own candidates and to complete DIF surveys for IT, as well as for their own candidate processes. IT SMEs are also invited to score the UC recommendations. By having UC and IT SMEs score each other's candidates, we balance the perspectives for each candidate and ensure that only those opportunities that best represent the needs of the organization are ranked highest.

Average DIF Scores

When IT and UC SMEs have completed DIF surveys for all candidate processes, the scores are averaged. The result is that each candidate process, whether introduced by IT or users, will have a single, overall DIF score.

Select According to Score

It is a straightforward process to rank candidate processes based on their overall DIF score. At this point, the project leader can add a weight based on extenuating factors. For example, extra weight is applied to all candidates that only require known, available resources to complete. This is a critical feature of our implementation since it empowers project leaders to have input into the entire process.

Submit to Management

This is the final step in the process—submitting a recommendation based on quantifiable, statistically valid scoring. However, in addition to using the overall weighted score, recommendations should include any process interdependencies as well. The combination of statistically valid scoring, weight accommodation and process interdependencies provides management a conscious approach for identifying the starting point of a project as well as laying out the subsequent iteration cycle.

Dysfunctional

Dysfunctional refers to how bad the processes are in terms of effectiveness and efficiency. To measure each process objectively, use questions such as:

- To what degree does the time to accomplish the process exceed the industry benchmark (or the time it takes similar companies to get it done)?

- Is the net result of the process actually being used?
- How would you grade the quality (or reliability) of data in the end product of the process?
- Are re-do's necessary in order to produce an acceptable report or end product?
- Is there duplicate or redundant data in the reports or end products?
- Does the end product or report need significant data to be manually typed in?
- Is the data consistently available?
- Just how dependent are user communities on information technology in order to get at their data (i.e., to do ad hoc reports)?
- Is the stored data that is used in the process normalized?
- Are there data integrity problems in the stored data?

On a scale from 0 to 5, a zero would mean that a process is considered to be *least* dysfunctional, whereas a five would mean that it is considered to be *most* dysfunctional.

Impact

Impact refers to how many other processes, applications, and user groups can be affected by making changes to the process under consideration, and it can be measured by answering the following questions:

- If this particular process was completely redesigned or a new one was implemented, what percentage of the overall process flow would be simplified or reduced?
- How many applications would be simplified or reduced?
- What would be your rough estimate of user community pain (family time or personal appointments missed; "I must get a life" sort of complaints; non-motivating work. . .) that can be reduced?
- In terms of percentages, what would be a rough estimate of cost reduction that could be achieved?
- What would be your rough estimate of how much reduction in person-hours devoted to this process could be achieved?

With the same scale as before, a zero grading would mean that a process has the *least* impact, whereas, a five would mean that it has the *most* impact.

Feasibility

Feasibility specifically attempts to quantify how likely we are to succeed in simplifying a particular process or process flow given the following:

- What is the probability of successfully carrying out a complete redesign of the process within three months?

- Do you consider that the business rules to carry out the process are well defined?

- Do you consider that the necessary technology to carry out a significant improvement exists?

- Do you believe we have the knowledge and understanding to complete a redesign or implement a new process?

A zero would mean that redesigning this particular process or creating a new one has the *least* feasibility, whereas a five would mean that it has the *most* feasibility.

DIF Matrix Results

Once you have identified and prioritized all the opportunities, you can use a model like that in Figure 3.10 to establish a formal procedure to complete the analysis of candidate processes. As illustrated, the model incorporates all the traditional means to flesh out and document requirements, including use case, class diagrams, and interaction diagrams. The purpose of the documentation is to understand the process under consideration and to determine how best to implement a solution.

This model results in one of three outcomes per candidate:

Quick fix.   The candidate process can be quickly addressed.

Redesign.   The candidate process will require a full redesign or new implementation plan, including analysis, design, and implementation.

Gradual improvement.   Even after analysis there is still much unknown about the process, and consequently, the candidate process must be approached via a pilot project.

Once all the DIF values are collected from both IT and the User Community, then an average score is calculated and published in the DIF Matrix (see Figure 3.11).

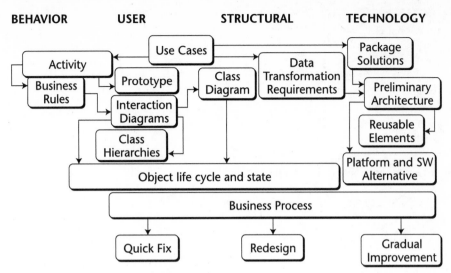

Figure 3.10   Candidate process analysis.

	Score		
	Dysfunction	**Impact**	**Feasibility**
Candidate Process	IT Avg.: ##.# UC Avg.: ##.# Average: ##.#	IT Avg.: ##.# UC Avg.: ##.# Average: ##.#	IT Avg.: ##.# UC Avg.: ##.# Average: ##.#
Candidate Process	IT Avg.: ##.# UC Avg.: ##.# Average: ##.#	IT Avg.: ##.# UC Avg.: ##.# Average: ##.#	IT Avg.: ##.# UC Avg.: ##.# Average: ##.#

Figure 3.11   DIF Matrix.

Dysfunctional Weight	#
Impact Weight	#
Feasibility Weight	#

Figure 3.12   Adding weights to the DIF calculation.

For additional control over the procedure, we have provided for a weighted average to be applied. The project leaders should reserve the ultimate decision on what those values will be. Figure 3.12 shows one example.

The following example illustrates the proposed calculation. Let's say that for a specific process, the sum of DIF scores provided by five UC SMEs is 19, 10, and 20. The average DIF is then calculated and the appropriate weights are applied. As shown in the following, the Overall Average Weighted Compound Score in this case is 4.93. The range of scores will be largely dependent on the number of SMEs and the applied weight factors. However, in order to constrain the range, we have opted to include only 0 through 5 as the scoring scale:

Dysfunction: 19 sum score / 5 UC SMEs = 3.8 avg. * 1.0 weight = 3.8

Impact: 10 sum score / 5 UC SMEs = 2.0 avg. * 1.5 weight = 3.0

Feasibility: 20 sum score / 5 UC SMEs = 4.0 avg. * 2.0 weight = 8.0

Overall Average Weighted   4.93
    Compound Score

This approach successfully identifies, defines, and quantifies candidate processes. We were able to clearly establish criteria for the executive steering committee to base their decisions on regarding a work schedule. This is quite a coup since there are always many BI opportunities to address within a highly disparate environment with several different agendas, business requirements, data, and technologies. The DIF Matrix allows you to keep the team above the fray.

Planning Subsequent Iterations

After the first iteration of your warehouse, all subsequent iterations become more focused on addressing the business requirements and less on laying out technical and data architecture foundations. This means there can be a significant difference in terms of time, costs, and resources. Where the first iteration may take 6 months, subsequent iterations of the BI environment may take as little as 6 to 9 weeks. The following sections highlight some of the key processes that you need to consider for subsequent iterations.

Defining the Scope

While it seems simple, defining the scope for warehouse iterations is problematic. With competing demands from user communities and the propensity for warehouse teams to want to accommodate requirements, it is not unusual for project planners to find themselves tackling a larger project than would be recommended.

There are at least three ways to scope data warehouse iterations:

Source availability. When planners use this to scope warehouse efforts, they are essentially saying, "We will start here because this is the best, most reliable source of data." It is certainly not the best way to scope an effort, but it is not uncommon.

Subject area. Another approach is to scope the iteration by subject area. For example, planners may simply point to Finance or Sales or Marketing and ask the warehouse team to start addressing their particular requirements. And just like using available data sources to scope your effort, this approach is less than desirable.

Strategic business question. This is the best way to scope any warehouse iteration. It is a rifle approach when compared to the first two methods. A good, strategic business question not only provides business requirement precision but also serves as an excellent analysis and design guide.

Although we will address the strategic business questions in this section, that does not mean you cannot or should not consider using the other approaches. You may even apply more than one approach to scope your efforts.

Identifying Strategic Business Questions

There is an endless supply of business questions that must be addressed in any enterprise. The endless supply is good for warehouses, since it means there is always some aspect of the business that must be dealt with. Project planners, however, must identify those questions that are most suitable for a warehouse. One quick technique is to categorize business questions into one of two groups: strategic or tactical.

Strategic business questions deal with issues such as forecasting and trend analysis. These types of questions embrace integrated data with historical perspectives and analysis not readily available in operational systems. Strategic questions include:

- What is the sale trend for Ford car parts over the past six quarters?
- What is the expected gross profit for each sales region over a 3-month period?
- What monthly premium should we charge for high-risk drivers?

Conversely, *tactical* questions focus on the day-to-day operations of a business and are handled in traditional applications such as inventory control, accounting, or sales order processing. Examples of tactical questions might be:

- What is the total dollar amount in Ford car parts in stock?
- How much gross profit did I make last month?

So why should warehouse planners focus on strategic business questions? As suggested earlier, there are several reasons:

- Warehouses maintain significant historical data and perspectives.
- Warehouses maintain complete and cleansed data.
- Warehouse information is based on integrated source data.
- Warehouses are aligned with the corporate strategy.

Answering tactical questions does not exploit the historical perspectives of a warehouse, nor do they represent corporate strategies. There is, however, a temptation by user communities and project planners to take advantage of the integrated, cleansed data of the warehouse for tactical purposes. And even though a warehouse can address some tactical questions, it is recommended that you refrain from committing warehouse resources to do so. If you have a serious tactical reporting problem, there are far less expensive ways to deal with them on the operational side. Or, you can build an ODS or reporting platform for this purpose.

Elements of good business questions are pointed out in Figure 3.13. From the example, an experienced architect readily detects constraints of analysis such as date (monthly), customers, products, and stores, as well as

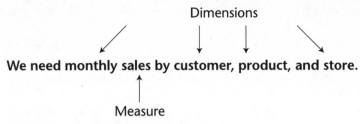

Figure 3.13   Business question components.

the measures/metrics/facts to be analyzed. A good business question serves to define the fundamental scope of the warehouse iteration. It describes much of the data needed and the potential analytical landscape to be considered.

Implementing a Project Approach

There are several formal, well-documented approaches for implementing warehouse projects. In this section we will review the following:

- BI hacking approach
- Bill Inmon's approach
- Business Dimensional Lifecycle approach (Ralph Kimball)
- The spiral approach
- IBM's approach

The list is not exhaustive. We have only selected a few approaches in order to illustrate the variety available to project planners. Of all the approaches we've listed, the spiral approach will be covered in more detail for three reasons. First, there is very little information about applying this approach to warehouse and BI efforts. Second, this approach is the only one that can be used to complement any of the other approaches mentioned, as well as others not listed. Finally, there exists mountains of readily available information on the Inmon and Kimball approaches that readers can research. We conclude this section with an overview of choosing the right approach.

BI Hacking Approach

In traditional software application development, hacking software means developing applications without sufficient planning and management. This is similar to the hacking found in warehouse efforts, which, unfortunately, is alive and well.

There are many opportunities in BI efforts to hack your way through development. Following are a few of the most common scenarios:

- No formal, permanent plan for effectively cleansing source data is implemented before moving forward with loading and access tasks.

- Rogue departments willing to sponsor their own warehouse efforts, usually under the guise of wanting to help IT. A telling signal of this is when the sponsor says, "IT is very busy, so we want to get this going ourselves. When IT has time, we will let them take it over."

- No executive sponsorship exists, and the warehouse team finds itself meandering from one iteration to the next, hoping the funding will not dry up.

Hacking is frowned upon by most professional developers, but too often is implemented by rogue or inexperienced individuals.

The Inmon Approach

Bill Inmon is often referred to as the father of data warehousing. It is his design that we follow for the atomic layer of the data warehouse. Inmon (like Kimball, in the next section) suggests that the warehouse be built iteratively—in small, fast bursts of development.[2] To do so, Inmon believes that you need to use a development life cycle that is essentially the reverse of the Systems Development Life Cycle (SDLC). Its name, CLDS, simply emphasizes that it represents the reverse of the SDLC. Where SDLC starts with requirements, the CLDS starts with data. Table 3.4 highlights the components of each.

Table 3.4   Comparison of Life Cycles

SDLC	CLDS
Requirements gathering	Implementation
Analysis	Integrate data
Design	Test for bias
Programming	Program against data

[2] Inmon, W.H. *Building the Data Warehouse, 3rd Edition* (New York: Wiley Publishing, Inc., 2002).

Table 3.4   *(Continued)*

SDLC	CLDS
Testing	Analyze results
Integration	Understand requirements
Implementation	

Business Dimensional Lifecycle Approach

Ralph Kimball is the leading voice for techniques and technologies related to dimensional data and its subsequent analysis. As such, it is not surprising that Kimball's project management perspective is referred to as The Business Dimensional Lifecycle[3] (TBDL) model. As with other development approaches, TBDL begins with the definition and scope of the project effort. This usually includes readiness assessment, business justification, resource planning, task assignments, duration, and sequencing. The resulting plan is then used to drive three tracks of effort:

Data track.   This path is focused on dimensional modeling, physical design, and the design and development of data staging.

Technology track.   There are two areas of concentration in this track. First, the architect formalizes the technical architecture. Then the technology is selected, purchased, and installed.

Application track.   The tasks of this track are focused on the specification of the end-user application and the subsequent development of that application.

The three tracks are run in parallel with each other, and once completed, they converge into a deployment phase. The Business Dimensional Lifecycle approach ends with a Maintenance and Growth stage. Of course, it is important to remember that Ralph Kimball views the warehouse as being developed in iterations, and therefore the model is used over and over with each new warehouse effort.

The Spiral Approach

The spiral approach is a unique risk mitigation tool that can be used to drive the entire project iteration or overlaid with your in-house life cycle development steps. The spiral approach contains four sections:

[3] Kimball, Ralph, *The Data Warehouse Lifecycle Toolkit* (New York: Wiley Publishing, Inc., 1998).

Quadrant 1—Determine objectives and constraints.   This quadrant is designed for project planners to examine the objectives of the particular round, along with any constraints that might be associated with it.

Quadrant 2—Risk analysis, alternatives, and prototypes.   Here is where risk is explicitly addressed. The quadrant is formally defined in order to ensure project planners identify the means by which risk can be mitigated specific to the round being implemented. For example, if we have known data quality issues that will confront us on a particular warehouse iteration, we can define and initiate a spiral round to address just that issue. Perhaps we know that integrating sales data from 20 disparate locations is going to be difficult. To address the integration risks, we would conduct a quality analysis and build an ETL prototype to see if we can achieve the level of integration necessary or come up with alternative solutions.

Quadrant 3—Develop the solution.   This is where we would blend the results of our risk analysis with development requirements in order to create the needed solution. In the preceding example, we may have identified an alternative approach to integrating sales data, which in this stage is being developed into a formal ETL process.

Quadrant 4—Plan the next phase.   As you conduct the risk analysis and adapt those results into your formal development, you potentially change how the next tasks of your overall project may be conducted. Let's say our initial plans called for nightly updates of integrated sales. After we conduct a test of the integration, we determine that updates could only be done weekly. This new information changes how subsequent tasks of the overall project iteration may be approached. This is the quadrant where you adjust your next steps.

A detailed discussion of the spiral approach goes beyond the scope of this book. The bibliography lists additional reading material. Next we discuss a recommended format to follow while using the spiral approach for your warehouse iterations.

Reducing Risk

The best process model for implementing warehouse iterations is the spiral approach. The rationale is simple: The spiral approach is the only process model that is risk-driven. All other process models and software development methods are document-driven. What's the difference? Document-driven processes assume that complete, formal documentation can be obtained. Unfortunately, to obtain clear, concise documentation, the solution must be clearly understood and defined. Therein lies the problem. Anyone with experience in warehouse-centric iterations knows that having a clear solution accurately defined prior to development is seldom the case.

How many times have warehouse planners asked users what type of strategic analysis or reporting they require only to have users respond, "Well, I need a weekly report that tells me this or that." And, the minute you deliver that report, the users say, "Good. But can you summarize this column or add another column?" Why does this happen? It's because users are not entirely sure of the decision support requirements until they see something. Then and only then will they be better able to clarify their requirements. This has always been the problem with analytical applications. Users are never sure of what they need until they have something in front of them to work with. Therefore, planners are never 100 percent sure that what they are building addresses the requirements until it is already built. This characteristic of analytical applications creates a significant amount of project risk. And it is the project risk that must be addressed, as opposed to naively attempting to build detailed, formal documentation based on a best guess. In general, the spiral approach:

- Fosters the development of specifications that are not necessarily uniform, exhaustive, or formal.
- Incorporates prototyping as a natural part of risk reduction.
- Encourages rework in the early development stages as better alternatives are discovered.

The flexibility of the spiral model to accommodate your requirements is one of its strengths.

The Spiral Approach and Your Life Cycle Model

The power of the spiral approach is not just the fact that it is risk-driven. The flexibility of the spiral approach is in its ability to be adapted for various iterations, as well as to accommodate your preferred life cycle development method. For example, your company may have spent thousands of dollars building its own in-house development life cycle. You can simply use those exact life cycle tasks, except implemented using the spiral approach. This means you get a double benefit. First, you are using a life cycle model you and your team are most comfortable with. Second, you are controlling the project iteration with an approach that explicitly addresses risk.

Warehouse Development and the Spiral Model

N5 DW Spiral is a standard format that you can follow for data warehouse iterations. Figure 3.14 illustrates the components of the approach. In it, there are four quadrants to each spiral, as well as five recommended core spiral rounds that can be planned, including a feasibility study or readiness assessment, an ETL prototype, an access prototype, complete first iteration, and all subsequent iterations. Each of these core spiral rounds are covered in the following sections.

Round 0: Feasibility Study

The entire spiral effort starts with a feasibility study. This provides an opportunity for project planners and sponsors to evaluate the organization's ability to take on a warehouse effort. It can be used to examine such issues as iteration priority, data quality, access alternatives, and cultural aspects of the organization, as well as the skill of IT and user communities. It also gives the organization a chance to better understand its warehouse requirements and the relevant impact on costs and other resources. (See Figure 3.15.)

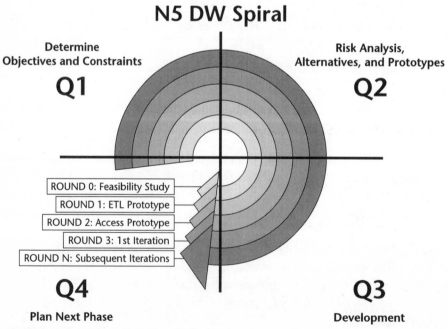

Figure 3.14 A data warehouse spiral.

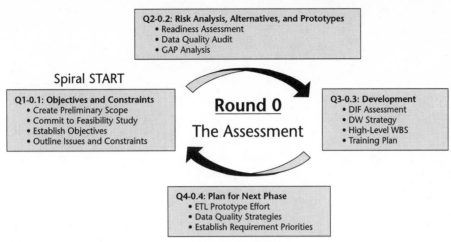

Figure 3.15   Round 0.

Round 1: ETL Prototype

This spiral round is designed as a discovery effort to clarify the most challenging issues regarding the extraction, transformation, and loading of source data. This prototype might take the form of detailed data quality evaluation and identification of alternative sources or cleansing strategies. On the other hand, you may have decided that loading large data sets within a limited window might be of greater concern, and therefore, ETL process chains might be tested for providing an optimum load time. Irrelevant of the type of ETL prototype, its range must be kept within the scope agreed to by planners. (See Figure 3.16.)

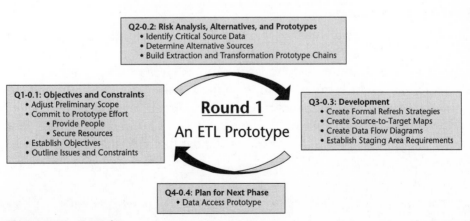

Figure 3.16   Round 1.

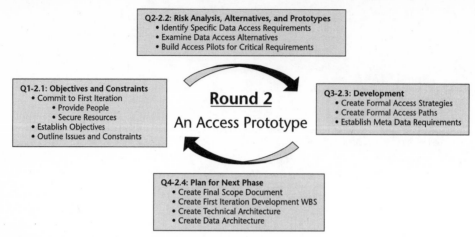

Figure 3.17   Round 2.

Round 2: Data Access Prototype

A spiral round dedicated to data access ensures that end users are given a chance to understand the technology and the type of decision support they can expect. Moreover, it affords users active participation in the requirements and design process, which is critical in analytical applications. This risk mitigation ensures that project planners do not deliver a solution unacceptable to the target user community. (See Figure 3.17.)

Round 3: The First Iteration

The first iteration of a warehouse effort deserves a unique spiral round of its own. In this iteration, planners and architects are required to lay the foundation for all future warehouse iterations. Here is where fundamental strategies and architectures are implemented. This includes identifying the hardware and software, procuring and implementing the technologies, and training staff. Because of all the extra work required during the first iteration of a warehouse, this round will most likely be the longest one to implement. (See Figure 3.18.)

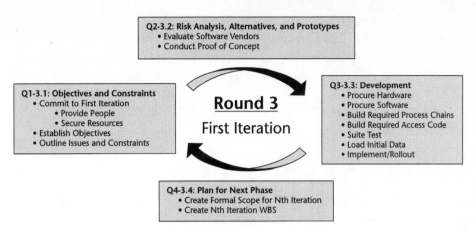

Figure 3.18 Round 3.

Round *N*: Subsequent Iterations

This round should be considered the most common spiral of your warehouse effort. This is the round that is designed to deal with all subsequent iterations once the foundation of the technology is implemented, data architecture has been adopted, and warehouse strategies defined. That is not to say that you will never implement other technology nor want to execute a pure access or ETL prototype round if necessary. However, the *N*th round is designed for short delivery cycles to ensure that users are able to quickly gain benefit from the warehouse efforts. (See Figure 3.19.)

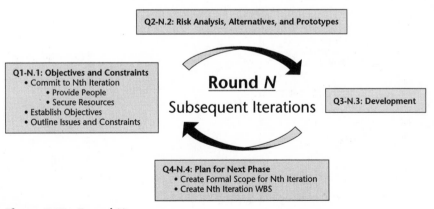

Figure 3.19 Round *N*.

The most important thing to remember when implementing the spiral approach is to be flexible and creative and to adapt the approach to the circumstance. The spiral approach is a process model. Its purpose is to help you define the entry and exit criteria between tasks and phases. Most importantly, it consciously blends risk assessment into the process before you develop or create anything. But beyond defining criteria and integrating risk assessment, the model is flexible. Exploit it.

Flattening Spiral Rounds to Time Lines

A question that invariably arises with project planners is how to apply the spirals to a time line. Although there are several approaches, one is simple and effective: V-W staging.[4] There is not much documentation on the technique, but Figure 3.20 gives you an example for placing spiral rounds onto a time line.

Figure 3.20 shows how a single round of a spiral is represented over a time line. The round is a 12-week effort, with the objectives covered in 2 weeks, risk analysis conducted in 4 weeks, development completed in 5 weeks, and next-round planning done in 1 week. You can scale the time line and the quadrants as necessary. In Figure 3.21, we see how multiple rounds are laid onto a time line. In this case, four rounds are planned over a 12-month period. As you lay each round of the spiral, you see where the name V-W comes from.

VW Staging a Spiral Round

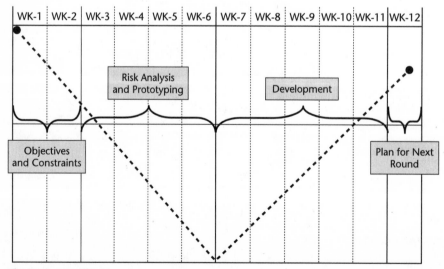

Figure 3.20   The V.

[4] Cockburn, Alistair, "Using 'V-W' Staging to Clarify Spiral Development," Salt Lake City, Utah: MethodJournal.com - http://www.methodjournal.com, 2001.

V-W staging is simply a method to address the notions of iterative, spiral, and prototyping strategies. The technique allows project planners to uncurl each spiral, arrange the spirals onto a time line to ensure continuity and manage deliverables. Following are the core benefits of implementing V-W staging:

Uncurl.   Each spiral round and its activities can lie flat against the project time line.

Arrange.   Iterations, including risk-reducing activities (i.e., prototypes), are formally tracked without sacrificing the notion of continuous progress.

Derive.   Progress is measured by delivered function as opposed to just "phase deliverables."

Manage.   Delivered increments and not just phase deliverables can be managed.

Get.   In the words of Alistair Cockburn, ". . .get the value of 'gestalt round-trip' without having to study Zen."

There is obviously more to V-W staging, but only a general understanding is necessary for our purposes.

VW Staging Multiple Rounds

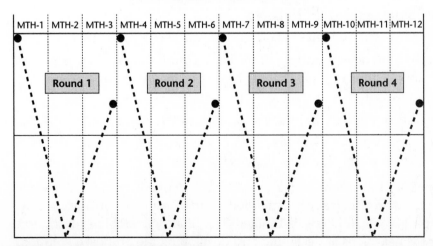

Figure 3.21   Staging multiple rounds.

The IBM Approach

The IBM approach to data warehouse and BI efforts is based on the experience of IBM's Global Services. BI engagements may encompass the entire model known as BI Solution Delivery. As shown in Figure 3.22, the model can be broken down by BI solution components, such as:

- Strategy, design, and planning
- Data warehouse development
- Decision optimization

The model starts with a Strategy engagement. This is designed to assist the client and IBM in developing an understanding of the fundamental business issues before embarking on a business intelligence project. It incorporates complete problem and solution definition, impact analysis, cost/benefit analysis, and high-level planning. Objectives concentrate on determining the requirements and focus areas, both for the short-term and longer-term. This BI engagement proposes alternative solutions to help address the priority areas including recommendations for the next steps for further, more comprehensive BI projects. The BI Strategy engagement combines activities from the IGS Method Business Intelligence Engagement Model phases of Business Discovery, Infrastructure Planning, and Solution Outline. It provides the structure to conduct the initial analysis of business requirements and then to outline plans of how business intelligence can address those requirements. It identifies the business challenges or opportunities and sets the objectives for subsequent business intelligence iterations. The main steps of the engagement plan are to:

1. Perform a high-level analysis of the business areas appropriate for the business challenge proposed.
2. Review client's business, data, and technical environments.
3. Develop an understanding of the background of the business to gain an appreciation of what the business is, what it does, and how it can be improved.
4. Identify and prioritize business opportunity focus areas.
5. Develop alternative solutions, along with a set of recommendations to address the business challenges identified.

This provides the client with a list of clearly defined business issues and solution focus areas and a recommended solution approach, including business impact, value, and cost estimates. The final deliverable is an outline plan for the next steps of designing and developing the proposed solution.

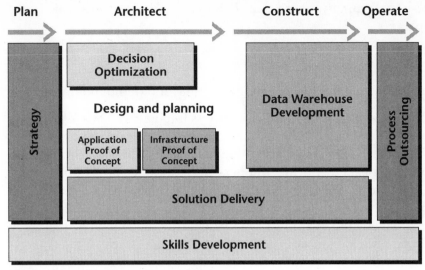

Figure 3.22   The IBM project model.

A business intelligence design and planning engagement is usually the second engagement type performed for a client. This engagement plays an important role in fully defining and planning business intelligence solutions before the implementation stage. The scope of the solution should be based on the following requirements of the organization:

- Availability
- Quality
- Accessibility
- Consistency

A Design and Planning engagement produces a high-level design for the data mart/data warehouse environment and the initial business user applications, and it defines the data needs that must be addressed. This engagement is specifically limited to the creation of a high-level system design and project plan. The work is preparatory to the implementation of a business intelligence solution based on a data warehouse infrastructure. Engagement plan steps include:

1. Develop the solution requirements, including user profiles, business rules, business terms, meta data strategy, use cases, and nonfunctional requirements.
2. Design the solution logical data model, the architecture model, and the meta data design.

3. Assess data quality, infrastructure impact, and organizational impact.

4. Develop data map and data migration plan, and design extract, transform, verification, and load processes.

5. Specify the initial release, training, testing, and deployment plans.

The third engagement is usually a Business Intelligence Data Warehouse Development engagement. It typically follows the strategy engagement and an associated design and planning. During a BI Data Warehouse Development engagement, practitioners design, build, and implement a scalable, enterprisewide data warehouse environment that might include any combination of the following components: an operational data store, a centralized data warehouse, one or more departmental data marts, and the supporting data warehouse infrastructure. The main steps of the engagement plan are to:

1. Complete the detail design specifications for the application, the data, the user interface, and the architecture.

2. Build the solution application, data, and infrastructure components.

3. Design test specifications, build the test environment, and perform all levels of testing.

4. Define the training and user support requirements, build training and support materials, and conduct training.

5. Deploy the solution.

Often organizations want to explore the benefits of data mining by undertaking a feasibility workshop, a trial, proof of concept, or a data mining quick start. These result in a Business Intelligence Decision Optimization consulting engagement, which can help you:

- Leverage industry-specific and business-specific techniques in order to provide actionable business information.

- Unearth previously unknown connections between related records and small clusters that contain unusual or suspicious records.

- Solve a variety of business issues, such as target marketing, customer segmentation, attrition prevention, churn management, loyalty management, cross-selling, product bundling, payment delinquency, fraud detection, claims prediction, defect prediction, yield maximization, channel prediction, and customized advertising.

Business Intelligence Proof of Concept engagements are often employed to test a technical aspect of a solution or to get buy-in to a solution concept.

Business Intelligence Solution Delivery engagements are typically an iterative packaging of Business Intelligence Design and Planning activities with the Business Intelligence Data Warehouse Development activities for delivering data marts and their associated applications after the data warehouse and infrastructure are in place.

Choosing the Right Approach

There are as many project approaches to data warehouse iterations as there are tools to choose from. Choose the approach that fits your requirements and level of skill. For small shops, stick to project management plans that don't require a highly skilled project management team to administer. For large shops with large project efforts, choose a project planning approach and dedicate resources to learn, implement, and administer the approach. Then establish the use of the approach to ensure consistency of application over successive iterations of your warehouse.

If you have the skill and project management resources available, consider implementing your life cycle model of choice with the spiral approach. It is a sure method for directly addressing and minimizing the risk ubiquitous to all BI efforts.

Summary

Project planners must always be aware of how a specific iteration affects the overall BI vision and how the overall vision must guide each iteration. When creating your plans and designs, consider lessons from the object-oriented crowd. There are valuable procedures and tools matured by this group that lend themselves to warehouse-centric applications. For example, use case, realization, or swim lane diagrams are a few of the well-documented techniques that communicate high-level requirements and yet serve as the basis and framework for further requirements detail and meta data gathering. Architects and planners should not constrain themselves to minimally effective techniques for requirements definition like source-to-target maps.

The DIF Matrix is one of those rare tools that, with a little practice, will become invaluable to any BI iteration. It provides a statistically valid method to prioritize iterations, which means that you and your team are no longer caught between competing interests and political agendas when determining where to start your warehouse effort or in which sequence to address the iterations. It is a method that users, project planners, and sponsors can use to understand how iterations will be prioritized and addressed. The approach can be implemented at a high level for the enterprise, allowing all the executives to determine the priority of the business requirements across your organization. Or, the approach can be implemented for a specific functional or business unit, where senior management of that unit contribute to the business requirements list, and by their own scoring, determine the priority of those business requirements in terms of dysfunction, feasibility, and impact. Moreover, the approach allows you to periodically reshuffle the business requirements deck. For example, a business requirement that is 4 months old may not be as critical to the company or even the requesting user community. The DIF Matrix can become a routine procedure conducted periodically in your organization to ensure the right business requirements are being addressed.

Analytical applications by their very nature deliver solutions that will require changes as soon as they arrive on the user's desk. Why? Because it is extremely difficult to clearly define all the requirements for an application where users cannot clearly describe to you all they need until they can see and use the application. BI applications are often considered "killer apps"—not because they represent the next technology wave, but because they are impossible to fully specify. Consequently, reducing risk is critical and should be your top priority. By experimenting and practicing with the spiral approach, you can customize a project process to your warehouse iterations that increases the likelihood of success.

Business Intelligence Architecture

Designing the Data Architecture

Key Issues:

- Several architectural design choices are available. The challenge is to select the one that best represents your requirements, corporate culture, skills, and available resources.

- Building an atomic layer is critical to most enterprisewide efforts, and there are a few alternatives to choose from. Although the traditional atomic layer is implemented in third normal form (3NF), there are successful sites implementing the atomic level in relational stars or MOLAP cubes.

- Creating an atomic layer with normalized structures with a dimensional server on top—and essentially covering the enterprise need for multidimensional data—has some tantalizing benefits.

Do not underestimate the importance of the architectural design. Your choice will dictate the future success of your warehouse. It will determine how well your warehouse can adapt to ever-changing business requirements, the scalability your environment can tolerate, the manageability of your environment, and its capability to deliver the necessary information content for user analysis.

Making a poor architectural choice early in your implementation will lead to a rigid environment that may, at best, serve the needs of the original project sponsor, but little else. You can readily identify poor architectural choices because they often lead to:

Project failures.   These are projects that never achieved what was originally intended for the sponsor and were essentially stopped. From the perspective of data architecture, project failures occur because of too much or too little complexity. Either the architect attempted a complex architecture for which the organization had little skill or resources to implement or there was no architecture considered except for buying into vendor hype about their implementation solution.

Data silos.   We all understand what a data silo is, but from an architectural point of view, the silo is not a failure to the specific user community it services. The architectural failure is apparent when attempting to share informational content or perform analysis across the silos.

Orphaned structures.   These structures or platforms are implemented for a particular project, with specific technology and techniques. The project met with minimal or even great success, but now the warehouse planners find that they must change direction for successive iterations. Perhaps the group learned so much during the iteration that they now realize the shortcomings of their architectural choices. Or, it may simply be that new management has arrived and the direction has suddenly shifted. Any previous efforts are left as-is to continue supporting user communities while the warehouse team moves toward new architectures. Of course, the plan is always to re-engineer those orphaned applications back into the new warehouse. But there is an old saying that applies to warehouses: There is nothing as permanent as a temporary solution.

Warehouse architects are challenged to build a warehouse environment that addresses the requirements outlined by executive sponsors while dealing with the realities of source systems, corporate culture, existing resource skill levels, and technical architecture limitations. Because of these many issues, an architect will typically rely on established and proven architectures to serve as the foundation of his solution.

The right data architecture must fit your organization. You cannot assume that reading this book, or any other, and implementing exactly what the author outlined is the right approach for your company, its goals, and its objectives. Instead, your data architecture must be personalized, customized to your world. This means that requirements identified by corporate sponsors, corporate culture, risk management, implementation time lines, and available resources must be factored into the architecture design. At the same time you must protect the information asset that will be created over the life of the warehouse.

Considering the variations of warehouse architectures being implemented, there are only a few viable architectural templates to consider when building your BI organization, all of which are born of literally decades of hard-won experience. The data architecture of the BI organization found in Figure 4.1 is considered a traditional, engineered approach to data warehousing. It includes all the important data structures used in warehousing:

- Operational data store (ODS)
- Staging area
- Atomic layer
- Data dart

We've discussed the characteristics of each data structure in Chapters 1 and 2. Here we want to explore the blending of relational and multidimensional structures, as well as varied data delivery alternatives. The chapter starts with a broad discussion of traditional data architectures from which project planners can choose, including different types of atomic layers, data marts, and combinations of the two. We then examine the data models necessary to design your choice of architecture, as well as the expected deliverables of that design effort. The chapter ends with a recommendations matrix to help you decide which data architecture is right for your organization.

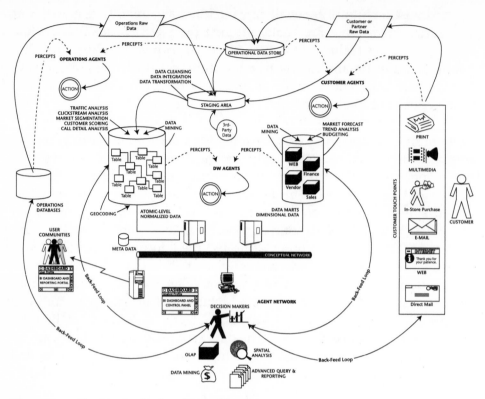

Figure 4.1 The BI organization data architecture.

Choosing the Right Architecture

As technology advances it presents us with new architectural opportunities. In the past there were clear choices driven mainly by the technology. You could implement your warehouse as a centralized data warehouse in a relational database, or you could implement a MOLAP warehouse using RDBMS mainly for staging and ETL efforts. And, of course, you could blend the two technologies into a single, cohesive solution for your organization. But as technology marches on, the variations of architectures change as well. Leading database vendors continually siphon off the technological advantages of niche players, and this practice serves as a catalyst for niche players to relentlessly pursue other differentiators. The data architect is left to decipher the vendor hype and the real technology benefits from its shortcomings.

An extract of the fundamental data structures for our BI organization is in Figure 4.2, which shows an atomic layer implemented in a relational database in third normal form. The diagram also includes data marts that can be implemented as star schemas, MOLAP cubes, or stars with cubes. The first step in the data propagation is from the operational systems (production systems as well as the ODS) into the staging area. Once staged, all necessary data is first populated into the atomic layer of the warehouse. From the atomic layer, data is distributed to all subsequent BI applications and data structures, such as the data marts pictured in Figure 4.2. Reporting and analysis is conducted against either the atomic layer or the data marts.

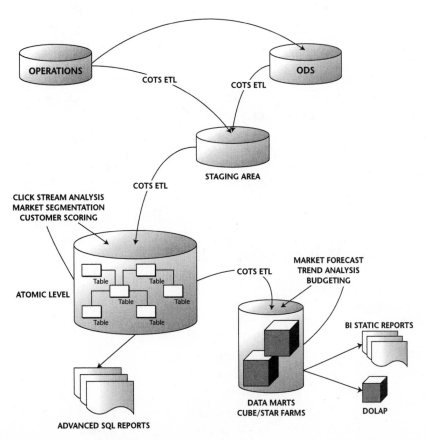

Figure 4.2 Traditional high-level data architecture.

This is probably the most common form of enterprisewide data architecture for warehousing. It is often referred to as an "architected" data warehouse with dependent data marts. The basis of enterprisewide data is found in the atomic layer. All multidimensional content is found at the data mart level in star schema data structures or MOLAP cubes or both. These structures represent the transformation point from normalized atomic data to dimensional data. And, if that data transformation is at the natural grain of the organization, then multidimensional analysis will be capable to the lowest meaningful level, within the scope of the subject area covered by that star or cube. Moreover, these structures can serve as the source of multidimensional data for subsequent OLAP-centric uses.

This traditional structure of a normalized, enterprisewide atomic layer and subject-area-specific data marts creates a data dependency. As the data cascades from one structure to another, it mutates, evolving toward the informational content suited for that structure. From staging to atomic to dimensional data and ultimately to user reporting and analysis, there exists a dependency among the data structures themselves and the data they serve up. (See Figure 4.3.)

As effective as this architecture is for enterprise deployment of BI, it is not the only viable architecture available. In Chapter 2 we discussed the characteristics of each data structure. Here we want to explore the blending of relational and multidimensional structures, as well as data delivery alternatives that might better support your efforts.

Data Structure Dependency

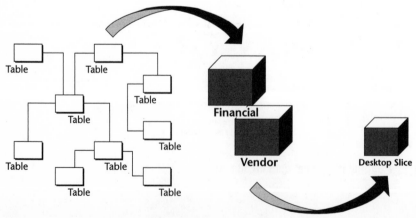

Figure 4.3   Data structure dependency.

Atomic Layer Alternatives

For many, the only architecture for an enterprise atomic layer is a normalized model implemented in an RDBMS. There does exist a significant history of success with this type of architecture. However, multidimensional atomic layers have also met with success. Investigating this option includes multidimensional data stored in either relational technology using star schemas or MOLAP cubes using technology such as DB2 OLAP Server.

Figure 4.4 shows an atomic layer implemented using proprietary cube technology in a pure MOLAP environment or a farm of relational data structures implemented as stars with conformed dimensions and fact tables. In this structure the cubes/stars themselves represent the scope of subject areas covered by the warehouse. They can be physical cubes as well as cube views of physical cube data. As for the stars, they can be implemented in classical structures and snowflakes. They can include aggregated tables, SQL views, and any number of techniques used in relational environments to improve performance and functionality. The technologies and techniques in both stars and cubes provide significant flexibility and coverage of your multidimensional data.

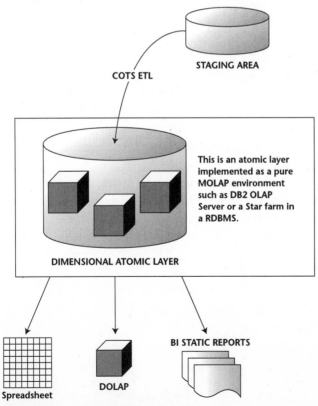

Figure 4.4   Dimensional atomic layer.

Implementing your atomic level in MOLAP does not preclude you from implementing OLAP technology further downstream, nor does it eliminate the possibility of building departmental data marts, as shown in Figure 4.4. As a matter of fact, a MOLAP atomic layer implemented with DB2 OLAP Server makes an obvious foundation of multidimensional analysis by any variety of leading data access techniques and technologies. DB2 OLAP Server has native driver support in leading OLAP-centric technologies such as Cognos, Business Objects, Brio, and Microsoft Excel. It is arguable that such an atomic layer can actually enhance and facilitate OLAP usage.

A multidimensional atomic layer can also be implemented as stars in a relational database using the "bus" architecture of conformed dimensions and fact tables. Properly implemented, this architecture, purposed by Ralph Kimball, can be a successful alternative to multidimensional data implemented in proprietary structures. Of course, star schemas are not MOLAP or ROLAP. Instead, a star schema superimposes multidimensional data in a relational database. Consequently, you still need OLAP-centric technology to fully benefit from the structures themselves and the multidimensional data they serve.

There is another alternative for creating your atomic layer, which is a combination of atomic layer data with a dimensional engine that sits on top—a dimensional cap, if you will, for the atomic layer as illustrated in Figure 4.5. This cap is more than a data mart farm implemented in persistent data structures like star schemas or pure MOLAP technology that is fed warehoused data from your atomic level. This cap is established specifically to serve up multidimensional data to the enterprise by exploiting the actual data stored at the atomic layer, thus minimizing, if not eliminating, the need for data propagation from atomic data stores to multidimensional data stores.

At first glance you might be thinking we are recommending two atomic layers. That's not so. We are recommending only a single atomic layer in 3NF or star schemas (depending on the vendor you select to implement for your dimensional cap) with a multidimensional server on top. This server can be a platform implemented as ROLAP or HOLAP technology. Why? Well, having an atomic level is a proven, widely accepted technique to ensure enterprisewide warehouse data at the natural grain of your business. Furthermore, OLAP is a critical component to your analytical landscape. Implementing the two is not an option for many organizations. The only issue remains how to optimize the process to ensure atomic-level data across the enterprise while serving up timely dimensional data to a broad and hungry audience.

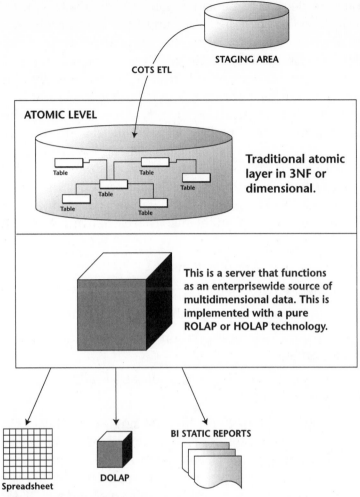

STAGING AREA

COTS ETL

ATOMIC LEVEL

Table

Table

Table

Table

Table

Table

Traditional atomic layer in 3NF or dimensional.

This is a server that functions as an enterprisewide source of multidimensional data. This is implemented with a pure ROLAP or HOLAP technology.

BI STATIC REPORTS

DOLAP

Spreadsheet

Figure 4.5   A dimensional cap.

Atomic data provides a solid foundation and is an excellent source of informational content for many BI-centric applications, but often further processing must be done to ready the data for dimensional analysis. To that end, we usually implement physical star schemas or MOLAP cubes (or both) to serve as a middle layer of persistent data structures to address the transition from atomic data to OLAP analytics. We build ETL processes that take the atomic data and propagate it into these structures and attempt to make the disparate data stores (atomic and data marts) act as one syn-chronized environment.

There are several inefficient and inherent problems with this traditional architecture, as well as several benefits. You can argue that the physical movement of data from one structure to another may introduce potential problems to the data. This issue is not likely for the professional architect. Nevertheless, some vendors like to feed this fear to clients. In reality, the single biggest issue with multiple data structures is the batch window necessary to keep them all effectively updated. It is the necessary size of this batch window that constrains the time lines of available data for final BI applications.

Until recently, technology to support an enterprisewide dimensional cap was not in place. There have been technologies that served up multidimensional data to a wide audience, but the data was typically handicapped with performance and scale problems. That is not the case with today's technology, which provides:

- Support for a full range of BI applications

- A robust development environment

- Support and administration for potentially thousands of users

- Centralized, enterprisewide administration of the entire multidimensional implementation

- A seamless integration for OLAP-centric applications and the data on which they are based

Note that this technology is not the brainchild of a single company or the next killer application. Instead, it represents an industry trend, migrating from BI tools and applications toward BI, enterprisewide platforms.

You have two primary alternatives to creating a dimensional cap to your atomic layer data: a ROLAP platform on a 3NF atomic layer and a HOLAP platform on a star Schema atomic layer. We describe these approaches in the following sections.

ROLAP Platform on a 3NF Atomic Layer

The first option is exemplified by technology from MicroStrategy. In its current release, the MicroStrategy Intelligent Server provides ROLAP functionality to a broad array of OLAP-centric and standard reporting tools and dynamically facilitates the transition from normalized atomic-level data to OLAP analysis without having to implement, maintain, and support interim persistent data structures.

A MicroStrategy implementation involves a combination of ROLAP and MOLAP-centric technology. It has earned its reputation as a strong ROLAP engine; however, with their concept of caching the requested data once a report is requested, it can afford similar performance of MOLAP technology for popular requests. It is reasonable for users to assume that the analysis will often remain within the domain of the original report requested even though data pivoting, slicing and dicing, and rollup/drilldown are being conducted. So even though the implementation of MicroStrategy is often associated with a pure ROLAP solution, in fact, the Intelligent Server exploits sufficient technologies that resemble the functionality found in HOLAP solutions.

Although MicroStrategy can work with either normalized or denormalized data, it is often best implemented on top of a normalized data source. Therefore, it is recommended that MicroStrategy be on your short list of dimensional cap technology if you plan a 3NF atomic layer.

HOLAP Platform on a Star Schema Atomic Layer

The second option is to use HOLAP technology to serve up multidimensional data to your enterprise. Under this scenario, the data architect implements a dimensional cap that provides a blend of MOLAP and ROLAP-centric technology. This option provides the same functionality as found with the ROLAP cap, except here we have a blended approach between the best of MOLAP characteristics with the scalability of ROLAP-centric capability.

The technology for this platform is DB2 OLAP Server Version 8.1, using hybrid analysis that sits on a dimensional source of atomic data. Architects can define how much of the data is stored in MOLAP form and how much analysis will be left for the star schema tables, using ROLAP to access the required data. DB2 OLAP Server will retrieve the "cells" from the relational database (star schema tables) as if they physically resided on the cube storage. Hybrid analysis eliminates the need to load and store members and their data with the physical cube itself, combining the efficiency of mass data scalability with the sophisticated data analysis and rapid reporting of a MOLAP server.

Similar to the way MicroStrategy is often typecast as only a ROLAP solution, DB2 OLAP Server is too often associated with only MOLAP technology. In fact, both MicroStrategy Intelligent Server and DB2 OLAP Server are migrating toward an enterprisewide solution for dimensional data. The only difference is that MicroStrategy relies on the strength and experience of ROLAP, and IBM relies on the MOLAP strength of DB2 OLAP Server. In either case, DB2 OLAP Server or MicroStrategy Intelligent Server provide a means to fully exploit atomic layer data, with no use of additional persistent structures in the case of MicroStrategy or minimal use of additional persistent structures in the case of DB2 OLAP Server.

Data Marts

Data marts are yet another area of dispute among warehouse practitioners. There seems to be constant debate regarding the implementation of star schemas in an RDBMS versus proprietary cube technology. Certainly, the star structure makes up for the shortcomings of cubes such as scalability. However, cubes are the solution to the single most glaring issue with stars because they actually provide you with OLAP functionality (the slicing/dicing, rollup/drill-down functionality that everyone gets all excited about). Stars by themselves are not OLAP. If implemented correctly, a star will serve up denormalized, symmetrical data that is outstanding for OLAP analysis, but you still need some means for performing the online, analytical processing. This can be achieved to some extent with SQL; however, the most robust OLAP environments employ OLAP technology from leaders like Cognos, Business Objects, and IBM.

So, we know that for OLAP-centric applications, we need OLAP technology if we implement star schemas. But if we are implementing OLAP technology, why would we need to implement stars? Actually, stars bring exceptional value to architectures. Some of the primary benefits found in staging data in a star schema for supporting OLAP applications include the following:

Integrated.   Data stored in star schemas is already integrated, either as a result of being imported from the atomic-level data warehouse or from ETL processes directly from staged data. Once the data is correctly populated in the stars, all subsequent SQL extractions for data headed to cubes will be valid. This eliminates the potential problems of using SQL generated by report writers, for example, to make the jump from atomic layer source data, or worse, operational systems.

Summarized/precalculated/derived.   Much of the aggregation, precalculation, and derived data requirements of the subsequent OLAP applications can be completed within a star data mart. For example, if your OLAP tool does not allow you to implement limited prequery calculations to the cube, you can use a SQL statement to extract and precalculate data from the star and put the results in a launch table or file for loading into the cube. Another illustration of a star's value has to do with aggregation flexibility. If the cube analysis normally works from monthly data and requires daily-level granularity only once in a while, using a star could facilitate the flexibility required. You can have SQL statements that extract and pre-aggregate your monthly data and place it in aggregated fact tables or launch tables/files as needed.

Adjusted for business rules.   The star is a perfect environment to implement security access, accountancy issues (for example, currency), or organizational/operational/legal structures. That does not mean that this functionality is not available in OLAP technology. However, each OLAP vendor addresses these issues with varying degrees of success. The architect can adjust the dimensional data for business rules at the star level and not worry about the limitations of the various OLAP technologies that might be implemented in their environment.

Extensive attribution.   MOLAP cubes frequently contain less attribute information about members than that found in star schemas. There is a technical reason for this: Cubes suffer from inflation. Consequently, cubes will refrain from heavily attributed data to ensure a minimum cube size. That does not mean that the attributes are not important to OLAP analysis. A star schema can maintain all the attributes required for OLAP applications, which means that the OLAP technology can select attributes as necessary.

Historical integrity.   When properly designed, star schemas can deal extensively with historical data, whereas MOLAP cube technology differs greatly in its ability to address history. For example, if you have built a cube for analyzing monthly sales and you want to add a new month, you may need to drop and re-create your cube with the new data. DB2 OLAP Server does the best job of incrementally updating the cubes. But there are many other vendors whose OLAP tools do a very poor job at handling incremental updates—if they handle them at all. Stars can readily be designed for incremental updates.

Drill-through/Drill-down.   A star facilitates the use of dimensional analysis even if a drill-through is required from a cube application into the relational data store or drill-down is necessary for more granular, dimensional analysis. DB2 OLAP Server with Hybrid Integration Services is one such example of this technique.

Of course, one of the greatest advantages for exploiting stars is that the architect must go through the challenge of correctly building and loading the star itself. This effort ensures that the data stored is symmetrical, equally available, cleansed, and complete. Consequently, this guarantees that all subsequent uses of the data are based on a solid foundation. Moreover, the star will provide a "single version of the dimensional truth," irrelevant of the variety of OLAP technology that might be implemented across your organization.

Atomic Layer with Dependent Data Marts

Building an atomic layer with dependent data marts is most effective for an enterprisewide effort. Often referred to as an *enterprise data warehouse*, the design creates an environment that exploits the flexibility and scalability of a normalized atomic layer founded on principles espoused by Inmon, while establishing an effective analytical landscape afforded by data marts based on star schemas defined by Kimball. This structure epitomizes the blend of best-of-breed strategies for data warehousing.

Together, Inmon's and Kimball's methods provide an effective means for enterprises to methodically tackle the volumes of potentially disparate source data while remaining nimble to strategically adjust the warehouse direction. Figure 4.6 illustrates the elements of this design. As shown, the foundation of the entire warehouse is the atomic layer, which serves as the wellspring from which all data in the warehouse will be propagated and made available for reporting and analysis. The data flows from the atomic layer into departmental data marts, either Star schemas or proprietary cube technology. From there, slices of dimensional data are served up to the user communities.

This architecture ensures a centralized, persistent data structure (atomic layer) that grows by iterations, essentially becoming a "sum of its parts," where advanced SQL reporting can be applied across the enterprise—as opposed to merely a subject area. It is an engineered approach that ensures historical integrity, referential integrity, and central control of meta data.

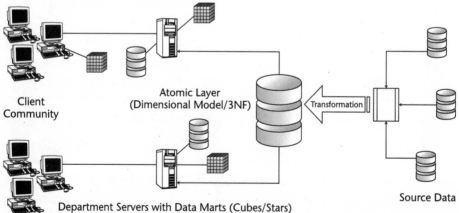

Figure 4.6 Atomic layer with dependent data marts.

Each data mart iteration requires that source data be loaded into the atomic layer first. Then that data becomes available for use at the data mart level. This requires not only additional work and sufficient time for implementation but also corporate discipline. The organization must be prepared to adhere to the engineering discipline in order to fully exploit the benefits of this structure—a task that is often easier said than done.

Organizations drive executives to BI building agendas that may not tolerate the time frames required to implement a more methodical warehouse structure, even though that structure would best serve the enterprise as a whole going forward. Consequently, executives too often decide to build "interim" solutions in order to get the results they seek quickly and avoid the disciplined approach. They rationalize this strategy by describing their solution as only "interim" with the idea that they will allow IT to incorporate the permanent solution in the future. This, of course, creates the potential for orphaned structures discussed at the beginning of this chapter.

Independent Data Marts

For those warehouses with only one or two well-defined and constrained subject areas, perhaps independent data marts are appropriate. The obvious difference between this approach and the dependent data mart strategy described previously is the lack of an atomic layer as illustrated in Figure 4.7.

The single most influential factor for selecting independent data marts is implementation speed. These types of warehouse structures can be implemented very quickly and, therefore, generally at a cost savings when compared to the atomic layer with dependent data mart strategy described previously.

This warehouse approach principally suffers from a lack of meta data control and, therefore, integrity. This may not be much of an issue if there is only one small data mart. However, when another data mart is built, they do not share a centralized pool of precleansed and integrated data with consistently applied business rules. Instead, each data mart extracts, integrates, cleanses, and maintains its own business rules. This creates an environment where reports from each data mart containing similar elements—for example, profit—may have completely different values. This leads to another problem with independent data marts: stovepipes. Each data mart built in this manner is essentially a disparate data silo disjointed from every other data mart.

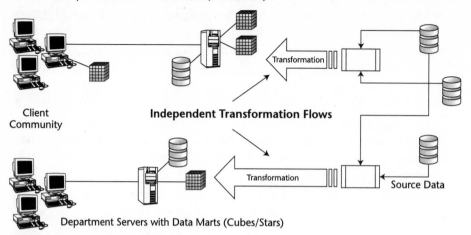

Figure 4.7 Independent data marts.

It may have been widely known to warehouse architects that Inmon is against building independent data marts. However, what many may not be aware of is that Kimball is equally critical of this type of architecture. The warehouse, according to Kimball, is a union of data marts organized around a bus architecture made of conformed dimensions and fact tables. This bus allows queries to traverse multiple data marts, and it therefore eliminates the problem of stovepipes.

Data Delivery Architecture

Message broker technology—like MQSeries from IBM—is another data architecture component that you should have in your arsenal and must be considered for enterprisewide reporting architecture design. This is the technology that enables enterprise application integration (EAI). Whether you called it EAI or message brokering, this is a core data delivery mechanism for your enterprise BI efforts.

The basic premise for considering the implementation of a message broker is to eliminate the classic spaghetti code challenge of developing and maintaining point-to-point integration. Spaghetti code is just one symptom of disparate data. Other effects include the following:

- Disparate data makes ad hoc reporting difficult, if not impossible. This is indigenous to environments where applications are implemented without an enterprise reporting strategy.

- Disparate data creates system complexity and therefore prohibits the fostering of power users, since programmers may be the only means for performing the reporting tasks.

- The lack of integrated and accurate data sources complicates management reporting.

- Disparate data creates a heavy reliance on IT for reporting requirements and consequently creates a bottleneck for user communities.

- IT projects never seem to reach closure, since disparate data creates hidden complexities that are often overlooked during project planning.

Highly disparate data leads to complex integration. When you consider that each application has to share some type of data with every other system in the network, your integration points and problems grow geometrically as you add applications. To further complicate matters, consider integration issues such as operating systems, file structures, and network communications, as well as the fact that each integration point probably contains several individual subcomponents. To hard-code programs to deliver specific data between two applications, a strategy known as point-to-point integration is an unsupportable endeavor destined to fail.

Ultimately, any successful approach to resolving data integration among disparate sources must adhere to one simple objective: reducing the complexity. The most efficient means to reduce complexity is to implement an infrastructure that replaces hard-coded, point-to-point solutions with a standardized messaging system that transports data from application to application and from data sources to target databases. Establishing this foundation cuts the integration requirements in half. Instead of writing code for each point-to-point requirement, you only need to attach a candidate application to the message system. Therefore, each application in the enterprise requires one integration point with all other applications. That integration point establishes the application's connectivity with the enterprise instead of to a particular application. Applications gain independence from each other, but the architecture provides the conduit for data to flow freely between applications. IT staff can now readily fit new applications into the message broker environment by focusing only on the integration requirements to the message queue. By the same token, they can easily remove applications from the broker environment without compromising the movement of enterprise data. This is known as *single-point integration*.

There are additional benefits of a message broker environment that go beyond eliminating point-to-point complexity. This type of technology establishes a centralized meta data repository that ensures information about the data being transported around the enterprise is formally documented and centrally administered. If there are any changes to business rules, IT staff can go to a single place to make that adjustment, rather than searching lines of spaghetti code.

The centralized control of meta data, coupled with the capability to move, cleanse, and transform data through the enterprise, makes an EAI architecture a perfect launch site for both tactical data structures and the data warehouse itself. You simply attach the necessary components (such as the staging area for the warehouse or the ODS or reporting database) to the message queue as you would any other application. All of the established meta data and queuing technology is exploited by the warehouse effort. For example, a warehouse team would normally have to collect and document the business rules that define how to handle the application data; the message broker architecture provides this information in a centralized meta data repository.

Figure 4.8 shows a single-point integration model for data delivery. As shown, the message broker technology serves as a data delivery platform, servicing the applications of the enterprise, as well as all the enterprisewide reporting, both tactical and strategic. The warehouse ODS can enjoy a simple single-point integration with the balance of the enterprise community.

In essence, the message broker can be divided into four distinct components:

Network.   This is the tangible hardware needed to ensure that the data can be accessed from one point and populated at a target destination.

Message.   A message is similar to a data record except that the message contains not only the data but also instructions on what to do with the record in hand.

Connectors.   Message brokers typically maintain a wide array of native driver support for connecting data sources to the message broker environment.

Administrator.   An advantage of a message broker environment is that it is centrally controlled. From a single command station, IT personnel can define a message and the relevant process chain, including transformations and target destinations. Consequently, a single meta data repository is established that documents the source data that impacts enterprise reporting.

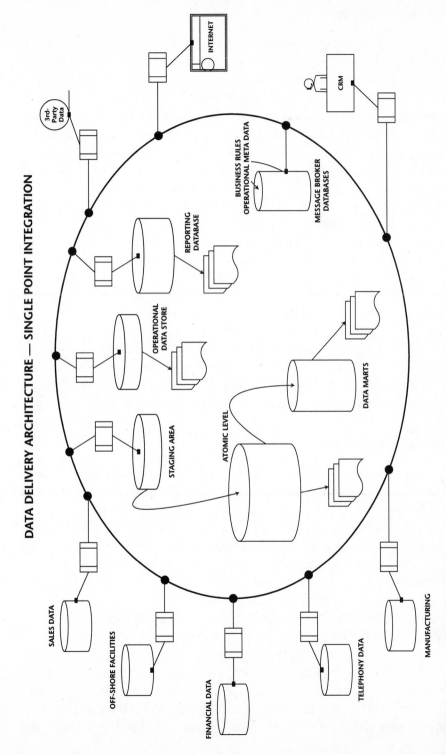

Figure 4.8 Data delivery architecture.

EAI and Warehousing

From a pure warehouse perspective, there are plenty of benefits to using EAI technology. For instance, you can capture and move data at the event level. This means that the warehouse can stage data using the "drip method," such that as the message queue moves data, data tagged for the warehouse is placed into a staging area one record at a time. Data needed to refresh the warehouse is collected at the time of the event; consequently, there is no need to batch volumes of data across the enterprise. This is an important aspect of EAI that can help you establish zero-latency in your BI environment.

Another reason to consider this technology is its ability to move atomic data. Refer to the following section, *Comparing ETL and EAI*. With this granular data you create a perfect place to determine whether the data being moved is different from the data already recorded in the warehouse. This process is referred to as "finding the delta." It can be a resource-intensive task, but the EAI structure becomes that front line of technology that can assist without adding much overhead to the movement of data.

Finally, EAI can perform light transformation and cleansing. This is a boon for those concerned with batch windows. The message queue can capture data, tag delta data, do light transformation, and stage the data for the warehouse refresh programs, taking a considerable load off your nightly batch processes and therefore expanding your window.

Comparing ETL and EAI

ETL and EAI solutions differ considerably in their functionality and approach to moving and transforming data. ETL tools are set-oriented technology; they are primarily designed to take source data and integrate, transform, reorganize, and ultimately populate this evolved data set into target structures—for example, an atomic-level warehouse. These tools are designed to work on large sets of data that require complex integration and transformation. ETL is typically characterized as affording a synchronous one-way movement of data in a batch process.

EAI tools, on the other hand, represent technology designed to provide automated and seamless data movement. The objective of EAI technology is to guarantee acquisition, distribution, and delivery of data from a source to target. And, because message (data set) acquisition can be controlled at a granular level, the implementation of EAI can ensure minimal data latency. In other words, the movement of data can be driven by time or events. If you choose event-driven movement of data, your EAI implementation can monitor specific events in your enterprise that trigger the technology into action. EAI tools are essentially built to deal with random, singular business events.

The difference between these two technologies is not trivial. It is important to refrain from making the message broker your ETL tool and vice versa.

Expected Deliverables

Several deliverables are expected when you design your data architecture. Not only must you decide on the overall data architecture of your warehouse environment, but then you must begin creating and compiling all the necessary models to support your decision and subsequent iterations. This section examines the modeling techniques and diagrams employed to support the effort. We start by outlining the expected deliverables.

You will notice that the vast majority of deliverables are models or diagrams used to assist the data architect's understanding of the subject area and to provide unique views of the target data. The major purpose of modeling is to communicate the end users' view of the organization's data to those who will design the system. Models answer questions such as:

- How fast and how frequently do users want to access the data?
- Where does the source data come from?
- With what frequency is the source data being updated?
- What transformations will be required to the source data to meet the requirements of the target structure?
- What calculations and derived data will be required?
- What are the capacity requirements on the target systems?
- What are the relationships between business entities?
- What checks and constraints are in place to enforce known business rules?

Although the models should not be tied to a particular technology, or product, the types and number of models you use in warehouse efforts will nevertheless be dictated by the target architecture.

It is recommended that you utilize a combination of the models presented. Each model builds upon the other, giving the architect more and more layers of detail. Your modeling effort culminates with a formal foundation that demonstrates a design that meets user requirements.

Table 4.1   Core Models Required

MODELS	ARCHITECTURES		ATOMIC LEVEL WITH DEPENDENT DATA MARTS
	CENTRALIZED ATOMIC LEVEL	INDEPENDENT DATA MARTS	
Business logical model	X	X	X
Atomic-level model	X		X
Dimensional model		X	X
Star schema		X	X

At the very least, there are two distinct assets that are a necessary result of your data architecture:

Atomic-level model.   The atomic level is the front line of your warehouse. Therefore, the model is used to describe and define the core set of data structures that will be utilized to store and manage the most fundamental data, cornerstone to all subsequent warehouse-centric uses of that data.

Data mart models.   If you choose an architecture that uses data marts, you will generally want to create two models that support the data mart: dimensional models and the star schema. A matrix in Table 4.1 illustrates the models necessary.

Another model that may or may not be required is the business logical model (BLM). It is discussed later in the chapter; however, for now, it is important to recognize that this may also be necessary as a deliverable. All models that directly relate to the atomic or data mart levels are discussed in the following sections of this chapter.

In addition to the traditional models describe previously, there are several information assets that are helpful to the architect and project planners:

Metric map.   Building a metric map provides designers with meta data and insight into the calculation of derived data. Architects often find that users differ on how derived data is calculated. For example, "cost" might be calculated one way for the finance department and another way to compute sales commissions. Going through the exercise of developing metric maps will isolate those inconsistencies. Figure 4.9 is an example of a metric map.

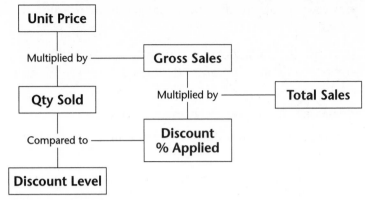

Figure 4.9   Metric map.

Source-to-target map.   Here is a common method to document the extraction and transformation required to go from source to the target data store. Typically implemented in a spreadsheet, it is used to show the transformation requirement to extract and source data elements and load them into a target data structure.

Data flow diagram (DFD).   Unlike the source-to-target mapping method, a DFD is actually a modeling technique as well as a data dictionary. This model is explicitly designed to address data issues at the design level as opposed to leaving it up to developers during the actual construction of the code.

Metric maps, source-to-target maps, and DFDs all provide a formal understanding of the source data required and transformed into the target data structures defined by the chosen architecture.

Modeling the Architecture

During the mid to late 1980s, there was considerable debate over the two data warehouse architectures prescribed by Bill Inmon and Ralph Kimball. Many believed that Inmon was a proponent of building an atomic layer and Kimball emphasized independent data marts. In fact, both Inmon and Kimball believe that an atomic layer is critical to the long-term viability of any warehouse effort. The difference between the two approaches is in terms of how that atomic layer would be implemented. Inmon is a proponent of a normalized atomic layer, whereas Kimball believes in an atomic layer implemented as a denormalized model consisting of conformed dimensions and fact tables.

We will use the Inmon approach to the atomic layer in this chapter. It is characterized as follows:

- The atomic layer contains the lowest level of granularity of the entire data warehouse and subsequently dictates the lowest possible level of analysis.

- The atomic-layer data is often at the transactional level.

- The atomic layer initiates and maintains historical integrity for the entire warehouse.

- Data architecture is normalized to ease data integration and provide extensibility and flexibility for future warehouse iterations.

- The atomic layer represents the front line of source data integration, transformation, and cleansing for the entire warehouse.

- The atomic layer maintains static data that is refreshed according to business requirements.

The atomic-layer model is derived from a business logical model for the subject area defining the warehouse iteration at hand. Consequently, when modeling your atomic level, the best place to start is with a BLM. This begs the question, where do you get one?

Business Logical Model

The BLM is considered a composite of two subordinate diagrams: high-level diagram and attributed relational diagram. Although the high-level diagram is considered optional, it does help a data architect go through the discovery process in order to document an organization's entities and their relationships based on business rules. If the organization has an enterprise model, the high-level diagram can be derived from that body of work. If no enterprise model exists, the data architect has three alternative strategies:

- Build the high-level BLM by reverse engineering production systems relevant to the subject area.

- Conduct modeling sessions with subject area experts and business analysts to identify entities pertinent to the subject area.

- Use business forms (order, invoices) and reports relevant to the subject area to discern the business entities for the BLM.

Generally, there are two steps to building a high-level BLM diagram. First, the architect must identify the high-level business entities that fall under the scope area for the warehouse iteration. Usually these entities are business objects of importance, for example: customers, orders, products, and so on. It is common to collapse entities together when creating the diagram from existing production models. For example, the CONTACT table may become part of the CUSTOMER entity in the BLM. The second step is to define the relationship between the business entities, for example, one-to-one, one-to-many, and so on.

A fully attributed BLM, also referred to as a mid-level relational diagram, is your real goal (see Figure 4.10). This model requires the architect to expand the high-level diagram in the following ways:

- Identify all relevant entities for the subject area.

- Add entities that help resolve many-to-many relationships, if necessary.

- Identify primary key and foreign key relationships.

- Normalize the content and include supertype/subtype and domain entities.

- Include all attributes for each entity.

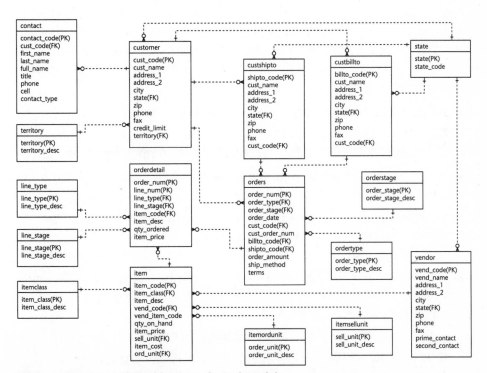

Figure 4.10   An attributed business logical model.

Copyright © 1999. The Focus Group, Ltd.

Atomic-Level Model

Once you have created the BLM for the subject area, you are now ready to develop the atomic-level model (see Figure 4.11). This process consists of the following steps:

1. Include all data necessary to exploit the warehouse iteration effort.
2. Remove operational data.
3. Add time to entity key values as well as non-key attributes.
4. Collapse nonhistorical entities.
5. Include derived data.
6. Include aggregated data.

Dealing with derived and aggregated data may entail additional diagrams typically associated with data marts, including the dimensional model and metric maps.

Of data necessary for the atomic layer, you should consider loading only data that adds analytical value for the warehouse effort. This seems obvious, but invariably ETL jockeys tend to bring over more data than needed for the task at hand. And, of course, this introduces all sorts of issues, such as data quality, cleansing, and integration. Moreover, your warehouse will grow disproportionately between the data actually being used and data being stored. When thinking about data to pull into the atomic layer, consider the following:

- All required data for the project scope should be included.
- Supplemental data should be considered only if the cost of inclusion is minimal and lack of data would result in compromised usability.
- If cost of supplemental data is high and lack of data would result in compromised usability, consider expanding the project scope.
- Remove operational data that provides no analytical value to the data warehouse. For example, a login may be useful for the production system, but it would normally not provide analytical fodder.
- Add time-variant data in order to maintain historical integrity. Time must be incorporated as part of the key structure as well as a non-key attribute. (See Chapter 2.)
- Consider geocoding address data. Refer to Chapter 16 for more information regarding spatial data and analysis.

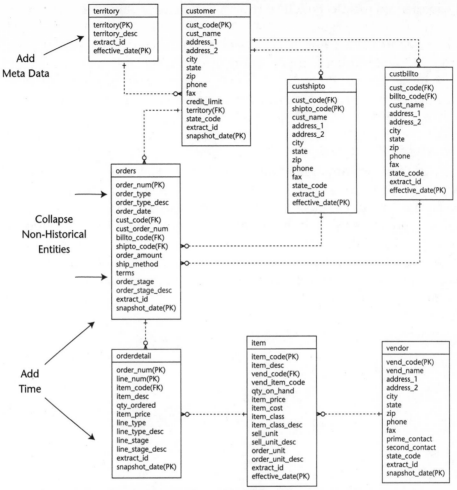

Figure 4.11 Atomic-level data warehouse model.

Modeling the Data Marts

The atomic-layer model neutralizes the complexities of the source feeder systems and serves as the front line for data integration and preparation. However, it is the dimensional model that formalizes the target data structures that will support the analysis necessary to address many of the strategic business questions brought forward by user communities. Ralph Kimball dominates the strategy, structure, and technique for implementing a data mart.

Experienced architects will start with a dimensional model when building data marts (see Figure 4.12). This is true whether the ultimate data mart is a star schema or a proprietary cube or both. The conceptual model is best created in a top-down manner. In other words, the data architect should conduct sessions with subject matter experts and business analysts. Together, session participants attempt to define entities from which to conduct multidimensional analysis. It is a perfect tool for architects to perform walk-through reviews with users, demonstrating the various data interrogation paths available within the scope of the subject area.

In addition, top-down modeling should be based on strategic business questions. This ensures that the design of the target data structure reflects the business requirements of the sponsoring user communities. The alternative approach is to use bottom-up modeling, where existing production models such as entity relationship diagrams are used to discern the dimensional requirements. This is an important choice for the architect. It is entirely possible that a dimensional model from a top-down design will differ significantly from a bottom-up approach.

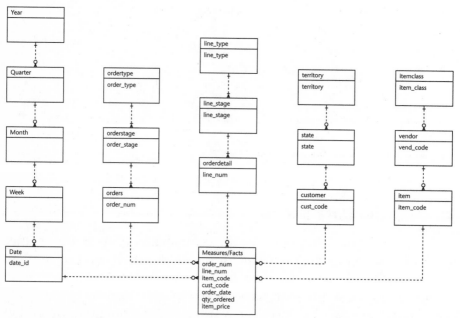

Figure 4.12   Dimensional model.

Business Question Components

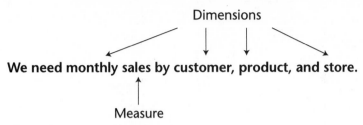

Figure 4.13   A good business question.

The approach for building an effective dimensional model starts by creating a conceptual or high-level dimensional model. This effort is best implemented in front of a user audience. The architect quickly diagrams a high-level model by exploding the documented business questions from the users. Figure 4.13 shows the components of a business question.

A good business question contains clues for the type of dimensions that will be required, as well as the measures/facts to be analyzed. For example, the business question in Figure 4.13 suggests that a date dimension will be required because of the reference to "monthly" values. Additionally, customer, product, and store are all likely candidates for dimensions. The measure to be analyzed seems to be "sales" dollars, but it could also be referring to units sold. In either case, the data architect has many clues to the type of data mart or cube necessary to answer the business question.

A dimensional model starts at a conceptual view and develops into a logical view. As a conceptual diagram, relevant entities that constitute a particular dimension are defined, as well as the root measurements/facts to be analyzed. This provides a high-level understanding of the dimensions, their hierarchies, and required measurements. At this stage, the dimensional diagram can serve as a means to communicate and confirm the analytical landscape users expect. The steps include the following:

1. Define dimensions for the subject area.

2. Add hierarchical entities.

3. Identify measurements/facts.

4. Identify entity relationships.

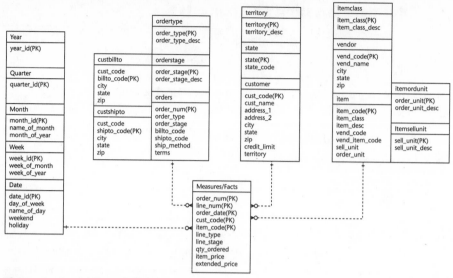

Figure 4.14   Attributed dimensional diagram.

To evolve the conceptual model into a logical model like that shown in Figure 4.14, the architect simply adds notation such as indexes for each dimension involved. He or she would then perform the following steps:

1. Add descriptions to each entity.

2. Add all candidate attributes to each entity represented.

3. Identify and define derived data.

4. Define the overall granularity.

Once a fully attributed dimensional model has been defined, it is a straightforward process to create the logical star schema. Figure 4.15 shows the results of the following steps:

1. Collapse dimensional entities into a single table. For example, Territory, State, and Customer entities are all represented in the dimensional model as being a part of the same hierarchy. These entities must be collapsed into a single entity and table when you are designing the star schema.

2. Eliminate duplicate dimensional attributes. The architect must decide if any duplicate attributes can be removed as part of the process of collapsing entities into a single dimension. For example, the entities CUSTSHIPTO and CUSTBILLTO both have a CUST_CODE (customer code). Only one is needed for the final, single-dimension table.

3. Add time to dimensions.

4. Add extraction meta data.

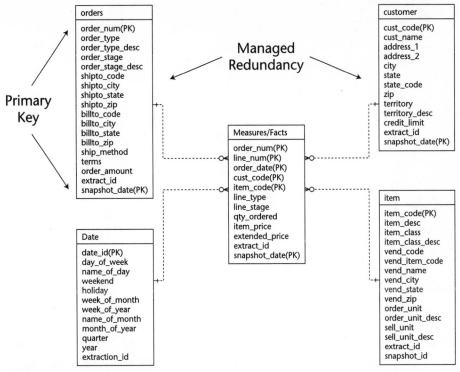

Figure 4.15   A star schema.

Comparing Atomic and Star Data

The preceding sections focused on modeling atomic and star structures. So, what is the net difference between them? This section examines how the data is stored in these two structures by using Figure 4.16 as an example.

On the left side of the exhibit are two tables: orders and orderdetail. These tables reflect the process used to build target data structures for an atomic level. As illustrated, the orders table has a one-to-many relationship with orderdetail, and the information stored in each contains denormalized domain entities of the BLM. For example, the orderdetail table has collapsed entities such as line_type and line_stage into the orderdetail table itself, as opposed to creating and maintaining the data in distinct tables at the atomic level. The same is true for the orders table, where the order_type and order_stage domains have been collapsed into orders. This partial denormalization of atomic-level data is generally done to keep complexity to a minimum while still maintaining much of the flexibility afforded by normalization rules.

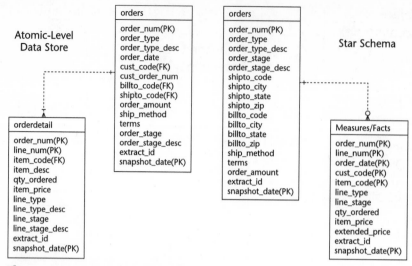

Figure 4.16   Comparing target schemas.

The orders dimension table and the related fact table of the star schema are shown on the right side of the exhibit. The star schema offers even more denormalization than that found in the atomic layer. For example, examining the orders dimension reveals that all customer ship-to and bill-to information has been collapsed into the single table. Ship-to and bill-to data found in the atomic level are still maintained in separate tables, with only a shipto_code and billto_code used to join the tables together. As for the fact table, it resembles the orderdetail table of the atomic level. In the example, the descriptions for line_stage and line_type have been removed. This is done for scale issues, since the fact table can and often does grow to contain millions of records. For efficiency's sake, the architect would use a simple, lookup table to reference the line_type and line_stage descriptions. This technique could also be applied at the atomic layer.

Operational Data Store

The operational data store is another data structure often associated with data warehouse efforts that requires some discussion. Architects and other warehouse practitioners are often confused regarding its application. Figure 4.17 shows the typical architecture of an ODS. This section attempts to distinguish the ODS from traditional warehouse efforts.

An ODS can be characterized as follows:

It is subject-oriented.   An ODS is designed to address the specific requirements of a subject area.

It contains integrated data.   One of the primary purposes of the ODS is to serve up integrated data.

It is current.   There is essentially no history maintained in an ODS.

It is dynamic.   ODS data is dynamic.

Given the preceding characteristics, it should be obvious to architects that the ODS has a different agenda than that of the data warehouse. Yes, an ODS contains integrated data just like that found in a DW. For that reason an ODS is a potential supply for source data fed into the warehouse. But that is where the similarity ends.

An ODS is also subject-oriented. Now it is true that the warehouse grows by iterations constrained by subject areas, but each subject area is layered into the atomic layer, and over the course of time, the atomic layer can potentially represent the entire enterprise. This is not true for an ODS. You may build an ODS to show current sales figures across the enterprise, but its application will be to publish sales figures—that's it. The goal of the ODS is not to be the wellspring of tactical data for the entire warehouse.

Another difference is history. The warehouse is designed to handle historical data and lots of it. This is completely different from an ODS, whose data is only maintained as long as it is considered current. What is "current" depends on the application, but it is often not more than 30 days. In other words, there is no such thing as history in an ODS.

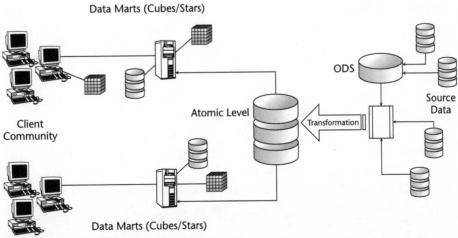

Figure 4.17   An operational data store.

A final difference between the warehouse and an ODS has to do with dynamic versus static data. An ODS is designed to deal with data that is constantly being updated and changed. This is not true for a warehouse, where static data is maintained and refreshed as part of a known cycle.

So why build an ODS? It is built to provide tactical information based on integrated sources of current data given a particular subject area. If you have several sources of disparate sales data, an ODS might be a great solution to integrate and make available current sales data.

And why is an ODS important to a warehouse effort? There are only two reasons that an ODS should be considered under the umbrella of warehousing:

- It is a great source of integrated data. If the warehouse is considering a sales iteration and an ODS already exists for sales, using the ODS as a source of data makes sense. It is likely that the ODS has done much of the integration work already.

- It is not unusual for users to require extensive tactical reporting as well as strategic analysis. Data architects cannot design the warehouse to address all tactical reporting without compromising the characteristics of the warehouse structures. Therefore, two project efforts may be initiated. The first is an ODS for integrating the data for tactical purposes. Once complete, a warehouse effort follows to use that current, integrated data stored in the ODS as a source for the warehouse requirements to address the strategic analysis.

Data Architecture Strategy

Given the variety of data architecture components and the combinations in which they can be implemented, how do you choose what is appropriate for your organization? This is not an easy question to answer. We propose a simple matrix that might help to guide you in your decision process. The operative words are "simple," "might," and "guide". The data architecture matrix in Table 4.2 associates core characteristics of warehouse initiatives with established, formal data architectures.

First, you need to understand the characteristics and the architectures being linked. The characteristics are listed down the right side of the matrix, while the architectures are identified across the top. In the following, we define each characteristic and architecture outlined in the matrix:

Scope.   Is the BI effort an enterprisewide initiative or a department project?

Integration. Are there numerous, disparate data sources that must be integrated, or is the source data from a single source system?

Cleansing and transformation. Will you need to perform intensive cleansing and transformation of the sourced data, or is it relatively clean and ready for the target warehouse applications being addressed?

OLAP. Does the environment expect OLAP applications?

Latency. How critical is it that your data quickly be made available for analysis? Is nightly batch processing acceptable, or do you need the data ASAP?

Data architectures include the following:

Atomic. A centralized, atomic-level warehouse with no other structures necessary

Atomic with cap. An atomic-level warehouse with a dimensional cap

Atomic with DDM. An atomic-layer with dependent data marts

IDM. Independent data marts with no atomic layer

EAI. Specialized data delivery

Table 4.2 Data Architecture Matrix

CHARACTERISTICS OF INITIATIVE		ATOMIC	ATOMIC WITH CAP	ATOMIC WITH DDM	IDM	EAI
Scope	Enterprise	X	X	X		X
	Department				X	
Integration	Light				X	
	Complex	X	X	X		X
Cleansing and transformation	Light				X	
	Complex	X	X	X		
OLAP required	None	X				
	Light			X	X	
	Advanced		X	X	X	
Latency	Batch			X		
	Near zero		X			X

Now that we know what the edges of the matrix represent, let's review the associations themselves. You should consider starting from a centralized atomic-level architecture only if the scope of the warehouse effort is enterprisewide, the integration of data is complex, the cleansing and transformation required is complex, and most importantly, no OLAP is required. This is not unusual. For as much mind-share as OLAP receives in our industry, static, advanced SQL reporting is still king.

An atomic-level warehouse with a dimensional cap is a viable option if your effort is enterprisewide, with complex integration and cleansing required and advanced OLAP solutions expected. The atomic layer will address the issues of integration, cleansing, and transformation across the enterprise. The dimensional cap can deal directly with an enterprisewide need for advanced OLAP applications. By placing a single dimensional server on top of your atomic data, you can ensure a single source of the truth for dimensional data applications, irrelevant of the user's tool of choice—of which you will find many. It is not unusual to find DB2 OLAP Server geeks who swear by the sophistication of the tool, as well as the users who have grown to know and love spreadsheets, and still others who live and die by Business Objects or Cognos, all under the same roof of your enterprise. The dimensional cap provides a single administrative environment to apply complex aggregation and hierarchy structures, thus buffering individual user communities from these issues and eliminating the burden of IT attempting to deal with these issues within each OLAP technology used.

The dimensional cap is a solid approach to deal with data latency. Since the dimensional server works directly from data found in the atomic level, there are no additional ETL steps necessary to propagate data from the atomic layer to persistent dimensional structures. This minimizes latency of the data.

An atomic layer with dependent data marts should always be evaluated as a potential architecture, given the same characteristics that trigger the consideration of a dimensional cap. Although dependent data marts represent a proven, traditional approach, they do entail more effort to maintain than dimensional caps. This is especially true when you are expecting to implement many data marts. However, the flexibility to implement data marts on an as-needed basis avoids complex implementation of server technology that must be considered an initial part of a dimensional cap. This means that dependent data marts can be implemented even for light use of OLAP across an enterprise. The light use of OLAP might be from the perspective of only one department requiring the technology. Or light use can be defined by requiring simple OLAP applications published in a single technology—even to a large audience.

The persistent data structures, atomic layer, and data marts (star/cubes) require additional batch processing to maintain and keep current the data. This translates into a larger batch window for propagating data into the atomic layer first and then to the dependent data marts affected by the data. Therefore, this architecture is best for those environments where batch processing of data on a nightly basis is not a problem.

Independent data marts are those OLAP-centric structures that are not dependent on atomic-level data. This means you do not have the benefit of a single source of integrated, cleansed data. This can result in a disparity between reports from different data marts. Consequently, you should only consider this architecture for initiatives constrained to a department with nominal integration and cleansing requirements.

Finally, let's review the EAI architecture. For warehouse efforts, EAI represents a specialized data delivery mechanism that can minimize the complexity of moving data between disparate source systems. As such, EAI should always be considered when you are dealing with an enterprisewide initiative with complex integration requirements and the need for minimizing the latency of the data.

The data architecture matrix is a simple guide. It should be used to give the reader a general sense of when and why to apply specific architectures. There are, of course, many other issues to consider when examining the best architecture for a particular environment, including skill resources, budget, project time lines, executive-level commitment, and existing technologies, just to name a few.

Summary

A variety of architectural designs are available. To fully appreciate the alternatives, you must completely understand what each data structure is used for and when to implement it. Once you feel comfortable with the architectural components, you can apply the components or combination of components to your BI efforts. This is an important point. As sad as it sounds, it is not unusual to see warehouse planners confused because they still don't understand the difference between star schemas and cubes, for example.

That said, it is not enough to be a great DBA with normalizing skills. Warehouse environments are not OLTP data structures. Each warehouse data structure is uniquely designed for a particular function, so you will need to accommodate those structure characteristics in your modeling efforts. The atomic layer is often normalized with the exception of domain entities for which you require no history. Stars or cubes require dimensional models to ensure granularity and symmetry of your structure. Data flow diagrams are the real modeling approach to ETL, not enormous source-to-target spreadsheets.

Like other vendors, IBM likes to remain nimble. If the client chooses to build an enterprisewide solution complete with atomic layer and dependent data marts, then IBM can respond with DB2 UDB V8 for both the atomic level and star schemas for the data marts, as well as DB2 OLAP Server as the dimensional cap for the enterprise. On the other hand, if a client runs to IBM saying, "Help! I need a quick OLAP solution," IBM can rush in with just DB2 OLAP Server and quickly create an independent data mart.

Of course, it is one thing to be nimble, but quite another to be completely naive or unaware of the future consequences given the architectural design. It is fair to conclude that IBM's preference is a fully engineered, traditional enterprise approach to data warehousing with a normalized atomic layer and dependent data marts.

CHAPTER 5

Technical Architecture and Data Management Foundations

Key Issues:

- The technical architecture implemented for any warehouse effort is as critical to the success of your warehouse effort as the data architecture chosen and the approach taken.

- The skills required to research and define your proper technical architecture encompass the selected RDMBS, OS, computer hardware (CPU, memory), disk storage, and networking. Consequently, a formal technical architecture often requires the talents of many individuals. This is substantially different from the data architecture, where the skills required can be found in one seasoned individual.

- Any warehouse of scale will exploit technical advances in data partitioning at both a hardware and software level, as well as the technical advances in parallelism, both at a system level and with regard to software utility.

- Creating the technical architecture is an iterative process that grows as your BI environment unfolds. However, the first iteration of the warehouse will probably require a disproportionate investment in the technical architecture.

We defined and described the persistent data structures of your data architecture in the previous chapter. This chapter explores the technical considerations for implementing that data architecture and to support your overall BI and warehouse goals. We review the numerous technical components necessary to create a formal technical architecture that complements and supplements your data architecture. Figure 5.1 is an example of a diagram created to illustrate components of the design.

Let's assume, for example, that your data architecture requires a centralized atomic layer with dependent data marts distributed onto platforms specific to the departments they serve. This data architecture provides much of the guidance to the technical design. In this case, you will need one platform as a server for your atomic level. This server must scale to the predicted size of your central atomic layer. Symmetric multiprocessing (SMP), massively parallel processing (MPP), and cluster technology are all viable hardware options to consider. Data partitioning and techniques to implement fast loads and ensure high availability will drive your architecture requirements.

Another type of platform will probably be necessary to support the individual data marts being implemented. This set of servers (potentially one for each data mart) will be sized and tuned differently than that of the atomic level. Additionally, the type of data mart implemented will further dictate the design requirements. If you are planning to build a star with large dimensions (10 million rows or more) and a large fact table (500 million rows), then partitioned tables and indexing will be critical. On the other hand, if you are planning to implement a large cube (50 GB or more), memory may be of greater concern.

Then there are the technical aspects of staging areas, development, and test platforms that must be a natural part of your overall architecture. The point is this: Each structure of your data architecture will directly impact the type of technical architecture you need to implement. You must be able to answers questions like:

- What technology is required for your overall effort?
- How much of this technology is required for your first iterations?
- How do you plan to integrate the technology into a synchronized data delivery system for BI analysis?

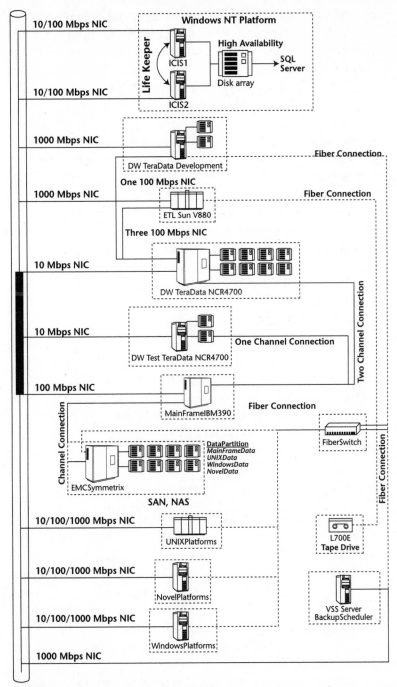

Figure 5.1 Technical architecture diagram.

Finally, the technical architect is not just hardware. It includes the operating systems, network middleware, RDBMS, cube technology vendor, make and version of the report writer, and any other software layer required to support your environment. Since the technical architecture is a broad, diverse topic, we will only focus on the customary components that must be evaluated. Unfortunately, the components can warrant a book's worth of discussion, so we recommend that readers use the following content to conduct deeper research where appropriate to your efforts.

This chapter begins with an examination of broad technical architecture decisions that project planners must make, including whether to build a centralized or distributed environment, whether to implement parallelism, and what data partitioning might be required. Next, the chapter reviews the technical architecture issues to consider for atomic-layer and star schema implementations using DB2 V8. We then detail the architectural essentials for DB2 that cover SMP, MPP, static, and dynamic parallelism and other technology for building high-availability warehouse environments.

Broad Technical Architecture Decisions

In this section we examine broad technical considerations for your environment. Following are discussions regarding centralized warehousing to distributed environments and the introduction of concepts such as parallelism and data partitioning. Each of the four topics covered in this section are done so from the technical perspective. And all have a direct impact on your architecture of choice.

Centralized Data Warehousing

DB2 offers a number of features that are critical to the centralized warehousing model. A centralized warehouse can grow to tens, potentially hundreds, of terabytes, supporting thousands or tens of thousands of queries per day. In a centralized warehouse, user demands and the related service level agreements (SLAs) are often in conflict with one another. DB2 provides a number of features to allow the support of conflicting, frequently shifting user requirements with a minimum of administrative effort. To understand how DB2 supports data warehouses, we must first understand some basic DB2 architectural concepts.

A single copy of DB2 running on a hardware platform is called an *instance*. Each instance can have one or more databases. This hardware platform can consist of one or more physical servers (or nodes). Each node can contain one or more processors. DB2 supports single-processor, SMP, cluster (shared disk), and shared-nothing (MPP) hardware architectures.

Combined with DB2's ability to support a true shared-nothing software model, this ensures scalability from the smallest to the largest implementations, with linear query performance, high user concurrency, and high query throughput. In every case, DB2 is managed as a single system image, making administration of the largest environments as simple as the smallest. When multiple nodes (including very large SMP nodes, such as IBM's Regatta class machines) are run using one of IBM's interconnects (SP switch or Colony), the operating system and physical server settings are also controlled as a single system image.

A database consists of multiple schemas, physical collections of database objects (tables, indexes, etc.). Schemas can be used to simplify administration, application development, and user access. As an example, consider a case with a single schema for the core, highly normalized atomic level warehouse tables. This model can contain hundreds of tables with myriad relationships between them. While some power users may be able to navigate this data maze, for most users this complexity is daunting. So a second schema may be used to represent a collection of views and summary tables for a specific group of users or applications. These views would then access the normalized tables, but present to the users and application developers a consistent, simple-to-understand view of the business. Another advantage of this approach is that as changes are required to the underlying table structures (such as adding a new data element), they can be made to the base tables, with the user views and aggregates updated but existing applications and queries left untouched. If we have users that demand access to multiple views of the data, single queries or user views can always access data from multiple schemas.

Summary tables, as noted earlier, make sense when a query is frequently repeated. While summaries reduce the amount of processing power and memory required (by executing all or part of repeated queries exactly once), they do increase storage requirements. In general, the business impact of having faster answers and the saving in processor and memory requirements will more than make up for the summaries. But in a traditional environment, the administrative overhead required to create and maintain the summaries and rewrite queries to utilize them can cause the expected cost savings to quickly evaporate. To address this problem, DB2 introduced a concept called materialized query tables (MQTs). An MQT is a summary table, or a projection of one or more underlying tables. As such, it may contain joins and aggregates.

The advantage to this approach is in the automatic portion. Once created, the optimizer will automatically redirect queries to the summary when the query can leverage it. Suppose we notice we have a lot of queries that aggregate sales by week. We create an MQT on sales by week. Now all queries are eligible to use the new structure without rewrite. The optimizer will determine if it makes sense for each application. The optimizer can use the MQT as it would any other table—in other words, it can join it to additional tables, aggregate it further, and even combine multiple MQTs in a single query. So, our sales-by-week MQT could be used as an intermediate step to sales by month. In other words, a materialized view does not have to contain the entire answer set for a particular query to be of value to that query.

The other part of the automatic portion regards maintenance. DB2 understands when data is added, changed, or deleted in one or more base tables, and it can automatically update the impacted MQT. So if we added another day of transactions to our sales table, our sales-by-week materialized view would automatically be updated to reflect these changes. There are two options for this: delta change or full refresh. At creation time, the DBA can determine if it makes more sense to propagate only the changed rows to the MQT or to clear it and reload the entire MQT. This is strictly a performance decision.

Of course, some environments require certain tables be updated in real time (or near real time). Users of the summary tables may not require this up-to-the-minute currency of data, and updating their MQT could introduce performance problems or transient inconsistencies. To allow for this, DB2 offers both refresh-immediate and refresh-deferred options for MQTs. With refresh-immediate, all changes to any base table are immediately reflected in the materialized view. With refresh-deferred, the updates are queued until a refresh command is received (through a DBA command, a daemon process, a batch trigger, or other mechanism).

In an MPP or cluster environment, you may not want multiple schemas running on the same collection of nodes. Or within a schema, you may want to isolate one or more summaries. Isolation of specific portions of a database to specific nodes is generally done to ensure SLAs can be met. While MPP architectures often force you to group all tables into the same "big bucket" of partitions, DB2 supports a concept called partition groups. A partition group is a collection of logical data partitions. A single partition can be part of one or more partition groups.

Again, let's consider an example where this might be used. DB2 always has a default partition group that contains all nodes in the configuration. Normally, this is where your centralized warehouse's data structures are stored. Now assume we create a summary (generally an MQT) table that supports a specific user community, say, the CEO's office. By default, this summary table would be on the same partition group as the underlying table structures. But the CEO is likely to have very specific reporting requirements and an SLA that demands immediate access. If a power user executes a long-running, ad hoc query, it can consume tremendous system resources. Even with the lowest possible prioritization setting, this can disrupt time-critical SLAs, such as our CEO's. With partition groups, we can "carve out" a specific set of partitions for this summary. Let's say we decide to add a physical node (or an LPAR on a Regatta-class system) for this purpose. While other queries, including the ad hoc requests, run on the larger partition group, the CEO's office can run its queries in isolation. We can meet both SLAs simultaneously, with no manual intervention beyond the original table specification.

Partition groups offer us a number of advantages to a traditional shared-nothing environment. If we place all the tables the CEO's office is likely to require on the same partition group, we can assign a logon point directly to this partition group to further improve performance.

Because multiple partition groups can exist in the same database, they are all administered as a single database image, greatly reducing the administrative effort required. Also, even though we default them to a specific partition group through table assignment and login point, the users are free to access any and all structures they have security rights to, across the entire database.

We can place multiple summaries or user groups on the same partition group. To simplify administration, schemas can be set to a default partition group. Thus, we could develop a schema specifically for the CEO's summaries and default it to the required partition group. All summaries we create in this schema would then go to the nodes we wanted. Again, the goal is to simplify long-term administration. If we require more computing power to support our isolated summaries, we simply increase the size of our SMP node or increase the number of nodes in the partition group.

Using MQTs to define these summaries also makes administration simpler. The MQT concept means that the summaries can be automatically updated or refreshed whenever data in the base tables is changed, even though the data is on separate partition groups. And, as with all MQTs, the optimizer is able to automatically pass through requests to the underlying tables, if it determines the available summaries cannot meet the new request.

Sometimes it makes sense to have the summaries located on a server closer to the user—in other words, as a traditional dependent data mart. This can be done in a variety of ways, one of which is to again leverage the concept of MQTs. In Version 7, IBM introduced a concept called *nicknamed MQTs*. A nicknamed MQT is a materialized view that contains data from one or more tables in one or more separate databases. For a centralized data warehouse, nicknamed MQTs allow us to build a summary on a separate physical server and have it automatically maintained as the base tables are updated. For our CEO summary, we could locate a dedicated server close to the CEO's office for reduced communication costs and improved performance. The local users could then be given exclusive access to this server. The only restriction on nicknamed MQTs over traditional MQTs is that delta updates are not allowed. Nicknamed MQTs can only be updated through a complete refresh.

Key to the success of any data warehouse is the optimization capabilities of the DBMS. In the 1990s, IBM undertook a massive project to develop the most sophisticated database optimizer in the world, one capable of sophisticated optimization of complex queries and complex, extensible data structures. Called Starburst, this optimizer has the ability to examine every possible alternative that could be used to satisfy a query. DB2's Starburst optimizer will examine queries, looking for ways to make it more efficient before analyzing any possible paths. Queries can be entirely rewritten to take advantage of more effective (but equivalent) constructs.

The DB2 optimizer takes into account table and index cardinality through statistics collected after the load process. It also accounts for the types of processors used and the speed of the disk subsystem. Some optimizers rely on hints from the DBA to function properly. Others use a combination rules/cost approach but do not allow any alterations: If you come up with a bad query plan, you have no choice but to live with it or redesign your database. DB2 does not require, nor in fact even allow, hints. Nor does it force you to live with a sub-par plan. DB2 has a tunable parameter, set at the database level for the amount of effort put into the optimization. The lower the number (valid numbers are between 0 and 9), the faster the optimization itself will occur. The higher the number, the more plans that DB2 will consider, hence the longer it may take to produce an optimal plan. In a data warehouse environment, most clients set the default optimization level from 5 to 7. At 5, all possible paths are evaluated and costed. For troublesome queries, the level can be raised (for that query only) to 9 by adding the runtime parameter "OPTLVL = 9" to the SQL statement. With level 9 optimization, Starburst will invoke advanced statistical predictive heuristic methods developed by IBM Research to develop the best plan possible. While other optimizers may sometimes produce a good plan, DB2 can always produce the best plan.

Distributed Data Warehousing

Distributed data warehousing can arise from a variety of technical or political situations within a company. Recognizing this, IBM has built a number of features into DB2 to support this approach.

There are several ways to implement distributed data warehousing under DB2. The simplest model is to have the individual subject areas (star schemas, domain segmented tables, or other departmental structures) stored on a single copy of DB2. The partitioning keys (see the next section, *Parallelism and the Warehouse*) can then be used to collocate data and minimize redistribution, improve performance, and improve throughput. This model makes the most sense if the underlying subject areas are frequently joined together.

Another approach is to store the data in the same database, but maintain each of the independent subject areas in separate schemas. MQTs can then be used to present more integrated views of the data to those users who require them. This makes the most sense when the subject areas are under conflicting SLAs, as each can be isolated to a unique partition group for performance.

The third approach is through truly distributed databases, where each subject area resides on a separate server. In this case, nicknamed MQTs may be used to present a consistent view of the data where required, with minimal data transfer (data transfer is required only when the nicknamed MQTs are loaded). This approach makes the most sense when the data cannot be collocated, but there are users who require frequent access to large volumes of data from multiple data marts.

Alternatively, DB2 provides a feature called DB2 Relational Connect. With DB2 Relational Connect, a copy of DB2 can catalog data from remote databases and use these data in queries. A single query can access data from a variety of servers. User views can be created that rely on data elements from different sources.

Consider the case where a large organization has offices in multiple states (or other jurisdictions), each of which develops its own suite of products and prices based on its local regulations. This organization is likely to have local analysts within each organization, local reporting requirements for the regulators, and possibly a localized data warehouse. At the corporate headquarters, however, are higher-level users (finance, risk management, product planning, etc.) who need to analyze the same data across various jurisdictions. DB2 Relational Connect allows each local office to maintain independence while providing seamless access for those users who require it.

DB2 Relational Connect provides read and update access to DB2 databases under UNIX, Linux, Windows, OS400, and OS390. It also provides read access to Oracle databases, and can optionally be ordered to provide update access to Oracle, as well as read access to SQL Server or other ODBC-compliant DBMSs.

But DB2 Relational Connect is more than simply pass-through access. It will take queries that were designed for DB2 and convert the SQL to a form compatible with the source DBMS. In many cases, it can recognize certain SQL constructs that may cause performance problems for the source and rewrite them into better-performing constructs. For those requiring additional data sources, DataJoiner, a standalone product that works in conjunction with DB2, provides access to a wider variety of database platforms.

Another place to consider using DB2 Relational Connect or DataJoiner is when a specific application requires data that would not normally be part of the data warehouse. Take a customer-facing call center application, which could reasonably require data from the data warehouse and the operational data store (i.e., up-to-the-minute data that has not yet been put through any significant cleansing or transformation processes). DB2 Relational Connect can access these data sources seamlessly, providing a single, timely view of the customer.

Obviously, some degree of performance and capacity planning is required when using this feature, as it would be very costly to move terabytes of data from platform to platform for various queries. However, DB2 Relational Connect is a very powerful tool when used appropriately.

Parallelism and the Warehouse

As data volumes grow, user communities expand, and query demands increase, parallelism has become the method of choice for ensuring performance and scalability. But everyone implements parallelism differently. DB2 implements parallelism on a variety of levels simultaneously.

The first level of parallelism is achieved through data partitioning. Tables (and by implication their associated indexes) can be partitioned in DB2. A single physical node (server) can contain one or more partitions, but a partition can exist on exactly one node.

DB2 uses a shared-nothing partitioning model, meaning each database partition has exclusive control of its data. Thus, if Partition 0 contains Row A, and Partition 5 needs to read Row A, it must be read by Partition 0 and passed to Partition 5. If Row A is to be altered in any way, it can only be done by Partition 0. This model eliminates the control/locking problems the shared data model encounters as data volumes grow. It also has significant impact on how we choose our partitioning keys.

To partition a table, DB2 uses a *hash map*, that translates hash buckets into controlling partitions. A *partitioning key* is determined for each table. The value of this key is divided by a large prime number, and the resulting remainder (residue class) is used to determine which hash bucket the row falls into, and, consequently, which partition will own the row. The partitioning key may be chosen independently of any physical index considerations.

Choosing the partitioning key is a matter of three primary factors. First, we need a key that has reasonably even data distribution across its domain. Date of sale is likely not a good candidate, as most companies experience considerable variance in their sales volumes from day to day. As all sales from a single day would end up on the same partition, we would have poor, or "lumpy," data distribution. Second, we need a key that allows a high degree of uniqueness. Even though it has a reasonably even distribution, sex, with a maximum of two values, is not a good candidate, as all the rows would end up in only two partitions. Third, we need a key that takes into consideration how the tables are used together. Queries demand that rows be joined together. But the only way you can match rows (or sometimes determine if there even is a match) is to have them on the same partition. In a shared-nothing model, this means data must be moved based on some common criteria—specifically, the join columns. This means at least some of the rows of one or both tables in a join may have to be physically sent to another partition. If the rows are already partitioned based on the join columns, however, we can eliminate this relatively expensive step. This can be found by examining the primary/foreign key relationships of various tables and considering how frequently they will be used, the data volumes involved, and the criticality of the join. The first thing to consider is how data is loaded into the partitions, and how parallelism impacts load performance. We will discuss the DB2 Autoloader process, although it should be noted that third-party load products also exist for DB2. Data is collected at the source and, usually, put through an ETL process.

To speed loading, DB2 splits the transformed data into multiple load files, with each load file matching a specific partition. This is done through a utility called DB2SPLIT. DB2SPLIT can be run on the source (mainframe, UNIX, or Windows) or target (UNIX or Windows) platforms. For faster performance, multiple DB2SPLIT processes can be run in parallel against a single load source. Next, the load files are sent to the load utility. This load utility works against empty files and files that already contain data. All partitions are loaded in parallel. Autoloader automates this process by invoking the split and load utilities in sequence and managing the data movement between them.

Suppose we find ourselves in a situation where we have a candidate partitioning key that is perfect in almost every respect. We have a large table, and our candidate partitioning key has a high degree of uniqueness. In addition, it is frequently used to access smaller tables, but it is somewhat lumpy in its distribution. With most shared-nothing systems, you would have to accept the lumpy distribution or choose an alternative partitioning key, even if it did not match the business model as well. DB2 has a unique way to deal with this. By running the large table through the DB2SPLIT process using the CREATE MAP option, we can create a unique hash map that better reflects the reality of our business environment. The advantage is we can use the partitioning key that makes the most business sense. The disadvantage is we may need to occasionally monitor the data distribution to ensure our demographics have not significantly changed.

Now that our tables have data in them, let's look at how parallelism is applied to a query. DB2's Starburst optimizer will determine the level of parallelism to be applied in any given circumstance. There is no DBA or user intervention required. With queries, DB2 may choose to invoke multiple simultaneous levels of parallelism.

Frequently, a query requires the manipulation of multiple rows from a table or intermediate workspace. If these rows are spread across multiple partitions, DB2 requests that each partition retrieve the requested rows they own in parallel. This is known as *inter-partition parallelism*. Thus, for an N-partition system, we could have up to N inter-partition parallel processes running for a single query. Note that DB2 can execute parallel requests for a variety of operations, including table scans, direct index retrievals, index range scans, joins, and aggregations.

Within a partition, DB2 can also assign "degrees of parallelism" for certain operations. This is known as *intra-partition parallelism*. For example, if a specific partition was doing a full table scan, DB2 might detect that this query would become I/O bound based on the expected number of qualified rows. DB2 could then direct that query step to use additional scans in parallel against subsets of its partition. If DB2 instructed every partition in an N partition configuration to use X degrees of parallelism, we could now have $N \times X$ parallel tasks running to satisfy this single request.

While intra-partition parallelism can speed up a variety of queries, it has another purpose as well: workload balancing. Even if we have created a perfectly balanced system, imbalances will occur as queries are executed. For example, earlier we said date of sale was not a good candidate partitioning key, as sales volumes are very uneven from day to day. However, users still need to report on daily sales. This means data will be redistributed to group by day, and the temporary work files will become imbalanced. DB2 can recognize these dynamic imbalances and compensate for them by assigning the appropriate number of parallel tasks to each partition.

Of course, some queries rely on indexes to satisfy their queries. Consider a star schema, where the fact table is accessed through a variety of indexes around the dimension tables. Traditionally, a DBMS would look at the most selective index, followed by the next most selective, and so on to generate an access plan to the fact table. But these indexes are often unrelated to one another, except they happen to intersect in the fact table. DB2 can access multiple indexes for the same table in parallel. And, of course, these indexes can be accessed using both inter-partition and intra-partition parallelism.

Another parallelism feature can be found in the way DB2 treats multiple query steps. Consider the query "Select t from A, B, C, where A.y = C.x and C.y = B.z. "For simplicity, suppose DB2 has decided to scan all three tables and do two merge joins. Traditionally, a DBMS would scan one table, then a second. Next, it would run the merge join, then scan the third table, and finally run the second merge join. DB2 can choose a variety of alternatives here. It may choose to scan A and C at the same time, then scan B while the A:C merge join is running. Or it may decide the most efficient method is to scan all three tables at once. Of course, these operations can be done using inter-partition and intra-partition parallelism.

DB2 also makes extensive use of pipeline parallelism. Consider the preceding simple query. Assume DB2 had decided to scan all three tables at once, then do the merge join on A:C. The results of this merge join could then be pipelined to the B merge join as rows were qualified. In other words, because the final join step does not require the previous join to be completed before it can begin, DB2 can run them in parallel.

Finally, DB2 supports parallelism at the I/O level. Modern RAID (redundant array of independent disks) controllers support parallel I/Os across their platters, and DB2 fully leverages this feature.

Partitioning Data Storage

At the physical level, DB2 is a set of tablespaces. One or more tables are assigned to each tablespace.

Tablespaces consist of containers. A *container* is a directory within the operating system's file system, a file under the OS's file system, or a physical device. Containers are made up of extents, the lowest level of space allocation.

DB2 provides two types of storage management: system-managed storage (SMS) and database-managed storage (DMS). The use of SMS or DMS tablespaces is not mutually exclusive within a database; SMS and DMS can be mixed within the same environment.

SMS relies on the OS's file management system and is the simplest to create and manage. When using SMS, each container is a directory within the OS's file structure. This space is not pre-allocated to any single tablespace (hence table) but grows and shrinks as the database requires. When using

SMS, all objects associated with a given table must be stored in the same tablespace. SMS offers excellent performance, and its simple administration makes it the space management method of choice for many installations.

DMS provides the maximum in performance and control, but it requires some knowledge of the hardware, database, and operational environment. With DMS, containers are either physical files or a storage device (logical or physical). If the container is specified as a file, the file is of a fixed size and is pre-allocated to the tablespace. If the container is a storage device, it must use the entire device.

One of the advantages of using DMS is it provides the ability to split certain portions of a file structure from one another. For example, if we frequently can satisfy queries using indexes (with or without INCLUDE columns), or if we want to effectively lock a frequently used index in memory, with DMS we can place these indexes in a separate tablespace and dedicate a bufferpool to them. Similarly, we can create a separate tablespace and bufferpool for large objects. This provides DB2 with additional optimization options to avoid reading or carrying large data objects through the query.

As mentioned previously, a single database is not limited to either SMS or DMS. It is possible to use SMS for the majority of your tables and use DMS for a table that has a number of large objects in it or other unique performance characteristics.

Technical Foundations for Data Management

Data management is much more than simple building and table maintenance. There is a significant amount of effort that must go into how data is propagated and stored throughout your environment. Here we will examine the various functions and features of the DB2 Universal Database with regard to the persistent data structures you plan to implement.

DB2 and the Atomic Layer

In this section we address the physical storage of atomic-level data structures. Examined are several storage techniques with related technical aspects as they pertain to implementation and performance.

Redistribution and Table Collocation

You must remember to keep a number of things in mind when implementing the atomic-level physical model with DB2. Foremost is the relationship between the various tables. For rows from two tables to be joined, they must first be located on the same partition. In many cases, this means the data must be moved from the owning partition to the processing partition. This process is called *redistribution*.

Redistribution occurs in a relationship between two tables, specifically:

- When two tables are being joined but they are not partitioned the same. For example, when they use the same partitioning key.

- When two tables are partitioned the same but are joined using a different set of columns.

Let's say we have a table called Customer, partitioned by Customer_ Number, and another table called Sales, partitioned by Transaction_ Identifier. Now we want to run the following query:

```
SELECT Customer.Customer_Name, Sales.Sale_Date, sum(Sales.Sale_Amount)
FROM Customer, Sales
WHERE Customer.Customer_Number = Sales.Customer_Number
AND Customer.Customer_State = -CA
GROUP BY Customer.Customer_Name, Sales.Sale_Date
```

For Customer and Sales to be joined, corresponding rows must first be located on the same partition. In this case, they must first be collocated according to Customer_Number. There are a number of ways to accomplish this task:

- The Sales table could be redistributed based on Customer_Number.

- The Customer table could be read based on Customer_State = "CA", and the qualified rows redistributed to every partition.

- The qualified rows, once distributed, could be used to drive an indexed read of Sales.

Luckily for us, the DB2 optimizer will choose the most effective one.

Only the columns required to satisfy the join are moved using any of the preceding methods. The rows are then qualified and the remaining columns are picked up at the end of the query. This is likely to happen if the size of reported nonqualified columns is high and the join will result in relatively few rows remaining at the end.

The redistribution process must read the row from the owning partition, pass the data to the requesting partition, store it temporarily locally, and, depending on the query and current workload, possibly move it to virtual memory and back out for processing. As illustrated in Figure 5.2, this is obviously inefficient and costly.

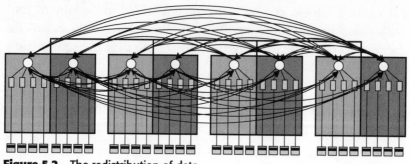

Figure 5.2   The redistribution of data.

One objective of the atomic-level physical model, then, is to reduce the frequency of required redistributions. To do this, the DBA must not only map the primary and foreign key relationships but also understand how frequently those relationships will be used in the course of a day. In our example it might make more sense to partition the Sales table by Customer_Number. In this case, the table would be collocated by Customer_Number. The caveat here is that the Sales table is likely to be very large. In that situation, the partitioning by Customer_Number may result in uneven data distribution, at which point you, as the architect, must choose between the lesser of the two evils, or determine if a system-generated customer hash map is in order.

Replicated Tables

An additional partitioning option exists when you are dealing with smaller tables. A state lookup table is an example, albeit a small one. In the case of the state table, we have few realistic choices but to partition according to the state lookup code. This table is likely to be used in two ways: as an indexed lookup table for a handful of reported states or as a full table lookup to report all states. In the latter case, the optimizer is likely to simply redistribute all rows of the table to all partitions, so every partition ends up with a complete copy of the table. While simple and effective for a single query, it quickly becomes a major waste of resources to do this for thousands of queries a day. A DB2 replicated table maintains a complete copy of the entire table on every partition within the partition group. This way, the tables can always be accessed locally. Figure 5.3 is a simple illustration of this replication.

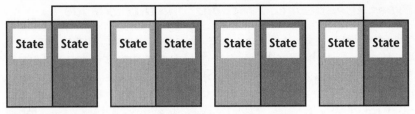

Figure 5.3   Replicated state table within partition group.

Indexing Options

The next thing to determine is which columns make suitable indexes. DB2's index structure is an effective dual-chained B*Tree. This means the indexes can be traversed in either ascending or descending order, reducing the need for redundant indexes.

In a partitioned environment, the index entry for any row will be on the same partition as the row. This eliminates the need for redistribution or other cross-partition communication to locate the actual row.

If data are frequently accessed in the same order as a specific index, a clustering index may be in order. A clustering index tells DB2 to store the underlying data in the same sequence as the index. In addition to improving query performance, this can also reduce or eliminate the need for data reorganization.

In some cases, the entire row may not be retrieved frequently with an index, but selected columns might be. For example, the state lookup table might contain more than simply the state code and state name, such as a state flower, state bird, an image of the state flag, or an image of the state seal. In this case, the state name is far more likely to be the item used in a query than a graphic of the state seal. We can create an index on the state abbreviation but specify that a copy of the state name is to be stored with the index. The extra columns do not impact the organization of the index.

Multidimensional Clusters as Indexes

Multidimensional clusters (MDCs) not only define how data is stored, but because the DB2 optimizer is aware of these block structures, they can also be used as effective indexes. DB2 can quickly locate data when only specific times or dates are required. This is achieved by addressing only the potentially relevant blocks within each hash partition.

Defined Types, User-Defined Functions, and DB2 Extenders

We must also consider if we will be using only traditional data types, or if special data types are to be used. Special data types may be defined types or part of a DB2 Extender (see Chapter 6). Defined types, also known as user-defined types (UDTs), are generally designed by a particular user and implemented for a specific use. *User-defined functions* (UDFs) are stored processes that allow the data to be processed in a consistent manner. DB2 Extenders are developed by IBM or partners and packaged for sale with DB2. DB2 Extenders include the specialized data types and the specialized functions to effectively process them. For example, the DB2 Image Extender allows you to store image data and run advanced queries on them using Query By Image Content (QBIC). A discussion of the available DB2 Extenders can be found in Chapter 6.

UDTs can enforce specific business rules on a column. We could define a UDT called Customer_Number to ensure that the definitions within our Customer and Sales tables are identical. We can also make certain that two customer numbers can be compared, but not allow arithmetic operations to be performed against them.

Having the same column definitions is a great way to enforce consistency, but more is needed to guarantee consistency of functional domains between tables. For this, we must consider what referential integrity (RI) constraints will be applied. For example, we might choose to allow a customer number to be entered in the Sales table only if the same customer number exists in the Customer table, or we may choose to automatically update all pertinent transactions in the Sales table if we should alter a customer number in the Customer table.

RI constraints can have a performance impact when running large loads, as every loaded row might have to be checked against multiple reference points. To allow referential constraints to be applied but still have guaranteed batch windows, DB2 allows the restrain checks to be deferred until after the load process is complete.

Hierarchical Storage Considerations

The traditional way to store data that is managed by an RDBMS is on magnetic disk drives. In the BI environment, there are situations where some data might be of value, but infrequently used or simply difficult to justify maintaining from a return-on-investment perspective. DB2 has an alternative in these situations, and it impacts how we implement our physical model.

DB2 offers tight integration with IBM's Tivoli Storage Manager through a feature called Hierarchical Storage Management (HSM). HSM allows us to place data that is most critical or most frequently used on traditional disk drives and place less critical data on alternative, less expensive devices, such as optical media or tape. (See Figure 5.4.)

There are a variety of ways we could use HSM. Following are three examples:

- Let's say you own a property and casualty insurance company. Records of claims are kept; in addition, audio, graphics, video, or document data are stored with each claim. Using HMS, we allocate magnetic storage for the data and indexes. For the table that contains the large objects, we define the containers on optical jukeboxes. We present a single view of the data back to the user through a view. Now we can store large volumes of these critical but ancillary data at a fraction of the traditional cost and retain full relational access to them.

- Suppose you deal in antiquarian books. There are certain things about your inventory that are analyzed and queried on a regular basis, for example, book title, condition, and publication date. The information is stored as non-index columns, but with the index as INCLUDE columns. There is a lot more data on the book such as history and authentication that is infrequently reported or analyzed. We define the index and primary data tablespace containers as magnetic and the ancillary data tablespace containers as optical. This places the most frequently used and time-critical data on the fastest devices.

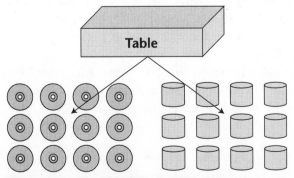

Figure 5.4 Hierarchical Storage Management.

■ Suppose you are a retailer selling everything from videotapes to washers and dryers. For most items we want to keep 1-year-plus-1-quarter of sales history, considered a standard for most retailers. However, for appliances we want to keep 10 years of history. For this example, you would develop HSM rules for DB2 that create containers for the 10-year history on a tape device. Then you can define the functional domain for appliances to DB2 for HSM migration after the standard retention time has passed, at which point DB2 automatically moves the appliance history to tape.

DB2 recognizes the nature of the underlying device type and optimizes accordingly. DB2 knows that some data is on disk, some on optical media, and some on tape and understands the performance characteristics of each. Entirely new classes of applications become financially viable with HMS.

DB2 and Star Schemas

When DB2 encounters a star schema structure, it has a variety of optimization options. It can use any of the standard optimization and parallelism techniques available, as well as an exclusive approach called *STARjoin*.

The STARjoin optimization method accesses the dimension tables and fact table indexes to drive the final result. This option is generally chosen if the fact table has secondary indexes corresponding to at least some of the dimension tables and the selectivity into the fact table is reasonably high. STARjoin selects an appropriate dimension table, qualifies the rows to be used, and does a "semi-join" with the fact table. A *semi-join* accesses only the index columns in the fact table and returns only the qualified row IDs from the fact table. The row IDs are then hashed into memory, and a dynamic bitmap index is built. The next dimension table is then accessed, and a semi-join done. The row IDs are again hashed, and another dynamic bitmap is constructed. When DB2 has generated the bitmaps it wants, they are joined using an AND construct. The resulting row IDs are then used to gather information from the fact table for the final report. Figure 5.5 demonstrates the STARjoin process.

The use of STARjoin is completely up to the optimizer. Moreover, the DBA does not have to specify anything unique to indicate a star schema is present. The optimizer will make its decision based solely on the cost of the query plans.

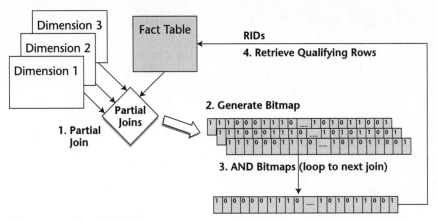

Figure 5.5 The STARjoin.

Nevertheless, you do have some choice in the physical implementation of a star schema. The most straightforward physical model approach is to store the fact and dimension tables as you would store other data warehouse tables, using standard partitioning. When this approach is used there is likely to be some redistribution, since the dimension tables may have far less information available for effective partitioning than the fact table. If we have a dimension table that is quite large in comparison to the other dimensions, and the dimension is frequently used to access the fact table, you might consider co-locating these tables by partitioning the fact table using the same partitioning key as the large dimension table. This would eliminate many of the larger redistributions.

A number of other options exist that might be of use for star schemas. For smaller dimension tables, consider using the replicated table option. This stores copies of the entire dimension table on every partition, thus improving performance and throughput. If the star schema is relatively contained—for instance, the queries accessing the star do not generally join the star to other database objects—then consider isolating it onto a separate nodegroup. This provides more consistent performance for the star users by isolating them from other users of the system.

DB2 Technical Architecture Essentials

As with any DBMS, there are some essential facts on the architecture and features to keep in mind during implementation. DB2 Universal Database is no exception. In this section we address the following:

- SMP, MPP, clusters
- Shared-resource versus shared-nothing
- Static and dynamic parallelism
- Catalog partition
- High availability
- Extensibility

SMP, MPP, and Clusters

Symmetric multiprocessing, massively parallel processing, and clusters are hardware architectures. Each is illustrated in Figure 5.6.

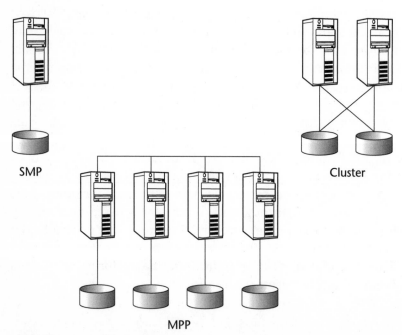

Figure 5.6 SMP, MPP, and clusters.

SMP systems consist of multiple processors sharing common resources, for instance, memory, bus, and operating system. The advantages of SMP systems are simplicity of administration and price/performance. Disadvantages are limited high-end scalability, diminishing improvements (nonlinear scalability) as processors are added (depending on the application, operating system, hardware architecture, and underlying DBMS), and limited recoverability/availability options.

Clusters consist of multiple systems (sometimes called servers, sometimes called nodes) sharing disk resources. The nodes communicate with one another using an interconnect technology that can be as simple as an Ethernet network or as complex as IBM's Colony Switch. Each of these nodes is generally an SMP system. Clusters are often implemented to increase the overall system throughput by allowing more queries to run on separate processors. Moreover, they provide additional recoverability and availability alternatives. For example, if one node goes down, the others in the cluster may be able to take over its workload. Clusters provide excellent data and performance scalability, but only when used with a shared-nothing DBMS architecture.

Finally, MPP systems consist of multiple systems (usually called nodes) that do not share resources. As with clusters the nodes are generally SMP systems. Modern MPP systems often use collections of clusters to ensure high availability. (This topic is covered in more detail later in this section.) The primary advantage of an MPP system is that it promises and, with an effective shared-nothing DBMS, can deliver linear scalability to a practically unlimited number of nodes. There are disadvantages, however:

- They are relatively expensive when compared to large SMPs in that they require additional cabinetry, interconnect points, and operating system copies.

- Without the proper management software, MPP systems can be difficult to effectively administer. Modern MPP systems come with built-in cross-node management software that make all nodes appear as a single system image.

- MPP systems have an inherent reliability problem. If the mean time between failure (MTBF) of the underlying SMP system is X hours, then the MTBF of an N node MPP environment is X/N hours.

The most modern systems combine the price/performance of large-scale SMP systems with the unlimited scalability of MPP systems. IBM's Regatta and its kin provide an excellent building block to construct powerful MPP systems. When multiple large SMP systems are planned to be connected by a single IBM switch, the large systems can still be managed and controlled as though they were a single AIX system. This greatly simplifies management of the largest environments.

In addition to providing better price performance for large MPP systems, using large SMPs as the building blocks also reduces the need for MPP environments. Many traditional MPP systems have less power than a single 32-way Regatta class machine. These customers could easily move their environments to a single SMP server. There are several benefits to this strategy:

- Increased reliability, as fewer parts equal higher MTBF
- Reduced cost by:
  - Reducing the number of O/S copies
  - Reducing the need for an interconnect
  - Reducing the need for additional utility license fees
- Simplified administration

To ensure maximum scalability on large SMPs, DB2 uses database partitions to effectively treat the hardware as a logical collection of smaller nodes.

The critical piece of knowledge here is that DB2 effectively supports all of these hardware types, and it has special features to overcome many of their inherent limitations.

Shared-Resource vs. Shared-Nothing

Shared-resource and shared-nothing represent forms of software architectures. In a shared-resource model various processes in the DBMS have access to all the system resources, including the data. In the shared-nothing environment, separate DBMS resources divide up the workload, each responsible for its own data, memory locations, and other resources.

DB2 UDB follows a shared-nothing model. Data is partitioned according to a partitioning key. Rows are assigned to a partition, and each partition has total control of that row. If another partition wants to read or update a row, it must send the request to the owning partition. The owning partition then executes the command on behalf of the requestor.

The shared-nothing model greatly simplifies things like resource contention, including memory, locks, and processors. Implemented properly, it offers unlimited scalability. As new rows or data sources are added, more partitions can be added. The workload on any individual partition remains the same.

DB2 on Hardware Architectures

Figure 5.7 illustrates the three hardware architectures with DB2 instances, including SMP, MPP, and clusters. For SMP servers, DB2's shared-nothing approach allows more linear scalability than a shared-resource DBMS. DB2 can treat the SMP server as a collection of smaller servers, dividing the workload among multiple concurrent processes.

For clusters, DB2 treats the servers and storage as though they are MPP components; in other words, even though they may share physical connections, each partition controls its own segments of the disk subsystem. This avoids the contention, locking, and ownership problems associated with shared resources. DB2 also works closely with standard high-availability clustering software, like High Availability Cluster Multi-Processing (HACMP). (More on HA options is provided later in the chapter.)

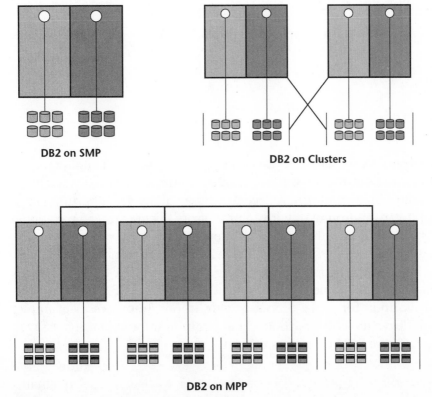

Figure 5.7 Hardware with DB2 instances.

In an MPP environment, DB2 exploits the shared-nothing hardware environment completely. Because DB2 is fault-tolerant, it can continue running even if underlying components, including complete servers, fail. Many shared-nothing DBMSs are fault-resilient, meaning if a node in an MPP or cluster is lost, the entire environment shuts down and then restarts, and all work must start over.

In both a cluster and MPP environment, DB2 is a single system image, no matter how large the environment grows.

Static and Dynamic Parallelism

In a traditional MPP model, parallelism is achieved when the various database partitions work on pieces of the same problem, at the same time. This model, called *inter-partition parallelism*, is completely dependent on the number of partitions available to the DBMS. In other words, it represents static parallelism.

While DB2 employs static parallelism across its partitions, it also uses intra-partition, or dynamic, parallelism. Dynamic parallelism allows the optimizer to assign a specific number of parallel tasks within each partition, based on individual query requirements.

This approach has a number of implications. Fewer partitions are needed because parallel query performance is not constrained by the number of partitions. Consider the impact on a simple query:

```
SELECT A.x
FROM A, B
WHERE A.y = B.y
```

Assume no indexes can help this query. Each table has 1 million rows, and they are not partitioned on "y." In an environment that relies solely on static parallelism, a vendor may recommend as many as 16 partitions per processor. In an environment with 16 processors this means 256 partitions. Each partition will have to send at least one message to each of the other partitions for each table. Consequently, the minimum number of messages sent is 65,280. With dynamic partitioning, we can assign far fewer partitions per processor. While it varies with the workload, IBM often recommends 1 partition for every processor pair. In our 16-processor example, this would leave us with 8 partitions and a minimum number of messages of only 56. Figure 5.8 emphasizes this difference.

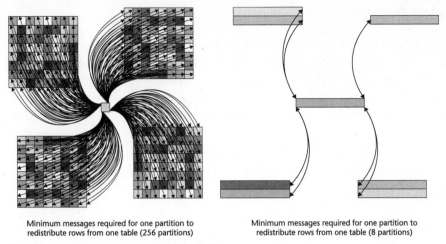

Minimum messages required for one partition to
redistribute rows from one table (256 partitions)

Minimum messages required for one partition to
redistribute rows from one table (8 partitions)

Figure 5.8   Static and dynamic parallelism.

In addition to reducing the overall workload, there is a dramatic difference in the join processing between static and dynamic parallelism. It is very likely that the partitions in each case will end up with uneven distribution. With static partitioning, each partition will process the join at the same speed. The partition with the largest number of rows to compare will end up with the most work, and the others will wait for it to complete. Conversely, dynamic parallelism with DB2, as illustrated in Figure 5.9, can dynamically assign additional parallel tasks to assist the partitions with more data.

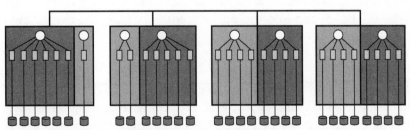

Figure 5.9   Dynamic parallelism after redistribution.

Catalog Partition

The meta data about the database objects is stored in the system catalog. While traditional shared-nothing DBMSs distribute the catalog objects across all partitions, DB2 uses an exclusive partition for the catalog. Catalogs are small, rarely exceeding 5 GB of data. It's simply not rational to have the overhead of the cross-partition messages for all queries. For performance, DB2 does keep some frequently used portions of the catalog locally on all partitions.

High Availability

Today's BI systems are mission-critical environments. Recognizing this, IBM has constructed DB2 as part of a high-availability environment. When considering high availability, you need to define outages. There are essentially two types of outages: planned and unplanned. While the unplanned get the most attention, planned outages are rarely less disruptive. To minimize the number of required planned outages, DB2 offers a number of features, discussed in the following sections.

Online Space Management

In addition to improving performance for certain types of queries, clustering indexes also reduce the need for reorganizations by keeping the data in the same order as a sequenced index. If you find you need additional space in an SMS tablespace, it will be automatically allocated online. If you find you need more space with a DMS tablespace, you can add additional containers while the environment is online. Index and data defragmentation (reorganization) can be done while the system remains online. For space recovery, containers can be dropped while the system remains online.

MDC's block index structure can also eliminate the need for reorganizations, as data will be loaded into the proper sequence from the beginning.

Backup

Backups are a critical part of the overall batch window. To reduce the time required for backups, DB2 offers a number of options, including incremental backups, as demonstrated in Figure 5.10. Incremental backups allow you to only back up the data that has changed since the last backup. DB2 backups can also be defined to a fine granularity, down to the partition or individual tablespace. This reduces the amount of time required to make a backup and yet ensures that the critical data is stored. In addition, backups can be run while the system remains online.

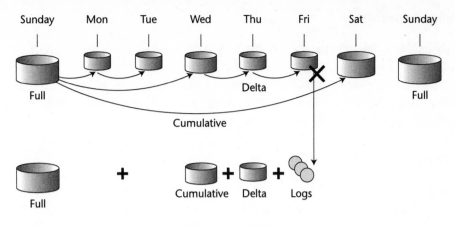

Incremental Backup

Figure 5.10   Incremental backup.

DB2 also supports the ability to keep multiple mirrored copies of the data. (See Figure 5.11.) When a disk mirror is used, the mirror can be split from the primary copy to create an immediate backup copy. The mirror image can then be used to create a complete backup without impacting the production environment. Using Tivoli Storage Manager, DB2 can also create copies of data structures on secondary storage devices.

Every once in a while a mistake happens. One of the most damaging can be the accidental dropping of a production table. Rather than requiring the table be rebuilt and the data recovered from backups, DB2 allows you to recover dropped tables if you have not reused the space.

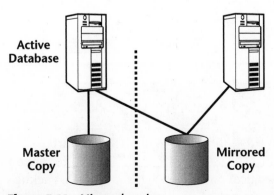

Figure 5.11   Mirrored copies.

Parallel Loading

The DB2 Loader is capable of loading all partitions in parallel, as shown in Figure 5.12. This technology reduces the amount of time required for the load process. Indexes are created and populated in parallel across all partitions as well. The Loader also allows read access to the tables while the load is running, which sustains the objective of high availability.

Online Load

As part of the loader, DB2 has the ability to load while queries are running against the table. The loaded rows are not visible to users until explicitly activated by a daemon process or the DBA. This allows us to keep the system active for user queries while we load the data. In a nightly load environment, it also gives us an option of capturing transactions throughout the day, running them through an ETL process, and loading them to the data warehouse as they become available. Then, at the end of the day, we can activate the entire day's loads through a single command, eliminating our nightly load batch window.

Multidimensional Clustering

DB2 provides a feature called multidimensional clustering (MDC). MDCs are block index structures present within each hash partition across the system. The MDC has a number of implications for system loads and availability.

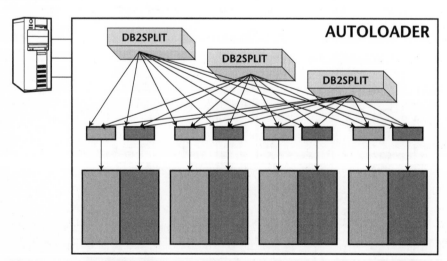

Figure 5.12 Parallel loading.

To create an MDC, the DBA defines the columns to be used for clustering. Data is loaded to the current cluster, in parallel and across hash partitions. Using online load, the entire cluster remains transparent to the user until it is activated. Activation can occur through a daemon process or through a DBA-initiated command. There are three core benefits that MDC technology brings to high availability:

Reduced resource requirements.   Because the clusters can be directly addressed, separate index reads and full or partial table scans can be avoided.

Elimination of reorganizations.   Because data are loaded in the proper sequence at all times, the need for reorganizations is eliminated.

Allows elimination of the batch window.   While online load can allow us to effectively load data with no batch window, MDC provides very fast deletes of the oldest data. With Type 2 indexes, DB2 can allow concurrent reads and deletes without false lock contention.

Unplanned Outages

DB2 also incorporates a number of features to help avoid unplanned outages or at least to minimize their disruption. DB2 starts with a highly available RDBMS, using industry-leading software development practices to ensure the best-possible code quality. Still, things can go wrong. So, DB2 allows you to have both hardware and software redundancy.

Let's examine software redundancy first. DB2 uses a watchdog program to allow partitions on different nodes to monitor the health and status of other partitions, as well as cleanup agents to clean up the work in case of a failure. These features are designed to work in conjunction with the hardware takeover features.

Because there are so many components within an MPP environment, component failure is a primary concern. There are a number of layers to hardware redundancy to address this issue. Starting at the storage level, we use RAID to protect against disk failures. DB2 also supports full disk subsystem mirroring. In the case of operating system or hardware failure, DB2 works with industry-standard clustering technologies, including IBM's HACMP, Sun Cluster, VERITAS Cluster Server, Qualix HA, Microsoft Cluster Services, Service Guard, and SteelEye LifeKeeper to ensure maximum uptime. When you are using clustering services, a number of takeover options are available to recover from node failure. Node failure can occur as a result of a nonrecoverable operating system error or hardware error in the node itself. In each case, DB2 will act as a partially fault-tolerant environment. In-flight work that was not using the crashed node will continue uninterrupted; in-flight work that was using the crashed node will be rolled back. If we used Query Patroller or MQSeries to submit the work, it can be automatically resubmitted when DB2 recovers.

The mechanism for recovery for DB2 partitions is a graceful shutdown on the failed node and an automatic restart on the takeover node.

In each of the following cases, the takeover nodes must have access to the disk used by the failed node. To accomplish this, we group the nodes within an MPP environment into one or more clusters.

Idle Standby

Idle standby is when a single node acts as a "hot spare" in case any node in the configuration crashes. In this situation, all of the work from the failed node is redirected to the hot standby, as shown in Figure 5.13. The advantage of this approach is that there is no degradation in performance. The disadvantage is that it is relatively expensive to have nodes sitting around not doing work, waiting for the off chance that a component will fail.

Active Standby

Active standby occurs when a node that is running a production workload is used as the go-to point in case of node failure. Here you would likely configure the takeover node with more capacity or a lighter workload than other nodes in the configuration. Either approach has some negative implications. You will either experience possible performance degradation when running with a down node (which could be high, if the recovery node is not powerful enough to absorb the entire workload) or a much higher node cost if it is properly configured to handle the extra workload. (See Figure 5.14.)

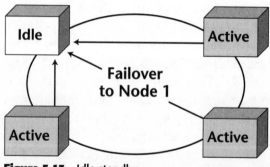

Figure 5.13   Idle standby.

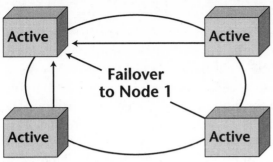

Figure 5.14   Active standby.

Mutual Takeover

Mutual takeover is yet another approach to addressing unplanned outages. In this situation, every node is assigned a "buddy" node. If one of the nodes fails, the buddy automatically takes over its workload. The advantage is that it allows for a very high rate of failure; you could lose half the nodes in an MPP configuration and continue running. The disadvantage is significant performance degradation when running with a down node. Because one node would now have twice the workload of the others, the majority of nodes will have to wait for the busiest node to complete, even with DB2's dynamic parallelism. Figure 5.15 illustrates this configuration.

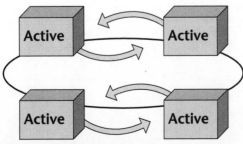

Figure 5.15   Mutual takeover.

Cascade Takeover

The final option, and the one used most frequently in an MPP configuration, is the *cascade takeover*. Each node will likely have multiple DB2 partitions. With a cascade takeover, the other nodes within the cluster serve as multiple takeover points. So, if we have four nodes with three partitions on each node, each node would be configured to take over one partition. The advantage is it allows us to maintain a balanced workload, even when running with diminished capacity. The disadvantage is it takes some planning to determine the optimal number of nodes per cluster in a very large MPP environment. (See Figure 5.16.)

When the partition is restarted on its takeover node, it must be given access to its data. This means the takeover node must be given access to the data. This can be the longest part of the recovery process. On AIX systems, DB2 works with the Concurrent Resource Manager (CRM) to minimize the recovery time required. Figure 5.17 illustrates the difference when utilizing CRM. With CRM, all disks can be designated available to all nodes within the cluster. DB2's shared-nothing architecture will only allow access to the data from the owning partition. When the partition is restarted on the takeover node, it will have immediate access to its data.

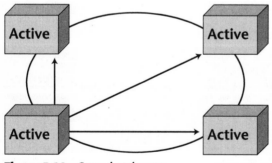

Figure 5.16 Cascade takeover.

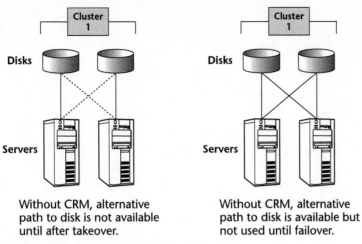

Figure 5.17   Concurrent Resource Manager.

Sizing Requirements

Estimating your data size requirements continues to be part technical application and part ability to accurately assess your current data needs, as well as to estimate their growth. Moreover, there are different kinds of data structures that you must size. For instance, in our BI architecture we have an ODS, DW staging area, atomic layer, and data marts of stars and cubes.

Nevertheless, these are a few of the issues that impact your sizing estimates. For example, you may be able to use the source system platform to perform much of your required transformations. That would mean, among other things, that you need less staging area. Another issue is associated with how you receive the data to be transformed and loaded into the warehouse. If you receive only the needed records, then your transformation space can be significantly smaller, as opposed to receiving a wholesale dump of data and having to determine the delta. Other issues affecting size estimating include storage technology, mirroring, archiving, and history required.

Figure 5.18 shows several variables that must be included, or at least considered, when you calculate sizing requirements. Of those identified, three require further discussion:

Percent of staging. You must remember two issues when dealing with staging areas. Your first concern should be with the initial load. Often the staging area is estimated on the ongoing transformation cycles, but the initial load is considerably larger than any period cycle you may have. The second issue has to do with being able to deal with the largest table in your effort. For example, the staging area needs to consider rebuilding the index for the largest tables in your warehouse or data mart. Estimating staging area is very difficult and must be periodically reviewed.

Percent of meta data. Gartner has estimated that warehouses maintain 10 to 25 percent of the space requirements for meta data. Your value will be based on the amount and type of meta data you plan to maintain and the tools you implement.

Statistical row size. To understand the "real" size of a row, the architect must take the time to get a statistical average of production rows, as opposed to merely taking the physical schema of the source table and use that as the basis for warehouse storage requirements. Many production systems have large fields with fixed lengths—for example, address line 3, with 50 characters, when in reality, 90 percent of the values in the field are less than 20 characters.

Formula Variables	Description
Period Measurement	Daily, Weekly, Monthly, Quarterly
Period of Row Growth per Period	The value is dependent on business requirements and calculated against initial load.
Percent of Aggregation	The value could be as much as 100% of base tables.
Percent of Staging	The value is dependent on business requirements, system environment and experience with data.
Percent of Meta Data	10% to 25% of base tables.
Percent of Contingency	The estimate is largely dependent on experience with the data being transformed and stored. A typical contingency is 15% to 25% of base tables.

Figure 5.18 Estimation issues.

Table Values	Dim 1	Dim 2	Fact	Initial Totals
Initial Rows Loaded	100,000	50,000	10 million	
Statistical Row Size (Bytes)	1,000	1,500	100	
Index Size (Bytes)	20	20	15	
Initial Load Size (MB)	102	76	1,150	1,328 MB
Percent of Aggregation (30%)				398.4 MB
Percent of Staging (15%)				199.2 MB
Percent of Meta Data (10%)				132.8 MB
Percent of Contingency (20%)				265.6 MB
			Initial Load Estimate	2,324 MB

Figure 5.19 Estimation calculation.

A template calculation is provided in Figure 5.19. The template is intended only as a general guideline to highlight those issues pertinent to attempting to estimate warehouse-centric database size. It is highly recommended that the data architect and project planners invite experts in the chosen technology to participate in sizing estimation. These experts should cover database administration, computer system, and disk storage. You will need the input from all of these areas to create a reasonable estimate of the initial size of your warehouse and the expected size of your warehouse over the next several months.

Even as you make your predictions of warehouse size, do not go out and immediately purchase disk capacity for the expected size of your warehouse in 2 years. This is not only a waste of disk space but of money. Purchase a sufficient amount of disk that gives you room for several months, perhaps a year. And plan to go back to the money well for disk storage in the next budget cycle. By that time you will have a much clearer understanding of your disk requirements.

Summary

Establishing an effective technical architecture for your warehouse environment is an ongoing challenge that requires constant monitoring and tuning. It is incumbent on the technical staff to be active participants in this effort and the technical architect to solicit the contribution of selected vendors. The document produced is a unique work requiring an array of skills that cover everything from systems engineering to disk storage. Furthermore, it is a living document. As new hardware and software is implemented or upgraded, the architecture document will continue to be updated through the life of your warehouse and BI environment.

Data Management

DB2 BI Fundamentals

Key Issues:

- BI drives the need to accommodate different types of information content. It is not sufficient to simply address the management of structured data. Architects and project planners must ensure that text, spatial data, images, and other video objects can be blended into the warehouse.

- As the need for 24x7 BI becomes widespread, it demands that the database engine provide a means to load and maintain data with minimum impact to the availability of the information to user audiences. Batch window processing must become the exception and no longer the rule.

Plenty of books document SQL syntax and other typical RDBMS functions. This chapter avoids the SQL trap and instead focuses on five fundamental themes that best represent the DB2 V8 features and functionality that support BI:

- High availability
- Administration
- SQL and other programming features
- Performance
- Extensibility

In this chapter, we define and illustrate each of these concepts. All of them lend themselves to a stable, scalable, and flexible BI environment. That is not to say that these are the only important aspects of DB2 V8, but these provide a secure foundation for all your subsequent BI efforts. Some of these features are covered in greater depth elsewhere in this book. For example, here we introduce materialized query tables (MQTs), but in Chapter 7 we go into MQTs in considerable detail. Another example is the Spatial Extender. This chapter includes it as part of the extensibility of DB2, but Chapter 16 provides a much broader overview of the technology.

High Availability

As data warehouses and business intelligence systems continue to move into the mainstream, availability has become critical. In the past it was possible to update a system through a nightly, weekly, or even monthly refresh process, a process that could take the system away from the users for extended periods. Today, with real-time updates, real-time decisions, and user communities spread across the globe, this is simply not feasible. To this end, DB2 has a large number of features designed to ensure high availability for the data warehouse, for example:

- Multidimensional clustering
- Online loads
- Real-time updates
- Batch window elimination
- Elimination of table reorganization
- Online load and MQT maintenance
- MQT staging tables
- Online table reorganization

- Dynamic bufferpool management
- Dynamic database configuration

These features are described in the following sections, along with discussions on logging and storage considerations.

Multidimensional Clustering

Multidimensional clustering (MDC) is the basis for a number of high-availability features. An overview of MDC is shown in Figure 6.1. MDCs are clusters of data within each hash partition across the system. For certain types of applications, the MDC has a number of implications for system loads and availability. Prior to MDC:

- All indexes were row-based.
- Clustering was in one dimension only.
- Clustering was not guaranteed, since it degrades once page free space is exhausted.

With MDC:

- Tables managed by block according to defining clustering dimensions.
- Clustering is guaranteed, since it inserts an existing block that satisfies all dimensions or creates a new block.
- Dimension indexes are block-based, which results in smaller indexes and allows row-based indexes to be supported.
- Queries in clustering dimensions only do I/Os absolutely necessary for selected data.

To create an MDC, the DBA defines the columns to cluster on and the data that will be in each:

```
CREATE    TABLE
                SALES (Customer VARCHAR(80),
                       Region       CHAR(5),
                       Year          INT)
           ORGANIZE BY DIMENSIONS (Region, Year)
```

Data is loaded to the current cluster (in parallel, across hash partitions).

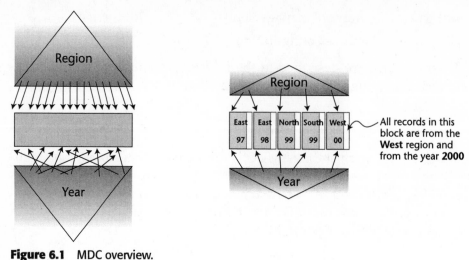

Figure 6.1 MDC overview.

Online Loads

DB2 supports online loads, for example, data can be loaded to a table while users continue to access the table. New rows will not be available to the users until explicitly activated, either through an automated process or by the DBA.

To accomplish this, DB2 places a marker indicating the end of the most recently activated segments. Queries will only read up to this marker. When a new load segment is activated, the marker is moved. In this way, data can be loaded without worrying about dirty reads or other data currency impacts.

Let's look at an example of using MDCs and online loads. Say you are a telecommunications provider running a fraud detection application on credit card calls. To have maximum impact, you need to look at current data. You can create an MDC with the hour and minute of the transaction as one of the defining dimensions. Every minute's data will be placed in a new set of clusters (depending on the other clustering columns). Every minute, the transactions can be activated at the end of the load cycle.

In other words, MDC complements online loads. Because the new clusters are transparent to running applications, loads can proceed with no locking and minimal "dirty read" considerations. Refer to Figure 6.2.

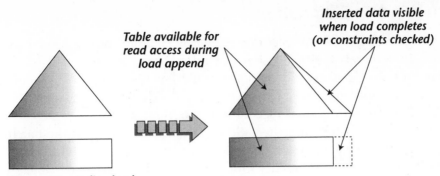

Figure 6.2   Online load.

Load From Cursor

The DB2 Loader allows data to be loaded from a cursor. This cursor can be part of an existing application, or it can be directed to an existing table. Suppose we want to load data into the data warehouse directly from an ODS or our OLTP system. The cursor can reference a table on a separate system, running under a different copy of DB2 or Oracle. By using a cursor against a table that is tied to MQSeries, rows from an MQSeries Integrator queue can be directly loaded in real time.

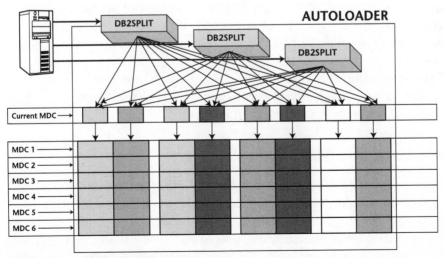

Figure 6.3   AUTOLOADER with MDC.

Batch Window Elimination

Most every business has at least one or two very large transaction tables that tend to dominate the nightly batch window. Suppose you want to significantly reduce (or essentially eliminate) your batch window. With online load, you can populate these tables throughout the day—or, for that matter, populate the entire warehouse piecemeal throughout the day.

Online load and MDC together allow virtual elimination of the batch window. Consider a situation where we want to maintain a nightly load process but eliminate our batch window. We use the transaction date as one of the clustering columns for our MDC. We can load to the current cluster as transactions become available throughout the day using online load, keeping the loaded data transparent to the user. At the end of the day, we run a simple command to activate the daily partition. At the same time, we run a process to eliminate the oldest rows. While the rows will be deleted using standard SQL transactions, because the MDC will cluster the rows together (because we used the load date as part of the cluster definition), it is possible to delete the oldest rows very quickly. (This speed is enhanced considerably by the DB2's use of type-2 indexes, covered later in this section.) Of course, queries that are not impacted by rows being deleted can be run while the deletes are executing. The batch window, the biggest recurring cause of planned outages, is effectively eliminated.

Elimination of Table Reorganization

Many times tables have specific groups of columns that are used to cluster the data. As rows are loaded to and deleted from the table, the rows can get out of sequence, forcing reorganization (reorg). With MDC, you can eliminate the need for many reorgs.

When you define the columns you want to cluster the data on, you ensure the data is physically stored in sequenced order. Thus, you eliminate the need for reorganizations on the table.

Online Load and MQT Maintenance

Materialized query tables are dependent on the data in the underlying tables, as shown in Figure 6.4. When these tables are part of a real-time load environment, the impacts on an MQT using check constraints could be tremendous. For example, suppose you are running loads in 15-second intervals on the transaction table. An MQT has been set up to summarize transactions by week. The process to create this summary takes 10 seconds for every 15 seconds of data. Obviously, it is hard to keep up with this rate of change, particularly in the middle of the day, when the system is likely to be running its most intense workload.

To offset this, DB2 offers the option of deferred checking of MQT to base table check constraints. Users must be aware, however, that there may be data currency issues between the source table and the MQT when this feature is used. See Chapter 7 for more information.

MQT Staging Tables

When real-time updates are applied against an MQT, it is possible for contention hot spots to form, particularly when multiple MQT source tables are being updated at the same time. Suppose we are doing near real-time loads to two base tables used to create an MQT. Of course, while we are attempting to apply these changes, read-only queries are also running against the MQT. In this situation, a high level of contention on the rows can quickly occur, and the same row in the MQT might end up being updated multiple times.

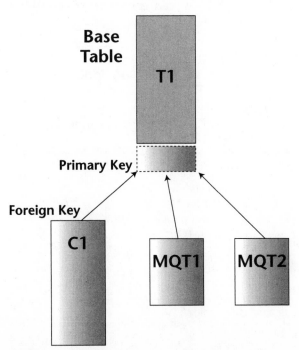

Figure 6.4   MQT maintenance with online loads.

To avoid these hot spots, DB2 uses staging tables (Figure 6.5). The staging table receives the real-time updates and applies them, and the resultant changes can then be applied to the MQT as an incremental refresh. In this way, the user is never impacted by contention from multiple real-time update sources, and we don't waste resources with multiple intermediate updates.

Online Table Reorganization

In some cases, we want to define an MDC on a table in a way other than how we need to order the data physically. For example, we want to cluster by date (to optimize our deletes, minimizing our batch window), but we want to order the table by customer number, as many of our reports are run this way. Or, there are tables where we have decided an MDC is simply not a reasonable solution.

These tables may become fragmented over time. DB2 lets you reorganize fragmented tables without shutting down the tablespace. Table reorgs are done within the existing tablespace, eliminating the need for excessive storage. Each moved row leaves behind a "reorg pointer" indicating its new location. This ensures rows are not read (or even reorged) more than once. Once the reorganization is complete, the pointers are removed. Refer to Figure 6.6.

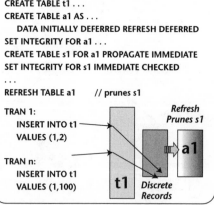

Figure 6.5 MQT staging table versus no staging table.

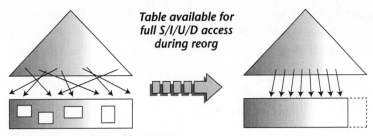

Figure 6.6   Online table REORGs.

As shown in Figure 6.7, online table reorganization can be run in two modes:

- Reclustering mode reorganizes the clustering index and the underlying data together.

- Space Reclamation mode, used with tables without a clustering index, works backward through the table to reclaim unused space.

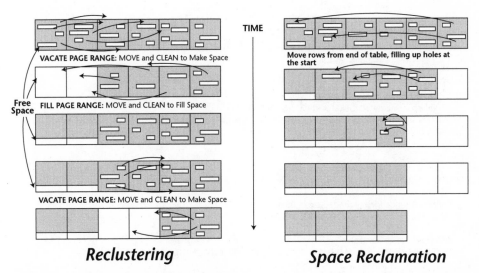

Figure 6.7   Online table reorganization modes.

Online table reorganization operates in a trickle mode, as a low-priority task (see Figure 6.8). This ensures the reorganization does not significantly impact query execution. If faster reorg execution is required, the DBA can alter this priority.

Dynamic Bufferpool Management

On rare occasion, bufferpools need to be added, dropped, or expanded. Suppose a pressing business need dictates we analyze years of data to produce an ad hoc report for a regulatory agency. The amount of data being scanned and moved into one of the bufferpools far exceeds our normal usage patterns, creating a thrashing situation (as bufferpool pages are moved from real to virtual memory and back).

DB2 allows this and other bufferpool alterations to be done online. We can expand the impacted bufferpool to meet the current needs without shutting down the system, and we can return it to its normal state when we are done, again online.

The syntax for bufferpool maintenance is shown in Figure 6.9.

```
REORG {TABLE table-name Table-Clause | INDEXES ALL FOR TABLE table-name
Index-Clause} [On-DbPartitionNum-Clause]

Table-Clause:
    [INDEX index-name] [[ALLOW {READ | NO} ACCESS]
    [USE tablespace-name] [INDEXSCAN] [LONGLOBDATA]] |
    [INPLACE [ [ALLOW {WRITE | READ} ACCESS] [NONTRUNCATE TABLE]
    [START | RESUME] | {STOP | PAUSE} ]]

Examples:
    // Recluster data, allowing write access always
    REORG TABLE t1 INDEX i1 INPLACE ALLOW WRITE ACCESS NOTRUNCATE TABLE

    // Reclaim all embedded unused space in the table
    REORG TABLE t1 INPLACE ALLOW WRITE ACCESS

    // Reclaim space on partition 5
    REORG TABLE t1 INPLACE ALLOW WRITE ACCESS ON DBPARTITIONNUM 5
```

Figure 6.8 Online REORG syntax.

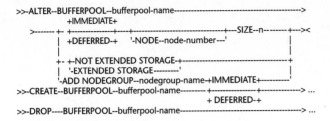

```
>>-ALTER--BUFFERPOOL--bufferpool-name--------------------------------------->
           +IMMEDIATE+
   >------- +- +---------------+----------------------------+---SIZE--n-------+---><
           |  +-DEFERRED-+    '-NODE--node-number---'                        |
           |                                                                |
           +- +-NOT EXTENDED STORAGE-+--------------------------------------+
           |  '-EXTENDED STORAGE---------'                                  |
              '-ADD NODEGROUP--nodegroup-name-+IMMEDIATE+----------'
>>-CREATE--BUFFERPOOL--bufferpool-name--------- +----------------+-------------> ...
                                               + DEFERRED-+
>>-DROP----BUFFERPOOL--bufferpool-name---------------------------------------> ...
```

Figure 6.9 Dynamic bufferpool maintenance.

Dynamic Database Configuration

On rare occasions you might want to reset database configuration parameters. The syntax is shown in Figure 6.10. Suppose we need to alter a major configuration parameter because it was set incorrectly, or the Health Center has indicated a potential problem in the works. DB2 allows this to be done while the database remains online.

Database Managed Storage Considerations

If you choose to have the DBMS, rather than the operating system, manage storage, you must monitor the storage (or, more precisely, have the Health Center, which is discussed separately in this chapter, monitor it and alert you to impending problems). Of course, manipulating the underlying storage system could produce significant outages. To avoid this, DB2 allows you to alter the containers and stripe sets without taking the system offline. You can add stripe sets to a database-managed storage (DMS) container or add another disk to the same stripe set in order to increase the available storage. (See Figure 6.11.)

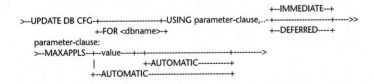

```
                                                       +--IMMEDIATE--+
>--UPDATE DB CFG-+--------------------+-USING parameter-clause,..-+---------------------+----->>
                 +-FOR <dbname>-+                          +--DEFERRED----+
     parameter-clause:
     >--MAXAPPLS--+--value----+--+------------------------------+----------->
                  |              +-AUTOMATIC-----------+
                  +--AUTOMATIC------------------------------+
```

Figure 6.10 Online database configuration parameters.

Figure 6.11   Add stripe sets.

You can also drop containers, as shown in Figure 6.12, from an active DMS storage space—provided, of course, you leave enough space to store the data.

Logging Considerations

As data warehouses are incorporating more and more real-time data, logs are becoming an increasingly critical feature of the DBMS. DB2 provides a number of features to improve logging performance and recovery time.

A number of log features are designed to prevent or minimize outages. DB2 can track which tablespaces have changes within each log file. You can turn on and off the logs using the following setting.

```
Db2set DB2_COLLECT_TS_REC_INFO=OFF
```

If a tablespace needs to be recovered, DB2 will only read the logs that have an impact on the recovery process, dramatically reducing the recovery time.

DB2 provides for infinite logging. When activated, space for logs that have already been archived is automatically reclaimed and reused. This can reduce the amount of log maintenance required in data warehouses (or other systems) with a high update volume, and it can prevent unexpectedly long transactions from having a negative performance impact due to log overruns. Syntax is shown in Figure 6.13.

Figure 6.12   Drop container.

```
>--UPDATE DB CFG-+-----------------------+-USING LOGSECOND  -1
                 +-FOR <dbname>-+
```

Figure 6.13   Enabling infinite logging.

DB2 allows mirrored logs to be kept on separate physical devices, ensuring recoverability in the event of a complete device failure. The syntax is shown in Figure 6.14.

Administration

Data warehouses are inherently complex, supporting an ever-changing mixture of data demographics, user requests, and the resultant conflicting workloads. Adding to this mix are increasing use of real-time loads, integration of remote data sources, and user communities that are demanding new forms of data delivery.

Managing and tuning a system with these inherent levels of volatility can be a daunting task. But the amount of time a DBA has in the day is finite. To reduce the level of effort required and allow DBAs to expand their control, IBM has invested heavily in the eLiza program. For DB2, the SMART project has had the most direct impact on the product.

eLiza and SMART

The Self Managing and Resource Tuning (SMART), represents a database effort that is part of IBM's broader eLiza project for self-managing servers. SMART is a long-term project designed to make database management and tuning simple and automatic, with the eventual goal of full autonomic computing. The items discussed in this section encompass many of the newest administration features of DB2, but because of the resources IBM has committed to the eLiza project, you should be aware that rapid advances in this area are quite possible. You should therefore check with IBM for the latest information.

```
>--UPDATE DB CFG-+-----------------------+-USING LOGSECOND  -1
                 +-FOR <dbname>-+
```

Figure 6.14   Enabling mirrored logging.

Automated Health Management Framework

The Automated Health Management Framework, shown in Figure 6.15, allows the DBA to set thresholds for specific database events, including performance- or availability-related items. When the threshold is reached, a predetermined action is taken (e.g., a report produced, an email or page sent). When the alert is received, the DBA can log into the Health Center to view details and the Health Center's suggested actions. The DBA can then take one or more of the recommended actions or create his or her own desired action. Through this proactive, automated approach, potential problems can be dealt with before they become critical.

AUTOCONFIGURE

The AUTOCONFIGURE option allows DB2 to automatically configure a number of critical system performance parameters, including memory allocation percentages and bufferpool resizeability, automatically. The AUTOCONFIGURE option can be defined through the CREATE DATABASE command or the CLP. The syntax is shown in Figure 6.16.

Initial studies from IBM show that a few minutes of answering questions for the AUTOCONFIGURE expert system can replace weeks of performance tuning by a human DB2 performance expert.

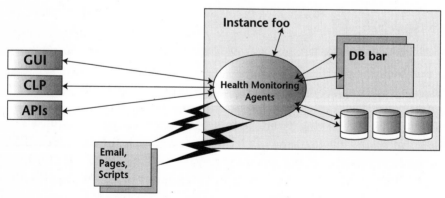

Figure 6.15   Automated Health Management Framework.

```
AUTOCONFIGURE [USING config-keyword value [{, config-keyword value}...]]
   [APPLY {DB ONLY | DB AND DBM | NONE}]

config-keyword:
   MEM_PERCENT, WORKLOAD_TYPE, NUM_STMTS, TPM, ADMIN_PRIORITY,
   IS_POPULATED, NUM_LOCAL_APPS, NUM_REMOTE_APPS, ISOLATION, BP_RESIZEABLE
```

Figure 6.16   AUTOCONFIGURE.

Administration Notification Log

The Administration Notification Log provides a single, easy-to-read log file for all administrative messages. The syntax is diagrammed in Figure 6.17. DBAs can set the notification level (1 to 4) to the level of message they wish to have reported, along with a customized message indicating the severity they associate with each level.

Maintenance Mode

Sometimes it is necessary to place a DB2 instance into a known and stable state before performing certain administrative tasks. To allow this, D2 provides a quiesce mode. When an instance is quiesced, the users can be immediately forced off, or new logons/attachments can be disallowed. When the latter option is used, the quiesce will take place when all active users have logged off. Specific users (such as the DBA) can still be allowed to access a database that is being quiesced. The syntax for quiesce is shown in Figure 6.18.

```
>--UPDATE DBM CFG---USING NOTIFYLEVEL [1|2|3|4]

1 :  Critical        " It's Too Late! "
2 :  1+Urgent        " Immediate Action Required "
3 :  2+Important     " Important Information, But No Immediate Action Required "
4 :  3+FYI           " For your information "
```

Figure 6.17   Notification log.

QUIESCE DATABASE IMMEDIATE [FORCE CONNECTIONS]

QUIESCE INSTANCE instance-name [USER user-name | GROUP group-name]
IMMEDIATE [FORCE CONNECTIONS]

UNQUIESCE DATABASE

UNQUIESCE INSTANCE instance-name

Figure 6.18   Quiesce.

Event Monitors

Event monitors can now be targeted to individual tables, and deadlock monitors can provide the exact SQL statements that caused the deadlock. The syntax for monitoring UDB events is diagrammed in Figure 6.19.

SQL and Other Programming Features

As business intelligence environments become more complex, features are implemented which can make the development of applications simpler.

INSTEAD OF Triggers

For some situations it is desirable to have triggers perform actions instead of standard SQL INSERT, UPDATE, or DELETE functions. INSTEAD OF triggers allow the DBA to define case-by-case substitutions for standard SQL operations. The code for using this function is shown in Figure 6.20. Say we have data that is coming from a variety of source systems, and the rules for updating these systems are different. When a change comes to the data warehouse, we can use INSTEAD OF triggers to indicate different processing depending on the original source system.

```
CREATE EVENT MONITOR myevmon FOR DEADLOCKS WITH DETAILS WRITE TO TABLE
SET EVENT MONITOR myevmon STATE 1
// deadlocks occur
FLUSH EVENT MONITOR myevmon
SELECT dlconn_myevmon.deadlock_id, stmt_text FROM dlconn_myevmon, deadlock_myevmon
    WHERE dlconn_myevmon.deadlock_id=deadlock_myevmon.deadlock_id
```

deadlock_id	stmt_text
4	lock table t1 in exclusive mode
4	lock table t2 in exclusive mode

Figure 6.19   Event monitors.

```
CREATE VIEW EMPV (EMPNO, FIRSTNAME, MIDINIT, LASTNAME, PHONENO, HIREDATE, DEPTNAME)
   AS SELECT EMPNO, FIRSTNME, MIDINIT, LASTNAME, PHONENO, HIREDATE, DEPTNAME
   FROM EMPLOYEE, DEPARTMENT WHERE EMPLOYEE.WORKDEPT = DEPARTMENT.DEPTNO

CREATE TRIGGER EMPV_INSERT INSTEAD OF EMPV
REFERENCING NEW AS NEWEMP DEFAULTS NULL FOR EACH ROW MODE DB2SQL
INSERT INTO EMPLOYEE (EMPNO, FIRSTNME, MIDINIT, LASTNAME, WORKDEPT, PHONENO, HIREDATE)
   VALUES (EMPNO, FIRSTNAME, MIDINIT, LASTNAME,
          COALESCE ((SELECT DEPTNO FROM DEPARTMENT AS D WHERE D.DEPTNAME = NEWEMP.DEPTNAME),
                  RAISE_ERROR ('70001', 'Unknown department name')),
          PHONENO, HIREDATE)

CREATE TRIGGER EMPV_UPDATE INSTEAD OF UPDATE ON EMPV
REFERENCING NEW AS NEWEMP OLD AS OLDEMP DEFAULTS NULL FOR EACH ROW MODE DB2SQL
BEGIN ATOMIC
   VALUES (CASE WHEN NEWEMP.EMPNO = OLDEMP.EMPNO THEN 0
            ELSE RAISE_ERROR ('70002', 'Must not change EMPNO') END);
   UPDATE EMPLOYEE AS E SET (FIRSTNAME, MIDINIT, LASTNAME, WORKDEPT, PHONENO, HIREDATE)
     = (NEWEMP.FIRSTNAME, NEWEMP.MIDINIT, NEWEMP.LASTNAME,
        COALESCE ((SELECT DEPTNO FROM DEPARTMENT AS D WHERE D.DEPTNAME = NEWEMP.DEPTNAME),
                RAISE_ERROR ('70001', 'Unknown department name')),
        NEWEMP.PHONENO, NEWEMP.HIREDATE)
     WHERE NEWEMP.EMPNO = E.EMPNO;
END

CREATE TRIGGER EMPV_DELETE INSTEAD OF DELETE ON EMPV
REFERENCING OLD AS OLDEMP FOR EACH ROW MODE DB2SQL
DELETE FROM EMPLOYEE AS E WHERE E.EMPNO = OLDEMP.EMPNO
```

Figure 6.20   INSTEAD OF trigger code.

Let's consider an example. Suppose we have a table that is part of our system of record. Because of this, we must keep historically accurate views of the data. A user with proper access issues a DELETE command. Rather than delete the entry, we want to create a new row that cancels out the original transaction. Using an INSTEAD OF trigger, we can specify this reversing transaction be applied instead of the standard SQL DELETE command.

DML Operations through UNION ALL

DB2 Version 7 provided full UPDATE and DELETE functionality to views that contain one or more UNION ALL statements in their bodies. DB2 Version 8 extended this capability to include INSERTs. Now, all data manipulation commands are common across tables and views, including those views with UNION ALL statements in their bodies.

INSERT through UNION ALL has a number of potential applications, including the ability to insert data into a view that includes tables that have been migrated to tertiary storage by a Hierarchical Storage Manager (HSM). In this case, we may have identical table structures on RAID devices for the most recent data, and the same table definitions on optical for the oldest data. We may need to update rows in some of these tables. INSERT through UNION will send the updates to the appropriate table. The code syntax is shown in Figure 6.21.

```
CREATE TABLE Q1(order DATE, item VARCHAR (10), CHECK (MONTH (order) BETWEEN 1 AND 3)
CREATE TABLE Q2(order DATE, item VARCHAR (10), CHECK (MONTH (order) BETWEEN 4 AND 6)
CREATE TABLE Q3(order DATE, item VARCHAR (10), CHECK (MONTH (order) BETWEEN 7 AND 9)
CREATE TABLE Q4(order DATE, item VARCHAR (10), CHECK (MONTH (order) BETWEEN 10 AND 12)

CREATE VIEW V (order, item)
AS SELECT * FROM Q1
    UNION ALL
    SELECT * FROM Q2
    UNION ALL
    SELECT * FROM Q3
    UNION ALL
    SELECT * FROM Q4

INSERT INTO V VALUES ('2000-01-06', 'Shoes'), ('2000-06-17', 'Socks')
```

Figure 6.21   INSERT through UNION ALL.

Informational Constraints

Referential integrity constraints do not have to be enforced by the DBMS. In some cases, the source applications are used to enforce compliance between tables. Still, in these cases, the DB2 optimizer could benefit from knowing there is a constraint enforced between the tables. The CHECK CONSTRAINT command, as outlined in Figure 6.22, provides an option to allow the constraint to be exploited by the optimizer, but not checked by the DBMS. This is called *informational constraints*.

```
CREATE TABLE H1 (MONTH INT, DATA INT)
CREATE TABLE H2 LIKE H1
ALTER TABLE H1 ADD CONSTRAINT CHK1 CHECK (MONTH BETWEEN 1 AND 6) NOT ENFORCED
ALTER TABLE H2 ADD CONSTRAINT CHK2 CHECK (MONTH BETWEEN 7 AND 12) NOT ENFORCED

CREATE VIEW FY AS SELECT * FROM H1 UNION ALL SELECT * FROM H2

SELECT * FROM FY WHERE MONTH IN (1, 2, 3)
```

Figure 6.22   Informational constraints.

User-Maintained MQTs

In some cases, we may have applications or users that maintain summary or other derived tables. Consider an example where an application suite calculates and stores all standardized corporate calculations for profitability. Still, we would like these summary tables to be available to the optimizer for automatic substitution at query execution time.

User-maintained MQTs allow us to tell the DB2 optimizer that a table is calculated using certain commands, based on specific tables. DB2 will use this information in its optimization process, even though it is not responsible for creating or maintaining the MQT.

Performance

Performance, of course, is one of the most critical aspects of a data warehouse environment. The faster a query can execute, the faster the business response can be enacted. The fewer resources a process takes, the more resources that are freed for other tasks. Better performance translates directly into faster actions and lower costs.

Connection Concentrator

Each user who is logged on to the system requires a certain level of resources from the DBMS. DB2 uses an agent/sub-agent approach to dispatch specific commands throughout the system. At any given time, these users or tasks have down cycles that could be used for other processing.

The Connection Concentrator allows multiple users to share critical resources, including agents (agents coordinate the query and finalize the result set in a shared-nothing environment) and sub-agents (processes that carry out the actual execution of the query steps). Figure 6.23 illustrates the concept.

Think of the connection concentrator as a multiplexer for query execution steps. By allowing multiple users to share database resources, the overall demands on the system can be dramatically reduced, and the need for process context switching can be greatly reduced.

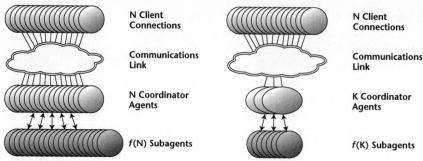

Figure 6.23   Connection Concentrator.

Compression

One of the truths about any data warehouse is that some columns are sparsely populated. These columns can take considerable space in the data warehouse. A method to effectively squeeze the unused space out can save money and improve efficiency.

DB2 allows compression on specific columns. While this saves space (and, hence, storage costs), it can also improve query performance by allowing more rows to fit into each page, and hence be retrieved by each I/O. Compression can be specified on "null" for any null column or on a default value for any column. The compressible defaults are blank for character type fields and zero for numeric. For each row where the compressed value is found, a compression byte is stored in place of the data. When the column is retrieved by a query, DB2 will substitute the default value.

Figure 6.24 illustrates noncompressed versus compressed data.

Type-2 Indexes

To ensure the highest level of concurrency, DB2 provides type-2 index structures. These prevent false lock contention on the surrounding row values. Type-2 indexes use a pseudo-delete algorithm, where rows that are deleted will be left in the table but marked as deleted. The rows will be physically removed when the transaction is committed. All indexes created in DB2 V7 or lower will be Type 1 indexes; all indexes created in DB2 V8 or higher will be type-2 indexes. Both index types are compared in Figure 6.25.

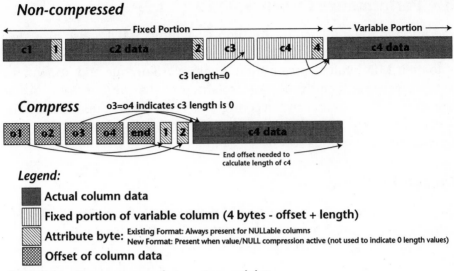

Figure 6.24 Non-compressed vs. compressed data.

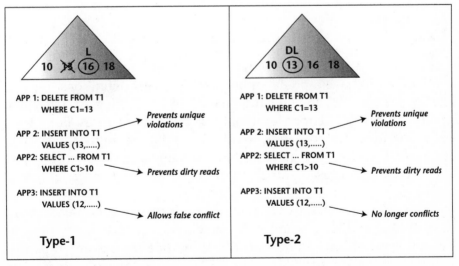

Figure 6.25 Index types.

MDC Performance Enhancement

In addition to the implications for high availability, MDCs also provide a significant performance boost. Data are kept in clusters, or blocks, according to their MDC value. Because these values are unique and known, the optimizer can use them to quickly isolate rows that pertain to a specific request. MDCs maintain rows in contiguous order. In addition to reducing the need for reorgs, this also means more effective physical I/Os, as each page contains contiguous rows.

Blocked Bufferpools

When the DB2 pre-fetchers read data from a table (or index) into the buffer-pools, they use the first available space they find. Because data is removed from the bufferpool based on spoiled rows, then via an LRU algorithm, the available space at any given time can be spread across the bufferpool. This can have a negative impact on performance.

DB2 allows you to define a bufferpool as blocked. A blocked bufferpool maintains contiguous memory in block sizes that match the associated tablespace. As blocks of pages are read by the pre-fetchers, they are moved into contiguous memory. In this way, data is not only available to the application when it needs the data, it is also available in the most effective manner possible.

Extensibility

One of the key features of DB2 Universal Database is its extensibility. Traditional RDBMSs have a predetermined set of object definitions (integer, character, decimal, etc.) and operations (add, subtract, string, etc.) that they support. DB2 certainly supports all of these standard features. But it goes well beyond these features and provides the ability to support new data types (spatial, image, XML, and custom, to name a few) and operations (PMML Scoring, discussed at the end of the chapter, data mining, spatial analysis, etc.).

Incorporating advanced functionality at the engine level is the necessary step for IBM to address a seamless integration of BI functionality. Only at the engine level of the RDBMS can you truly tune for maximum performance and consolidate administration. The extensions of DB2 UDB include MQSeries Extender, Spatial Extender, Text Extender and Text Information Extender, Image Extender, XML Extender, Video Extender, Audio Extender, and Net Search Extender. In addition, a number of mining functions like

DB2 Scoring, as well as access to MQSeries Integrator, are implemented using these extensibility features. All of these bring to the core of your database advanced features and functionality that enhance the capabilities of your RDBMS and your ability to deliver broad informational content to your user communities and their analytic applications.

Spatial Extender

The DB2 Spatial Extender allows you to store graphical information, index it, and explore the relationships among various objects. This topic is discussed in greater detail in Chapter 16. For now, we will only briefly mention the extensions functionality.

Say you work for a bank and your user community wants to look at the performance of your various branches and ATMs. In a tabular report you can see that one of our ATMs is underperforming, but there is no immediate indication of why this might be. On the spatial version, you can readily see the issue: there are natural boundaries preventing customers from reaching this ATM. Spatial analysis allows you to quickly see relationships that would be difficult to find in a traditional tabular format. Images can be viewed and analyzed using tools from ESRI. As illustrated in Figure 6.26, analysts can quickly discern the outlet performance in comparison to the competition.

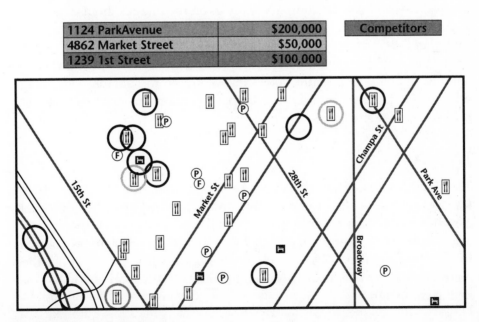

Figure 6.26   Spatial analysis.

Text Extender and Text Information Extender

The DB2 Text Extender provides linguistic indexing and search capabilities in 22 languages. It includes the ability to run a number of different search types, including free text and fuzzy searches. Synonyms and similar spellings can be checked in all 22 supported languages. In addition to traditional documents, the Text Extender allows users to search in HTML and XML texts.

Suppose we work for a property and casualty insurance company. The Text Extender would allow us to easily store and analyze document-based data pertaining to claims, for example, police reports on accidents and damage reports from field agents. Using the fuzzy search capabilities, we can find similar documents even when different descriptions were used.

The DB2 Text Information Extender provides mode sophisticated search techniques, but does not have the range of language support that the Text Extender does.

Image Extender

The DB2 Image Extender allows you to store image data and analyze it using IBM's Query By Image Content (QBIC). QBIC allows us to query images for matches using colors or texture patterns from a sample image. With DB2 Image Extender, we can do more than simply store and retrieve images, we can perform complex analysis on the images themselves.

Let's switch our example to a health insurer. A health insurer could keep all patient records, including radiograph, ultrasound, and MRI images. This data could then be offered as a value-added service to health care professionals. The doctor could take an MRI, search the database for images with similar patterns, and receive a report on diagnosis and treatment efficacy for similar situations.

XML Extender

The DB2 XML Extender allows us to categorize and index XML-based data for easy analysis. Tags and text within an XML record can be automatically assigned to database columns.

Say you are an online retailer, and you collect a lot of data on your customers. You can use XML to track their privacy restrictions and use these restrictions as part of your criteria on including them in an upcoming marketing campaign.

Video Extender and Audio Extender

The DB2 Video Extender and DB2 Audio Extender allow storage and retrieval of audio and video images. Say you are an analyst for a major league sports team of a game, such as basketball, with a timed environment. You want to analyze the progress of other teams' players for competitive purposes and your own players for improvement purposes. You can collect statistics on how the players perform under specific circumstances. Using the Video Extender, coordinated with the official time clock used in the events, you can use actual game footage to precisely demonstrate the trends and tendencies you are examining.

Net Search Extender

The DB2 Net Search Extender allows high-speed Boolean and fuzzy searches against very large indexes. Returning to the online retailer example, suppose you want to give our customers access to your inventory, even when they use very imprecise search criteria. Using Net Search, you can provide "Internet speed" search capabilities to their queries.

MQSeries

DB2 can view MQSeries Integrator queues as tables in the database. In this way, DB2 can place data onto the queue by simply writing to the table, and take data off of a queue by simply reading the table.

Let's consider an example. Suppose you are a bank, and you want to know every transaction your customer has made so you can position the correct offer in front of him at any time. You need to understand everything he has done with up-to-the-second accuracy. You define an MDC of one second. You search the incoming MQSeries queue for new entries constantly. When one is found, you use the DB2 loader's ability to load directly from another table (load from cursor) to load into your MDC directly from the MQSeries Integrator queue. Every second, your data warehouse is refreshed with the latest view of your customers.

DB2 Scoring

Implemented using DB2 Extender technology, DB2 Scoring is based on the Data Mining Group's (DMG, www.dmg.org) Predictive Model Markup Language (PMML). PMML is an industry standard for creating and using scoring models. Once developed, PMML models can be deployed across any PMML-compliant software. Data mining is explored in greater depth in Chapter 14.

In a traditional data mining environment, a risk management expert would develop the scoring models, and the business area experts would decide how to treat customers within each score group. Moreover, typically the customers would be scored in a batch process and the results pushed out to the customer-facing employees.

To clarify this, let's return to the bank scenario. A customer calls the service center to request a new credit line. He provides the customer service agent with updated financial information. The agent puts the new data in, and DB2 Scoring returns a score. Based on this score, the customer service agent can give the customer an almost immediate answer.

What happened behind the scenes is the risk manager still defined the scoring process, and the business area experts decided on the appropriate actions to take based on the score. The scoring model was implemented as a DB2 function. When the customer service agent input the new data, the model used a standardized approach to determine a score and returned an action based on these business rules. Without even realizing it, the customer service agent executed a real-time data mining exercise. (See Figure 6.27.)

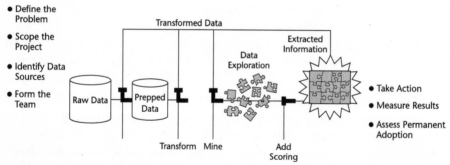

Figure 6.27   DB2 Scoring.

Summary

Today's BI environments are increasingly demanding. From zero-latent techniques to Internet portal technology to global enterprise logistics, current BI systems are stressed to their maximum. That is why IBM has designed DB2 V8 for maximum uptime, efficient administration, and extensibility. DB2 provides many of the fundamental features and functions to support the most demanding requirements for data management in both warehousing and BI applications.

CHAPTER 7

DB2 Materialized Query Tables

Key Issues:

- Materialized query tables (MQTs) are an excellent example of BI analytics blended into the database engine and its optimization process.

- Significant performance can be experienced using MQT technology for complex, long-running decision support queries over large data sets.

- DB2 V8 MQTs are a significant improvement over previous implementations of automatic summary tables (ASTs).

Materialized query tables were introduced in DB2 UDB Version 5 and have been continually enhanced with new capabilities since then. Their objective is to address the performance problems known to exist with automatic summary tables. Prior to DB2 UDB V8, MQTs were called ASTs. In DB2 V8, this feature has been extended to include a larger variety of materialized views that do not contain summary data and therefore a more generalized term than AST was required. ASTs can be considered a subset of the generalized MQT.

The motivation for materialized views came from the performance problems associated with analyzing large amounts of data repetitively with minor variations to the query predicates. The results of these queries are almost always expressed as summaries or aggregates. For example, a query might request the number of items belonging to a consumer electronics product group sold in each month of the previous year for the western region, while another query may request the same kind of information for only the month of December for all regions in the United States. A third query might request monthly information for laptops for all regions in the United States over the past 6 months. The underlying data could easily involve millions of transactions stored in one or more tables that would need to be scanned repeatedly to answer the queries. Consequently, query performance is likely to be poor. MQTs address performance problems by:

- Allowing a DBA to precompute and materialize into a table an aggregate query. This summary table contains a superset of the information that answers a number of queries that have minor variations.

- Enhancing the DB2 optimizer to automatically rewrite a query against the base tables to target the materialized view instead (if appropriate) to satisfy the original query. And since the materialized view contains precomputed values, it is generally much smaller in size than the base tables, causing significant performance gains to be achieved.

A real-world example is a client that requires a query to compute the total sales for all product categories for the year 1998. In this particular case, the query involves joining 1.5 billion transaction rows in a fact table with three dimension tables. The query has to touch at least 400 million rows in the transaction table. Without an MQT, the response time on a 22-node SP was 43 minutes. With an MQT, the response time has been reduced to 3 seconds! DB2 essentially touches at least 4,000 times fewer rows and avoided a join. The benefits achievable with MQTs largely depend upon your own unique workload.

Materialized view functionality is somewhat similar to the role of a DB2 index, which provides an efficient access path that the query user is typically unaware of. But unlike an index, a user may directly query the MQT. This is not generally recommended, however, since it would detract from the appeal of an MQT being a black box that an administrator creates and destroys as required to deliver superior query performance. Figure 7.1 provides an overview of the materialized view concept.

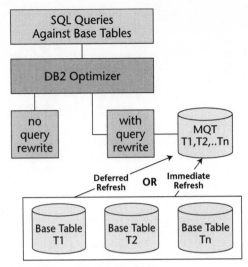

Figure 7.1   Materialized view.

The materialized view concept can also be exploited for better performance in an e-business environment. For example, in e-commerce, product catalog information can be cached on mid-tier servers to significantly improve the performance of catalog browsing. MQTs can be used to cache back-end database product information on a mid-tier. DB2 supports such caching by allowing MQTs to be defined over nicknames that are used to define a remote table. Populating the MQT involves pulling data from the remote table and storing it locally, resulting in significant performance benefits. Note that this only applies to deferred refresh MQTs.

The single-table MQT example described in Figure 7.2 is replicating the CUST table in a partitioned database environment to all the partitions. This is done in order to improve the performance of joins with the TRANS table, which is partitioned across a number of partitions. Single-table MQTs are primarily used to isolate hot data for improved access performance. Such MQTs can have indexes created on them that may not be viable on the underlying tables on which the MQT is based. The join MQT example is similar in concept to the single table MQT except that it involves a join of two tables.

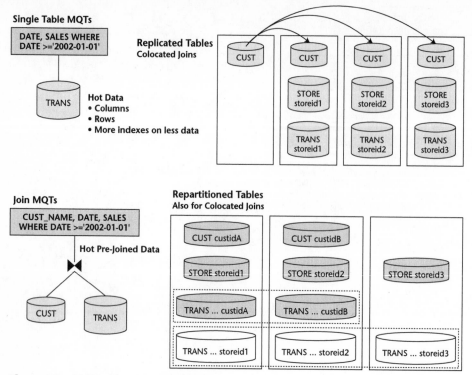

Figure 7.2   MQT without aggregation.

Implementing MQTs requires you to determine the acceptable latency of data for the query. For data warehouses and strategic decision making, there can be (and in some cases needs to be) a certain latency, such as end-of-day, end-of-week, or end-of-month information. In such cases, the materialized view need not be kept in sync with the base tables. DB2 supports a deferred refresh of the MQT for such scenarios. With regard to OLAP and tactical decision making, any MQT latency may be unacceptable, and DB2 supports an immediate refresh of the MQT in such cases. Note that there could be significant performance overheads on the base tables when the volume of update activity is high in these scenarios.

Other issues to consider for using MQTs include implementation and tuning. For implementation you must identify the materialized views that need to be created and the refresh approach to be adopted. Similarly, MQTs that are no longer required should be identified and dropped. Tuning requirements for optimal performance of your MQTs is another concern—for example, executing RUNSTATS, creating referential integrity constraints, choosing appropriate refresh approaches, and creating appropriate indexes. The main syntax elements of creating an MQT are shown in Figure 7.3.

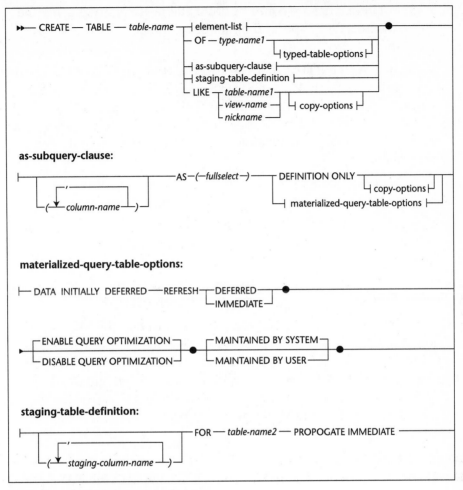

Figure 7.3 Main MQT syntax elements.

For brevity, other issues that impact your implementation and execution of materialized views are outlined in the following:

- When DEFINITION ONLY is specified, any valid fullselect that does not reference a typed table or typed view can be specified. The query is used only to define the table. The table is not populated using the results of the query, and the REFRESH TABLE statement cannot be used.

- When the CREATE TABLE statement is completed, the table is not considered a materialized view. The columns of the table are defined based on the definitions of the columns that result from the fullselect. If the fullselect references a single table in the FROM clause, select list items that are columns of that table are defined using the column name, data type, and nullability characteristic of the referenced table.

- With the DATA INITIALLY DEFERRED option, data is not inserted into the table as part of the CREATE TABLE statement. The MQT has to be populated using the SET INTEGRITY command or a REFRESH TABLE statement, or some other user-determined mechanisms, depending upon whether the MQT is system-maintained or user-maintained.

- The ENABLE QUERY OPTIMIZATION parameter allows the MQT to be used for query optimization. This is the default option.

- The DISABLE QUERY OPTIMIZATION ensures that the MQT is not used for query optimization. However, it can still be directly queried.

- The MAINTAINED BY SYSTEM option indicates that the data in the MQT is maintained by the system and it is the default.

- The MAINTAINED BY USER option indicates that the MQT is user-maintained. In this case, the user is allowed to perform UPDATE, DELETE, or INSERT operations against the user-maintained MQT. The REFRESH TABLE statement, used for system-maintained MQTs, cannot be invoked against user-maintained MQTs. Only a REFRESH DEFERRED MQT can be defined as MAINTAINED BY USER.

Figure 7.4 shows the syntax of the REFRESH statement that refreshes the data in an MQT. The INCREMENTAL and NOT INCREMENTAL options are covered later in the chapter.

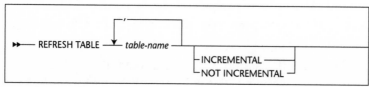

Figure 7.4   REFRESH TABLE statement.

Initializing MQTs

Three steps are necessary to initialize an MQT: creating, populating, and tuning. And, of course, you will need to drop MQTs from time to time. We discuss each in the following sections.

Creating

Assuming that the user has determined what the materialized view should look like, the following occurs when the MQT creation DDL is executed. First, since the MQT is not populated at the time of creation, it is placed in CHECK PENDING NO ACCESS state regardless of whether it is a system-maintained or a user-maintained MQT. No SQL read or write access is permitted against tables in a CHECK PENDING NO ACCESS state. Second, the dependencies regarding the underlying tables and the MQT are recorded in SYSCAT.TABLES, SYSCAT.TABDEP, and SYSCAT.VIEWS, just as in any other table or view definition creation. All packages that access the underlying tables on which the materialized view is built are invalidated if the REFRESH IMMEDIATE option is chosen or it is a staging table. This is because the SQL compiler must add appropriate operations in the package to support the refresh immediate MQTs or staging tables. When the package is first accessed after invalidation, an automatic rebind ensures that the package has been updated to support the MQT or staging table.

EXPLAIN of this package will highlight the additional SQL operations being performed to support MQTs.

Populating

Populating may be achieved in one of three ways: a SET INTEGRITY statement, a REFRESH TABLE statement, or a user-managed technique:

SET INTEGRITY.   The following statement causes the MQT to be populated, and results in the CHECK PENDING NO ACCESS state being reset on successful completion.

```
SET INTEGRITY FOR tablename IMMEDIATE CHECKED
```

REFRESH TABLE.   The following statement causes the MQT to be populated and the CHECK PENDING NO ACCESS state to be reset on successful completion.

```
REFRESH TABLE tablename
```

There is no semantic difference between using the SET INTEGRITY or the REFRESH TABLE syntax; both are treated identically.

User-managed.   In the user-managed approach, it is left to the user to populate the MQT and then reset the CHECK PENDING NO ACCESS state. The user is responsible for ensuring the consistency and integrity of the MQT. Typically, the user would first make the underlying tables read-only. Then the user would extract the required data from the underlying tables and write it to an external file, at which point the user can IMPORT or LOAD the data into the MQT. Either of these operations are permitted on a table in CHECK PENDING NO ACCESS state. Finally, the user would reset the CHECK PENDING NO ACCESS state using the following statement:

```
SET INTEGRITY FOR tablename ALL IMMEDIATE UNCHECKED
```

This action is recorded in the fifth position of the CONST_CHECKED character array (value 'U') in the catalog table SYSCAT.TABLES column, indicating that the user has assumed responsibility for data integrity of the MQT. The SET INTEGRITY statement also applies to staging tables.

To use SQL INSERT statements, you must first take the MQT out of CHECK PENDING NO ACCESS state, if appropriate. However, you must first disable optimization before resetting the CHECK PENDING NO ACCESS state via the DISABLE QUERY OPTIMIZATION option in the DDL to ensure that a dynamic SQL query does not accidentally optimize to this MQT while the data in it is still in a state of flux. This warning applies to user-managed MQTs with the DEFERRED REFRESH option. Once the materialized view has been populated, the optimization needs to be enabled and the underlying tables need to be made read/write using the SET INTEGRITY command.

Note that at any time a system-maintained MQT can be put back in CHECK PENDING NO ACCESS state using the SET INTEGRITY FOR tablename OFF statement. The 'REFRESH TABLE tablename NOT INCRE-MENTAL' can be used if you want DB2 to fully refresh the MQT.

Using the SET INTEGRITY or REFRESH TABLE approaches to populate the MQT involves using SQL INSERT subselect-type processing, which may result in excessive logging when very large MQTs are being populated. Users may want to avoid this logging overhead by refreshing the MQT using the preceding approach.

Another mechanism of using LOAD via cursors may be used to populate materialized views as well. For more information on this logic, please refer to the redbook titled "DB2 UDB's High Function Business Intelligence in e-business" published by IBM.

Tuning

The tuning of an MQT is a straightforward process. This involves creating appropriate indexes and executing the RUNSTATS utility on the MQT to ensure optimal access path selection. For more details regarding the tuning of MQTs, refer to the section *MQT Tuning* toward the end of the chapter.

MQT DROP

When an MQT is dropped, all dependencies are dropped and all packages with dependencies on the MQT are invalidated. Views based on dropped MQTs are marked inoperative.

MQT Refresh Strategies

As mentioned, DB2 supports both a deferred refresh as well as an immediate refresh of the MQTs. We discuss both of these options in the following sections.

Deferred Refresh

This approach is used when the MQT need not be kept in sync when the underlying tables on which it has been defined are updated. The data could be refreshed when appropriate as deemed by the administrator. Such MQTs are called REFRESH DEFERRED tables. There is one restriction: MQT optimization does not occur for static SQL statements with REFRESH DEFERRED tables. Figure 7.5 provides an overview of the deferred refresh mechanism.

The SQL for creating a REFRESH DEFERRED MQT could look like:

```
CREATE SUMMARY TABLE dba.summary_salesAS (SELECT ..........)
DATA INITIALLY DEFERRED
REFRESH DEFERRED
```

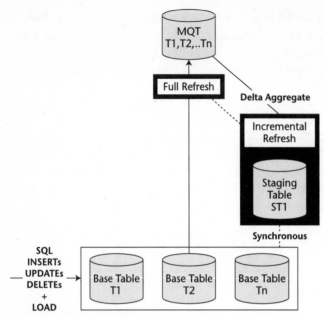

Figure 7.5   Deferred refresh.

REFRESH DEFERRED tables can be updated in one of two ways:

- Issue a full refresh command:

```
REFRESH TABLE dba.summary_sales NOT INCREMENTAL
```

The NOT INCREMENTAL option specifies a full refresh for the table by recomputing the MQT definition. When this is done, all existing data within the table is deleted and the query defining the materialized query table is computed in its entirety.

- Perform an incremental refresh:

```
REFRESH TABLE dba.sales_summary INCREMENTAL
```

The INCREMENTAL option specifies an incremental refresh for the table by considering only the appended portion (if any) of its underlying tables or the content of an associated staging table (if one exists and its contents are consistent). If DB2 detects that the MQT needs to be fully recomputed, then an error condition is returned.

If neither INCREMENTAL nor NOT INCREMENTAL is specified, the system will determine whether incremental processing is possible. If not possible, full refresh will be used.

There are three considerations for staging tables:

- If a staging table is present for the MQT that is to be refreshed and incremental processing is not possible because the staging table is in a pending state, an error is returned.

- Full refresh will be performed if the staging table is inconsistent and the staging table is pruned.

- Incremental refresh will be performed using the contents of a valid staging table and the staging table will be pruned.

Incremental refresh for update operations other than LOAD requires the creation of a staging table. In the following example, assume that sales_summary has been defined with the REFRESH DEFERRED option. The staging table is created as follows:

```
CREATE TABLE sales_stage
FOR sales_summary
PROPOGATE IMMEDIATE
```

For this to be successful, even though the sales_summary table was defined with the REFRESH DEFERRED option, it must satisfy all the conditions of a REFRESH IMMEDIATE MQT.

The schema of the staging table looks much like the MQT for which it has been defined. The difference is that the staging table may have two or three more columns than its associated MQT. These are as follows:

globalTransid CHAR(8).   Global transaction ID for each propagated row.

globalTransTime CHAR(13).   The timestamp of the transaction.

operationType SMALLINT.   Values -1, 0, and 1 for SQL DELETE, UPDATE, and INSERT, respectively.

There is a restriction: Each column name in the staging table must be unique and unqualified. If a list of column names is not specified, the columns of the table inherit the names of the columns of the associated summary table. If a list of columns is specified, it must include the required extra columns.

For replicated MQTs and nonaggregate query MQTs, the staging table contains three more columns than the associated MQT. Otherwise, the staging table only contains two extra columns, with the operationType column being omitted.

The PROPAGATE IMMEDIATE parameter indicates that any changes made to the underlying tables as part of an INSERT, DELETE, UPDATE operation are immediately added to the staging table with additional information generated in the three extra columns of the staging table. This is done as part of the same SQL statement. If the staging table is not marked inconsistent, its content, at any point in time, is the delta changes to the underlying table since the last REFRESH TABLE statement.

The target MQT has not yet been updated and still contains data corresponding to the previous refresh operation. When the following refresh statement is issued:

```
REFRESH TABLE dba.summary_sales
```

assuming DB2 uses the data in the staging table to update the target MQT, it prunes the applied data in the staging table as part of this process.

The rows in the staging table are grouped and consolidated as required, before the changes are applied to the MQT. DB2 takes a z-lock on the MQT and the staging table (if one exists) during the REFRESH TABLE statement. If the staging table is unavailable for extended periods of time because of a lengthy refresh, it has the potential to negatively impact update activity on the underlying table. Similarly, having the MQT unavailable for an extended period because of refresh times can negatively affect the performance of queries accessing the MQT.

The frequency of execution of the REFRESH TABLE statement has an impact on the following:

Latency of the data.   The tolerance for latency depends on the application.

Logging overhead against the MQT.   This is because more frequent refreshes have the potential to involve more updates against the MQT. Less frequent refreshes may result in fewer updates because data consolidation may occur either on the staging table or underlying table. On the other hand, less frequent refreshes could result in a large volume of data in the staging table that needs to be pruned and logged.

Following are several issues that you should examine when considering deferred refresh:

- Logging space can be of concern when large volumes of data are involved in refreshing an MQT. The following approaches may alleviate this problem:

- Temporarily make the MQT look like a regular table so that it can be populated directly using LOAD or suitably batched insert statements with sub-selects corresponding to the query used to define the MQT. When the entire table is populated, convert this table back to an MQT using the SET SUMMARY option in the ALTER TABLE statement.

- Use the ALTER TABLE statement with the NOT LOGGED INITIALLY option to avoid logging during the refresh. This is probably the option of choice for the following reason: By limiting the unit of work to the REFRESH TABLE statement, the probability of an inadvertent rollback due to an error is quite small. In the unlikely case that a rollback does occur, the MQT can be refreshed again. However, only a full refresh occurs in such cases (no incremental refresh is possible), and the database administrator must drop and re-create the MQT DDL definition, since the rollback will result in the MQT being placed in the DELETE ONLY state.

- As mentioned earlier, using LOAD via cursors may be used to populate materialized views as well. Since LOAD does not log data, this is an effective mechanism to overcome the logging issue.

- The data in the MQT can be refreshed at any time using the REFRESH TABLE statement. The data in the table only reflects the result of the query as a snapshot at the time the REFRESH TABLE statement is processed.

- System-maintained MQTs defined with this attribute do not allow INSERT, UPDATE, or DELETE statements.

- User-maintained MQTs defined with this attribute do allow INSERT, UPDATE, or DELETE statements, but the REFRESH TABLE statement cannot be issued against such MQTs.

NOTE When experiencing performance problems, you can choose to increase the space for active logs by simply increasing the number of secondary log files available. Another option for expanding active logs is to set the number of secondary log files to -1. This is interpreted as infinite log space to DB2. This does not imply additional disks as long as log archival is used. With log archival, the active log is migrated to tertiary storage. In the event of a rollback, recovery that requires log data from the archived log may take an extended amount of time.

Immediate Refresh

This approach is used when the MQT must be kept in sync with any changes in the underlying tables on which it has been defined. Such MQTs are called REFRESH IMMEDIATE tables. Given the synchronous nature of the immediate refresh capability, the atomic requirement for the change propagation can have a negative impact on transactions updating the underlying tables on which the MQT is based. The maintenance overhead of a REFRESH IMMEDIATE must only be implemented under extreme circumstances that truly warrant the technique.

Not all MQTs can be defined to be REFRESH IMMEDIATE. What determines which MQT can be defined with REFRESH IMMEDIATE is dictated by the ability to compute the changes to the MQT from the delta changes to the underlying tables and any other base tables involved. MQT optimization occurs for both static and dynamic SQL statements with REFRESH IMMEDIATE tables.

The SQL for creating a Refresh Immediate materialized view could look like this:

```
CREATE SUMMARY TABLE dba.summary_sales
AS (SELECT ...........)
DATA INITIALLY DEFERRED
REFRESH IMMEDIATE
```

REFRESH IMMEDIATE tables are synchronized with the underlying tables in the same unit of work as the changes (inserts, updates, or deletes) to the underlying tables. For this to be an efficient process, there are limitations on what can be defined as a REFRESH IMMEDIATE table. These are discussed in the section *MQT Limitations* at the end of this chapter.

An incremental update mechanism is used to synchronize a REFRESH IMMEDIATE MQT whenever an update, delete, or insert is done to an underlying table. The process involved is shown in Figure 7.6.

The following steps occur when an SQL statement modifies a row in the underlying table. Note that this processing occurs at statement execution time as opposed to occurring at commit time:

1. The modified row is captured.

2. The query defining the MQT is computed based on the modified row, computing the delta joins and delta aggregation to generate the data necessary to update the materialized query table.

3. The delta is applied to the MQT.

Immediate Refresh of MQT

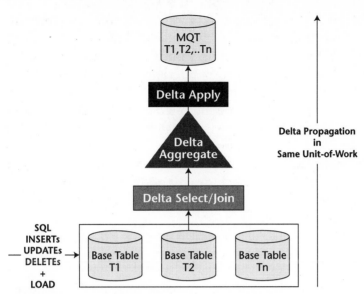

Figure 7.6   Immediate refresh.

For illustration, let's say you have an MQT that has data grouped by month. Assume that the data was up to and including the month of June. If a sales entry is made for the month of June, the delta change to the aggregation is computed so that the row in the materialized query table is updated to reflect the newly inserted row in the underlying sales table. If a row happens to be inserted into the sales table for the month of July, a new row would be inserted in the MQT, since one did not exist before for July.

DB2 may use pipelining or temporary tables to effect this operation. And, since this entire operation is atomic, any error encountered while updating either the underlying table or the MQT will roll back all the changes during the unit of work. This guarantees the synchronization of the MQT with the underlying tables.

Loading Underlying Tables

The underlying tables of the MQT may be updated either through SQL statements or via the LOAD utility. The LOAD INSERT appends rows after the last pages of the table. The following discussion applies to REFRESH IMMEDIATE MQTs and staging tables.

In DB2 V7, when a LOAD is performed on the underlying tables, all the corresponding materialized views are put in a CHECK PENDING NO ACCESS state until complete synchronization of the MQT and underlying tables has been accomplished via the SET INTEGRITY or REFRESH TABLE statements. When the tables involved are very large, the time to refresh may be very large, since the entire underlying data is scanned, not just the recently appended data. This can result in very poor response times since MQT optimization would be inhibited with the MQT being in a CHECK PENDING NO ACCESS state (see *Matching Criteria* coming up in the chapter for details of matching limitations).

In DB2 V8, functionality has been added to reduce the impact of loading data into the underlying tables. This includes the addition of new states, as well as new options to LOAD and SET INTEGRITY. Each is discussed in the sections that follow.

New States

Three new states have been added in DB2 V8 that reduce loading impact:

CHECK PENDING NO ACCESS state.   The state is similar to the previous CHECK PENDING state.

CHECK PENDING READ ACCESS state.   This allows read access to tables in such a state, but only up to and not including the first page loaded.

NO DATA MOVEMENT state.   This ensures that the RID of a row cannot change. Consequently, operations such as REORG or REDIS-TRIBUTE or an update of a partitioning key or of a key in an MDC table will all be inhibited. SQL INSERT, UPDATED (except those just mentioned), and DELETE operations do not change the RIDs and are therefore permitted.

New LOAD Options

Two new options have been added to the LOAD:

CHECK PENDING CASCADE DEFERRED | IMMEDIATE.   CAS-CADE DEFERRED specifies that descendent foreign key tables and descendent refresh immediate and staging tables are not put into CHECK PENDING NO ACCESS state, but left in normal state.

ALLOW READ ACCESS | NO ACCESS.   ALLOW READ ACCESS specifies that all the data prior to the first page appended can continue to be read, but not updated.

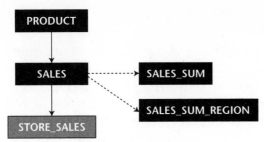

Figure 7.7 LOAD application sample.

SET INTEGRITY new option.   There has been one significant option added to SET INTEGRITY referred to as FULL ACCESS. This option specifies that full read-write access is allowed on the table. This is true even if there are dependent MQTs for the table that have not yet been refreshed with the newly load appended data. If this option is not specified, the table has the NO DATA MOVEMENT mode set on it.

Let's examine the scenario given in Figure 7.7. Here SALES is the underlying table on which two MQTs, SALES_SUM and SALES_SUM_REGION, are defined. The SALES table has check constraints in its definition, such as region code checking, and it is also involved in referential integrity constraints with the PRODUCT and STORE_SALES tables.

In this scenario, we will assume that LOAD insert is performed on SALES with the CHECK PENDING CASCADE DEFERRED option set:

```
LOAD INSERT INTO SALES .....
CHECK PENDING CASCADE DEFERRED...
ALLOW READ ACCESS...
```

This causes data to be appended to existing data in the table. If LOAD replace is done, the entire contents of the table are deleted and replaced by the new data. The CHECK PENDING CASCADE DEFERRED option can still be used for LOAD REPLACE, but the ALLOW READ ACCESS option cannot be used for LOAD REPLACE.

Now, let's assume a LOAD insert is performed. The following events will occur:

- LOAD issues a SET INTEGRITY SALES OFF, which causes SALES to be put in CHECK PENDING READ ACCESS state because of the ALLOW READ ACCESS option, and the data is loaded.

- STORE_SALES, PRODUCT, SALES_SUM, and SALES_SUM_REGION are left in normal state because of the CHECK PENDING CASCADE DEFERRED option. SQL statements will only be able to access the SALES table data prior to the beginning of the first loaded page because of the ALLOW READ ACCESS option. They can also use SALES_SUM and SALES_SUM_REGION for optimization because they are still synchronized. This has expanded the window of availability of the MQT and underlying table data.

- At the end of the load, SALES still has the CHECK PENDING READ ACCESS state set on.

- Next, a SET INTEGRITY SALES...IMMEDIATE CHECKED is issued to verify the integrity of the new data loaded. This takes an exclusive lock on SALES and puts it into a NO DATA MOVEMENT state. Also, the SALES_SUM and SALES_SUM_REGION MQTs are placed in a CHECK PENDING NO ACCESS state. STORE_SALES will remain in normal state, since the rows added do not affect the referential integrity relationship with STORE_SALES. The PRODUCT table is also unaffected by the rows added to SALES and is therefore left in normal state. The SET INTEGRITY step is not required if the underlying table has no parent tables, descendent tables, check constraints, or generated columns. SET INTEGRITY SALES will cause local check constraints to be verified, as well as referential integrity violations checked against the PRODUCT table. These checks may fail, which would result in states being rolled back to the way it was at the end of the load. At this point, MQT optimization will be suspended because both the SALES_SUM and SALES_SUM_REGION MQTs are in CHECK PENDING NO ACCESS state.

- Assuming a successful SET INTEGRITY SALES step, we issue a REFRESH TABLE SALES_SUM statement. This results in an incremental update using only the data after the first loaded page, which is a faster operation than scanning the entire underlying table. This increases the availability of the SALES_SUM MQT as well. When this refresh is completed, the CHECK PENDING NO ACCESS state is reset on SALES_SUM, but not on SALES_SUM REGION, which has yet to be refreshed. SALES will continue to be in the NO DATA MOVEMENT state. SALES_SUM MQT is now available for optimization, while SALES_SUM_REGION is not, since it is still in CHECK PENDING NO ACCESS state.

■ Now a REFRESH TABLE SALES_SUM_REGION causes the table to be taken out of CHECK PENDING NO ACCESS state and therefore is available for MQT optimization. Since this is the final MQT on SALES, the NO DATA MOVEMENT state is reset on SALES.

If the FULL ACCESS option is chosen on the SET INTEGRITY step, then the NO DATA MOVEMENT state is not set on the SALES table. This means that full read-write access is permitted on SALES, and therefore incremental update is no longer possible on the SALES_SUM and SALES_SUM_REGION tables. When a REFRESH TABLE is issued against these tables, a full refresh is done, which has a negative impact on availability of the MQT. The decision to use FULL ACCESS is therefore an implementation choice.

The preceding steps outline the significant feature improvements in DB2 V8. These improvements of data loads for MQTs exemplify the scalability and performance of subsequent queries and data availability.

Using DB2 ALTER

The ALTER statement can be used to convert a materialized view to a regular table, and vice versa. The following statement converts an existing MQT into a regular table. This results in all the packages dependent on this MQT being invalidated.

```
ALTER TABLE tablename SET SUMMARY AS DEFINITION ONLY
```

The following statement converts an ordinary table into an MQT, where the summary-table-definition defines the query and refreshable-table-options:

```
ALTER TABLE tablename SET SUMMARY AS summary-table-definition
```

ALTER may be used for several reasons. You may choose to implement it for correcting the MQT options to address changing requirements over time. There may be a need to temporarily take MQT optimization offline for maintenance, such as creating indexes. Or you may decide to take it offline to avoid logging overhead as described in the *Deferred Refresh* section earlier in the chapter.

When changing a regular table into an MQT, the regular table must not.

■ Already be an MQT.

■ Be a typed table.

- Have any constraints, unique indexes or triggers defined on it.
- Be referenced in the definition of another MQT.

Keep in mind you cannot ALTER a regular table into a staging table or vice versa.

Materialized View Matching

The DB2 SQL Compiler analyzes user queries and produces an optimal access path to produce the desired results. Figure 7.8 illustrates the process flow of optimization. There are two key components to this process that are most relevant to MQTs as follows:

- Query-rewrite component that analyzes the query and, if appropriate, rewrites this query into another form that it believes will perform in superior fashion to the one written by the user. This capability frees users from having to deal with different syntactic representations of the same semantic query and allows them to instead focus on using syntax they are most comfortable with. Part of this query-rewrite process is the task of considering MQTs for optimization. This includes checking for specific states and matching criteria.

- Cost-based optimizer component, which performs a cost analysis of MQT processing versus underlying table access and decides on the optimal access path.

State Considerations

The following state considerations apply for DB2 to even consider MQT optimization:

- MQT must be created with the ENABLE QUERY OPTIMIZATION parameter.

- The CURRENT MAINTAINED TABLE TYPES FOR OPTIMIZATION register must enable optimization of the particular table type. This register can be set to:

```
SET CURRENT MAINTAINED TABLE TYPES FOR OPTIMIZATION =
ALL|NONE|SYSTEM|USER
```

- For REFRESH DEFERRED materialized views, the CURRENT REFRESH AGE register must be set to ANY as follows:

```
SET CURRENT REFRESH AGE ANY|0
```

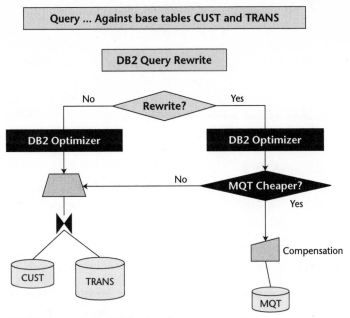

Figure 7.8   MQT optimization flow.

- REFRESH IMMEDIATE MQTs are always current and are always candidates for MQT optimization regardless of the CURRENT REFRESH AGE register setting.

- For dynamic and static SQL, the QUERY OPTIMIZATION level must be set to 2 or greater than equal to 5. The default value is 5, and this default can be changed in the DFT_QUERYOPT parameter in the database configuration file. The level can be changed as follows:

```
SET CURRENT QUERY OPTIMIZATION LEVEL 7
```

- MQT cannot be in a CHECK PENDING NO ACCESS state.

Matching Criteria

Matching is the process of reviewing the user query and evaluating the potential use of an MQT for query rewrite. Assuming that the state criteria are not inhibitors, the query-rewrite component reviews the following criteria to determine the viability of using the MQT in the query rewrite. We discuss these criteria as:

- Matching permitted
- Matching inhibited

Quite often an MQT may not exactly match the user query, and DB2 may have to incur some extra processing to massage the MQT data to deliver the desired result. This extra processing is called *compensation*. Both of the matching issues are discussed in the following sections.

Matching Permitted

MQTs will be considered for optimization in the following cases: Superset predicates and perfect matches, queries with aggregations and grouping columns, extra tables in the query and, finally, extra tables in the MQT. Let's review each of these in more detail.

Superset Predicates and Perfect Matches

This is the simplest case where the user query has the same number of tables as in the MQT and the same expressions, and the user requests an answer that can be fully met with the data in the MQT. Here, the predicates involved in the MQT must be a superset of those involved in the query. In DB2 V7, predicate analysis to detect this was limited. Only exact matches or simple equality predicates and IN predicates were considered. In DB2 V8, the analysis has been expanded to cover a broader range of predicates. Consider the following MQT example:

```
CREATE SUMMARY TABLE custtrans AS
(
SELECT cust_id, COUNT(*) AS counttrans
FROM trans
GROUP BY cust_id
)
DATA INTITIALLY DEFERRED REFRESH DEFERRED
```

A query that looks like the following will be considered matching for materialized view optimization purposes:

```
SELECT cust_id, COUNT(*)
FROM trans
WHERE cust_id > 1000
GROUP BY cust_id
```

Following is another MQT example for your consideration:

```
CREATE SUMMARY TABLE custtrans AS
(
```

```
SELECT cust_id, COUNT(*) AS counttrans
FROM trans
WHERE cust_id > 500
GROUP BY cust_id
)
DATA INTITIALLY DEFERRED REFRESH DEFERRED
```

A query that looks like the following will be considered matching for MQT optimization purposes:

```
SELECT cust_id, COUNT(*)
FROM trans
WHERE cust_id > 1000
GROUP BY cust_id
```

Query with Aggregation Functions and Grouping Columns

Aggregation collapses related groups of rows, resulting in a smaller size of the MQT. It is not necessary to define different MQTs for each type of user grouping. DB2 can decide to use an MQT even if the MQT's grouping is different from that of the user query under certain conditions. For instance, if the materialized view has a GROUP BY on a finer granularity, DB2 can compute the result of a coarser granularity GROUP BY by doing further aggregation (also known as compensation) on top of the MQT, as shown in the following example. Consider this MQT, which has one row for every month of every year:

```
CREATE SUMMARY TABLE dba.trans_agg AS
(
SELECT ti.pgid, t.locid, t.acctid, t.status,
year(pdate) as year, month(pdate) AS month,
SUM(ti.amount) AS amount, COUNT(*) AS count
FROM transitem AS ti, trans AS t
WHERE ti.transid = t.transid
GROUP BY YEAR(pdate), MONTH(pdate)
)
DATA INITIALLY DEFERRED REFRESH IMMEDIATE
```

The following query with a GROUP BY on YEAR can be computed from the preceding MQT by aggregating all the months of a year:

```
SELECT ti.pgid, t.locid, t.acctid, t.status,
YEAR(pdate) AS year, MONTH(pdate) AS month,
SUM(ti.amount) AS amount, COUNT(*) AS count
FROM transitem AS ti, trans AS t
WHERE ti.transid = t.transid
GROUP BY YEAR(pdate)
```

This capability allows the DBA to optimize by only defining one MQT at the month level. This is the simplest form of matching handled by DB2 as far as grouping columns are concerned. The number of MQTs can be minimized by using complex constructs, including grouping sets, such as ROLLUP and CUBE operators. Following are examples using grouping sets:

```
CREATE SUMMARY TABLE MQT1 AS
(
SELECT .....GROUP BY GROUPING SETS
((customer_id, product_group_id), YEAR(date_col), MONTH(date_col))
)
DATA INITIALLY DEFERRED REFRESH IMMEDIATE;
```

The DB2 query-rewrite engine would consider matching any one of the following queries against the above MQT, assuming there are no other inhibitors:

```
SELECT ..... GROUP BY customer_id, product_group_id
SELECT ..... GROUP BY customer_id
SELECT ..... GROUP BY product_group_id
SELECT ..... GROUP BY YEAR(date_col)
SELECT ..... GROUP BY MONTH(date_col)
```

If the grouping columns are NULLABLE, it may be necessary to add the GROUPING in the output of the MQT. Following is another example:

```
CREATE SUMMARY TABLE MQT2 AS
(
SELECT store_id, cust_id, year, month, COUNT(*) as cnt
FROM Trans
GROUP BY GROUPING SETS
(
(store_id, cust_id, year),
(store_id, year),
(store_id, year, month),
(year)
)
)
DATA INITIALLY DEFERRED REFRESH IMMEDIATE
```

The following query can be satisfied from the preceding MQT by simply filtering out the rows pertaining to the other entities in the grouping set:

```
SELECT store_id, year, COUNT(*) as cnt
FROM Trans
WHERE year > 1990
GROUP BY store_id, year
```

In this case, assuming that the columns are defined as NOT NULL columns, the DB2 query-rewrite engine transforms the query automatically internally as follows:

```
SELECT store_id, year, cnt
FROM MQT2
WHERE store_id IS NOT NULL AND
year IS NOT NULL AND
cust_id IS NULL AND
month IS NULL AND
year > 1990
```

The following extra predicates are the only compensating predicates needed to make use of the MQT:

- The cust_id IS NULL predicate ensures that nothing will qualify from the (store_id, cust_id, year) grouping.
- The month IS NULL predicate will filter out the rows pertaining to the (store_id, year, month) grouping.
- The store_id IS NOT NULL predicate will ensure that nothing will qualify from the (year) grouping, as well as the empty grouping ( ).
- The two predicates store_id IS NOT NULL AND year IS NOT NULL ensure that all the rows from the (store_id, year) grouping are retrieved.

More complex scenarios might require further grouping.

Similar examples can be shown using the ROLLUP and CUBE operators to satisfy user queries having many different combinations of column groupings. Such complex MQTs not only save disk space but also can save refresh times, since a single scan of the underlying tables is sufficient to populate the MQT. Creating multiple MQTs, on the other hand, would require individual REFRESH statements to be executed for each MQT and thereby individual accesses against the underlying tables.

GROUPING SETS, ROLLUP and CUBE are effective ways of defining MQTs that could be exploited by queries aggregating over a variety of groupings available in the MQT as part of these super aggregates.

For the purpose of understanding these super aggregates, it is useful to consider the equivalent result set broken down into a union of simple groupings:

```
GROUP BY GROUPING SETS ((a,b), (c, d))
```

is equivalent to:

```
SELECT .... GROUP BY a,b
UNION ALL
```

```
SELECT .... GROUP BY c,d
UNION ALL
SELECT .... GROUP BY ( )

GROUP BY ROLLUP (a,b,c)
```

This could also be expressed as a statement involving several UNION ALL clauses or is equivalent to:

```
GROUP BY GROUPING SETS
(
(a,b,c)
(a,b)
(a)
()
)

GROUP BY CUBE (a,b,c) is equivalent to
GROUP BY GROUPING SETS
(
(a,b,c)
(a,b)
(a,c)
(b,c)
(a)
(b)
(c)
()
)
```

Extra Tables in the Query

DB2 can match user queries that contain more tables than those defined in the MQT when the join predicates to the underlying tables can be replaced by join predicates between the MQT and the additional tables.

Consider the following MQT:

```
CREATE SUMMARY TABLE dba.trans_agg AS
(
SELECT ti.pgid, t.locid, t.acctid, t.status,
YEAR(pdate) AS year,
MONTH(pdate) AS month, SUM(ti.amount) AS amount,
COUNT(*) AS count
FROM stars.transitem AS ti, stars.trans AS t
WHERE ti.transid = t.transid
GROUP BY YEAR(pdate), MONTH(pdate), ti.pgid, t.locid, t.acctid, t.status
)
```

```
DATA INITIALLY DEFERRED REFRESH IMMEDIATE
```

A user query that looks like the following can be considered matching the preceding MQT even though it has an additional location table stars.loc included:

```
SELECT YEAR(pdate) AS year, loc.country,
SUM(ti.amount) AS amount, COUNT(*) AS count
FROM stars.transitem AS ti, stars.trans AS t, stars.loc AS loc
WHERE ti.transid = t.transid AND t.locid = loc.locid
AND YEAR(pdate) BETWEEN 1990 and 1999
GROUP BY YEAR(pdate), loc.country
```

The stars.loc is joined on the locid column to stars.trans. The locid column is one of the GROUP BY columns of the MQT. DB2 can use this column to join the relevant rows of the MQT after applying the YEAR predicate with the stars.loc table. The aggregated results can then be further consolidated by grouping on the YEAR(pdate) and country.

Extra Tables in the MQT

DB2 can match user queries against MQTs that have more tables than defined in the query in certain cases involving system-maintained referential integrity. Consider the following MQT:

```
CREATE TABLE dba.PG_SALESSUM AS
(
SELECT l.lineid AS prodline, pg.pgid AS pgroup,
loc.country, loc.state, YEAR(pdate) AS year,
MONTH(pdate) AS month, SUM(ti.amount) AS amount,
COUNT(*) AS count
FROM stars.transitem AS ti, stars.trans AS t,
stars.loc AS loc, stars.pgroup AS pg, stars.prodline AS l
WHERE ti.transid = t.transid AND ti.pgid = pg.pgid
AND pg.lineid =l.lineid AND t.locid = loc.locid
GROUP BY loc.country, loc.state, year(pdate),
month(pdate), l.lineid,pg.pgid
)
DATA INITIALLY DEFERRED REFRESH IMMEDIATE
```

A user query as follows can be considered as matching the preceding MQT even though the MQT has two more tables (pgroup and prodline) than in the user query:

```
SELECT YEAR(pdate) AS year, loc.country,
SUM(ti.amount) AS amount, COUNT(*) AS count
```

```
FROM stars.transitem AS ti, stars.trans AS t, stars.loc AS loc
WHERE ti.transid = t.transid AND t.locid = loc.locid
AND YEAR(pdate) BETWEEN 1990 and 1999
GROUP BY YEAR(pdate), loc.country
```

The preceding query references three tables, while the MQT has five. It would appear at first glance that these additional tables, pgroup and prodline, would affect the result of the preceding query if that MQT were used in the query rewrite. This would be true unless DB2 was aware of a referential integrity relationship involved. For instance, if the pgroup and prodline tables were related to the other tables through referential integrity, it would not affect the number of rows in the result. They could be considered as lookup tables that are merely adding columns to the output. System-maintained referential integrity lets the query-rewrite component know if this is the case, and since these additional tables are guaranteed not to add or remove rows in the result, the query-rewrite engine can proceed with the MQT matching optimization and ignore these tables.

In the preceding example, the transitem table is joined to the pgroup table on column pgid. If pgroup.pgid is the primary key in the referential integrity relationship, every value of transitem.pgid has one and only one value in pgroup. Furthermore, if the prodline table has a referential integrity relationship with the pgroup table, where prodline.lineid is the primary key, this join is also a join that does not affect the number of rows in the output. The MQT can now be used for applying the query predicate, selecting the columns required by the query, and consolidating the aggregation by further grouping on only the columns required in the query.

Referential integrity may either be system maintained or provided as informational constraints. This is new in DB2 V8 and uses the NOT ENFORCED constraint attribute when defining the constraint. With informational referential integrity constraints, the onus is on the DBA to guarantee the integrity of reference, since DB2 makes no attempt to enforce referential integrity. Informational referential integrity constraints help the DB2 query rewrite engine make superior decisions about matching user queries that have fewer tables than those defined in the materialized view.

Matching Inhibited

The query-rewrite component currently does not consider materialized view optimization in the following cases:

- Query includes the following constructs.
- MQT is missing columns that are in the query.

- MQT contains predicates more restrictive than in the query.
- Query contains an expression not derivable from a materialized view.
- Friendly arithmetic.
- Isolation mismatch.

Each of these conditions is described in the following sections.

Query Constructs

A query that includes the following constructs will not be considered for MQT query rewrite:

- An underlying table in the MQT is itself a target of an UPDATE.
- Recursion or other complex constructs.
- Physical property functions like NODENUMBER.
- Outer join.
- UNION.
- XMLAGG.
- Window aggregation functions. These are aggregate functions specified with the OVER clause.

This is not a comprehensive list. Also, some of these restrictions may be removed in future releases. As an example, while earlier versions of DB2 V8 needed an exact match of CASE expressions in the MQT and the query, some CASE expressions are now handled with more flexibility. Refer to DB2 UDB's redbook titled: *High Function Business Intelligence in e-business*.

Fewer Columns

If the MQT is missing columns that exist in the underlying tables and the query references those columns, then the MQT will be ignored for optimization. Consider the following MQT:

```
CREATE SUMMARY TABLE custtrans AS
(
SELECT cust_id, COUNT(*) AS counttrans
FROM trans
GROUP BY cust_id
)
DATA INTITIALLY DEFERRED REFRESH DEFERRED
```

A user query that looks like the following will result in the MQT being ignored for optimization purposes. This is because the trans_date column has not been defined in the MQT:

```
SELECT cust_id, COUNT(*)
FROM trans
WHERE trans_date > '2002-01-01'
GROUP BY cust_id
```

Expression Not Derivable

Even if the expression used in the MQT is not identical to that used in the query, it might be possible to derive the expression used in the query from that in the MQT. However, it is possible for some "obvious" matching cases to be ignored by DB2 because of precision or other issues, which will eventually be handled in the future. Following is an example:

```
CREATE summary table custtrans AS
(
SELECT cust_id, SUM(sale_price) AS total, COUNT(items) AS countitems
FROM trans
GROUP BY cust_id
)
DATA INTITIALLY DEFERRED REFRESH DEFERRED
```

A user query that looks like the following will result in the MQT being ignored for optimization purposes, since the expression could not be derived by DB2:

```
SELECT cust_id, SUM(sale_price * 0.15) / COUNT(items)
FROM trans
GROUP BY cust_id
```

Friendly Arithmetic

The database configuration parameter DFT_SQLMATHWARN NO | YES sets the default value that determines the handling of arithmetic errors and retrieval conversion errors as errors (unfriendly) or warnings (friendly) during SQL statement compilation. For static SQL statements, the value of this parameter is associated with the package at BIND time. For dynamic SQL statements, the value of this parameter is used when the statement is prepared. The default is NO (unfriendly). It is rare for this option to be changed after initial database creation, since the ramifications may be significant. (Refer to the DB2 Administration Guide for more details.)

The MQT will *not* be considered for query rewrite if the query demands unfriendly arithmetic and the MQT supports friendly arithmetic. The MQT will be considered for query rewrite when the query and MQT have identical arithmetic requirements, and also when the query demands friendly arithmetic and the MQT supports unfriendly arithmetic.

Isolation Mismatch

The isolation level of the MQT must be equivalent to or higher than that demanded of the user query. For example, if the MQT is defined with ISO-LATION of CS, then a query that requests either UR or CS can match with the MQT, whereas RS or RR will not be considered for matching. It is important to know the ISOLATION under which the MQT was created. The CLP command CHANGE ISOLATION TO may be used to set the ISO-LATION level before creating the MQT.

MQT Design

Materialized views have the potential to provide significant performance enhancements to certain types of queries and should be a key tuning option in every DBA's arsenal. However, MQTs do have certain overhead characteristics that you must carefully consider when designing MQTs. These include:

- Disk space due to the MQT and associated indexes, as well as stag- ing tables.
- Locking contention on the MQT during a refresh. With deferred refresh, the MQT is offline while the REFRESH TABLE is executing. The same applies to a staging table, if one exists. Update activity against underlying tables is impacted during the refresh window. With immediate refresh, there is contention on the MQT when aggregation is involved because of SQL INSERT, UPDATE, and DELETE activity on the base table by multiple transactions.
- Logging overhead during refresh of very large tables.
- Logging associated with staging tables.
- Response time overhead on SQL updating the underlying tables when immediate refresh and staging tables are involved because of the synchronous nature of this operation.

The objective should be to minimize the number of MQTs required by defining sufficiently granular REFRESH IMMEDIATE and REFRESH DEFERRED MQTs that deliver the desired performance while minimizing their overhead. To that end, the following information needs to be available in order to determine the most effective MQTs to build:

- Collect all the static SQL queries that are performing poorly and can benefit from MQT optimization. Note their response time, frequency of execution, priority, and data latency tolerance.

- Collect all the dynamic SQL queries that are performing poorly and can benefit from MQT optimization. Note their response time, frequency of execution, priority, and data latency tolerance.

- Group the queries that need to be satisfied by a REFRESH IMMEDIATE MQT, and those that can be satisfied by a REFRESH DEFERRED MQT.

- Based on matching criteria knowledge, identify a minimal number of REFRESH DEFERRED and REFRESH IMMEDIATE MQTs of appropriately fine granularity to satisfy multiple user queries.

- Create and populate the MQT along with RUNSTATS and indexes.

- Execute the grouped queries against this MQT and use EXPLAIN to verify MQT optimization has occurred. Note response time improvement of the queries, and consider whether any performance tuning of the MQT or rewriting of the user query would help.

- If EXPLAIN indicates that query rewrite of the MQT has not occurred, it may be due to one of three problems: state, matching criteria, or costing. Determining state problems is easy enough, but honing in on the other two reasons will have to be a trial-and-error exercise, since there is no deterministic method to determine the reason for the lack of MQT optimization. Once the cause has been identified, appropriate corrective action can be taken.

You may need to consider converting static SQL queries to dynamic SQL queries in order to exploit REFRESH DEFERRED MQTs after weighing the appropriate pros and cons.

The aforementioned steps describe a process that requires skilled professionals using trial-and-error techniques in order to design effective MQTs and drop them when they are no longer beneficial. The process is both time-consuming and error-prone.

MQT Tuning

Since the MQT is a just another table, normal tuning considerations apply, such as ensuring RUNSTATS is current and appropriate indexes exist. Two broad categories of tuning considerations apply to materialized views as follows:

- User query related: These are the considerations related to improving the performance of user queries against base tables that get routed to the materialized view. This includes ensuring that RUNSTATS is current, and that appropriate indexes exist on the materialized view.

- Materialized view maintenance related: These are considerations related to improving the performance of materialized view maintenance by DB2 when updates occur on the underlying tables. The following guidelines are recommended:

  - Create a non-unique index on the materialized view columns that guarantee uniqueness of rows in a materialized view. In the case of a partitioned materialized view, the partitioning key should be a subset of the columns described above.

  - Do not create an index on the staging table, since such indexes will degrade the performance of appends to the staging table.

  - Create an informational or system enforced referential integrity (RI) constraint on joins in a materialized view if appropriate, since DB2 takes advantage of these constraints to optimize the maintenance of materialized views.

  - Partition the staging table according to the partitioning of the materialized view to promote collocated joins.

In choosing indexes, you should also take into account any joins necessitated by REFRESH IMMEDIATE and staging MQT maintenance operations that must be included in packages updating the underlying tables. An EXPLAIN of such packages will identify these maintenance operations, which might benefit greatly from appropriate indexes on the joined columns. Note that unique indexes cannot be defined on a materialized view.

Refresh Optimization

REFRESH TABLE operations can have the following negative impact:

Refresh takes a z-lock on the MQT, thus making it unavailable for access by SQL queries.   Performance can be significantly impacted for queries depending on MQT optimization during the refresh window.

Refresh also takes a z-lock on the staging table (if one exists).   This can have a negative impact on updates to the underlying tables (they will not succeed) if refresh takes an extended period of time, since the staging table is updated in the same unit of work as updates to the underlying table. Refresh causes logging to occur as a consequence of updates to the MQT, as well as pruning of the staging table. Refresh also consumes CPU, I/O, and buffer pool resources, which ultimately impacts other users contending for the same resources. Refresh resource consumption can be reduced by combining multiple MQT refreshes in a single REFRESH TABLE statement. DB2 uses "multi-query optimization" to share joins and aggregations required of each MQT in order to reduce the resource consumption against underlying tables shared by the MQTs.

Illustrated in Figure 7.9 is the refresh process. MQT1 is an MQT based on tables TRANS, STORE, and CUST, while MQT2 is based on tables TRANS and STORE. Issuing the statement REFRESH TABLE MQT1, MQT2 causes DB2 to attempt to match the MQT queries to formulate a common "subsumer" query (CS), which is executed on the underlying tables. The results are then suitably predicated to update MQT1 and MQT2, respectively. This approach optimizes resource consumption against the underlying tables and staging tables. It has a positive impact on the performance of SQL queries and updates of underlying tables associated with staging tables.

```
INSERT INTO MQT1                          INSERT INTO MQT2
SELECT store_name, cust_name,             SELECT store_name, year,
    SUM(sales) AS ss, COUNT(*) AS cnt         SUM(sales) AS ss, COUNT(*) AS cnt
FROM CS                                    FROM CS
WHERE year = 2001                          WHERE year >= 1998
GROUP BY store_name, cust_name             GROUP BY store_name, year
```

```
        SELECT store_name, cust_name, year,
            SUM(sales) AS ss, COUNT(*) AS cnt
        FROM Trans T, Store S, Cust C
        WHERE T.store_id = S.store_id
            AND T.cust_id = C.cust_id           Common Subsumer CS
            AND T.year >= 1998
        GROUP BY store_name, year, cust_name
```

REFRESH TABLE MQT1, MQT2

```
MQT1                                       MQT2
SELECT store_name, cust_name,              SELECT store_name, year,
    SUM(sales) AS ss, COUNT(*) AS cnt          SUM(sales) AS ss, COUNT(*) AS cnt
FROM Trans T, Store S, Cust C              FROM Trans T, Store S
WHERE T.store_id = S.store_id              WHERE T.store_id = S.store_id
    AND T.cust_id = C.cust_id                  AND T.year >= 1998
    AND T.year = 2001                      GROUP BY store_name, year
GROUP BY store_name, cust_name
```

Figure 7.9   Multi-query optimization.

Considerations in grouping MQTs in a single REFRESH TABLE statement include the following:

- Identical or overlapping underlying tables.

- Identical latency requirements for both MQTs, or at least acceptable latency discrepancies between the MQTs.

- Large size of the underlying tables.

Materialized View Limitations

Like all other technologies, MQTs do have their limitations. For brevity, the core limitations are outlined in the following list:

- When REFRESH DEFERRED or REFRESH IMMEDIATE is specified, the fullselect cannot include the following:

  - References to a MQT, declared temporary table, or typed table in any FROM clause.

  - References to a view where the fullselect of the view violates any of the listed restrictions on the fullselect of the MQT.

  - Expressions that are a reference type or DATALINK type (or distinct type based on these types).

  - Functions that have external action.

  - Functions written in SQL.

  - Functions that depend on physical characteristics (for example, NODENUMBER, DBPARTITIONNUM, HASHEDVALUE).

  - Table or view references to system objects (explain tables also should not be specified).

  - Expressions that are a structured type or LOB type (or a distinct type based on a LOB type).

  - When REPLICATED is specified, there are two restrictions. First, the GROUP BY clause is not allowed, and second, the materialized view query must only reference a single table.

- The following limitations apply to REFRESH IMMEDIATE, as well as to queries used to create REFRESH DEFERRED tables associated with a staging table:

  - The fullselect must be a subselect, with the exception that UNION ALL is supported in the input table expression of a GROUP BY.

- The subselect cannot include the following:
    - References to a nickname.
    - Functions that have side effects or are nondeterministic.
    - Scalar fullselects.
    - Predicates with fullselects.
    - Special registers like CURRENT TIMESTAMP.
    - SELECT DISTINCT
- The supported column functions are SUM, COUNT, COUNT_BIG, and GROUPING (without DISTINCT). The select list must contain a COUNT(*) or COUNT_BIG(*) column. If the MQT select list contains SUM(X) where X is a nullable argument, then the MQT must also have COUNT(X) in its select list. These column functions cannot be part of any expressions.
- If the FROM clause references more than one table or view, it can only define an inner join without using the explicit INNER JOIN syntax.
- All GROUP BY items must be included in the select list.
- GROUPING SETS, CUBE, and ROLLUP are supported. The GROUP BY items and associated GROUPING column functions in the select list must form a unique key of the result set. Thus, the following restrictions must be satisfied:
    - No grouping sets may be repeated. For example, ROLLUP(X,Y),X is not allowed because it is equivalent to GROUPING SETS((X,Y),(X),(X)).
    - If X is a nullable GROUP BY item that appears within GROUPING SETS, CUBE, or ROLLUP, then GROUPING(X) must appear in the select list.
    - Grouping on constants is not allowed.
- A HAVING clause is not allowed.
- If you are dealing with a multiple partition database partition group, then the partitioning key must be a subset of the GROUP BY items.
- If REPLICATED is specified, the table must have a unique key.
- When a GROUP BY clause is not specified, the following uniqueness related restriction applies: The materialized view's non-duplicate requirement is achieved by deriving a unique key for the MQT from one of the unique key constraints defined in each

of the underlying tables. Therefore, the underlying tables must have at least one unique key constraint defined on them and the columns of these keys must appear in the select list of the MQT definition.

Certain operations cannot be performed on the underlying tables of an MQT that needs to be incrementally maintained:

- IMPORT REPLACE cannot be used on an underlying table of an MQT.
- ALTER TABLE NOT LOGGED INITIALLY WITH EMPTY TABLE cannot be done on an underlying table of an MQT.
- MQTs cannot be used as exception tables to collect information when constraints are being validated during bulk constraints checking (during LOAD or executing the SET INTEGRITY statement).

Summary

It is not uncommon for the initiated to implement MQTs to address specific performance problems for a particular BI solution. This is certainly something DBAs and data architects have available to them. The problem is that implementing MQTs on an as-needed basis is dependent on the database person having the foresight and knowledge to exploit the technology. This invariably leads to great performance gains for very specific applications and only for limited durations. In other words, the value of MQTs is limited when implemented in a haphazard manner.

The correct approach for MQT technology is for data architects and DBAs to blend the use of MQTs as a natural part of the overall BI effort. This means establishing standards and procedures regarding when they should be applied and how they must be monitored and tuned, as well as when they must be removed when they provide no more value. To that end, data architectures and DBAs must take the lead in understanding the application of this important technology with regard to decision support applications and DB2.

Warehouse Management

Warehouse Management with IBM DB2 Data Warehouse Center

Key Issues:

- ETL technology must include a wide variety of robust transformation processes from which programmers can choose. This is not always the case with some ETL tools where preprogrammed transformation processes are painfully limited. Application programmers are forced to write custom programs even for common process steps.

- Preprogrammed processes for statistical analysis, OLAP, and mining provide an environment for warehouse planners to tackle advanced BI applications.

- Warehouse management cannot be fulfilled without meta data applications which gather and publish meta data to user communities.

- Warehouse management must be able to address relational database targets as well as OLAP cubes within the same environment so that cohesive, centralized control of data propagation can be achieved.

IBM DB2 offers the IBM DB2 Data Warehouse Center, which is an integrated component of the DB2 Control Center, providing the graphical user interface for defining, automating, processing, and maintaining the data warehouse. Specifically, the IBM DB2 Data Warehouse Center (DWC) is used to define the processes that extract, cleanse, and transform data for the warehouse. Moreover, once the processes are defined, DWC is used to schedule, maintain, and monitor these processes.

IBM DB2 Data Warehouse Center is a warehouse management system that can build multi-tiered data warehouses and is totally driven by meta data. It can support various sources of relational databases, open database connectivity (ODBC) sources, replication tables, OLE-DB sources, and application sources such as WebSphere, MQSeries message queues, and SAP R/3.

The primary graphical interface of DWC is the process modeler that is used to design and model the warehouse processes with regard to data movement, transformation, and loading into the warehouse, data marts, and OLAP cubes. These target structures can be implemented in DB2 relational tables including nicknames, DB2 OLAP Server, and Hyperion Essbase Server cubes, as well as via exports to flat files.

This chapter provides an overview of data warehousing, warehousing meta data, warehousing components, and warehousing tasks.

IBM DB2 Data Warehouse Center Essentials

There are fundamental components of DWC important for you to understand. Administrators must understand what subject areas mean to DWC as well as warehouse source and target structures. You should also understand the concepts of steps, processes, task control flow, security, and task scheduling. Each of these is defined in this section.

Warehouse Subject Area

A subject area identifies and groups related processes to a logical area of the business. For example, if you are building a warehouse of wholesale and retail data, you define a Wholesale subject area and a Retail subject area. You then add the processes that relate to wholesale under the Wholesale subject area and add the definitions that relate to the retail data under the Retail subject area.

Warehouse Source

Warehouse sources identify the tables and files that will provide input data to your data warehouse. The source definition is stored in the data warehouse meta data, which can be exported to other warehouse partner meta data. DWC uses the specifications in the warehouse sources to access the data. The sources supported in the data warehouse include a wide range of relational and nonrelational sources that have connectivity to your warehousing environment and network—for example, database tables, views, ASCII files, replication enabled tables, SAP business objects, OLE DB, and MQSeries message queues.

Warehouse Target

Warehouse targets can be DB2 database tables or local files that contain data that has been transformed. Similar to a warehouse source, users can use warehouse targets to provide data to other warehouse targets. A central data warehouse can provide data to departmental servers, or a main fact table in the data warehouse can provide data to summary tables.

Warehouse Server and Logger

Warehouse server and logger are available on Windows and AIX operating systems. Each warehouse server comes with a default agent.

Warehouse server interfaces with the warehouse client and Work In Progress to direct the warehouse requests to the appropriate warehouse component to execute the task. Once the task is completed, the task status is returned to the warehouse client or Work In Progress. Most of the warehouse tasks related to and building warehouse targets are sent to the specified warehouse agent for execution.

The warehouse server also has a built-in scheduler that is capable of scheduling and dispatching your warehouse tasks based on the time interval and task control flow that you specify.

The warehouse server directs all the warehouse message resolution and logging to the warehouse logger.

Warehouse Agent and Agent Site

Warehouse agents manage the flow of data between the warehouse sources and the warehouse targets. Warehouse agents are available on the AIX, AS/400, Linux, OS/390, Windows NT, and Sun Solaris. The warehouse agents use ODBC drivers or DB2 Call Level Interface (CLI) to communicate with different data sources.

Multiple warehouse agents can be used to handle the transfer of data between sources and target warehouses. The number of warehouse agents that you use depends on your existing connectivity configuration and the data volume that you plan to manage in your warehousing environment.

Additional instances of a warehouse agent can be generated if multiple warehouse processes require concurrent data extraction, transformation, and loading.

Warehouse agents can be local or remote. A local warehouse agent (including the default warehouse agent) is an agent that is installed on the same operating system as the warehouse server. A remote warehouse agent is an agent that is installed on a different operating system from the warehouse server. There must be network connectivity configured between the warehouse agent system and the warehouse server system.

An agent site is a logical name for an operating system where the warehouse agent software is installed. The agent site name does not have to be the same as the TCP/IP hostname. You can define multiple agent sites with different agent user IDs on a single operating system or an IP address. A logical name identifies each agent site in DWC.

The default agent site, named the *default DWC agent site*, is a local agent on the same operating system as the warehouse server; this default agent site is defined during initialization of the warehouse control database.

Warehouse Control Database

Warehouse meta data can be stored in a DB2 database that is local or remote from the warehouse components. The warehouse control database can be initialized at warehouse server and logger installation or use the Warehouse Control Database Management tool on Windows or AIX. The warehouse client, warehouse server, and logger maintain active connections to the warehouse control database to store and retrieve warehouse operational data.

IBM DB2 Data Warehouse Center provides the graphical user interfaces for you to import warehouse meta data from a tag file in IBM DB2 Data Warehouse format, common warehouse metamodel format, ERwin, MQSeries, and Trillium. You can export the warehouse meta data to a tag file in IBM DB2 Data Warehouse format, common warehouse metamodel format, and OLAP Integration Server. The IBM DB2 Data Warehouse Center meta data and OLAP Integration Server meta data can also be published to IBM Information Catalog.

IBM DB2 Data Warehouse Center provides additional interfaces for users to exchange warehouse meta data with IBM partners and vendor tools. These partners and vendor tools include Evolutionary Technologies International, Ascential, ERwin, Trillium, Brio, Business Objects, Cognos, and Hyperion OLAP Server CWMI compliant.

Warehouse Process and Step

A warehouse *process* contains a series of warehouse steps that perform data extract, transformation, and loading for a specific warehouse use. In general, a process can retrieve source data, and populate warehouse targets. With data that is aggregated, summarized, and cleansed for warehouse use.

A *step* is the definition of a single operation within the warehouse. By using SQL statements, Replication, DB2 utilities, warehouse built-in transformers, or user-defined programs, steps define how you move data and transform data. When you run a step, a transfer of data between the warehouse source and the warehouse target, or any transformation of that data, can take place.

A step is a logical entity in the IBM DB2 Data Warehouse Center that defines:

- A data link to its warehouse source.
- The definition of and a data link to the warehouse target table or local file.
- The definition of the transformation using SQL, Replication, warehouse transformers, DB2 utilities, or user-defined programs involved in the population of the output table or file.
- The processing options and schedule by which the output file or table are to be populated, such as appending to the warehouse target or replacing the warehouse target entirely.

Suppose you want IBM DB2 Data Warehouse Center to perform the following tasks:

- Extract data from different data sources.
- Convert the data to a format required by your user analysts to do data mining or analysis.
- Write the data to a warehouse target table.

You would create a process that contains several warehouse steps. Each warehouse step performs a separate task, such as extracting the data from a source table or converting it to the desired format. You might need to create several steps to completely transform and format the output data and put it into its final warehouse target table.

When a warehouse step or process runs, it can affect the warehouse target in the following ways:

- Replace all the data in the warehouse target with new data.
- Append the new data to the existing data.
- Append a separate edition of data.
- Update only the changed source data in the warehouse target.

You can run a step on demand, or you can schedule a step to run at a specified time. In addition, you can schedule a step to run one time only, or you can schedule it to run repeatedly, such as every month. You can also schedule steps to run in sequence via the step task flow mechanism provided in DWC, so that when one step finishes running, the next step begins running based on the step task flow conditions specified. You can schedule steps to run unconditionally upon completion of another step, or on success or failure.

If you schedule a warehouse process, the root step (or root steps) in the process runs at the process's scheduled time. The individual step's schedules will not be used for the warehouse process run. You can also cascade a process on success, on failure, or on completion (unconditional).

The common processing steps are SQL, replication, program, transformer, Web site analysis programs, and user-defined. Each of these is defined in the section that follows; however, for more detail on each step, refer to Chapter 9.

SQL Step

A *SQL step* uses a SQL SELECT statement to extract and transform from a warehouse source using a range of DB2 built-in functions and generates an INSERT or UPDATE statement to insert or update the data into the warehouse target table. You can also perform your own data type mapping in the SQL step column-mapping page. The IBM DB2 Data Warehouse Center also gives you the choice of using a pre-existing warehouse target or having the warehouse target generated based on the selected warehouse source columns.

Replication Step

A *replication step* uses the IBM Replication Capture and Apply technology to either refresh the entire warehouse target or to just apply the changed data. There are five different types of replication steps supported in DWC:

- A *base aggregate replication step* creates a target warehouse table that contains summarized data for a source appended at specified intervals.

- A *change aggregate replication step* creates a target warehouse table that contains aggregated data tracking the changes in the source between each program cycle.

- A *point-in-time replication step* creates a target warehouse that matches the source table, with a timestamp column added.

- A *staging table replication step* creates a table with data from committed transactions; that table, also called the consistent-change-data table, can be used as the source for updating data to multiple target warehouse tables.

- A *user copy replication step* creates a target warehouse that matches the source table exactly at the time of the copy.

DB2 Utilities Step

You can use IBM DB2 utilities on Windows platform, AIX, SUN, Linux Intel, iSeries, and z/OS to export data to a file, load data from a file to the warehouse target, reorganize the warehouse target, and run statistics against the warehouse target.

Use these utilities instead of the IBM Data Warehouse Center's SQL processing when there is a substantial amount of data to load. Experiment to see which one is more efficient for you.

The bulk load and export utilities operate on a data file and a DB2 database. The database server does not need to reside on the agent site, but the source or target file must reside on the agent site.

OLAP Server Program Step

You can use these warehouse OLAP programs to automatically refresh an OLAP Server database. The Data Warehouse Center allows you to schedule three types of operations with an OLAP Server. To execute these programs, you must install Essbase Server or IBM DB2 OLAP Server software.

- Loading data into the OLAP Server database.

- Updating dimensions of update an OLAP Server outline from a source flat file using load rules, or from an SQL source using load rules.

- Running calculations using default calculation or calculation with OLAP calculation rules.

File Program Step

You can use these warehouse file programs to copy a file using FTP, export ODBC source data to a file, run a FTP command file, or submit an MVS JCL jobstream to an MVS system for execution.

Transformer Step

Transformer steps are DB2 stored procedures and user-defined functions that specify statistical or warehouse transformers that you can use to transform data. You can use these transformers to clean, invert, and pivot data; generate primary keys and period tables; and calculate various statistics.

When you run the process, the transformer step writes data to one or more warehouse targets.

User-Defined Program Step

A *user-defined program step* is a logical entity within the IBM DB2 Data Warehouse Center that represents a business-specific transformation that you want DWC to start. Because every business has unique data transformation requirements, businesses can choose to write their own program steps or use tools such as those provided by ETI or Ascential.

For example, you can write a user-defined program that will perform the following functions:

- Export data from a table.

- Manipulate that data.

- Write the data to a temporary output resource or a warehouse target.

IBM DB2 Data Warehouse Center Launchpad

IBM DB2 Data Warehouse Center has a built-in launchpad that guides you through the process of building a data warehouse. This launchpad provides an easy-to-use step-by-step wizard to walk you through each key step with instructions.

Let's go through a simple scenario of building a warehouse to store the entire manager's annual income in a DB2 data warehouse. Before you start building a warehouse, there are a few setup steps that you need to perform.

Setting Up Your Data Warehouse Environment

When setting up your warehouse environment you need to consider three general issues: defining and creating your warehouse database, identifying the source data, and establishing your warehouse access. Let's look at each of these considerations.

Creating a Warehouse Database

You need to allocate a database for your data warehouses. You may have one or more databases depending on your installation's configuration and size. It is highly recommended that you build a data warehouse on the same machine as the warehouse agent that populates your target warehouses for performance improvement. In our example, we will use the sample database on Windows and use the warehouse agent on the same Windows system. After you have created your warehouse database, you need to register this database as an ODBC system data source. The warehouse agent on Windows uses ODBC to access the source data and the target warehouse tables. You can use the Microsoft ODBC Data Source Administrator to register the warehouse database and perform a test against the registered database to verify the connection is successful.

Browsing the Source Data

Source data is not always well structured or ready for analysis; you may need to transform or cleanse it to make it more usable. In our example, we will use the EMPLOYEE and DEPARTMENT tables from the DB2 SAMPLE database to construct a warehouse target table containing the manager's personnel data and the annual income. It is important to identify what your user analysts need to see in the warehouse target so that you can collect the source operational data correctly and efficiently.

IBM DB2 Data Warehouse supports a variety of relational and non-relational source data such as an ASCII file. For DB2 source data, you can use the IBM Control Center to sample the content of the source data: Select Start → Programs → IBM DB2 → General Administration Tools → Control Center. For ASCII file source data, you can use any editor to view the content and the format of the file. After the source data has been defined in DWC, you can then sample the data immediately from DWC.

Establishing IBM DB2 Data Warehouse Center Security

To start IBM DB2 Data Warehouse Center, you can use the IBM DB2 Business Intelligence Tools Data Warehouse Center. To log on to DWC, you must be a registered IBM DB2 Data Warehouse Center user. At installation time, a default user is defined and that is the same user ID that you use to initialize the IBM DB2 Data Warehouse Center control database. In the Logon Window, click on the Advanced button to verify the name of the control database that is known to your Windows Client and the name of the Warehouse Server host. Once you have logged on to the IBM DB2 Data Warehouse Center, you can define additional users.

There is also a default security group defined at installation time and it has Operations and Administration authority; the default user is assigned to this group. You may later define additional security groups and users to manage the security of your warehouse objects via the IBM DB2 Data Warehouse Center's Administration folder. (See Figure 8.1.)

Building a Data Warehouse Using the Launchpad

Figure 8.2 shows the nine tasks that you can follow to build the data warehouse. Each task has a context help to give you an overview of what the step does. The graphic representation of these nine tasks will also be refreshed to highlight the warehouse objects that you are currently operating.

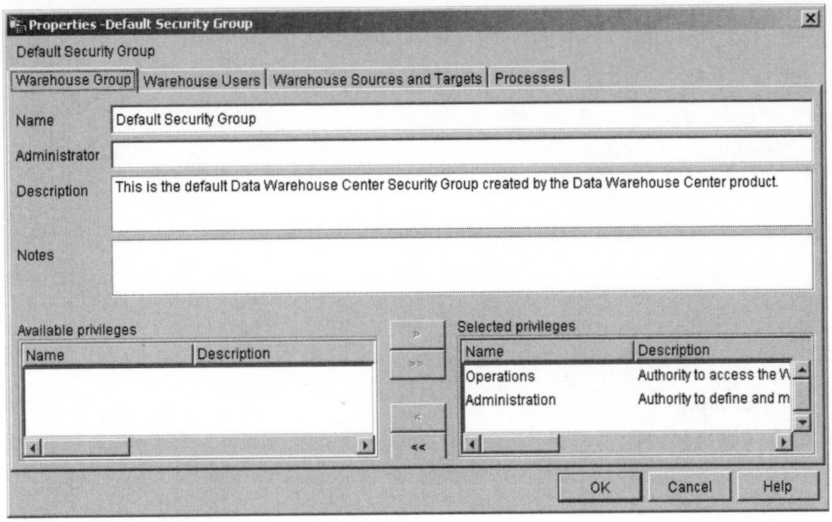

Figure 8.1   Default security group.

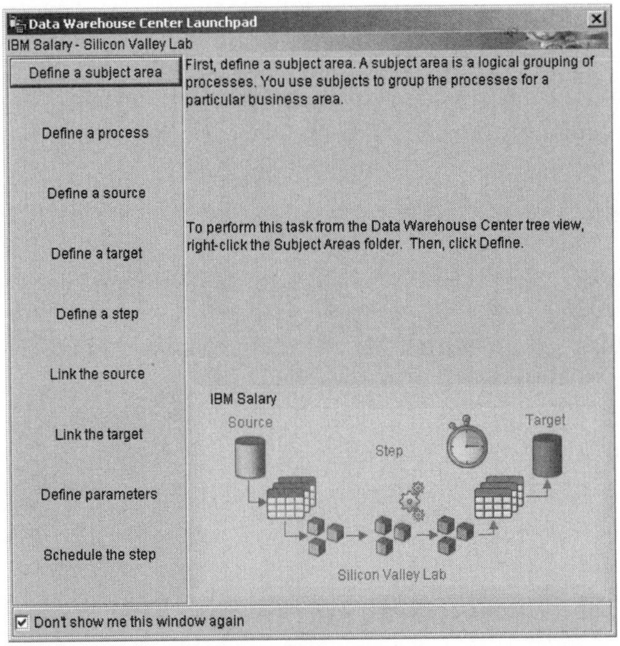

Figure 8.2   IBM DB2 Data Warehouse Center launchpad.

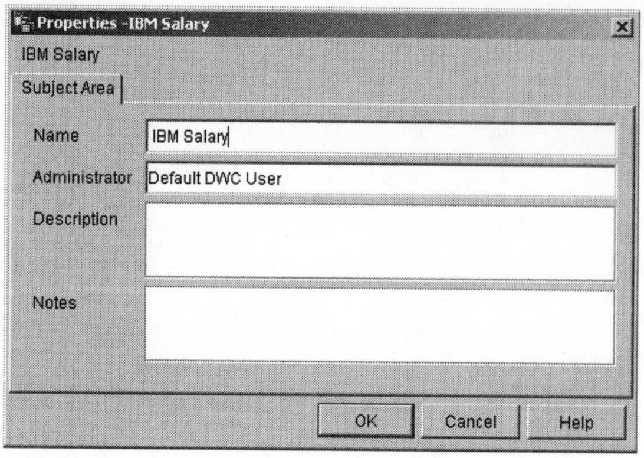

Figure 8.3   Subject area.

Task 1: Define a Subject Area

A *subject area* is a place where you can group the related processes, and it can be used to represent a certain business area in your data warehouse environment. If you are building a warehouse of sales and marketing data, you define a Sales subject area and a Marketing subject area. (See Figure 8.3.)

Task 2: Define a Process

As illustrated in Figure 8.4, you can now define a process that contains your data warehouse sources, targets, and steps to extract and transform the source data into your target data warehouse in a data format that meets your user analysts' requirements.

You can assign user security to manage your warehouse objects at a process level. You can also add warehouse users or groups to access the warehouse objects in this process. In addition, you can insert process description and additional notes to help you organize this process. (See Figure 8.5.)

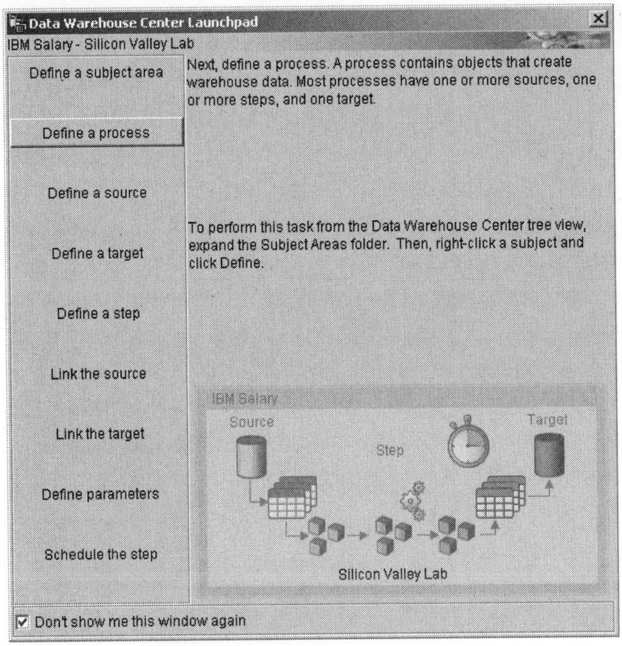

Figure 8.4   Define a process.

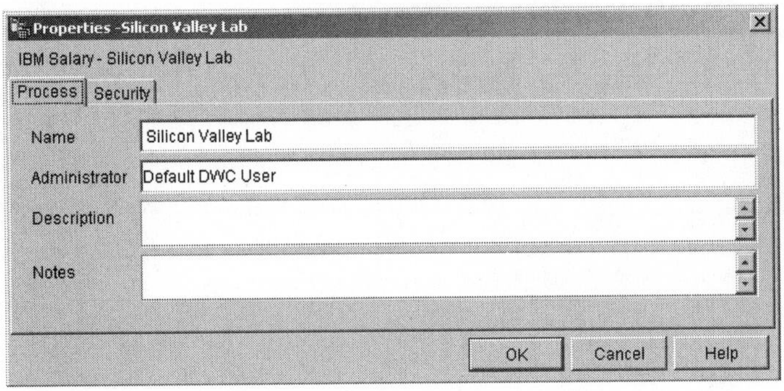

Figure 8.5   Process properties.

Task 3: Define a Warehouse Source

You can define relational and non-relational data sources to be used in your process. Figure 8.6 lists the supported data source that you can manage in the IBM DB2 Data Warehouse Center. Only the definition of the source is read and stored into the data warehouse meta data.

Shown in Figure 8.7 is an example of a DB2 source called "Employee" that can contain one or more tables or views residing in the same database. There is a list of operations that you can perform against the tables, such as "sample the contents of the source." When you define a source, you need to provide a data source name, user ID, and password to connect to the data source, and the connect information is used by the agent site specified. Therefore, you need to make sure the database is accessible from the agent site. Again, the access to this source can be granted to warehouse users or groups. You can also have multiple agent sites with different authorization IDs access this source.

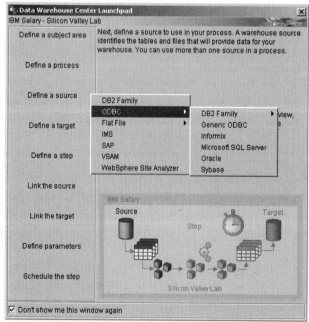

Figure 8.6 Define a source and source types.

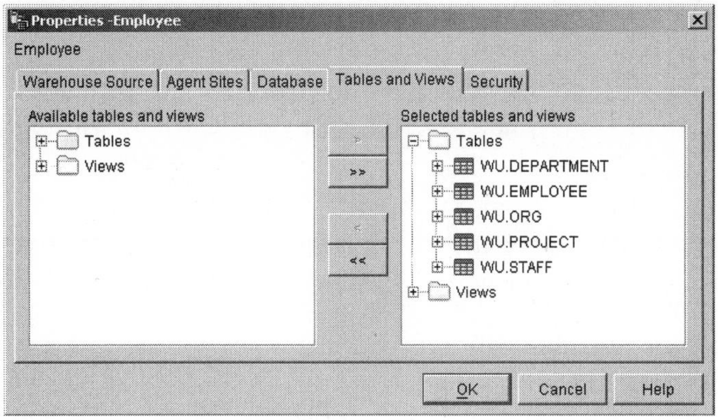

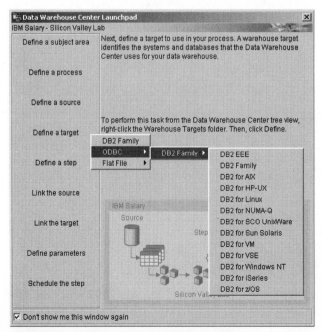

Figure 8.7   Employee DB2 source.

Task 4: Define a Warehouse Target

You can define a warehouse target that will store the transformed source data for analysis or for further data transformation such as building a cube. Figure 8.8 lists the supported warehouse target types.

Figure 8.8   Define a target and target types.

Defining a warehouse target (Figure 8.9) is similar to defining a warehouse source, except that the warehouse target's role in a warehouse step is to store the transformed data. You will have to provide the same data source connect string for the agent site to connect to the source. You can also authorize other warehouse users and groups to access this target. In addition, you can have multiple agent sites with different authorization IDs to access this target. If you want to use the warehouse transformers, you can register and enable them in the warehouse target database.

Task 5: Define a Step

You can use a variety of warehouse steps (Figure 8.10) to transform and cleanse your data. Your own program can even be defined as a step to further customize your warehousing needs; these user-defined programs do not always require a warehouse source or target. You have total flexibility to tailor your data extract, transformation, and loading process. You can further define step cascade links to set conditions for the successor steps to run on success, on failure, or on completion.

In our example, we have chosen the SQL step to extract the manager salary data from the EMPLOYEE and DEPARTMENT warehouse source tables. SQL step provides an SQLAssist Wizard for you to build the appropriate SQL statement to filter, extract, and join source data. Figure 8.11 illustrates the types of step types and subtypes available.

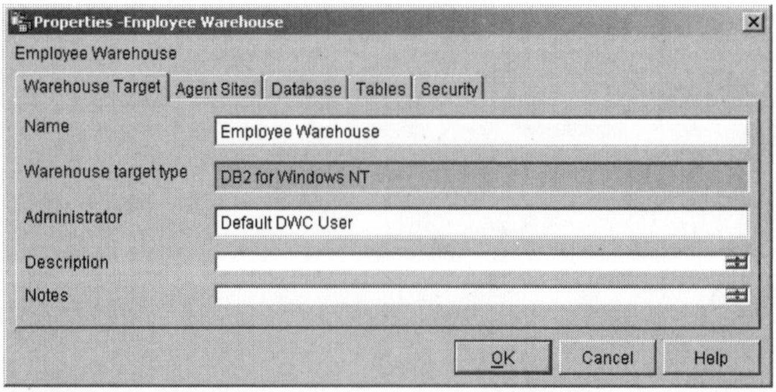

Figure 8.9 Target properties.

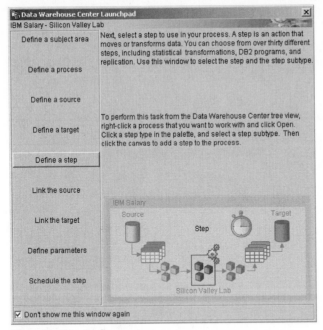

Figure 8.10   Define a step.

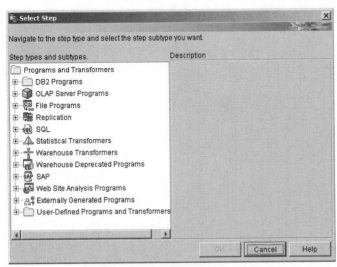

Figure 8.11   Step types and subtypes.

Task 6: Link a Source to a Step

Depending on the warehouse step type that you have chosen, the step may require you to link a warehouse source as input to the step, (see Figure 8.12.) In our example, we have two warehouse source tables feeding into the SQL step.

Figure 8.13 shows the warehouse source tables being selected and linked to the SQL step we defined earlier. From the process modeler, you can also draw a data link from a warehouse target as input to another compatible warehouse step.

Task 7: Link a Step to a Target

Again, depending on the warehouse step type that you have specified, a warehouse target may or may not be required. In our example, the SQL step requires a warehouse target. (See Figure 8.14.)

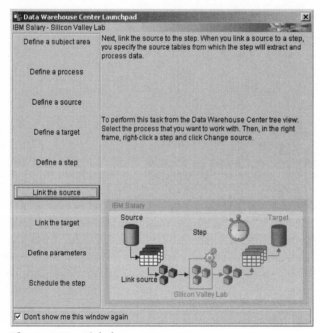

Figure 8.12   Link the source.

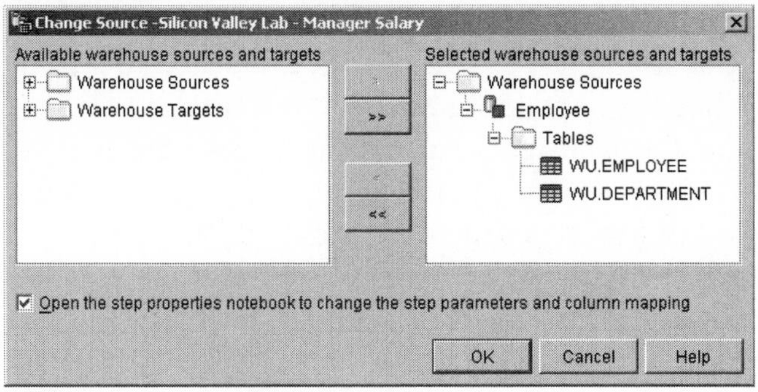

Figure 8.13 Warehouse sources.

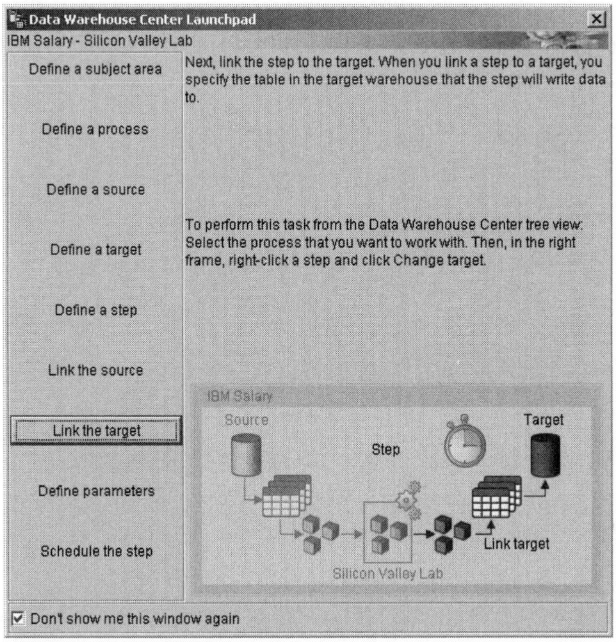

Figure 8.14 Link the target.

If you only need the warehouse target to store staging data to feed into another compatible warehouse step type, you may link the step to a transient warehouse target. When the successor step is done with the transient warehouse target as input, the transient warehouse target data will be removed. The step that generates the transient warehouse target is called a *transient step*. However, you cannot schedule a transient step in DWC.

In our example, we have defined a DB2 warehouse target table called IWH.MANAGER_SALARY in the Employee Warehouse. (See Figure 8.15.)

Task 8: Define the Step Parameters

Each warehouse step has different parameters required to do the data extract, transformation, and loading. Figure 8.16 shows the menu option to initiate the process to define parameters.

In our example, the warehouse source tables are joined, filtered, aggregated, and ordered before the SQL step populates the selected data into the warehouse target. This is done via the Build SQL button (where the SQLAssist Wizard is opened). You can also edit or test generated SQL. Refer to Figure 8.17 for the IBM DB2 Data Warehouse Center interface.

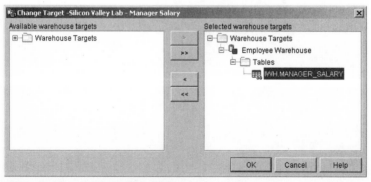

Figure 8.15 Warehouse targets.

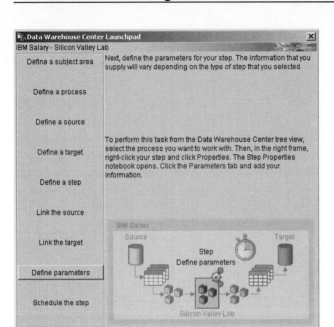

Figure 8.16   Define step parameters.

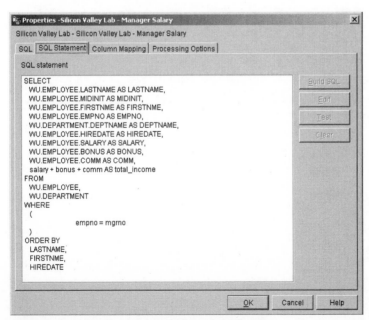

Figure 8.17   Building SQL Statement for the step.

Task 9: Schedule a Step to Run

Once you have tested the step, you can add schedules to the step and move it to production. Figure 8.18 shows the menu option to start this process.

You can schedule a step (except for a transient step) or a process based on certain run intervals or run frequency. If you have defined a step task flow for this step, only the first step in the task flow stream needs to be scheduled. Figure 8.19 shows the parameters available to scheduling steps. After the first step is executed, the step task flow will be executed based on the next step in the task flow condition. Also, mail notification can be added to a step so that email can be sent to the DBA when the step completed with certain conditions that require your DBA's attention.

Defining Keys on Target Tables

If your warehouse target is generated by the warehouse step, you may choose to define a primary key for the target table to improve data access performance. You can also define additional indexes for your target table to optimize the data retrieval performance.

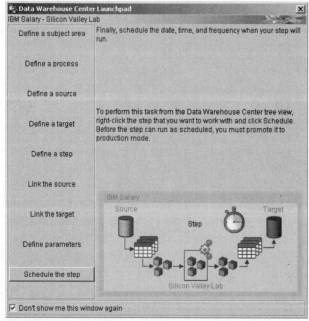

Figure 8.18   Schedule a step.

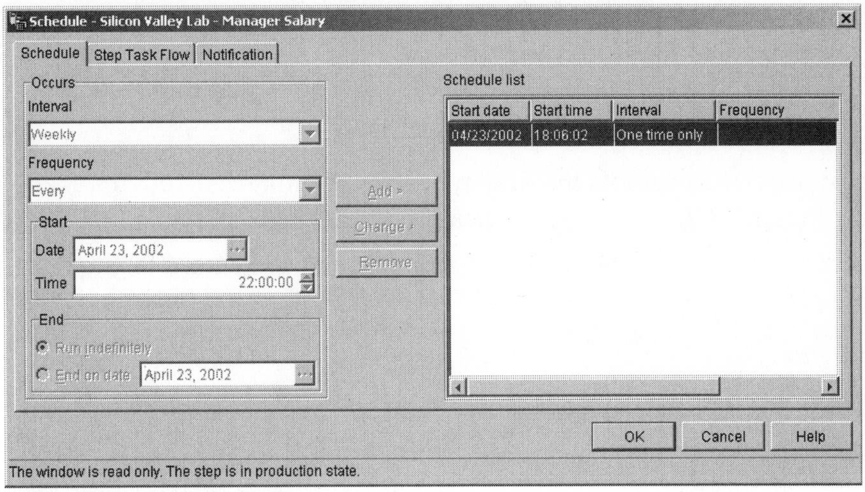

Figure 8.19 Schedule types.

Maintaining the Data Warehouse

DB2 table statistics provide information about the physical and logical characteristics of a table and its indexes. You must periodically collect these statistics so that DB2 can determine the optimal access path to your data. If extensive inserts, updates, and deletes are made to the data in your warehouse target table, and the last collection of statistics no longer reflects the actual table data, then data access performance can diminish. You should always update statistics after major changes are made in your data warehouse.

Reorganize a table rearranges the data in its physical storage; thus eliminating fragmentation, and ensuring that the table is stored efficiently in the database. You can also use reorganization to control the order in which the rows of a table are stored by adding indexes. You should drop the table indexes before reorganizing your warehouse table and re-create them after the data is loaded back to the warehouse table in the proper physical order.

DB2 Performance Monitor provides information about the state of DB2 and the data that it controls, and it alerts users of unusual situations. The information is provided in a series of snapshot switch groups, each of which represents the state of the system, databases, or application at a point in time. You can control the frequency of the snapshots and the amount of information collected.

The information that is collected by the performance monitor is returned in performance variables. These performance variables are a defined set of elements:

Counter.   Counts the number of times something has occurred, for example, the number of rows written.

Gauge.   Returns the current value, for example, the number of applications currently connected.

Timestamp.   Represents the time when something occurred, for example, the time when the last application completed.

Watermark.   Records the highest value reached, for example, the maximum size of the database heap.

Authorizing Users of the Warehouse

IBM DB2 Data Warehouse Center provides security groups and users to operate and administer warehouse objects. Once the warehouse target tables are created in the target database or operating system, you need to grant the proper database authorities or file privileges to the users to access the warehouse data.

Cataloging Warehouse Objects for Users

You can catalog the warehouse objects (such as warehouse sources, targets, subject areas, processes, and warehouse schemas) for use by the end users. You catalog the objects by publishing IBM DB2 Data Warehouse Center meta data in the IBM Information Catalog Manager (ICM). (See Figure 8.20.) ICM manages business meta data that helps users identify and locate data and information available to them in the organization. For example, users can look up the information catalog to locate the tables that contain the data that they need to query.

After you publish the warehouse meta data to the ICM, you need to update it periodically to refresh the changes that have been made in the IBM DB2 Data Warehouse Center. To transfer DWC meta data updates to the information catalog, you use Publish Metadata → Data Warehouse to Information Catalog. For more information regarding meta data control, see Chapter 10.

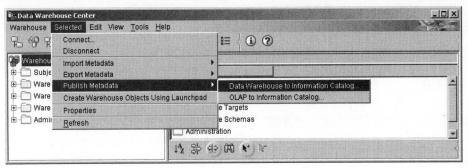

Figure 8.20 Publish meta data.

Process and Step Task Control

Task flow control for steps and processes is the method for controlling their sequence in DWC. The task flow for a step or a process can be one of the following:

On success. The predecessor step has to complete successfully before the successor step can run.

On failure. The predecessor step has to fail before the successor step can run. This task flow can be used to do error handling for a failing step.

On completion. The successor step will run unconditionally.

In a warehouse process, you may have multiple step task flow. Each step task flow may contain one or more warehouse steps. Sometimes it is desirable to wait for a set of warehouse steps to finish before executing the next set of warehouse steps. Once the related steps have been configured, you can use the process task flow to manage how you want to execute successor processes.

Each warehouse step or process can be scheduled. IBM DB2 Data Warehouse Center administrators can specify when a step or a process will run and how often. The schedule defined for a step will be activated when the step is promoted to *production* mode. The schedules defined for a process, however, will be activated when the process is enabled. If an enabled process is scheduled to run, only the steps in *production* mode will be run. Only the first process in the process task flow needs to be scheduled and enabled. All the subsequent processes in the process task flow need to be enabled only. There is no concept of development, test, and production modes for a warehouse process.

A number of rules are used to determine the completion code of a process. Each step task flow identified in a process will have a *root* step and a *terminal* step. The root step is predetermined while the terminal step is the last step executed in the step task flow. The root step must be a step defined physically in the current process and must not be a *shortcut* step or a *transient* step. The completion status of the terminal step in each step task flow is used to calculate the final completion status of the entire process. It is important to compute the final completion status of the process so the decision can be made as to whether the process task flow should be followed.

When you define task flows for your warehouse steps, the successor steps will perform a data dependency check to ensure the warehouse source is *current*. You may optionally turn it off if data dependency checking is not desirable. This may be the case when you first develop steps for your warehouse and the data dependency is not available or required. You may later turn it back on when you are ready to go to production.

If your step requires both warehouse source and target, the DWC agents available to run your step will be those that are common to both the warehouse source and target. You should choose an agent that is on the same physical machine as your warehouse target so that the data insert or load to the warehouse target obtains the best performance.

Scheduling

When you have completed the testing of your warehouse steps, you may schedule the step using the warehouse scheduler. Note that your step must not be in production mode when you are adding a schedule. If you have steps grouped into multiple warehouse processes, you may schedule the steps at the process level. If you have schedules associated with both the warehouse step and process and you want to run a process, only the process schedule will be observed.

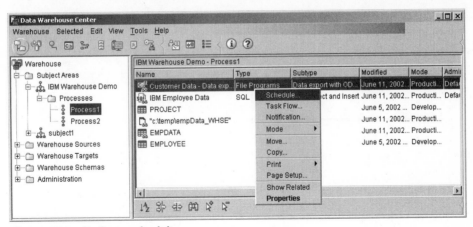

Figure 8.21   Define a schedule.

To add a schedule to your warehouse step using the IBM DB2 Data Warehouse Center scheduler, right-click on the step from the navigator and select Schedule, as shown in Figure 8.21. Note that the process schedule has the same schedule options as the step schedule.

Once selected, the window shown in Figure 8.22 appears. Here you can add the schedule to the selected warehouse step. Within the window are a few parameters to set as follows:

- *Interval* is the time interval that you want a task to run. It can run only once or by Minutes, Hourly, Daily, Weekly, Monthly (Dates), Monthly (Days), or Yearly.

- *Frequency* defines how frequently you want to run the task. For a weekly schedule, for example, the frequency can be Every, Every 2nd, Every 3rd, . . ., or Every 8th.

- *Start Date and Time* determines when you want the schedule to take effect. Note that if your interval value is One Time Only, the Start Date and Time must be a future time.

- *End* indicates when you want the schedule to stop. You can let the schedule continue indefinitely or end on a specified date.

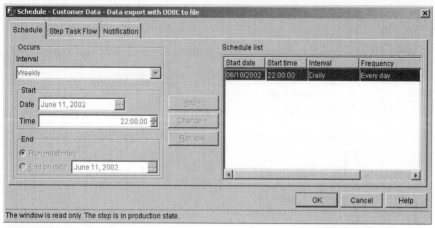

Figure 8.22   Add a schedule.

You may use the Add button to define multiple schedules to run your task. Or you can also change or delete the schedule entries in the Schedule List later. However, note that the schedule for a step can only be added, changed, or deleted when the step is in nonproduction mode. Once the step is promoted to production mode, you will not be able to make any changes to the step schedule, because the IBM Data Warehouse Center has already started to track and to maintain the schedules that you defined for the tasks.

You can add a step task flow to a predecessor step or a successor step by selecting the Step Task Flow notebook tab and right-clicking on white space. You can also add a process task flow to a predecessor process by opening the Process Task Flow notebook tab and clicking on the white space. The condition for a step or process task flow can be: Starts on Success, Starts on Failure, or Starts on Completion. (See Figure 8.23.) If you have chosen to add both Starts on Success and Starts on Failure for the same predecessor and successor, the IBM DB2 Data Warehouse Center will consolidate both conditions to Starts on Completion.

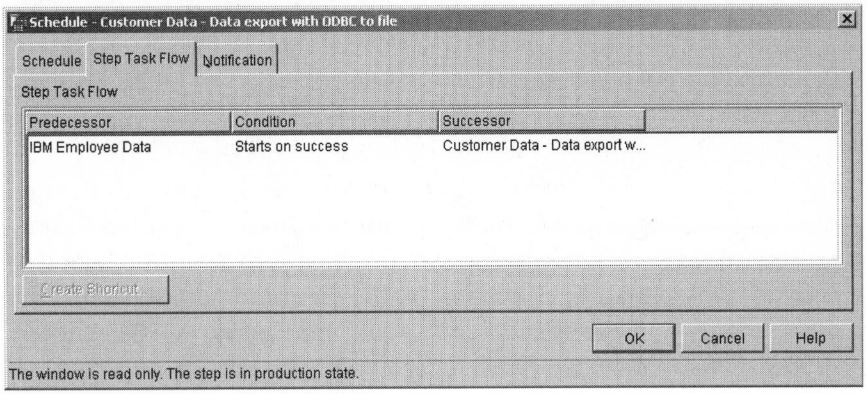

Figure 8.23 Define a step task flow.

You can also specify a predecessor or a successor step from another process. To do this, click on the Create Shortcut button to identify which step from another process you want to reference in the current process. The button brings up a navigator to guide you to the warehouse subject, process, and step that you want to reference.

Once you have added the shortcut to this process, you can again right-click on the white space to add a new task flow condition. The shortcut step appears in the predecessor and the successor selection list. Figure 8.24 shows the selection list.

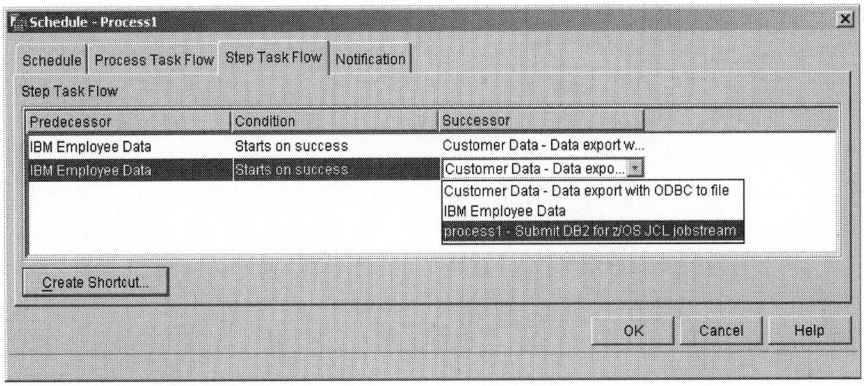

Figure 8.24 Adding predecessor and successor steps.

Notifying the Data Administrator

Upon the completion of a warehouse step, you can send an email message to notify the appropriate parties about the status of the step or the process execution. Figure 8.25 shows the notification parameters to set. This is particularly useful when the warehouse step or warehouse process fails and the system programmer or data administrator needs to be notified to handle the failure in order for the production job stream to continue. Another use is to notify the responsible parties upon the completion of the entire job stream so that other non-warehouse processing may continue or resume.

You can send email to a warehouse user when this step or a process has completed (unconditionally), succeeded, or failed. You may also include additional text by clicking on the Edit button. Once you have completed the editing of the message, you can click on the Add button to add a new message. You may change or remove the message later. You may also add more users on the Notification List.

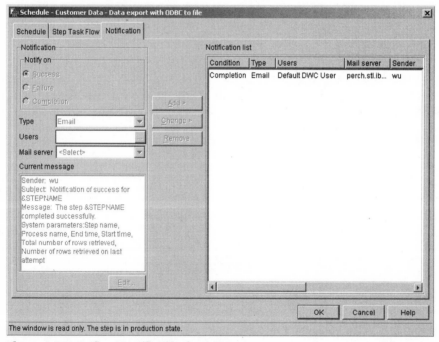

Figure 8.25 Define a notification for a step.

Scheduling a Process

If you have grouped a set of related steps in a process, you may want to schedule a process to run instead of scheduling the individual steps. You may also arrange your steps in multiple processes so that you may have certain steps in the successor processes to wait for those steps in the predecessor process to run. This new feature allows the user to customize and control the step flow.

For example, if you have three steps—Step 1, Step 2, and Step 3—and Step 1 and Step 2 must complete successfully before Step 3 can be run, you can group Step 1 and Step 2 into Process 1 and define Step 3 in Process 2. Then you can add a process task flow between Process 1 and Process 2. (See Figure 8.26.)

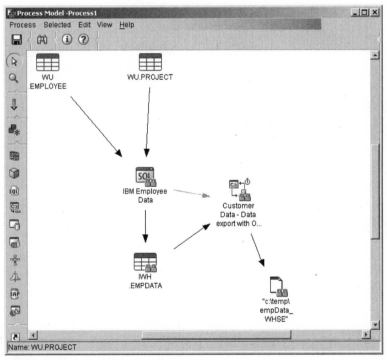

Figure 8.26   Grouping steps into a process.

Process 1 contains two steps, and these two steps must be completed successfully before the successor process starts. You may also notice that there is a step task flow defined between the steps. This step flow appears green to indicate that the successor step will run only if the predecessor step is completed successfully.

Process 2 will wait for Process 1 to complete before it starts. In this process, there is only one step, and there is a red arrow pointing to it. This indicates that the step will retry *indefinitely* if it fails. You should use this approach with caution. (See Figure 8.27.)

You can schedule Process 1 to run and promote all the steps to production mode, as shown in Figure 8.28. The process will be enabled and the scheduling starts. You can monitor the scheduled task in the Warehouse Work in Progress window. The process schedule has the same graphical user interface as the step schedule.

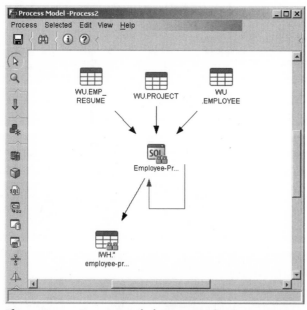

Figure 8.27 Recommended step grouping in a process.

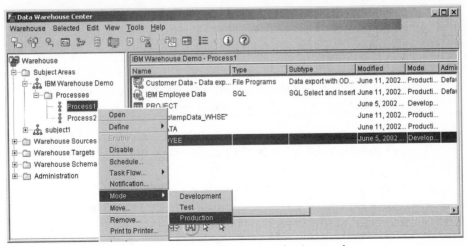

Figure 8.28   Promoting all steps in a process to production mode.

Figure 8.28 illustrates a process that is in Enabled mode. Any schedule defined for this process will be honored until you click on Disable on the Process pop-up menu. The Process pop-up menu has several submenus that help you manage the process:

Schedule.   You can open the process schedule to add, change, or delete the schedules defined for the process.

Task Flow.   You can open the process or the step task flow to add, change, or delete the task flow for the process or the steps in the process. Each task flow entry contains a predecessor and a successor. The successor can be run when the predecessor is completed, succeeds, or fails.

Notification.   You can add warehouse users to the mail notification list when the process has completed.

Mode.   You can promote the steps in the process to *test* or *production mode*. You can also demote the steps in the process to *test* or *development mode*.

Move.   You can move the current process to another subject.

Remove.   You can remove the current process from the IBM DB2 Data Warehouse Center. All steps in the process must be in development mode.

Locate.   You can locate warehouse objects including steps, files, tables, views, and columns in the IBM Data Warehouse meta data store based on the search criteria specified.

Properties.   You can use the properties notebook to add or change the process description and manage the security of the process such as assigning warehouse security groups to access this process.

There are certain rules applied to using the process scheduling with the multiple wait function. Understanding these rules will help you to determine how to group your steps in a process.

First, we need to identify the "root" step in a process, since all the root steps will be started by the process schedule concurrently. The criteria for a root step include the following:

- The step must not have a predecessor step within the same process.

- The step must be physically defined within the current process— that is, a shortcut step coming from another process will not be taken into consideration.

- The step must be in production mode. Any step that is not in production mode will not be run as part of the process.

- The step must be a step that produces persistent warehouse data or has data dependency from the predecessor step.

Next, we need to determine terminal steps in a process. The completion status of the terminal steps will be used to calculate the process exit status. It is very important to determine the process exit status in order for the process task flow to be evaluated and to be followed. The terminal step in a process must satisfy the following conditions:

- It has no successor step that is in production mode and is physically defined in the current process.

- It has no matching condition to cascade down to the successor step that is in production mode and is physically defined in the current process.

Triggering Steps Outside IBM DB2 Data Warehouse Center

You can populate a warehouse target in the IBM DB2 Data Warehouse Center by running a step manually in the process modeler or schedule a step to run automatically. On certain occasions you may want to initiate the step execution outside DWC, and a fixed schedule for the step does not quite serve the purpose. The IBM DB2 Data Warehouse Center allows you to send a request to the warehouse server to promote, populate, or demote a warehouse step via a Java interface with the program called XTClient. You may embed this XTClient in your application or script file to trigger a particular warehouse step to run upon demand. This gives you total flexibility to run a scheduled or nonscheduled warehouse step based on your own local warehouse requirements. You may run your system and database backups before triggering the first warehouse step in your nightly production run. After the first production warehouse step is executed, the task flow defined for that warehouse step is observed and followed.

The external trigger program is composed of two components: *XTClient*, just mentioned, and *XTServer*. The XTServer is installed with the warehouse server, while the XTClient is installed with the warehouse agent on all the supported warehouse agent platforms. They are written in Java and therefore require the appropriate level of the Java Development Kit (JDK) to be installed on the system where you start the XTServer and XTClient. You may also use the JDK that comes with the IBM DB2 Data Warehouse Center and Control Center.

Starting the External Trigger Server

You must start the XTServer so that it is listening from a known TCP/IP port before you invoke the external trigger client. Once the XTClient is started, a request is sent to the XTServer to do the work. When the work is completed, the XTClient is notified.

The syntax for starting the external trigger server is as follows:

```
java db2_vw_xt.XTServer TriggerServerPort
```

where *TriggerServerPort* is the TCP/IP port assigned to the external trigger server. This value can be available for TCP/IP ports in your operating system such as 11003 or 11004. Since the XTServer is going to listen from this port for any incoming XTClient requests, you should ensure this port is not used by other applications on the system where you start your XTServer.

Starting the External Trigger Client

You need to make sure the XTServer is listening from its TCP/IP port. You can issue the command NETSTAT-A on the XTServer system to verify the listening port.

The syntax for starting the external trigger client is as follows:

```
java db2_vw_xt.XTClient ServerHostName ServerPort DWCUserID
DWCUserPassword StepName Command  WaitForStepCompletion RowLimit
```

The parameters are as follows:

ServerHostName.   This is the TCP/IP hostname for the system on which the warehouse server is installed. You should specify a fully qualified hostname.

ServerPort.   This is the TCP/IP port assigned to the warehouse server. The external trigger client must use the same port as the external trigger server.

DWCUserID.   This is the user ID with IBM DB2 Data Warehouse Center Operations privileges.

DWCUserPassword.   This is the password for the user ID.

StepName.   This is the name of the step to process. The name is case-sensitive and should be enclosed in double quotation marks ("") if it includes blanks, such as " My First Warehouse Step ".

Command.   This can be one of the five values described below. Note that the user ID under which you run the external trigger program must be in the same warehouse group as the process that contains the step.

1. Execute the step.
2. Promote the step to test mode.
3. Promote the step to production mode.
4. Demote the step to test mode.
5. Demote the step to development mode.

WaitForStepCompletion.   This optional parameter indicates whether the external trigger program is to return the results of the step processing. You can choose one of the following values:

- 1 is to wait for step completion. 0 is returned if the step is successful; a nonzero value is returned if the step fails.
- 0 or blank does not wait for step completion.

RowLimit.   This optional parameter indicates whether the external trigger program is to extract all the rows of the source table or a subset of the rows. You can use this parameter to quickly test the steps that extract a large amount of data. Note that this parameter is valid only when the step is in test mode. You can choose one of the following values:

- 0 or blank will fetch all rows.
- N will fetch n rows.

Monitoring Strategies with IBM DB2 Data Warehouse Center

Many strategies and approaches are available to monitor the activities of the warehouse. We discuss each in this section, from tools that monitor the ETL data propagation of DWC to DB2 V8 to replication monitoring.

IBM DB2 Data Warehouse Center Monitoring Tools

A crucial task in building and maintaining a successful data warehouse environment consists of monitoring the data warehouse. This monitoring process covers two very distinct activities: monitoring the data warehouse *population* and monitoring the data warehouse *usage*.

Typically, data warehouse administrators are often faced with the following questions:

- How much data is being extracted and loaded into a specific target table?
- How long does it take to populate a specific target table?
- Does the amount of data being processed significantly vary between different runs of the same transformation?
- Do some agents have a much bigger workload than others?
- When should some transformation steps be assigned to a different agent for better load balancing?
- What would be the performance impact of assigning the execution of a transformation step to a different agent?
- Are there peak times during the day when a certain agent is overloaded?
- Did all the transformation steps complete successfully?
- Do transformation steps complete successfully on the first try, or after how many tries?

- Are there concurrency problems?

- What is the approximate percentage of execution failures that can be attributed to communication problems, or to a service that has not been started?

- Which steps whose execution results in a failure can be associated with bad source data?

- Which part in the step execution takes the longest to complete?

- Should a table in the data warehouse be transient or not? What are the trade-offs?

- Should some steps be redesigned; for example, should an SQL step be replaced with a DB2 load step?

All the questions are strictly related to the data warehouse population process. Statistical information and logging information kept under the Work in Progress GUI of DB2 Warehouse Manager hold the key to answering all these important questions. A sample statistical data warehouse could be built very simply to automate the process of collecting a variety of statistics and to deliver statistical reports to the data warehouse administrator.

The second aspect of data warehouse monitoring relates to the usage of the data warehouse by the end users. To ensure optimal usage of resources, this monitoring is indispensable, since it enables you to address these critical questions:

- Which tables in the data warehouse are the least used?

- Are some tables only used around certain dates—for example, during the first 3 days of the month?

- Do users need to receive the latest information in the table, or is data that was retrieved an hour ago still meaningful?

- Which users should have higher priority to have their requests executed?

- Should limits be imposed on the resources allocated to execute a request?

- Should different resource limits be allocated to different groups of users?

- How could resource usage and user activity be tracked and reported?

- How could a fair chargeback policy be implemented?

- How to balance resource usage across nodes?
- How to set and monitor thresholds for query concurrency?
- How to identify data archival candidates?

This kind of monitoring, although not restricted to a data warehouse environment, provides influential information in a data warehouse environment. Its results can guide the data warehouse administrator in deciding how the data warehouse should evolve and be restructured. This monitoring can certainly give accurate hints regarding the need for:

- Dropping an unused table in the data warehouse
- Modifying an existing transformation step to filter the data truly needed by end users
- Creating automatic summary tables
- Redistributing the data warehouse over multiple nodes

Monitoring Data Warehouse Population

During the execution of any transformation step, DB2 Warehouse Manager collects a variety of statistical and logging information, which is stored in the control database. This information is available to users belonging to a group that has been assigned Operations privileges. Any user with Operations privileges has the authority to access the *Work in Progress functions* by following the menu options in Figure 8.29. The Work in Progress environment is launched from the main IBM DB2 Data Warehouse Center window.

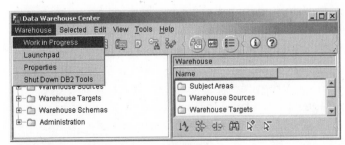

Figure 8.29   Starting Work in Progress.

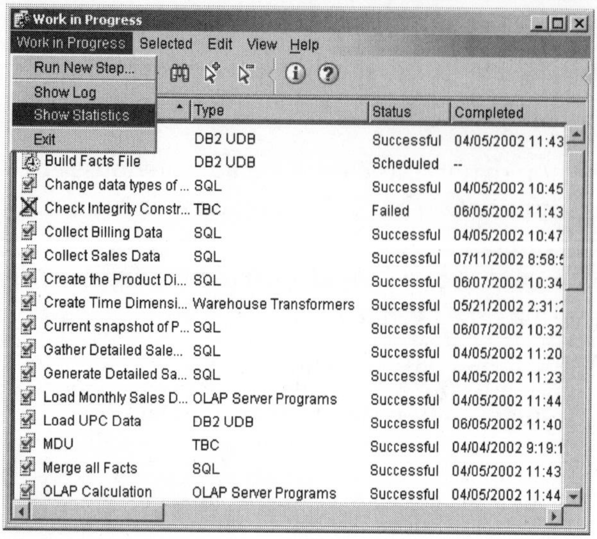

Figure 8.30   Monitoring steps and processes.

From the Work in Progress GUI shown in Figure 8.30, three types of monitoring capabilities are available. You can view statistics associated with transformation steps or browse the log information associated with transformation steps. You can examine the status of transformation steps and processes. Finally, you can view the warehouse source and warehouse target import activities and errors.

Statistics related to the execution of transformation steps are kept at a detailed level and a summarized level:

- The summarized statistics hold the average elapsed time needed to execute the step, and the average number of bytes transferred. However, these values are not computed for each type of transformation.

- For an SQL transformation step, if the source and the target are located on different systems, both the average elapsed time and the average number of bytes transferred are computed.

- For an SQL transformation step, if the source and the target reside on the same system, or if the step receives data from other steps, then only the average elapsed time is computed; the column holding the average number of bytes displays the not-applicable symbol (—) in this case.

■ The average elapsed time, expressed in seconds, includes the time to complete all processing steps, including connection time, disconnection time, and the time that it took to commit changes.

Figure 8.31 illustrates the high-level statistics available for examination. Detailed statistics can also be retrieved for an individual step. This detailed statistical information is shown in Figure 8.32 and includes:

■ Number of times the transformation step was successfully and unsuccessfully executed since the statistics were last reset for that step.

■ Date and time of completion of the first execution of the step since the last statistics reset.

■ Average elapsed time to complete the execution.

■ Average number of rows and number of bytes extracted during processing; this information is available only for SQL transformation steps.

■ Average number of rows and bytes extracted per minute.

■ Number of rows and bytes extracted, the elapsed time as well as the date and time of completion for executions with the following characteristics:

Name	Type	Average elapsed time	Average bytes
Search Institution Customers	SQL	00:00:08	8,650
Load UPC Data	DB2 UDB	00:00:00	0
Create Time Dimension	Warehouse Transfo...	00:00:00	0
Create Holiday Schedule	SQL	00:00:05	393
Reformat the date	SQL	00:00:04	--
Update Time Dimension	TBC	00:00:00	0
Check Integrity Constraint	TBC	00:00:00	0
Current snapshot of Product ...	SQL	00:00:03	--
Create the Product Dimensio...	SQL	00:00:03	--
Collect Sales Data	SQL	00:00:22	109,289.33
Change data types of Orders	SQL	00:00:09	--
Collect Billing Data	SQL	00:01:03	549,226
Pivot Billing Data	Warehouse Transfo...	00:00:00	0

Figure 8.31   Step statistics.

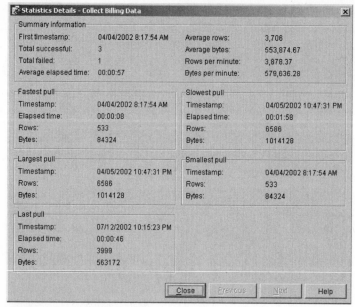

Figure 8.32   Detail statistics.

- Fastest execution
- Slowest execution
- Execution with the smallest number of bytes extracted
- Execution with the largest number of bytes extracted
- Last execution of the step

Some of the detailed statistical information may not be available depending on the type of the transformation step. For SQL steps, the information about the number of bytes extracted is not available if the source and target of the step are the same database. For non-SQL steps, no statistical information is being kept. All statistics for a step (or a set of steps) can be reset to zero; this may be an appropriate action when new statistics are collected for a step from a specific point in time.

Besides statistics, log information is also available to monitor the data warehouse population. You can display log information by selecting the Show Log item from the Work in Progress menu, shown in Figure 8.33. The log window displays log messages that were written to the log during a run of a step and can be particularly useful to help troubleshoot problems for a step. Only steps that have a status of Successful, Failed, Warning, or

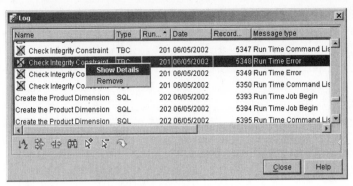

Figure 8.33 Log entries for a step.

Canceled will have logs. Many records may be written to the log during the run of a single step. These logs have a tendency to grow fast, and the warehouse administrator might need to adjust the maximum number of log entries that should be displayed in the log window. This value can be adjusted in the Server page of the IBM DB2 Data Warehouse Center Properties notebook by changing the value in the Purge Log When Total Records Equal field.

Detailed information about each log record can be displayed by selecting the Show Details item from the menu for a selected log record. (See Figure 8.34.)

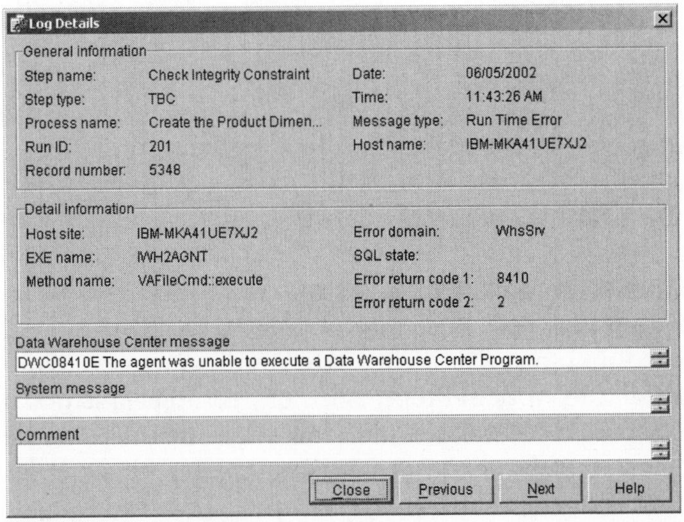

Figure 8.34 Log detail.

The Log Details window contains three areas of information: general, detail, and message. The general information identifies the step, the identifier of the step edition (run ID), the record number of the log record, and the log message type, which identifies the event or error that occurred. Detail information shows additional data about the event that is represented by the message type, including:

- The name of the program (*.exe name*) that encountered the error
- The name of the subsystem (*Error Domain*) that originally encountered the error (such as Windows 32, Sockets, ODBC, or the IBM DB2 Data Warehouse Center)
- The unique DWC return code displayed in the Error Return Code 1 field and documented in the Message Reference section in the Information Center (refer to DWC messages)
- The return code that is issued by the subsystem that originally encountered the error, displayed in the *Error Return Code 2* field
- SQLSTATE code that corresponds to an SQL statement if an error occurred during execution of the statement

Finally, the detailed message area provides even more detail about the log. This section contains information such as:

- Message text that corresponds to the error Return Code 1
- System message, supplied by the subsystem that encountered the error, showing the message text that corresponds to the error Return Code 2
- Comments that may contain additional information that the IBM DB2 Data Warehouse Center provides for the message type

Even for steps that have executed successfully, logging information is generated. In this case, the fields related to error messages are not filled; the useful logging information displays the commands that have been executed to run the step.

The status of the Transformation Steps and Processes, displayed in the main Work in Progress window, provides information about the steps and processes that are scheduled to run, are currently running, or have completed running. Note that the Work in Progress is not a complete historical record of every step or process that has run; it only retains entries for the last occurrence of each step or process. In addition, an entry for a step or process is not kept in the Work in Progress window if:

- The step is a transient step. A transient step populates a transient table and is executed when another step is executed that uses the transient table as input. Data in a transient table is not stored permanently and is automatically removed when the dependent step has completed its execution. The entry for a transient step only appears in the Work in Progress window while the step is being executed.

■ There are multiple steps that populate the same target. In this case, only the step that was executed most recently to populate that target will have an entry in the Work in Progress window.

Several status labels can be assigned to transformation steps. These include the following:

Scheduled.   The value in the Scheduled field shows the date and time when the step is scheduled for execution; the Completed field is not filled, since the step has not executed yet. If multiple execution schedules have been defined for the step, one entry appears for each schedule defined. The step must be in production mode for the entry to appear in the Work in Progress window.

Populating.   The step is currently being executed.

Retrying.   The step execution has started but could not complete and is in a retry mode; a step will be in a retry mode, for example, when there is a network connection error between the warehouse server and warehouse agent at the time of step execution. A step can only be in a retry mode if in the Processing Options page of the step definition the retry count is greater than zero. The execution of the step will be retried automatically up to the number specified in the Retry Count field, as long as it cannot complete successfully; the interval between retries is also specified in the Processing Options page of the step definition. If the step still does not complete successfully when the maximum number of retries is reached, its status is switched to Failed.

Successful.   The last execution of the step was successful.

Failed.   The last execution of the step failed.

Warning.   The last execution of the step completed with a warning. The warehouse administrator can control what constitutes a warning; the Processing Options page of the step definition lets you specify how to treat an SQL warning and the case of No rows returned. These situations can be treated as a success, a failure, or a warning. Note that these options are only available for steps of type SQL.

Canceled.   This identifies a step that was canceled by the warehouse administrator while it was being executed.

Canceling.   A step is in the process of being canceled; its execution is being terminated before completion.

Purging.   Only steps that have a status of successful, failed, warning, or canceled can be purged. Purging a step with a status of *warning* or *successful* results in the data being deleted. Purging a step with a status of *failed* results in the log records being deleted.

Monitoring Data Warehouse Usage

The Query Patroller tool is aimed at monitoring the usage of a database. Its main capability is proactive governing. The tool prevents runaway queries from even beginning. To detect such queries, it calculates the query's cost and compares that cost to thresholds set by the DBA for each user or group of users. The Query Admin component of the tool lets the administrator set the following parameters:

- Maximum number of simultaneous queries
- Maximum cost of any individual query (User Threshold)
- Maximum time that may elapse before a query is aborted
- Maximum number of rows that may be in the result set before the result set gets truncated or the query is aborted

When the cost thresholds are violated, the query is put into a hold state, and the administrator can decide when to put it back on the queue. There are five core aspects to usage monitoring:

Priority queuing.   When the query passes the cost threshold test, the query ends up in one of possibly several priority queues and is run when the server is ready. The administrator can set three different priority levels (low, normal, high) for a user or group. When a user submits a query, a dialog box appears, letting the user specify which priority level he or she wants to assign for the query, and whether the query should run now or be scheduled for later execution.

Result caching.   Since in a warehouse environment at least some of the data may not be updated very frequently, Query Patroller takes advantage of that fact and implements a result caching technique. So, if the same query is submitted several times between cache cleanups, the results are only computed the first time after cache cleanup, and for the subsequent requests, the result is immediately delivered to the user. When a user submits a query, a dialog box appears, asking the user whether he or she accepts a cached result or if the query should be run again to get a fresh result. The user does not have to tie up the application for the result to come back; another dialog box lets the user release the query, in which case the control returns to the application, and the user receives an email when the query finishes running. The result is then obtained by resubmitting the query.

System monitoring.   All users can monitor the progress of their own queries, and administrators can monitor and manipulate the progress of all users' queries. The System Monitor window displays a list of jobs, their associate state (running, queued, done, aborted, held, canceled), the name of the user who submitted the job, and the start and completion time.

Historical analysis.   Query Patroller logs information about every query it traps. The administrator can then get reports on what tables and columns are being requested the most, what time of the day the system is busiest, how many rows are being returned, and which users are requesting data from which tables and columns. From that kind of information, the administrator can decide, for example, on which tables new indexes should be built.

Dynamic load balancing.   On EEE systems, Query Patroller dynamically load balances by looking at the CPU activity of every node and distributing the work evenly among them.

DB2 Monitoring Tools

DB2 also provides the Snapshot Monitor and the Event Monitor to help you collect database activities and statistics while you are populating your warehouse targets. The Snapshot Monitor can be turned on to collect the following database statistics:

- Bufferpool activity information (BUFFERPOOL)
- Lock information (LOCK)
- Sorting information (SORT)
- SQL statement information (STATEMENT)
- Table activity information (TABLE)
- Unit of work information (UOW)

You can use the collected Snapshot statistics to:

- Measure the workload, resource contention, lock escalation, and buffer pool usage in the target database.

- Evaluate the progress of the warehouse population via the Warehouse Agent by the number of reads and writes, cursors being held, and the elapsed time.

- Monitor the database activities for the Warehouse Server and Logger against the Warehouse control database, or for the Warehouse Agent against the source and target databases.

You can use the DB2 command LIST APPLICATIONS to list the DB2 application name, handle, ID, and database name for Warehouse Server (IWH2SERV.EXE), Warehouse Logger (IWH2LOG.EXE), and Warehouse Agent (IWH2AGNT.EXE) processes to filter the Snapshot Monitor statistics collected in different SNAPSHOT switch groups. To help diagnose poor system and application performance, you can use the LOCK switch group to trace deadlocks and determine resource conflicts among Warehouse Agent, Warehouse Server, Warehouse Logger, and other database applications running on the system that lead to overall system performance degradation. Additionally, you can examine the amount of time the Warehouse Agent processes spent waiting for locks and which application is holding these locks, as well as identify the applications that fail to commit their transactions and release the held database resources.

Replication Center Monitoring

You can use the Replication Center Monitoring tool to monitor the Replication Capture and Apply activities and set threshold values to alert responsible parties. When the specified threshold value has been reached, you may choose to send an email to the system programmer or data administrator to take the appropriate actions. Monitoring the Capture and Apply activities is vital to the performance of running the warehouse replication steps. Refer to Figure 8.35 for menu options.

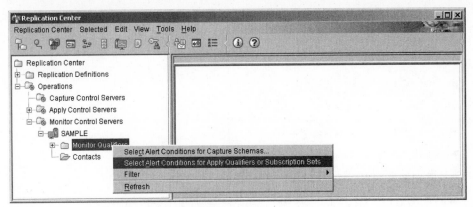

Figure 8.35 Replication Center Monitor.

The following Capture alert conditions can be set per Capture schema in the specified Capture server:

- Status down
- Status last committed
- Errors
- Warnings
- Current latency
- Historic latency
- Memory used

The following Apply alert conditions can be set per Apply schema in the specified Apply server:

- Apply status
- Errors
- Warnings
- Subscription sets failed
- Subscription sets delayed
- Inactive subscriptions sets
- Full refresh occurred
- Transactions rejected due to update anywhere conflict
- Number of rows reworked
- End-to-end latency

Once you have the Capture and Apply alert conditions defined and the Replication Monitor started, you may display and examine the alert status. Figure 8.36 illustrates the options. You can also filter the alerts based on the specified time interval.

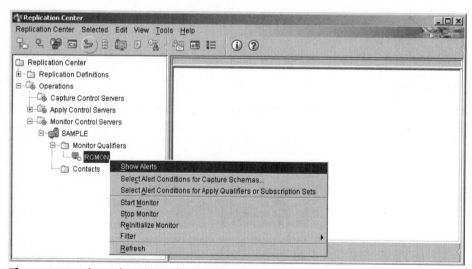

Figure 8.36   Show alerts in Replication Center Monitor.

Warehouse Tuning

IBM DB2 Data Warehouse Center provides additional functions via DB2 utilities to tune your warehouse. From this tool you can update statistics, reorganize your data, and tune the overall database performance. Each of these components as well as others are detailed in this section.

Updating Statistics

You can use the DB2 Run Statistics Utility shown in Figure 8.37 of the DB2 Control Center to schedule RUNSTAT against your warehouse sources and targets to update the DB2 access plan. This should be run after many changes have been done against your warehouse sources and targets so that table statistics managed by DB2 will be aware of the changes.

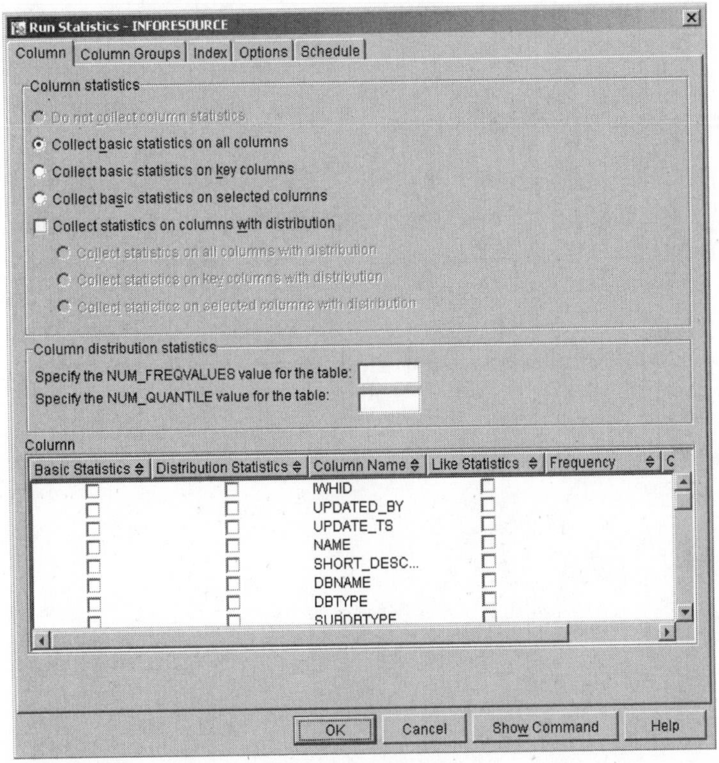

Figure 8.37   DB2 RUNSTATS parameters.

Reorganizing Your Data

The DB2 REORG utility can be invoked from the IBM DB2 Control Center that allows you to reorganize your data when excess fragmentation has been caused by frequent insert, update, and delete activities against your warehouse sources and targets. The REORG utility will affect all the nodes in the node group. After each REORG, you should do a RUNSTAT to update the table statistics and rebind the packages that use this reorganized table; you may also want to re-create the indexes so that the optimized access path is updated and can be used against the reorganized data.

If the table is a partitioned table residing on multiple nodes, and the REORG fails on one or more nodes, only the failing nodes will have the table reorganization rolled back. If the REORG fails, you should keep the temporary files so that DB2 can reuse these files for database recovery.

You can also define a warehouse user-defined program to invoke a REORGCHK script to monitor your warehouse table after each warehouse data population, especially for the warehouse target populated by a Select and Update SQL step.

Using DB2 Snapshot and Monitor

You can use DB2 Snapshot Monitor in the IBM DB2 Control Center to turn different DB2 SNAPSHOT switches to collect statistics on bufferpool usage, unit of work, application, and lock. Events can be set to accumulate statistics for specific groups of performance data, and the Event Analyzer can be used to display and drill down the snapshot data. The available event types that you can monitor are illustrated in Figure 8.38.

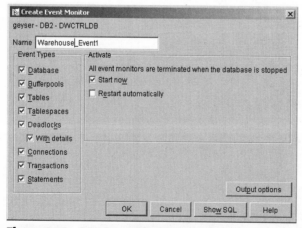

Figure 8.38 DB2 Event Monitor parameters.

Once the performance statistics are collected, you can open the Analyze Event Monitor Records to analyze the data.

Using Visual Explain

You can use the Visual Explain in the IBM DB2 Control Center to display and analyze the data access paths for an SQL statement you use in a Warehouse step such as SQL Select and Insert. The access path is displayed in an easy-to-read graphical format, shown in Figure 8.39.

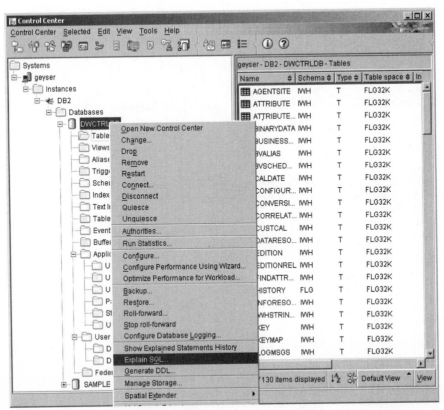

Figure 8.39   DB2 Explain SQL statement.

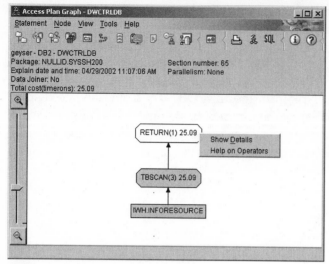

Figure 8.40   DB2 access plan graph.

An example is shown in Figure 8.40. It shows a graphic in Visual Explain for the following SELECT statement.

```
SELECT * FROM IWH.INFORESOURCE
```

By highlighting the objects of the map, you can see more details, as shown in Figure 8.41.

Table Statistics - INFORESOURCE
geyser - DB2 - DWCTRLDB
Table: IWH.INFORESOURCE
Explain date and time: 04/29/2002 11:07:06 AM
Current date and time: 04/29/2002 11:11:39 AM

Statistics	Explained	Current
CREATE_TIME	04/23/2002...	04/23/20...
STATS_TIME	Statistics n...	Statistic...
CARD	1(default)	-1
NPAGES	1(default)	-1
FPAGES	1(default)	-1
COLCOUNT	44(default)	44
OVERFLOW	0(default)	-1
TABLESPACE	FLG32K	FLG32K
INDEX_TABLESPACE	FLG32K	
LONG_TABLESPACE		
VOLATILE	No(default)	No

[Reference Columns] [Column Groups] [Indexes] [Save As...] [Print...] [Close] [Help]

Figure 8.41   DB2 operator details.

Tuning Database Performance

To help tune for performance of building and populating your warehouse data, the IBM DB2 Data Warehouse Center provides the Export and Load utility steps to help manage the movement of large amounts of data, along with the replication steps to update the warehouse target with the changed data.

DWC can be tuned like other DB2 application programs using the Snapshot Monitor data. Based on the findings on the statistics collected, you may update certain DB2 database manager and database configuration parameters.

For example, if you have been experiencing deadlocks or excessive lock escalation, you may consider tuning the following DB2 database configuration parameters:

- Max storage for lock list (4KB) (LOCKLIST)
- Interval for checking deadlock (ms) (DLCHKTIME)
- Percent of lock lists per application (MAXLOCKS)
- Lock timeout (sec) (LOCKTIMEOUT)
- Block log on disk full (BLK_LOG_DSK_FUL)

Another example is the space management for the primary and secondary logs. You need to size the amount of data being extracted and populated to the warehouse targets so that these DB2 logs will have sufficient space for all the concurrent warehouse steps to run:

- Log buffer size (4KB) (LOGBUFSZ)
- Log file size (4KB) (LOGFILSIZ)
- Number of primary log files (LOGPRIMARY)
- Number of secondary log files (LOGSECOND)

Maintaining IBM DB2 Data Warehouse Center

You can configure IBM DB2 Data Warehouse Center to meet your needs by providing various configuration and default parameters that will be used during IBM DB2 Data Warehouse Center function execution. DWC configuration utility allows you to set the following information by updating the properties of the following:

- Trace levels for each DWC component to help you with problem determination

- Default actions for the warehouse server to determine how to process missed or interrupted transformation schedules such as the warehouse server restart type on the Windows platform.

- Timeout-related information when communicating with other warehouse components

- The default number of times the warehouse server is to retry the execution of a step that failed

- The default action the warehouse agent is to take when it encounters warnings or situations where no data is returned

Log History

The IBM DB2 Data Warehouse Center logs the run status of all the warehouse sources, steps, and targets in a log table in the warehouse control database. Depending on your installation need for log history, you may schedule an archive of these log records or prune the log history accordingly. You may access this log history table from an application or script to ensure it is operating at an optimal state.

Control Database

There is a set of warehouse tables that keep track of the warehouse objects defined by the users and the relationships among these objects. These objects may change dynamically. It is crucial to ensure the data integrity of these control tables. You may want to schedule regular backups for these tables, especially after major changes made to the warehouse sources, steps, and targets. Since these control tables are being changed when you define or operate against the warehouse objects, you may want to do a regular RUNSTAT or REORG against these control tables to ensure the best performance when you perform your day-to-day warehouse operations.

DB2 Data Warehouse Center V8 Enhancements

Although there are numerous enhancements in IBM DB2 Data Warehouse Center Version 8.1, we think it important to draw the reader's attention to some of the most significant. In the following list we identify nine:

Warehouse server on AIX.   The warehouse server that interfaces with the client and the warehouse meta data to create and schedule steps to run at the designated agent site is now available on the AIX platform with the very same functions as the warehouse server on the Windows platform. This enhancement totally removes the dependency on the Windows platform for the IBM DB2 Data Warehouse Center. For example, you can set up your warehouse clients, warehouse server, and warehouse agent all on the same AIX system and take advantage of the power of the AIX machine.

Warehouse agent on Linux.   The data warehouse agent that interfaces with the data sources and targets to extract, transform, and load the warehouse data is now available on the Linux Intel platform. This is one of the key UNIX platforms for IBM DB2 and its tools. The Linux warehouse agent can take advantage of direct access to the local warehouse residing in DB2 Linux.

Wait for multiple steps.   In the warehousing environment, users often must wait for certain steps to complete before running the next steps. The solution to this requirement must be to take care of the waiting step so that it does not run more than necessary. A simple step-to-step cascade link may run the waiting step multiple times, and the generated target warehouse may not be desirable. The enhancement ensures the waiting step is run properly—that is, the waiting step will not be run more than necessary. Users can organize their steps to be waited on and group them in processes. A process can be enabled to run using the defined schedules for the process. Enabling a process will activate the process schedule and to execute the steps that are in production mode within this process. Users can cascade the process on success or on failure or on completion using the Process → Define Schedule → Task Flow pull-down menu. Note that each step may have its own schedule, but the process does not take the individual step's schedules into consideration when the process is scheduled to run. Furthermore, a process may have steps in different modes (development, test, and production); only the steps in production mode will be run by the process's schedules. When the steps in a process are running, the user can monitor the scheduled process and steps in the Work In Progress window.

Select from source and update target warehouse.   Building a warehouse may be time-consuming because of the large volume of data involved and refreshing the entire target warehouse each time is not very efficient. This enhancement introduces a new warehouse step type to allow the user to select from the source warehouse data and update the target warehouse based on the user-specified UPDATE criteria, which include the selected source columns, column mapping between source and target, and key mapping between source and target. With this change, the time to refresh your target warehouse can be minimized to just refreshing the changed data. Since the target warehouse is updated on a regular basis, you should consider reorganizing the target warehouse. This ensures optimum performance when users access the data. You may schedule a DB2 REORGCHK script and a DB2 RUNSTATS script to run after populating an updated warehouse target.

Client Connect, direct access to data source from client. This enhancement allows the user to access the DB2 sources, including IBM federated server, directly via the DB2/Java database interface from the data warehouse client system. This allows the user to gain access to certain data types, and functions that are supported by DB2 only and federated server nicknames. Warehouse sources defined via Client Connect will not use the warehouse server or the warehouse agent. The DB2 data source and target must be cataloged at the warehouse client system. If you use this Client Connect source as input to an SQL step and Client Connect target as output from that step. You must also catalog the same DB2 source and target on the warehouse agent system.

DB2 LOAD utility for parallel load. The DB2 script step for LOAD has been enhanced to support parallel load. Refer to Figure 8.42 for more information.

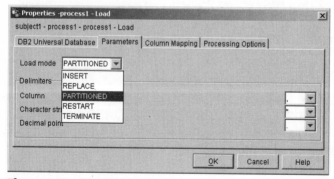

Figure 8.42   DB2 LOAD types.

Publish warehouse meta data to the IBM Information Catalog Manager and OLAP via the warehouse client. You can publish IBM DB2 Data Warehouse (DWC) meta data objects such as warehouse subjects, processes, steps, sources, targets, and star schema objects to the IBM Information Catalog Manager and OLAP via a graphical user interface. When an object is published from DWC to the Information Catalog Manager, the objects, object types, relationships, and relationship types then become visible both the IBM DB2 Data Warehouse Center and the Information Catalog Manager. The IBM DB2 Data Warehouse Center application will remain the owner of the published objects. Information Catalog Manager users, including the administrator, will have only read access to the published objects, object types, relationships, and relationship types. Published objects will be allowed to have additional related objects created in the Information Catalog Manager. For example, a published table can have a comment added to it in the Information Catalog Manager. A published database can be added to an Information Catalog Manager-created business subject area. DWC-created relationships between published objects cannot be changed or removed through the Information Catalog Manager.

Improved usability.   There are additional column mapping functions that allow the user to map the source and target columns more efficiently. There are also usability enhancements done with the process modeler for rearranging warehouse objects layout, undoing arrangement, opting step shortcuts, and highlighting information area of process model for errors. The user can also have a new default option to create primary key for the warehouse-generated target tables, to disable dependency checking, and to customize agent trace levels for individual DWC steps.

Improved integration with Control Center and Replication Center. The interface with Control Center utility functions has been improved to generate DB2 scripts to be run on the warehouse agent system. In addition, an improved integrated Replication interface in the DWC now supports the V8 replication APIs.

Summary

IBM DB2 Data Warehouse Center is competitive with many of the leading ETL tools in the market. As such, it goes beyond traditional ETL and addresses the broader notion of warehouse management, including meta data control, high availability, and warehouse monitoring. It can be implemented in heterogeneous environments with disparate data sources and database target tables and operating system files. It encompasses all the core components necessary to support and manage a warehouse environment, and continues to be improved.

IBM DB2 Data Warehouse Center is significant for the IBM community not because it is competitive with other leading technology of the same genre. IBM DB2 Data Warehouse Center is important because it is especially tuned to work with other IBM products such as DB2 V8, Replication Server, and DB2 OLAP Server. This is important to remember when considering ETL-centric applications. If you are an IBM shop or are considering an investment in IBM technology, then IBM DB2 Data Warehouse Center must be on your short list for evaluation.

CHAPTER 9

Data Transformation with IBM DB2 Data Warehouse Center

Key Issues:

- Automating the transformation steps ensures process consistency, data integrity, and meta data control.

- Preprogrammed transformation steps save significant time and resources.

- ETL tools must not simply provide a process framework with little true transformation capability.

- Any ETL process requires integration with a range of applications, including your own in-house applications and those from a number of vendors. Any ETL environment should provide transparent integration with leading vendors in the ETL or data-quality space, as well as leading applications such as SAP and PeopleSoft.

The design of your warehouse takes many factors into account. We have already discussed several of these issues in previous chapters, such as data and technical architectures. For this chapter, however, we now turn our attention to the factors that influence the extraction, transformation, and loading of data from sources to warehouse targets. Since we have already debated the philosophical issues, like whether or not to implement an atomic level, we will simply dive into the details. To that end, there are several factors to consider, for example:

- Where is your data stored and what format is it in?
- How will you access that data?
- Do you need to manipulate the data in any way?
- Will you need a staging area to supply data to multiple data marts off of the main warehouse?
- What is the frequency with which you need to refresh the data in the warehouse or data mart?
- What is the final format in which you want to present the data to your end users?
- How will you let users know what is available for their use?

These and many other questions should be discussed among the data administrators, the warehouse architects, and the end users so that you can produce a warehouse that contains the data needed to address your end user's business requirements.

For example, suppose you have an operational system with sales information, and you have warehouse requirements to analyze the data using OLAP processing each day. The system and warehouse requirements consist of the following:

- The source sales data is in their operational CICS system on MVS (CICS stands for Customer Information Control System; MVS for Multiple Virtual Storage).
- Nightly batch jobs are run that extract data from the CICS system.
- The data needs to be cleansed, summarized, and stored in a local DB2 UDB for SUN OS database.
- Cleansed and summarized data needs to be loaded into DB2 OLAP Server for end-user analysis.

To process this data, you need to determine the best-possible approach to get the data into its final end-user format. Using our preceding simple example, the warehouse administrator would need to determine which functions of the IBM DB2 Data Warehouse Center (DWC) should be used versus external functions. The types of questions should include the following:

- Should an MVS scheduler handle the execution of the batch jobs, or should the jobs be managed by warehouse?

  - Who will be responsible for initiating the nightly MVS jobs? Data Warehouse Center provides functions to start MVS jobs and wait for their completion; however, in many cases, security policies at a customer environment do not allow non-MVS schedulers to initiate MVS jobs.

- Should the data sets be pushed from the MVS system to Sun, or should they be pulled on some timed basis?

  - How will the extracted data get to the Sun system? As part of the MVS job itself, the last step of the job could be to FTP the file to Sun once the data is extracted successfully and then trigger the IBM DB2 Data Warehouse Center to start processing those files. Or you could use the warehouse functions to wait for the files to appear on the MVS system and then pull those files down to Sun.

- Should the data be loaded into DB2 using the load utilities, or should they be treated as open database connectivity (ODBC) data sources?

  - Will the data be directly loaded into the staging tables with minimal processing, or do you want to do some preprocessing (using SQL) prior to loading the data? If no preprocessing of the data is required, you could choose to do a fast load of the data using the DB2 LOAD utility (driven by the IBM DB2 Data Warehouse Center). This option is the fastest way to get the data into DB2, since it can provide parallel loads into partitioned tables with minimal logging. If you decide that preprocessing of the data is needed as it is loaded in the staging table (e.g., data filtering or adding timestamp information), you may want to treat the file as an ODBC source so that you can use SQL to manipulate the data, or add an additional date column to the staging table as the data is loaded.

- What types of summarization and aggregation do you need to have done on the data?

  - Will you need to do extensive cleansing on the data prior to it being loaded into the OLAP cubes? IBM DB2 Data Warehouse Center provides "clean" transformers for basic cleansing of the data. However, if you need more extensive cleansing capabilities (e.g., name and address matching), you might consider using a cleansing tool that IBM supports via the IBM DB2 Data Warehouse Center, such as Ascential.

■ Is the data written to the DB2 staging tables in a format of facts and dimensions, or will the data need to be loaded into the cube based on a set of rules? The IBM DB2 Data Warehouse Center allows you to define the data to best suit your needs. If the data is stored in the format of facts and dimensions, you can then use IBM DB2 Data Warehouse Center's integration with the Hyperion Integration Server to load the data from this format directly into the cubes for use by the end user. If the data is not stored in a dimensional schema, it can be loaded into the cubes using SQL-based load rules. IBM DB2 Data Warehouse Center can then direct DB2 OLAP Server to build and populate the cubes using the load rules. Alternatively, you could first export the data from the DB2 staging tables into files and then drive the DB2 OLAP Server load process.

As you embark on the task of designing your warehouse, you will need to know what functions are available directly through the IBM DB2 Data Warehouse Center. Based on this information, you can begin the design of your warehouse transformation processes. In some cases, you may need additional functionality not provided by the IBM DB2 Data Warehouse Center and therefore look to outside vendors to provide the transformations that you require. Fortunately, the IBM DB2 Data Warehouse Center provides an interface allowing vendor applications to hook their transformation applications directly into the Data Warehouse Center. Doing so allows you to have a single management interface to control all of your warehouse processing, from data access to final end-user formatting.

This chapter defines and describes the core data transformation and integration steps provided by the Data Warehouse Center. Each step represents a robust and efficient means to implement complex ETL processes in a single development environment.

IBM DB2 Data Warehouse Center Process Model

The IBM DB2 Data Warehouse Center provides many different ways to extract, transform, and load data, depending on your needs. The basic model of working with the IBM DB2 Data Warehouse Center follows these steps:

1. Identify the sources of data that you will be using to populate the warehouse.

2. Identify where the atomic layer, data marts, or OLAP cubes will be stored.

3. Identify the types of transformations that need to be applied to your data.

4. Identify a means of grouping those transformations together for easy maintenance.

5. Identify the schedules that transformations are to run on.

6. Identify task flows between transformations.

To illustrate the basic model, we will continue with the scenario we started earlier and walk you through the various steps outlined in the next three sections: *Identify Sources and Targets*, *Identify the Transformations*, and *The Process Model*.

Identify the Sources and Targets

The first two steps in the basic model are to identify the data sources that are required for populating the warehouse and identify the warehouse targets. Figure 9.1 shows the screen interface used in IBM DB2 Data Warehouse Center that provides the necessary functionality to do so. Figure 9.2 is a screen shot of the IBM DB2 Data Warehouse Center dialog box for defining warehouse targets.

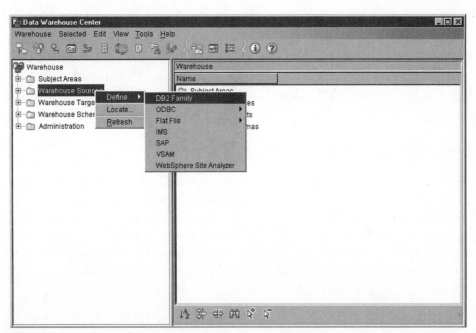

Figure 9.1 Define a source.

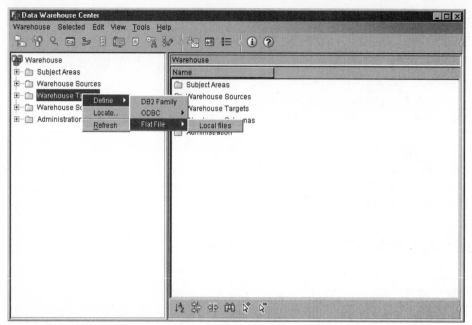

Figure 9.2 Define a target.

In our scenario, we will be using staging tables in DB2 to cleanse and aggregate the data prior to loading it into the OLAP cubes. As part of this example, we identify the DB2 Sun system as a target warehouse. We also identify the files that will be used by the warehouse. This includes the files that are the results of a CICS extract that will be downloaded to the Sun machine.

Identify the Transformations

Once your sources and targets have been defined, you can begin to define the transformations that your data needs to go through. To do so, you first must define a subject area. The menu option is shown in Figure 9.3. The *subject area* is a logical grouping of warehouse processes that transform the data from its source format to its target format. These subject areas are generally created to identify a specific set of warehouse processes for a particular area (for example, "Populate the sales department warehouse").

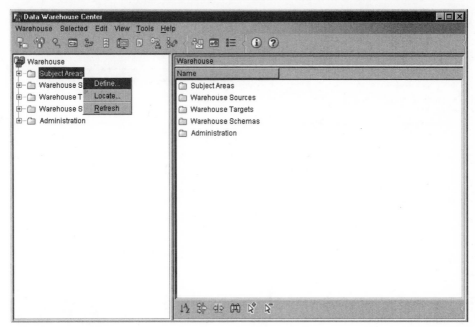

Figure 9.3 Subject areas.

The subject area groups together related warehouse processing using another logical grouping called a *process*. (See Figure 9.4.) A process groups together individual transformations that produce all or some part of the warehouse target. Processes can identify all of the individual transformations that must be completed (individually or together) before the process is considered successful. You can also link processes together such that when one process completes, another process starts in order to provide additional transformations.

Continuing with our example, you will want to create a subject area that groups a set of processes that takes the data from MVS, transforms the data, and loads into OLAP cubes. One process may be defined to run the MVS jobs to produce files and then FTP those files to the Sun system, another process may be defined that loads those files into DB2 and cleanses the data, and a third process might take the data from DB2 and load it into OLAP cubes. Remember that we are merely reviewing a simple example. Hopefully, you will not simply create a bunch of independent data marts; instead, you will build and populate an atomic layer, which then serves as the source for loading a cube like the one in our example.

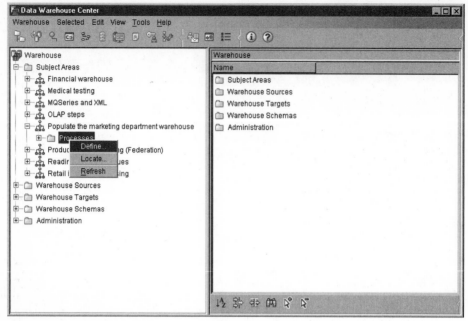

Figure 9.4 Define a process.

Once you have defined the processes, you can begin to identify the transformations you want to perform on the data as you move it into your warehouse. In our example, you can add the "Extract MVS data and move to Sun" process in a way that the IBM DB2 Data Warehouse Center transformations execute MVS jobs and, upon completion, FTP those files to Sun.

The Process Model

The basis for defining the transformations is the *process model*. The process model is used to define the actions and transformations that will occur, the order in which the transformations are to take place, the schedule those transformations are to run under, and the task flow between the transformations.

When you open up the modeler on a process, you are presented with a pallet of transformations and actions that you use to define the transformations called IBM DB2 Data Warehouse Center steps. Figure 9.5 illustrates the pallet. The modeler allows you to define the steps, the input and output data that is used by a step (referred to as *sources and target* and *data links*), the schedule a step is to execute on, and the task flow (called *warehouse cascade links*) between steps.

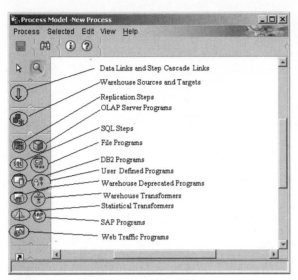

Figure 9.5   Warehouse steps pallet.

To use the process modeler, you simply drag and drop a data object or transformation object from the pallet to the canvas and link them together with the link tool. Using our example, you will want to drag and drop the following:

- Two transformation steps that submit jobs on MVS
- Two transformation steps that FTP files from one system to the other
- Two objects to represent the files produced by the MVS jobs
- Two objects that represent the FTP files from MVS to Sun

To provide the data flow between the steps, you would link the first two files representing the MVS files as sources to the FTP steps and link the second pair of files representing the Sun files as targets of the FTP steps using the *data link* tool.

To provide the scheduling and task flows between the steps, you would add a schedule to each of the steps that execute the MVS jobs and then link these steps so that if they complete successfully, the IBM DB2 Data Warehouse Center will process the FTP steps. In all cases, if any of the steps fail, you may want to link to a step that pages the console operator. Task flow is accomplished via the *cascade link* tools.

The final results of the process model would resemble Figure 9.6.

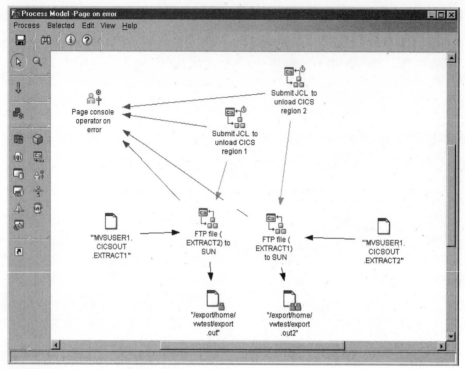

Figure 9.6 Sample process model.

IBM DB2 Data Warehouse Center Transformations

As we have discussed before, a significant portion of your time will be used determining which transformation types to use under which circumstances. This section covers all the warehouse steps that you can use to transform the source data into your DB2 target warehouse. Each step has unique characteristics that are designed to meet different user requirements. Some steps allow you to have multiple warehouse sources and warehouse targets. Depending on the selected step type and your warehouse configurations, you can extract and transform a wide range of data sources, including the IBM DB2 family, Oracle, Sybase, Informix, Microsoft SQL Server, OLE DB, MQSeries queues, ASCII files, VSAM files, and so on. Some warehouse step types provide wizards to help you customize your extract and data transformation using the SQL built-in functions, stored procedures, and so forth. Table 9.1 outlines the steps of IBM DB2 Data Warehouse Center and provides some guidance as to the pros and cons of each transformation step identified.

Table 9.1 Transformation Step Types

STEP TYPE	PROS	CONS	NOTES
SQL steps Select/Insert Select/Update	Full power of SQL Full database logging Incremental commit Rollback capabilities Platform independent Edition support Data dependency checking	Performance Data volumes	SQL steps allow you to process data at a record level and give you the full power of the source's SQL support. However, because this is using the source database application interface, the performance will be affected.
Utility steps LOAD EXPORT RUNSTATS REORG	Performance Parallelism File output Error handling Data volumes Data dependency checking Native database utility	No logging Minimal transformations on load Platform-dependent	The DB2 utilities provide a mechanism to quickly load, unload, or organize information in DB2. The LOAD utility can be set up to exploit the parallel nature of DB2. The utility's key feature is performance, but because of this, there is minimal logging, and if a severe error should occur, the transactions cannot be rolled back. You will need to restore the data from a prior backup.

(continues)

Table 9.1 Transformation Step Types *(Continued)*

STEP TYPE	PROS	CONS	NOTES
Warehouse steps	Integrated transformations Platform-independent Basic data cleansing and formatting Key and period generation Data inversion and pivoting Data dependency checking	Java stored procedures Geared toward smaller data volumes Data cleansing limited to SQL manipulation	Java stored procedures may have performance impacts with large amounts of data. Additional cleansing capabilities may require vendor products such as Ascential's INTEGRITY or Trillium's Batch System.
Statistical steps	Integrated transformations Platform-independent Analysis of variances Basic statistical functions Popular statistical analysis Data dependency checking	Java stored procedures Geared toward smaller data volumes	Java stored procedures could have performance implications.
Replications steps	Only changed data need to be moved Performance Capture outside the warehouse	Initial loads are having performance implications. DB2 sources only	Use the SQL or Utility transformation steps to initially populate data in warehouse, then use replication transformations to move only changes.

Table 9.1 *(Continued)*

STEP TYPE	PROS	CONS	NOTES
	Integration of replication subscription services into warehouse	Capture administration and management outside of warehouse control	
	Data dependency checking		
OLAP steps	Allows the loading of cubes after warehouse processing complete	Administration of cube done outside warehouse	
	Data loading	No ESSCMD or MaxL support	
	Cube calculations	z/OS support remote	
	Outline updates		
	Integration within warehouse		
	Data dependency checking		
SAP steps	Integration within warehouse	Performance on large amounts of data	
	Column maps from SAP business object to target DB2	No IDOCS support	
	Transform data while moving	Need basic understanding of GetDetails and GetCode BAPI calls to do column mapping	
	Hide low-level details of BAPI calls from user	No z/OS or iSeries support	
		Administration outside of warehouse	

(continues)

Table 9.1 Transformation Step Types *(Continued)*

STEP TYPE	PROS	CONS	NOTES
Web traffic steps	Allows you to bring in WEB data for analysis by warehouse Integration within warehouse Transform data while moving to target	Administration outside of warehouse No z/OS or iSeries support	
User-defined steps	Flexible architecture to add any transformation (user or vendor written) to warehouse Feedback to warehouse about processing status Utilized warehouse vendors such as: ETI, Ascential, Trillium, and Hyperion. Platform-independent Language of choice Black box processing Data dependency checking	In some cases, user must write and maintain code. Meta data about the transformation is not externalized in ICM	The architecture of the warehouse allows a user or vendor to write an application that can then be managed by the IBM DB2 Data Warehouse Center. The user/vendor needs to specify the application to execute, as well as the meta data that is needed by the application. After the application completes its processing, the application can pass back processing reports and statistics to the warehouse so that they can be viewed by the user.

In addition to the selection of your transformation steps, there are other considerations that impact your process model. The additional issues for you to evaluate are described in the following sections.

Refresh Considerations

If your plans call for completely replacing existing data in a warehouse, or you are creating a new data warehouse, you might consider using warehouse step types such as SQL Select and Insert with the Replace option. These are easy-to-use and easy-to-implement transformation types that readily address wholesale refresh of warehouse data. For the initial load of the warehouse, you might consider the DB2 Export and Load Scripts or the Replication User Copy step to do the initial population of the target warehouse.

You can also use a SQL Select and Update to refresh the target warehouse table. For example, use SQL Select and Insert to make the initial load from any supported data sources to a warehouse-generated default target table. Then you can update the generated default target table using the SQL Select and Update step. The SQL Select and Update step has a user-friendly interface to help you construct an UPDATE statement to extract only the data records that have changed at the source and move them into the target warehouse table.

On the other hand, if you plan to refresh your target warehouse with the changed source data only after the initial load, you might consider using the IBM Replication technology. This particular feature is integrated in the IBM DB2 Data Warehouse Center using the Warehouse Replication User Copy step. You can then take advantage of other warehouse replication steps to apply only source data changes to your target warehouse. Note that the replication steps in the IBM DB2 Data Warehouse Center support replicated changes from DB2 source tables only.

After you have created the target warehouse, you may start building indexes to optimize the data access by the end users. When loading data into multiple tables, the warehouse does not consider constraints and you may run into constraint errors. It is recommended indexes be dropped prior to loading and then rebuilt after the data has been loaded. This increases the performance of the load because the indexes will not need to be updated on each insert.

Data Volume

Another issue to consider is data volume. For reasonable amounts of data (based on data volumes and machine characteristics), you can use the SQL Select and Insert steps to populate the source into a target warehouse. Remember that this type of step selects data from the source (16 rows at a time in most cases) and then inserts the block of data to the target. The good thing about this type of transformation step is that it can exploit the power of the source system. On the other hand, there are additional over-head issues that have a direct impact on system performance. As a result, SQL Select and Insert steps are only recommended for small to medium data volumes.

For larger volumes of data you may want to use the warehouse DB2 UDB Export step to export data from a source table into a file—at which point you can take that file and load it into the target warehouse table using a warehouse transformation Load step. These step types use the DB2 utilities for exporting and importing data, and the performance can be significantly faster than that of a SQL Select and Insert step. When using the warehouse Load step, you need to consider a few features that may affect your deci-sion—for example, the use of parallel loading of data for partitioned tables, as well as the lack of logging for recoverability and error handling.

Manage Data Editions

You should consider using SQL Select and Insert steps in append mode if you want to have the warehouse manage how much data is in the target table. IBM DB2 Data Warehouse Center has a concept called *editions* that allows you to define how many copies of the data you want in the target table before the oldest data is purged. For example, if you are interested in keeping a year's worth of historical information about sales in your target table, and you are loading that information each month, you can tell the warehouse that you want 12 editions of the data in the target table when you define your step. When the step is run each month, the warehouse determines how many times the step has run before. In this example, the first 12 times that the step runs, it adds the new sales information for that month to the target table. When the step runs for the 13th time, the ware-house adds the new sales information to the target table, and if that completes successfully, it then deletes all the rows of sales data associated with the first run of the step. From this point on, each time the step is run, it appends the newest sales data to the table, then deletes the oldest sales data from the table. This feature allows you to keep rolling historical information within the warehouse, totally managed by the warehouse.

User-Defined Transformation Requirements

In some cases, you may need to write your own application to provide a specific transformation. Once you have written and tested your application, you can register the application to the warehouse so that it can be used just like any other step type. The application can even pass back processing status and statistical information to the warehouse, making it available to other warehouse users and process steps.

Multiple Table Loads

At times, you will want to load data into multiple tables within the same target warehouse. In this case, you will probably want to consider activating the database prior to the execution of the first step.

When the warehouse processes a step, it first connects to the database where the source data resides, connects to the target database where the target table is being loaded, runs the transformation, and then disconnects from the source and target databases. When moving small amounts of data during the transformation, the time it takes to connect and disconnect from the database may be a significant portion of the total processing time.

If you *activate* the database prior to the first step executing, you will significantly reduce the connect and disconnect times for all subsequent steps using that database. Of course, you must remember to *deactivate* the database as the last action of the warehouse processing. Otherwise, resources may not be freed up appropriately. The ACTIVATE and DEACTIVATE commands need to be created as user-defined steps to the warehouse.

Ensure Warehouse Data Is Up-to-Date

If you want to make sure that your data is always up-to-date, you might consider using a function called *transient* data when defining your target table. Transience is a concept that allows the user to indicate to the warehouse that the source data needs to be refreshed prior to it being used by a step.

For example, suppose you are designing a warehouse that pulls a subset of operational data from an Oracle database and loads it into a staging table in DB2. That data is subsequently processed by another warehouse step to cleanse and aggregate the data prior to a final export and load into an OLAP cube. However, you should make sure that the data in the DB2 staging table is always the most current prior to the final processing.

Using the transient concept allows you to define the target table of the step that pulls from the Oracle database as *transient* and then use that transient table as a source to the step that cleanses and aggregates the data. You would then schedule only this second step (unlike the case where the first step does not produce a transient table and you would schedule the first step). When this second step is executed, prior to doing any processing, it executes the first step to make sure the latest Oracle data is in the transient staging table. Once the transient table has been successfully loaded, the second step continues its processing.

Transient tables are very useful in the case where the data being pulled is used by more than one subsequent step. If you do not use transient tables, you need to make copies of this step for each process that uses that data. Figure 9.7 shows the differences between using transient and non-transient tables.

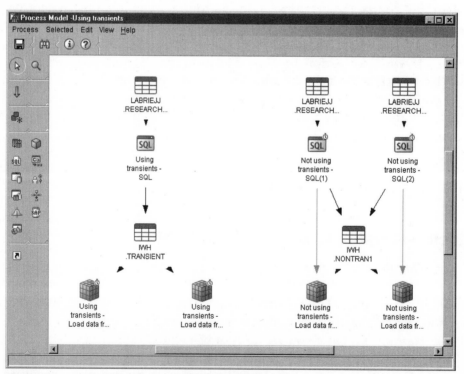

Figure 9.7 Using transient and nontransient tables.

In the first process flow in Figure 9.7 (left flow), the target of the "Using transients-SQL" step is defined as a transient table called TRANSIENT. This table is then used as a source to the two OLAP steps that populate two different cubes. Now as each of the OLAP steps executes, prior to them loading the cube, it will run the "Using transients-SQL" step, and once complete, the OLAP steps will complete. In this case, you will notice that the schedules are not on the "Using transients-SQL" step, but on each individual OLAP step indicated as by the small clock icon. In fact, if you were to schedule a step that produces a transient table, you would get a runtime error.

In contrast, the second process flow (right flow) shows how you would accomplish the same task, using two SQL steps that load the same data into the target table and run that at the different schedules, and then on successful completion (links between the SQL and OLAP steps) of the SQL step, it would execute the OLAP load step. To define the target table as transient, you need to specify this on the step's target output table definition. Refer to Figure 9.8 to see the dialog interface.

There is an alternative to transient tables called *dependency checking*. You should use this feature when you are concerned about the data being current prior to the execution of a transformation. Using this function, IBM DB2 Data Warehouse Center checks to make sure that the data in the table being used as a source is valid.

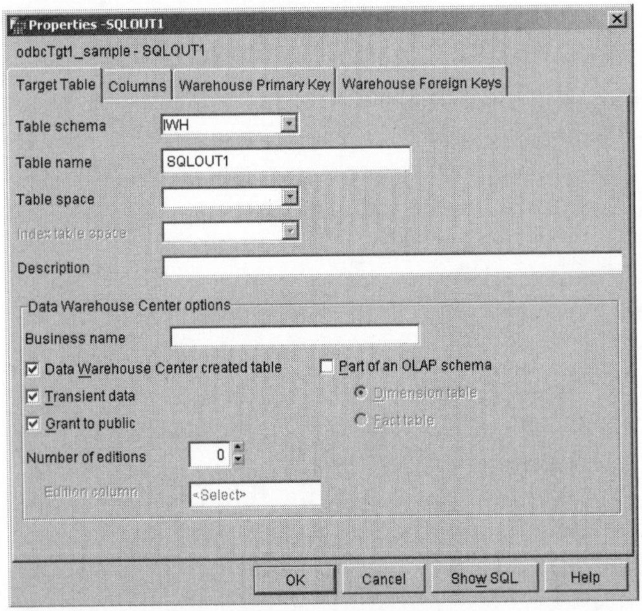

Figure 9.8   Define a transient target.

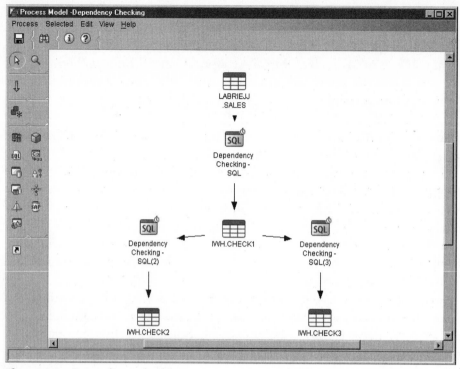

Figure 9.9 Dependency checking.

Dependency checking is possible to do with transient data as described previously, but transients cannot be used in all cases. For example, suppose we need to define a process that contains three transformations, where the second and third transformations use the data produced by the first step. Also, we need to have each of these three transformations run on its own schedule with no task dependency between them.

In some cases, if the first transformations were to fail—for example, the data at the source was bad—then the target of the first transformations may contain invalid or no data. This is especially true when transformations run independently of the first transformations, leading to the possibility of subsequent transformations pulling data that is invalid.

With the data dependency checking feature of the IBM DB2 Data Warehouse Center, the user can indicate that the second and third steps should check to make sure that the step that populates the table it uses as a source completed successfully during its last run. If the step completed successfully, these dependent steps will begin execution. If the step failed, the second and third steps will not start and a runtime error will be logged indicating that the data dependency check failed and that the user needs to take corrective action to make sure the first step runs successfully.

As shown in Figure 9.9, dependency checking occurs each time the steps "Dependency Checking-SQL (2)" or "Dependency Checking-SQL (3)" execute. Dependency checking makes sure that the last execution of "Dependency Checking-SQL" produced valid results in the target table called IWH.CHECK1.

Retry

IBM DB2 Data Warehouse Center provides you the ability to retry a step if a communications error occurs when the warehouse server is starting a warehouse agent. This capability is called *retry* and is specified at the step level. If the step fails because of a communications error, the server retries the step for the user-specified number of times. As long as the step is being retried, the Work In Progress indicates that the step is in retry status.

The user can also specify a retry interval. A time interval can be established and used by the warehouse server that specifies the time to wait between each retry. The default value for this is to retry the step three times once every 30 minutes. If the step continues to fail after all retries are exhausted, the step fails with an error.

SQL Transformation Steps

SQL step types allow you to use the relational features of your source systems to access and transform necessary data. Using SQL steps, you have full SQL language supported by the source to query and transform your data and move it to the target warehouse. Of course, data architects and ETL programmers need to understand what SQL is supported by the source systems before it can be coded in your SQL step.

When you define an SQL transformation using the SQL step, you select the SQL step type from the process modeler pallet and drop it onto the process modeler canvas. The next step is to link up the sources that you will be extracting data from and, optionally, the target where the extracted and transformed data will be loaded. Linking the source to the SQL step and the SQL step to the target on the process modeler canvas is done with the process modeler link tool.

Two types of SQL query steps allow you to extract, transform, and load the source tables to the target table. You can define these steps using the SQL Step icon from the processor modeler. Figure 9.10 illustrates the options.

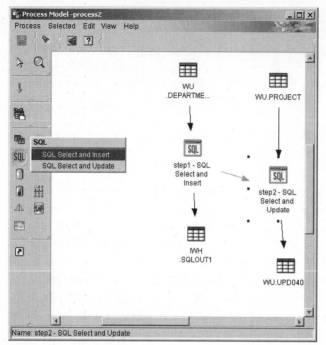

Figure 9.10   SQL step types.

Some points to remember about SQL step types are as follows:

- You can only join multiple source tables from the same physical database for non-federated sources. For federated sources, you may join heterogeneous data source types.

- You can only write to one target table.

- The warehouse agent that executes the SQL step must have connectivity to both the source and target databases.

- The columns that are output as a result of the SELECT statement are those that are mapped to the target.

- The target table can exist and be mapped in the step's properties page, or it can be generated by the warehouse as a result of a default mapping and the columns resulting from the SELECT statement.

- Data in the target table can be appended to or completely replaced, except for SQL Select and Update steps.

- You can have the warehouse incrementally commit the new records of data after a user-defined number of records have been written to the target table.

Let's look at each of the two SQL step types.

SQL Select and Insert

This IBM DB2 Data Warehouse Center step type allows you to select the source data and do a full insert into the user-defined or warehouse-generated target table. You have an option to append to or replace the content of the target table. When you choose the APPEND option, you may also keep multiple editions of the load data in the target table.

On the SQL page there is an SQL wizard called SQLAssist to help you customize a SELECT statement against the warehouse sources so that you can filter and transform the source data according to your specific warehouse needs.

On the Column Mapping page, map the output columns (resulting from the SELECT statement you generated) to columns of your target table. Column mapping allows you to create an explicit data type mapping between the source and target columns.

When creating SQL steps with edition functionality based on usage, you should consider creating a nonunique index on the edition column to speed up the performance of deleting editions. This option is critical for large warehouse tables, since it can impact row insertion into target tables.

If you want IBM DB2 Data Warehouse Center to generate the target table based on the source data, the IBM DB2 Data Warehouse Center will do an automatic data type mapping from the selected source columns to the output target columns. (See Figure 9.11.)

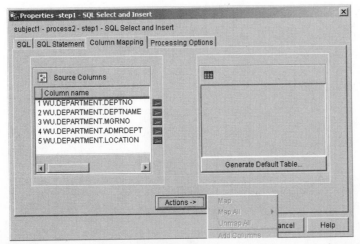

Figure 9.11   Generate default table.

Incremental commit is an option that is available for all SQL Select and Insert steps. It allows you to control the commit scope of the data that is managed by the IBM DB2 Data Warehouse Center. Incremental commit can be used when the volume of data to be populated by the DWC agent is large enough that the DB2 log files may fill up before the entire warehouse step transaction is complete, or when you want to save partial data. SQL steps will complete with an error if the amount of data being populated exceeds the DB2 maximum log file size that has been allocated. Incremental commit is specified on the step processing options page as illustrated in Figure 9.12.

The incremental commit option allows you to specify the number of rows (rounded to the nearest factor of 16) to be processed before a commit is performed. The agent selects and inserts data, committing incrementally until it completes the data population to the warehouse target successfully. When the data population completes successfully, outdated editions are removed if the warehouse target has multiple editions and the target table is defined with more than one edition.

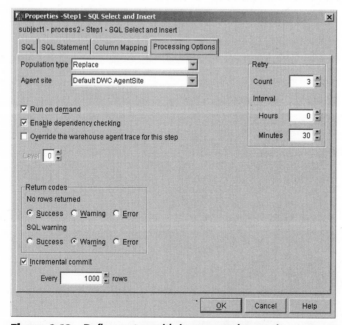

Figure 9.12 Define a step with incremental commit.

SQL Select and Update

This warehouse step type allows you to select the changed source data and update the target table. For example, if you have a warehouse target that contains the current inventory in stock, you may first do an initial load to populate the source operational data into the warehouse target. At the end of each business day, you can run the defined SQL Select and Update step to update the warehouse target to reflect the changes in the current inventory in stock without doing a full reload to your target warehouse.

Since the target table is updated each time you run the defined SQL Select and Update step, you should schedule a RUNSTATS against the warehouse target to keep DB2 table statistics up-to-date for optimal data access performance. Also, you can schedule a REORG against the warehouse target table to make sure it is done when necessary so the access performance on the warehouse target will not deteriorate.

When you configure the update criteria for the warehouse target, you must provide key mapping between the source and target tables. You can also define the column mapping between the source and target like Select and Insert Step type. The same capability as the SQL Select and Insert step is available to edit the SQL statement and to choose the processing options, except that IBM DB2 Data Warehouse Center does not generate the default target tables for updates. Note, you should not have multiple editions of the target table. (See Figure 9.13.)

Figure 9.13 SQL Select and Update.

DB2 Utility Steps

IBM DB2 Data Warehouse Center tightly integrates with the DB2 V8 utility functions. This integration is such that DB2 V8 utility scripts generated by warehouse are executable by a warehouse agent. You manage these DB2 Utility steps just like other warehouse step types and schedule them to run based on your warehouse needs.

Export Utility Step

The Step Properties notebook for DB2 export is used to create a step to export data from a DB2 table or view to a file located at the agent site. Figure 9.14 shows the interface.

The source database does not need to be on the same system as the warehouse agent. However, the target file must be local to the warehouse agent. You must specify the name of the target file as it is used on the warehouse

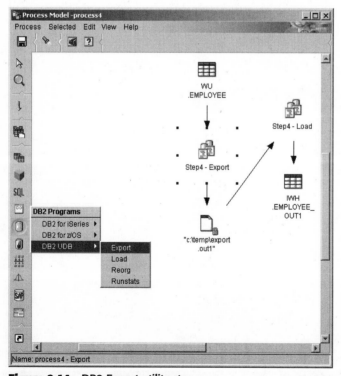

Figure 9.14 DB2 Export utility step.

agent system. The DB2 export utility creates a target file if it does not exist or replaces it if it exists. Note that the created target file will be owned by the user ID that the warehouse agent executes under. Consequently, consideration should be taken to authorize this target file to the appropriate users.

To use an Export Utility step, the source table or view must be linked to the step in the process modeler and the step must be linked to the warehouse target file.

LOAD Utility

You can use the supplied warehouse programs to efficiently move large quantities of data into newly created tables, or into tables that already contain data, including DB2 on Windows, Unix, DB2 for iSeries, and DB2 for z/OS database. Indexes for the load table are rebuilt upon successful data load. The input file to the LOAD utility must be authorized to the warehouse agent and it must be local to where the warehouse agent is. The input file can be in either character delimited, fixed-length, or PCIXF format. The LOAD Utility step provides an option for you to bypass the DB2 logging for high-speed data loading to the target DB2 table. The load modes supported are the following:

INSERT. Append the data in the input file to target DB2 table.

REPLACE. Replace the content of the target DB2 table with the data in the input file.

PARTITIONED. Load the input file data into a partitioned DB2 table using parallel loading. The loading process takes advantage of multiple processors or multiple storage devices available on the operating system, such as in a symmetric multiprocessor (SMP) environment.

RESTART. Restart a previously suspended LOAD utility. The loading process resumes from the last consistency point.

TERMINATE. Terminate a previously suspended LOAD utility and rolls back the operation to the point in time at which it was started, even if consistency points were passed. The tablespaces where the warehouse target table is will be reset to normal, and all table objects in these tablespaces will be marked consistent again.

Figure 9.15 shows all the DB2 LOAD utility options identified in the preceding list.

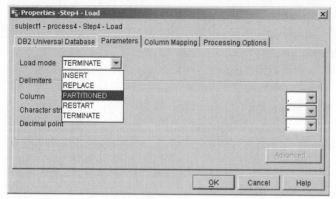

Figure 9.15 DB2 LOAD utility step.

Warehouse Transformer Steps

IBM DB2 Data Warehouse Center provides a rich set of basic data transformations grouped under the warehouse transformers and statistical transformers. To run these transformers, you should register them in your target warehouse database and enable them in the warehouse meta data. This can be accomplished by opening the Warehouse Target notebook's Database page, and checking the box named "Enable target for transformers".

Cleansing Transformer

Use this transformer to perform rules-based find-and-replace operations on a target table. The transformer finds values that you specify in the data columns of the source table that your step accesses. Then the transformer updates the corresponding columns with the replacement values that you specify in the table to which your step writes. You can select multiple columns from the input table to carry over to the output table. This transformer does not define rules or parameters for the carry-over columns.

Before you can use this transformer, you must create a rules table for your clean type. A rules table designates the values that the Clean Data transformer will use during the find-and-replace process. The rules table must be in the same database as the input table and output table. Note, the output table must exist and be identified as the warehouse target before the cleansing step is defined.

The transformation options for the Clean Data transformer include the following:

Find and Replace. Locate the input value from the rules table and replace it with the value specified in the rules table. If a match is not found and you have turned on the error processing options, the entire input row is written to the error table along with the RUN_ID of the execution.

Carry Over.   Copy the input column directly to the output table without modification.

Clip.   The rules table contains replacement values for numeric-only data that fall below a lower bound or exceed an upper bound.

Discretize.   The rules table contains one column with the low value, one column with the high value, and one column with the replacement value; if the input value is in one of the ranges specified (between low and high values), it is replaced with the value specified in the rules table.

Convert Case.   Convert the character-only value to upper- or lowercase

Encode Invalid Values.   Convert the invalid values to the predefined correct values stored in the specified rule table.

At a minimum, a rules table must contain at least two columns. One column contains the values to be searched for, and the other column contains the values to be replaced.

If a match is found, the corresponding replacement value will be copied to the target table. If you specify a differentiator column for both the rules and the source table, the values in the differentiator column must be identical for the match to be successful. If you specify an order column for the rules table, the find and replace operation matching order will follow the ascending order of values in the order column.

If a match is not found and you have turned on the error processing option by selecting the multiple match option, write to error table, or by enabling error processing, the entire input row will be written to the error table along with the RUN_ID of the execution.

If you allow nulls for this clean type, you must put a null value in the Find column of the rules table. (See Figure 9.16.)

For example, suppose your company receives syndicated data on a periodic basis for each retail store that sells its products. Data from different stores is provided by several different syndications, each of which, while supplying the needed sales data, provides it in slightly different formats. You can use the Clean DB2 stored procedure to modify and convert the input data into a standard format for further propagation of the data into the warehouse environment.

The clean utility has a few constraints. For instance, the input must be a column in the warehouse source table and it cannot be a computed value from the warehouse source table.

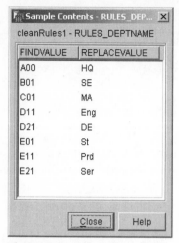

Figure 9.16 Clean Data-find and replace rules table.

To illustrate, let's define a Clean Data transformer step. We will use a table called EMPLOYEE and cleanse the WORKDEPT using Find and Replace, SALARY using Clip, and COMM using Discrete, and leave the EMPNO, LASTNAME, and FIRSTNAME unchanged using Carry Over. Figure 9.17 shows the clean data step parameters.

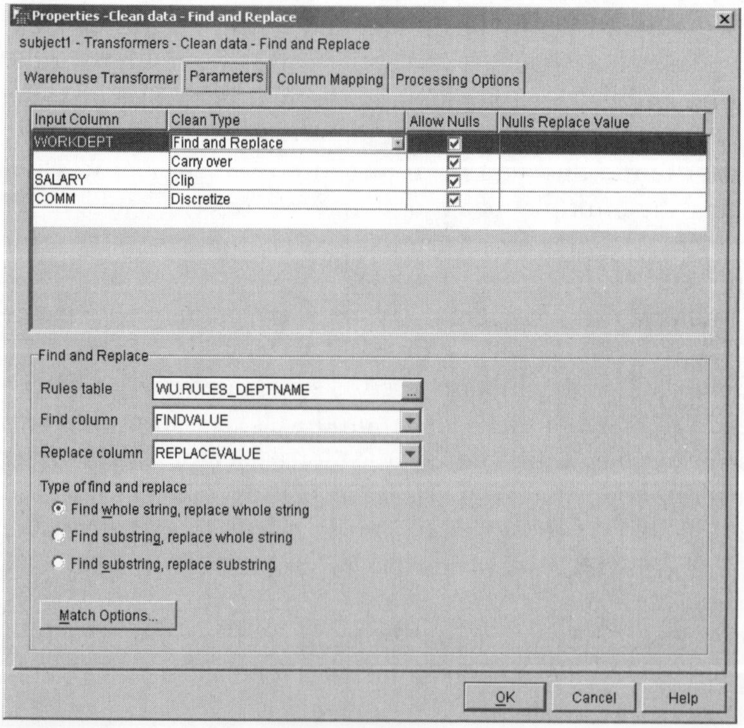

Figure 9.17 Clean data step parameters.

Generating Key Table

Use this transformer to create and insert unique keys into a warehouse table. After you have built your warehouse target table, you may want to add a key column to uniquely identify each record in your warehouse target table. You can alter the warehouse target table to add the new key column definition and the new column must be defined with NULLs accepted. Alternatively, the key column may have been created initially with the table; the initial values could be NULL or a default value. Then you can run the Generate Key Table transformer against the modified warehouse target. You can populate one key column to the target warehouse in each step.

The generated key values can either replace null values via an Update step or can be inserted into a newly defined key column using the Replace step option.

Starting key values can be explicitly specified or calculated from the maximum existing value of a column in the same or another table.

This transformer uses the warehouse target table as both input and output, and it writes the customized key values into the target table. If you want to alter the customized key properties, the Generate Key Table transformer step must be in development mode. However, you may change the step properties such as the starting key values when the step is in nonproduction mode.

When you select Update the Value in the Key Column, the transformer updates only those rows in the table that do not have key values. When additional rows are inserted into the table, the key values are null until you run the transformer again.

Figures 9.18 and 9.19 show the property pages necessary to define the Generating Key Table step.

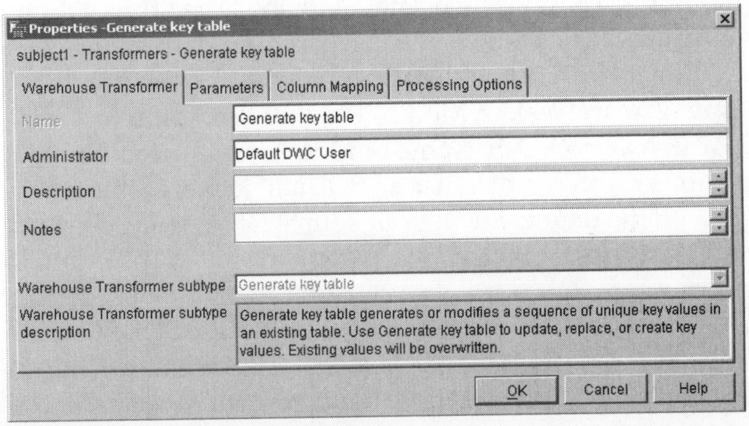

Figure 9.18 Generate Key Table step.

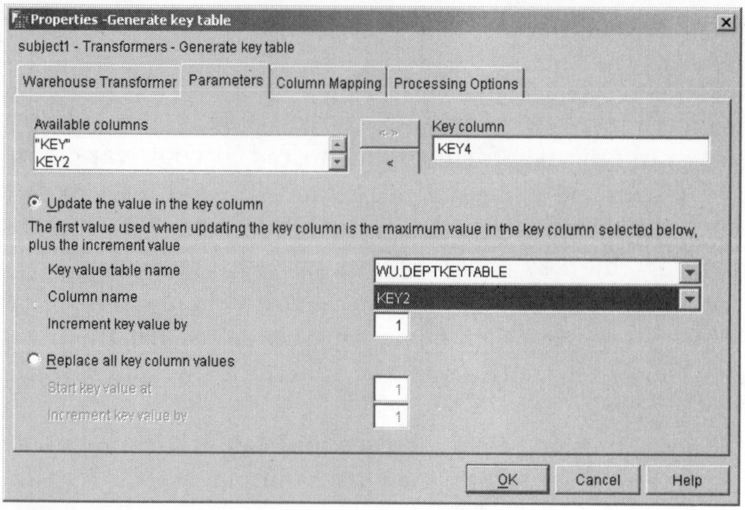

Figure 9.19 Generate key table parameters.

Generating Period Table

This transformer is designed to create a period table that contains columns of date information that you can use when evaluating other data, such as determining inventory on stock within a certain period of time. There is no input table required for this transformer. Output values are computed based on the parameter values specified in this transformer, and placed into an empty output table in predefined columns. You can specify the Start and End values using date and time values or number of rows. One column of data type Date, Time, or Timestamp is required. Values are generated based on the resolution parameter, including: Day, Week, Month, Quarter, Year, Two weeks, Four weeks, Hour and Minute. Figure 9.20 illustrates the resolution options as well as other parameters available to warehouse planners.

Optional period related columns associated with the Date/Time column value can be populated. For instance, you can associate date values with up to 14 different formats including Julian Day, Hour in Day, Day in Week, Day of Month, Day of Year, Week of Month, Week of Year, Month of Year, Quarter of Year, Year, Name of Day, Name of Month, and Period Number plus a sequence number. You can then use an SQL join to merge this generated period table with the date value in your source tables using the Date column to create a warehouse target.

Let's assume a company has a number of product data tables that all include a DB2 date column. The company would like to use SQL SELECTs against these tables using various period-related values rather than just date. You can use the Generate Period Table transformer to populate a table of period-related columns containing value types of interest.

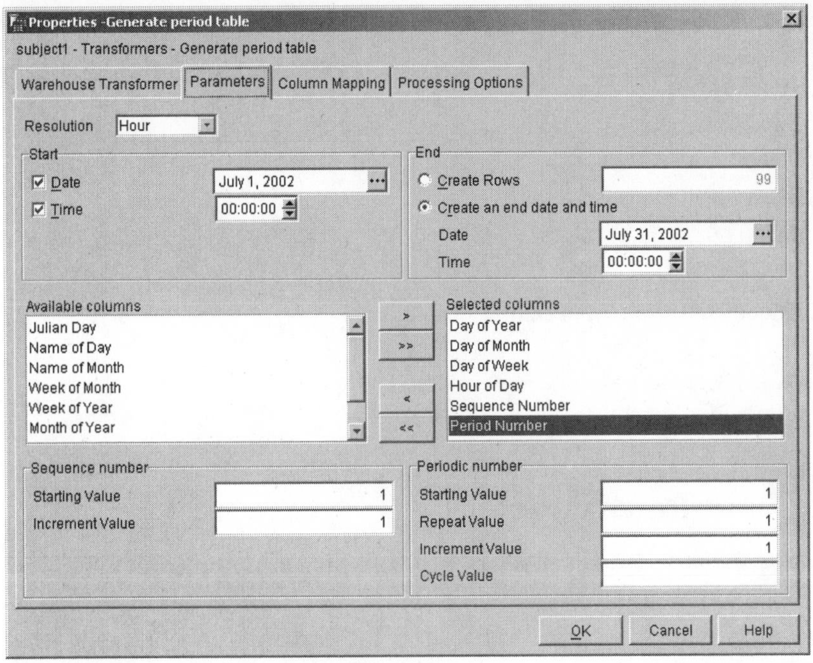

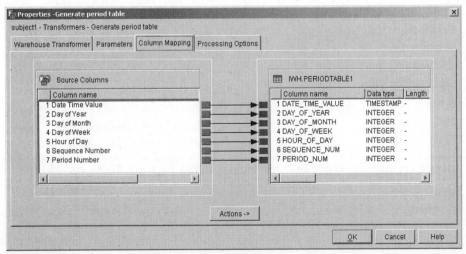

Figure 9.20   Generate period table parameters.

Mapping the selected date format to the warehouse target is shown in Figure 9.21. After the transformation is executed, the target table will contain the generated date values, as illustrated in Figure 9.22.

Figure 9.21   Generate period table column mapping.

DATE_TIME_VALUE	DAY_OF_YEAR	DAY_OF_MONTH	DAY_OF_WEEK	HOUR_OF_DAY	SEQUENCE_NUM	PERIOD_N
2002-07-01 00:00:00.000000	182	1	2	1	1	1
2002-07-01 01:00:00.000000	182	1	2	2	2	1
2002-07-01 02:00:00.000000	182	1	2	3	3	1
2002-07-01 03:00:00.000000	182	1	2	4	4	1
2002-07-01 04:00:00.000000	182	1	2	5	5	1
2002-07-01 05:00:00.000000	182	1	2	6	6	1

Figure 9.22 Generate Period Table sample output.

Inverting Data Transformer

Use this transformer to invert the order of the rows and columns in a table. When you use this transformer, the rows in the source table are transformed to columns in the output table, and the columns in the input table are transformed to rows in the output table. The order of data among the columns, from top to bottom, is maintained and placed in rows, from left to right. For example, consider the input table as a matrix. This transformer swaps the data in the table around a diagonal line that extends from the upper left of the table to the lower right. Then the transformer writes the transformed data to the target table.

Before you begin this task, you must connect a source table from the warehouse database to the step. You can also specify a target table that the step will write to, or you can designate that the step create the target table. The desired output columns must be created manually in a step-generated warehouse target table. This transformer drops the existing database table and re-creates it during each run. Each time you run a step using this transformer, the existing data is replaced, but the tablespace and table index names are preserved.

The input table is expected to be either homogenous or of types all related to each other through automatic promotion. That is, all the table data is of the same or promotable type except for the first column if that is to be used as the pivot column. Other constraints include the following:

- All data in the pivot column must be less than 18 characters wide.

- The number of rows in the source table should be less than the maximum number of table columns supported in the version of DB2 that is running this transformer.

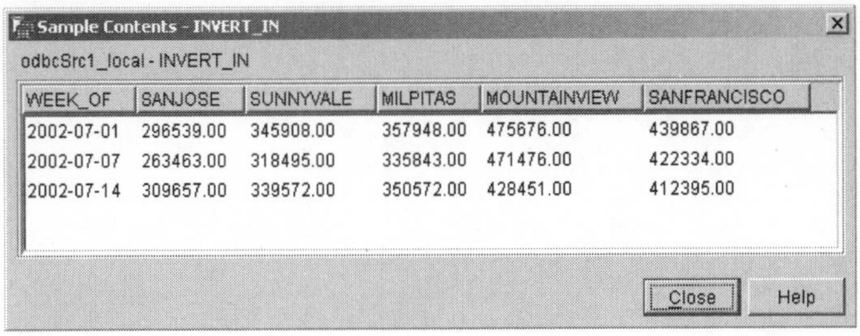

Figure 9.23   Invert Data–sample source table.

Each time this step is run, the column names or the number of columns may change. These columns will not be displayed when the target table data is sampled; however, you may import the warehouse target table after the transformer is executed.

Figure 9.23 shows a sample source table where the WEEK_OF column will be inverted and the target table will be generated based on the input parameters.

This transformer is useful because it is much simpler and easier to issue an SQL statement against the resulting table than against the original table. For example, after the table has been inverted, it is very easy to select the highest value for the week of July 1st.

When setting the parameters of the invert, you should indicate the column you want to invert on. In our example we plan to invert on the WEEK_OF column, as shown in Figure 9.24.

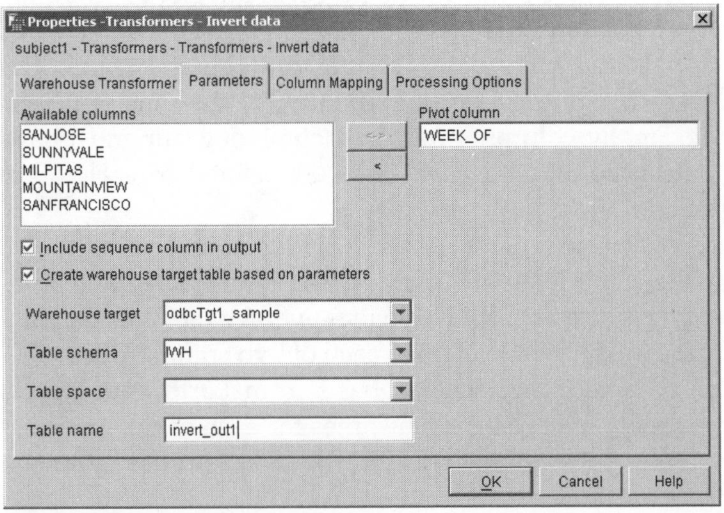

Figure 9.24   Invert data parameters.

Figure 9.25   Invert data sample output.

The data displayed in Figure 9.25 is the output results once the transformer has executed.

Pivoting Data

Often there is a requirement to group related data from selected columns in the source table, which are called *pivot columns*, into a single column, called a *pivot group column*, in the target table. The Pivoting data transformer can create this regrouping of data even if you need to create more than one pivot group column.

When using this transformer, you must keep in mind several considerations. First, you can select multiple columns from the source table to carry over to the output table, but the transformation will not change the data itself. This transformer uses an existing target table in the same database or creates a target table in the same database that contains the warehouse source. Also, you can change the step definition only when the step is in development mode. Finally, columnar data in each pivot group must have either the same data type or data types that are related to each other through automatic promotion.

To illustrate, let's use an example. Figure 9.26 shows source data that we want to pivot from the TransGalactic Company. The source data has a database table representing Space Craft Maintenance average repair times for 4 lines, described by the propulsion system in each of two craft families (Passenger and Cargo) collected on a weekly basis from Earth and Earth's Moon. The DBA wishes to aggregate repair times for each of the two craft families so that she can perform statistics on the craft families either by week, repair site, or craft line.

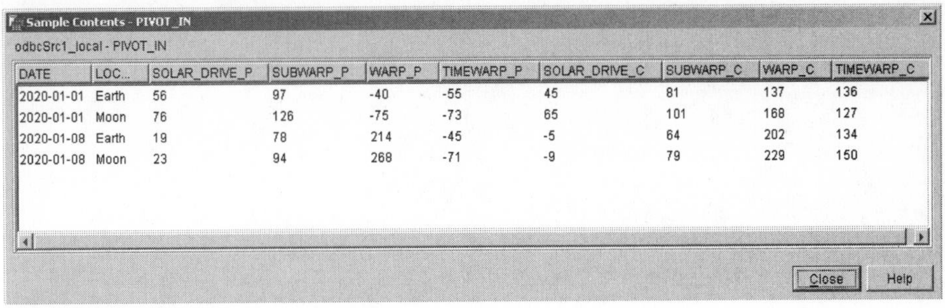

Figure 9.26   Pivot data–sample input.

To start this pivot process, we first need to identify the carry-over columns and the pivot groups as shown in Figure 9.27.

Next, we want to set the grouping characteristics of the source data. Note that the number of pivot columns must be divisible by the number of groups. Figure 9.28 demonstrates the grouping interface.

Finally, the source columns must be mapped to their corresponding target columns as shown in Figure 9.29.

After the transformation is executed, the warehouse target contains the data shown in Figure 9.30. You can create other SQL steps to query this pivot_out table by date, location, or spacecraft.

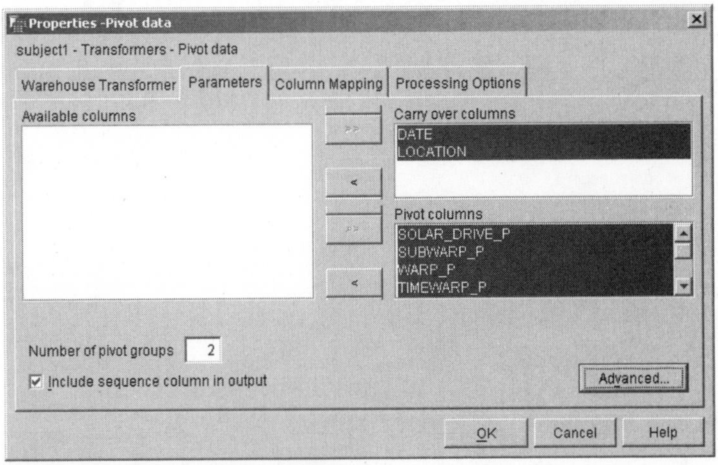

Figure 9.27   Pivot data parameters.

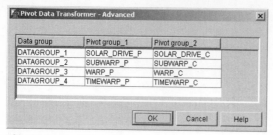

Figure 9.28 Pivot data grouping.

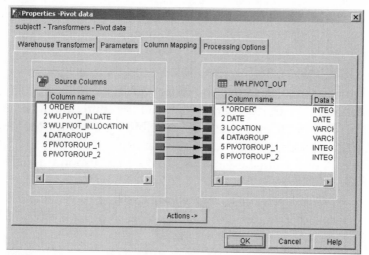

Figure 9.29 Pivot data column mapping.

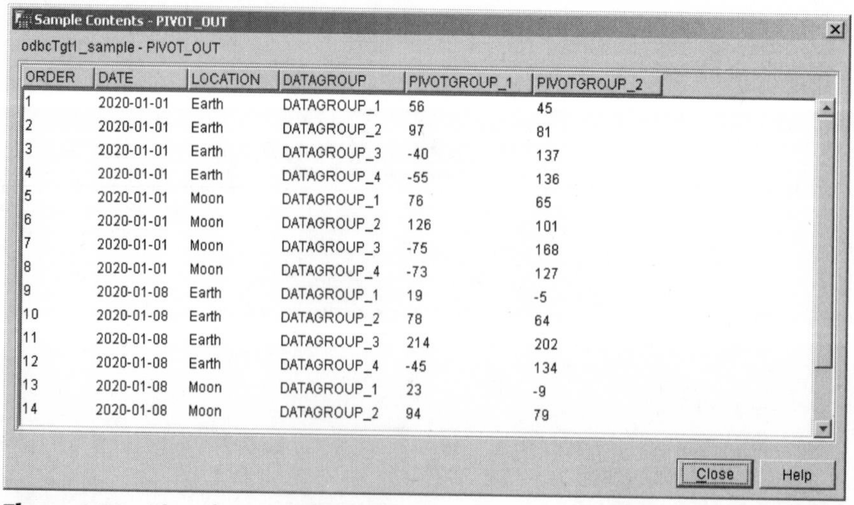

ORDER	DATE	LOCATION	DATAGROUP	PIVOTGROUP_1	PIVOTGROUP_2
1	2020-01-01	Earth	DATAGROUP_1	56	45
2	2020-01-01	Earth	DATAGROUP_2	97	81
3	2020-01-01	Earth	DATAGROUP_3	-40	137
4	2020-01-01	Earth	DATAGROUP_4	-55	136
5	2020-01-01	Moon	DATAGROUP_1	76	65
6	2020-01-01	Moon	DATAGROUP_2	126	101
7	2020-01-01	Moon	DATAGROUP_3	-75	168
8	2020-01-01	Moon	DATAGROUP_4	-73	127
9	2020-01-08	Earth	DATAGROUP_1	19	-5
10	2020-01-08	Earth	DATAGROUP_2	78	64
11	2020-01-08	Earth	DATAGROUP_3	214	202
12	2020-01-08	Earth	DATAGROUP_4	-45	134
13	2020-01-08	Moon	DATAGROUP_1	23	-9
14	2020-01-08	Moon	DATAGROUP_2	94	79

Figure 9.30 Pivot data sample output.

Date Format Changing

For easy and efficient transformation of date field formats, use this transformer. It converts the format of a date field in your source table to a desired date field format in your target table. You can run this transformer with any other transformer or warehouse program.

Numerous standard date formats are available with this transformer that you can specify for the input and output columns. If a date in the input column does not match the specified format, the transformer writes a null value to the output table.

This transformer runs as a function called FormatDate against the input date column for each row in the table, and the formatted output date is placed in the output date column (which must exist). The format of the input and output dates are chosen from menu lists of date and time formats. Optionally, a user can specify his or her own input or output date format using the listed data formats. Figure 9.31 shows the FormatDate interface.

Illustrated in Figure 9.32 is the SQL code generated when using the FormatDate UDF.

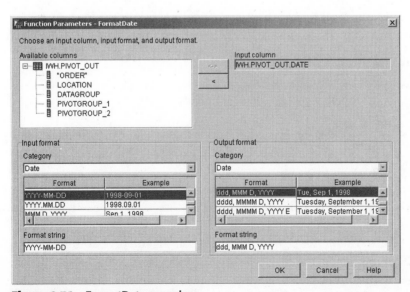

Figure 9.31 FormatDate mappings.

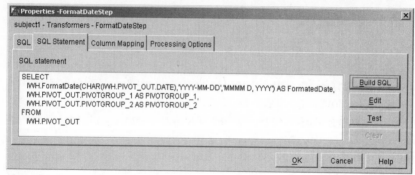

Figure 9.32 Using FormatDate in an SQL statement.

Statistical Transformers

Several statistical analysis tools are available through IBM DB2 Data Warehouse Center. Being able to include complex, statistical algorithms as a natural part of your ETL processing is powerful. However, any discussion of their applicability is beyond the scope of this book. We present these transformers to ensure complete coverage for the reader. It will be up to the reader to discern their application.

Analysis of Variance (ANOVA)

The ANOVA transformer produces statistical calculations in two tables based on a small number of parameters. There are three types of ANOVA:

- One-way
- Two-way
- Three-way

The transformer obtains two independent estimates of variance. The first estimate is based on variability between groups, while the second estimate is based on variability within groups.

After the ANOVA step computes the estimates, it calculates their ratio. A family of distributions, the Fisher-F distributions, describes the significance of this ratio.

The process also calculates a p-value. The *p-value* is the probability that the means of the two groups are equal. A small p-value leads to the conclusion that the means are different. For example, a p-value of 0.02 means there is a 2 percent chance that the sample means are equal. Likewise, a large p-value leads to the conclusion that the means of the two groups are not different.

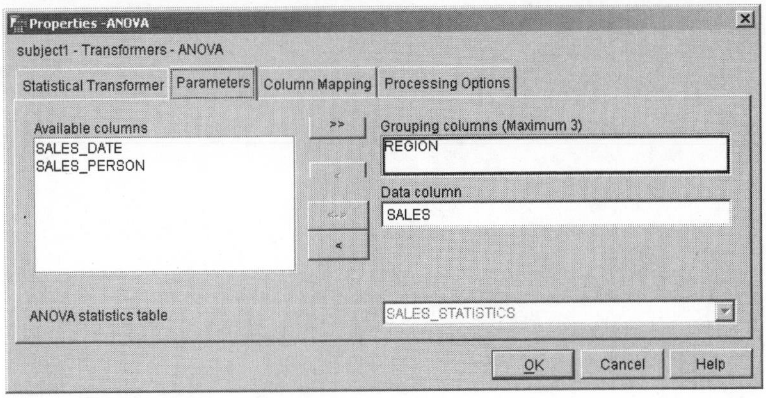

Figure 9.33 ANOVA properties.

Many industry sectors rely upon this kind of statistical analysis, such as finance and insurance, where ANOVA is used to detect, prevent, and reduce fraud and error, and the medical and scientific community, where ANOVA is used to identify populations with certain particular characteristics.

Let's use a sample SALES table as the input table to ANOVA and generate the summary and statistics table. Figure 9.33 shows the ANOVA properties interface.

When we select the Column Mapping tab, we are prompted to enter both the summary and statistics warehouse target table names. Figure 9.34 illustrates a straightforward movement of columnar data from the source to target columns.

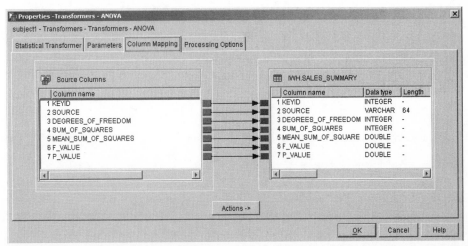

Figure 9.34 ANOVA column mapping.

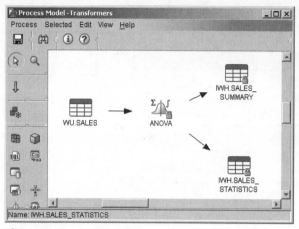

Figure 9.35 ANOVA step.

Once we have identified and mapped the source to target tables in our process, we now need to add the ANOVA step to our process model. Figure 9.35 demonstrates how the ANOVA step is implemented in our example where the output summary and statistics tables are generated.

The summary table is called SALES_SUMMARY, and the statistics table is SALES_STATISTICS. Once the ANOVA step is executed, the summary data is stored in the SALES_SUMMARY table as shown in Figure 9.36. The output displays six columns of data, each with a maximum of three rows. The columns include the following:

- Source
- Degrees of freedom (DF)
- Sum of squared deviations from the mean (SS)
- Mean sum of squared deviations from the mean (MSS=SS/DF)
- F-value (MSS (between groups)) / MSS (within groups)
- P-value (Pvalue_function (DF, F-value))

Sample Contents - SALES_SUMMARY

odbcTgt1_sample - SALES_SUMMARY

KEYID	SOURCE	DEGREES_OF_FREEDOM	SUM_OF_SQUARES	MEAN_SUM_OF_SQU...	F_VALUE	P_VALUE
1	Between Groups	3	14	4.84217171717172	0.331498876...	0.8025956...
2	Within Groups	36	525	14.6069023569024		
3	Total	39	540			

Close   Help

Figure 9.36 ANOVA sample output summary.

The statistics data is store in, SALES_STATISTICS, shown in Figure 9.37, that contains five calculated statistics: Count, Sum, Average, Variance, and Standard Deviation.

Calculating Statistics

The Calculating Statistics transformer calculates numerous descriptive statistics on any number of data columns from a single table, including the following:

COUNT.   Number of items

SUM.   Total when numbers are added together

MINIMUM.   Smallest number

MAXIMUM.   Largest number

RANGE.   Difference between largest and smallest number

AVERAGE.   Sum divided by the number of items (i.e., mean)

VARIANCE.   Average squared deviation from the mean

STANDARD DEVIATION.   Square root of the variance

COEFFICIENT OF VARIATION.   Standard deviation as a percentage of the mean

STANDARD ERROR.   Standard deviation divided by square root of the number of items

This transformer writes summary information into relational tables that can be queried directly or used as input for further statistical analysis.

KEYID	VARIABLE	COUNT	SUM	AVERAGE	VARIANCE	STDDEV
1	Manitoba	11	41	3.7272727272...	8.41818181818...	2.766386191764..
2	Ontario-North	4	9	2.25	0.916666666666...	0.829156197588..
3	Ontario-South	13	52	4.0	13.33333333333...	3.508232077228..
4	Quebec	12	53	4.4166666666...	25.35606060606...	4.821105221373..
5	Total	40	155	3.875	13.85576923076...	3.675510168670..

Figure 9.37   Calculating statistics–sample output.

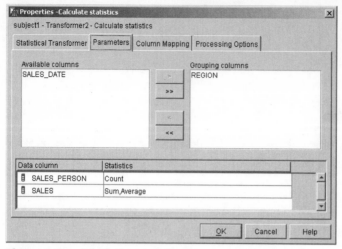

Figure 9.38   Calculating statistics step parameters.

Defining the transformation step is straightforward, using the customary properties interface. Figure 9.38 illustrates the parameters necessary to define the step.

In our example we are calculating the number of sales people (COUNT) for each region, and we are deriving statistical SUM and AVG against the source column SALES. The results of these statistics are mapped to a target table as shown in Figure 9.39.

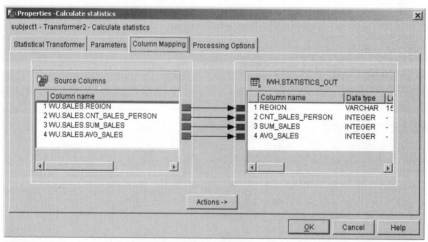

Figure 9.39   Calculating statistics column mapping.

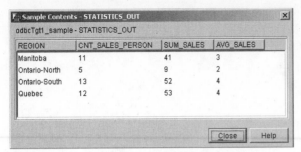

Figure 9.40 Calculating statistics sample output.

The output of our statistical transformation step is shown in Figure 9.40.

Calculating Subtotals

Use this transformer to calculate the running subtotal for a set of numeric values grouped by a period of time. This particular feature is invaluable in warehouse data propagation, since much of the ETL work has to do with creating running subtotals. The transformer allows subtotals to be calculated in these increments: weekly, semimonthly, monthly, quarterly, or annually.

To illustrate, we will take an accounting perspective. In accounting it is often necessary to produce subtotals of numeric values for basic periods of time. This is frequently encountered in payroll calculations where companies are required to produce month-to-date and year-to-date subtotals for various types of payroll data.

There are a few issues to remember during the setup. First, the subtotal values are placed into the input table in predefined output columns. Second, the output columns must already exist. To put it simply: The input table is the output table. Finally, there must exist a primary key column.

The first step to defining a subtotal transformation is to complete the properties parameters as shown in Figure 9.41.

For example, a company has employee payroll data where employees are paid semimonthly and would like to collect the monthly subtotal. The primary key is CHECKID, and we plan to map the subtotal of SALARY_Month to the column name SUBTOTAL in the output as shown in Figure 9.42.

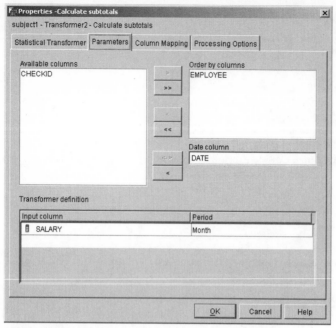

Figure 9.41 Calculating subtotals step parameters.

The final output is shown in Figure 9.43. The subtotal column in the payroll table contains the employee monthly subtotal.

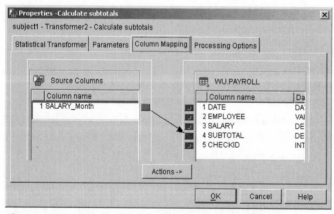

Figure 9.42 Calculating subtotals column mapping.

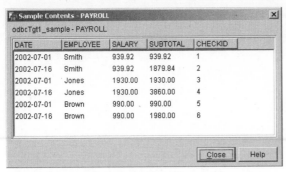

Figure 9.43   Calculating subtotal sample output.

Chi-Squared Transformer

The Chi-Squared transformer performs the Chi-Square test on columns of numerical data. Additionally, it is possible to supply expected values to the Chi-Squared transformer, rather than having them calculated. This is called the *Chi-Square goodness-of-fit test*. The results show how the observed data differs from statistical expectations. Both of these tests, however, are nonparametric tests. You can use the statistical results of these tests to make the following determinations:

- Whether the values of one variable are related to the values of another variable
- Whether the values of one variable are independent of the values of another variable
- Whether the distribution of variable values meets your expectations

This transformer produces one or two output tables. One table is the Chi-Square output table, which reports degrees of freedom, the Chi-Square value, and the p-value. A second table is referred to as the Expected Output Values, which shows the goodness-of-fit values for each cell used in the Chi-Square by the transformer. This table is optional when running the standard Chi-Square test.

To illustrate the process, we start with sample data shown in Figure 9.44.

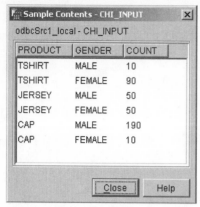

Figure 9.44 Chi-Square sample input data.

Next, we need to set parameters as identified in Figure 9.45. The *Column of row definition* contains the names of the rows in the conceptual table. The *Column of column names* specifies the names of the columns in the conceptual table. The *Observed frequencies column*, which must be numeric, contains the cell counts used to compute the chi-square statistics. And, finally, the *Expected frequencies column* is optional. If it is specified, it must be numeric and contain the expected cell counts; it then calculates the goodness-of-fit.

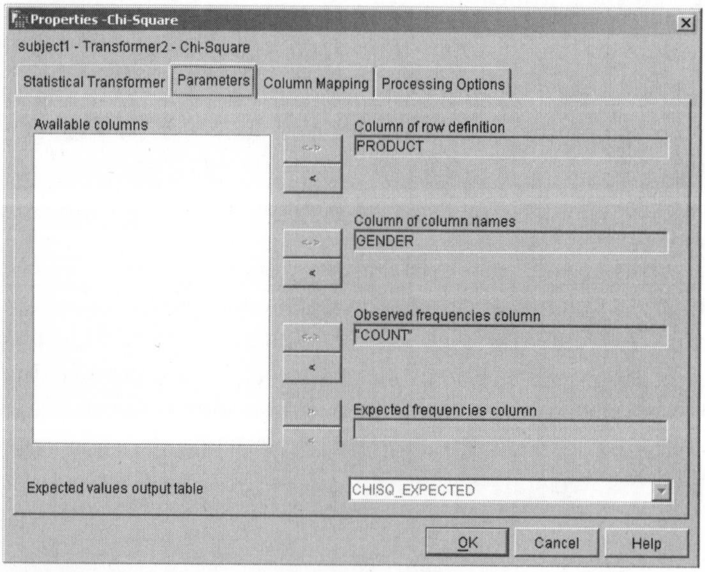

Figure 9.45 Chi-Square step parameters.

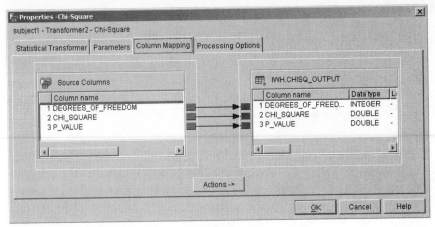

Figure 9.46   Chi-Square column mapping.

Once we have defined the necessary parameters, the next step is to map the source columns to target output. (See Figure 9.46.)

After the Chi-Square transformer is defined, it must be included in the process model. As shown in Figure 9.47, there is a single input table and two output tables. The first output table is referred to as CHISQ_OUTPUT, and the second is CHISQ_EXPECTED.

A sample of the calculated results in both the output tables is shown in Figures 9.48 and 9.49.

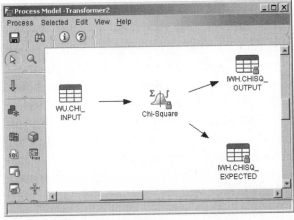

Figure 9.47   Chi-Square step.

Figure 9.48 Chi-Square–observed data.

Sample Contents - CHISQ_EXPECTED

odbcTgt1_sample - CHISQ_EXPECTED

ROWCOL	COLCOL	DATACOL	EXPCOL
TSHIRT	MALE	10.0	62.5
TSHIRT	FEMALE	90.0	37.5
JERSEY	MALE	50.0	62.5
JERSEY	FEMALE	50.0	37.5
CAP	MALE	190.0	125.0
CAP	FEMALE	10.0	75.0

Figure 9.49 Chi-Square–expected data.

Correlation Analysis

Correlation analysis is used to determine the extent to which changes in the value of an attribute (such as length of employment) are associated with changes in another attribute (such as salary). The data for a correlation analysis consists of two input columns. Each column contains values for one of the attributes of interest. The Correlation transformer can calculate various measures of association between the two input columns. You can select more than one statistic to calculate for a given pair of input columns.

The data in the input columns also can be treated as a sample obtained from a larger population, and this transformer can be used to test whether the attributes are correlated in the population. In this context, the null hypothesis asserts that the two attributes are not correlated, and the alternative hypothesis asserts that the attributes are correlated.

This transformer calculates any of the following correlation-related statistics on one or more pairs of columns:

- *Correlation coefficient* is a measure of the linear relationship between two attributes (columns) of data. It is also known as the Pearson product-moment correlation coefficient. It ranges from -1 to +1 and is independent of units of measurement. A value near 0 indicates little correlation; a value near +1 or -1 indicates a high level of correlation.

- *Covariance* is a measure of the linear relationship between two attributes (columns) of data ranges from -infinity to +infinity. A value too small or too large is represented by a null value. It is dependent on the units of measurement.

- *T-value* is the observed value of the T-statistic that is used to test the hypothesis that the two attributes are correlated. It ranges from -infinity to +infinity. A value near 0 is evidence that there is no correlation between the attributes (null hypothesis). A value far from 0 is evidence that there is correlation between the attributes. T-Value = r * SQRT($(n - 2) / (1 - r * r)$) where r is the correlation coefficient, n is the number of input value pairs, and SQRT is the square-root function.

- *P-value* is the probability, when the null hypothesis is true, that the absolute value of the T-statistic would equal or exceed the observed value (T-value). A small p-value is evidence that the null hypothesis is false and the attributes are correlated.

We start at the same place as defining other transformers, the properties parameters tab, as shown in Figure 9.50. Points of interest are the Grouping Columns that group related rows for each statistical calculation. The Data columns you select must be numeric and must contain input values for the calculations. Particular statistics are chosen for each row through a secondary dialog box.

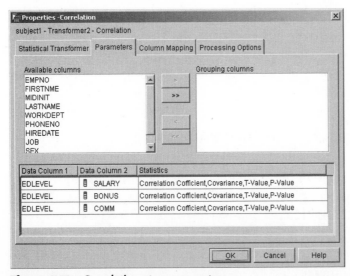

Figure 9.50 Correlation step parameters.

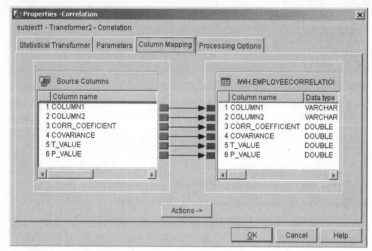

Figure 9.51 Correlation column mapping.

In our example we are trying to determine if there is a correlation between the sample table EMPLOYEE education level and the corresponding salary, bonus, and commission earned. We will choose all the available statistics for Data Column2. All mapping from the source to target is done under the Column Mapping tab of the properties interface, as shown in Figure 9.51.

The calculated results are shown in Figure 9.52.

Moving Average

Use this transformer type to calculate simple and exponentially smoothed moving averages, which can often predict the future course of a time-related series of values. Moving averages are widely used in time-series analysis in business and financial forecasting. Rolling sums have other widely used financial uses.

You can use this transformer to calculate the following values:

Simple moving average.   This is a standard moving average calculation. SMA [row i] = SUM (data values for last N rows) / N.

Exponential moving average.   An exponentially smoothed moving average is often more precise than a simple moving average. EMA [row i] = (Value [row i] * K) + (EMA [row i - 1] * (1 - K)), where K = 2 / (N + 1).

Rolling sum.   This is a standard rolling sum. RS [row i] = SUM (data values for last N rows).

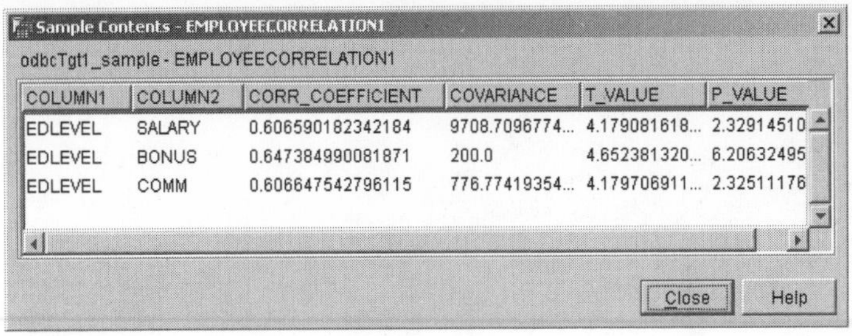

Figure 9.52 Correlation sample output.

Figure 9.53 shows the parameters tab of the properties page that must be completed. The *Order by column* defines how to sort the source data for the moving average calculations. You must specify at least one order column. *Input columns*, which must be a numeric data type, contain input values for the moving average. The specific statistics are chosen for each row through a drop-down list. Finally, the *Period* determines the size of the "window" in terms of the number of rows.

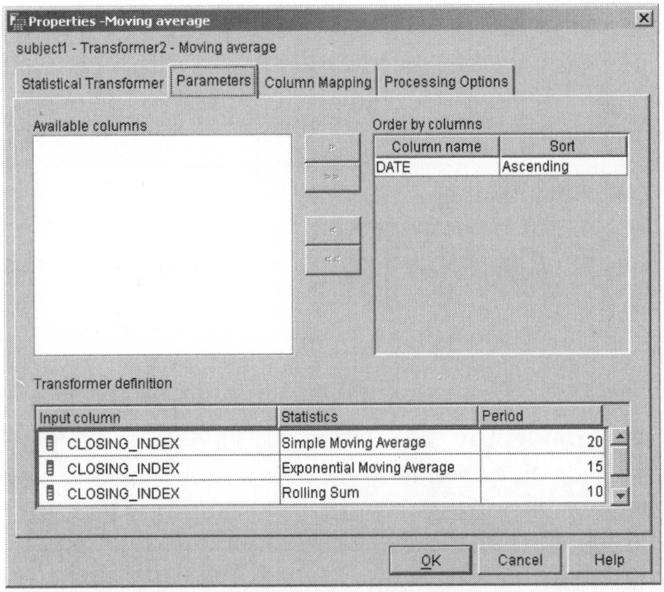

Figure 9.53 Moving average step parameters.

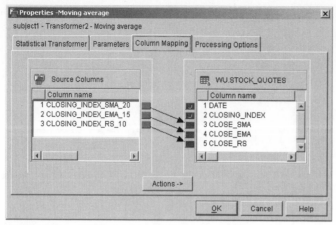

Figure 9.54 Moving average column mapping.

Following are some constraints to remember when using this transformer:

- The table must contain a primary key (it was DATE in this example).

- The table must contain at least one numeric column. An Order By column is required.

- You cannot use the Order By columns as input columns (on the parameters page) or as output columns (target columns on the column mapping page).

- A column may be used multiple times as an input column (CLOSING_INDEX in this example).

- It is possible to replace the values in an input column with a calculated moving average, provided this column is not used as an input in another row in the table.

In our example we are demonstrating how to calculate the moving average of a stock quote. The columnar mapping is shown in Figure 9.54. Note that the input table STOCK_QUOTES also contains the output columns CLOSE_SMA, CLOSE_EMA, and CLOSE_RS.

Regression Analysis

Regression analysis is used to identify the relationships between a dependent variable and one or more independent variables, and to show how closely they are correlated. You can use this transformer to show the effect of a change in pricing on demand for a product, to show the effect of location on the response to advertising, or to show how closely two seemingly random sets of data are related.

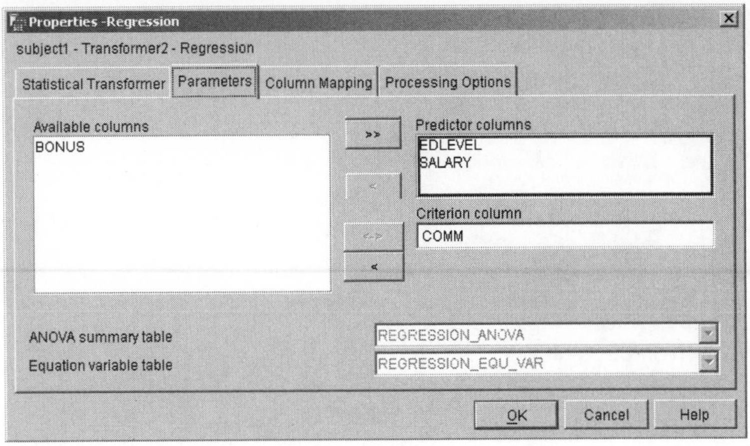

Figure 9.55 Regression step parameters.

This transformer performs a backward, full-model regression. This method starts with all independent variables in a model but removes the least-important independent variables one at a time until only significant independent variables remain in the model. The Regression transformer produces two additional output tables: the ANOVA summary table and the Equation variable table.

Figure 9.55 shows the parameters that must be set for regression analysis. There are a few areas of interest that need to be considered. First, only numeric columns will be shown on the parameters page. The *Predictor columns* are the independent variables of interest. In our example we are using EDLEVEL (education level) and SALARY. And, finally, the *Criterion column* is the dependent variable that is presumably related to the independent variables. In our case the COMM column is the dependent variable.

In our example we will use the EMPLOYEE table as our input, and the analysis will produce three separate outputs. Figure 9.56 identifies the three as Multiple correlation coefficient table, ANOVA summary table, and Equation variable table. And, as always, we must map the source columns to target output.

The actual results of the regression transformation are found in three tables. Figure 9.57 shows the output for the Regression variable table.

Figure 9.58 displays the sample results of the Regression ANOVA table.

And, finally, Figure 9.59 shows the results found in the Regression correlation coefficient table.

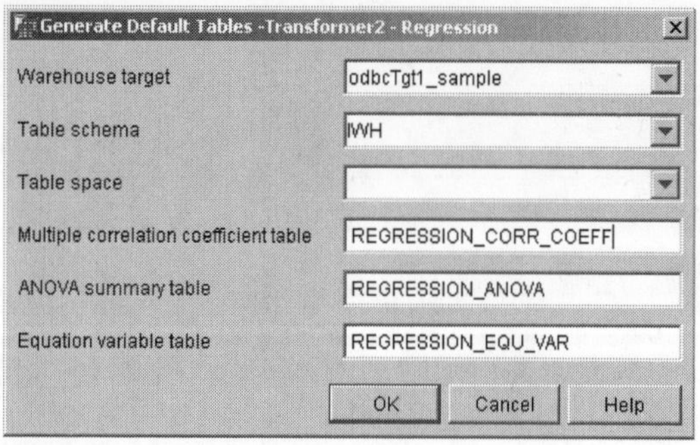

Figure 9.56 Regression–output tables.

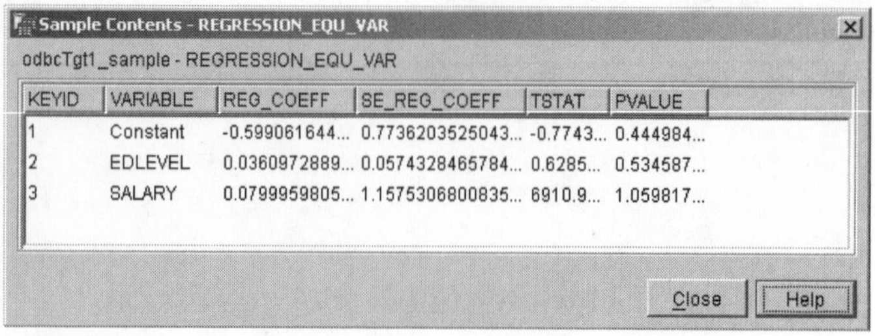

Figure 9.57 Regression–equation variable output table.

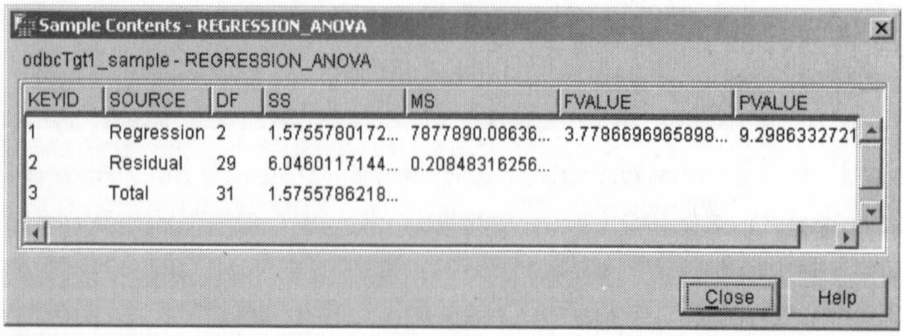

Figure 9.58 Regression ANOVA–summary output table.

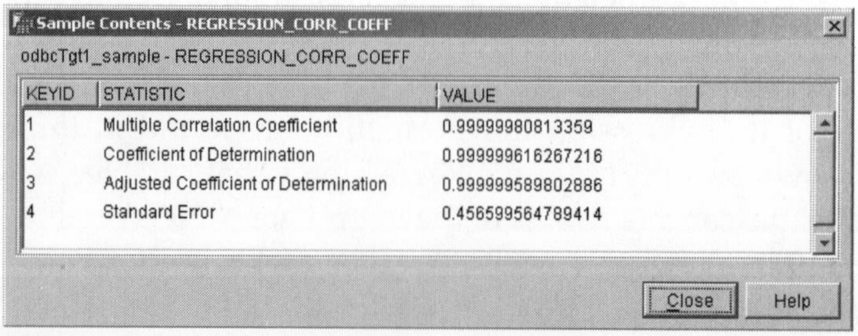

Figure 9.59 Regression–multiple correlation coefficient output table.

Data Replication Steps

Replication is a process of copying specific changes from one location (source or capture) to another (target or apply) and synchronizing the data in both locations. The source and target can be located on the same or different machines in a network. IBM DB2 Data Warehouse Center provides replication capabilities via replication steps, which will replicate changes or do a full copy between any two tables in DB2 databases. To define a replication step, you must belong to a warehouse group that has access to the process in which the step will be used.

There are five types of replication steps to consider. Each is shown in Figure 9.60 and defined in the following list:

User copy. Generates a complete and condensed copy of the source table. "Condensed" implies the target table has a primary key with which updates are made. User copy tables look like regular source tables and are the most common type of replication target tables.

Point in time. Generates a complete and condensed copy of the source table at a certain point in time. It differs from a user copy table in that it has an additional timestamp column to keep track of when the transaction occurred.

Base aggregate. Produces a history table in which new rows are appended for each subscription cycle using the result of a calculation (via an SQL column function) against the source (or the base) table.

Change aggregate. Generates a table similar to base aggregate except that new rows are based on the Changed Data (CD) table that contains recently changed data as opposed to the source table.

Staging table. This is also called a Consistent Change Data (CCD) table, because it reflects changes from a committed transaction. The output table generated can be condensed or non-condensed and completed, or non-completed. Following are the data types:

- *Condensed:* The table contains a primary key and the most current value for a row. Updates are made using the primary key, and it is useful for staging changes to remote locations and for summarizing updates before replicating to a target table.
- *Noncondensed*: The table does not contain a primary key, only a history of changes to a row. Updates are done via appending rows to the table, and it is useful for auditing purposes.
- *Complete:* The table contains every row in the source table.
- *Non-complete:* The table contains only changes made to the source table for insert, update, and delete.

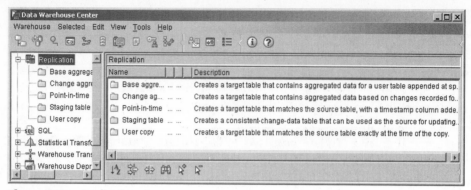

Figure 9.60 Replication steps.

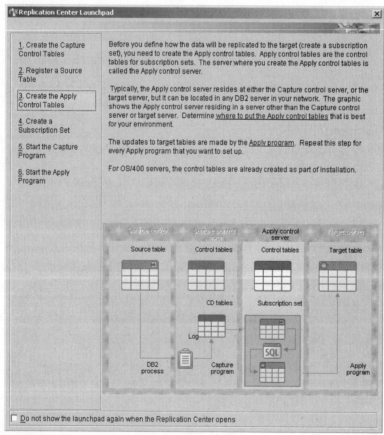

Figure 9.61 Replication Launchpad.

Changes can only be made to a replication step in development mode; promoting it to test mode will create the target table and generate the subscription set in the replication control table. A full refresh will be made the first time a replication step is run. Promoting a replication step to production mode enables the schedules that have been defined.

Setting Up Replication

Before you can import the replication source into the IBM DB2 Data Warehouse Center, you need to create the replication control tables using the Replication Center. Replication control tables must exist in both the control and target databases before the replication steps can be run.

To start, you use the Replication Center, where you would see the interface shown in Figure 9.61, the Replication Launchpad.

The launchpad is extremely verbose and therefore relatively easy for technicians to follow. It is highly recommended to keep the launchpad visible to users until you establish proficiency on the various options available using replication services.

If you elect not to use the Launchpad, then you can use the Replication Center to accomplish the same task, as shown in Figure 9.62. At this point you should expand the folders as shown until you have opened the Custom option. This will lead you to the Create Capture Control Tables interface shown in Figure 9.63.

In the Create Capture Control Tables window, select the Capture control database, override existing options if necessary, and click on OK. If you didn't check the option Use This Server as Both a Capture and Apply Control Server, then repeat these steps to create the replication control tables in the warehouse target database (apply server).

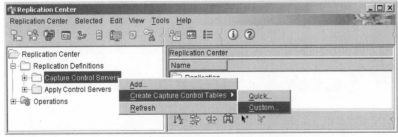

Figure 9.62   Open Create Capture Control Table Custom window.

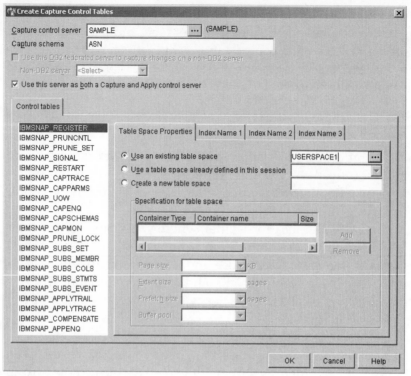

Figure 9.63   Create Capture and Apply control Tables.

Under the same Replication Center interface, you will now need to register the source tables for the replication process. Figure 9.64 shows the menu options to select.

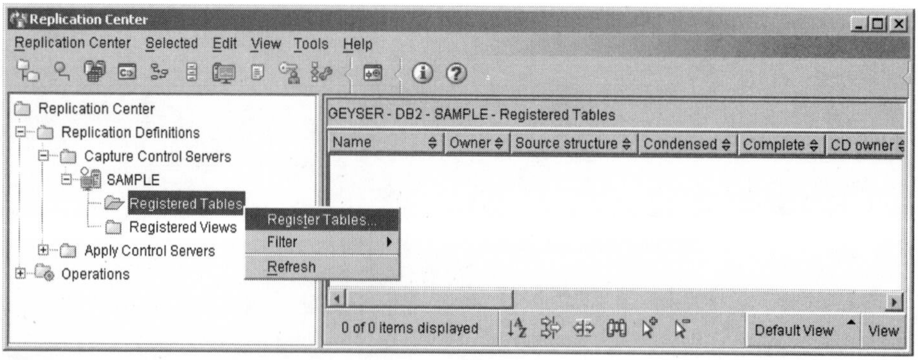

Figure 9.64   Register Replication source tables.

A table or view must be defined as a replication source using the Replication Center before it can be used as a replication source in the IBM DB2 Data Warehouse Center. Again, you can use the Replication Launchpad or expand the Capture Control Server folder, select the appropriate control server, right-click on Registered Tables, and select Register Tables. These steps take you to the screen shown in Figure 9.65.

When you define a replication source table in the Replication Center, you must choose which before-image and after-image columns to replicate (see Figure 9.66). These columns are then defined in the replication CD table, with the before-image columns starting with a special prefix (usually an X). In IBM DB2 Data Warehouse Center, you then define a replication source in the same way that you define other DB2 sources; just be sure to mark the check box to retrieve replication source tables and specify the correct capture schema. *Note:* If you need to change the before- and after-image columns, you must change them in the IBM DB2 Replication Center and then re-import the replication source into the IBM DB2 Data Warehouse Center.

Defining Replication Steps in IBM DB2 Data Warehouse Center

Remember that the replication subtype and subtype description fields, which are noneditable, are different for all step types. However, except for the Row Filtering page, all other pages of the replication step notebooks are the same for all five types of replication steps.

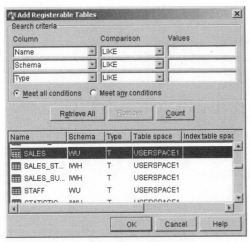

Figure 9.65 Add registerable tables.

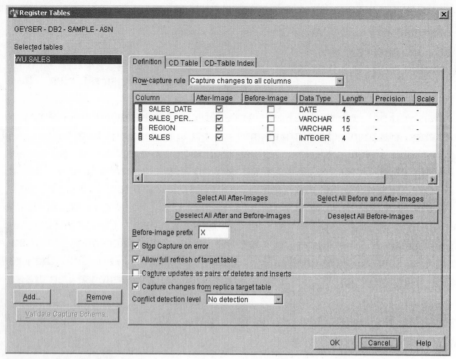

Figure 9.66 Register tables.

The first tab of the Replication step notebook displays general information about the step type. (See Figure 9.67.) Only the name field is mandatory, and a default name is supplied.

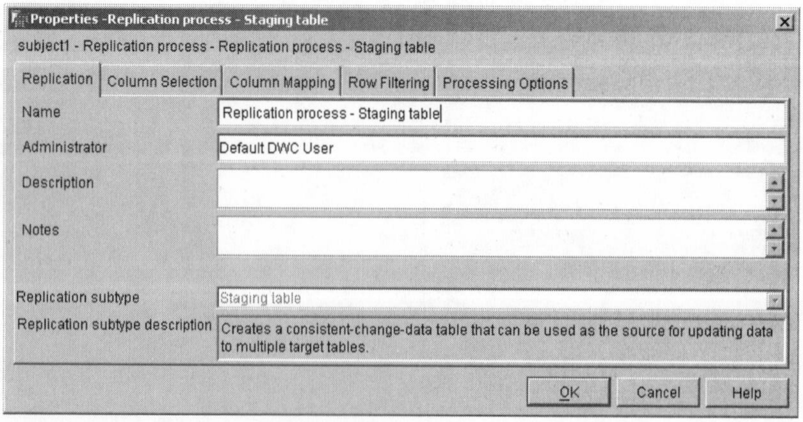

Figure 9.67 Replication staging table step.

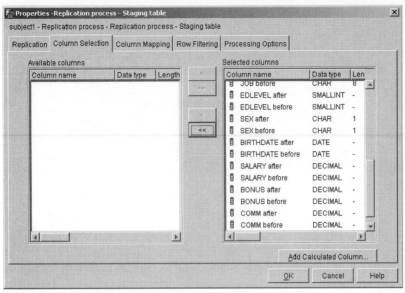

Figure 9.68 Replication column selection.

The second tab, Column Selection, shows the columns that are available or selected for replication. Note that only the columns that are defined for change capture will appear in the available columns list. Figure 9.68 displays the Column Selection tab.

Shown in Figure 9.68 is an option to add a calculated column. If selected, this option takes you to an expression builder. (See Figure 9.69.) The user can type the expression directly into the Expression text area or can build the expression by double-clicking on columns, operators, functions, and expressions. Note that the resulting column will have a default type of CHAR; it's up to the user to make sure that the corresponding column in the target table is of the correct data type.

The Column Mapping page, shown in Figure 9.70, is the same as that for the other steps in the IBM DB2 Data Warehouse Center. After the default target table is generated, the user can edit the attributes of any of the target columns that are mapped to calculated columns if so desired, or they can be edited directly in the columns mapping page.

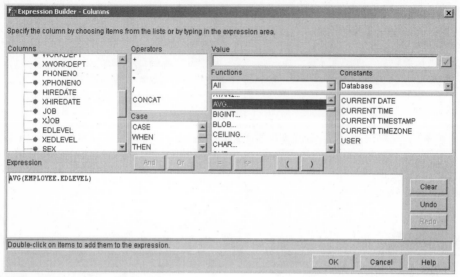

Figure 9.69 Expression Builder.

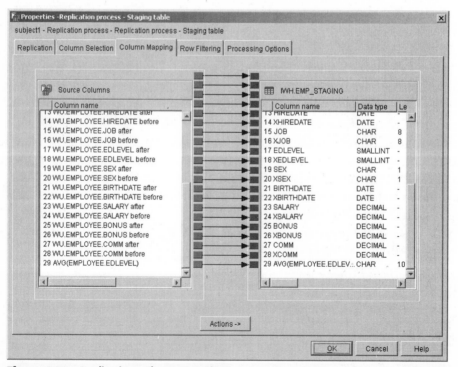

Figure 9.70 Replication column mapping.

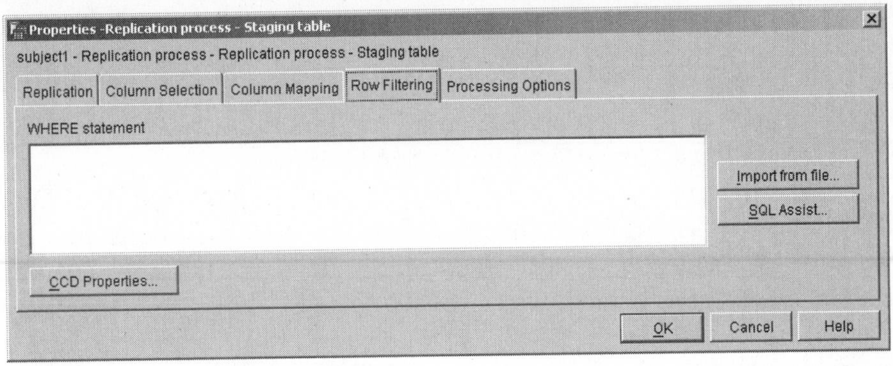

Figure 9.71 Replication row filtering.

The fourth tab in the step notebook for Replication is row filtering. The row filtering tab allows the user to specify the SQL WHERE clause that will be used to sub-select rows from the source table. Figure 9.71 shows the tab.

The row filter code can be directly entered into the text area. Or, as shown in Figure 9.71, you can import an SQL script from a file. Another option is to use the SQL Assist tool to help you build your query.

There is a final option under the Row Filtering tab called CCD Properties. The term stands for Consistent Change Data properties and should only be present and considered when you are dealing with staging replication tables. By selecting this option, a window will appear as shown in Figure 9.72.

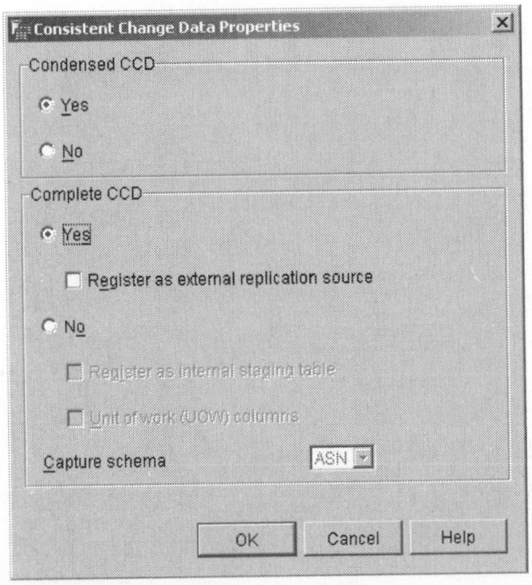

Figure 9.72 CCD.

The CCD options allow you to specify whether your staging table contains only current data or historical changes. It allows you to define whether your staging table is appended to or empty when you start your replication process. For information on all combinations, refer to the IBM DB2 Data Warehouse Center Administration Guide.

Other than the properties that are common to all step types in IBM DB2 Data Warehouse Center, the Replication Step Processing Options tab also allows the user to specify replication options such as Apply Control Server Alias, Database Type, User ID, Password, and so on. Even though Apply Qualifier is not a mandatory field, it's still a good idea to specify a unique name, since otherwise the system will generate a unique cryptic name. (See Figure 9.73.)

Once the Replication step is defined and configured, you can execute the step. This can be done by promoting the step and starting the capture program in the Replication Center or by typing the following in a command prompt:

```
ASNCAP CAPTURE_SERVER=source_DB STARTMODE=WARMSI
```

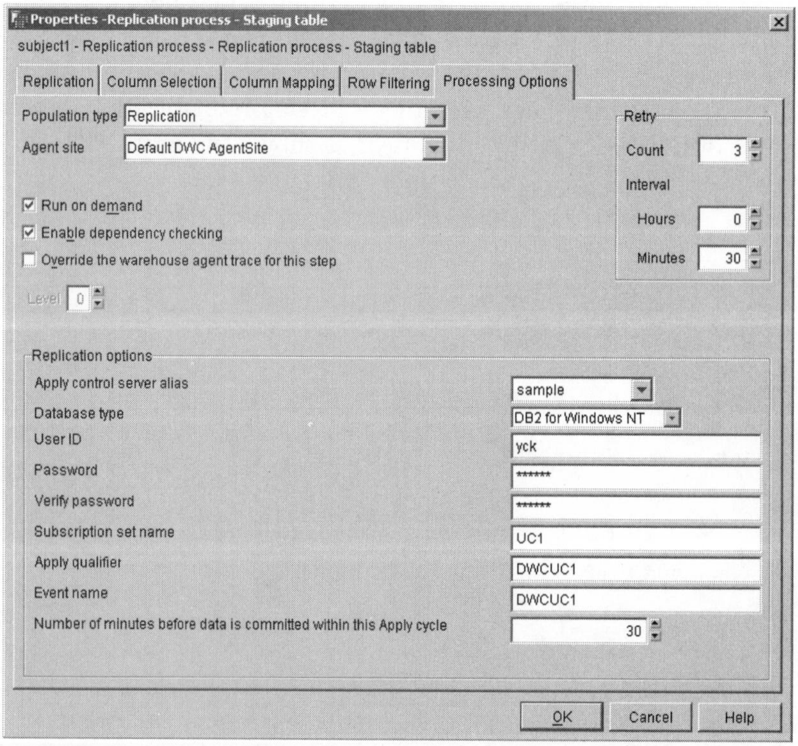

Figure 9.73 Replication step processing options.

The STARTMODE=WARMSI parameter specifies an initial COLD start that deletes any existing data in the CD tables; subsequent starts are warm starts.

Before you test or run the step, make sure that the encrypted password file has been created for the replication step. This is done using the replication program ASNPWD. Data Warehouse Replication steps assume that the password file is found in the VWS_LOGGING directory and have a filename of applyqual.pwd, where applyqual is the Apply Qualifier in the Processing Options page of the replication step. Finally, you can test the step, which involves updating the event record in the IBMSNAP_SUBS_EVENT table, marking the subscription record in IBMSNAP_SUBS_EVENT active, and calling the agent to start the Apply program. After the test runs successfully, you can then schedule and promote the step to production mode.

MQSeries Integration

The IBM DB2 Data Warehouse Center enables you to access MQSeries messages as character strings which are fixed length, character-delimited format or XML documents. You do this by generating a DB2 user-defined table function to access the MQSeries message data and creating a DB2 view against this user-defined table function in the IBM DB2 Data Warehouse Center.

This provides powerful capabilities to the warehouse in that the MQSeries support provides access to application data in queues and presents them to warehouse users as regular relational views. This functionality allows you to join application data on a queue with data you may have in a relational database.

For example, suppose a chemical company has an application where, when a test of a chemical compound completes, the test results are written to an MQSeries message queue. In your warehouse, you need to have the test results joined with the chemical information to provide your users a view of all the testing done by your company. Using the warehouse and MQSeries, you can join the test information on the queue with the chemical information in your DB2 database and write those results to a warehouse target table. No special application coding is needed in order to provide this function to your warehouse users.

MQSeries supports two types of message on the queue in its integration with DB2 and the warehouse:

- If the MQSeries message is in fixed-length or character-delimited format, you can use the wizard provided by the IBM DB2 Data Warehouse Center to transform the MQSeries messages into a DB2 view. Each supported MQSeries message is treated as a string, which is parsed according to your specification and returned as a result row of the view. You can use the created DB2 view as a warehouse source for an SQL step or user-defined step.

- If the MQSeries messages are XML documents, you can use IBM DB2 Data Warehouse Center to import meta data from the MQSeries message queue with a DB2 XML Extender Document Access Definition (DAD) file. A warehouse user-defined step is generated to do the data transformation. When this step is executed, it parses the XML documents according to the user-defined DB2 XML Extender DAD file and populates the target table containing the result data.

Accessing Fixed-Length or Delimited MQSeries Messages

You can use the IBM DB2 Data Warehouse Center to access fixed-length or character-delimited messages from MQSeries. Figure 9.74 shows the straightforward process for invoking a wizard.

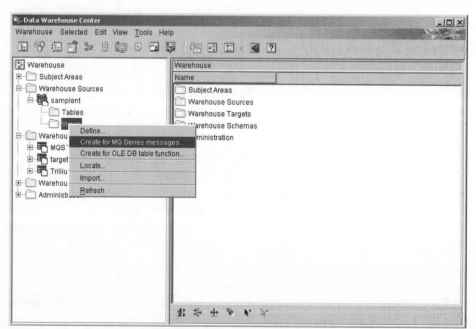

Figure 9.74   Invoking MQSeries wizard to create MQSeries table function.

The wizard guides you through the task of creating user-defined functions for reading or retrieving messages from MQSeries. You can further create a DB2 view using the DB2 user-defined table function.

When you are finished with the wizard, the DB2 user-defined functions are registered in the target database. The wizard also creates a DB2 view using the user-defined function as a warehouse view source, which is available for you to reference in an SQL or user-defined step. This DB2 view has the same characteristics as any other DB2 view defined in the IBM DB2 Data Warehouse Center.

The wizard creates table functions that give the relational look to the queue. Following is an example of the table function and view definition that can then be used within the warehouse. This table function is called DRUG_READ(), and it will provide a relational view of the queue with the correlation ID of the message in the queue, as well as parse out the message (using the DM2MQ built-in function called DB2MQ.GETCOL()) in the queue to return the drug code, proper drug name, drug manufacturing location, and a description about the drug.

```
CREATE FUNCTION DRUG_READ()
RETURNS TABLE
            (CORRELID  varchar(24),
            DRUG_CODE varchar(10),
            DRUG_NAME varchar(20),
            DRUG_MAN_LOC varchar(30),
            DRUG_DESC varchar(50) )
    LANGUAGE SQL
            NOT DETERMINISTIC
            EXTERNAL ACTION
            READS SQL DATA
            RETURN
    SELECT
            CORRELID,
            VARCHAR(DB2MQ.GETCOL(T.MSG,',',1),10),
            VARCHAR(DB2MQ.GETCOL(T.MSG,',',2),20),
            VARCHAR(DB2MQ.GETCOL(T.MSG,',',3),30),
            VARCHAR(DB2MQ.GETCOL(T.MSG,',',4),50)
            FROM TABLE (DB2MQ.MQREADALL()) AS T
            WHERE CORRELID = 'Drugs';
```

In this example, there is a queue that contains drug information (rather than it being in DB2 tables already). As new drugs are created, they are added to the queue. Say that you want to use this information to determine which researchers and projects utilize which drugs. The research and project information is stored in DB2 tables, so you want to be able to join the queue data with the DB2 data. After the wizard described previously has executed, the result is the definition of a table function and a view.

The view is then simply created as a SELECT * from the table function:

```
Create view drug_read as select * from table(drug_read()) t;
```

Once this view has been created, you can import this view definition as a source into the warehouse, just like any other view. The view can then be used in any step that requires a relational table or view. This mechanism provides a powerful tool for treating queue data as a warehouse source.

Using DB2 MQSeries Views

Figure 9.75 is a screen shot showing the view created from the preceding code and defined as a warehouse source.

A process model is shown in Figure 9.76, where MQ views and relational tables are used within SQL type transformations. The LABRIEJJ.DRUG_READ source object is an MQSeries message queue that will be joined with other data sources to create the IWH.COMPOUND target table.

The MQSeries view is also available for use in complex SQL statements. Figure 9.77 demonstrates the integration of MQSeries views and SQL. This SQL statement joins the MQSeries queue (DRUG_READ view) to other DB2 tables to get the list of all researchers working with compounds that the drug is made up of.

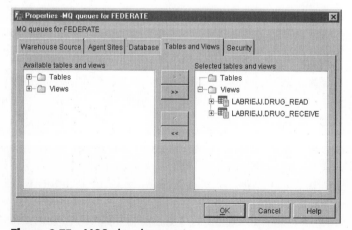

Figure 9.75   MQSeries views.

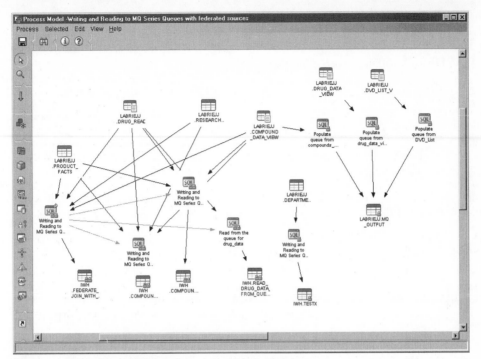

Figure 9.76 Using MQSeries views in warehouse steps.

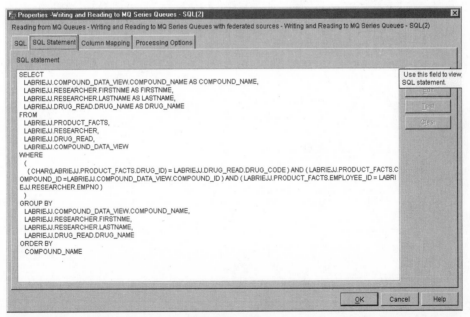

Figure 9.77 Extracting data from MQSeries view.

Accessing XML MQSeries Messages

The following are the steps required to import MQSeries meta data into the IBM DB2 Data Warehouse Center:

1. Prepare a warehouse target for the MQSeries XML document:

   a. Define a warehouse target, and register and enable the transformers in this warehouse target.

   b. Enable the DB2 user-defined functions for MQSeries XML document Support.

   c. Enable the warehouse target for DB2 XML Extender. Refer to the IBM DB2 XML Extender documentation for more information.

   d. Create an XML Extender Data Access Definition (DAD) file to specify the mapping between the XML documents content and warehouse target tables.

   e. Enable an XML collection using the DAD file for the database. Refer to the IBM DB2 XML Extender Release Notes for more information.

2. Import the MQSeries XML document meta data:

   a. Right-click on the Warehouse folder in the navigator, and click on Import Meta data. Select MQSeries to open the Import Meta data window. (See Figure 9.78.)

   b. Click on OK to create a user-defined program step. When this step is executed, the Data Warehouse MQSeries stored procedure extracts the XML document from the queue and transforms the data into the target tables as specified in the DAD file. (See Figure 9.79.)

Figure 9.78   Import MQSeries XML document metadata to a DB2 target table.

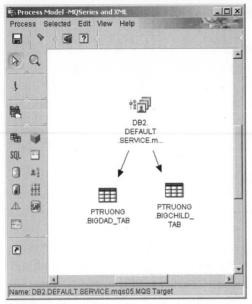

Figure 9.79   MQSeries step–import XML document to DB2 target tables.

User-Defined Program Steps

You can use user-defined programs to use the best extract and transformation software for your warehouse needs while providing a single point of control to administer your warehouse. You can manage and schedule these user-defined programs like other warehouse step types.

For example, suppose you have a data cleansing program that you want to use on your warehouse tables. You can define the data cleansing program as a user-defined program and run a step for that program that starts after a step that populates the warehouse tables.

First you would create a user program group before you define a user-defined program to the IBM DB2 Data Warehouse Center. A *user program group* is a logical group that contains related user-defined programs. The supported user-defined program types include the following:

- Executable
- Command program
- Dynamic load library (on Windows only)
- Stored procedure

You can use the Warehouse System parameters and tokens as program parameters in your user-defined programs. These parameters will be substituted at execution time based on the source or target linked to the user-defined program and your current IBM DB2 Data Warehouse Center configuration.

To define a user-defined program, open the Warehouse → Administrator folder. Then select Programs and Transformers → User-Defined Programs and Transformers → your program group → Define Program. (See Figure 9.80.)

Once you have defined the program, you can create instances of the program in your user-defined program step in the process modeler. You need to make sure the proper warehouse agent and warehouse groups and users are authorized to access this program. Furthermore, the warehouse agent is the one that will execute the program; you must make sure the PATH, library PATH, and CLASSPATH (if necessary) required for this program are known to the warehouse agent. On Windows, you can add the path directories to the system environment variables. On UNIX, you need to add the path directories to the IWH environment file.

Figure 9.81 is an example that defines a user-defined program with one output parameter.

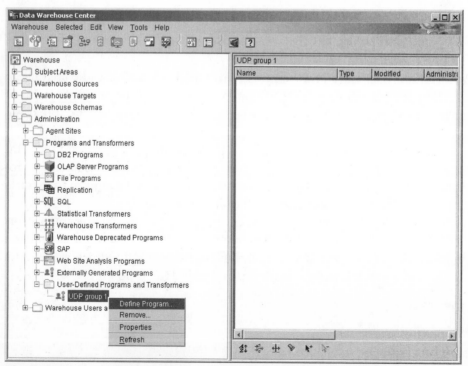

Figure 9.80 User-defined programs.

After your program runs, it should return a return code to the warehouse agent that executed the program. The return code should be a positive integer. If your program does not return a zero return code, the step using the program will fail. The IBM DB2 Data Warehouse Center displays the return code in the Error RC2 field of the Log Details window when the value of Error RC1 is 8410. If the value of Error RC2 is 0, then the program ran successfully without errors.

To return additional status information to the warehouse agent, your program must create a file, called a *feedback file*, that contains the additional status information about the execution of the user-defined program. The directory path and filename for the feedback file is specified in the system environment variable VWP_LOG, where the warehouse agent sits before it calls the warehouse program. Your program must read the value of this environment variable to create the feedback file. After the user-defined program finishes running, the warehouse agent checks whether the feedback file exists. If it exists, the warehouse agent reads and processes the feedback file.

Otherwise, the warehouse agent will not report the errors generated in your program other than the operating system return code that resulted from invoking your program. If the user-defined program cannot create the file, you can continue to run without an error reporting mechanism in your program.

The following shows an example of the feedback file:

```
<RC>20</RC>
<ROWS>0</ROWS>
<MSG>The parameter type is not correct</MSG>
<COMMENT>Please supply the correct parameter type (PASSWORD
NOTREQUIRED,GETPASSWORD,ENTERPASSWORD)</COMMENT>
<BYTES>0</BYTES>
<WARNING>0</WARNING>
<SQLSTATE>12345</SQLSTATE>
```

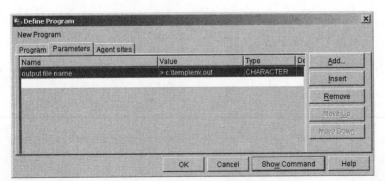

Figure 9.81 Define a user-defined program parameter.

This feedback indicates to the warehouse agent that an error occurred (<WARNING>0</WARNING>), no rows of data were processed (<BYTES>0</BYTES> and <ROWS>0</ROWS>), the message (in the <MSG> element) should be displayed in the warehouse monitoring tool, and RC2 should be set to 20 (<RC>20</RC>) overriding the value returned to the agent. If you do not return a feedback file to the warehouse agent, all nonzero return codes returned to the agent will be treated as an error, and only default messages will be displayed.

Vendor Integration

IBM DB2 Data Warehouse Center supports many processes to transform your data from its original source format to those that meet the requirements of your warehouse end users. These transformations provide a GUI interface to define the parameters of the transformation, as well as a process modeler to help you visualize both data and task dependencies.

In some cases, the warehouse-supported transformations may not meet your needs because of platform or transformation limitations. To address this, the warehouse can manage transformations generated by ETL vendors such as ETI, Ascential, Trillium, and Microsoft, to name a few. The user who is already set up and configured to run in these vendor's environments can easily bridge their tool to seamlessly operate in the Data Warehouse environment.

This section discusses the details of the vendor's transformation processes integration into the IBM DB2 Data Warehouse Center.

ETI•EXTRACT Integration

ETI provides large-scale transformation tools to extract data from multiple sources, transform that data, move it across systems, and then load it to the target warehouse. ETI•EXTRACT is the ETI tool that provides the interfaces and utilities to define and coordinate these transformation (ETL) steps. Once the steps have been defined via the interface, the ETI•EXTRACT product generates applications (in the language of the user's choice) that performs the actual transformations. The basic output of ETI•EXTRACT includes the ETL-generated applications and a "conversion plan." This conversion plan describes the system, order, and error condition logic for the transformation to occur. For example, if a user wanted to pull data from his ordering system in Oracle on a Sun system, transform that data, and move the data to a z/OS system to be loaded into a DB2 for z/OS database, the conversion plan would be something like:

- Query the ORACLE database and transform the data.
- Write output from transformation to a temporary file on Sun.
- FTP the file from Sun to the z/OS system.
- Delete the temporary file on Sun.
- Populate the DB2 for z/OS database with the flat file that was just transferred using the DB2 load utilities.
- Delete the temporary file on z/OS.

Once the ETI•EXTRACT user has defined and tested the transformations that need to take place and a conversion plan has been generated, the ETI•EXTRACT user can then register this conversion plan to the IBM DB2 Data Warehouse Center so that it can manage the scheduling and execution of the ETI•EXTRACT transformation processes. This is accomplished when the ETI•EXTRACT user chooses the function to register the conversion plan to IBM DB2 Data Warehouse Center and provides information such as the system where IBM DB2 Data Warehouse Center resides, the user ID and password for warehouse, and other information.

When the user has entered all of the required information and chooses to register the conversion, ETI•EXTRACT connects to the IBM DB2 Data Warehouse Center system specified, transfers the conversion plan and associated meta data to that system, and then invokes an IBM DB2 Data Warehouse Center function to convert this information into a format usable by the IBM DB2 Data Warehouse Center. Once the transfer and function invocation completes, the ETI•EXTRACT user is notified of the completion status of this request.

ETI•EXTRACT remotely invokes the IBM DB2 Data Warehouse Center function to convert its meta data from an ETI•EXTRACT format to an IBM DB2 Data Warehouse Center format. This function reads the conversion plan and meta data, and based upon this information, it generates IBM DB2 Data Warehouse Center meta data that mimics the conversion plan, but in a format that the IBM DB2 Data Warehouse Center can understand. This ETI•EXTRACT information is converted into IBM DB2 Data Warehouse Center meta data that represents the sources (warehouse sources), targets (warehouse targets), intermediate files (warehouse targets) and generated transformation program (warehouse processes and steps) and data/task flows (data links and step completion actions) and it is imported into the IBM DB2 Data Warehouse Center. Business-oriented meta data can also be optionally imported into the Information Catalog Manager so that your business end users can understand what ETI•EXTRACT transformations are taking place, as well as determine the lineage of their data targets.

After the meta data has been imported into the IBM DB2 Data Warehouse Center, the function returns the processing status to the ETI•EXTRACT user. The phase of the meta data registration is now considered complete, and the IBM DB2 Data Warehouse Center has almost all the information it needs to run the ETI•EXTRACT transformations. If the transfer and conversion completes successfully, the warehouse administrator needs to provide some additional information in order for these transformations to execute properly. This information includes the following:

- Any warehouse user that needs to view/modify these conversions must be added to the generated ETI•EXTRACT security group.

- The passwords for the source and target systems where the data resides.

- Optional descriptive meta data that will further embellish the meaning of the transformation.

- Schedule information for the root transformations (Step 1 in the conversion plan described previously) must be provided so that IBM DB2 Data Warehouse Center knows when to execute the ETI•EXTRACT transformations.

- Optional step flows to other warehouse-managed transformations (e.g., when the last ETI transformation takes place, as in Step 6 in the conversion plan, and completes successfully, start another warehouse step that may then pull from the DB2 for z/OS database and populate an OLAP cube).

Now that all the information has been successfully added/updated in the IBM DB2 Data Warehouse Center, the warehouse steps reflecting the ETI•EXTRACT conversions can be executed on demand or when the specified schedule is met.

To support the ETI•EXTRACT conversions, IBM DB2 Data Warehouse Center provides a set of applications that know how to process the ETI•EXTRACT transformation steps:

ETIEXMVS. Calls ETI•EXTRACT conversions on a z/OS (MVS) system.

ETIEXUNX. Calls ETI•EXTRACT conversions on a UNIX or Windows system.

ETIDLMVS. Deletes intermediate files from a z/OS (MVS) system.

ETIDLUNX. Deletes intermediate files from a UNIX or Windows system.

ETIRCMVS. FTPs an intermediate file on a z/OS (MVS) system to another system.

ETIRCUNX. FTPs an intermediate file on a UNIX/Windows system to another system.

These applications are defined as "user-defined programs" to the IBM DB2 Data Warehouse Center, and the parameters passed to these programs are generated from the meta data sent during the registration process. The parameters to these programs include information such as:

- Host system where the ETI transformation is to execute
- User ID and password to the host system
- ETI program, script, or Job Control Language (JCL) that is to be executed in order to perform the transformation
- ETI transformation type:
    - QUERY—Pulls information from the source systems and writes to an intermediate file
    - POPULATE—Loads the data in the intermediate file to a target system
    - COPY—Copies the intermediate file from the source system to the target system
    - DELETE—Deletes the intermediate files
    - MERGE—Merges multiple intermediate files together into a single intermediate file
    - SORT—Sorts an intermediate file
    - QUERY/POP—Pulls data from a source system and loads it in a target on the same system without intermediate files
- Intermediate files to be deleted

Once all the ETI•EXTRACT transformations have been registered to IBM DB2 Data Warehouse Center and the required meta data has been updated, the user does not modify any of the parameters of the IBM DB2 Data Warehouse Center step other than any required password parameters.

As mentioned earlier, when the first ETI•EXTRACT conversion plan registration occurs, the IBM DB2 Data Warehouse Center administrator must add any other warehouse users to the ETI•EXTRACT security group. This is done by opening the Warehouse → Administration folder, expanding the Groups folder, and adding all the users that need access to the ETI•EXTRACT information to the ETI•EXTRACT Security Group.

When IBM DB2 Data Warehouse Center users connect to GUI and open the Subject Areas folder, they will see that the registration process has created a warehouse subject area. The subject area is named based on the ETI•EXTRACT conversion plan name. For each time the conversion plan is imported into Data Warehouse Center, a new warehouse process is created that contains all of the IBM DB2 Data Warehouse Center steps necessary to complete the ETI•EXTRACT conversion. The processes are named based on the ETI•EXTRACT conversion plan name and the timestamp of when the registration occurred. This allows for the ETI•EXTRACT user to have multiple versions of the same conversion plan so that IBM DB2 Data Warehouse Center will support development, test, and production environments. The production version of the process is usually the process that has schedules and follow-on task flows associated with it.

A sample screen shot is shown in Figure 9.82, which shows the tree view (navigator view) of the warehouse subject area that was created, as well as the warehouse process object as a result of the registration process. The right side of the screen shot shows all of the individual warehouse steps and warehouse source and target objects in the warehouse process.

Right-clicking on the warehouse process object in the tree and selecting Open causes the DWC process modeler to display all of the DWC steps, along with their sources, targets, and data/task relationships in a graphical view.

For example, in Figure 9.83, we can see that the registration process created three warehouse steps that will run the actual ETI•EXTRACT transformations. In this example, QUERY, POPULATE, and DELETE steps were generated. These steps will call the appropriate warehouse application to

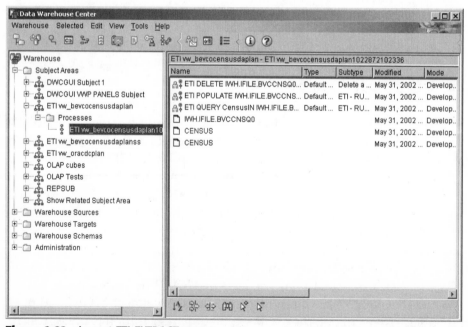

Figure 9.82 Import ETI•EXTRACT steps.

invoke the ETI•EXTRACT transformation on the proper platform. The following example also shows the data lineage (e.g., the CENSUS file is a source to the QUERY step, which produces an intermediate file called IWH.FILE.BVCCNSQ0, which is used as input to the POPULATE step, which will load a different file called CENSUS). Lastly, the registration process determines the appropriate task flow between the warehouse steps (e.g., "on successful completion of the QUERY, start the POPULATE, and upon successful completion of the POPULATE, clean up by calling the DELETE step"). Again, all of this information has been generated based upon the conversion plan and other meta data sent during the registration process.

Note that all functions of IBM DB2 Data Warehouse Center are available on these objects. For example, if you wish to see the columns of the CENSUS file as well as the source database that it has been defined in, you can right-click on the CENSUS object and select Open. This displays all of the meta data associated with the CENSUS file. You can also do this to each warehouse step to view the details of each of those steps.

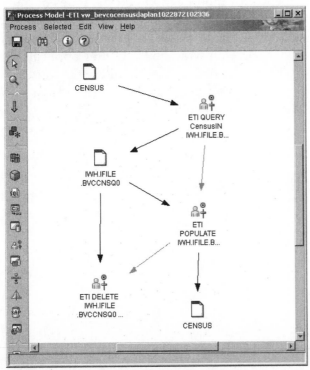

Figure 9.83 Imported ETI•EXTRACT steps.

Also, from this interface, if you wish to change the task flow (e.g., add another warehouse step that pages your administrator and that will be executed in the case where the QUERY or POPULATE fails) or add the schedule to when the root (QUERY) step is to execute, you can do that from this interface.

When you right-click and select Open on one of the steps, a dialog box appears that gives all of the details of the step. The first page of the step notebook shown contains general information about the step. (See Figure 9.84.)

For example, if you open the QUERY step, a step dialog box appears that shows all of the meta data associated with this step. You will notice that this is a *user-defined program* type of step. This is because of the way the integration between IBM DB2 Data Warehouse Center and ETI•EXTRACT was designed. The meta data includes the following:

- The name of the step
- Descriptive information about the step (which can be modified)
- Contact information

All ETI•EXTRACT step types contain similar information and can be modified as necessary. The means for modification and the types of meta data are the same for these steps.

Switching to the Parameters page allows you to modify the parameters that will be passed to the IBM DB2 Data Warehouse Center applications that invoke the ETI•EXTRACT transformation. You should not modify any parameters other than the password parameter and the return code parameter. These parameters contain the information about the ETI•EXTRACT transformation programs that were generated by the ETI•EXTRACT user.

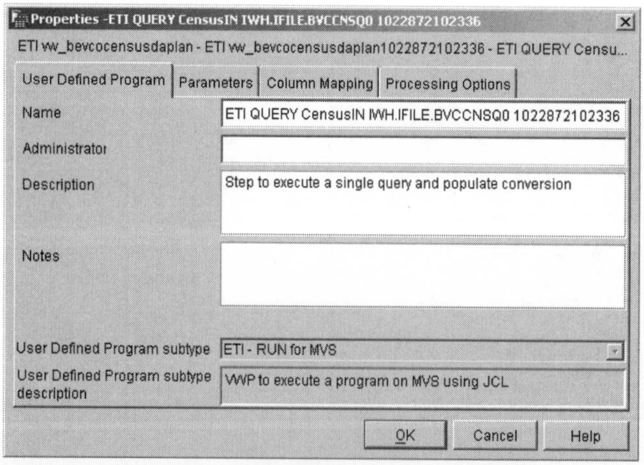

Figure 9.84 Imported ETI•EXTRACT step properties.

Figure 9.85 displays the following parameters:

- Name of the system where the ETI•EXTRACT-generated program is to be executed.

- Name of the program to execute (Windows batch file, UNIX scripts, or MVS JCL).

- Where messages are to be written.

- Type of password to the host system, as well as the password itself; this can be a password or the name of a program that will generate the password.

- Highest return code that is considered successful. IBM DB2 Data Warehouse Center will use the value of this parameter to determine whether the ETI•EXTRACT transformation completed successfully. This has implications for follow-on tasks; if the return code returned from the ETI•EXTRACT conversion is greater than the value specified in this parameter, the transformation is considered a failure, and only "On Failure" or "On Completion" steps will be executed. The IBM DB2 Data Warehouse Center Work in Progress (WIP) dialog box will also show this step as failed. If the value returned from the ETI•EXTRACT transformation is less than or equal to the value of this parameter, the step will be considered a success, and only "On Success" or "On Completion" steps will be executed.

The Column Mapping page is not relevant to this transformation program, since this meta data is embedded in the ETI•EXTRACT transformation itself. In addition, the Processing Options page contains the same options as all other user-defined Processing Options pages.

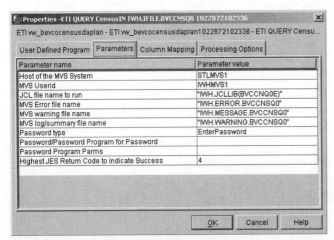

Figure 9.85   ETI•EXTRACT step parameters.

All steps generated from the ETI•EXTRACT registration process are treated like any other step in the IBM DB2 Data Warehouse Center; that is, you can schedule these steps, change the task flows, change the parameters (where recommended), and enhance the descriptive information. Even though there are seven different types of ETI•EXTRACT transformations managed by the IBM DB2 Data Warehouse Center, the properties of the generated warehouse steps for all of these transformation types are the same, except for the parameters page. The parameters page contains different parameters based upon the ETI•EXTRACT transformation that needs to be executed.

Including the types of transformation expands the breadth of the transformations that the IBM DB2 Data Warehouse Center can provide, since it gives you the full power of ETI•EXTRACT to integrate high-end, complex transformations into the data. Remember that these transformations and steps are generated based upon the information you specified in the ETI•EXTRACT. Therefore, you should only need to modify the password information on the parameters page. Modifying any other parameter may cause the step to fail during execution.

Trillium Integration

The Trillium Software System is a name and address cleansing product that reformats, standardizes, and verifies name and address data. The IBM DB2 Data Warehouse Center has integrated these Trillium cleansing functions by reading the Trillium control files and create the corresponding Trillium source, target, and step definition into the warehouse metadata to produce cleansed output data files. You can manage these name and address cleansing warehouse objects inside the IBM DB2 Data Warehouse Center and take advantage of warehouse facilities such as step control flow, the scheduler, warehouse object management, and monitoring. These cleansing steps can be scheduled to run, and the cumulative results can be monitored via the Work in Progress dialog box.

You can use the cleansing functions in the IBM DB2 Data Warehouse Center by starting the Trillium Batch System programs from a user-defined program. The user-defined program is added to the warehouse navigator tree when you import the meta data from the Trillium Batch System script or JCL. The warehouse agent can execute a Trillium Batch System script on various platforms, including AIX, Solaris, Windows/2000, Windows/NT, and z/OS.

To import Trillium meta data into the IBM DB2 Data Warehouse Center, you first create a Trillium Batch System (TBS) script or JCL to execute the TBS commands to perform the desired name and address cleansing. The script/JCL should have been verified to run successfully. Next, use the Import Trillium Meta Data dialog box from the IBM DB2 Data Warehouse Center to create the Trillium name and address cleansing step. (See Figure 9.86.)

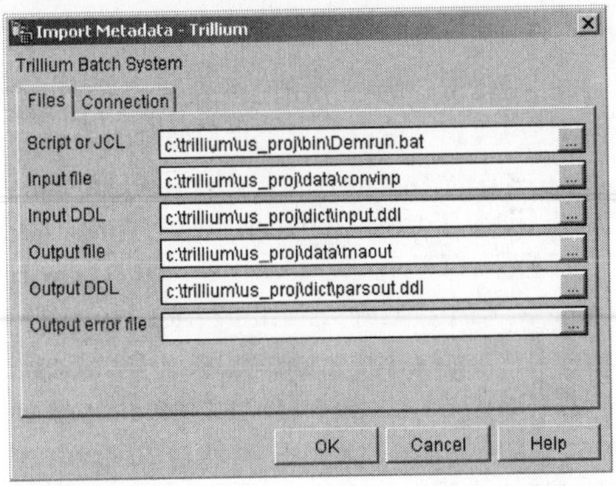

Figure 9.86   Importing Trillium metadata to create a warehouse step.

Once the input files and script are read into the IBM DB2 Data Warehouse Center, the Trillium name and address cleansing step is automatically created in the specified Warehouse process. Figure 9.87 illustrates a process model with Trillium integration. You can promote the step and run the test to execute the TBS script or JCL to do the name and address cleansing.

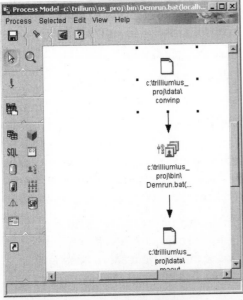

Figure 9.87   Imported Trillium steps.

Ascential Integration

Ascential INTEGRITY is another data cleansing tool that is integrated into the IBM Data Warehouse Center. The INTEGRITY tool allows you to cleanse and re-engineer your data, taking one or more input files and producing one or more "cleansed" output files. The integration between IBM DB2 Data Warehouse Center and INTEGRITY includes the exchange of meta data between the two products and the management of the INTEGRITY cleansing routines.

The warehouse administrator can define the various source and target data sources using the base functions of IBM DB2 Data Warehouse Center. Once these have been defined to IBM DB2 Data Warehouse Center, that meta data can then be exported to an interchange file on disk. Once the warehouse meta data has been exported, the Ascential INTEGRITY (INTEGRITY) tool can read that interchange file and load it into its own private meta data store. Once the meta data is in INTEGRITY, the INTEGRITY user can then use the tool and the imported meta data to define all of the INTEGRITY procedures required to perform the cleansing required.

Once the INTEGRITY procedures have been defined and tested, they can be exported back to the warehouse and used in the warehousing process. The IBM DB2 Data Warehouse Center administrator can schedule these steps (when imported into the warehouse, the INTEGRITY procedures become warehouse steps) and cascade to and from them as any other warehouse transformation. Once these steps are executing, you can use IBM DB2 Data Warehouse Center functionality to monitor the progress of the execution, such as the Work in Progress dialog box.

Ascential INTEGRITY supports the following (noninclusive) types of cleansing and reengineering:

Investigation. Analyzes free-form and single-domain fields. During this process, free-form fields are parsed, patterns revealing field formats are created and the meaning of data in free-form text fields is determined.

Super STAN. Performs the data standardization, formatting, and validation of the data. It may involve converting free-form text into fixed fields and manipulating data to conform to standard conventions.

Super Match. Groups related records and performs matching with external reference files. The matching process involves performing statistical matching, which involves calculating a score based on the probability of a match between two records

Survivorship. Handles conflict resolution and creates a format for data loading.

Ascential INTEGRITY also provides a set of operators that you can use in the INTEGRITY procedures:

Transfer. Copies all or part of input data to the output file.

Collapse. Produces a unique list of values for a data field.

Sort. Reorders the data file.

Parse. Separates free-form text fields to individual fixed fields.

Build. Generates a single record from multiple records from the PARSE operator.

Unijoin. Matches fields to a reference file to perform statistical matching.

Business Name Abbreviator. Converts data in business name fields to abbreviated name keys for use in a matching procedure.

Microsoft OLE DB and Data Transformation Services

You can access data from an OLE DB provider as a DB2 database view. IBM DB2 Data Warehouse Center provides an interface to the IBM DB2 OLE DB Wizard to assist you in creating a DB2 OLE DB table user-defined function. This table user-defined function is responsible for extracting data from the OLE DB source in table format. You can further define a DB2 view against this table user-defined function and access the OLE DB data via this DB2 view.

Microsoft Data Transformation Services (DTS) allows you to import, export, and transform data between OLE DB sources and targets to build data warehouses. DTS is installed with Microsoft SQL Server. All DTS tasks are stored in DTS packages that you can run and access using Microsoft OLE DB Provider for DTS Packages. You can also create DB2 views with the Data Warehouse OLE DB Assist Wizard for DTS packages. When you access the DB2 view, the DTS package is also executed; the target table generated by the DTS package becomes the created DB2 view.

After you create a DB2 view for the OLE DB or DTS in the IBM DB2 Data Warehouse Center, you can use it like any other DB2 view. For example, you can join a DB2 table with an OLE DB source from the same source database in an SQL step. When you use the created DB2 view in an SQL step, the DTS provider is called and the DTS package runs automatically.

Accessing OLE DB

To access OLE DB source in the IBM DB2 Data Warehouse Center, you need to create a DB2 user-defined function and then create a DB2 view against it (see Figure 9.88):

1. From the IBM DB2 Data Warehouse Center navigator, expand the Warehouse Sources tree.

2. Expand a DB2 warehouse source.

3. Right-click on the Views folder, and click on the Create for OLE DB table function. The OLE DB Assist Wizard opens. The wizard walks you through the task of creating a new DB2 view in the Warehouse Source database. This includes building the OLE DB connection string and specifying the table in the OLE DB provider.

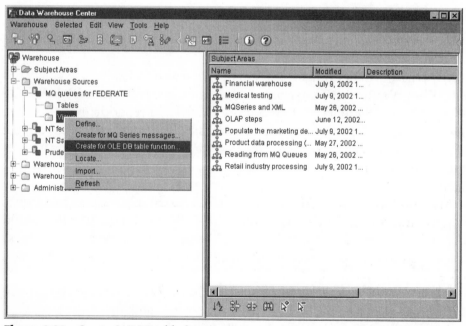

Figure 9.88 Create OLE DB table function.

Accessing DTS Packages

To access a Data Transaction Services (DTS) package, you need to create a view for the DTS package:

1. From the IBM DB2 Data Warehouse Center window, expand the Warehouse Sources tree.

2. Expand the warehouse source that is to contain the view.

3. Right-click on the Views folder, and click on Microsoft OLE DB Provider for DTS Packages.

4. The OLE DB Assist Wizard opens. The wizard walks you through the task of creating a new view in the warehouse source database. This includes helping the user create the OLE DB connection string and identify the desired table in the OLE DB provider.

There are several considerations when accessing DTS packages. For example, to identify a specific table from a DTS package, you must select the DSO Row Set Provider check box in the Options tab of the Workflow Properties window of the Data Pump Task that creates the target table. If you turn on multiple DSO row set provider attributes, only the result of the first selected step is used. When a view is selected, the row set of its target table is returned and all other row sets that you create in subsequent steps are ignored. When you enter the table name for the wizard, use the step name, which is shown on the Options page of the Workflow Properties notebook for the task.

Summary

The IBM DB2 Data Warehouse Center transformation steps are essential to any warehouse iteration. The most frequently used transformation steps are SQL, DB2 utilities, and Replication. For maximal flexibility and performance, user-defined programs (for example, stored procedures) can be invoked as transformation steps. The IBM technology also provides predefined transformations that are critical to the success of any ETL process, for example, generating surrogate keys and period tables to support the foundations of the atomic data warehouse. With transformations to support data pivoting and data inversion, architects can quickly transform data into meaningful information slices as dictated by user communities. It is important not to underestimate transformations such as these. Without the support of the IBM DB2 Data Warehouse Center, ETL programmers would need to use OLAP tools to create the pivot or inversion and then propagate that data back into the warehouse for use by a broader audience. If this is your only alternative, you will most likely never repopulate the warehouse with the data pivot and instead keep all of that information in the data silo of the OLAP tool. The IBM DB2 Data Warehouse Center ensures that we can create informational content and store it in data structures most accessible by all warehouse participants, the RDBMS itself.

The same holds true for transformers such as Correlation, Subtotals, and Moving Average. These transformers empower the warehouse architects to readily create information content at the atomic level, content that was traditionally the domain of other tools.

If there is a tool that supports the evolution of the enterprise information asset, it is the IBM DB2 Data Warehouse Center. With it, we can create more information content, store it at the atomic level, and make it available to the broadest possible audience.

CHAPTER 10

Meta Data and the IBM DB2 Warehouse Manager

Key Issues:

- Warehouse efforts still do meta data poorly. It seems that warehouse project managers continue to relegate the effort to a secondary status rather than as a necessary primary component of any warehouse iteration.

- Although warehouse planners seem adamant to invest heavily in vertical technologies such as ETL or access tools, they often seem less dedicated to investing just as heavily in a technology that horizontally has broad impact on the entire enterprise warehouse effort: a central meta data repository.

The planning effort involved in a repository implementation should be, in many respects, similar to the planning of the data warehouse itself. The same discipline and diligence should be undertaken. This planning should occur synchronously with the warehouse planning, not as an afterthought.

We examine several aspects of meta data in this chapter, starting with a definition of meta data, its repository, sources, and types. We also examine various considerations pertaining to the maintenance of a healthy meta data repository. Then we focus on IBM software that is most responsible for capturing and maintaining meta data, including Information Catalog and Data Warehouse Center. We end the chapter with details on how IBM warehouse meta data can be enriched with meta data from vendor products.

What Is Meta Data?

Meta data is most commonly defined as "data about data". A *repository* is a place where this data is managed and maintained. These are high-level abstract definitions that are generally undisputed but may vary somewhat depending on whom you ask. Attempts to define this broad concept in greater levels of detail and specificity result in greater ambiguity. The principal reason for this is that there are no universal industrywide standards regarding meta data. The intent of this section is to describe a meta data repository in the context of a data warehouse.

An enterprise data warehouse normally includes data from a multitude of sources. These sources include operational data as well as third-party external data. Meta data can be extracted from the various tools, applications, and vendor solutions that are used to supply data to the warehouse. Internal custom applications, relational database management systems (RDBMSs), modeling tools, and enterprise resource planning (ERP) systems are all examples of and important contributors to meta data.

As the data is stored and propagated throughout a typical warehouse environment, each physical data store adds more meta data. For example, the meta data captured at the atomic level will not be the same as that captured at the star or cube level—even for the same subject area. Moreover, the data of a BI environment is both structured (e.g., spreadsheets, relational databases, multidimensional cubes) and unstructured (e.g., Word documents, images).

Another influence on meta data are the core components of warehousing, including ETL, data management, and data access. Each component impacts the type of meta data being generated. For example, as raw data is extracted from source systems, it is cleansed and transformed by applying business rules. The ETL process and the rules themselves are excellent meta data.

It is imperative that the warehouse system and warehouse planners understand the characteristics and properties of the data under the warehouse's care so that the warehouse can be intelligently used. This is the role that a meta data repository plays in the enterprise data warehouse.

Meta data can be as varied as the original data that it attempts to describe. The more accurately and completely we can describe the data in the warehouse, the more we can maximize its success and effectiveness. Following are some examples of meta data that could be appropriate to capture and maintain for a data warehouse:

- Source information describing where the data came from
- Lineage information showing historic data movement
- Column names
- Alias names
- Column sizes
- Transformation rules
- Logic rules
- Transformations task flow
- Update schedules
- Access patterns
- Ownership
- Data quality load results

These are only some of the types of meta data and their sources that can be stored in a meta data repository. There is no universally agreed upon list or standard that indicates which meta data is appropriate for a given enterprise warehouse.

The meta data structures the information in the data warehouse into categories, topics, groups, hierarchies, and so on. As shown in Figure 10.1 and outlined in the following list, meta data provides information about the data within a data warehouse:

- Meta data is "subject-oriented" and is based on abstractions of real-world entities, for example, "project," "customer," or "organization."
- Meta data defines how the transformed data is to be interpreted, for example, whether 5/9/99 means September 5, 1999 (British) or May 9, 1999 (U.S.).

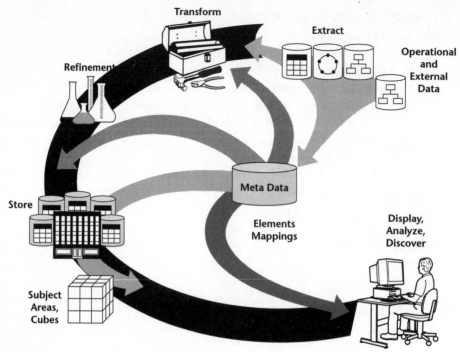

Figure 10.1 Meta data sources.

- Meta data gives information about related data in the data warehouse.
- Meta data estimates response time by showing the number of records to be processed in a query.
- Meta data holds calculated fields and precalculated formulas to avoid misinterpretation and contains historical changes of a view.

The data warehouse administrator's perspective of meta data is a full repository and documentation of all contents and processes within the data warehouse; from an end user perspective, meta data is the road map through the information in the data warehouse.

Classification of Meta Data

Meta data can be categorized in several ways. In this section we discuss three: by type of user, by its degree of formality at origin, and by the context in which it is used.

Meta Data by Type of User

It is not unusual for some to split meta data by user audience. In this case there would be two broad audiences. The first is a technical audience represented by data modelers, DBAs, ETL, and access programmers or even power users. These types of individuals look for information to support ongoing maintenance and growth of the data warehouse. Without technical meta data, the task of analyzing and implementing changes to a decision support system is significantly more difficult and time-consuming. The second user of meta data is the business community. This audience is primarily made up of executives or business analysts. This group needs to have the warehoused data defined for them in business terms—for example, what reports, queries, and data are in the data warehouse; location of the data; reliability of the data; context of the data; what transformation rules were applied; and from which legacy systems the data was sourced.

Meta data users can be broadly placed into the categories of business users and technical users. Both of these groups contain a wide variety of users of the data warehouse meta data. They all need meta data to identify and effectively use the information in the data warehouse. To that end, three traditional categories of meta data that address the requirements of these two audiences exist:

Technical meta data describes the technical attributes of warehouse data.   Examples include data types, source systems, and internal column names. Obviously, IT gains the most benefit from this type of meta data. Technical meta data provides accurate information regarding the data within the domain of the data warehouse and BI environment itself. IBM refers to this meta data as *definitional meta data*.

Operational meta data describes the process-related attributes of warehouse data.   Examples include access patterns, update schedules, and data quality results. This type of meta data is valuable to IT resources as well as business users.

Business meta data describes the business-related attributes of warehouse data.   Examples include load schedules, data ownership, and business rules. This meta data is used primarily by business users and provides a link between the data warehouse and the business community. Business meta data provides users with a road map for access to the data in the data warehouse.

Although meta data can be separated into different categories, with different audiences that benefit, the objective remains the same: better understanding of the warehouse data.

Meta Data by Degree of Formality at Origin

Business, operational, and technical meta data for an organization come from a wide variety of sources and support. The sources range from very formal to completely informal.

First, let's examine formal meta data sources. These sources of meta data have been discussed, defined, documented, and agreed upon by the decision makers of the enterprise. Formal meta data is commonly stored in tools or documents that are maintained, distributed, and recognized throughout the organization. These formal meta data sources populate both technical and business meta data.

Informal meta data consists of corporate knowledge, policies, and guidelines that are not in a standard form. This is the information that people already know and is located in the "company consciousness" or perhaps in a note on a key employee's desk. It is not formally documented or agreed upon; however, the information is every bit as valuable as that in the formal meta data sources. Often, informal meta data provides some of the most valuable information, because it tends to be business related. Note that in many cases much of the business meta data is really informal. As a result, it is critical that this meta data be captured, documented, formalized, and reflected in the data warehouse. By doing this, you are taking an informal source of meta data and transforming it into a formal source. Because every organization differs, it is difficult to say where your informal sources of meta data are; however, the following is a list of the most common types of informal meta data:

- Data stewardship
- Business rules
- Business definitions

Formal meta data is obviously the most readily available to warehouse planners. Even so, there is no standardization of these sources, and, therefore, collecting and keeping current this meta data in one repository still requires significant effort and commitment.

The hardest meta data to collect and keep current is the informal stuff. This type of meta data source fluctuates dramatically, from well-documented sources to Post-it notes. This inconsistency presents real challenges to warehouse planners. Collecting this type of meta data is also labor-intensive. But failure to collect and reconcile this type of meta data into the warehouse may greatly weaken the benefits of building the warehouse in the first place.

Meta Data by Usage Context

Earlier we defined meta data as "data about data." What project planners often miss is that meta data in one context may just be viewed as plain data in another context. The distinction between data and meta data can become very fuzzy.

Let's use two examples to debate whether the user sees data or meta data. In a warehouse implementation, dimension tables will very likely be created. A market dimension may contain columns with the countries, regions, and cities where products are being marketed. The content of this dimension constitutes *data* for warehouse users. When this information is transferred to the OLAP environment to update the outline of a DB2 OLAP Server cube, the data is used to populate the members of the market dimension. For an OLAP user, this information is clearly *meta data*.

For our second example, let's take a product lookup table composed of two columns: one column with the product code and the other with the product name. In the operational environment, product codes are used; however, warehouse users need more explicit information and want to deal with real product names. There will be a transformation required to perform this operation in the warehouse. The lookup table can be considered as meta data, since it expresses the transformation rule, and at the same time it also contains data in the traditional sense.

The point is that it is not crucial to make a very precise distinction between meta data and data itself. However, it is just as important to keep the integrity between meta data and the data it describes as it is to keep relational integrity in a database. An environment where the meta data would not reflect the exact status of the data is not only useless, but it may greatly jeopardize the effectiveness of decision making.

What Is the Meta Data Repository?

Now that we have an understanding of meta data, we need to further discuss what is the repository. As noted previously, the repository provides a place to store meta data. There are several implications that can, and should, be made regarding the characteristics of a meta data repository. In addition to the obvious requirement of a physical area to accommodate meta data, the repository should be capable of managing and maintaining this meta data such that it can be used to better understand the contents of the data warehouse. It should be architected such that the contents of the meta data repository are continually synchronized with the data in the enterprise data warehouse. This means that any structural change to the actual data is also reflected in the repository. Structural changes could include changing a calculation or size for a given column, for example. Some vendors prefer to use the term meta data store rather than meta data repository because the latter tends to formally imply an automated, integrated set of well-managed processes. However, this material will refer to the more commonly used term: meta data repository.

The scope of the meta data repository should include any data that is contained in the enterprise data warehouse. The meta data repository and the data warehouse should be tightly coupled to gain maximum value. All data in the warehouse should be accounted for in the repository. This should include both internal and external data, structured and unstructured.

From an IBM perspective, there are two places where warehouse meta data is being stored. The first is the Data Warehouse Center control database, which keeps the warehouse technical meta data generated during the definition of the warehouse and the warehouse transformations. It can also receive meta data from third-party ETL tools. The second place, the Information Catalog, can be viewed as the central business meta data repository. However, this repository does not generate or refresh any meta data in and of itself. It is merely a persistent database for the storage, maintenance, and publication of meta data. It is fed meta data by other IBM tools, as well as by third-party applications. The most significant contributor to the catalog repository from the IBM world is the Data Warehouse Center, which controls much of the data propagation throughout the warehouse environment.

Feeding Your Meta Data Repository

Different techniques can be used to feed the meta data repository, and many terms have been used in the literature to describe the population of meta data into the repository, such as meta data import and export, meta data exchange, meta data transfer, meta data publication, meta data sharing, and meta data integration. Following are definitions of these terms:

Meta data import.   This operation consists of bringing meta data from a remote environment into the local environment. The system issuing the request for import is the receiver of the meta data. So, it is a pull mechanism.

Meta data export.   This operation consists of sending local meta data to a remote environment. The system issuing the request for export is the sender of the meta data. So, it is a push mechanism.

Meta data transfer.   This refers to the moving of meta data to another environment. It can be implemented via a meta data import or export operation.

Meta data exchange.   This is the ability to move meta data in both directions between two environments. This term is often mistakenly used to express a simple transfer in only one direction. We will use this term only to convey the idea of movement in both directions.

Meta data publication.   This operation consists of moving technical meta data from the Data Warehouse Center control database or from OLAP to the Information Catalog.

Meta data sharing.   This operation does not result in any physical transfer of meta data between environments; it describes the ability to point to meta data stored in another environment. Under this scenario, the central meta data repository does not keep a physical copy of the meta data generated by the other tool.

Meta data integration.   This refers to seamless movement of meta data across environments. True meta data integration is far from being a reality in today's environment.

Unfortunately, manual input of meta data is another important component of the meta data repository feeding process that should not be underestimated.

Benefits of Meta Data and the Meta Data Repository

Enterprise data warehouses have proven to be very valuable in a number of corporations. The time and expense consumed in developing, implementing, and maintaining a data warehouse is usually a significant investment. In fact, the meta data repository is arguably one of the most important components of an enterprise data warehouse. A well-managed, well-architected meta data repository helps protect this investment in several ways, directly and indirectly. The important benefits of a meta data repository include the following:

Enhances the value and usability of the warehouse.   With nearly any product you use, an information or user's guide helps you better understand the product and how to gain the maximum usage. When and if the product changes, the user's guide should change also. The meta data repository is analogous to a user's guide; it must be dynamic, not static.

Improves the quality of the warehouse by helping keep data consistent and accurate for analytical purposes.   Quality business decisions need to be fueled by quality data and quality data usage. The meta data repository helps to keep the warehouse consistent with data in the source systems. Poor decisions made based on a lack of understanding of the data in the warehouse can be costly.

Saves time and money.   Structural changes to the warehouse often require the participation of several resources, including business analysts, database administrators, and data warehouse developers. A meta data repository speeds the systems development process and reduces development costs. This is achieved by better understanding the data in the warehouse and how it is being used.

Involves minimal disruption when IT and business users change positions.   In today's work environment, employee transfers, terminations, promotions, and job changes are common. The meta data helps provide knowledge continuity as key players leave and change their positions.

Provides a consistent, neutral, unbiased understanding of the data. A meta data repository fosters the concept of having a single version of definitions. The enterprise consists of resources from multiple departments, each with its own perceptions of the data. Documenting the "enterprise" perception in the meta data repository helps to eliminate the confusion and misunderstandings that typically occur in these environments.

Increases competitive advantage by the ability to change systems at the pace of business change.   Business changes, such as mergers, acquisitions, product changes, and initiatives to gain market share, are predictable and typically frequent. When these changes occur, the data warehouse structure needs to change. The ability to make data warehouse changes in a timely manner so that there is no adverse impact on the business is crucial. An effective means to complete an impact analysis is often a prerequisite to these changes.

So who benefits from having a meta data repository? The simple answer is everyone involved with implementing, maintaining, and using the data warehouse. The beneficiaries are both internal and external to a corporation. Following are some examples:

- Database administrators
- Auditors
- Business analysts
- Warehouse developers
- Suppliers, customers, stockholders
- Business executives and decision makers

Attributes of a Healthy Meta Data Repository

The meta data repository is one of the most valuable components in an enterprise data warehouse. It is virtually a user's guide for those who access data in the data warehouse. Establishing and maintaining a meta data repository would be useless if users could not access the information stored. Therefore, the information in the meta data repository should be readily available to anyone using the warehouse (business meta data), as well as those who manage and maintain the warehouse (technical meta data).

Meta data repositories are as diverse as data warehouses. There are no universal standards for their content or for their publication. However, some important publication criteria to consider include the following:

Accessible. The meta data repository and its corresponding interface must be accessible to all consumers of both technical and business meta data. Having a meta data repository that is difficult to use or understand will greatly limit the repository's effectiveness.

Secure. Given the broad scope of data contained in the repository and the diverse group of potential users, the repository should appropriately limit access to those who should have it. Additionally, those who have access should only be allowed to view content within their domain.

Consumer-sensitive. Both technical and business meta data is resident in the repository. Although they are both meta data, the publication should reflect the relevant consumer. Interfaces and content, for example, will be very nontechnical and business-oriented for the presentation of business meta data.

Accurate. The data warehouse user trusts that the data contained in the warehouse is accurate in order to make quality decisions. This same level of trust must exist for all those who access and use information from the meta data repository.

Complete. A meta data repository may have a broad range of data, from database schemas to query information to quality information. All relevant information must be made available to meta data users as necessary.

Dynamic. The meta data repository must reflect on a timely basis the changes that have occurred in the definition and description of the warehouse and the warehouse transformations.

Maintaining the Repository

Once established, the meta data repository must be continually upgraded to reflect the current, accurate state of all data warehouse elements.

Although some of the data in the repository will be relatively static (i.e., not requiring frequent updates), some data will be updated constantly. These updates to the repository may be either manual or automated. Following are important considerations for meta data maintenance:

- Updates must be timely.
- Updates should originate from the appropriate source.
- Updates should be driven from the business or system.
- Ideally, maintenance should be performed on integrated meta data.
- A link between technical and business meta data maintenance should be present.
- Changes to any and all meta data elements should be under version control.

There are several additional considerations to remember to ensure a healthy meta data environment. First, avoid meta data hiccups by always having the latest available fix pack. Remember, the more you prolong that upgrade to the latest fix pack, the further behind you will be with the fixes and software enhancements.

Second, make timely backups. It is always a good idea to back up the control database regularly, so you can go back to a recent earlier state of the control database in case anything goes wrong. You should also back up the control database before applying changes via a tag file, since there is no way to undo changes applied via a tag file.

Third, update regularly the statistics with the RUNSTATS utility, and reorganize the data with the REORG utility, so that the meta data about the tables adequately reflects the current status of your tables. This will also ensure optimal performance when accessing the data.

Finally, do not commit the cardinal sin of using SQL to modify meta data. The Data Warehouse Center GUI manipulates the control database to keep the meta data in a consistent state. The only other safe way to manipulate meta data would be through the meta data utilities. Note what this implies: Under no circumstance should any SQL scripts be used to manipulate meta data in the control database directly. This could leave inconsistent meta data, which will cause steps to fail. The bottom line is this: Never manipulate data in the control database directly.

Challenges to Implementing a Meta Data Repository

Having a data warehouse offers a number of advantages to a business in terms of analysis and decision making. As noted previously, the meta data repository supports the data warehouse in many ways. Despite this seemingly mutually convenient arrangement, there are several issues that make implementing a successful, effective meta data repository a challenging endeavor.

The very nature of data warehousing calls for source data from a variety of different platforms, vendors, and applications. Ironically, this goal is very difficult to achieve when you are implementing meta data. There are many reasons for this, but the central reason is that applications and tools may maintain their own repositories—which do not communicate well with each other. Because of a lack of industrywide standards and proprietary formats, islands of meta data usually result with no seamless way to integrate. A number of ETL, ERP, RDBMS, and business intelligence vendors provide meta data repositories that are tool-specific. This results in a disparate, fractured, and inconsistent meta data environment. The most common way to "share" meta data is to bridge these islands with meta data interchange mechanisms.

Despite the market hype, no one solution integrates all the various meta data from different applications and tools—although some vendors attempt to lead potential buyers to believe otherwise. Even within the same company, many vendors have not provided a fully integrated meta data environment. Sadly, this means that enterprise data warehouses in most instances are not fully exploited.

Both corporations and vendors recognize the missed opportunities of not having a fully centralized meta data repository or at least a set of standards to enable meta data sharing. To this end, IBM has led a workgroup that came up with a meta data interchange proposal called the Common Warehouse Meta Data Interchange (CWMI). Unisys, Hyperion, Oracle, and NCR were also involved. This proposal evolved into a standard called the Common Warehouse Metamodel (CWM).

Another challenge to implementing a meta data repository is identifying and documenting the required business meta data. Technical meta data can be extracted from most systems and imported into another meta data system. Business meta data, on the other hand, is principally retained in the minds of various corporate employees. Attempting to extract this information is time-consuming and fraught with the attendant human imperfections (such as interpretational bias).

IBM Meta Data Technology

IBM has a suite of warehouse-centric tools that help create, manage, maintain, and monitor DB2 data warehouses. At the core of this robust technology is a central control database that stores meta data from its own tools, as well as from other non-IBM tools. Selected IBM partners and vendor tools can interchange meta data in this environment. IBM offers several tools to support the data warehouse environment. This section describes the individual tools that are relevant to meta data processing: the Information Catalog, Data Warehouse Center, and third-party partner tools.

Information Catalog

The Information Catalog, a component of the DB2 Warehouse Manager, is the physical database that stores meta data. It is a DB2 Universal Database of persistent data structures that is created and maintained. Beyond the actual table structures, the Information Catalog has search and navigational capabilities to allow meta data managers and user communities to access the meta data stored. Also, the catalog can receive meta data from a number of sources such as the IBM DB2 Data Warehouse Center (DWC) and IBM QMF for Windows, as well as several non-IBM products, including Brio, Business Objects, and Cognos.

Access to the Information Catalog is available via the Information Catalog Center, through a Web interface, or through the Information Catalog Manager API.

IBM DB2 Data Warehouse Center

The IBM DB2 Data Warehouse Center, a component of DB2 Universal Database, is a meta data-driven interface used to actually build the data warehouse. It defines warehouse processes, transforms data, and manages the warehouse. Each operation defined in the Data Warehouse Center results in the generation of technical meta data stored in the warehouse control database, which is a DB2 Universal Database. For more information on the Data Warehouse Center, please refer to chapters 8 and 9.

The IBM DB2 Data Warehouse Center manages the warehouse transformation using the meta data acquired from users and other applications that is stored in its control database. The meta data that is maintained and managed by DWC includes information about the following:

- Authorized users of the warehouse center and their privileges
- The source databases and files that the user will be pulling data from during the execution of warehouse processes
- The target databases and files that the user will be writing to during the execution of warehouse processes
- The transformation algorithms that will be applied on the data as it is being transformed
- User-defined applications that the warehouse center is to manage
- The systems where transformations are to be executed

Tight integration between DWC and the Information Catalog is provided through a publication mechanism invoked by DWC. The mechanism performs an extraction of specified technical meta data stored in the control database and loads the meta data into the Information Catalog database. During this process, the structure of the meta data is transformed to a format and content geared toward the business user community.

DWC can also exchange meta data with other vendor products, using various protocols and standards, such as:

Interchange file.   This is a meta data interchange format that is supported by the IBM DB2 Data Warehouse Center. A tag language file, which is a file containing the meta data for the objects to import, is an example of an interchange file; the tag language, fully documented in the "Data Warehouse Center Application Integration Guide," allows you to create DWC objects with an application in a programmatic fashion.

MDIS.   Meta Data Interchange Standard, a standard developed in the mid-1990s.

CWM.   Common Warehouse Metamodel, a modern standard for interchange of technical warehouse meta data based on XML.

IBM API.   Import and export routines that can be invoked from user scripts and programs.

The protocols or standards available to interchange meta data depend on the products involved. If several protocols are supported for a particular product, the meta data transferred may be slightly different depending on the protocol chosen.

IBM DB2 Data Warehouse Center can be the recipient of meta data stored in the following products:

- Ascential INTEGRITY
- Ascential DataStage
- CA ERwin
- ETI (Evolutionary Technologies International) ETI•EXTRACT
- Evoke Axio
- DB2 OLAP Integration Server and Hyperion Integration Server
- Other IBM DB2 Data Warehouse Center instances

IBM DB2 Data Warehouse Center meta data can be propagated to the following products:

- Ascential INTEGRITY (file definitions)
- DB2 OLAP Integration Server and Hyperion Integration Server
- IBM DB2 OLAP Server and Hyperion Essbase
- IBM's Information Catalog
- Other IBM DB2 Data Warehouse Center instances

Meta Data Acquisition by DWC

Meta data can be loaded into the warehouse using the following general techniques:

- Manual user input via a Java-based GUI; the definition of any object in the warehouse via the IBM DB2 Data Warehouse Center GUI results in the creation of meta data.

- Retrieval of existing source and target database schemas; from the DWC GUI, functions are provided to pull (via ODBC or CLI connectivity) existing meta data stored within those data systems catalogs. The imported meta data includes the definition of tables, as well as files in the source or target database selected.

- Any CWM-compliant warehouse application that supports the following:

  - Source and target definitions

  - Transformation and step definitions

  - Workflow between warehouse transformations

- Any application that can generate the IBM DB2 Data Warehouse Center's interchange file format.

Additionally, specific interfaces have been designed to collect meta data from several ETL and data modeling tools. The process of collecting meta data into IBM DB2 Data Warehouse Center may be implemented via an import process initiated by DWC or by an export process initiated by the other tool. Table 10.1 gives a summary of the meta data that can be collected from specific tools into IBM DB2 Data Warehouse Center, as well as the operation invoked to perform the transfer and standard used.

Table 10.1 IBM DB2 DWC Meta Data Acquisition from Various Tools

SOURCE	STANDARD	OPERATION	SOURCE OBJECTS
ETI•EXTRACT	MDIS	Register Conversion	Conversion
INTEGRITY	IMF +Interchange file	Export Procedure	Procedure
DataStage	Interchange file	Export to DWC	Job
Erwin	Interchange file	Import .er1 file	ERwin physical or logical model
Axio	CWM	Import CWM	Mapping
OLAP/Hyperion Integration Server	Interchange file	Export to DWC	Script to update the outline and to load data in cube
DWC	Interchange file	Import	Subject, Process, Source, Target, Schema, Program

Collecting Meta Data from ETI•EXTRACT

The ETI•EXTRACT tool from ETI is used to define conversions, which represent mappings and data transformations to be applied between source and target environments. Once the conversion is defined, several programs and scripts are generated. The source code programs contain the code required to perform the transformations and mappings specified in the conversion; the execution scripts as well as information on how to run the generated programs in the right sequence.

To collect the meta data about an ETI•EXTRACT-generated conversion into IBM DB2 Data Warehouse Center, you must first install the ETI•Meta Scheduler for Data Warehouse Center, which is an optional priced feature of the ETI•EXTRACT toolset. Then, after the conversion has been defined and the conversion programs have been generated and executed to verify that the conversion executes successfully, you have the choice between two commands to send the information about an ETI conversion, as shown in Figure 10.2.

The TRANSFER CONVERSION TO DATA WAREHOUSE CENTER HOST command performs the following tasks:

- Takes the information produced during the program generation phase of the conversion and translates it into the standard MDIS format.

- Transfers the MDIS-produced file from the ETI workstation environment to the IBM DB2 Data Warehouse Server host.

- Transfers the execution plan to the Data Warehouse Center Server host. The execution plan for Visual Warehouse (VW) is one of the execution plans generated during the generate program phase of the conversion. It contains an ordered list of instructions (programs) to execute.

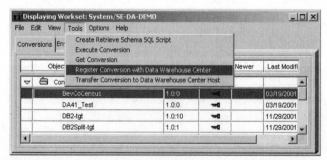

Figure 10.2   ETI•EXTRACT commands to transfer/register conversion.

The REGISTER CONVERSION WITH DATA WAREHOUSE CENTER command performs the same operations as the transfer command but also populates the Data Warehouse Center and the Information Catalog with the meta data related to the conversion.

While the Register Conversion command provides a single operation approach for sending meta data to the IBM DB2 Data Warehouse Center, the preferred approach might be to split this transfer of meta data into two operations. The first operation is performed by ETI•EXTRACT issuing the TRANSFER CONVERSION command. This generates an MDIS file and an execution plan with the necessary meta data about the conversion. Notice that the meta data is not stored at this point in IBM DB2 Data Warehouse Center. The second operation, performed at the discretion of the DWC administrator, invokes the FLGNMVE0 routine, which imports the meta data stored in the MDIS file and the execution plan into DWC and the Information Catalog.

Figure 10.3 shows the meta data flow between ETI•EXTRACT and IBM DB2 Data Warehouse Center. Note that the REGISTER CONVERSION command also generates meta data in the Information Catalog; this activity is detailed later in this chapter.

The MDIS file produced by the TRANSFER CONVERSION or REGISTER CONVERSION operation contains the following information:

- A list of database sources and targets used by the conversion. Within each database, the MDIS file has a description of records, mapped to units in ETI and corresponding to tables, files, or IMS segments. For each record, the MDIS file has a technical description (data type, length, position) of each element, mapped to a part in ETI and corresponding to columns or fields.

- The mapping between source and target, represented in the MDIS file by the object type relationship. Each such object is identified as a three-part name composed by the ETI source part, the word <derived>, and an ETI target part. The relationship expression field in MDIS contains the definition of the filter applied by ETI.

- ETI annotations are included in the MDIS file as Long Description.

In ETI•EXTRACT, conversion properties, schema properties, and filters can be attached to a database, a unit, and a part. The meta data representing the conversion property, the schema property, and the filters appear as application data in the MDIS file. The application data is associated to each database, record, and element in the MDIS file.

Table 10.2 shows how objects in an ETI conversion are mapped into the MDIS file.

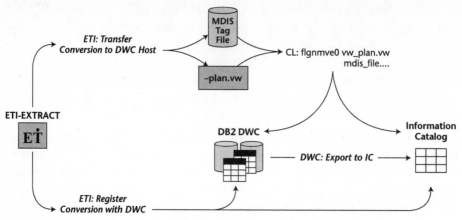

Figure 10.3 Meta data flow: ETI•EXTRACT to DB2 DWC.

Table 10.2 Object Mapping between ETI•EXTRACT and MDIS File

ETI•EXTRACT	MDIS FILE
Database (Source / Target) — name,	Database — name
Conversion properties,	ApplicationData ConvProps
Schema properties,	ApplicationData SchProps
Filters	ApplicationData FilterProps
Unit — name	Record — name, type
Conversion properties,	ApplicationData ConvProps
Schema properties,	ApplicationData SchProps
Filters	ApplicationData
Part / Virtual Part	Element
Name, type, length, annotation	Name, type, position, length, long description
Conversion properties	ApplicationData ConvProps
Schema properties	ApplicationData SchProps
Filters	ApplicationData FilterProps
Map	Relationship — expression

The REGISTER CONVERSION operation performs the same work as the TRANSFER CONVERSION operation, but it adds another task: It uses the information in the execution plan file and the MDIS meta data file to generate meta data in the IBM DB2 Data Warehouse Center. The objects created in IBM DB2 Data Warehouse Center are as follows:

- The source database for the conversion, listed in the Sources notebook; detailed information about the source is found in the Files/Tables page of the notebook, along with a description of each field/column.

- The target database for the conversion, listed also in the Sources notebook; same detailed information about the table and columns, or file and fields, is provided.

- A subject area, which represents the conversion itself, with a name composed of three parts separated by blanks: ETI, the execution plan name, and a suffix of vw. The subject area contains one process named New Process (n); this process holds the list of steps related to the conversion, as well as the sources and the targets for each step. Each step corresponds to one instruction in the execution plan file. The name of the step is composed of up to five parts: ETI, the name of the instruction (query, populate, delete, sort, merge), the input file/table name, the output file/table name, and the time the object was imported in the Data Warehouse Center. If this is the second time this conversion is imported into DWC, a new process is created, and each step in the process has a name containing the time of the import.

- Each step contains information about the ETI program to call (e.g., ETIEXMVS if the instruction in the plan is "RUN, QUERY, mvshost, . . ."), the step to cascade on success (which is the next instruction in the execution plan), and the source. So, the complete sequencing for execution is available in DWC and is directly derived from the order of appearance of the instructions in the execution plan.

- The intermediate files created by the conversion appear in the Sources notebook, as "ETI intermediate files." In the files page, the intermediate filenames are listed.

Table 10.3 shows how objects in the MDIS file and the execution plan file are mapped to IBM DB2 Data Warehouse Center objects.

Table 10.3 Mapping between MDIS, Execution Plan, and DB2 DWC

MDIS AND EXECUTION PLAN	IBM DB2 DATA WAREHOUSE CENTER
Database (Source/Target)	Warehouse Sources
Name, type	Name, type
Record	Files/Tables
Name	Name
Element	Fields/Columns
Name, type, length,	Name, type, length,
long description	description
Execution plan	Subject Area
Filename	(Name: ETI execution plan name)
	Process—New Process
Instruction	Step—name (ETI QUERY)
(e.g., QUERY source target)	Source, target, task flow
i-files	Warehouse Sources
	ETI intermediate files

The commands that can be invoked to transfer meta data from ETI•EXTRACT into IBM DB2 Data Warehouse Center are summarized in Table 10.4.

Table 10.4 Commands to Transfer Meta Data from ETI•EXTRACT to DB2 DWC

SOURCE	TARGET	GUI	COMMAND LINE
ETI•EXTRACT	DB2 DWC	ETI•EXTRACT:	
		Workset>Open MetaStore	
		> Select Conversion	
		> Tools	
		> Register Conversion	
		with DWC	

Table 10.4   *(Continued)*

SOURCE	TARGET	GUI	COMMAND LINE
ETI·EXTRACT	MDIS file + execution plan	ETI·EXTRACT: Workset>Open MetaStore > Select Conversion > Tools > Transfer Conversion to DWC Host	
MDIS file + execution plan	DB2 DWC		flgnmve0

Collecting Meta Data from INTEGRITY

The INTEGRITY product, initially developed by Vality and acquired by Ascential, is a comprehensive development environment for achieving data quality. The tool provides a set of integrated modules for accomplishing data reengineering tasks such as data investigation, data conditioning, data matching, relationship building, conflict resolution, and data formatting. The successive phases of this re-engineering process generate procedures that analyze and transform data in a source file and produce after several phases one or more files with re-engineered data.

Meta data about the procedures generated by INTEGRITY and about source files and generated files can be transferred to IBM DB2 Data Warehouse Center. However, before meta data can be transferred, INTEGRITY extension software must be installed. There are two components to install: the Ascential Extensions for Buildtime and the Ascential Extensions for Data Warehouse Center. The Extensions for Buildtime are stored on the INTEGRITY client workstation. The Extensions for Data Warehouse Center are stored by default in the IBM\sqllib\bin subdirectory on the Warehouse Manager server.

Two types of INTEGRITY procedures can be defined and exported to IBM DB2 Data Warehouse Center:

Prebuilt procedures.   These are provided with the INTEGRITY code; they incorporate a number of data re-engineering operations into one procedure. Prebuilt procedures provided are Investigation, Super-STAN, SuperMATCH, and Survivorship.

Built procedures.   These are constructed by the user and are composed of a number of basic INTEGRITY operations.

When an INTEGRITY procedure is exported to IBM DB2 Data Warehouse Center, the following activities take place:

1. Meta data associated to the procedure is stored into an IMF (INTEGRITY Meta data Format) file on the local INTEGRITY file system.

2. The IMF meta data file is transferred to the DB2 Data Warehouse Center platform.

3. The IMF file is converted into a tag language file (tag file).

4. The tag language file, which contains the meta data describing the procedure, is imported into DWC.

For each procedure exported from INTEGRITY, a step and a process are created in IBM DB2 Data Warehouse Center. The step can then be promoted and scheduled for execution.

The following tasks must be performed in order to export the meta data about the procedure to DWC:

1. From INTEGRITY, stage each procedure you want to export. To stage a procedure, choose a procedure name, and select Run. From the Run options window, select Stage. The staging step creates on your client the required files to execute the run procedure, and it transfers the files to the INTEGRITY server using FTP. It also builds a JCL or shell script. This staging operation is part of the normal INTEGRITY process, even when the procedure is not exported to DWC.

2. From INTEGRITY, select the Export Built Procedures, or Export Prebuilt Procedures item on the Data Warehouse Center menu; and then select the procedures to export.

3. Before the export starts, INTEGRITY displays an Export Profile, set up previously, along with the location of the IBM DB2 Data Warehouse Center directories and the login information. A run profile must also have been defined previously.

If the procedure was already exported, and the corresponding step in IBM DB2 Data Warehouse Center is in test or production mode, then re-exporting the procedure results in an error. For the export to be successful, the step must be demoted to development mode first.

Table 10.5   Object Mapping between INTEGRITY and IBM DB2 DWC

ASCENTIAL INTEGRITY	IBM DB2 DATA WAREHOUSE CENTER
Project—Name, description	Subject Area—Name, description
Procedure	Process—New Process (n)
Procedure—Name, description	Step—Name, description
Input Data Files—Name, description	Source(s)—Name, description
Result Data Files—Name, description	Target(s)—Name, description
Procedure	Program Group—Vality
	Program—Name, description
Project—Name, description	Warehouse Target—Name, description
Data Files—Name, description	Files—Name, description
Fields—Name, start, length, description, type	Fields—Name, start, length, Description, type

Table 10.5 shows the mapping of objects between Ascential INTEGRITY and IBM DB2 Data Warehouse Center, as well as the meta data transferred. In Ascential INTEGRITY, the main object types are as follows:

Projects.   These are composed of data files and procedures to re-engineer the data files.

Data files.   These are used as input and output of the re-engineering process.

Procedures.   These describe the re-engineering activity.

When an Ascential INTEGRITY procedure is exported to IBM DB2 Data Warehouse Center, there is also some additional contextual meta data information that is being transferred, such as the project the procedure belongs to and the files that are used as input and output to that procedure. Note that each procedure being exported results in the creation of a separate process in DWC. The detailed description of each of the operations used by the procedure is not part of the meta data transferred. Information about the order in which the procedures should be executed is not explicitly transmitted as part of the meta data. However, the warehouse administrator can discover the correct order by using the Show Related feature for each target file, which shows the name of the step using this file as input. With this information, it is easy to define how the steps should be cascaded.

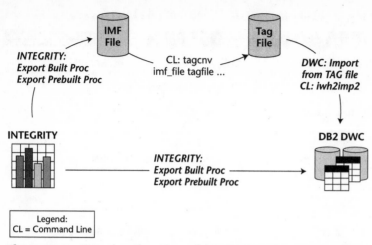

Figure 10.4 Meta data flow: Ascential INTEGRITY to IBM DB2 DWC.

Figure 10.4 shows the meta data flow between Ascential INTEGRITY and IBM DB2 Data Warehouse Center. Note that meta data can also be transferred from IBM DB2 Data Warehouse Center into Ascential INTEGRITY. This is detailed later in the *Transmission of DWC Meta Data to Ascential INTEGRITY* section.

Table 10.6 provides a summary of the commands available either from the GUI or from the command line to perform the transfer of meta data from Ascential INTEGRITY into IBM DB2 Data Warehouse Center.

The transfer of meta data between INTEGRITY and IBM DB2 Data Warehouse Center can be done in one single operation, or it can be decomposed into multiple tasks. The INTEGRITY administrator can just export the meta data about a procedure into an IMF file. Please note that specifying an invalid hostname in the Export profile results in the interruption of the execution just after the IMF file is produced on the INTEGRITY system. The IMF file can be converted into a tag file by using the tagcnv routine (refer to the INTEGRITY documentation for a complete explanation of the parameters to provide). The tag file can eventually be imported by the DWC administrator using either the Data Warehouse Center GUI or the command-line interface.

Table 10.6   Commands to Transfer Meta Data from INTEGRITY to DB2 DWC

SOURCE	TARGET	GUI	COMMAND LINE
INTEGRITY	DB2 DWC	INTEGRITY: Data Warehouse Center > Export Procedures	
INTEGRITY	.imf file	INTEGRITY: Data Warehouse Center > Export Procedures	
.imf file	.tag file		tagcnv
.tag file	DB2 DWC	DB2 DWC: Warehouse > Import Meta Data > Tag Language > Import File name	iwh2imp2 tagfile

Collecting Meta Data from DataStage

The DataStage product, developed by Ascential, consists of a set of tools for designing, developing, compiling, running, and administering applications that perform ETL operations. Extracting data from sources, performing data transformations, and loading a target with the resulting data are examples of the operations defined by DataStage.

A user typically creates DataStage jobs using the DataStage Designer GUI. A DataStage job consists of a series of individual stages, linked together to describe the flow of data from a data source to the data warehouse. A stage describes a particular operation performed on the data, such as an extraction from a data source or a data transformation.

Meta data about the ETL jobs created in DataStage can be transferred into IBM DB2 Data Warehouse Center. This meta data transfer involves the following activities:

1. DataStage jobs, created with the DataStage Designer tool, are exported as DataStage Export files (DSX).

2. DSX files are converted into tag files.

3. Tag files are imported into IBM DB2 Data Warehouse Center.

Before such a transfer can be initiated, you must install the IBM DWC Interface, which can be found on the Ascential DataStage Server CD-ROM. The IBM DWC Interface installation has two parts:

■ A client installation, performed on the DataStage client workstation. It is here where the DWC export is initiated.

■ A server installation, performed on the platform where the DataStage server and the DWC agent are located.

The transfer of meta data about DataStage jobs is activated using the DataStage Manager tool, as shown in Figure 10.5. A wizard helps you define the parameters required for this meta data transfer.

Table 10.7 shows the mapping of objects between Ascential DataStage and IBM DB2 Data Warehouse Center, as well as the meta data transferred.

When a DataStage job has been transferred to IBM DB2 Data Warehouse Center, a process and a step are created. Their name is composed of three parts: the name of the DataStage job, the word "Process", and a timestamp.

The process is put in the subject area specified on the DWC Export Wizard page used to define the subject area name. This subject area is created in the IBM DB2 Data Warehouse Center if it did not exist already.

A warehouse source or target is created for each table or file used as a source in the DataStage stage, or file used as the output of a stage, respectively. The name is composed of three parts: the name of the DataStage job, the name of the table or the file, and a suffix (SRC for a source and TGT for a target). Each warehouse source or target contains the name of one table or file.

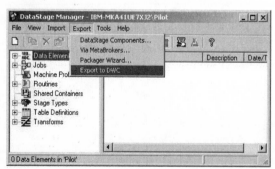

Figure 10.5 Export of a job to IBM DB2 DWC from DataStage Manager.

Table 10.7   Object Mapping between Ascential DataStage and IBM DB2 DWC

ASCENTIAL DATASTAGE	IBM DB2 DATA WAREHOUSE CENTER
Job—Job name	Process—JobName_ Process_Timestamp
	Step—JobName_Process_Timestamp
	Warehouse Source—JobName_SourceName_SRC
	Warehouse Target—JobName_TargetName_TGT

If they do not already exist, a DataStage program group, named DataStage, and a program template, named DataStage Server Job Executor, are also created with attribute values specified in the DWC Export Wizard.

Note that information about the individual stages of the job is not transmitted as part of the meta data export.

The meta data transmitted is mainly intended for allowing the warehouse administrator to schedule DataStage jobs within the IBM DB2 Data Warehouse Center and to link these jobs with other IBM DB2 Data Warehouse Center steps for execution.

Collecting Meta Data from ERwin

IBM DB2 Data Warehouse Center provides functionality to read CA's ERwin 3.5.2 models and format that meta data for import into IBM DB2 Data Warehouse Center. A modeling expert can define the target and source schemas using ERwin's modeler. Both the physical and the logical models can be created in the tool. Once an ERwin model is completed, the DWC administrator can use IBM DB2 Data Warehouse Center functionality to read that model and import that meta data into DWC. Once the meta data is in DWC, it is treated as any other source and target definitions and can be used in any step that requires a table definition.

Figure 10.6 shows the menu options in IBM DB2 Data Warehouse Center for importing meta data from ERwin.

The transfer of meta data from Erwin to IBM DB2 Data Warehouse Center can be performed using the DWC GUI, as shown in Figure 10.6, or it can be achieved in two separate steps using the following commands:

1. The FLGERWIN command takes as input an .er1 file and produces a tag file.

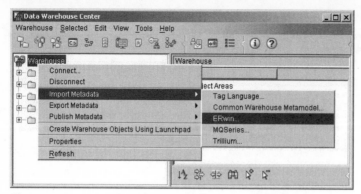

Figure 10.6 Importing ERwin meta data into IBM DB2 DWC.

2. The IWH2IMP2 command takes the tag file just created and imports the meta data into DWC. It is also possible to do this import from the DWC GUI by selecting the Tag Language option in the Import Meta Data menu.

Figure 10.7 presents the commands available either from the DWC GUI or from the command line to perform the transfer of meta data.

Table 10.8 shows the mapping of objects between ERwin and IBM DB2 Data Warehouse Center, as well as the meta data transferred.

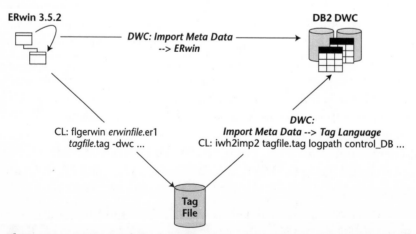

Figure 10.7 Commands for importing meta data from ERwin into IBM DB2 DWC.

Table 10.8 Object Mapping between Erwin and IBM DB2 DWC

CA ERWIN	IBM DB2 DATA WAREHOUSE CENTER
Database	Warehouse Target
Name, version, description	Name, type, description
Tables	Tables
Name, owner, comment	Name, schema, description
Columns	Columns
Name, type, length,	Name, type, length,
scale, nulls, comment	scale, allows nulls, description
Diagram	Warehouse Schema
Name, author, definition	Name, administrator, description
Entities	Tables
Name, definition	Name, description
Attributes	Columns
name,	name,
key group membership	warehouse primary/foreign key

Collecting Meta Data from Axio

The Axio product, developed by Evoke, automates the analysis of existing data sources through a process called *data profiling*. Data profiling includes column profiling, data dependency discovery, and redundancy analysis, and it results in the automatic generation of a data model in third normal form that expresses the desired business rules. The resulting data model is stored in the Evoke Repository. The knowledge acquired with data profiling is leveraged by Axio to create a new database design fully supported by the source data and to generate accurate source-to-target mapping and transformation specifications.

The meta data associated to this source-to-target mapping and the transformation specifications can be transferred to IBM DB2 Data Warehouse Center. The meta data stored in the Evoke Repository is first exported to a CWM conformant XML file. This XML file can then be imported into IBM DB2 Data Warehouse Center in one of two ways:

- Using the DWC GUI, by selecting in the Warehouse folder menu: Import Meta Data>Common Warehouse Metamodel.

- Using the CWMImport command, from the command line.

A successful import of meta data results in the creation of the following objects in IBM DB2 Data Warehouse Center:

- A Subject Area.
- A Process in that Subject Area.
  - Transformation steps: Each step is a program that maps and transforms a column of the source table (or file) into a column in the normalized target table (or file).
  - Source tables (or files) and normalized target tables (or files).
- A Warehouse Target, which contains the definition of all the source tables (or files) and normalized target tables (or files). For each table (or file), the complete definition of each column (field) is also provided.
- A Program Group, named "Mapping between Columns," which contains one program that the Axio product invokes to perform the mapping.

Collecting Meta Data from IBM OLAP Integration Server

The IBM OLAP Integration Server product and Hyperion Integration Server product provide a suite of tools to transform a relational data source into a multidimensional structure of an OLAP database. The process involves the following:

- Building an OLAP model, which presents a dimensional view of the relational data source schema
- Developing a metaoutline, which defines the dimensions and the semantic levels (the hierarchy of members) within the dimensions of a DB2 OLAP Server outline
- Creating a DB2 OLAP Server outline and loading data into a DB2 OLAP Server database

The metaoutline is an abstraction of an outline that defines domains such as GEOGRAPHY, REGION, and CITY. From a metaoutline, one or more outlines can be generated containing the specific instances in each domain. For more information regarding the DB2 OLAP Server outline, refer to Chapter 11.

Based on the specification of the metaoutline, scripts are automatically generated by the tool to load the members in the outline and to load the data in the DB2 OLAP Server database. These scripts can be saved and then run periodically to update the outline and load the data in the cube.

The meta data associated with the generation and loading of cubes can be transferred to IBM DB2 Data Warehouse Center. Once this OLAP meta data (cube information, the tables used by the cubes, and the applications that generate the cubes from the tables) is in IBM DB2 Data Warehouse Center, the DWC administrator can then include those OLAP applications as part of the warehouse building process.

For example, if you are building a warehouse from multiple sources that will eventually end up as OLAP cubes for business users to analyze data, you can define the transformations that will take the data from the source systems, transform it, and write it to dimension and fact tables in a warehouse. Once the data is in the warehouse, you can then execute the OLAP applications that read from the warehouse and generate the cubes used by the business user.

Having this type of processing managed by warehouse assures the warehouse users that the cubes contain the latest information from their sources. Again, this type of functionality is possible because the warehouse pushes meta data about the target tables it is managing to the OLAP tools. And the OLAP tools push the meta data about the applications that it generates back to DWC. The DWC administrator can control, via scheduling and task flow, how and when the cubes are regenerated (see Figure 10.8).

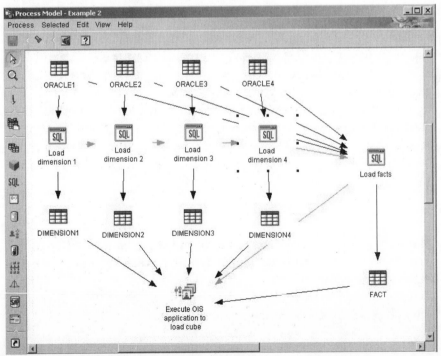

Figure 10.8 OLAP meta data process model.

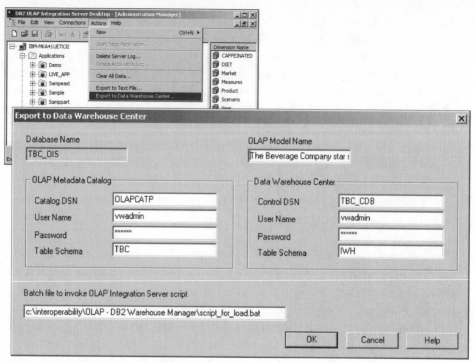

Figure 10.9 Export OLAP Integration Server meta data to IBM DB2 DWC.

The transfer of meta data is initiated on the DB2 OLAP Integration Server system, using the FLGNXOLV command from the command line, or the "Export to Data Warehouse Center" action item in the DB2 OLAP Integration Server GUI, as shown in Figure 10.9.

Notice that the export interface requests a batch file; the interface does not directly use the name of the scripts generated by the OLAP Integration Server tool. This batch file is very easy to construct. It contains one line with the OLAPICMD command to invoke the generated script in the following format:

```
OLAPICMD  < script_filename  > log_filename
```

For the export to complete successfully, the dimensions in the model must already have been defined as tables within a warehouse source in the IBM DB2 Data Warehouse Center.

The objects created in IBM DB2 Data Warehouse Center after the export completes successfully are as follows:

- A Subject Area, named "OLAP cubes."

- A process, with a four-part name identifying the cube; the four-part name is composed of the OLAP server system name, the application name, the database name, and the outline name.

- One step, which is a user-defined program that takes as parameter the batch program file mentioned during the definition of the export.

- One or more tables, as sources for the step; these tables, which contain the data to build the outline and load the data in the cube, had to be defined beforehand as part of a warehouse source.

- A user-defined program group, named OLAP Integration; this program group contains one program subtype named "Build OLAP Cube," which executes the HISEXNT.exe program, with the name of the batch file as parameter.

Exchanging Meta Data between IBM DB2 Data Warehouse Center Instances

One of the tasks that comes with every warehousing project is to manage the meta data associated with it. IBM DB2 Data Warehouse Center stores all its meta data in the control database that is initialized by the user. Meta data management is done via the DWC GUI. The GUI manipulates the control database to reflect the changes made by the user and keeps the meta data in a consistent state. So, for a single-system warehouse installation, hardly any meta data management is required, except for perhaps regular backups of the control database, which is part of the DBA's regular activities. However, implementation of warehousing projects typically involves a test system and a production system. Processes are developed on the test system, tested, and then moved to the production system. Some situations involve various satellite data marts that need to reflect, onto the main server, the changes in the changing dimensions. Another situation involves the addition of new data marts, whose meta data may need to be combined with the meta data on the main warehouse. Either way, in many cases there is a need to move meta data between two or more warehouse installations.

Following are some general tips on the best way to manage meta data, along with some of the utilities available to move meta data between two or more Warehouse Manager installs.

Maintaining Test and Production Systems

Once the processes are developed and tested on the development system, they must be moved to the production system. A good way to start is to duplicate the control databases. This can be done using the db2move export/import utility. Here are the steps involved:

1. Export the development control database using the db2move utility:

   ```
   db2move devdb export
   ```

2. Create the control database on the production machine:

   ```
   create db proddb
   ```

3. Import the development control database into the production system:

   ```
   db2move proddb import
   ```

You should then use the warehouse control database management utility to initialize this database (proddb) as the control database on the production system. Next, using the DWC GUI, you must change the source, target, and agent site definitions in the production system to point to the production sources. From the warehouse meta data perspective, it is important for the administrator to understand when to use the db2move export/import utility as opposed to warehouse meta data export/import. The rule is simple: Whenever the whole control database needs to be duplicated into another system, db2move should be used. For any other incremental changes to warehouse processes, sources, targets, and so on, warehouse meta data export/import should be used. The meta data export and import utility retrieves and updates existing objects from the control database if they already exist and validates the meta data being updated to ensure that the changes via the tag or XML file leave the meta data in a consistent state. The downside to this is that warehouse meta data export/import is slower than db2move; however, it offers more granularity.

Meta Data Exchange Formats

Warehouse meta data export and import utilities support two formats: IBM's tag language and Object Management Group's (OMG) CWM format, which is in XML. When the tag export format is used, a file containing object definitions is generated, and this file is in IBM's proprietary tag language format. With CWM export, an XML file that conforms to CWM standard is generated.

Tag Export and Import

The tag export and import utilities are useful to move definitional meta data between data warehouse installations. Meta data objects like processes, agent site definitions, warehouse schemas, user-defined program definitions, and source/target definitions can be moved from one installation to another. The Warehouse Export panel allows you to select objects that are to be exported and launch the utility with the selected options. Figure 10.10 shows the menu choices to access the tag dialog box, and the tag export box itself is shown in Figure 10.11.

Alternatively, you can use the command-line version of the same. This is documented in the "Application Integration Guide." The generated tag file and associated binary files (files with numerical extensions) can be moved to another system where the IBM DB2 Data Warehouse Center client is available and then be imported. They can also be moved across platforms (currently supported on Windows, AIX, and Solaris). When files are being moved across platforms, you should use ASCII mode for the tag and .inp files, and binary mode for the files with the numerical extensions.

When using export and import utilities, you should keep a couple of things in mind. Because these utilities do a lot of in-memory processing and repeatedly access the control database, they are very memory- and CPU-intensive. It is a good idea to limit other activities on the system. Also, since the memory buildup can be considerable, it is better to export and import meta data in smaller installments instead of one huge export and import.

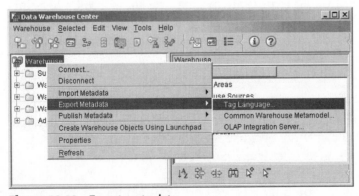

Figure 10.10   Export meta data.

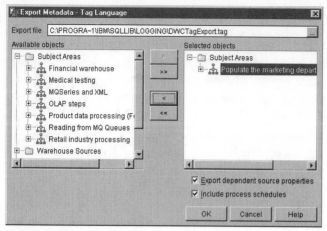

Figure 10.11 Tag language export.

When an export is being processed, there may be more objects included in the tag files than just the ones selected during the export specification. Indeed, the tag file is complete in itself: For example, all the referenced objects are automatically included and exported. So if you select a process to export, the sources and targets used by the steps, as well as dependent steps and processes, are automatically included. You have the option to exclude the source definitions during export; however, the target system should have those sources defined in order to be able to import that tag file. Otherwise, the user will get an error.

Exporting meta data to produce smaller tag files is a little tricky, though, and should be done with two issues in mind: data dependency and cascading.

You need to be aware that Export always exports steps that have a data dependency. For example, let's say Process P1 has Step S1 that populates T1, and Process P2 has Step S2, which has a source T1 such that the following dependency is established:

```
S1 -> T1 -> S2 -> T3 ....
```

Given this scenario, if you export only Process P2, then P1 will be exported in the tag file as well, because S2 is dependent on S1 for its data. The data dependency goes backward. So, even if you export P2 only, P1 will be included in the tag file as well. In these cases exporting P1 and P2 separately will not help. You might as well export them together.

The second issue is cascading. If a step S1 in Process P1 cascades a step S2 defined in process P2, then step S2 is considered to be a shortcut step in process P1. In this case, if process P1 is selected for export, then process P2 will also be exported.

Before importing a tag file, you should understand that the import utility applies whatever is in the tag file to the control database. So you need to be extra careful to ensure that the correct tag file is imported into the control database. You should also do a backup of the control database before running the import utility.

Initially we mentioned that meta data export and import utilities move only definitional meta data. This means that any meta data that is relevant to changes as a result of running a step is not carried as part of the tag file: For instance, no runtime meta data is included in the tag or XML file. Therefore, if transformers were enabled for target definitions from the system where the tag file is generated, the user will explicitly have to enable transformers wherever the tag file is imported.

Additionally, when importing meta data about a process more than once, you must consider the notion of promotion. If the steps in that process have been promoted, and the process is reimported, the import will fail. Therefore, it is first necessary to demote all the steps in that process at the production location before the process can be re-imported.

CWM Export and Import

Most of what has been said for the tag export and import utility in terms of behavior is true for CWM as well. The main differences between the two utilities are the language of interchange, which is XML for CWM, and, more importantly, the conformance to CWM 1.0 DTD. This facilitates exchange of meta data between vendors who support the CWM standard. However, it is important to realize that meta data in IBM DB2 Data Warehouse Center is composed of a richer set of object types and properties than what is specified by CWM. The way this is handled is that all the standardized objects are exported as CWM objects and the rest are exported as tag value pairs. Any other warehouse vendor that would like to utilize this (CWM-conformant) XML file would understand the CWM objects and will ignore the tag value pairs, thus facilitating exchange of meta data. The same process works vice versa, when IBM DB2 Data Warehouse Center needs to capture meta data from other warehousing tools.

Transmission of DWC Meta Data to Other Tools

Meta data within IBM DB2 Data Warehouse Center can be propagated to other tools using the following:

- Any CWM-compliant warehouse application supporting the following:
  - Source and target definitions

- Transformation and step definitions
- Workflow between warehouse transformations
- Any application that can read the DWC's interchange format—the tag language that allows you to read the definition of Data Warehouse Center objects with an application in a programmatic fashion for use within that application

Specific interfaces have been provided to facilitate the transmission of IBM DB2 Data Warehouse Center meta data. The process of meta data transmission to other tools may be implemented via an export command initiated by DWC or by an import command initiated by the other tool. Table 10.9 gives a summary of the type of meta data transmitted to specific tools, as well as the operation invoked to perform the transfer and the standard used.

Transmission of DWC Meta Data to IBM Information Catalog

Data Warehouse Center provides built-in functions that allow a DWC administrator to publish selected meta data to the IBM Information Catalog so that it can be viewed by typical (non-DBA) end users. The functions include a GUI for selecting various source data, target data, transformation processes, and warehouse schemas. Once the data is selected, the administrator may publish that meta data to a specific Information Catalog. The meta data is converted to a more "end user" format, such that users can see all of the meta data about the warehouses that IBM DB2 Data Warehouse Center is managing and, if necessary, can drill through the meta data to determine the lineage and transformations of the data as it was transformed from the original source to the final warehouse target format. (See Figure 10.12.)

Table 10.9 IBM DB2 DWC Meta Data Transmission to Various Tools

TARGET	STANDARD	OPERATION	SOURCE OBJECTS
Information Catalog	Interchange file	Publish meta data	Subject, Process, Source, Target, Schema
OLAP/Hyperion Integration Server	Interchange file	Export meta data	Warehouse Schema

Table 10.9 *(Continued)*

TARGET	STANDARD	OPERATION	SOURCE OBJECTS
DB2 OLAP Server	–	Update outline step	Dimension table
INTEGRITY	Interchange file	Import data dictionary	Source files
DWC	Interchange file	Export	Subject, Process, Source, Target, Schema, Program

IBM DB2 Data Warehouse Center also provides the capabilities to synchronize the technical meta data in DWC with an Information Catalog so that changes made to the meta data in IBM DB2 Data Warehouse Center are reflected in the Information Catalog. The DWC administrator can determine the frequency with which these changes are synchronized. The Information Catalog also keeps track of the last time each object in the Information Catalog was updated and the time the catalog initially created the object.

The following example illustrates how the meta data about a process (Figure 10.13) in the IBM DB2 Data Warehouse Center is presented in the IBM Information Catalog (Figure 10.14). The data lineage is represented in Figure 10.15. It provides information on how the transformation steps are being cascaded, as well as the complete tree of transformations leading back to the data sources.

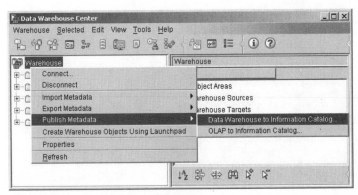

Figure 10.12   Integration with ICM.

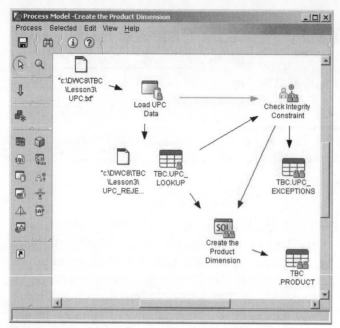

Figure 10.13   Example of a process in IBM DB2 DWC.

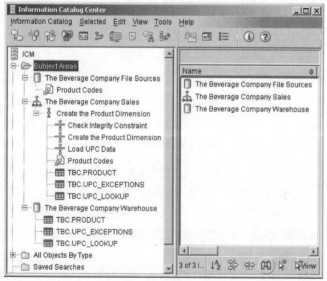

Figure 10.14   Meta data about the process in the Information Catalog Center.

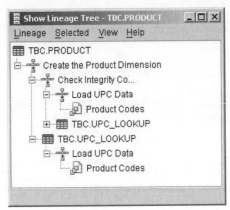

Figure 10.15   Data lineage displayed in the Information Catalog Center.

Transmission of DWC Meta Data to OLAP Integration Server

IBM DB2 Data Warehouse Center provides built-in functions that allow a DWC administrator to publish meta data about the target tables and star schemas defined in the warehouse to the IBM OLAP Integration Server and Hyperion Integration Server (OLAP) products. These functions take the target schema definitions from IBM DB2 Data Warehouse Center and write that meta data to the meta data structures of each product. The warehouse schema in DWC is converted into an OLAP model in the Integration Server product. Target schema information, as well as all relevant relationships between the targets, can then be used by these OLAP products to define metaoutlines, as well as define and build OLAP cubes. Figure 10.16 shows the menu options for the OLAP Integration Server Export utility.

Remember that you must create a warehouse schema that shows the relationships between the tables before you can export this meta data to IBM DB2 OLAP Integration Server (OIS) or Hyperion Integration Server (HIS). Figure 10.17 illustrates a warehouse star schema defined in IBM DB2 Data Warehouse Center. Figure 10.18 shows how this star schema is represented as a model in the DB2 OLAP Integration Server product after the meta data has been exported.

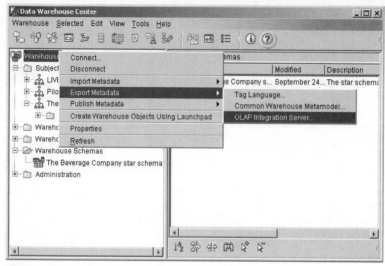

Figure 10.16   OLAP Integration export utility.

The function used to export the meta data about a warehouse schema to the Integration Server product can be invoked from the IBM DB2 Data Warehouse Center GUI, as shown in Figure 10.16, or from the command line using the FLGNXHIS command. Table 10.10 provides a summary of the commands available either from the GUI or from the command line to perform the transfer of meta data.

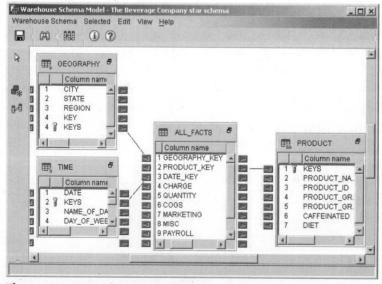

Figure 10.17   Warehouse star schema.

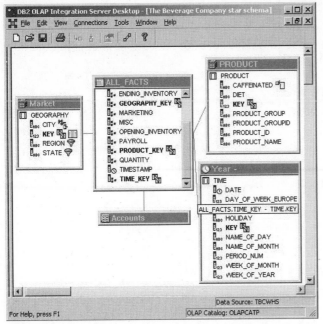

Figure 10.18 OLAP model in DB2 OLAP Integration Server.

Transmission of DWC Meta Data to IBM DB2 OLAP Server

When dimension tables are built in the warehouse, the tables can be used to populate the content of the outline in the OLAP environment. IBM DB2 Data Warehouse Center provides transformations to update the outline in OLAP based on data in a dimension table or in a file. The execution of the DWC step results in the outline being updated in IBM DB2 OLAP Server. This is a situation where the transfer of warehouse data results in the creation of meta data. The outline is considered meta data that describes the cube in the IBM DB2 OLAP Server environment.

Table 10.10 Commands to Transfer Meta Data from IBM DB2 DWC to OLAP Integration Server

SOURCE	TARGET	GUI	COMMAND LINE
DB2 DWC	OLAP Integration Server	DB2 DWC: Warehouse	flgnxhis
		> Export meta data	
		> OLAP Integration Server	

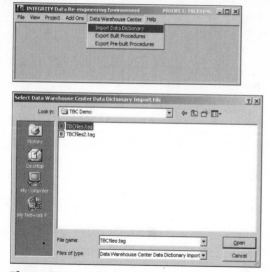

Figure 10.19   Import of file meta data in INTEGRITY.

Transmission of DWC Meta Data to Ascential INTEGRITY

One of the first tasks to perform with the Ascential INTEGRITY tool is to provide a definition for the files that will need to be reengineered. If these files have already been defined in the warehouse, it is possible to extract the definition of these files from IBM DB2 Data Warehouse Center and to import their definition into Ascential INTEGRITY.

This transfer of meta data is done by executing an import function using the Ascential INTEGRITY GUI, as shown in Figure 10.19. The meta data is imported from a tag file that had to be prepared ahead of time by the DWC administrator. This file is generated as the result of an export of a Warehouse Source issued from the IBM DB2 Data Warehouse Center GUI.

Transferring Meta Data In/Out of the Information Catalog

As described earlier, the IBM Information Catalog is the central business warehouse meta data repository. A lot of the meta data contained in the Information Catalog comes from the IBM DB2 Data Warehouse Center. A publication mechanism provides the means of transferring the meta data, as well as reorganizing the meta data according to the needs and expectations of business users.

In typical organizations, business meta data is spread within a variety of tools. For efficiency and consistency, it makes sense to try to consolidate all that meta data information into a single repository.

The Information Catalog can acquire meta data from a wide range of other products and transmit its own meta data to other vendor tools. Table 10.11 shows the most important tools with which the Information Catalog (IC) interacts, along with the commands to invoke for collecting meta data from other tools into the Information Catalog and for populating other tools with meta data stored in the Information Catalog.

Table 10.11 Transfer of Meta Data between IBM Information Catalog and Various Products

PRODUCT	COMMANDS TO POPULATE INFORMATION CATALOG WITH OTHER PRODUCT META DATA	COMMANDS TO POPULATE PRODUCT WITH IC META DATA
DB2 DWC	Publish meta data	—
Information Catalog	1. Export (to tag file)	1. Export (to tag file)
	2. Import (from tag file)	2. Import (from tag file)
Brio	Register to IBM Information Catalog	Connect to IC
		Connect to data source
BusinessObjects	Use BO IBM Metadata Bridge	Use BO IBM Metadata Bridge
Cognos	Update DataGuide Business subject area	Update impromptu Catalog
ERwin	1. flgerwin (to tag file)	—
	2. Import (from tag file)	
QMF for Windows	Register objects to Information Catalog	—
ETI•EXTRACT	Register conversion	—
DB2 OLAP Server	Publish meta data > OLAP to IC (issued from DWC)	—

Acquisition of Meta Data by the Information Catalog

Numerous tool are available that generate meta data in the BI space. This section explains how meta data can be collected from several leading vendor products, including IBM's.

Collecting Meta Data from IBM DB2 Data Warehouse Center

This operation is performed from DWC using the Publish Meta Data function, described earlier in this chapter in the section *Transmission of DWC Meta Data to IBM Information Catalog*.

Collecting Meta Data from another Information Catalog

Meta data can be exchanged between two instances of Information Catalog. This exchange is performed in two separate operations: One operation consists of exporting meta data objects from the Information Catalog to a tag file, and the second operation is an import of the tag file to the other instance of the Information Catalog. The import operation can be performed using the Information Catalog Center GUI, or the command line via the command DB2ICMIMPORT.

Accessing Brio Meta Data in the Information Catalog

The interface with Brio works quite differently than the other tools; specifically, no meta data is physically exchanged. Instead, the setup consists of establishing a connection to the other meta data environment. Since no meta data is copied, you will always see the most current meta data.

The setup required to access Brio meta data from the IBM Information Catalog includes the following tasks that are executed in the BrioQuery environment:

1. Establish a connection to the Information Catalog database, using the Brio Database Connection Wizard. This operation results in the creation of an OCE file.

2. Create the Brio control tables in the Information Catalog database. This operation is activated by selecting the Administer Repository option on the Tools menu of BrioQuery Designer. It results in the creation of nine control tables—all starting with the name Brio—in the Information Catalog.

3. Create the new object types related to Brio objects. This is done by selecting the Administer IBM Information Catalog item on the Tools

menu of BrioQuery Designer. The object types that can be created are Brio Enterprise Document and OnDemand Server Document. New tables will be created (bqy and bqods) in the Information Catalog, as well as new programs that can be launched against objects of these types.

4. Grant administrator authority to the user who will be assigned to register Brio objects in the Information Catalog. This operation is performed in the Information Catalog Center.

5. Create a business subject area in the Information Catalog. This business subject area will contain the Brio objects that the user will register. This completes the initial setup. Now Brio objects can be registered in the Information Catalog.

6. Register a Brio object. For example, to register a BrioQuery document, open the document using BrioQuery Designer, and select Register to IBM Information Catalog.

Once objects have been registered in the Information Catalog, the Information Catalog user can perform a search for objects of type *Brio Enterprise Document*, for example. Each Brio document listed as the result of the search in Information Catalog can then be viewed directly by selecting the Start Program function, which automatically launches the BrioQuery Designer application.

Collecting Meta Data from BusinessObjects

To transfer meta data between BusinessObjects and IBM Information Catalog, it is necessary to install the Business Objects IBM Metadata Bridge software, which can be obtained from Business Objects.

The transfer of meta data from BusinessObjects to IBM Information Catalog involves the following tasks, performed from the Business Objects IBM Metadata Bridge GUI and shown in Figure 10.20:

1. Establish a connection to the BusinessObjects repository.

2. Establish a connection to the Information Catalog.

3. Specify the type of meta data to extract from BusinessObjects. If a BusinessObjects universe is extracted, an object of type database is created in the Information Catalog, and it contains the tables defined in the universe. If a BusinessObjects report is extracted, an object of type document is created in the Information Catalog.

Table 10.12 shows the mapping between BusinessObjects objects and Information Catalog objects.

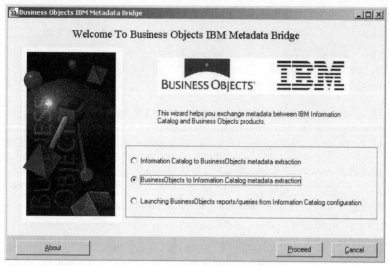

Figure 10.20 Business Objects IBM Metadata Bridge.

Once the transfer has completed, the Information Catalog user can look at the description and content of the databases that represent universes and launch on BusinessObjects Documents the BusinessObjects program that will display the report associated to the document.

Table 10.12 Object Mapping between BusinessObjects and IBM Information Catalog

BUSINESSOBJECTS	INFORMATION CATALOG
Universe	Databases
name, description, owner, . . .	name, description, owner, . . .
Classes	Tables
name, description, owner	name, description, owner
Objects	Columns
name, description, . . .	name, description, . . .
Document (Report)	BusinessObjects Documents
name	name, associated program

Collecting Meta Data from Cognos

To enable the exchange of meta data between the Cognos Impromptu Catalog and the IBM Information Catalog, you must first install the DataGuide Impromptu Bridge utility. The name DataGuide refers to the Information Catalog as it was named a few years ago.

The DataGuide Impromptu Metadata Bridge utility can be used to perform the following tasks:

- Extract meta data from the Cognos Impromptu Catalog and import it into a Business Subject Area in the Information Catalog.

- Extract meta data from a Business Subject Area in the Information Catalog and update the Cognos Impromptu catalog.

A graphical user interface, shown in Figure 10.21, leads you through the steps required to exchange the meta data.

Object types whose meta data can be transferred from Cognos to the Information Catalog are as follows:

- Impromptu folders stored in the Impromptu Catalog
- Impromptu reports
- PowerPlay reports
- PowerPlay cubes

Table 10.13 shows the mapping between Cognos objects and Information Catalog objects.

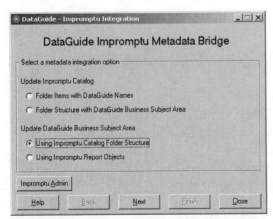

Figure 10.21   DataGuide Impromptu Metadata Bridge.

Table 10.13 Object Mapping between Cognos and IBM Information Catalog

COGNOS	INFORMATION CATALOG
	Business Subject Area
Impromptu Catalog (.CAT)	Impromptu Catalog
Folders	Impromptu Folders
Columns	Columns
	Business Subject Area
Impromptu Reports	Impromptu Reports
	Business Subject Area
PowerPlay Reports	PowerPlay Reports
	Business Subject Area
PowerPlay Cubes	PowerPlay Cubes

Once the transfer has completed, the Information Catalog user can look at the description and content of each folder that represents an Impromptu Catalog folder and launch from the Information Catalog the Cognos program that will display the Impromptu or PowerPlay report.

Collecting Meta Data from ERwin

In the section earlier in the chapter named *Meta Data Acquisition by DWC*, we explained how ERwin meta data can be transferred to the IBM DB2 Data Warehouse Center. Meta data can also be transferred immediately from ERwin into the Information Catalog. The following two tasks must be performed:

1. Generate a tag file for the Information Catalog. This tag file is generated by executing the FLGERWIN command, which takes as input an ER1 file. Note that the tag file produced here is not the same as the tag file being used as input to the IBM DB2 Data Warehouse Center. The flag—ICM in the FLGERWIN command notifies the system that the tag file must be generated for input to the Information Catalog.

2. Import the tag file into the Information Catalog; the import operation can be performed using the Information Catalog Center GUI or the command line via the command DB2ICMIMPORT.

Table 10.14 shows the mapping between ERwin objects and Information Catalog objects.

Table 10.14 Object Mapping between ERwin and IBM Information Catalog

ERWIN	INFORMATION CATALOG
Database	Databases
Name, version, description	name, type, owner, . . .
Tables	Tables
Name, owner, comment	name, schema, description
Columns	Columns
Name, type, length,	name, type, length,
scale, nulls, comment	scale, allows nulls, description
Diagram	Case Model
name, author, definition	name, info, description
Entities	Entity
name, notes,	name, for further information,
definition, owner	description, owner
Attributes	Attribute
name, notes, definition,	name, for further info, desc,
data type, length	data type, length

Collecting Meta Data from QMF for Windows

QMF for Windows is an IBM query and reporting tool. QMF objects (QMF queries and QMF forms) can be registered in the IBM Information Catalog; once registered in the Information Catalog, these QMF objects can be accessed directly from the Information Catalog.

The registration of a QMF object in the Information Catalog can be done when the object is initially created, by checking the Register the Object in the Information Catalog box. It can also be done after the object has been saved at the server; in that case, multiple objects can be selected and be registered in the Information Catalog, using the Register in Information Catalog item on the List menu in QMF.

Registration can be either a one-step operation or a two-step operation. By choosing the Register Immediately option, the QMF object definition is transferred immediately in Information Catalog. Choosing the Register Later option results in the creation of a tag file; this tag file can then be imported at a later time to the Information Catalog, using the Information Catalog Center GUI, or the command line via the command DB2ICMIMPORT.

Figure 10.22 shows the interface used in QMF for Windows to register objects in the Information Catalog.

The mapping between QMF for Windows objects and Information Catalog objects is represented in Table 10.15.

QMF objects in the Information Catalog are associated with QMF programs that can be launched directly from the Information Catalog; different types of programs are associated to different QMF object types. Three types of programs can be invoked for an object of type QMF query:

Run QMF query with QMF for Windows.   The result of the query is displayed in a table format.

Run QMF query unattended with QMF for Windows.   The query is executed, but the result is not displayed on the user's screen.

View QMF query with QMF for Windows.   The QMF query definition is displayed, but the query is not executed.

The program associated to a QMF form object is "View QMF Form with QMF for Windows"; this program displays the structure of the form. Data resulting from the execution of a QMF query can then subsequently be used as input for the form to be filled.

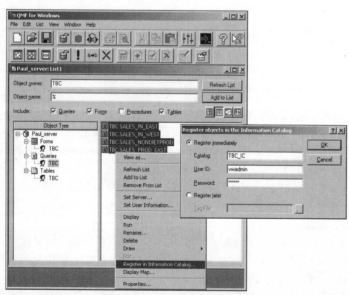

Figure 10.22   Registering QMF for Windows objects in the Information Catalog.

Table 10.15 Object mapping between QMF for Windows and IBM Information Catalog

QMF FOR WINDOWS	INFORMATION CATALOG
Server	QMF Server—Server name
Queries—Name	QMF queries on Server name
	QMF query—Name, owner
Server	QMF Server—Server name
Forms—Name	QMF forms on Server name
	QMF form—Name, owner

Collecting Meta Data from ETI•EXTRACT

In the *Meta Data Acquisition by DWC* section earlier in the chapter, we explained how ETI•EXTRACT meta data can be transferred to the IBM DB2 Data Warehouse Center. Meta data can also be transferred immediately from ETI•EXTRACT into the Information Catalog.

The Register Conversion operation transfers meta data in both the IBM DB2 Data Warehouse Center and the Information Catalog. If a Transfer Conversion operation is used, an MDIS meta data file is created; then the flgnmve0 procedure can be executed. It takes the MDIS meta data file as input and delivers meta data information to the IBM IDB2 Data Warehouse Center and the Information Catalog.

Table 10.16 summarizes the meta data carried over to the Information Catalog and the mapping with objects in the MDIS meta data file.

Table 10.16 Mapping between MDIS Meta Data File and Information Catalog

MDIS META DATA FILE	INFORMATION CATALOG
	Column—Name of target object
Relationship— Identifier, expression,	Transformation—Name, expression
SourceObj, TargetObj	Column—Name of source object
Database (Source/Target)—	Databases—Name, type
Name, type, ApplicationData	ETI Conversion Data— ApplicationData

(continues)

Table 10.16   Mapping between MDIS Meta Data File and Information Catalog *(Continued)*

MDIS META DATA FILE	INFORMATION CATALOG
Record—Name, ApplicationData	File—Name
	ETI Conversion Data—ApplicationData
Element—Name, type, length, null, long description,	Columns—Name, type, length, null, description
ApplicationData	ETI Conversion Data—
	ApplicationData

The objects created in the Information Catalog are as follows:

- Database objects, which represent the source and target databases. Under the database object are listed the tables/files in that database, and the columns/fields in each table/file.

- ETI Conversion Data objects. Such an object is created for each database, table/file, and column/field. The ETI Conversion Data objects contain Application Data such as the conversion property, the schema property, and the filters applied on the database, table/file, and column/field.

- A transformation object for each column/field on which a mapping has been applied. The transformation name corresponds to the relationship identifier in the MDIS file. The tree structure in the Information Catalog shows the column/field that results from the transformation and the column(s)/field(s) that are the source of the transformation. The filter expression is shown in the expression property of the transformation.

Note the information that is *not* imported in the Information Catalog:

- The description of each ETI instruction, each of which is mapped to a step in the IBM DB2 Data Warehouse Center.

- The lineage of transformations—that is, how the transformations cascade each other.

- The description of the intermediate files.

This information can, however, be published if needed into the Information Catalog from the IBM DB2 Data Warehouse Center. Most of the time, this technical information will be too detailed to be required in the Information Catalog.

Collecting Meta Data from DB2 OLAP Server

This transfer of meta data from DB2 OLAP Server to the Information Catalog is implemented by defining a warehouse transformation step that uses a predefined warehouse program to synchronize an OLAP meta data outline definition from OLAP with the Information Catalog meta data. Before the synchronization can be activated, the outline must first have been identified through a registration in the Information Catalog.

To initially register an outline in the Information Catalog, you can use the Data Warehouse Center GUI or the command-line interface.

- In the Data Warehouse Center, the Publish Meta Data command in the Warehouse folder menu enables you to publish OLAP meta data to the Information Catalog. (See Figure 10.12.) A control file containing the name of one or multiple outlines that you want to publish must be provided; each outline must be specified as a four-part name composed of the Essbase server name, the Essbase application name, the Essbase database name, and the Essbase outline name; the component names are separated by a dot. Each outline to be registered in the Information Catalog must appear on a separate line in the control file.

- From the command line, the FLGNXOLN routine can be used to perform the same operation. A control file must also be specified to identify the outlines to register.

Once the information about the outline to publish in the Information Catalog has been defined, an execution schedule can be associated to the publication step, as shown in Figure 10.23. After the publication step is promoted to production, the meta data in the Information Catalog is resynchronized with the OLAP outline according to the execution schedule.

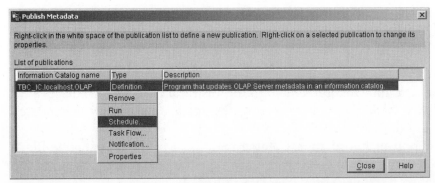

Figure 10.23 Associating a schedule to an OLAP-to-IC publication step.

Table 10.17   Mapping of an OLAP Outline in the Information Catalog

DB2 OLAP SERVER	INFORMATION CATALOG
Database—Name	Multidimensional DB—Name, description
Dimension—Name, type, alias	Dimension—Name, type, Dim name
Member—Name, alias,	Member—Name, member name
calc string, attributes	derived from, attributes

Several parameters can be specified during the outline registration definition to control how updates and deletes of members in the outline should be reflected in the Information Catalog. The *Delete existing object* flag provides a way to keep a history of the outline in the Information Catalog, if the flag is not set.

Table 10.17 defines the mapping between the objects in the OLAP outline and the objects in the Information Catalog.

Transmission of Information Catalog Meta Data

Information Catalog meta data can be transmitted to another Information Catalog instance and to other OLAP end-user tools. Objects of any type in the Information Catalog can be exported; during the definition of the export, the administrator can control whether the objects related to the object exported should also be exported. Related objects include the objects in the hierarchical relationship (e.g., database—table—columns), the objects in peer-to-peer relationship, the objects in support relationship (mostly objects providing additional documentation, such as a contact person), and the objects in precedence relationship (e.g., cascade of step).

The interchange file (tag file) is the format used to interchange meta data with other tools, as well as with another Information Catalog instance.

Transmitting Meta Data to Another Information Catalog

Meta data can be exported from one Information Catalog instance to another. The Information Catalog administrator can decide the level of granularity desired when exporting the meta data and which related objects to export.

The export of Information Catalog meta data to the interchange file is activated using the Export function available in the catalog menu of the Information Catalog Center. (See Figure 10.24.)

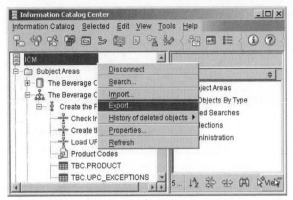

Figure 10.24 Exporting Information Catalog objects to a tag file.

The export results in the creation of the tag file, which contains all the meta data associated to the objects being exported, and the related objects, if desired. The tag file can then be used as a source of import into the other instance of the Information Catalog, as explained in the previous section.

Enabling Brio to Access Information Catalog Meta Data

The setup required to access IBM Information Catalog meta data from Brio includes the following tasks executed in the BrioQuery environment:

1. Establish a connection to the Information Catalog database, using the Brio Database Connection Wizard, as described earlier in the chapter.

2. Create a connection to a data source, using the Brio Database Connection Wizard; for example, that data source could be the data warehouse built with the DB2 Data Warehouse Center; the meta data about this database had to have been published to the Information Catalog, since Brio only interacts with the Information Catalog.

3. Specify the connection file that must be used to access this data source; this is the connection file specified in Step 1. This file provides information to connect to the Information Catalog.

4. Access the data source directly from BrioQuery; in that data source, all the tables that are defined in the Information Catalog can be accessed by the BrioQuery tool. In addition to the column names in the table, the BrioQuery tool has direct access to the following meta data: a description of the table, the contact name, and the date it was last refreshed. A query can then easily be defined with BrioQuery Designer using any of the tables in that source.

Transmitting Information Catalog Meta Data to BusinessObjects

Installation of the Business Objects IBM Metadata Bridge Software is a pre-requisite. The BusinessObjects to Information Catalog meta data extraction option (see Figure 10.20), selected on the main Metadata Bridge GUI page, lets you define the basic operations needed to transfer meta data from the Information Catalog into BusinessObjects. These operations consist of the following:

- Establishing a connection to the Information Catalog
- Selecting in the Information Catalog a Database (Subject) containing the tables of interest to BusinessObjects
- Connecting to the BusinessObjects Repository
- Selecting the tables and columns to include in the universe
- Specifying the name of a new BusinessObjects universe
- Creating a connection to the universe domain in which to store the universe

As a result of this meta data transfer, the definition of the tables and columns to be used in the universe is stored in BusinessObjects. Some complementary information may have to be specified in BusinessObjects Designer to fully characterize the universe:

- After the meta data transfer, all the columns are considered to be dimensions; for multidimensional analysis, some columns must be treated as measures. So, the property of appropriate columns should be changed to Measure.
- The tables are not linked together; choose the relevant columns in each table to define the table joins.
- The hierarchies within each table also need to be defined.

Table 10.18 defines the mapping between the objects in BusinessObjects and the objects in the Information Catalog.

Table 10.18   Object Mapping between BusinessObjects and Information Catalog

INFORMATION CATALOG	BUSINESSOBJECTS
Databases—Name	Universe—Name
Tables—Name, description	Classes—Name, description
Columns—Name, description	Objects—Name, description

Transmitting Information Catalog Meta Data to Cognos

The installation of the DataGuide Impromptu Metadata Bridge is a prerequisite. In the previous section, we showed how to transfer the meta data about Impromptu folders into an Information Catalog Business Subject Area.

A likely scenario would be for the Information Catalog administrator to rename some of the objects in the folder, or to change the structure of the folders, and then to propagate these changes back to the Cognos Impromptu Catalog.

Here again the bridge utility lets you easily transfer back to Cognos Impromptu Catalog:

The folder structure.   Any new folder not already in the Impromptu Catalog is added. If columns under the folder object in the Information Catalog are not in the Impromptu Catalog, you can choose to add or ignore them by selecting or clearing the Create Meta Data Objects box.

The folder items (columns) can be updated.   All column names in the Impromptu Catalog are replaced with the corresponding column names in the Information Catalog.

Summary

Meta data is a broad concept that encompasses all aspects of data warehousing and can be found throughout the organization. So it is not surprising that the exact definition of meta data varies. The most common definition of meta data is that it is "data about data." This very broad, highly generalized definition is great for a concise understanding of the term, but it falls short of providing the needed specifics.

To understand a meta data repository, we must define it in terms of a data warehouse. A warehouse combines data from internal and external information systems. This data is extracted, transformed, loaded, and combined into the data warehouse. Rules and logic are applied to this data to elevate its meaning to an enterprisewide perspective. The meta data repository provides the framework and processes to ensure that the data brought into the warehouse is kept consistent and accurate for analytical purposes.

This repository or "place" where descriptive information is stored can vary greatly in terms of origin, structure, and content. A number of vendors provide meta data repositories that are tool-specific. Examples can be found in ETL, relational database, data quality, and business intelligence tools. Conceptually, a meta data repository is a managed collection of information that describes the data in the warehouse. But maintaining meta data in separate, tool-specific repositories does not address the user requirements for meta data. These independent meta data structures only ensure that information regarding warehoused data remains fragmented.

What warehouse planners should focus on is building a centralized repository. This structure would be the recipient of meta data from each of these tool-centric structures and also serve as a point from which to publish a single view of warehouse data to all user communities.

OLAP and IBM

CHAPTER 11

Multidimensional Data with DB2 OLAP Server

Key Issues:

- DB2 OLAP Server is virtually the same product as the leading multi-dimensional server from Hyperion, Essbase. All features and functionality enjoyed by Essbase users is made available in DB2 OLAP Server.

- DB2 OLAP Server is just that: A database that serves up multidimensional data. As such, DB2 OLAP Server is more than a simple OLAP tool for your desktop. It can be the source of all dimensional data across your enterprise.

- DB2 OLAP Server pre-computes metrics to achieve query response times that are not attainable by relational database systems.

- DB2 OLAP Server is one of a few multidimensional database servers that can actually build and maintain MOLAP cubes of 100 GB and more. And, with Hybrid OLAP, scaling to larger multidimensional data sets is available.

- The outline is the database. This is a critical distinction between DB2 OLAP Server and relational database implementations of multidimensional data. The power to readily create and manipulate the database via a simple user interface understood by business analysts is core to the success of this product and essential to successful OLAP.

- The multidimensional data of DB2 OLAP Server is natively accessed by all leading OLAP and reporting vendors in the industry, including Cognos, Business Objects, Crystal Decisions, Brio, and many more.

- Hybrid OLAP is the direction IBM is taking to ensure that their RDBMS and Multidimensional Database (MDD) provide a seamless integration between the data and the analytical tools, as well as a transparent access to all the necessary data for OLAP business requirements. The blending of these two technologies addresses the ever-growing expectations of user communities for greater scale of multidimensional data sets.

DB2 OLAP Server is a multidimensional analytic database server platform that enables business analysts to analyze, manage, and steer their respective businesses. We define OLAP technologies as integral to BI and data warehouse initiatives, as well as complementary to data mining and other BI-centric technologies.

Arbor Software introduced their Extended Spreadsheet Services database (Essbase) in the early 1990s. Although multidimensional databases existed before, Arbor's chief contribution was to provide a version for the client/server environment. The software combined user-friendly, spreadsheet client functionality with client/server modality. From its introduction, Essbase was fast, interactive, and available for users within the current Windows desktop environments. Arbor very quickly achieved market dominance.

IBM entered the OLAP marketplace in 1997 by licensing and reselling Essbase from Arbor Software. In February 1998, IBM delivered DB2 OLAP Server V1.0 based on Arbor Essbase V5.0. This first release was available for Windows NT, OS/2, and AIX platforms. IBM called the product *DB2 OLAP Server* because multidimensional data was stored in the DB2 relational database, while the Essbase product stores data in multidimensional arrays only.

While arrays provided optimized performance, this was not considered an open storage format. IBM provided the option to store data in relational DB2 tables as a means of opening up the data storage platform. IBM's port of Essbase to DB2 OLAP Server subsequently evolved to support both storage formats. DB2 OLAP Server V8, the relational storage option, has been superceded by the Hybrid Analysis features of Essbase, which was jointly designed by IBM and Hyperion Solutions. Today, the Hyperion (who purchased Arbor Software) and IBM products remain virtually identical, except that IBM has added an OLAP mining utility for DB2 OLAP Server (Refer to Chapter 14 for more information on OLAP Mine).

OLAP technology and its related applications have surely captured the mind-share of most user communities and BI implementation teams—and for good reason. OLAP is an excellent analytic tool. Of course, when most people think about OLAP, including architects and project planners, they typically think of the desktop applications; Excel pivot tables or Cognos PowerPlay cubes are the front-end tools that people commonly refer to as OLAP. This perception is understandable, since that is the part of OLAP that is in front of the user and where IT delivers those sexy graphs and pie charts. However, OLAP is much more, and DB2 OLAP Server should not be confused with a data access tool. Instead, when architects and project planners think of DB2 OLAP Server, they should be thinking about an enterprisewide dimensional server platform from which Cognos Power-Play, Brio, Business Objects, Alphablox, and even Microsoft Excel can source quality dimensional data.

Figure 11.1 shows the conscious inclusion of multidimensional data in our BI organization. Several elements of our BI environment are impacted by dimensional data (identified by number):

1. **Data marts.**   The simple cubes suggest that architects often build several dimensional structures, referred to as "farms," to support user requirements.

2. **OLAP analysis.**   The cube graphic shown next to the analyst is one of the most important analytical tools available in the power user's tool chest and therefore a critical part of your BI deployment.

3. **Customer touch points.**   One of the best benefits of OLAP analysis is its trend-spotting and forecasting abilities. Accurately identifying trends helps you better respond to customers. This response might be adjusting inventory levels at stores or improved target-marketing through advertisements and coupon redemptions.

4. **User community reporting.**   OLAP is also an excellent way to service a broad audience of users via portal or other Web-enabled technology. The analysis for these communities is less remarkable than that needed by power users. Nevertheless, these users are equally excited about OLAP. Why? Because some of the fundamental analytical value of OLAP, such as slicing and dicing, pivoting and rollup, and drill-down capabilities. Such functions are incredibly valued by broad audiences.

5. **Back-feed loop.** OLAP has been a key contributor to analytical output that serves as input into production systems. The technology is often treasured by financial analysts for budget forecasting. Once the budgets are finalized, they are returned to the corporate financial systems.

6. **Meta data.** Mountains of meta data must be maintained for OLAP functionality. It is not that meta data for OLAP is more important than other BI-centric reporting technologies; however, OLAP seems to better facilitate complex calculations and aggregations. The calculations definitely require formal control of meta data. When CFOs compare profits for the same period from last year versus this year, they need to be able to determine how the profit was calculated. Therefore, historical integrity of meta data is especially important to OLAP applications.

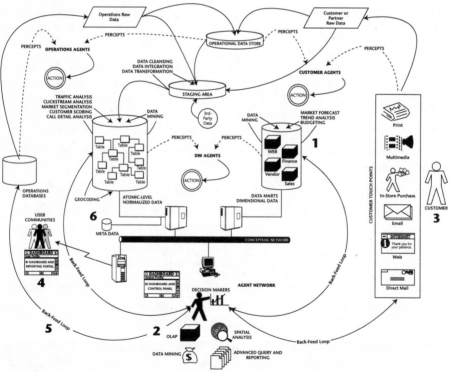

Figure 11.1 OLAP and the BI organization.

NEW FUNCTIONALITY IN DB2 OLAP SERVER V8.1

Released in July 2002, version 8.1 of DB2 OLAP Server provides some significant additional functionality to OLAP Server. For a complete discussion of DB2 OLAP Server release 8.1, please see the IBM Redbook *DB2 OLAP Server 8.1 Using Advanced Functions*, First Edition (April 2002). Following are summary descriptions of the important additions:

Hybrid analysis.   Hybrid Analysis accesses data from a relational database as if it resided in the multidimensional cube. It constructs SQL queries dynamically allowing total flexibility of access to the relational database from a DB2 OLAP Server multidimensional database. The MOLAP cube is pre-calculated and detailed relational data is accessed dynamically at user query execution time.

OLAP Miner.   OLAP Miner enhances the reporting capabilities of DB2 OLAP Server, combining IBM Data Mining with DB2 OLAP Server technology. It uses the calculated data that is created with DB2 OLAP Server to identify atypical or deviant values automatically. OLAP Miner is a free cost feature only of DB2 OLAP Server.

Advanced administrative functions.   Version 8.1 incorporates significant improvements in performance by exploiting multiple processors. Improvements were made to support the task of managing multiple OLAP servers, applications, and databases.

Parallel calculations, data load, and export.   Many critical operations (loading, calculating, exporting) can be run in multi-threaded mode to take advantage of multiprocessor hardware. This improves system performance and throughput, reducing batch windows when building and maintaining OLAP cubes.

Administration services.   Administration Services combines a single middle-tier point of administration with an easy-to-use wizard graphical interface. You can manage OLAP Server objects quickly, in a familiar visual setting. Administrators can now perform multiple tasks simultaneously, run processes in the background, do cross-server operations, and manage active user sessions and requests anywhere in the enterprise.

Security migration tool.   This tool automates the cross-server migrating OLAP security data as well as the migration of applications, databases, filters, users, and groups.

(continues)

NEW FUNCTIONALITY IN DB2 OLAP SERVER V8.1 *(Continued)*

Advanced enterprise services functionality. Enterprise Services enables DB2 OLAP Server-based applications to be more reliable and efficient in delivering the analysis needs to large numbers of web-based users. Enterprise Services allows administrators to cluster OLAP Servers, to balance OLAP Server workloads, and to provide connection pooling and high concurrency. It facilitates the maintenance of high availability OLAP Server environments.

External authentication. DB2 OLAP Server version 8.1 provides the option of using external authentication of DB2 OLAP Server users instead of native DB2 OLAP Server authentication. DB2 OLAP Server supports LDAP V3-compliant servers, Microsoft Active Directory Service and NT authentication as external authentication methods. You can even develop your own authentication modules and plug them into DB2 OLAP Server security infrastructure.

Not surprisingly, OLAP-centric architects argue that to fully exploit the power of DB2 OLAP, you should consider implementing the OLAP architecture across the enterprise in a manner similar to Ralph Kimball's bus architecture. This means that you would implement an atomic layer as a dimensional model as opposed to 3NF. Although we recommend a normalized atomic layer and dimensional data marts, you must evaluate the needs of your organization and decide what type of atomic layer best works for you. For a refresher of the architectural options, refer to Chapter 4.

This chapter dives deep into DB2 OLAP Server technology. At the risk of being redundant, we begin by defining OLAP analytics and the aggregation value the technology brings to your environment. Then we review the dimensional model and associate that model to the notion of an outline, as defined by DB2 OLAP Server. We then show how the outline represents the business requirements of your organization. Next, the chapter examines the technical architecture of DB2 OLAP Server, focusing on the components of the physical cube. The chapter ends with recommendations for sizing, tuning, and assessing the hardware requirements for maximum OLAP performance.

Understanding the Analytic Cycle of OLAP

As described in Chapter 1, OLAP stands for "online analytical processing." Coined by Dr. E.F. Codd in the early years of Arbor Software, the term alludes to OLTP (online transaction processing). OLAP is an online process as opposed to a batch process, which suggests having a dynamic rather than a static functionality. The objective of OLAP is to support the processing of business analytics and not business transactions. The coinage of the acronym really suggests that the speed of processing set off by relational database transaction processing systems is now available to business users for analyzing data.

The success of DB2 OLAP Server can be related to extending the speed analogy to apply to OLAP application development as well. No small part of the initial success of OLAP tools in general is because rapid deployment of departmental OLAP solutions provided an extremely fast return on investment (ROI) for organizations; departmental OLAP application deployment times generally range between 30 and 90 days. Unfortunately, departmental solutions remain disjointed and can fail across the enterprise—a point often missed by OLAP-centric developers. Just as unfortunate, however, is that seeing this disjointedness has led many IT professionals to the incorrect conclusion that OLAP tools are appropriate only for departmental initiatives and have a marginal place within enterprisewide initiatives. Providing OLAP across the enterprise brings to the entire organization what OLAP traditionally provides to departments: a controlled central data source for analytics. The ability to provide a "single source of truth" to the organization in the form of advanced dimensional analytics that DB2 OLAP Server delivers should be, at the very least, a provocative notion for IT.

To fully appreciate the value of OLAP, you must understand the term *analytics*. We find people in the marketplace often believe they know what OLAP is without having a sound understanding of what is meant by business analytics. Business analytics as enabled by DB2 OLAP Server are successful at measuring, understanding, and predicting business performance. But while this is a succinct definition, what does it really mean?

The old adage that you can't manage what you can't measure gives us a starting point. We measure business performance with metrics. At the most basic level, metrics are numbers that describe things. Business metrics become more useful when they measure things and events that experience has shown let us manage our business. For example, a metric called "sales" tells us the total sales dollars for quarter one. The ability to report this metric is of some interest, but it has limited value as a means of piloting a business. It may be necessary, but it is far from sufficient. However, if we pair "sales" with other metrics like "sales for last quarter," we now have a business measure useful for piloting the business. We can now measure progress. Let's add other metrics such as "sales for quarter one this year and quarter one last year as a percentage of year-to-date sales." We've now enriched our metric set with new information that will automatically enable us to ask and get answers to new questions like, "Why were we further ahead last year by this time than we are now?"

In fact, the process of asking questions of data is a sound-bite definition of what computer-based analysis is all about. And an analyst is an expert who knows both what questions to ask and how to formulate new questions. This heuristic iterative cycle of question asking and new question generation across business metrics defines what might be called the *analytic cycle*.

An OLAP technology is one that supports and empowers users through the analytic cycle. This is what is meant by OLAP. And the minimization of the duration of this analytic cycle across complex business metrics is what DB2 OLAP Server is all about.

Generating Useful Metrics

Our first business task is to generate useful metrics from our data. In the hands of experts, these metrics naturally enable the generation of new questions, which lead to new answers. So, what are useful metrics? Useful metrics are numbers that contain other numbers in "compressed form."

For example, a sum obviously adds up numbers by some criteria (e.g., "total sales for the second quarter for ISO channel products for the East Region"). This aggregate becomes very useful when compared with another aggregate, for example, the same criteria varied by time ("for last quarter") or when varied by geography ("for the West"). One way to describe basic OLAP that is not too misleading is that it is a technology for quickly comparing useful aggregates with other useful aggregates. It is, however, much more than that.

No business executive is going to pilot a business based solely on totals. The situation quickly becomes fascinating as people trained in quantitative analysis begin digging for metrics that will help them understand, change, and predict business performance, for example, ratios. Ratios are deceptively simple but highly useful tools for analyzing performance. For example: "What percentage of profit did our family x products deliver last quarter in the Asia Pacific region versus family y products?" Or, "What market share does brand y enjoy versus brand z?"

Talented executives and individuals trained in quantitative analysis can't wait to get their minds around different ways of looking at a business analytically. All of the numbers they generate in some way contain or represent other numbers in compressed form. Sums, averages, percentages—all are derived from base quantities and represent them in some more general way that allows comparing, contrasting, predicting, and understanding a business. The modern enterprise is so complex that if we did not have some way of compressing and representing events, we couldn't manage them.

Suggesting that OLAP metrics are numbers that represent other numbers in compressed form invites a comparison with classical statistical analysis. We find that the OLAP discipline and the discipline of statistics overlap and serve a similar purpose. Unfortunately, we also observe that statistical insights are not necessarily as compelling to decision makers as simple OLAP metrics. While DB2 OLAP Server can implement classic statistical measures like standard deviation and correlations, it can also implement simple ratios and percentages. Telling a decision maker "we lost money on footwear in Massachusetts last quarter but made money in New York State" is a lot more galvanizing than to say "the variance of profit in the Northeast was greater than in the Southwest in quarter one." Traditional statistics usually don't speak to an average businessperson. OLAP metrics do. While we'd like to see the day when statistical insight pervades all cultures, OLAP is pervasive now.

DB2 OLAP SERVER FUNCTIONS

To support calculations, DB2 OLAP Server has over 200 built-in functions in ten groupings and includes the ability to create user-defined functions. These functions include the following:

- *Allocation* functions, which allocate values that are input at the parent level

- *Boolean* functions, which provide expected analysis

- *Date and time* function, which converts date strings to numbers for use in calculations

- *Forecasting* functions, which manipulate data for the purpose of calculating future values

- *Mathematical* functions, which return calculated values based on specified parameters

- *Member set* functions, which return a list of members

- *Range and financial* functions, affording added flexibility to your analysis

- *Relationship* functions, which look up data within a database during a calculation

- *Statistical* functions, which calculate classical statistical metrics such as standard deviation

- *User-defined* functions, which enable users to create their own functions

OLAP Skills

In recent years BI products arose claiming to be MOLAP (Multidimensional Array Storage Supporting OLAP), ROLAP (Relational Storage Supporting OLAP), or HOLAP (Hybrid Storage Supporting OLAP) in nature. We intend to stay out of strict definitions of these differences in this discussion, except to point out that their relative positioning becomes clear when you evaluate the analytic world by skill set.

We stated that a systems analyst looks at column names, whereas a business analyst looks at business names. Exploring the differences between how systems professionals and business professionals see things is useful to help further understand OLAP. Consider Figure 11.2, which depicts perspectives of the BI world. The systems analysis perspective and the business analysis perspective apparently divide the BI world. The relevant academic degree on the left is from Computer Science, whereas the relevant academic degree on the right is from Business Science. Key business performance indicators drive the business analysts, while database or system application performance indicators drive the systems analyst/data architect. The view on the left is systems architectural in nature, whereas the view on the right is business logical in nature. Neither view is entirely correct. Or rather, both together are correct; that is, the skills differences between IT professionals and business management professionals cause them to understand analytic processing in different but essentially complementary ways.

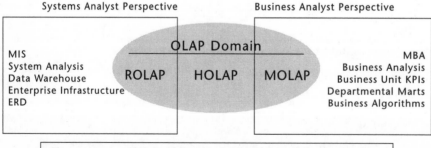

Business Intelligence/Data Warehouse

The way you view OLAP depends upon what side of the analytic space you come from. The whole "**ROLAP, HOLAP, MOLAP**" debate comes from this difference.

Figure 11.2 Skill domain of BI.

For the systems analyst or data architect, entity relationship diagrams rule the world, whereas for the MBA, business algorithms rule it. Many analysts think at the departmental level because business performance indicators are usually relevant to some specific task set that maps to a specific organizational subsystem. Architects and systems analysts, on the other hand, more often think at the corporate or enterprise level because data warehouses are thought of as corporate application assets, not departmental tools. Business analysts who do think at the corporate level have a particularly disquieting job. Metrics need to be defined and aggregated for the corporation as a whole and stored somewhere that permits asking OLAP questions of them. The physical location of this analytic cube in the corporate information structure has never been easy to define.

As in most things, "where you stand depends on where you sit." People skilled in business analytics are likely to be drawn to an OLAP tool that presents to them things they understand, like business names. People skilled in systems analysis are likely to be drawn to an OLAP tool that presents to them things that they understand, like column names. On the one hand, we do not want to comment on the appropriateness of any specific tool for any given task. Since pure objectivity on this matter is unlikely, it is useful to know the background from which tool recommendations are being made. However, we do want to suggest that there are more or less appropriate tools for every task and that it is the mandate of data warehouse architects to understand and implement tools that generate the largest ROI for their organizations.

In the final analysis, it makes as little sense to attempt to build a single OLAP cube and call it a warehouse as it does to populate summary tables at every possible intersection point, across every conceivable column combination in the DW and call it OLAP. The debate about relational versus OLAP technologies is misguided. It is time to recognize relational, OLAP, and data mining as complementary technologies.

Applying the Dimensional Model

Ralph Kimball seems to have been the first to systematically argue that normalized relational database schemas supporting transaction processes aren't appropriate for supporting analytic processes. His idea of a dimensional model stems largely from the fact that analytic processing requirements are not the same as transaction processing requirements, in the following ways:

■ A dimension business model is more easily understood by business users than a normalized business model. Users understand a star schema more easily than other modeling pictures.

■ Speed advances in transaction processing come from altering the schema. By properly configuring aggregation tables within these star schema structures, system response greatly improves.

So the net result of star schemas is a more responsive and user-friendly system. The relational database star provides the lion's share of analytic value to a large audience of business users. The advanced use of OLAP technology, on the other hand, is more precisely focused and targets those people in the organization who *manage* the business. It is focused on those whose job is to see that the business is viable and competitive.

Steering Your Organization with OLAP

We can illustrate this by extending an analogy Ralph Kimball uses in *The Data Warehouse Toolkit*, where he says that "users of an OLTP system turn the wheels of the organization" and that "users of a data warehouse, on the other hand, are *watching* the wheels of the organization" (Kimball, 3).

We propose that advanced OLAP users are the people who *steer* the wheels of the organization. They are looking at the biggest business questions possible: Are we profitable? Where? Why? Why not? The OLAP users are active. They decide where the enterprise is going, or provide information directly to people who do decide.

Speed-of-Thought Analysis

Ultimately, then, an analytic tool is a tool that enables business analysts to test different business models for the purpose of asking and answering OLAP-type questions. The speed at which this process occurs is critical. Does the analyst wait 1 second, 1 minute, 1 hour, or 1 day (or more) before viewing the results that will lead to the next question?

The answer is important. The duration between question and answer can be of such a length that the originating question needs to be recalled and reformulated before results can be optimally interpreted. The necessity of having to constantly replace results *in context* hinders the analytic process. Therefore, the OLAP functionality implemented by DB2 OLAP Server supports rapid question-and-answer response times and has been described as "analysis at the speed of thought."

A drill-down is much more than a movement down to a level of higher detail; it is a report that remains intimately connected to and answers the question that generated it. This is precisely why a drill-*up* is every bit as powerful for a business analyst as a drill-*down*; they both are question-answer reports in context. To repeat, a drill-down is a report in context. Each report is new, arrives instantaneously, and is not constrained by the boundaries of canned reports that use replaceable parameters. The rapid question-and-answer functionality that accrues to DB2 OLAP Server is truly definitive for the business analyst. It is difficult to overstate the analytic value of this functionality.

We are suggesting that the *quantitative* change in speed of answers makes a critical *qualitative* change in the ability to pilot the business. Because users can think more quickly, they are freed to think more deeply and in an unconstrained manner. They are able to be more creative. Using DB2 OLAP Server, you can steer the enterprise faster and better.

The Outline of a Business

The DB2 OLAP Server outline is a place where the data model and the business model are the same and are represented graphically. The DB2 OLAP schema is an "outline" of the business. The following discussion details how the outline drives the physical schema of the cube itself.

The relationship between a star schema and a DB2 OLAP outline (schema) is illustrated in Figures 11.3 and 11.4. This star schema is represented in the following DB2 OLAP Server database outline. As shown in Figure 11.3, the star has four dimensions that essentially surround a single fact table, thus the term *star*.

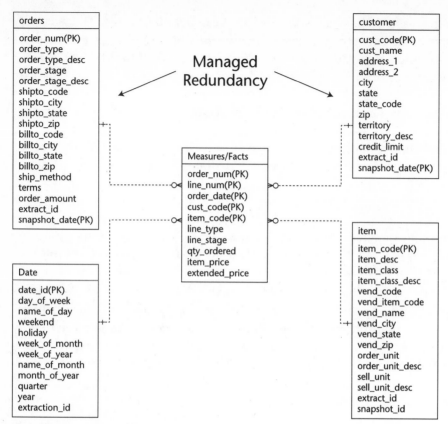

Figure 11.3 A star schema.

The DB2 OLAP Server outline shown in Figure 11.4 does not resemble a star schema at all. There are several differences between the two. First is the storage structure. As mentioned, the relational star has five tables (four dimension tables and a fact table), whereas the OLAP outline schema has five dimensions. Although it is correct to think about the five dimensions representing tables, the business itself is being modeled and stored differently in the resulting subsequent databases.

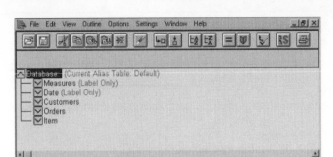

Figure 11.4 DB2 OLAP Server outline.

In the relational star schema, each business entity (for example, product code 100-1) is stored as part of the contents of a schema component (i.e., table). These contents are accessed using SQL. On the other hand, in the DB2 OLAP Server outline, instances of actual named business entities *are* the database schema. In the star schema, product code 100-1 is the name of a place where a specific item code is stored for each business event being managed. In DB2 OLAP Server, each specific item_code is an entry in the schema.

The DB2 OLAP Server schema is a way of picturing an enterprise that is closer to how businesspeople experience the business than are relational schemas. Business users experience specific named entities, like product 100-1. They don't experience the "categories" of entities, like a table column called item_code, which represent the core of relational modeling.

It is quite amazing to visit users and see that, day in and day out, they live with complex coding references. Everybody within the same work group would know that 100-55 is a *new* product for which the tooling hasn't been done yet, but the marketing brochures already tell the story. Users will exchange knowing glances during OLAP design sessions about specific arcane codes that even a close outsider from IT can barely understand. When users see their codes embedded in a DB2 OLAP Server "business model" (outline) they "get it" right away. That OLAP database meta data is composed of business entities, not database schema, is manifest by the fact that the best and most effective OLAP database designers are business users. (See Figure 11.5.)

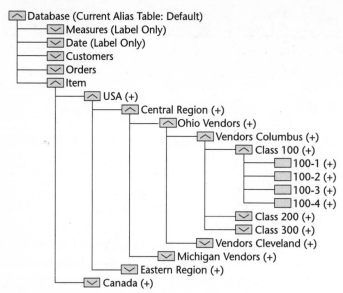

Figure 11.5 An expanded DB2 OLAP outline.

In a similar way, OLAP outlines make obvious the way the business aggregates. Note in the outline fragment shown in Figure 11.5 that the "form" given to the enterprise by the rollup structure is immediately obvious. This is important. Three inches of green bar paper of printed account codes is an organizational list, not an organizational structure. The DB2 OLAP Server outline, however, not only shows the list, but also affords the details to reveal the organizational structure.

Data processing people have long provided the ability to hide information in order to disclose form. The invention of the program subroutine and modular programming provided a way to isolate details but also to emphasize logical form. Programmers have long used this ability to understand the programs they write. This powerful capability is known as *information hiding* and has become such a staple of programming that it is no longer even mentioned.

In the same way that we can create computer programs we can't understand without help, we can create organizations we can't understand without help. In DB2 OLAP Server, double-clicking on an outline parent expands or collapses the information. Many users have never been able to visualize how account codes report to other account codes, but they can when they use a DB2 OLAP outline. The information-hiding ability of the

OLAP outline gives to business analysts the schematic clarity long available to data processing analysts.

In some OLAP modeling sessions, users will excitedly grab the input mouse and start moving schema objects around. This ability to move, reshape, and restructure the organization at the computer desktop is a core part of the online analytic processing experience that is provided by DB2 OLAP Server.

The business question "What if Alice's group reported to the Northeast?" can be modeled almost in one mouse-click. Users are close to their data and close to their organization's structure (i.e., multidimensional meta data). In a DB2 OLAP Server environment, by design, you are naturally close to both. This powerful organizational and analytic modeling is made possible by the pictorial nature of the OLAP schema, where the business model and the data model are identical.

The OLAP Array

The entity names in the OLAP Server outline are called *members*. The DB2 OLAP server stores a number at the intersection of every member by every other member in the outline, across all dimensions at all levels of hierarchy (see Figure 11.6). The storage structure supporting this is a multidimensional array. Accessing numeric data in a DB2 OLAP Server array is achieved by supplying appropriate coordinates or intersection points.

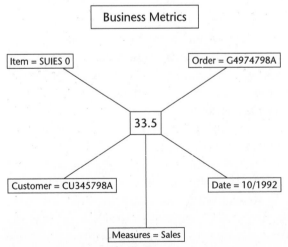

Figure 11.6   Business metrics.

IBM DB2 OLAP Server is a multidimensional OLAP (MOLAP) tool. As such, the array is defined to hold only numbers, and numbers only are *data* to the tool. Some relational data has become meta data to DB2 OLAP Server and is stored in a physically separate outline object. Pointers connect outline members to array storage locations. Much of the modeling quickness that OLAP Server provides is derived by this architecture. To manipulate the outline schema, you don't need to touch a vast data array. To manipulate the vast data array, you touch the outline as needed. The partnership between objects is intimate, patented, tested, and compelling.

Within the Item dimension, SKU-level members aggregate to class members, class members aggregate to vendor members, and so on. Organizational structure is therefore represented by the database schema and not as contents of the schema. The point still bears further emphasis and consideration, and we want briefly to sketch here what we perceive as a limit on the ability of relational modeling to successfully represent enterprise structure and business rules.

Relational Schema Limitations

A relational database schema (star or otherwise) approaches business logic asymptotically. This is because the business entities are really *contents* of relational database schema objects. Schema components reflect business logic according to the ways that they are related to each other. But the schema objects themselves are not business entities. Even though the suggestion that database schema objects (like tables and indexes) should represent business entities probably sounds idiotic to relational data modelers, that's precisely what DB2 OLAP array schema objects (like dimensions and members) do. Objects like array schema can also reflect relationships, as in the simple example of days aggregating to months. Indeed, very complex business relationships, or business logic, can be easily embedded in a DB2 OLAP Server schema. The array storage structure removes a level of abstraction and thus enables modelers to alter the schema and more efficiently and transparently create *new* business models.

Using our example from Figure 11.5, the level of abstraction that is removed is demonstrated in the OLAP Server outline. There simply is no column name called item_code whose contents instantiate the business structure (and rollups) to be modeled. This level of indirection, as it were, is eliminated. Users are directly connected to the business names they use daily. We suggest that column names containing instances of business names constitute an asymptotic limit to user understanding that relational modeling, as powerful and successful as it is, cannot, by definition, cross.

Derived Measures

Consider the DB2 OLAP schema extract in Figure 11.7, where the Revenues metric is calculated by multiplying the Quantity by the Price metric. The derived value (Revenues) is in no significant way different from other members and is also part of the database schema. Note that in the DB2 OLAP Server database, Revenues are calculated for every intersection point across each of the other dimensions in the database (i.e., every Item by every Order for every Customers by every Date.) However, Extended Price is calculated only (note the Boolean syntax within the formula) for members intersecting with the descendants of the Central Region Items. Finally, the Customer Revenue % Contribution formula relates the revenue contribution of each customer with its parent (as a percent). Once again, this calculation would occur across every other dimension in the database.

These are simple examples that illustrate the manner in which very complex business logic can be modeled using DB2 OLAP Server. By removing a level of abstraction present in relational dimensional modeling, we have dropped down into an arena where we manipulate business names directly in the picture object (outline) to help reveal the underlying business structure. We also add computations to the aggregations to reveal and test business rules. The point is that business analysts are very comfortable using DB2 OLAP Server to continue to manipulate business hierarchies and logic to create complex metrics to be used in piloting the business.

Business users are generally pleased to see that complex business analytics, typically hidden away in database programming logic, surface in the OLAP outline and are literally published for the entire user community to see, understand, and critique. "You can't manage what you can't measure" applies to the measures too.

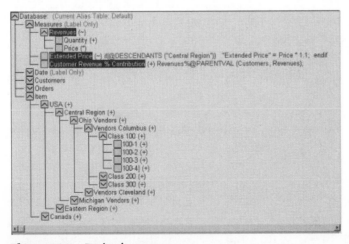

Figure 11.7   Derived measures.

Implementing an Enterprise OLAP Architecture

The preceding discussion made several observations that we now will briefly examine more closely:

- Many key performance indicators (KPIs) are relevant only within organizational subsystems.

- A star schema implies one OLAP cube and possibly many more.

- OLAP application development delivers rapid ROI.

- OLAP applications steer the business.

It follows from the first statement that there are metrics crucial to the management of departmental business units that are not appropriately stored within the DW. For example, at the corporate-level a bank does not care which customers make the best loan candidates. The bank only cares that the loan operation is profitable. The loans division of the retail banking department clearly does need to track loan customers at that level. Many departmental-level KPIs are different from the corporate-level KPIs that have to apply across the organization. The former properly needs to be derived within departmental data marts.

We have suggested that the departmental business analysts are experts at manipulating these metrics in order to test and steer their respective units, and, moreover, that OLAP technology really targets these individuals as the ideal advanced user group. Using the DB2 OLAP Server environment to provide complex, department-specific metrics for business analysts, we end up proposing an architecture that is really a variation on Kimball's bus architecture. The diagram in Figure 11.8 attempts to isolate BI/DW *data* structures. Nonhorizontal lines that link objects generally indicate data flow and move from the bottom up. The horizontal connecting lines between departmental marts indicate a conformed rather than a stovepipe relational data mart environment. OLAP Integration Server (OIS) is the MOLAP generating tool between relational star schema structures and DB2 OLAP cubes.

Note the corporate DB2 OLAP cubes. They are the same shade as the corporate warehouse because they contain metrics of interest at the corporate level but are created by connecting information contained in departmental DB2 OLAP cubes. This really illustrates that the proposed architecture is a variation of Kimball's bus architecture in that certain departmental or subject-oriented database metrics are brought together to compose a corporate perspective. (Chapter 4 also discussed implementing DB2 OLAP Server in the role of an enterprisewide multidimensional database it is intended to play.)

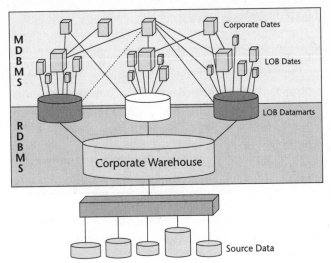

Figure 11.8 Enterprise OLAP.

The graphic should not be taken to prescribe any particular relational architecture. It is irrelevant, for example, whether the departmental marts in the picture taken together are considered the "warehouse" or the highly normalized database structure like that represented by the corporate warehouse. We consider DB2 OLAP Server as essentially neutral regarding relational architecture, except that OIS needs star schemas to perform efficiently.

We do not want to convey any ideas regarding the relative *importance* of MOLAP versus relational analytics. Space constraints make it difficult to adequately depict the important relational components that provide analytic reporting and underpin enterprisewide analytic (ROLAP or otherwise) applications. We want to emphasize where MOLAP resides within the BI/DW and position it as necessary and complementary technology.

In the production environment, organizational subsystem data is cleansed and scrubbed within the relational database. This cleansed data is used as source data that feeds star schema data marts. These data marts can be typical Kimball marts in every respect except that they will assume characteristics necessary to support DB2 OLAP Server cube creation and maintenance.

The debate concerning whether to begin constructing the entire warehouse or to begin building the data marts is very worn today. Clearly a coordinated effort is required to build a functional and efficient BI environment. But we want to point out that OLAP cubes quickly provide ROI by fulfilling business analytic requirements within a 30- to 90-day time frame. Moreover, cube schemas can be used to help define underlying star schema requirements that, in turn, can be used to refine source data requirements for the warehouse.

Prototyping the Data Warehouse

In this way, DB2 OLAP Server can have a powerful role in prototyping the data warehouse. Organizations have found that it is a relatively inexpensive, safe, and effective way to start a warehouse project. You deliver valuable business answers to grateful users while simultaneously discovering that your enterprise has five product master files, three general ledgers, and that "customer x" is spelled seven different ways. Since multiple meta data pointers to the same meta data entity (10 ways to spell "AT&T") will not pass edit in DB2 OLAP Server, you get to conform your designs as you quickly deliver individual actual working models. Then, the harder work of creating permanent data scrubbing and cleansing processes for overall warehouse use can begin, but in the context of a successful, though bounded, delivery of answers.

Sequentially adding OLAP applications while simultaneously conforming the dimensionality of the underlying relational data marts effectively implements (M)OLAP across the enterprise. A fully functional BI/DW can be implemented by coordinating the design of the OLAP supporting relational schemas with the relational warehouse schema that provides enterprisewide analytics using ROLAP or other SQL technologies. In other words, relational designs that support OLAP requirements can effectively be used to prototype the warehouse. More importantly, the warehouse is gradually constructed through the process of providing business-relevant metrics that are used to produce a rapid ROI for the organization.

Building a BI/DW environment through OLAP applications offers IT the ability to minimize application development time, maximize ROI and create a data repository that is conformed across the enterprise, and provide pertinent high- and low-level analytic functionality to business users from the start. Hence, it is our view that relational and OLAP development needs to be coordinated and done in parallel. Given this high-level description of enterprise OLAP, what are some of the practical considerations requisite to implementing DB2 OLAP Server?

Database Design: Building Outlines

There are three ways to build a DB2 OLAP Server outline:

- Manually build dimensions and members through the Application Manager GUI.
- Build a coordinated set of files and generate the outline in batch mode using the ESSCMD or MaxL utilities.
- Use OLAP Integration Server.

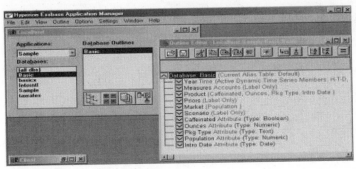

Figure 11.9   Application Manager.

> **NOTE** In Figure 11.9, Hyperion Essbase is printed on the screen shot of the DB2 OLAP Server Application Manager. This is because DB2 OLAP Server is a fully licensed, current version of Essbase. IBM has increased the functionality of Essbase but has not changed the base application itself.

Application Manager

Application Manager (App Man) is the central administrative tool for DB2 OLAP Server. It offers all administrative functions for building and maintaining DB2 OLAP applications and databases. Through App Man, administrators can modify database schemas by manually altering dimensions and dimension members. They can also:

- Create database calculation programs called *calc scripts*. (See Figure 11.10.)

- Create *rules files* for building dimensions and loading data. (See Figure 11.11.)

- Generate reports. (See Figure 11.12.)

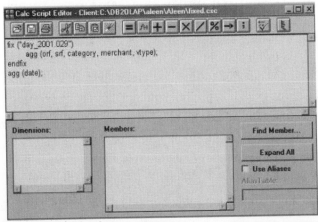

Figure 11.10   Calc Script Editor.

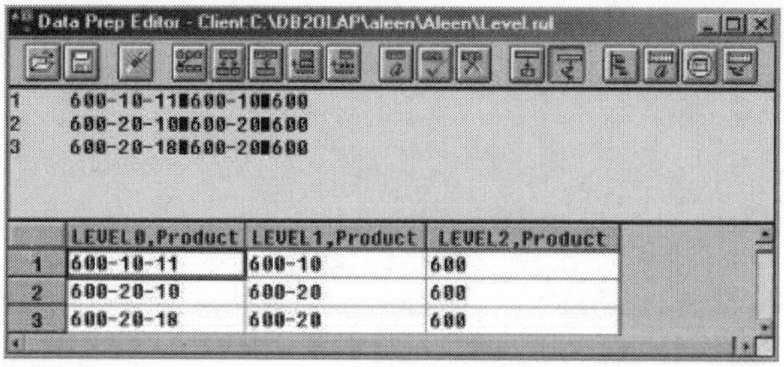

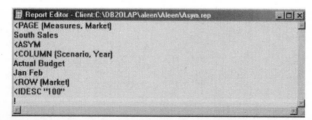

Figure 11.11   Data Prep Editor.

- Perform user security definition and maintenance. (See Figure 11.13.)

- Monitor database statistics reported at the database, application, and server levels, and perform routine database maintenance routines as required. (See Figure 11.14.)

ESSCMD and MaxL

The command-line utilities that support 100 percent of App Man functionality in batch mode are ESSCMD (pronounced "es command") and MaxL (pronounced "mac sel"). Traditionally, the database designer uses App Man to create rules files that enable external files (of specific design) to be used to build database dimensions (*dimension-build* rules files), as well as populate databases with data (*data-load* rules files). Users have the ability to load data from flat ASCII files, spreadsheets, or RDBMS tables using the optional SQL interface.

An administrator would be responsible for creating and configuring a batch environment to effect a lights-out production environment using ESSCMD or MaxL. (For a complete introduction to App Man, MaxL, and ESSCMD, refer to the documentation that accompanies DB2 OLAP Server.)

Figure 11.12   Report Editor.

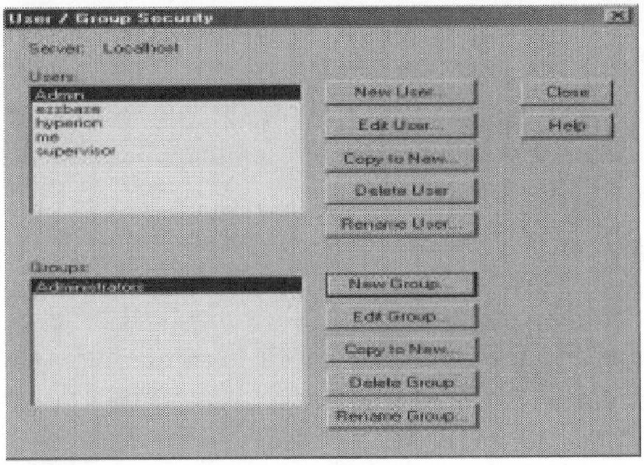

Figure 11.13   User/group security.

Application Manager, ESSCMD, and MaxL enable a powerful and flexible operating OLAP environment. Data can be loaded to a DB2 OLAP database from nearly every conceivable ODBC data source that includes flat files, RDBMS tables, and spreadsheets. Moreover, DB2 OLAP Server supports out-of-the-box database write capabilities. This functionality is crucial for supporting, for example, budgeting applications where the users need to be able to quickly adjust and readjust figures and test outcomes. In this process, users that have an appropriate security profile can write data to the database directly from (standard) spreadsheet client desktops.

Security can be maintained from providing users with full database access all the way down to having access to a single cell. DB2 OLAP Server supports development of a full complement of OLAP applications out-of-the-box, and applications can be completely user-defined and dynamic through the fully functional C and VB APIs.

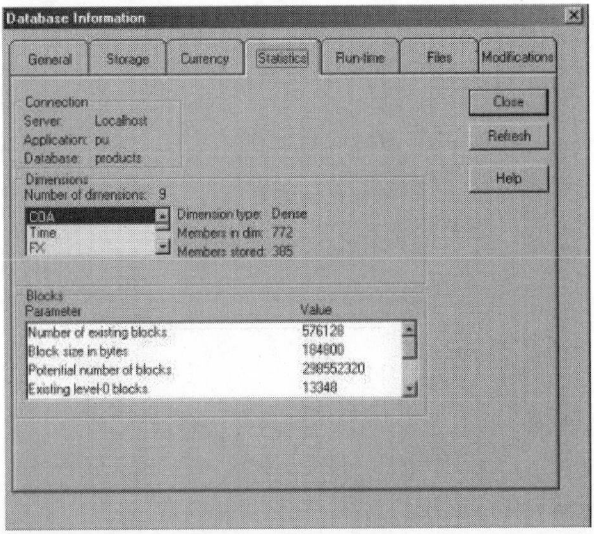

Figure 11.14   Database information.

The ability to build and load data from multiple sources eases prototyping efforts. Furthermore, the App Man outline development GUI can be used to function very effectively as a rapid application development (RAD) tool enabling business users to convey complex business notions to IT efficiently and with minimal effort.

Although the App Man, ESSCMD/MaxL tools represent a powerful OLAP application development setting, they really are best applied within small information systems environments. What works for application prototyping does not necessarily work in a production environment, and new OLAP application development here remains unfortunately tied to a cumbersome development process. New business models can be generated only after the newly defined set of supporting dimension-build and data-load files have been created. The result is an environment where a potentially chaotic proliferation of files and database tables has to be monitored and maintained. More often than not, these environments are decentralized and reuse of an object is more a result of luck than planning and design.

To bring OLAP to the enterprise, a tool is needed that effectively coordinates relational (star schema) meta data with OLAP meta data.

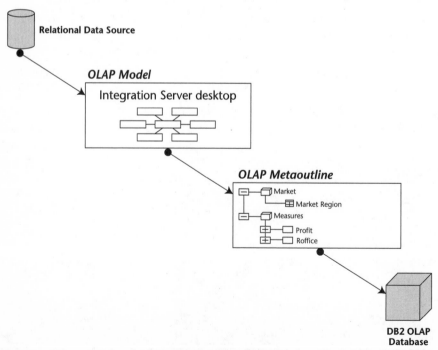

Figure 11.15   Relational to multidimensional data.

OLAP Integration Server

DB2 OLAP Integration Server very precisely fits the role as meta data coordinator. Using OIS, a user can create, populate, and then calculate databases directly from RDMS tables. Figure 11.15 shows the basic outline of the steps required to move relational data and meta data to multidimensional data and meta data.

Figure 11.16 shows this architecture in greater detail. The OLAP model "understands" source relational meta data. Users can select from a subset of the OLAP model objects to generate OLAP metaoutlines. From an OLAP metaoutline the user is able to generate a single DB2 OLAP database. The ability to create many OLAP metaoutlines from a single OLAP model enables users to efficiently create many OLAP cubes from a single relational star schema.

Relational data mart designers should take advantage of the one-to-many relationship between OLAP models and OLAP metaoutlines and design the relational database to support the generation of multiple OLAP databases. This means that data mart design and contents should be expressly expanded to let users take advantage of this functionality. For a concise overview of relational schema design techniques to support OIS-driven DB2 OLAP Server database development, refer to Appendix B, "Integration Server Implementation Guidelines" in the *IBM DB2 OLAP Server Theory and Practices Redbook*, IBM Inc., 2001.

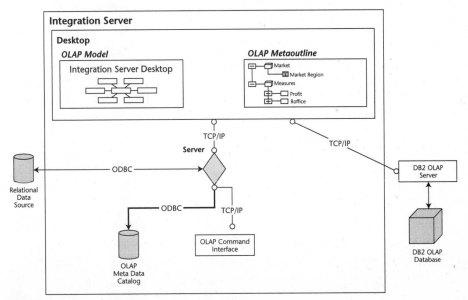

Figure 11.16 OLAP model and metaoutline.

Figures 11.15 and 11.16 show the correct flow of data and meta data but an incorrect ordering of development events. The best-practice OIS methodology actually works back to the relational star requirements from a set of OLAP requirements. Once the analytic requirements are sketched out for an OLAP database, star schema relational requirements can be developed. After the DBA has created the appropriate relational data source (star schema) to support OLAP model generation, DB2 OLAP databases can be created, populated, and calculated using the OIS OLAP metaoutline interface.

In fact, the OIS tool supports the database creation activities for power users, and the tool really aims at these individuals as its intended users. The advanced use of cube generation functionality is sometimes referred to as "cube-on-the-fly." This term attempts to convey that users can efficiently generate a new DB2 OLAP Server database for further analysis as a result of questions and issues generated while performing analysis in another cube. To support this, OIS enables users to select a subset of meta data (dimensions and members) and numeric data from the data mart and generate new OLAP databases.

However, the real enabler of cube-on-the-fly functionality is the design of the star schema that underpins cube generation. The relational schema must contain data that supports these ad hoc cube-creating excursions through data. For example, suppose that a key performance indicator (KPI) on an executive report prepared from data in a corporate cube for the CFO indicates a problem with sales in the Eastern Region for Diet Products. The CFO might pick up the phone and ask the Eastern Region Manager of Diet Products something like, "What is going on over there in the East?"

In a properly designed OIS/OLAP environment, a data analyst would quickly create a new OLAP metaoutline from an existing OLAP model. A new cube would be generated having a dimensionality and data that narrowly focuses on the details of Eastern Region and Diet Products. These details would not have been present in the corporate cube. Moreover, OIS can design cubes that enable a drill-back to even more granular relational detailed data stored in the star schema to further assist the analyst in her task. Once the investigation is completed to the CFO's satisfaction, the new cube can be thrown away. But the prerequisite would be that these Regional and Product details be available for use on demand in the star schema. Ultimately, then, everything rests on the details of the design.

To sum up, the concept of cube-on-the-fly and throwaway cubes really assumes an environment where the OLAP databases are being designed and generated by users. If so, then what is the role of IT within an enterprise OLAP environment if it is not to design and build the OLAP cubes to user specifications? After all, creating database schemas is not generally considered to be a user function.

Support Requirements

Let's examine the statement that DB2 OLAP Server meta data is composed of business entities. The most important implication that we want to draw here is that, with minimal technical training, business users can become excellent OLAP modelers. As we said earlier, users "get it" really fast.

Removing the layer of abstraction extant of the RDBMS schema components enables the organization to appropriately keep business logic in the hands of the business user and also put into their hands the ability to embed that business logic into a highly functional computer-based structure called DB2 OLAP Server. OLAP application development does *not* have to consist of transferring/translating business logic to a technician so that the technician can transfer that logic to a schema. In OLAP Server, business users build business models. The collaboration of IT and business users in an OLAP environment enables each to remain largely within the domains of their respective expertise.

Business users who build OLAP models (i.e., superusers) need to know what buttons to push and what keystrokes to make in OIS and App Man to enable them to achieve their objective. There are relational and multidimensional components that must be understood in order for users to meet these requirements.

To acquire this skill set, all that is really required is that they receive the appropriate end-user training. These users will need to understand enough about storage implications to be able to understand why they need to work very closely with IT in the database creation process.

Are business users being set free to run rampant within an enterprise infrastructure? No, they are not. The traditional role of IT is expanded in one way. Of course, IT needs to know in detail the hardware requirements necessary to support the entire OLAP environment. And to do this effectively, IT must know the details about the storage implications of DB2 OLAP Server databases. Someone in IT should follow the training path outlined for system administrators. But, in particular, they must understand in detail the concepts related to sparse matrix management as they pertain to DB2 OLAP Server. This is because OLAP storage constructs are, as will be seen in the next section, data-driven. In other words, the underlying sparse nature of OLAP data sets is a major factor in the resource requirements necessary to compute them.

DB2 OLAP Database as a Matrix

The notion that DB2 OLAP storage structures implement data storage as a matrix (or array) is perhaps the most important concept for a DB2 OLAP developer and IT resource manager. Figure 11.17 illustrates the array model. Understanding matrix management eventually will include an understanding of the corollary concept of sparseness. That is, as more dimensions are added to the matrix, proportionally fewer intersection points (or cells) across the matrix actually contain values.

Consider the following array declaration containing 21,370,660,375,680 intersection points:

DIM (172, 21, 27, 32, 209, 32765)

The DB2 OLAP Server allows dimensions to be tagged or defined as either dense or sparse. When a dimension is tagged as dense, it becomes part of the storage structure called the *data block*. Every data block that is created in the database has an identical structure. In our example, it contains precisely 172 * 21 * 27 = 97,524 cells, or intersection points. (See Figure 11.18.)

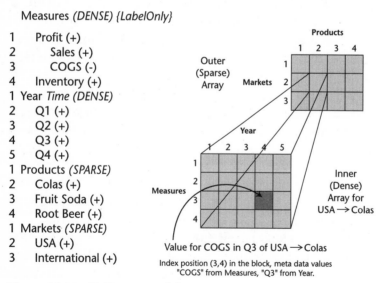

Measures *(DENSE) {LabelOnly}*

1 Profit (+)
2   Sales (+)
3   COGS (-)
4 Inventory (+)
1 Year *Time (DENSE)*
2   Q1 (+)
3   Q2 (+)
4   Q3 (+)
5   Q4 (+)
1 Products *(SPARSE)*
2   Colas (+)
3   Fruit Soda (+)
4   Root Beer (+)
1 Markets *(SPARSE)*
2   USA (+)
3   International (+)

Value for COGS in Q3 of USA → Colas

Index position (3,4) in the block, meta data values "COGS" from Measures, "Q3" from Year.

Figure 11.17 OLAP array model.

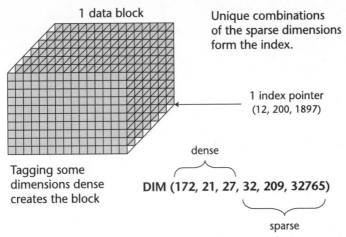

1 data block

Unique combinations
of the sparse dimensions
form the index.

1 index pointer
(12, 200, 1897)

dense

Tagging some
dimensions dense
creates the block

DIM (172, 21, 27, 32, 209, 32765)

sparse

Figure 11.18   OLAP storage structures explored.

All data blocks are stored on disk within the ESS*.PAG files. Addressing, or locating, blocks of data is provided by sparse member combinations. These combinations become part of the storage structure called the *index* and are stored on disk with the ESS*.IND files.

Enabling these two definitions of dimensions makes the matrix modular. The data block is a fixed format data structure, the existence of which is driven by data-relevant sparse member combinations in the index. By "data-relevant" we mean that only where business data actually exists across sparse member combinations will a data block be generated.

For example, if we do not sell any suntan oil in January in the Arctic, we do not reserve any space in our array for those intersection coordinates. One of the differences between the DB2 OLAP storage structures and relational ones is that a relational index is optional. In DB2 OLAP the index is not. Deleting an index for a relational table has no effect on the table data. Deleting the index from a DB2 OLAP database corrupts the database.

The small subcomponents of the array (the data block and its index address) are quite readily moved between disk and working memory. These structures mesh very well with the general user requirement of only being interested in sub-sets of information from the array at any one point in time.

Block Creation Explored

The database shown in Figure 11.18 contains six dimensions with the following DB2 OLAP configuration:

Dense dimension #1 containing 172 members

Dense dimension #2 containing 21 members

Dense dimension #3 containing 27 members

Sparse dimension #1 containing 32 members

Sparse dimension #2 containing 209 members

Sparse dimension #3 containing 32,765 members

Which data blocks are actually created depends upon unique sparse combinations that contain data. In our example, a block with address (12, 200, 1897) has been generated because a business event has occurred at that intersection point. We could convert or translate the index node into something like "A&P (customer 1897 of sparse dimension #3) sold colas (member 12 of sparse dimension #1) in New York (member 200 of sparse dimension #2.)"

Matrix Explosion

The three defining characteristics of a DB2 OLAP Server array are as follows:

- The number of dimensions
- The number of members within each dimension
- The hierarchical relationship of the members within each dimension

Data explosion can occur across each characteristic individually and concurrently having a combined (that is, Cartesian) impact. For example, if we increase sparse dimension #1 to include 5,000 members, the number of potential intersection points increases from $2.3 * 10^{13}$ to $3.3 * 10^{15}$! In similar fashion, adding a completely new dimension will explode the number of potential intersection points. We can do both at once, adding more members to an existing dimension at the same time as we add a completely new dimension to the database. (See Chapter 2 for more discussion regarding cell explosion.)

DB2 OLAP Server Sizing Requirements

Estimating the size of a DB2 OLAP multidimensional database is conceptually identical to estimating the size of any database, relational or otherwise. It essentially involves estimating final size based on numeric extrapolations derived from known characteristics of the data. The more precisely the characteristics of the data to be stored are known, the more accurate the estimation can be. Once we are confident that we know *what* has to be stored, we can more or less effectively gauge approximately *how much* of it we need to store. DB2 OLAP Server databases make this process very simple in some respects, in others not.

What DB2 OLAP Server Stores

As mentioned previously, DB2 OLAP stores only numbers at intersection points across a storage array. It stores floating-point numbers and needs 8 bytes per number. That's the easy part. You really do not have to worry about different data types. Moreover, there is an inherent sparseness of multidimensional data sets that the DB2 OLAP array has to deal with that creates overhead for the server, since some of those intersection points in the array contain no values. Illustrated in Figure 11.19 is a comparison between the DB2 OLAP outline and the storage of intersection points.

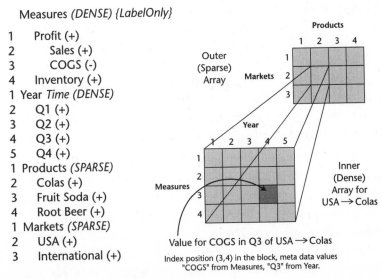

Figure 11.19 DB2 OLAP array.

DB2 OLAP Server uses a concept called *data blocks* to store intersection points. These data blocks contain a fixed configuration of intersection points called *data cells* where floating-point numbers can be stored. A properly configured database will be the one that generates the fewest number of data blocks with the greatest amount of data. You can create a reasonably accurate estimation of the overall database size if you can answer the following two questions:

- Approximately how many cells, on average, does a block contain?
- Approximately how many blocks are generated?

Using SET MSG ONLY: Pre-Version 8 Estimates

Prior to Release 8.1 of DB2 OLAP Server, SET MSG ONLY was a completely undocumented and unsupported command. It has a number of very significant uses. To use the command, a representative sample of production data is loaded into an empty database. Then a calculation of the database is initiated using the following script:

```
SET MSG ONLY;
CALC ALL;
```

This command, when specified in a calculation script or as part of the database default calc, will initiate a false-calculation of a database. This means that the DB2 OLAP Server engine will perform a calculation run-through of the database keeping track of the calculation process in terms of block creation. This information will be reported in the application log, and from it you can deduce the approximate number of data blocks that the database would have created as if you had actually calculated it.

If you can generate a reliable statistic regarding the total number of blocks that a model will create without having to create them, you can do two very valuable things:

Estimate database size. By keeping a record of the number of blocks created and database size in bytes directly after a representative level-0 data load to a database, you can divide the (total number of bytes) by the (number of loaded blocks) to derive an estimate of the average number of bytes per compressed block on disk. Multiplying that figure by the total estimated number of blocks gives you a very good approximation of the total size of your compressed database in bytes.

Estimate batch calculation time. Assuming that you now have a very good approximation of the total size of your database, you can divide that number by the DB2 OLAP throughput metric of your hardware to generate an estimation of the total time to calculate the model. Note that we are assuming here that batch calculation throughput is linear. Empirical observations repeatedly show that as calculations approach their completion, throughput on the DB2 OLAP server diminishes. This is especially evident when calculating very large databases containing many tens of millions of blocks.

What is Representative Data?

SET MSG ONLY reports block creation based on the nature of the data that was loaded. This is the hard part. It is not always possible to come up with a representative data sample. And if you only load some data, or fabricate data, you will only generate limited results, fabricated results, or both! To be reliable and accurate, you need to load real data across all of the dimensions in the model.

Thus, SET MSG ONLY enables you to get a very accurate estimation of the total number of blocks that a particular database (configuration) will generate in a very short amount of time. The word *estimation* is used because the algorithm will not take into consideration member formula or calculation scripts. This should be considered a qualification to any estimates generated by SET MSG ONLY.

Sizing Estimates for DB2 OLAP Server Version 8

As shown in Figure 11.20, there is a new support for DB2 OLAP Server V8.0 called ESTIMATEFULLDBSIZE. The command should be considered a replacement for SET MSG ONLY. Executed using esscmd.exe, this command provides an estimation of total block count.

A good estimate of database size can be calculated by multiplying the block count by the block size and compression ratio as follows:

```
102216 * 58464 * .03313 = 198 Meg
```

```
localhost: ccdemo: finance: essexer[1]->estimatefulldbsize 4;
EstimateFullDbSize:

Estimated count of blocks after full calculation = 102216
Time elapsed to calculate this estimation = 1.75 seconds
```

Figure 11.20 ESTIMATEFULLDBSIZE command.

	Parameter	Value	▲
1	Number of existing blocks	105440	
2	Block size in bytes	58464	
3	Potential number of blocks	1346018520	
4	Existing level-0 blocks	5750	
8	Compression Ratio	0.02778	

	Type	Size	Status	Name	▲
1	Index file	8216576	Open	D:\Essbase65bld	
2	Data file	180232192	Open	D:\Essbase65bld	

Figure 11.21   Estimate versus actual.

Figure 11.21 shows that the estimated database size is within 10 percent of the overall database size after calculation.

Database Tuning

We have already looked at the basics of the data storage structures and how dimension settings and member tags can be effectively used to offset the effects of sparse matrix management and the data explosion that can accompany multidimensional databases. But there are three more advanced issues to consider when tuning your database. These include two advanced DB2 OLAP functions and one feature that can also be employed to offset matrix explosion and to tune extremely large DB2 OLAP applications.

There are four major areas to concentrate on when performance tuning a DB2 OLAP database:

- Handling the characteristics of the dimensionality and embedded business logic.

- Implementing member tags.

- Handling outline/database consolidation and business formulae.

- Determining optimal dense/sparse settings.

All of these revolve around the single most important DB2 OLAP construct: the database outline. In a DB2 OLAP Server environment the database outline is the database schema. We have said it is a place where the business model and the data model are the same and are represented graphically. The storage characteristics of the outline are no less important to a multidimensional model than are the storage characteristics of the schema to a relational one. A relational schema tuned for OLTP or query processing will pay very different attention to the schema design and the associated storage structures to achieve the desired performance characteristics.

Goal Of Database Tuning

The goal of optimally configuring sparse-dense settings for a database tuning is twofold:

- Create as few blocks as possible.
- Create blocks that are as densely populated as possible.

Dense dimensions are implemented to reflect the *density* of the data set, and sparse dimensions are implemented to reflect, or reduce the effect of, the *sparseness* of the data set. We write *reduce* because it is not realistic to expect to be able to eliminate sparseness from a DB2 OLAP Server matrix. If the dense nature of a data set is not contained within the block (a dense dimension is tagged sparse), an explosion of the overall number of data blocks that the configuration generates will result. Conversely, large and empty data blocks indicate that sparseness has not been effectively eliminated from the data set.

Outline Tuning Considerations

There are three main considerations when tuning the outline:

How many dimensions are there?   Implementers are limited by the total number of dimensions that can be modeled, as well as by the hardware configuration on which the model is being developed.

How large are they?   The total number of members ultimately determines the sparseness of the data set.

How deep are they?   Database performance characteristics will also vary according to the depth of the hierarchies of the dimensions. Designers must be able to identify and adjust database configurations according to the demands of the specific (practical) database being developed.

Sparse or dense settings might have to be altered to accommodate specific client requirements—for example, to support member calculation or query retrieval requirements.

NOTE Database configurations will be optimal not necessarily according to the best sparse/dense configuration but according to requirements specific to the model at hand.

Databases that are incrementally updated across time almost by definition preclude the possibility of tagging the time dimension dense, even though it properly adheres to the density of the data set.

Batch Calculation and Data Storage

The batch calc process for DB2 OLAP Server databases optimizes runtime performance by making the vast majority of data set values persistent. The cycle of database build and refresh will regularly include time for loading data, as well as time to replenish derived and aggregation values along the dimensional hierarchies. The period of time required to refresh data is commonly referred to as the *batch window*. The batch calculation process will have significant disk storage implications. To help defray the cost of auxiliary storage and I/O, the objective of the database designer is to implement the database configuration that generates the least number of blocks that has the highest density.

Member Tags and Dynamic Calculations

DB2 OLAP Server enables users to tag members as dynamic calculations. Members that are tagged will have their calculation removed from the batch calculation process. They will be dynamically calculated for the user at query retrieval or runtime. Positive effects of implementing dynamic calculation member tags include:

- Reduced batch calculation window
- Reduced data block size
- Reduced overall database size

Member tags are not only implemented for storage implications. Tags also enable users to take embedded business logic coded in the DB2 OLAP Server calculation engine within the outline. The DB2 OLAP Server database has been coded to "understand" a certain amount of business logic.

For example, *time balancing* is the term DB2 OLAP Server uses to describe business quantities that do not aggregate over time. Having 5 headcount in January, 6 in February, and 10 in March does not mean we have 21 headcount for Quarter 1. The same is true for inventory items and (alas) for balance sheet items such as your checkbook. There is a critical business need to represent these metrics as desired at upper levels of time. They cannot be left to the standard engine aggregation. In DB2 OLAP Server, you click on a button in the outline to make a quantity "TB First" (said "Time Balance First"), or "TB Last," or "TB Average." This will cause the database engine to report correctly at upper levels of time the first period value, the last period value, or the average period value.

There are also ways to enable the database engine to calculate values according to business logic that either includes or skips values that are missing from the database—for example, to implement the business-relevant difference between the average revenue for all products and the average revenue for all products sold.

DB2 OLAP Server enables this business logic to be implemented by the database engine. Implementation is simple, intuitive, and a mouse-click away, and it works the same across all levels of time. The outline fragment illustrated in Figure 11.22 is a small sample of tagging capabilities of DB2 OLAP Server. Note first that the Measures dimension itself has been tagged as the Accounts dimension. This is a dimension tag that enables the implementation of other member tags like, for example, Expense Reporting. The Dynamic Calc tag indicates that member calculations are performed at query time rather than during batch window calculations. The Label Only tag causes DB2 OLAP Server to treat the member as a navigation point, and DB2 OLAP Server does not reserve any storage space for numeric data for these members. The TB First tag implements the time-balancing functionality discussed previously, and the Expense Reporting tag implements balance sheet expense account functionality. Finally, note that the Opening Inventory member has no less than three member tags, as well as a member formula associated with it.

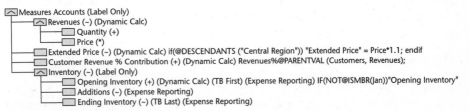

Figure 11.22   Tagging.

The small outline fragment helps illustrate why business users find it easy to use to build business models. The outline is, in the final analysis, a user-friendly object for business analysts. Users can be allowed (or disallowed) to view outline contents directly in order to understand the definition of metrics. The same user-friendly functionality cannot be said to apply to other OLAP products.

Disk Subsystem Utilization and Database File Configuration

We do not want to wade into ongoing debates on which RAID level offers optimal performance. We do want to offer some guidelines for storage experts to be aware of when considering how to configure disk arrays and subsystems. DB2 OLAP Server is disk I/O-intensive. It is write-intensive during database calculation events, and read-intensive during user query retrieval events.

DB2 OLAP Server offers administrators the ability to manage three sets of files differently. The first set we will refer to as database control files. These reside within the same directory structure as the DB2 OLAP Server executable files, but under a different subdirectory. Control files stored there include those associated with specific databases like the database outline (which need to be fully read into working memory), as well as transaction control files, and so on. By default, the data (ess*.pag) and data index (ess*.ind) files are also stored within subdirectories off of the installation directory.

Administrators can separate data and index files from each other, as well as from the control files along different disk I/O channels. Since every fetch from disk involves reading from both the index and data files, isolating these files from each other on separate disk I/O channels will be accompanied by a performance boost. An additional, though less significant, boost in performance can be achieved by isolating the database control files on an I/O channel separate, again, from both the data and data index files.

Database Partitioning

DB2 OLAP partitioning functionality potentially gives application designers the ability to implement a very large application across a multiple rather than single database architecture. Through partitioning, a designer can break up and divide a single database into smaller databases and then spread workload across the hardware infrastructure, thereby more efficiently utilizing disk and CPU resources.

We say *potentially* because use of the partitioning option in all but the simplest of cases involves very advanced understanding of DB2 OLAP storage structures, calculation, and query retrieval requirements. We almost hesitate to caution that database partitioning does not solve all issues concerning database scale.

We are bringing database partitioning to your attention because, properly configured, it can add real value to a DB2 OLAP Server implementation. For a more detailed discussion of DB2 OLAP partitioning, refer to the DB2 OLAP Server Database Administrator's Guide.

Attribute Dimensions

The third functionality that we deem important to mention in this context is the ability to use attribute dimensions in DB2 OLAP Server. An *attribute dimension* is essentially a dimension that describes another dimension directly and provides the ability for users to dynamically calculate values relative to the dimensional attribute at runtime.

For example, consider a product dimension where each individual product has the attribute of color, as shown in Figure 11.23. Users can have analytic functionality across the color attribute in one of two ways. The database can implement color analytics as a regular (or base) dimension. This solution has the Color dimension become part of the multidimensional storage array and will impact data storage and batch calculation requirements. The Color dimension would appear as a regular dimension, and every intersection point in the cube would have a member of the Color dimension as a reference point, or coordinate.

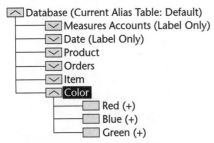

Figure 11.23   Color dimension.

On the other hand, color analytics could be implemented through an attribute dimension as shown in Figure 11.24. Here color is an attribute that describes members of the Product dimension. In the former case, all DB2 OLAP Server analytic capabilities are brought to bear on color, whereas as an attribute of product, DB2 OLAP Server offers only a subset of analytic capabilities. (For more information on the use of Attribute dimensions, see the DB2 OLAP Server Database Administrator's Guide.

If an attribute has no data storage or batch calculation requirements, why not use attributes all of the time? There are two main reasons for choosing to implement attribute dimensions cautiously:

■ Attribute dimension calculations are dynamically calculated for users at runtime, and, therefore, they can seriously impact retrieval performance. In fact, the only two scenarios that we are aware of where database tuning is required to support query retrievals involve both attribute dimensions and database partitioning.

■ An attribute dimension generally describes data at the lowest level of granularity. Products, for example, have attributes that disappear at the product-type level. For example, the size attribute for a particular cola SKU is 16 oz. However, the Colas product line does not have a single size attribute because the product line of Colas has potentially many size attributes. It perhaps warrants saying that product lines could have a suite of attributes and that these would *not* be applicable either below or above them along the product hierarchy.

Storing multidimensional data at a low level of granularity can expand tremendously the overall storage requirements of the OLAP database. As a result, we caution that the use of attributes, too, needs to be implemented by developers with advanced knowledge of DB2 OLAP Server storage structures and calculation requirements.

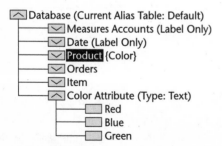

Figure 11.24   Attribute dimensions.

Assessing Hardware Requirements

Multidimensional technology is really only beginning to be delivered in enterprisewide contexts and management of an enterprise OLAP environment represents a nontrivial set of tasks. Databases and applications can grow to enormous proportions. For example, IBM manages and distributes their worldwide Corporate Planning application at their Apex center in Southbury, Connecticut. They scale over 1 terabyte of triple-mirrored OLAP data to over 6,000 users using 420 applications (500+ databases) delivered across 30 AIX nodes and it is available $24 \times 7 \times 365$.

Obviously, implementations with the magnitude of Apex require managing more than DB2 OLAP Server and perhaps defy attempts to prescribe hardware configurations. At the enterprise level it is quite out of the question to relegate OLAP functionality to that old out-of-service NT server. Enterprise BI/DW initiatives have assumed mission-critical status for organizations.

As mentioned, DB2 OLAP Server databases can be both CPU- and disk I/O-intensive, and you should expect a full-scale implementation of OLAP across the enterprise to be demanding of both types of resources. A number of questions can be asked that will assist you in determining hardware configuration definitions and requirements to support OLAP:

- Are the applications read-only?
- How many concurrent readers will likely be involved?
- Are applications read-, write-, and calculate-intensive?
- If so, how many concurrent calculations are likely to be involved?
- Are there also concurrent readers-only of these calculation databases?
- Are complex business algorithms involved in database calculations?

The answers to these questions will assist you in making a more or less accurate approximation of infrastructure requirements. In the absence of these answers, however, what can be done?

There is a way to make some more or less meaningful quantitative assessments about infrastructure requirements in advance of the availability of real data and detailed user requirements. For someone familiar with DB2 OLAP Server, the process involves making an assumption that might appear odd to someone not so familiar. The assumption is that platform utilization (essentially reducible to disk throughput) will be 100 percent during batch processing.

Experience has shown that the functionality offered by multidimensional databases is highly sought after within the business user community. The development of DB2 OLAP Server from its inception at Arbor Software until today can be read as the ongoing attempt to bring as much OLAP functionality to as much data as possible.

The result of satisfying this demand is that users generally end up pushing the OLAP envelope to its limit within the time frame of their particular batch-calculation environment (refer to the section *Batch Calculation and Data Storage*, earlier in the chapter). It is only a marginal exaggeration to say that each advance of DB2 OLAP Server that increases the ability of the engine to be more efficient at processing data is met with an equal increase in demand for more OLAP functionality.

At first, the demand for increased OLAP functionality takes the form of adding more dimensionality to the databases. This can cause the database sizes to explode. More refined and advanced OLAP environments will be populated with databases that vary in size from tightly focused small (hundreds of megabytes) databases serving precise business modeling purposes to larger (greater than 50 GB) generic reporting OLAP databases.

Consider, for example, what effect dynamic calculation member tags really brought to DB2 OLAP Server. When first introduced in Essbase version 5.0, dynamic member tags provided the ability to defer the calculation of certain metrics to occur at runtime. Because fewer members are being stored on disk, the database size is reduced. Because fewer members are being calculated during the batch process, the amount of time required to calculate data was also reduced.

The user community, however, did not respond by expressing delight at disk space saved or processing time reduced. Rather, they immediately began to look for ways to implement more OLAP functionality in their existing databases that still fit within the old batch window.

In a hypothetical but truly representative example, a batch calculation would be reduced from 8 to 2 hours and the database size reduced from 20 to 5 GB simply by implementing dynamic calculations. Once this performance boost was posted, users begin immediately to seek to implement *more* OLAP functionality. Implementing this increased functionality returns the batch calculation time back to 8 hours and grows the database back to 20 GB, but the "new" version of the "old" database will have nine rather than six dimensions, incorporating 100 rather than 10 business metrics!

In the final analysis, it can be expected that every gain in performance will be met with an equal user demand for an increase in OLAP functionality.

This user behavior, however, actually provides a way to back into an estimation of hardware requirements. These estimates involve at least being able to gather two pieces of user requirement information. The first is to get an estimate of the number of OLAP databases planned for implementation. The key component to the estimate, however, is determining how much time will be devoted to precalculating the databases.

CPU Estimate

Based on the assumption that user requirements will require each platform to be utilized 100 percent during batch processing, you can begin by assigning one CPU to support the calculation of each database. Factoring in the number of concurrent users that will be addressing OLAP enables you to refine CPU requirements. Query retrievals have supported multiple threading for a while, and in Version 8.1, each database can take advantage of up to four CPUs during calculation, so you can also factor assigning more than one CPU per database if necessary for calculation as well, if designed.

Disk Estimate

Since disk throughput continues to lag far behind CPU throughput, overall system performance remains directly related to the former. So, by factoring the overall OLAP disk throughput for a given platform across a strictly defined period of time, you can estimate how much disk space will potentially be required. You also have to take into account that certain DB2 OLAP Server maintenance routines will require double the amount of disk space, but you really only have to do so for the largest database. (The maximum largest database can be estimated by multiplying the amount of time for the batch window by throughput on a given platform.)

The following example represents a template for estimating OLAP throughput for a 4-hour OLAP database batch-process window:

```
Number of business units                          50
Cubes estimated per business unit              ×   4
Cubes (CPUs) for batch processing             200
Extra CPUs estimated for query processing     + 50
CPUs total                                    250
CPUs/Platform Server                          ÷   8
Total Platform Servers       (250/8)           32

Estimated OLAP Throughput (gigabytes/hour)      4
```

OLAP Auxiliary Storage Requirements

Total disk requirements to support 32 (discrete) servers can be calculated using the following formula:

```
Batch CalcTime * ThroughPut * NumberOFServers
4 hours * 4 gig/hour * 32 = 512 gigabytes
```

Add an additional 16 GB (per server) to support database maintenance routines (16 * 32 = 368):

```
368 + 512 = 880 gigabytes
```

Each cube averages (512 GB/200 cubes) 2.6 GB.

Is it reasonable to assume that the order of 0.9 terabytes of OLAP data will exist within an enterprisewide BI/DW? We think that the number is not too far out of line. The example *probably* overestimates when it assumes each database is roughly of equal size. Results will vary widely according to particular scenarios. The point is that the method provides a way to begin to define the scope of OLAP infrastructure requirements.

OLAP Backup and Disaster Recovery

Precisely which objects need to be backed up to support disaster recovery is what we want to consider OLAP disaster recovery when perceived from a slightly higher perspective.

In this chapter you have seen how DB2 OLAP Server functionality across the enterprise calls for the implementation of a tool called OLAP Integration Server. OIS is a sophisticated utility that enables users to map relational star schema data and meta data to DB2 OLAP Server data and meta data.

In such an environment, the source relational data that becomes meta data (i.e., dimension hierarchies and dimension hierarchy member names), as well as numeric (fact table) data for OLAP, are stored in an RDBMS. It is from the relational database that are generated both the structure and content of multidimensional DB2 OLAP Server databases.

A coherent backup and recovery strategy might be constructed around the notion that all that is required is to keep from disaster the data required to re-create or derive other values. In an OIS/DB2 OLAP Server environment, star schema data is the source from which multidimensional *databases* are derived. It seems to follow that only relational source data and OIS repositories, but not the derived values of multidimensional databases and their objects, need to be backed up.

In an OIS/DB2 OLAP Server environment, multidimensional databases are only loosely coupled with their relational source, and it is possible, and even sometimes desirable, for users to be able to alter the OLAP database schemas that OIS generates. We've argued that the ability to manipulate the multidimensional schema is a very important part of advanced user OLAP functionality. This functionality does infer, however, that the final form of OLAP databases may not be incipient with their relational sources.

In these cases, extra-database information needs also to be backed up for disaster recovery. And in all likelihood there will be other extra-database OLAP objects that need to be secured for a full disaster recovery program, for example, modified database outlines, user report definitions, and calculation programs (calc scripts).

Securing extra-database information is not the only reason to extend a disaster recovery strategy beyond RDBMS objects and contents. Efficiencies in the ability to restore user data and environments are also important. The ultimate factor in determining whether to extend backup strategies to include every OLAP object will be the amount of time it takes to *regenerate* the OLAP databases compared to the time it takes to *restore* them. The closer that users experience components of the BI/DW to be mission-critical, the more they will demand the fastest return to normal operations. You should expect OLAP users in particular to be very demanding in this regard.

Summary

DB2 OLAP Server is a MOLAP tool that enables analysts to steer the business. We defined OLAP as essential and integral to BI/DW initiatives. Its place is complementary to data mining and relational technologies within the BI/DW.

We provided a high-level architecture for implementing OLAP across the enterprise and argued for the strategic importance of using the fulfillment OLAP requirements to help IT prototype the data warehouse. Implementations of this type necessitate the coordination and cooperation of IT with business user personnel.

CHAPTER 12

OLAP with IBM DB2 Data Warehouse Center

Key Issues:

- ETL processes have an opportunity to blend OLAP-centric transformation steps into the environment, thus providing warehouse administrators and acquisition developers a single setting from which to control all data movement. And, although there are many ETL tools available, few focus on this aspect of data transformation—from relational technology to cube.

- Being able to load cubes is important; however, two characteristics of DB2 OLAP Server cubes must also be addressed. Warehouse administrators must be able to control the calculation of the cube as well as modify the cube structure itself.

IBM DB2 Data Warehouse Center (DWC) allows a user to manage and transform source data into a warehouse. Once the data is in the warehouse, it can then be used for loading into multidimensional (OLAP) databases such as DB2 OLAP Server.

OLAP integration is a natural fit for integration with the Data Warehouse Center. The base functions of the tool allow you to pull the data together from a variety of different sources and formats, clean and aggregate that data, and then take this atomic-level data at a predefined aggregate level and load it into OLAP cubes for use by end-user business analysts. For example, a process scenario could be like this:

1. Pull data from the ORACLE sales database and populate a DB2 warehouse.

2. Pull geographic information from the Human Resource database in DB2, cleanse it to remove any duplicate information, and blend it into the DB2 warehouse.

3. Summarize the data per salesperson to get the total sales for an individual.

4. Join the data together, sales and geographic information.

5. Import the data into DB2 OLAP Server for multidimensional analysis.

Resolving a lot of the data preparation at the atomic layer and then having OLAP-centric steps in IBM DB2 Data Warehouse Center to process that atomic level data into OLAP cubes for analysis ensures processing consistency.

We've already described OLAP in detail in various chapters. In Chapter 4 we defined the dimensional model and related OLAP structures, and in Chapter 11 we described the application of OLAP and the technical aspects of DB2 OLAP Server. In this chapter we describe how the Data Warehouse Center can support the propagation of data into the cube structures of DB2 OLAP Server. To that end, we start by defining the DWC step types specific to the support of OLAP transformations. The chapter then describes how these steps are added into your ETL process. Load and calc scripts are then specified for building your cubes, along with a review of steps to modify your cube outline.

IBM DB2 Data Warehouse Center Step Types

IBM DB2 Data Warehouse Center allows users to add OLAP processing of warehouse data to the warehouse process by having native OLAP support step types. Step types for OLAP are similar to those described in Chapters

8 and 9. As shown in Figure 12.1, these step types allow you to do a variety of processing on the data, including:

- Update the dimensions of outline of an OLAP cube from meta data stored in a file based on a rules file.

- Update the dimensions of outline of an OLAP cube from meta data in a relational table based on a rules file.

- Load the OLAP cube with a delimited file generated from the execution of a warehouse step using no rules file and using the OLAP load mechanism.

- Load the OLAP cube with a delimited file generated from the execution of a warehouse step using no rules file and using the OLAP lock and import mechanism.

- Load the OLAP cube with a file generated from the execution of a warehouse step using a rules file.

- Load the OLAP cube with data in a relational table generated from the execution of a warehouse step using a rules file.

- Execute the default calculation on an OLAP cube.

- Execute a calculation on an OLAP cube using a calculation script.

Each of these step types can be added to a warehouse process such that the steps can be executed after another warehouse process produces the data needed for the OLAP processing. All of the steps can be linked together so that the IBM DB2 Data Warehouse Center process can start with raw source data and only be considered successful when the OLAP cube is loaded.

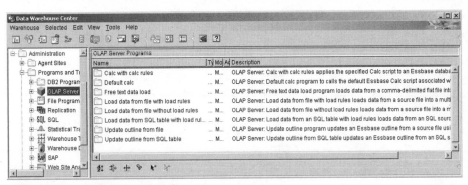

Figure 12.1   OLAP step examples.

Adding OLAP to Your Process

To include OLAP processing as part of your warehouse transformation, create or update a new subject area. Once you have created the subject area, you can create or update an IBM DB2 Data Warehouse Center process that will contain the warehouse transformations, or links to other transformation. Once you have created the process, open the process and begin defining the steps that pull and transform the data from its source systems and the steps to load the cubes. You can now begin to supply the information that DWC needs to execute the transformation.

To use OLAP steps in your process, you must perform the following steps:

1. Select the appropriate OLAP step type from the process modeler pallet and drop it onto the process modeler canvas.

2. Depending on the type of OLAP step you are using, you will also need to drop a Warehouse Source representing the data to be loaded into the OLAP cube.

3. Using the data link tool, connect the Warehouse Source to the OLAP step.

4. Right-click on the step and select Properties.

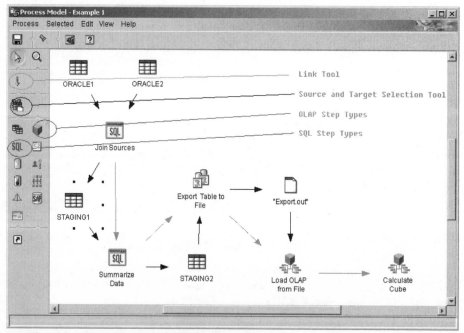

Figure 12.2   Process model with OLAP.

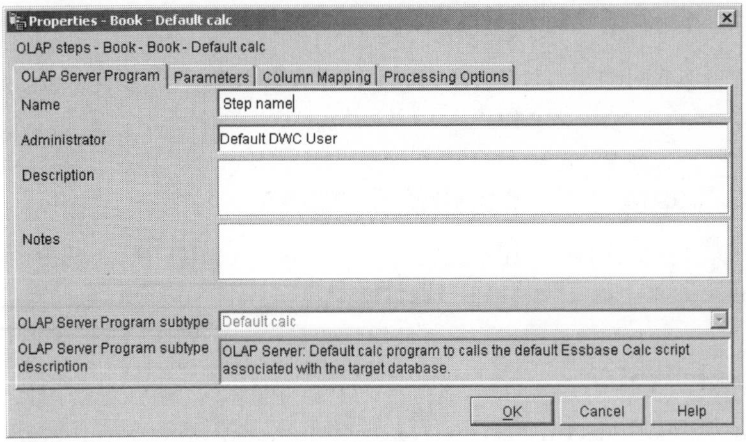

Figure 12.3   OLAP steps properties book.

Refer to Figure 12.2 to associate the preceding tasks with the process model interface. All of the OLAP steps contain similar meta data. The parameters page must be completed with the information needed for OLAP processing. Each page is reviewed in the following sections.

OLAP Server Main Page

The first page of all OLAP program steps contains general information about the step. Shown in Figure 12.3 is the main page, as well as the other three tabs to the property book, including Parameters, Column Mapping, and Processing Options.

Table 12.1 describes the information captured on the main page. Only the name is required.

Table 12.1   Main Page

PARAMETER	DESCRIPTION
Name	Step name. This must be a unique name across the warehouse and is required.
Administrator	The name of the warehouse administrator that maintains this step.
Description	A short description of the purpose of the step.
Notes	A longer description about what the step does.

OLAP Server Column Mapping Page

This page is not used for OLAP step types. The mapping information is defined by the OLAP processing program itself.

OLAP Server Program Processing Options

The Processing Options page of all OLAP programs contains information about how the step is to execute. Table 12.2 describes each option.

Other Considerations

There are several rules that you need to follow when any step parameters reference a location. First, you must be sure that the OLAP client of DB2 OLAP Server (or Hyperion's Essbase) is installed at the agent site where the steps will be executed.

Another consideration has to do with load files. If a file (either the file to be loaded into the cube, the rules file, or the calculation script) is used in one of the OLAP step types, you need to indicate where the file is physically located. If the file is located on the system where the agent (specified in the step's processing options) is executing, you need to specify the fully qualified filename, as well as indicate that the file is located at the agent system. If the file is located at the OLAP server's system, that file must not be fully qualified, nor should you specify the file's extension. The file on the OLAP server system must also be located in the directory structure associated with the OLAP database as specified by your OLAP system. Moreover, if a step requires a source file or table to be linked to the step, until that link exists, the entry fields on the parameters page will be disabled.

Table 12.2   Program Processing Options

OPTION	DESCRIPTION
Population type	Indicates how the step is to be populated. Since this is an OLAP program, it is considered program-controlled. This cannot be modified.
Agent site	Indicates the agent site where this step will execute. The agent site needs to have the OLAP client installed on this system.
Run on demand	Indicates that the step can be started manually from the WIP or from an external trigger.

Table 12.2   *(Continued)*

OPTION	DESCRIPTION
Retry	Indicates the number of times the warehouse server is to try to start the step in case there is a communications error with the agent.
Interval	Indicates how often the warehouse server is to try to contact the agent in case there is a communications error with the agent.

Each OLAP step type provides different options for the user. The processing is determined by the information specified on the parameters page in the step's properties notebook.

A final consideration is that all OLAP step transformations are available for the following operating systems:

- Windows NT
- AIX
- Solaris Operating Environment
- AS/400

OLAP Server Load Rules

You must examine several load rules for your OLAP steps. You can load free-form text to SQL tables, all with specific rules that define what to do with the data being loaded. The following sections describe each type of load.

Free Text Data Load

Use the OLAP Server free text data load warehouse program to load data from a comma-delimited flat file into a multidimensional OLAP Server database. The OLAP server can be a DB2 OLAP server or an Essbase server.

The free text data load warehouse program uses the file that is selected as a source for the step in the process. The step must have only one source file linked. The data in the source file must match the OLAP server outline values exactly. The selected source file must be on the agent site.

The file that is to be loaded is determined when you draw (using the link tool) a link between a file and this step. If a file source has not been attached to this step, the entry fields on this page are disabled. All parameters must be entered.

The properties page is shown in Figure 12.4. Table 12.3 lists the necessary page parameters.

File with Load Rules

Load data from file with load rules (ESSDATA2) warehouse program to load data from a flat file into a multidimensional OLAP Server database. The DB2 OLAP server or Essbase server can be used.

The warehouse program uses the linked file as a source for the step. The step must have only one source file linked. The name for the source filename must follow the conventions for specifying filenames on the client (agent system) or server of your OLAP server system. If the file location flag in your program indicates that the rules file is on an agent site, you must specify a fully qualified filename in the Load Rule File Name field on the Parameters page of the Step notebook.

Figure 12.5 is a properties page that requests information regarding where the load is to take place, as well as information about the files that will be used to load the OLAP cube. The file that is to be loaded is determined when you draw (using the link tool) a link between a file and this step. All parameters are required and are outlined in Table 12.4. Note, the load rules file must be built outside the IBM DB2 Data Warehouse Center.

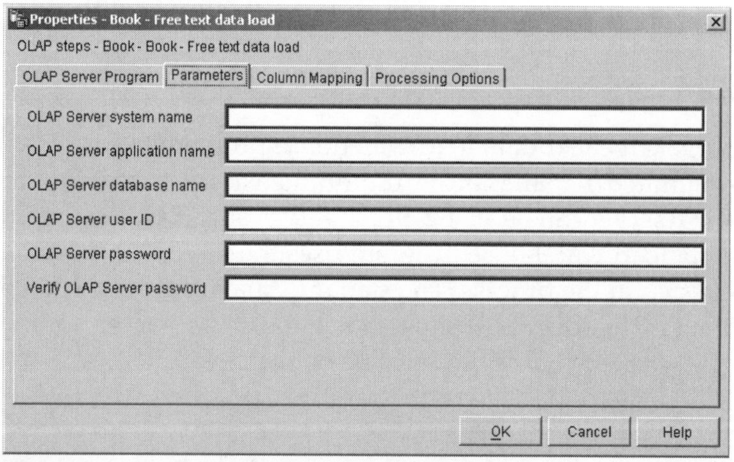

Figure 12.4 Free text data load properties page.

Table 12.3   Free Text Parameters

PARAMETER	DESCRIPTION
OLAP Server system name	Enter the name of the system where the OLAP server is installed.
OLAP Server application name	Enter the OLAP server application name that contains the database to be loaded.
OLAP Server database name	Enter the database name of the OLAP cube that is to be loaded.
OLAP Server user ID	Enter the user ID that the load is to run in behalf of. This must be a valid OLAP user ID.
OLAP Server password	Enter the password for the OLAP user that the load is to be run in behalf of.
Verify OLAP Server password	Re-enter the password for the OLAP user that the load is to be run in behalf of.

File without Load Rules

Use the load data from a file without using load rules (ESSDATA4) program to load data from a flat file into a multidimensional OLAP server database without using load rules. The OLAP server can be a DB2 OLAP server or an Essbase server. When you select a step that uses this warehouse program, link the source file to the step, but do not link the step to a target table.

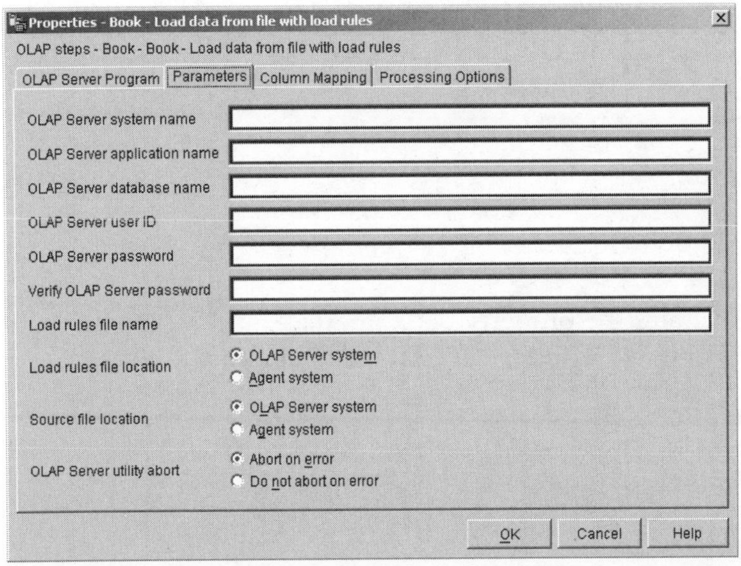

Figure 12.5   File load rules properties.

Table 12.4 File Load Parameters

PARAMETER	DESCRIPTION
OLAP Server system name	Enter the name of the system where the OLAP server is installed.
OLAP Server application name	Enter the OLAP server application name that contains the database to be loaded.
OLAP Server database name	Enter the database name of the OLAP cube that is to be loaded.
OLAP Server user ID	Enter the user ID that the load is to run in behalf of. This must be a valid OLAP user ID.
OLAP Server password	Enter the password for the OLAP user that the load is to be run in behalf of.
Verify OLAP Server password	Re-enter the password for the OLAP user that the load is to be run in behalf of.
Load rules file name	Enter the name of the file that contains the load rules. If the file location flag in your program indicates that the file is on the OLAP client (agent) site, you must specify a fully qualified filename.
Load rules file location	Indicate if the rules file resides at the OLAP client (agent) site or if it resides at the OLAP server site.
Source file location	Indicate if the source file to be loaded resides at the OLAP client (agent) site or if it resides at the OLAP server site.
OLAP server utility abort	Indicate what action the OLAP server is to take when it encounters an error.

Figure 12.6 illustrates the property book interface, and a description of the parameters is outlined in Table 12.5. All parameters are required.

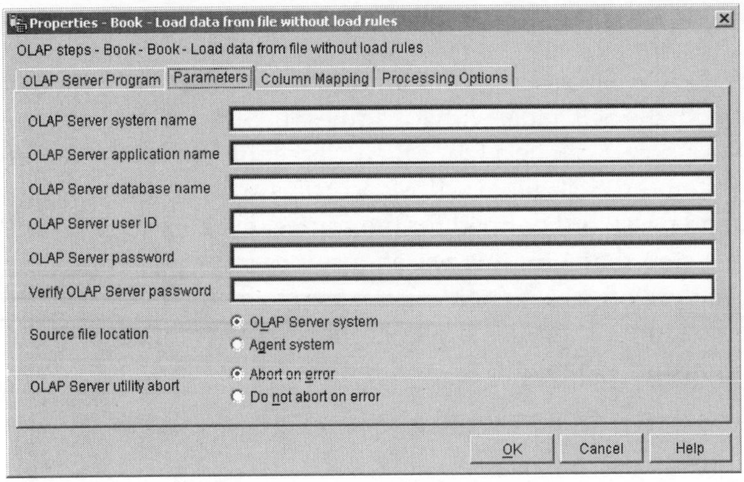

Figure 12.6 File without load rules properties page.

Table 12.5 File Load without Rules

PARAMETER	DESCRIPTION
OLAP Server system name	Enter the name of the system where the OLAP server is installed.
OLAP Server application name	Enter the OLAP server application name that contains the database to be loaded.
OLAP Server database name	Enter the database name of the OLAP cube that is to be loaded.
OLAP Server user ID	Enter the user ID that the load is to run in behalf of. This must be a valid OLAP user ID.
OLAP Server password	Enter the password for the OLAP user that the load is to be run in behalf of.
Verify OLAP Server password	Re-enter the password for the OLAP user that the load is to be run in behalf of.
Source file location	Indicate if the source file resides at the OLAP client (agent) site or if it resides at the OLAP server site.
OLAP server utility abort	Indicate what action the OLAP server is to take when it encounters an error.

SQL Table with Load Rules

Loading data from SQL tables into your multidimensional OLAP Server database is done with the SQL table with load rules (ESSDATA3) warehouse program. The OLAP server can be a DB2 OLAP Server or an Essbase server.

The load data from an SQL table with load rules warehouse program uses the user ID and password defined for the source database for the step. When you select a step that uses this warehouse program, you must link the source table to the step, but do not link the step to a target.

Figure 12.7 shows the properties interface page. The information you must enter is outlined in Table 12.6. All parameters are required.

Table 12.6 SQL Load Rules

PARAMETER	DESCRIPTION
OLAP Server application name	Enter the OLAP server application name that contains the database to be loaded.
OLAP Server database name	Enter the database name of the OLAP cube that is to be loaded.
OLAP Server user ID	Enter the user ID that the load is to run in behalf of. This must be a valid OLAP user ID.
OLAP Server password	Enter the password for the OLAP user that the load is to be run in behalf of.
Verify OLAP Server password	Re-enter the password for the OLAP user that the load is to be run in behalf of.
Load rules file name	Enter the name of the file that contains the load rules. If the file location flag in your program indicates that the file is on the OLAP client (agent) site, you must specify a fully qualified filename.
Rules file location	Indicate if the rules file resides at the OLAP client (agent) site or if it resides at the OLAP server site.
OLAP server utility abort	Indicate what action the OLAP server is to take when it encounters an error.

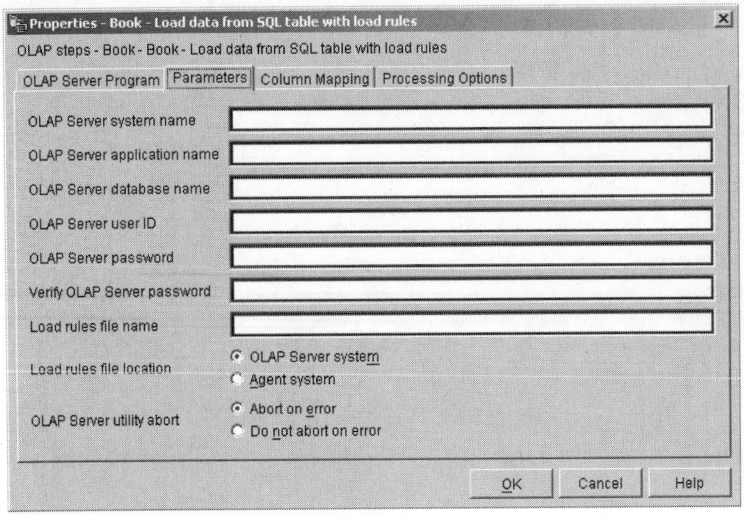

Figure 12.7   SQL load properties page.

OLAP Server Calculation

The intersection points of the cube can be calculated once the data is loaded into the multidimensional database. You can use the default calculations or define calculation rules. Let's look at each of these options.

Default Calculation

Use the default calc (ESSCALC1) warehouse program to call the default calc script that is associated with the target database. The OLAP server can be a DB2 OLAP Server or an Essbase server. When you select a step that uses the default calc warehouse program, do not link the step to a source or a target.

Figure 12.8 shows the properties page, and the information regarding the OLAP server where the default calculation is to take place is found in Table 12.7. All parameters are required.

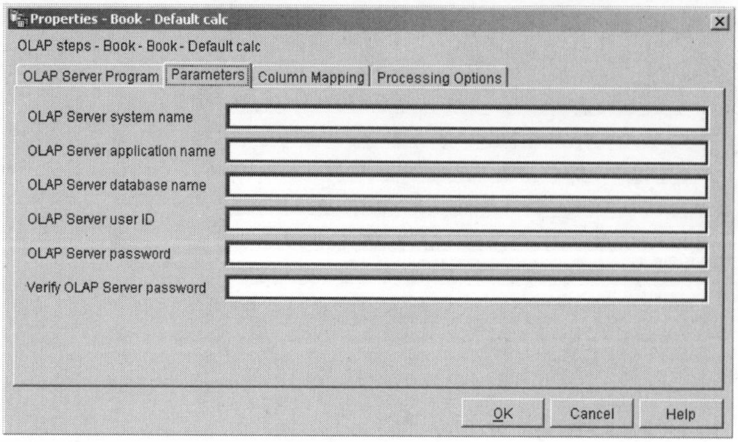

Figure 12.8 Default calc properties page.

Table 12.7 Default Calculation

PARAMETER	DESCRIPTION
OLAP Server system name	Enter the name of the system where the OLAP server is installed.
OLAP Server application name	Enter the OLAP server application name that contains the database to run the default calculation on.
OLAP Server database name	Enter the OLAP server database name of the OLAP cube that is to have the default calculation run.
OLAP Server user ID	Enter the user ID that the default calculation is to be run in behalf of. This must be a valid OLAP user ID.
OLAP Server password	Enter the password for the OLAP user that the default calculation is to be run in behalf of.
Verify OLAP Server password	Re-enter the password for the OLAP user that the default calculation is to be run in behalf of.

Calc with Calc Rules

The calc with calc rules (ESSCALC2) warehouse program is used to apply a specified calc script to an OLAP server database. The OLAP server can be a DB2 OLAP Server or an Essbase server. When you select a step that uses this warehouse program, do not link the step to a source or a target. (See Figure 12.9.)

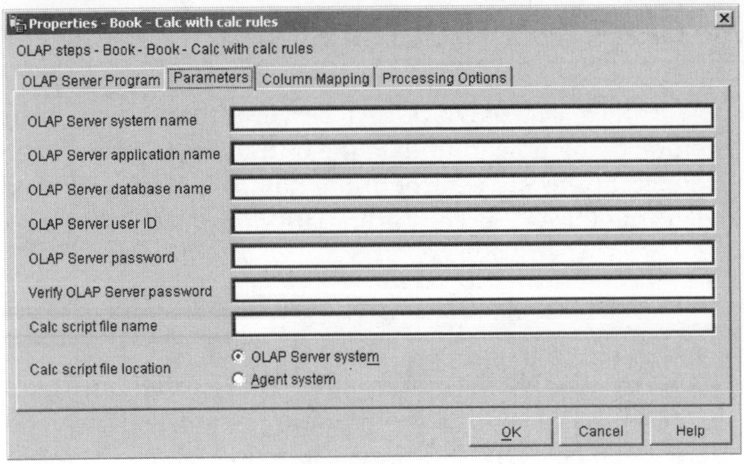

Figure 12.9 Calc rules properties page.

Table 12.8 outlines the parameters about the script file used to calculate the OLAP cube. All parameters are required. The calc script must be built outside the IBM DB2 Data Warehouse Center.

Table 12.8 Calculations with Rules

PARAMETER	DESCRIPTION
OLAP Server system name	Enter the name of the system where the OLAP server is installed.
OLAP Server application name	Enter the OLAP server application name that contains the database to run the calculation on.
OLAP Server database name	Enter the database name of the OLAP cube that is to have the calculation run.
OLAP Server user ID	Enter the user ID that the calculation is to run in behalf of. This must be a valid OLAP user ID.
OLAP Server password	Enter the password for the OLAP user that the calculation is to be run in behalf of.
Verify OLAP Server password	Re-enter the password for the OLAP user that the calculation is to be run in behalf of.
Calc script file name	Enter the name of the file that contains the calc scripts. If the file location flag in your program indicates that the file is on the OLAP client (agent) site, you must specify a fully qualified filename.
Calc script file location	Indicate if the calc script file resides at the OLAP client (agent) site or if it resides at the OLAP server site.

Updating the OLAP Server Outline

One of the most powerful aspects of DB2 OLAP Server is that the outline *is* the database. Therefore, being able to update the outline from either a file or SQL table adds flexibility to the control of the database itself. The two approaches to update the OLAP Server outline are discussed in the sections that follow.

Using a File

In this approach, you use the update outline (ESSOTL1) warehouse program to update an OLAP server outline from a source flat file using load rules. The OLAP server can be a DB2 OLAP server or an Essbase server.

The update outline warehouse program uses the linked file as a source for the step. The step must have only one source file linked, and the source filename must follow the conventions for your OLAP server for specifying filenames on the client or server. If the file location flag in your warehouse program indicates that the file is on the client (agent) site, you must specify a fully qualified filename in the Load Rules File Name field on the Parameters page of the Step notebook. If the file location flag indicates that the source file is on the OLAP server, you must specify the filename without an extension in the Load Rules File Name field on the Parameters page of the Step notebook.

When you select a step that uses this warehouse program, link the source file to the step, but do not link the step to a target table.

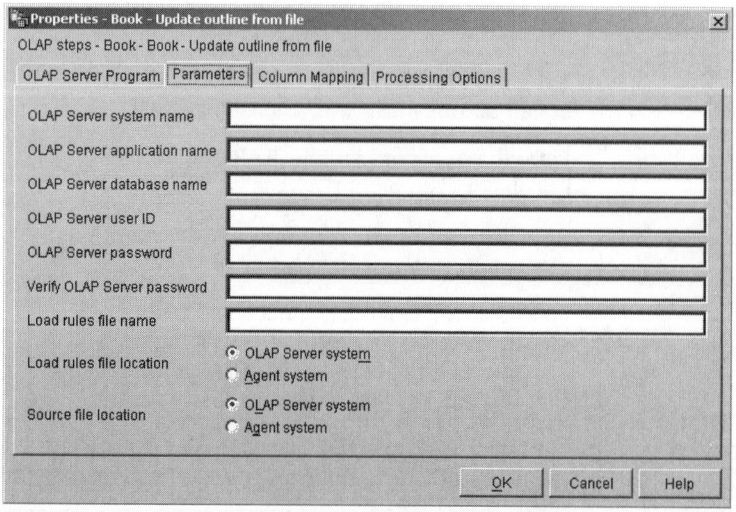

Figure 12.10   Outline update from file properties page.

Table 12.9   File Update to Outline

PARAMETER	DESCRIPTION
OLAP Server system name	Enter the name of the system where the OLAP server is installed.
OLAP Server application name	Enter the OLAP server application name that contains the database to have its outline updated.
OLAP Server database name	Enter the OLAP server database name of the OLAP cube that is to have its outline updated.
OLAP Server user ID	Enter the user ID that the update of the outline is to run in behalf of. This must be a valid OLAP user ID.
OLAP Server password	Enter the password for the OLAP user that the update of the outline is to be run in behalf of.
Verify OLAP Server password	Re-enter the password for the OLAP user that the update of the outline is to be run in behalf of.
Load rules file name	Enter the name of the file that contains the load rules. If the file location flag in your program indicates that the file is on the OLAP client (agent) site, you must specify a fully qualified filename.
Rules file location	Indicate if the rules file resides at the OLAP client (agent) site or if it resides at the OLAP server site.
Source file location	Indicate if the source file resides at the OLAP client (agent) site or if it resides at the OLAP server site.

Figure 12.10 shows the properties page. Table 12.9 identifies the parameters used for the outline process.

Using an SQL Table

Use the update outline from the SQL table (ESSOTL2) warehouse program to update an OLAP server outline from an SQL source using load rules. The OLAP server can be a DB2 OLAP server or an Essbase server.

When you select a step that uses this warehouse program, you must link the source table to the step, but do not link the step to a target table.

Figure 12.11 displays the properties page, and Table 12.10 identifies the parameters for defining a SQL table for outline update. All parameters are required.

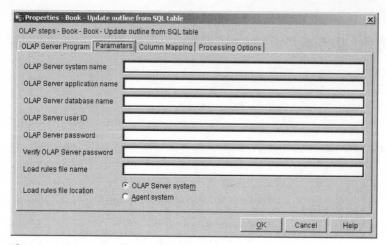

Figure 12.11 SQL outline update properties page.

Table 12.10 SQL Outline Update

PARAMETER	DESCRIPTION
OLAP Server system name	Enter the name of the system where the OLAP server is installed.
OLAP Server application name	Enter the OLAP server application name that contains the database to have the outline updated.
OLAP Server database name	Enter the database name of the OLAP cube that is to have the outline updated.
OLAP Server user ID	Enter the user ID that the update of the outline is to run in behalf of. This must be a valid OLAP user ID.
OLAP Server password	Enter the password for the OLAP user that the update of the outline is to be run in behalf of.
Verify OLAP Server password	Re-enter the password for the OLAP user that the update of the outline is to be run in behalf of.

Table 12.10 *(Continued)*

PARAMETER	DESCRIPTION
Load rules file name	Enter the name of the file that contains the load rules. If the file location flag in your program indicates that the file is on the OLAP client (agent) site, you must specify a fully qualified filename.
Rules file location	Indicate if the rules file resides at the OLAP client (agent) site or if it resides at the OLAP server site.

Summary

One of the biggest challenges of warehouse management is controlling the propagation of data from relational technology and related data structures to multidimensional technology and their physical structures. This control must be more than simple external calls to third-party loading and maintenance routines. The processing must be complete and robust within the warehouse management technology itself. IBM DB2 Data Warehouse Center is a rare warehouse tool that naturally blends two of the prominent technologies, relational and dimensional, into a central environment for maximum control for administrators.

One of the strengths that IBM DB2 Data Warehouse Center brings to warehouse management and ETL processing is the OLAP steps. These steps allow data warehouse administrators the opportunity to blend all physical structures of warehousing, relational as well as multidimensional, into a single cohesive process. This means that not only do administrators control the propagation of data between dissimilar structures, but they also control all meta data. It is a boon to any BI effort.

CHAPTER 13

DB2 OLAP Functions

Key Issues:

- DB2 UDB query-related functions are broadly classified into analytic and OLAP functions.

- Database-resident OLAP functions ensure a single point of truth and efficient management of dimensional data creation, propagation, and management.

OLAP is a critical BI technology that enables analysts and executives alike to gain informational insight through fast, reliable, and interactive access to a wide variety of views. The information of focus is transformed from raw data to reflect the real dimensionality of the enterprise as understood by the user and defined by the business itself. Typical enterprise dimensions are time, location/geography, product, and customer. For more information on OLAP, refer to Chapter 11.

While OLAP systems have the ability to answer "who" and "what" questions, it is their ability to answer "what if" and "why" that sets them apart. OLAP enables decision making about future actions.

OLAP functions provide the ability to return the following information in a query result:

- Ranking with RANK and DENSE_RANK

- Numbering with ROW_NUMBER

- Aggregation with existing column functions such as MAX, MIN, AVG, and so on

Key to DB2 OLAP functions is the ability to define a window that defines the set of rows over which the function is applied, and the sequence in which the function is applied. When an OLAP function is used with a column function, like AVG, SUM, or MAX, the target rows can be further refined, relative to the current row, as either a range or a number of rows preceding and following the current row. For example, within a window partitioned by month, a moving average can be calculated over the previous 3-month period.

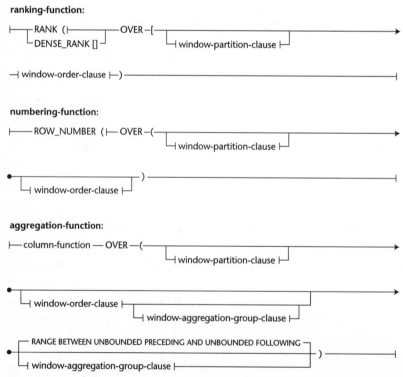

Figure 13.1 Ranking, numbering, and aggregate functions.

Besides windowing, the ability to group sets of rows is critical to OLAP functionality. ROLLUP and CUBE are extensions to the GROUP BY clause to provide OLAP functionality. ROLLUP and CUBE are called supergroups. We discuss OLAP functionality as:

- Ranking, numbering, and aggregate functions
- GROUPING capabilities, ROLLUP and CUBE

The syntax of OLAP functions is broadly defined in Figure 13.1. All of these functions and functionality are discussed in this chapter. We include examples for clarity.

OLAP Functions

The OLAP functions of DB2 V8 encompass a wide variety of applications to address the dimensional nature of most data. They include the following:

- RANK
- DENSE_RANK
- ROWNUMBER
- PARTITION BY
- ORDER BY

Another important class of OLAP functionality is incorporated under the window aggregation group clause. The windowing capability enables significant control of data grouping that enhances OLAP analytics. Figures 13.2 and 13.3 illustrate the overall syntax. In this chapter, we review the application of window aggregation group clause, as well as all the functions listed.

Specific Functions

Following are descriptions of each of the database-resident OLAP functions of DB2 V8.

RANK

The RANK function assigns a sequential rank of a row within a window. The RANK of a row is defined as one plus the number of rows that strictly precede the row. Rows that are not distinct within the ordering of the window are assigned equal ranks.

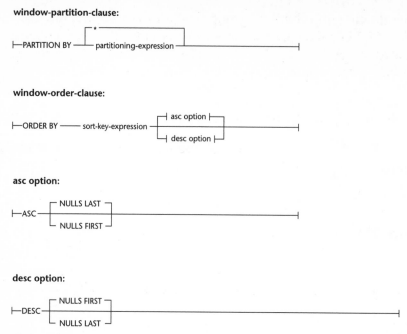

window-partition-clause:

window-order-clause:

asc option:

desc option:

Figure 13.2   Window partition and window order clauses.

If two or more rows are not distinct with respect to the ordering, then there will be one or more gaps in the sequential rank numbering. That is, the results of RANK may have gaps in the numbers resulting from duplicate values.

DENSE_RANK

Like the RANK function, DENSE_RANK assigns a sequential rank to a row in a window. However, its DENSE_RANK is one plus the number of rows preceding it that are distinct with respect to the ordering. Therefore, there will be no gaps in the sequential rank numbering, with ties being assigned the same rank.

ROWNUMBER

ROWNUMBER computes the sequential row number of the row within the window defined by an ordering clause (if one is specified), starting with 1 for the first row and continuing sequentially to the last row in the window. If an ordering clause, ORDER BY, is not specified in the window, the row numbers are assigned to the rows in arbitrary order as returned by the sub-select.

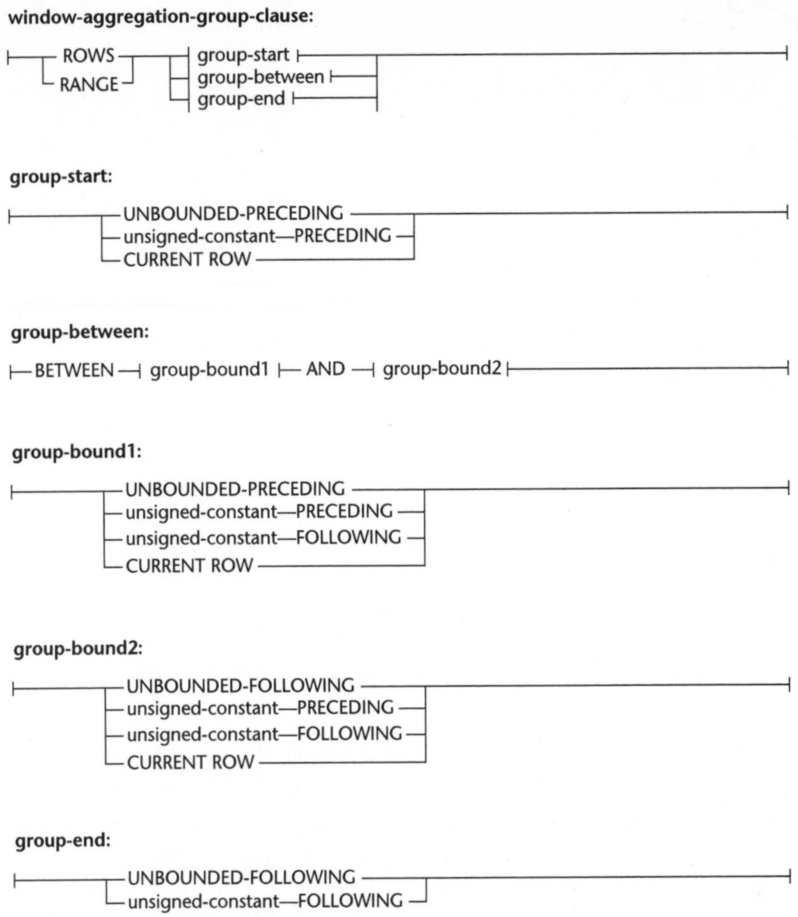

window-aggregation-group-clause:

```
┌─ ROWS ──┐ ┌─ group-start ──┐
├─────────┤─┤─ group-between ┤──────────────────
└─ RANGE ─┘ └─ group-end ────┘
```

group-start:

```
┌── UNBOUNDED-PRECEDING ──────┐
├── unsigned-constant—PRECEDING ─┤──────────────
└── CURRENT ROW ──────────────┘
```

group-between:

```
├─ BETWEEN ─┤ group-bound1 ├─ AND ─┤ group-bound2 ├──────────
```

group-bound1:

```
┌── UNBOUNDED-PRECEDING ──────────┐
├── unsigned-constant—PRECEDING ───┤
├── unsigned-constant—FOLLOWING ───┤──────────────
└── CURRENT ROW ──────────────────┘
```

group-bound2:

```
┌── UNBOUNDED-FOLLOWING ──────────┐
├── unsigned-constant—PRECEDING ───┤
├── unsigned-constant—FOLLOWING ───┤──────────────
└── CURRENT ROW ──────────────────┘
```

group-end:

```
┌── UNBOUNDED-FOLLOWING ──────┐
└── unsigned-constant—FOLLOWING ─┘──────────────────
```

Figure 13.3 Window aggregation group clause.

PARTITION BY

The PARTITION BY clause allows for subdividing the window into partitions. A *partitioning expression* is used to define the partitioning of the result set.

ORDER BY

The ORDER BY clause defines the ordering of rows within a window that determines the value of the OLAP function or the meaning of the ROW values in the window-aggregation-group clause (see the following section concerning the window-aggregation-group).

The ORDER BY clause does not define the ordering of the query result set. A *sort-key-expression* is an expression used in defining the ordering of the rows within the window. This clause is required when using the RANK and DENSE_RANK functions.

There are two sorting sequences:

ASC.   Sorts the sort-key-expression in ascending order. Null values are considered last in the order by default, since in DB2 nulls are considered high values.

DESC.   Sorts the sort-key-expression in descending order. Null values are considered first in the order unless NULLS LAST is specified.

Window Aggregation Group Clause

The window aggregation group clause defines the window to a set of rows with a defined ordering relative to the rows in the window:

- ROWS indicates the window is defined by counting rows.
- RANGE indicates the window is defined by an offset from a sort key:

  - group-start, group-between, and group-end: The group-start, between and group-end functions define the ROWS or RANGE window to be some number of rows or range of rows around the current row in the window. These functions make it possible to compute moving average types of calculations.

    - group-start: Specifies the starting point for this aggregation group. The window ends at the current row when UNBOUNDED PRECEDING or PRECEDING is specified (more coming up in the list). Specification of the group-start clause is the equivalent to a group-between clause of the form "BETWEEN group-start AND CURRENT ROW".

    - group-between: Specifies the aggregation group-start and -end based on either ROWS or RANGE that fit within the specified group-bound1 (beginning) and group-bound2 (endpoint).

    - group-end: Specifies the ending point of the aggregation group. The aggregation group start is the current row. Specification of a group-end clause is the equivalent to a group-between clause of the form "BETWEEN CURRENT ROW AND group-end". Figure 13.4 shows the relationships among the various window bounds that follow.

- Group-bounds one and two:
    - CURRENT ROW specifies the start or end of the window as the current row.
    - UNBOUNDED PRECEDING includes the entire window preceding the current row. This can be specified with either ROWS or RANGE.
    - UNBOUNDED FOLLOWING includes the entire window following the current row. This can be specified with either ROWS or RANGE.
    - PRECEDING specifies either the range or number of rows preceding the current row as being in the window. If ROWS is specified, then the value is a positive integer indicating a number of rows. If RANGE is specified, then the data type of the value must be comparable to the type of the sort-key-expression of the window ORDER BY clause.
    - FOLLOWING specifies either the range or number of rows following the current row as being in the window. If ROWS is specified, then the value is a positive integer indicating a number of rows. If RANGE is specified, then the data type of the value must be comparable to the type of the sort-key-expression of the window ORDER BY clause.

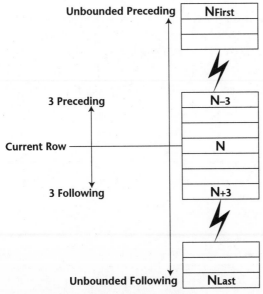

Figure 13.4 Windowing relationships.

GROUPING Capabilities: ROLLUP and CUBE

The result of a GROUP BY operation is a set of groups of rows. Each row in this result represents the set of rows for which the grouping expression is satisfied. Complex forms of the GROUP BY clause include grouping sets and supergroups.

For grouping, all null values from a grouping expression are considered equal. (See Figure 13.5.)

A *grouping set* specification allows multiple grouping clauses to be specified in a single statement. This can be thought of as a union of two or more groups of rows into a single result set. It is logically equivalent to the union of multiple sub-selects with the GROUP BY clause in each sub-select corresponding to one grouping set. A grouping set can be a single element, or it can be a list of elements delimited by parentheses, where an element is either a grouping expression or a supergroup:

```
GROUP BY a is equivalent to GROUP BY GROUPING SETS ((a))
GROUP BY a,b,c is equivalent to GROUP BY GROUPING SETS ((a,b,c))
```

In terms of OLAP functions we will confine our discussion to the two supergroups ROLLUP and CUBE. Shown in Figure 13.6 are the supergroup ROLLUP and CUBE functions.

ROLLUP

A ROLLUP group is an extension to the GROUP BY clause that produces a result set that contains *subtotal* rows in addition to the "regular" grouped rows. Subtotal rows are "super-aggregate" rows that contain further aggregates whose values are derived by applying the same column functions that were used to obtain the grouped rows. A ROLLUP grouping is a series of grouping sets. For example:

Figure 13.5   GROUP BY clause.

```
GROUP BY ROLLUP (a,b,c)
```

is equivalent to

```
GROUP BY GROUPING SETS
(
(a,b,c)
(a,b)
(a)
()
)
```

Notice that the n elements of the ROLLUP translate to $n+1$ grouping set. Another point to remember is that the order in which the grouping expressions are specified is significant for ROLLUP.

CUBE

The CUBE supergroup is the other extension to the GROUP BY clause that produces a result set that contains all the subtotal rows of a ROLLUP aggregation and, in addition, contains *cross-tabulation* rows. Cross-tabulation rows are additional super-aggregate rows. They are, as the name implies, summaries across columns if the data were represented as a spreadsheet.

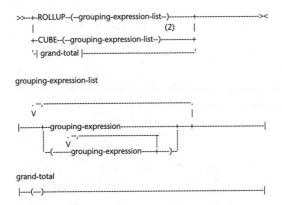

Figure 13.6 Supergroup ROLLUP and CUBE.

Like ROLLUP, a CUBE group can also be thought of as a series of grouping sets. In the case of a CUBE, all permutations of the cubed grouping expression are computed along with the grand total. Therefore, the n elements of a CUBE translate to $2n$ (2 to the power n) grouping sets. For instance, a specification of

```
GROUP BY CUBE (a,b,c)
```

is equivalent to

```
GROUP BY GROUPING SETS
(
(a,b,c)
(a,b)
(a,c)
(b,c)
(a)
(b)
(c)
()
)
```

Notice that the three elements of the CUBE translate to eight grouping sets.

Unlike ROLLUP, the order of specification of elements does not matter for CUBE, for example:

```
CUBE (DayOfYear, Sales_Person)
```

is the same as

```
CUBE (Sales_Person,DayOfYear)
```

CUBE is an extension of the ROLLUP function. The CUBE function not only provides the column summaries we saw in rollup but also calculates the row summaries and grand totals for the various dimensions.

Ranking, Numbering, and Aggregation

These functions are useful in determining ranks, positioning, sequences, and medians. They have been used by the following:

- Financial institutions to identify top profitable customers
- The International Olympic Committee (IOC) to rank contestants, assign medals, and determine leading-country medal rankings

Medians are useful in applications where the average is greatly influenced by a few extreme values called *outliers*. Companies want to build sales campaigns that hit the largest segment of their target population and not the average. The median metric is the midpoint of a set of data elements. For example, in the sequence 3, 5, 7, 8, and 37, the median is 8, and the average or mean is 12.

RANK Example

When specifying an OLAP function like RANK, DENSE_RANK, or ROW_NUMBER, a window is specified that defines the rows over which the function is applied, and in what order. This window is specified via the OVER() clause.

Assume we would like to rank employees by total compensation and list them alphabetically. The following SQL shows that the ORDER BY clause in the RANK () OVER statement controls only the ranking sequence and not output sequence:

```
SELECT EMPNO, LASTNAME, FIRSTNME,
SALARY+BONUS AS TOTAL_SALARY,
RANK() OVER (ORDER BY SALARY+BONUS DESC) AS RANK_SALARY
FROM EMPLOYEE
WHERE SALARY+BONUS > 30000
ORDER BY LASTNAME
```

The results of the query are shown in Figure 13.7.

EMPNO	LASTNAME	FIRSTNAME	TOTAL_SALARY	RANK_SALARY
000120	GEYER	JOHN	40775.00	4
000010	HAAS	CHRISTINE	53750.00	1
000120	HENDERS...	EILEEN	30350.00	9
000120	KWAN	SALLY	38850.00	5
000110	LUCCHESSI	VINCENZO	47400.00	2
000120	LUTZ	JENNIFER	30440.00	8
000120	PULASKI	EVA	36770.00	6
000120	STERN	IRVING	32850.00	7
999981	SMYTHE	CHRISTINE	53750.00	1
000120	THOMPSON	MICHAEL	41850.00	3
999982	VINO	VINCENZO	47400.00	2

Figure 13.7 Employee DENSE_RANK by total salary.

Since nulls collate high, nulls in RANK and DENSE_RANK functions are ranked first for descending rankings. This can be overridden with the "nulls last" parameter, RANK () OVER (ORDER BY salary desc nulls last) as ranking.

ROW_NUMBER, RANK, and DENSE_RANK Example

Since ROW_NUMBER creates a sequential numbering to the rows in the window, it can be used with an ORDER BY clause in the window to eliminate gaps or duplicates.

Without the ORDER BY clause, ROW_NUMBER assigns sequential numbers to rows arbitrarily as retrieved by the sub-select. Such a result is not related to ranking but merely assigns arbitrary numbers to rows.

The following example shows the differences between RANK, DENSE_RANK, and ROW_NUMBER:

```
SELECT EMPNO, LASTNAME, FIRSTNME,
SALARY+BONUS AS TOTAL_SALARY,
RANK() OVER (ORDER BY SALARY+BONUS DESC) AS RANK_SALARY,
DENSE_RANK() OVER (ORDER BY SALARY+BONUS DESC) AS DENSERANK,
ROW_NUMBER() OVER (ORDER BY SALARY+BONUS DESC) AS ROW_NUMBER
FROM EMPLOYEE
WHERE SALARY+BONUS > 30000
```

Figure 13.8 shows the results of such a query.

RANK and PARTITION BY Example

The following is an example of using the PARTITION BY clause, which allows you to subdivide the rows into partitions. It functions similarly to the GROUP BY function but is local to the window set, whereas GROUP BY is a global function.

EMPNO	LASTNAME	FIRSTNAME	TOTAL_SALARY	RANK_SALARY	DENSERANK	ROW_NUMBER
000010	HAAS	CHRISTINE	53750.00	1	1	1
999981	SMYTHE	CHRISTINE	53750.00	1	1	2
000110	LUCCHESSI	VINCENZO	47400.00	3	2	3
999982	VINO	VINCENZO	47400.00	3	2	4
000120	THOMPSON	MICHAEL	41850.00	5	3	5
000120	GEYER	JOHN	40775.00	6	4	6
000120	KWAN	SALLY	38850.00	7	5	7
000120	PULASKI	EVA	36770.00	8	6	8
000120	STERN	IRVING	32850.00	9	7	9
000120	LUTZ	JENNIFER	30440.00	10	8	10
000120	HENDERS...	EILEEN	30350.00	11	9	11

Figure 13.8 RANK, DENSE_RANK, and ROW_NUMBER comparison.

Assume we want to find the top four rankings of employee salary within each department. We need to use the RANK function with partition (ranking window) by department, along with a common table expression; otherwise, the reference to RANK_IN_DEPT in our sub-select is ambiguous. The SQL is as follows:

```
WITH CTE AS(
SELECT WORKDEPT, LASTNAME, FIRSTNME, SALARY,
RANK() OVER (PARTITION BY WORKDEPT
ORDER BY SALARY DESC NULLS LAST)
AS RANK_IN_DEPT
FROM EMPLOYEE )

SELECT WORKDEPT, LASTNAME, FIRSTNME, SALARY, RANK_IN_DEPT
FROM CTE
WHERE RANK_IN_DEPT <= 4 AND WORKDEPT IN
('A00','A11','B01','C01','D1','D11')
ORDER BY WORKDEPT, RANK_IN_DEPT, LASTNAME
```

Figure 13.9 illustrates sample results.

Initially, the employee table is partitioned by department. Then the ranking function is applied based on highest to lowest salary within the common table expression. Then the outer select chooses only the top four employees in the departments requested and orders them by department and rank in the department. Ties in rank are listed alphabetically.

WORKDEPT	LASTNAME	FIRSTNAME	SALARY	RANK_IN_DEPT
A00	HAAS	CHRISTINE	52750.00	1
A00	LUCCHESSI	VINCENZO	46500.00	2
A00	O'CONNELL	SEAN	29250.00	3
A11	SMYTHE	CHRISTINE	52750.00	1
A11	VINO	VINCENZO	46500.00	2
A11	WALKER	SEAN	29250.00	3
B01	THOMPSON	MICHAEL	41250.00	1
C01	KWAN	SALLY	38250.00	1
C01	NICHOLLS	HEATHER	28420.00	2
C01	QUINTANA	DOLORES	23800.00	3
D1	HOMEMAKER	SALLY	60000.00	1
D1	BOOKERN	DAN	50000.00	2
D1	WILLIE	SAMANTHA	48000.00	3
D1	BEGOOD	JOHN	45000.00	4
D1	DANCING	JEAN	45000.00	4
D11	STERN	IRVING	32250.00	1
D11	LUTZ	JENNIFER	29840.00	2
D11	BROWN	DAVID	27740.00	3
D11	ADAMSON	BRUCE	25280.00	4

Figure 13.9 PARTITION BY window results.

OVER clause example

With the OVER clause, you can turn aggregate functions like SUM, AVG, COUNT, COUNT_BIG, CORRELATION, VARIANCE, COVARIANCE, MIN, MAX, and STDDEV into OLAP functions. Rather than returning the aggregate of the rows as a single value, the OVER function operates on the range of rows specified in the window and returns a single aggregate value for the range.

Let's illustrate this function with an example. Assume we would like to determine for each employee within a department the percentage of that employee's salary to the total department salary. That is, if an employee's salary is $20,000 and the department total is $100,000, then the employee's percentage of the department's salary is 20 percent.

Our SQL would look like this:

```
SELECT WORKDEPT,LASTNAME,SALARY, DECIMAL(SALARY,15,0)*100/SUM(SALARY)
OVER (PARTITION BY WORKDEPT) AS DEPT_SALARY_PERCENT
FROM EMPLOYEE
WHERE WORKDEPT IN ('A00','A11','B01','C01','D1','D11')
ORDER BY WORKDEPT, DEPT_SALARY_PERCENT DESC
```

The SUM (SALARY) is ranged by the OVER (PARTITION BY...) clause to only those values in each department. Figure 13.10 shows sample results.

This same concept can be applied to determine product percentage of sales for various product groups within a retail store, bank, or distribution center.

ROWS and ORDER BY Example

You can also define the rows in the window function using a window aggregate clause when an ORDER BY clause is included in the definition. This allows the inclusion or exclusion of ranges of values or rows within the ordering clause.

Assume we want to smooth the curve of random data similar to the 50- and 200-day moving average of stock price found on numerous stock Web sites. The SQL for our example is

```
SELECT DATE,SYMBOL,CLOSE_PRICE,AVG(CLOSE_PRICE) OVER
(ORDER BY DATE ROWS 5 PRECEDING) AS SMOOTH
FROM STOCKTAB
WHERE SYMBOL = 'IBM'
```

WORKDEPT	LASTNAME	SALARY	DEPT_SALARY_PERCENT
A00	HAAS	52750.00	41.050
A00	LUCCHESSI	46500.00	36.186
A00	O'CONNELL	29250.00	22.762
A11	SMYTHE	52750.00	41.050
A11	VINO	46500.00	36.186
A11	WALKER	29250.00	22.762
B01	THOMPSON	41250.00	100.000
C01	KWAN	38250.00	42.279
C01	NICHOLLS	28420.00	31.413
C01	QUINTANA	23800.00	26.307
D1	HOMEMAKER	60000.00	13.636
D1	BOOKERN	50000.00	11.363
D1	WILLIE	48000.00	10.909
D1	DANCING	45000.00	10.227
D1	BEGOOD	45000.00	10.227
D1	KNOWSIT	44000.00	10.000
D1	NOTDANCING	43000.00	9.772
D1	MAKER	40000.00	9.090
D1	BAKER	35000.00	7.954
D1	JAMES	30000.00	6.818
D11	STERN	32250.00	14.520
D11	LUTZ	29840.00	13.435
D11	BROWN	27740.00	12.489
D11	ADAMSON	25280.00	11.382
D11	YOSHIMURA	24680.00	11.112
D11	PIANKA	22250.00	10.018
D11	SCOUNTTEN	21340.00	9.608
D11	WALKER	20450.00	9.207
D11	JONES	18270.00	8.226

Figure 13.10   Salary as a percent of department total salary.

The result is shown in Figure 13.11.

The equivalent result can be calculated using the RANGE instead of ROWS. ROWS works well in situations when the data is dense; that is, there are no values duplicated or missing.

Figure 13.12 shows a 5-day moving average.

ROWS, RANGE, and ORDER BY Example

Stock tables have the weekends missing. RANGE can be used to overcome gaps, as illustrated in the following example. Assume we want to calculate the 7-day calendar average with the intent of taking into account the weekends. We will compare the results of ROWS versus RANGE. The necessary SQL code is as follows:

DATE	SYMBOL	CLOSE_P	SMOOTH
1999-08-02	IBM	110.125	110.12500...
1999-08-03	IBM	109.500	109.81250...
1999-08-04	IBM	112.000	110.54166...
1999-08-05	IBM	110.625	110.56250...
1999-08-06	IBM	112.750	111.00000...
1999-08-09	IBM	110.625	111.10000...
1999-08-10	IBM	108.375	110.87500...
1999-08-11	IBM	109.250	110.32500...
1999-08-12	IBM	109.375	110.07500...
1999-08-13	IBM	108.500	109.22500...
1999-08-16	IBM	110.250	109.15000...
1999-08-17	IBM	108.375	109.15000...
1999-08-18	IBM	108.375	108.97500...
1999-08-19	IBM	109.375	108.97500...
1999-08-20	IBM	112.000	109.67500...
1999-08-23	IBM	113.125	110.25000...
1999-08-24	IBM	114.875	111.55000...
1999-08-25	IBM	115.500	112.97500...
1999-08-26	IBM	113.375	113.77500...
1999-08-27	IBM	115.625	114.50000...
1999-08-30	IBM	113.625	114.60000...
1999-08-31	IBM	112.875	114.20000...
1999-09-01	IBM	115.625	114.22500...

Figure 13.11   Five-day smoothing of IBM.

```
SELECT DATE, SUBSTR(DAYNAME(DATE),1,9) AS DAY_WEEK, CLOSE_PRICE,
DECIMAL(AVG(CLOSE_PRICE)
OVER (ORDER BY DATE ROWS 6 PRECEDING),7,2)
AS
AVG_7_ROWS,
COUNT(CLOSE_PRICE)
OVER (ORDER BY DATE ROWS 6 PRECEDING) AS COUNT_7_ROWS,
DECIMAL(AVG(CLOSE_PRICE)
OVER (ORDER BY DATE RANGE 0000006. PRECEDING),7,2)
AS AVG_7_RANGE,
COUNT(CLOSE(CLOSE_PRICE)
OVER (ORDER BY DATE RANGE 0000006. PRECEDING) AS
COUNT_7_RANGE
FROM STOCKTAB
WHERE SYMBOL='IBM'
```

The results shown in Figure 13.13 illustrate the difference in ROWS versus RANGE. Attempting to use ROWS in setting the window for 7 calendar days actually returns seven preceding rows. These seven rows span more than one calendar week. RANGE fixes this problem by recognizing the weekend gap. Therefore, RANGE is appropriate when there are gaps in the input data.

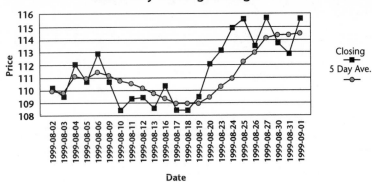

Figure 13.12   IBM 5-day moving average.

DATE	DAY_WEEK	CLOSE_P...	AVG_7_R...	COUNT_7...	AVG_7_RA...	COUNT_7...
1999-08-02	Monday	110.125	110.12	1	110.12	1
1999-08-03	Tuesday	109.500	109.81	2	109.81	2
1999-08-04	Wednesday	112.000	110.54	3	110.54	3
1999-08-05	Thursday	110.625	110.56	4	110.56	4
1999-08-06	Friday	112.750	111.00	5	111.00	5
1999-08-09	Monday	110.625	110.93	6	110.10	5
1999-08-10	Tuesday	108.375	110.57	7	110.87	5
1999-08-11	Wednesday	109.250	110.44	7	110.32	5
1999-08-12	Thursday	109.375	110.42	7	110.07	5
1999-08-13	Friday	108.500	109.92	7	109.22	5
1999-08-16	Monday	110.250	109.87	7	109.15	5
1999-08-17	Tuesday	108.375	109.25	7	109.15	5
1999-08-18	Wednesday	108.375	108.92	7	108.97	5
1999-08-19	Thursday	109.375	109.07	7	108.97	5
1999-08-20	Friday	112.000	109.46	7	109.67	5
1999-08-23	Monday	113.125	110.00	7	110.25	5
1999-08-24	Tuesday	114.875	110.91	7	111.55	5
1999-08-25	Wednesday	115.500	111.66	7	112.97	5
1999-08-26	Thursday	113.375	112.37	7	113.77	5
1999-08-27	Friday	115.625	113.41	7	114.50	5
1999-08-30	Monday	113.625	114.01	7	114.60	5
1999-08-31	Tuesday	112.875	114.14	7	114.20	5
1999-09-01	Wednesday	115.625	114.50	7	114.22	5

Figure 13.13   Calendar 7-day moving average.

GROUPING, GROUP BY, ROLLUP, and CUBE

Following are examples of OLAP functions using GROUPING, GROUP BY, ROLLUP and CUBE.

GROUPING, GROUP BY, and CUBE Example

Grouping is used in conjunction with the supergroup functions GROUP BY CUBE or ROLLUP. The purpose of the GROUPING function is to identify summary rows in the CUBE and ROLLUP query results. The GROUPING function returns a 1 or a 0 to indicate whether or not a row returned by the GROUP BY function is a subtotal row generated by the GROUP BY function.

A 1 means the row was the result of a subtotal, and a 0 means the row was not the result of a subtotal. The input to the GROUPING function can be any type, but it must be an item of the associated GROUP BY clause. For example:

```
SELECT SALES_DATE,
SALES_PERSON,
SUM(SALES) AS UNITS_SOLD,
GROUPING(SALES_DATE) AS DATE_GROUP,
GROUPING(SALES_PERSON) AS SALES_GROUP
FROM SALES
GROUP BY CUBE (SALES_DATE, SALES_PERSON)
ORDER BY SALES_DATE, SALES_PERSON
```

Sample results of the query are shown in Figure 13.14.

NOTE Figure 13.14 is output from the DB2 Command Line Processor. Here nulls are represented as "-".

The 1s in the DATE_GROUP column indicate the values in the UNIT_SOLD column are subtotal rows generated by the GROUP BY CUBE clause. Likewise, the 1s in the SALES_GROUP column indicate these rows are also subtotal rows. The last row, where DATE_GROUP and SALES_GROUP are both 1, indicates this row is a grand total row.

This function is used for end-user applications built to recognize SALES_DATE subtotal row by the fact that the value of DATE_GROUP is 0 and the value of SALES_GROUP is 1.

SALES_DATE	SALES_PERSON	UNITS_SOLD	DATE_GROUP	SALES_GROUP
12/31/1995	GOUNOT	1	0	0
12/31/1995	LEE	6	0	0
12/31/1995	LUCCHESSI	1	0	0
12/31/1995	-	8	0	1
03/29/1996	GOUNOT	11	0	0
03/29/1996	LEE	12	0	0
03/29/1996	LUCCHESSI	4	0	0
03/29/1996	-	27	0	1
03/30/1996	GOUNOT	21	0	0
03/30/1996	LEE	21	0	0
03/30/1996	LUCCHESSI	4	0	0
03/30/1996	-	46	0	1
03/31/1996	GOUNOT	3	0	0
03/31/1996	LEE	27	0	0
03/31/1996	LUCCHESSI	1	0	0
03/31/1996	-	31	0	1
04/01/1996	GOUNOT	14	0	0
04/01/1996	LEE	25	0	0
04/01/1996	LUCCHESSI	4	0	0
04/01/1996	-	43	0	1
	GOUNOT	50	1	0
	LEE	91	1	0
	LUCCHESSI	14	1	0
	-	155	1	1

Figure 13.14   Grouping result.

A SALES_PERSON subtotal row can be recognized by the fact that the value of DATE_GROUP is 1 and the value of SALES_GROUP is 0. A grand total row can be recognized by the value 1 for both DATE_GROUP and SALES_GROUP.

ROLLUP Example

In our sales data example in Figures 13.15 and 13.16, we want to summarize the sales data by salesperson and date with a rollup of sales to a day and week level for weeks 13 and 14 in 1996.

Our SQL looks like this:

```
SELECT WEEK(SALES_DATE) AS WEEK,
DAYOFWEEK(SALES_DATE) AS DAY_WEEK,
SALES_PERSON, SUM(SALES) AS UNITS_SOLD
FROM SALES
WHERE WEEK(SALES_DATE) IN (13,14) AND
YEAR(SALES_DATE) = 1996
GROUP BY ROLLUP ( WEEK(SALES_DATE), DAYOFWEEK(SALES_DATE), SALES_PERSON
)
ORDER BY WEEK, DAY_WEEK, SALES_PERSON
```

SALES_DATE	SALES_PERSON	REGION	SALES
1996-03-29	LUCCHESSI	Ontario-So...	3
1996-03-29	LUCCHESSI	Quebec	1
1996-03-29	LEE	Ontario-So...	2
1996-03-29	LEE	Ontario-No...	2
1996-03-29	LEE	Quebec	3
1996-03-29	LEE	Manitoba	5
1996-03-29	GOUNOT	Ontario-So...	3
1996-03-29	GOUNOT	Quebec	1
1996-03-29	GOUNOT	Manitoba	7
1996-03-30	LUCCHESSI	Ontario-So...	1
1996-03-30	LUCCHESSI	Quebec	2
1996-03-30	LUCCHESSI	Manitoba	1
1996-03-30	LEE	Ontario-So...	7
1996-03-30	LEE	Ontario-No...	3
1996-03-30	LEE	Quebec	7
1996-03-30	LEE	Manitoba	4
1996-03-30	GOUNOT	Ontario-So...	2
1996-03-30	GOUNOT	Quebec	18
1996-03-30	GOUNOT	Manitoba	1
1996-03-31	LUCCHESSI	Manitoba	1
1996-03-31	LEE	Ontario-So...	14
1996-03-31	LEE	Ontario-No...	3
1996-03-31	LEE	Quebec	7
1996-03-31	LEE	Manitoba	3
1996-03-31	GOUNOT	Ontario-So...	2
1996-03-31	GOUNOT	Quebec	1

Figure 13.15   Sales item detail for March.

The results are presented in Figure 13.17. The last row has no entry in the first two columns. These blanks are, technically speaking, nulls. The DB2 Command Center translates nulls to blanks in this case. (Other tools may display nulls differently.) This same behavior is seen in the DB2 Command Center output for CUBE.

The key to translating the format of the query results is to recognize the output format is controlled by the ORDER BY statement. In the preceding example, the output is sequenced first on week, then days within that week, and finally by salesperson for that day. Second, a summary or rollup row is inserted based on the order of the rollup statement. It is processed in reverse order. First, the rollup for each salesperson is given for the first day, then for that day a rollup is given. After that, all salesperson summaries for that day are presented. After all days in a week are processed in this manner, a rollup row for each week is given. This process continues until all weeks are processed. Finally, a rollup grand total is given.

SALES_DATE	SALES_PERSON	REGION	SALES
1996-04-01	LUCCHESSI	Ontario-So...	3
1996-04-01	LUCCHESSI	Manitoba	1
1996-04-01	LEE	Ontario-So...	8
1996-04-01	LEE	Ontario-No...	
1996-04-01	LEE	Quebec	8
1996-04-01	LEE	Manitoba	9
1996-04-01	GOUNOT	Ontario-So...	3
1996-04-01	GOUNOT	Ontario-No...	1
1996-04-01	GOUNOT	Quebec	3
1996-04-01	GOUNOT	Manitoba	7
1996-04-05	LEE	Manitoba	5
1996-04-05	LEE	Quebec	3
1996-04-05	LEE	Ontario-So...	3
1996-04-05	LEE	Ontario-No...	1
1996-04-06	LEE	Manitoba	3
1996-04-06	LEE	Quebec	2
1996-04-06	LEE	Ontario-So...	1
1996-04-06	LEE	Ontario-No...	1
1996-04-06	LUCCHESSI	Manitoba	2
1996-04-06	LUCCHESSI	Quebec	2
1996-04-06	LUCCHESSI	Ontario-So...	2
1996-04-06	LUCCHESSI	Ontario-No...	2
1996-04-05	LUCCHESSI	Manitoba	1
1996-04-05	LUCCHESSI	Quebec	1
1996-04-05	LUCCHESSI	Ontario-So...	2
1996-04-05	LUCCHESSI	Ontario-No...	1
1996-04-05	GOUNOT	Manitoba	5

Figure 13.16   Sales item detail for April.

To put it succinctly, rollup processing provides column summaries. This is demonstrated in Figure 13.18.

The results are best viewed as tables, spreadsheets, or bar charts. The objects are made by translating the results into commercially available spreadsheets and charting tools. Figure 13.19 demonstrates charting visualization.

CUBE Example

To calculate a CUBE in our previous example, we merely replace ROLLUP with CUBE in the GROUP BY clause as follows:

WEEK	DAY_WEEK	SALES_PERSON	UNITS_SOLD
13	6	GOUNOT	11
13	6	LEE	12
13	6	LUCCHESSI	4
13	6		27
13	7	GOUNOT	21
13	7	LEE	21
13	7	LUCCHESSI	4
13	7		46
13			73
14	1	GOUNOT	3
14	1	LEE	27
14	1	LUCCHESSI	1
14	1		31
14	2	GOUNOT	14
14	2	LEE	25
14	2	LUCCHESSI	4
14	2		43
14	6	GOUNOT	5
14	6	LEE	12
14	6	LUCCHESSI	5
14	6		22
14	7	LEE	7
14	7	LUCCHESSI	8
14	7		15
14			111
			184

Figure 13.17   Results of the ROLLUP query.

```
SELECT WEEK(SALES_DATE) AS WEEK,
DAYOFWEEK(SALES_DATE) AS DAY_WEEK,
SALES_PERSON, SUM(SALES) AS UNITS_SOLD
FROM SALES
WHERE WEEK(SALES_DATE) in (13,14) AND
YEAR(SALES_DATE) = 1996
GROUP BY CUBE ( WEEK(SALES_DATE),
DAYOFWEEK(SALES_DATE), SALES_PERSON )
ORDER BY WEEK, DAY_WEEK, SALES_PERSON
```

The query results are shown in Figure 13.20.

These results are more readily understood when translated into a three-dimensional cube (our three dimensions are weeks, days, and salesperson) or tables laid out one on top of another.

Week 14					
	Day 1	Day 2	Day 6	Day 7	
Gounot	3	14	5	0	
Lee	27	25	12	7	
Lucch…	8				
Subto…	15				
Total					74

Week 13		
	Day 6	Day 7
Gounot	11	21
Lee	12	21
Lucchessi	4	4
Subtotal	27	46
Total		73

Figure 13.18 ROLLUP visualization as tables.

In Figure 13.21, which shows a CUBE query result explanation, we have added labels to the sections of the query result to aid in the creation of the tables. Unlike the results in ROLLUP, which are column summary tables, the results of a CUBE are cross tabulation tables. The three tables based on our example are as follows:

- _ Units Sold by Salesperson by Day for Week 13
- _ Units Sold by Salesperson by Day for Week 14
- _ Units Sold by Salesperson by Day for Weeks 13 and 14

The tables are built using any commercially available spreadsheet tool. We simply follow the template provided in Figure 13.21 to create the three tables in Figure 13.22, which shows the CUBE query tables. In that figure, the super-aggregate rows are represented as the Total *column* in those tables. The Total *rows* in those tables are the row summaries referred to in the previous discussion on subtotal rows for the ROLLUP function.

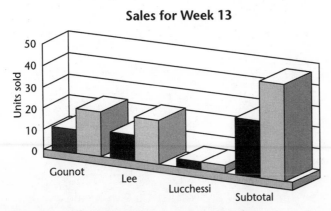

Figure 13.19 ROLLUP visualization as bar chart.

WEEK	DAY_WEEK	SALES_PERSON	UNITS_SOLD
13	6	GOUNOT	11
13	6	LEE	12
13	6	LUCCHESSI	4
13	6		27
13	7	GOUNOT	21
13	7	LEE	21
13	7	LUCCHESSI	4
13	7		46
13		GOUNOT	32
13		LEE	33
13		LUCCHESSI	8
13			73
14	1	GOUNOT	3
14	1	LEE	27
14	1		31
14	2	GOUNOT	14
14	2	LEE	25
14	2	LUCCHESSI	4
14	2		43
14	6	GOUNOT	5
14	6	LEE	12
14	6	LUCCHESSI	5
14	6		22
14	7	LEE	7
14	7	LUCCHESSI	8
14	7		15
14		GOUNOT	22
14		LEE	71
14		LUCCHESSI	18
14			111
	1	GOUNOT	3
	1	LEE	27
	1	LUCCHESSI	1
	1		31
	2	GOUNOT	14
	2	LEE	25
	2	LUCCHESSI	4
	2		43
	6	GOUNOT	16
	6	LEE	24
	6	LUCCHESSI	9
	6		48
	7	GOUNOT	21
	7	LEE	28
	7	LUCCHESSI	12
	7		81
		GOUNOT	54
		LEE	104
		LUCCHESSI	26
			184

Figure 13.20 CUBE query results.

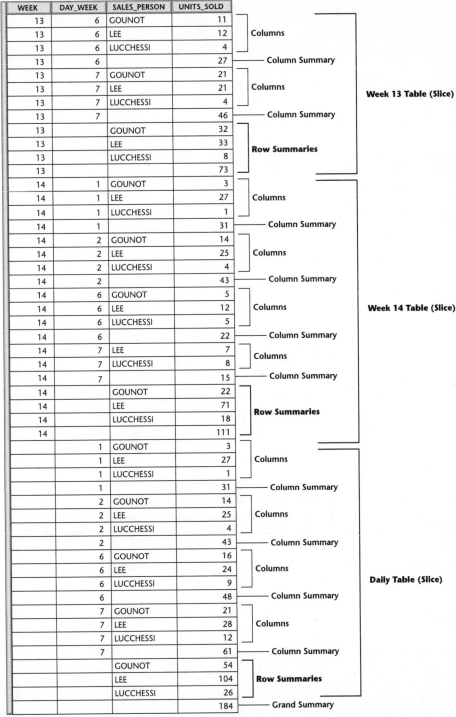

Figure 13.21   CUBE query results explanation.

Week 13/14	Day 1	Day 2	Day 6	Day 7	Total
Gounot	3	14	16	21	54
Lee	27	25	24	28	104
Lucchessi	1	4	9	12	26

Week 14	Day 1	Day 2	Day 6	Day 7	Total	184
Gounot	3	14	5	–	22	
Lee	27	25	12	7	71	
Lucchessi	1	4	5	8	18	
Total	31	43	22	15	111	

Week 13	Day 1	Day 2	Day 6	Day 7	Total
Gounot	–	–	11	21	32
Lee	–	–	12	21	33
Lucchessi	–	–	4	4	8
Total	–	–	27	46	73

Figure 13.22   CUBE query tables.

OLAP Functions in Use

To ensure readers understand the application of DB2 V8 OLAP functions, we have chosen two different business scenarios. Each scenario describes an application goal, the type of OLAP functions used, the SQL necessary, and the expected results.

Presenting Annual Sales by Region and City

This is a typical report reviewing sales results for planning budgets, campaigns, expansions/consolidations, and so forth. The SQL and OLAP functions defined here are simple implementations of complex and effective technologies.

Data

Input for this report is primarily transaction data, along with dimension information relating to date, product, and location. Attributes of interest include the following:

- Date of transaction, product purchased, product price, and quantity purchased
- Product code, product name, subgroup code, subgroup name, product group, and product group name
- Region, city

BI functions

The following functions are showcased:

- GROUP BY
- ROLLUP

Steps

Our data resided in a FACT_TABLE and a LOOKUP_MARKET table. The following SQL was run in DB2 Control Center:

```
SELECT b.region_type_id, a.city_id,
SUM(a.sales) AS TOTAL_SALES
FROM fact_table a, lookup_market b
WHERE YEAR(transdate)=1999
AND a.city_id=b.city_id
AND b.region_type_id=6
GROUP BY ROLLUP(b.region_type_id,a.city_id)
ORDER BY b.region_type_id, a.city_id
```

To reduce the size of the query result, the preceding SQL limits the query to region 6 and a transaction date of 1999. Table 13.1 shows the results of this query.

Table 13.1 Yearly Sales by City, Region

REGION_TYPE_ID	CITY_ID	TOTAL_SALES
6	1	81655
6	2	131512
6	3	58384

(continues)

Table 13.1   Yearly Sales by City, Region *(Continued)*

REGION_TYPE_ID	CITY_ID	TOTAL_SALES
...	...	...
...	...	...
...	...	...
6	19	77113
6	20	55520
6	21	63647
6	22	7166
6	23	92230
...	...	...
...	...	...
6	30	1733
6	31	5058
6		1190902
		1190902

Some rows of the result table were removed to fit on the page. The result shows ROLLUP of two groupings (region, city) returning three totals as follows:

- Total for region, city
- Total for region
- Grand total

Identifying Target Groups for a Campaign

The following example illustrates advanced OLAP functions used in combination with traditional SQL, as well as with statistical functions. The end result is an incredibly valuable SQL statement that epitomizes the power and relevance of BI at the database engine level.

The objective is to identify a particular group of customers from a larger set that will most likely respond to a marketing campaign, thus resulting in a better return on investment.

In our example, a financial institution would like to increase revenue by marketing mortgages to customers during the first quarter of the new fiscal year. Previous total coverage campaigns have been unsuccessful, and the company would like to focus on a particular city for better results.

Candidate target cities chosen are Palo Alto (eight branches) and San Jose (nine branches), since they are located in the Silicon Valley area, which has the highest average family income in the state of California. The rationale is that people with high incomes generally own their homes or would like to own homes and therefore are ideal targets for the campaign.

The decision to choose Palo Alto or San Jose as the target city was based on the following analysis steps:

1. Conduct a survey of the residents of Palo Alto and San Jose and analyze the results.

2. Using the Chi-Squared technique, infer from the results whether a relationship exists between where a customer lives and the product he or she will buy.

3. If such a relationship exists, use the Wilcoxon Rank Sum Test to prove that Palo Alto residents will likely buy mortgage loans.

Data

The main sources of data for this query are as follows:

- Cumulative distribution of the Chi-Square table
- Survey results in the form of contingency and survey tables
- Cumulative distribution of the Wilcoxon Rank-Sum Statistic Table

BI Functions

The following functions are showcased:

- SUM
- CUBE
- LOG(n)
- GROUPING
- RANK

Table 13.2 Survey Data Contingency Table

PRODUCT	PALO ALTO	SAN JOSE	TOTAL
Checking/savings	45	85	130
Visa	90	10	40
Mortgage	110	80	190
Total	185	175	360

Steps

We executed the following three steps to arrive at the answer:

1. We collected the survey data, documenting it in a Contingency table before loading it into a DB2 table called SURVEY. The survey asked Palo Alto and San Jose residents which products they will likely buy next and documented the results in the Contingency table shown in Table 13.2. This data was then loaded into the SURVEY DB2.

2. We then used the Chi-Squared technique to prove that there is a relationship between where a customer lives and the product he or she will buy by disproving the null hypothesis—in other words, by disproving that where customers live has no bearing on what products they buy. The formula for the "maximum likelihood" Chi-Squared test for independence is shown below:

```
Maximum Likelihood X = 2n log (n)
+ [2n11 log (n11) + ... + 2n rc
- [2n1+ log (n1+) + ... + 2nr+ log (nr+)]
- [2n+1 log (n+1) + ... + 2n+c log (n+c)]
Where:
nij: # in cell (i,j)
ni+: row i sum
n+j: column j sum
n: total # of user
```

NOTE Table lookups and complex calculations can be automated in DB2 via user-defined functions (UDFs).

The SQL query for calculation of the preceding Chi-Square (X) is as follows:

```
WITH c_table (prod_name, city, n, g1, g2) AS
(
SELECT prod_name, city, count(*),
2e0*(0.5e0-GROUPING(prod_name)),
2e0*(0.5e0-GROUPING(city))
FROM survey
GROUP BY CUBE (prod_name, city)
)
SELECT SUM(g1*g2*2e0*n*log(n)) as chi2
FROM c_table
```

NOTE When multiple division and multiplication operators are involved, consider using floating-point data type instead of INTEGER or DECIMAL to avoid arithmetic exceptions such as overflow.

The result of the preceding query is CHI2 = 34.1139

The *cumulative distribution* of the Chi-Square table (not shown here) shows that the probability of independence for Prob (X > 34.114) is less than 0.001 percent. Therefore, we conclude that there is a relationship between where a person lives and the products they will buy.

3. Here we use the Wilcoxon Rank Sum Test to prove that Palo Alto residents will likely buy more mortgages than the residents of San Jose. This, too, involves disproving the null hypothesis; that is, we disprove that customers in Palo Alto will not buy more mortgages than the residents of San Jose. This involves the following steps:

a. For each branch in Palo Alto and San Jose, collect the percentage of people who responded "yes" when asked whether they were likely to buy mortgages. Load the statistics to a table called SURVEY_MORTG. The columns in this table are as follows:

- Cityid—City
- Branchid—Branch within the city
- Percentyes—Percentage of branch customers who responded yes

b. Compute the Wilcoxon Rank Sum Test one-tail analysis for Palo Alto—also known as the "W statistic."

c. Look up the table of tail probabilities for this W statistic value, in order to determine whether or not the hypothesis is disproved.

d. Compute the W statistic for Palo Alto:

```
WITH ranked_mortg (city, ranks) AS
(
SELECT city, RANK() OVER (ORDER BY Percentyes)
FROM survey_mortg
)
SELECT SUM(ranks) as W
FROM ranked_mortg
WHERE city='Palo Alto';
```

The result of this query is a Wilcoxon W = 93.

Based on the table of tail probabilities for small values of ranks (not shown here), the probability of getting a rank sum of 93 is only 2.3 percent. In other words, the probability that Palo Alto residents will not buy more mortgages than San Jose residents is about 2.3 percent, which is quite low. We therefore conclude that Palo Alto residents will likely respond to our mortgage loan campaign as compared to San Jose residents.

Summary

OLAP is quickly becoming an integral part of the database engine itself. This migration of technology blurs the distinction between RDBMS and OLAP tools and effectively challenges the traditional role relational databases are often relegated to play with regard to dimensional data.

For years the OLAP functionality was the exclusive domain of OLAP tools. Leading database vendors such as IBM are working aggressively to blend that technology into the core of the database, thereby making OLAP a natural extension of database management.

To that end, DB2 V8 OLAP functions are a logical, effective expansion of SQL and its role in BI. If you have a background in SQL and an understanding of OLAP techniques, then becoming proficient with these functions will be fairly straightforward and intuitive. Moreover, once empowered with this technology, data architects and warehouse DBAs will readily recognize the opportunities to implement this technology to maximize performance for user communities.

Enhanced Analytics

CHAPTER 14

Data Mining with Intelligent Miner

Key Issues:

- Data architects and project planners must understand data mining to ensure a robust analytical landscape and rich informational content for their BI organization.

- Although query and reporting, as well as OLAP, are important tools in our BI war chest, they alone are not sufficient. Data mining is cornerstone to assessing customer risk, market segmentation, and prediction.

- It is not necessary for architects and IT personnel to become data mining experts. What is important is that architects understand the technology and techniques that are a part of a mining environment. Most importantly, architects must be able to recognize when a mining solution is required for a particular BI application.

■ Data mining is quickly being integrated into the database environment. A substantial step forward to this is the Predictive Model Markup Language (PMML) standard and the associated scoring functions. Among other things, this standard enables a shared use of mining models between vendors and gives your BI environment the flexibility that allows you to apply mining models wherever you can execute SQL.

In this chapter we concentrate on the practical issues of data mining. Specifically, we show you what is necessary to reliably mine your own business with results that you can put to use.

The use of scientific applications in commercial environments was the direct result of relational database technology that allowed companies to capture and store larger and larger volumes of data. The term *data mining* was coined as a phrase to encompass these different techniques when applied to very large volumes of data.

Some of the techniques that are used to perform data mining are computationally complex. In order to discover the patterns existing within large data sets, a large number of computations must be performed. In the last 10 years the growth in the use of large commercial databases (specifically, data warehouses), coupled with the need to understand and interpret this data, has led to an explosion in the use of data mining for a wide variety of commercial applications.

This chapter begins by defining how data mining fits in your BI effort and what is necessary for effective mining. We then detail the mining process itself by outlining the steps necessary for mining runs. As a departure from traditional mining application, we demonstrate how to exploit mining techniques to design more effective data warehouse structures and the informational content they store. The content also examines how mining should be deployed as an active participant in the decision-making and information cycle for analysts with products like IM Scoring and the new DB2 V8 features for modeling and visualization. The chapter ends with an introduction to new mining technology introduced by IBM for data discovery applications with DB2 OLAP Server.

Data Mining and the BI Organization

It is imperative that data architects understand the value data mining tools and techniques bring to any BI environment. Moreover, architects must be able to spot mining opportunities within the business requirements and understand what is necessary to effectively implement mining solutions to address those requirements.

Frankly, without mining, how can organizations with 24x7 worldwide operations keep pace with the critical monitoring and analysis of mountains of data in the constant quest of tuning the company's operations for maximum performance? Moreover how can CRM be effective without data mining playing an active, if not key, role?

The single biggest hurdle facing the broad adoption of data mining technology for warehouse-centric efforts is comprehension. But this does not apply to users; for them, the use of data mining is transparent. IT shops are the ones that need to understand the value of mining.

The information organization must include data mining as a natural, integral tool for the BI environment—that means everything from extraction, transformation and loading (ETL) to data management to data access and deployment. Figure 14.1 illustrates the information organization with regard to data mining. For brevity, each area influenced or impacted by mining is identified by a number, which is described in the following list:

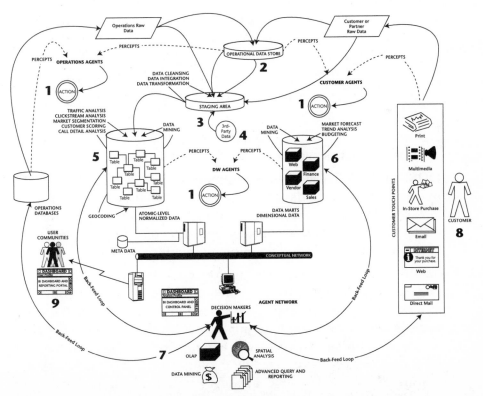

Figure 14.1 The influence of data mining on the information organization.

1. **Agent technology.** The objects used for blending agent-based technology into the BI environment are defined as *agents*. Each of these agent objects are a part of a broader agent network that reports findings and makes action recommendations to analysts. The agents can start as simple reflex agents that simply alert analysts of KPI thresholds—for example, "demand deposits are critically low." At the other extreme, the agents can be implemented as neural networks designed with mining tools that recommend actions, if not perform the necessary adjustments themselves. For example, suppose the customer agents are monitoring demand generated by a new banner ad campaign. The agent network contains several components. For instance, the network could monitor customer responses to a campaign and inventory levels, and use trend analysis from the warehouse to predict demand. If the demand starts to exceed the inventory necessary to meet fulfillment requirements, the agent network can either recommend to an analyst that more inventory should be purchased or it can place the necessary orders itself and notify the analyst that it has done so. Three agents are identified in the diagram:

   a. *Operations agent:* This object represents agent-based technology specifically designed and implemented to monitor operational systems.

   b. *Customer agent:* The object identified is for those agents designed and implemented to monitor customer systems and related touch points.

   c. *Data warehouse agent:* Agents identified in this role monitor data in atomic data structures as well as data marts.

2. **ODS.** The ODS object is the information organization's representative object for tactical data. That is not to say that there are not other tactical data sources, including production systems. For our purposes, the ODS epitomizes the use of tactical data in support of zero-latent analysis, of which data mining is a critical BI tool.

3. **Staging area.** For the information organization, any ETL efforts implemented should evaluate the requirements of any subsequent mining projects. For example, the ETL effort should ensure that a value exists for the income column. However, the ETL effort should go one step further, if necessary to a mining process, and bin the income into categories defined by mining, for instance, high, upper middle, middle, and low income bins. If this type of data preparation

is done as a natural part of our ETL, then the mining effort does not have to concern itself with this work. Moreover, if the ETL process adopts the work, multiple mining model efforts as well as reporting and OLAP will use similar source data from the atomic level of the warehouse.

4. **Third-party data.** It is not unusual for third-party data to be integrated with your own company data to enhance the information content for mining purposes. For instance, you may know little more than a customer's address. But with that address you could purchase third-party data that tells you a lot more about the area around that address, for example, age and income classifications, race, and population trends.

5. **Atomic level.** The atomic layer of the warehouse environment is an excellent source of mining data for several reasons. First, the atomic layer should represent the enterprise as a whole, thus allowing mining data to be sourced across subject areas. Second, the granularity of the atomic layer should be at the natural (lowest) grain of the business. This is not always the case for other warehouse structures such as stars or cubes. Third, the atomic layer should be where derived data is created and historical integrity is implemented and maintained.

6. **Data marts.** Star and cube farms are an excellent source of mining fodder. The dimensions of these structures are built by collapsing correlated data into a single table or entity construct. This is true for stars, and in the case of cubes, the construct is a resultant set of rows to be loaded into the cube technology. In either case, the correlated data stored in these structures readily lends itself to data mining, since mining often focuses on data correlation. To a large degree, if dimensional data is built correctly, it can be considered prepped data for mining.

There is another aspect of data marts that makes them important mining fodder. Cubes created to support OLAP can be incredibly large, making it difficult for analysts to notice nuggets of information hidden in the vast array of precalculated cells. Mining can be optimized to read the cube structures to search for trends that might be useful for an analyst to examine. This is definitely a task for mining: being sent out into a sea of data to return with any significant findings.

7. **Analysts.** The success of the information organization is determined by its ability to access BI-centric informational content. Data
mining is not only a critical contributor to that informational content, but it also has great impact on the value of analysis using other
BI tools. For example, scoring results of a mining model could be
incorporated into the data for an OLAP application or advanced
SQL reporting or even spatial analysis.

8. **Touch points.** CRM is all about being attentive to your customers
and adjusting operations to better serve them. CRM simply cannot
be successful without the contribution of data mining techniques
and technologies.

9. **User communities.** Although the general user community will
never create mining models, it benefits significantly from the efforts.
Usually reports or portal dashboards provide an excellent means to
publish pertinent mining results.

Although not numbered in the figure, it should be obvious that feedback
loops and meta data are necessary for your mining efforts. Actions taken as
a result of mining runs must be fed back into existing systems. These feedback loops ensure that the informational asset of the organization is nur-
tured and necessary adjustments to the organization are implemented.

One particularly important development with regard to Intelligent
Miner and the data mining arena in general is the establishment of standards for exchanging data mining models and the ability to deploy these
models directly into relational databases, such as DB2 Universal Database
and Oracle. The new standard is based on the Predictive Model Markup
Language. This standard provides for the exchange of analytic models like
linear regression, clustering, decision tree, and neural network. The most
important advantages are as follows:

- Mining experts on-site are not necessary.

- Computational resources are exploited efficiently.

- It allows real-time (event-triggered) processing, as well as batch
processing.

- It enables foreign software applications access to the modeling logic.

- It allows the generalization of any future model type.

- Mining models can be developed in one technology and deployed in
another.

The balance of this chapter discusses the types of business issues that can
be solved by data mining, the mining techniques employed, and how to
create a warehouse environment to support your mining efforts.

Effective Data Mining

The data collected about its customers is one of the greatest assets that any business has available. Buried within all this data is valuable information that can make a difference regarding how you do business. The challenge is how to unearth all the hidden nuggets of informational content buried under mountains of data. It is the ability to uncover the information hidden just beneath the data layer that mining brings to the BI table, thereby improving your ability to make better, well-informed decisions.

Data in itself provides no judgment or interpretation and therefore provides no basis for action. Putting data into context is what turns it into informational content. Where the context is well understood, BI enables the transformation from data to decision to become a routine process within your business. However, in today's highly competitive environment, which pushes the need for innovative ways to satisfy customer demands, the context of the data is not well understood. In these situations, data mining provides the tools and techniques to help you discover new contexts and hence new things about your customers. Armed with this knowledge, data mining also helps you to *predict* customer behavior and proactively adjust your interactions. The combination of discovery and prediction is the essence of data mining. This ability allows you to make decisions based on real knowledge of your business and customers, instead of just on gut feelings.

Data mining, for example, can address questions such as:

- What are the characteristics of my most profitable customers?
- What product mix should I keep in all stores in the NE region?
- Who is likely to respond to a certain campaign?
- Where should I open new stores?

The Mining Process

Data mining generally follows a process that begins with a precise, formal definition of the business problem. This dictates the data necessary to address the issues, as well as the appropriate mining technique. With the data and mining technique selected, miners will conduct test mining runs and inspect and evaluate the results. It is entirely possible that further iterations of data selection and the application of different mining techniques may be necessary to provide a final solution. Assuming that your mining effort effectively addresses the original business problem, it is necessary to deploy the results so that it leads to concrete actions taken.

You might think that you already are data mining by using standard statistical techniques or reporting tools to explore your database. In reality, what you are doing is making a hypothesis about a business issue that you are addressing and then attempting to prove or disprove your hypothesis by looking for data to support or contradict the hypothesis.

For example, suppose that, as a retailer, you believe out-of-town customers visit your larger inner-city stores less often than other customers. But when they do so they make larger purchases. To answer this type of question you can simply formulate a database query looking, for example, at your branches, their locations, sales figures, and customers, and then compile the average money spent per visit for each customer to prove your hypotheses. The answer discovered, however, may only be true for a small, highly profitable group of out-of-town shoppers who visited inner-city stores over a weekend. At the same time, out-of-town customers, perhaps commuters, visit the store during the week and spend exactly the same way as your other customers. In this case, your initial hypothesis test may indicate that there is no difference between out-of-town and inner-city shoppers.

Data mining uses an alternative approach that begins with the premise that you do not know what patterns of customer behaviors exist. In this case, you might simply ask the question: what are the relationships between what my customers spend and where they come from? You would leave it up to the mining algorithm to tell you about all of the different types of customers and the money they spend. Data mining provides answers without your having to ask specific questions. That is not to say that data mining is magic. You still have to understand the overall process.

To that end, the process starts with defining the business problem that you want to solve. Then a mining expert can concentrate on the right solution, that is, gather relevant data and discover hidden patterns using mining algorithms. Once the analysis is complete, the new knowledge extracted from the data must be put into action. Any mining investment only pays off when the net results are deployed in the day-to-day business.

There are seven steps to follow, as illustrated in Figure 14.2, for implementing a mining process:

1. Create a precise definition of the business issue.

2. Map the business issue to a data model and data requirements.

3. Source and preprocess the data.

4. Explore and evaluate the data.

5. Select the data mining technique.

6. Interpret the results.

7. Deploy the results.

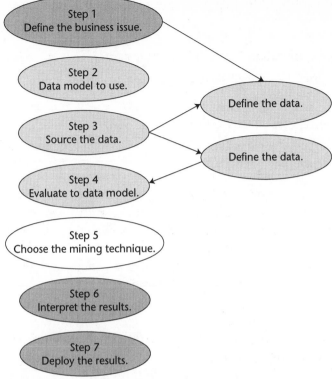

Figure 14.2 Seven steps of data mining.

Let's look at each of these steps more closely.

Step 1: Create a Precise Definition of the Business Issue

Data mining is about choosing the right tools for the job and then using them skillfully to discover the information in your data. We often have to use a combination of the tools at our disposal if we are to make real discoveries and extract the maximum value from our data. Therefore, the first step in our data mining method is to identify the business issue that you want to address and then determine how the business issue can be translated into a question, or set of questions, that data mining can tackle.

By *business issue* we mean that there is an identified problem to which you need an answer, where you suspect, or know, that the answer is buried somewhere in the data but you are not sure where. As you are formulating the business issue, you need to also think about whether you have access to the right data. It is important to recognize that the data you hold may not contain the information required to answer the question you are posing.

A business issue should fulfill the requirements of having:

- A clear description of the problem to be addressed
- An understanding of the data that might be relevant
- A vision for how you are going to use the mining results in your business

Each of these requirements is discussed in the following sections.

Describing the Problem

If you are not sure what questions data mining can address, the best approach is to look at examples of where it has been successfully used, either in your own industry or in related industries. Many business and research fields have been proven to be excellent candidates for data mining, for example, banking, insurance, retail, and telecommunications. There are many others, such as manufacturing, pharmaceuticals, biotechnology, and so on, where significant benefits have also been derived. Well-known approaches are customer profiling and cross-selling in retail, loan delinquency and fraud detection in banking and finance, customer retention (attrition and churn) in telecoms, and patient profiling and weight rating for diagnosis-related groups in health care. Some of these are depicted in Figure 14.3.

Figure 14.3   Data mining problems.

Even where the specific business issue you are addressing has not been addressed elsewhere, understanding how data mining can be applied helps to define your issue in terms that data mining can answer. You need to remember that data mining is about the discovery of patterns and relationships in your data. All of the different applications are using the same data mining concepts and applying them in subtly different ways.

With this in mind, when you define the business issue, you should think about it in terms of patterns and relationships. Take fraud as an example. Rather than ask the question, "Can we detect fraudulent customers?", you could ask the question, "Can we detect a small group of customers who exhibit unusual characteristics that may be indicative of fraud?" Alternatively, if you have identified some customers who are behaving fraudulently, the question is this: Can we identify some unique characteristics of these customers that would enable us to identify other potentially fraudulent customers?

Understanding Your Data

As mentioned previously, when you are formulating the business question, you need to consider whether you have the data necessary to answer the question. It is important to recognize that the data you hold may not contain the information required to answer the question you are posing. For example, suppose you are trying to determine why you are losing customers and you suspect the reason is that your competitors are undercutting you on price. If you do not have any competitor pricing data in your database, then clearly data mining is not going to answer whether this is the case. Although this is a trivial example, sometimes it is not so obvious that the data cannot provide the answer you are looking for. The amazing thing is how many people still believe that data mining should be able to perform the impossible. Where the specific business issue has been addressed elsewhere, then knowing what data was used to address the issue helps you to decide which of your own data should be used and how it may need to be transformed before it can be effectively mined. This process is termed the construction of a *common data model*. The use of common data models is a very powerful aid to performing data mining, as we show when we address specific business issues.

Using the Results

When defining the business issue that you want to address with data mining, you should carefully consider how you are going to use the information that you discover. Very often, considering how you will deploy the results of your data mining into your business helps to clarify the business issue you are addressing and helps you determine what data you are going to use. One approach is to assume you have already gotten the right results from your mining effort, then examine how they will apply or impact your business organization. Suppose, for example, that you want to use data mining to identify which types of existing customers will respond to new offers or services and then use the results to target new customers. Clearly, the variables you use when performing the data mining on your existing customers must be the same variables that you can derive about your new customers. In this case you cannot use the 6-month aggregated expenditure (*aggregated spend*) on particular products if all you have available for new customers is the expenditure from a single transaction. Thinking about how you are going to use the information you derive places constraints on the selection of data that you can use to perform the data mining and is therefore a key element in the overall process of translating the business issue into a data mining question.

Step 2: Map Business Issue to Data Model and Data Requirements

Where the data is being used routinely to support a specific business application, the data and meta data together form what we call a *data model* that supports the application. Typically the data model defines the following:

Data sources used.   Indicates the physical location where the data is stored or derived from.

Data types.   Defines how the data is structured, for example, CHAR, INT, DATE.

Data content.   Lists the tables or data files and the fields they contain.

Data description.   Delivers the names and description of the fields themselves.

Data usage.   Considers the ownership of tables and fields and how users use the content.

The data model essentially describes the data that it contains and that the users exploit. And like all other applications that require data models, data mining needs its own model as well. For most data mining applications, the data model required is in the form of a single file or database tables, with the record addressing whatever the target investigation requires.

Data mining techniques usually work with one huge input table. This doesn't mean that you have to physically store all data in one de-normalized table. Instead, it's common to define an appropriate SQL view that represents all the normalized tables. Each record can comprise one or many fields, where each field may be derived from a number of different data sources but all are tied to the same target or subject. For example, if the target/subject is your customers, then all data in the table should somehow relate to customers. In most business applications the most common data types are as follows:

Transactional data.   This is operational data generated each time some interaction occurs with the target. This data typically contains a time-stamp and some transaction identifier, as well as details of the transaction. Transactional data may, for example, relate to point-of-sales data for a customer in a supermarket or to the recording of information on a production line in a manufacturing application.

Relationship data.   This nonvolatile data contains relatively stable information about customers, products, equipment, items, and working processes.

Demographic data.   Demographic data comprises person-specific (customer, patient) data that usually comes from external or third-party sources. Typically this includes information on age, gender, postal code, and so on.

Defining data models for any application is often a complex task, and defining data models for data mining is no exception. Where the data model is required to support an application that has specific requirements (e.g., some form of business reporting tool), the data can be defined by asking the end users what types of information they require and then performing the necessary aggregations to support this requirement. In the case of data mining, the challenge is that very often you are not sure at the outset which variables are important and therefore exactly what is required. Generating data models for completely new data mining applications can therefore be a time-consuming activity.

The alternative is to use common data models that have been developed to solve business issues similar to the ones you are trying to address. While these types of models may not initially provide you with all of the information you require, they are usually designed to be extendable to include additional variables. The main advantage of using a common data model is that it provides you with a way of quickly seeing how data mining can be used within your business. In the following chapters we suggest some simple data models that can be used in this way.

Step 3: Source and Preprocess the Data

Data sourcing and preprocessing comprises the stages of *identifying, collecting, filtering,* and *aggregating* (raw) data into a format required by the data models and the selected mining function. Sourcing and preparing the data is the most time-consuming part of any data mining effort. These steps are similar to the steps associated with warehouse extraction, transformation, and loading discussed earlier in this book. Most mining projects start without having a data warehouse in place and therefore must deal with all the basic ETL steps initially. If your mining project can read the data from a well-organized data warehouse, you are lucky. It means that you can concentrate on the mining issues right away. However, even if you start with a well-managed data warehouse containing cleansed data, there is still additional data preparation necessary for mining. For example:

- Customer segmentation could require data where the number and dollar value of transactions are summarized per customer.

- Key performance indicators, such as an estimated lifetime value for customers, may be necessary for a mining run.

- Discretization of numeric values into common classes, such as age ranges, can make mining results easier to interpret.

Step 4: Explore and Evaluate the Data

Even after populating the mining model with data, we still have to make sure that the data used fulfills the requirements of completeness, exactness, and relevance. The purpose of this step is to perform an initial evaluation of the data. We start this step by browsing the input data with visualization tools, referred to as *visual inspection*. This may lead to the detection of *implausible distributions*. For example, a wrong join of tables during the data preparation step could result in variables containing values actually belonging to different fields.

During the initial exploration you can easily detect fields that have too many missing values or fields with many outlier values. Although most mining functions are able to deal with missing values, there may be default values that must be substituted as a "best guess." Sometimes a field has a rather skewed distribution of values; for example, there may be a few very big numbers. This is typical of data about personal income where a few people have extraordinary salaries. Another typical example is image data about the length of phone calls. Almost all calls are quite short, in the range of minutes, while a few phone calls may last an hour or more. Again, some mining algorithms are smart enough to deal with such data distributions, but transforming these fields can improve results. Let's say you take numeric income values and transform them into discrete tax brackets.

Finally, the *selection of features/variables* for the mining run is a natural part of this explore and evaluate step. Variables could be superfluous by presenting the same or very similar information as others but increasing the runtime. *Dependent*, or *highly correlated variables* could be found with statistical tests like bivariate statistics and linear and polynomial regression. Dependent variables should be reduced by selecting one variable for all others or by composing a new variable for all correlated ones by factor or component analysis.

Step 5: Select the Data Mining Technique

Data mining also includes the crucial step of selecting the best-suited mining technique for a given business issue. This step not only includes defining the appropriate technique or mix of techniques to use, but also the way in which the techniques must be applied.

In general, data mining techniques can be divided into two broad categories:

- Discovery data mining
- Predictive data mining

Each category is discussed in the following sections, as well as its relevant data mining techniques.

Discovery Data Mining

Discovery data mining applies to a range of techniques whose primary objective is to find patterns inside your data without any prior knowledge of what patterns exist. The following are examples of discovery mining techniques:

Clustering. This term is used for a range of techniques that attempt to group data records on the basis of how similar they are. A data record may, for example, comprise a description of each of your customers. In this case, clustering would group similar customers together, while at the same time maximizing the differences between the different customer groups formed. Clustering constructs, for example, customer segments by analyzing the characteristics represented in the data instead of starting with predefined assumptions. It will find the commonly known large segments and it will also find niche segments which may be overlooked.

Link analysis.   Link analysis describes a family of techniques that determine associations between data records. The most well-known type of link analysis is *market basket analysis*. In this case the data records are the items purchased by a customer during the same transaction, and because the technique is derived from the analysis of supermarket data, these are designated as being in the same basket. Market basket analysis discovers the combinations of items that are purchased by different customers, and by association (or *linkage*), you can build a picture of which types of product are purchased together. Link analysis is not restricted to market basket analysis. If you think of the market basket as a grouping of data records, then the technique can be used in any situation where there are a large number of groups of data records.

Sequence analysis.   Sequence analysis comprises of data mining techniques that are applied to the analysis of time-ordered data records or, indeed, any data set that can be considered ordered. These data mining techniques attempt to detect similar sequences or subsequences in the ordered data.

Predictive Mining

Predictive data mining is applied to a range of techniques that find relationships between a specific variable (called the *target variable*) and the other variables in your data. The following are examples of predictive mining techniques:

Classification.   This term describes the assignment of data records into predefined categories—for example, assigning customers to predefined market segments, risk classes, or product usage classes. In this case, the target variable is the category and the techniques discover the relationship between the other variables and the target category. When a new record is to be classified, the technique determines the category and the probability that the record belongs to the category. Classification techniques include decision trees and neural and radial basis function (RBF) classifiers.

Value prediction.   This concerns predicting the value of a continuous variable from the other variables in a data record—for example, predicting the likely expenditure of a customer from his or her age, gender, and income group. The most familiar value prediction techniques include linear and polynomial regression, and data mining extends these to other techniques, such as neural and RBF value prediction.

Step 6: Interpret the Results

The results from performing any type of data mining can provide a wealth of information that can be difficult to interpret. Therefore, this step often requires assistance from a business expert who can translate the mining results back into the business context. Because we do not expect the business analyst to necessarily be a mining expert, it is important that the results are presented in such a way that they are relatively easy to interpret. To assist in this process, you have at your disposal a range of tools that enable you to visualize the results and to provide the necessary statistical information necessary for facilitating the interpretation. Figure 14.4 illustrates one of the visualization techniques used by Intelligent Miner.

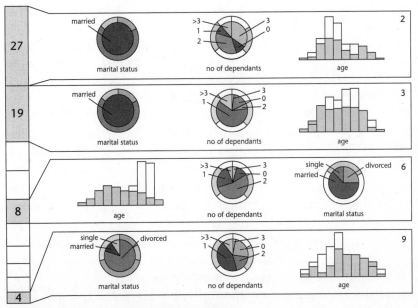

Figure 14.4   Intelligent Miner visualization.

Step 7: Deploy the Results

This step is possibly the most important of all: deploying the results of the data mining into your business. If you only see data mining as an analytical tool, you are failing to realize the full potential of what data mining has to offer. When you perform data mining you can both discover new things about your customers and determine how to classify or how to predict particular characteristics or attributes. In all these cases data mining creates mathematical representations of the data that we call models. They contain the rules and patterns found by the mining algorithm. These models are very important for two reasons:

- They provide you with a deeper insight of your business.
- They can be deployed in or used by other business processes, for example, your CRM systems.

When embarking on any data mining activity, you should think carefully about how you intend to use the data mining results and where in your business the results will have the greatest impact.

Integrating Data Mining

While data mining is often performed using a stand-alone workbench tool, there are many cases where the data mining functions should be integrated as an additional function in another business application. Most notably, this is true for scoring. DB2 provides a feature called IM Scoring that implements the deployment of predictive mining as SQL extensions. For example, a call center application can easily be enriched by an indicator for the *churn risk* of a customer. When a customer calls in, the application will look up the customer profile data and compute the predicted risk score on the fly. Or think of a Web application where product recommendations are placed dynamically when a visitor clicks to the next page. Based on customer profile data and also on the user's recent online activities, a scoring function will pick the campaign that is most likely to be of interest to the online user. This real-time scoring method always uses up-to-date information about the customer. Often the input data is read from an Operational Data Store (ODS). Contrast this with an environment where a mining expert launches a workbench tool and once in a while produces an output table containing the scores for all customers. With batch processing, the mining results are outdated by the time they are actually used. Real-time scoring is the best method for closing the loop between back-office analysis and front-office operations.

The functions of IM Scoring are tightly integrated with the SQL interface of the database engine. They read standard PMML models as input, and the models are managed and updated as simple values in database tables. A particular benefit is that any database application can easily be adapted to invoke scoring. The application doesn't even have to know the mining functions because they can be hidden behind regular VIEW. Furthermore, scoring can be called within triggers or by agents, thus enabling trigger-based campaigns where certain rules are activated as soon as an indicator or predicted score reaches some threshold.

The integration of data mining into business applications is not restricted to scoring. In fact, the modeling functions creating a new customer segmentation or training a new classification model are available as DB2 extenders. Visualization tools are provided as pluggable components as well. This opens up a whole new area where customized mining processes can be integrated into a solution, thereby enabling business users to drive a predefined mining process. For example, a tailored solution for detecting fraudulent behavior of stock traders or detecting data quality issues in a daily ETL process can be built by calling the database mining functions internally. The solution is able to better detect unusual patterns in the most recent data. The end user does not have to know the technology and does not need to depend on a mining expert after the solution has been designed and implemented.

Skills for Implementing a Data Mining Project

Successfully implementing a data mining project using the preceding method requires a mix of skills in the following areas:

- Data manipulation (for example, SQL)
- Knowledge of mining techniques
- Domain knowledge or ability to communicate with domain experts
- Creativity

These skills are normally not incorporated into one person, and therefore mining requires a team effort. Such a team will comprise the following:

- A marketing analyst who is informed in the branches of businesses that have been selected for data mining.
- An IT analyst who is experienced with data management procedures within your business.
- A data engineering team who will have the lead and the experience in all data mining topics.

- A business user or users who can check the usability of the mining result and evaluate the deployment from a solely business perspective. Many data mining projects run into problems by underestimating the efforts of searching and delivering raw data with a reasonable degree of quality necessary for the deployment of mining.

- A project owner who is normally the head of a branch inside the company to support the work and help to resolve problems.

Whether or not these are different individuals clearly depends on the mix of skills that they have, but in general the team must be able to accomplish the following:

Understand the data source.   There are two aspects of understanding the data source: knowledge about the physical data situation in the company and the usage of the data proposed for data mining. Normally, the data mining expert is not the data administrator, who is responsible for the all data repositories. In this case, the interaction with the database owner and the mining expert must be guaranteed.

Understand the data preparation.   Data preparation requires a lot of expertise in creating new data input (for example, SQL programming skill) and a good understanding of the given raw data. An excellent data miner may not be successful if he or she lacks expertise in the business field under discussion.

Understand the algorithms.   Using algorithms means being able to adapt the setting for the various mining runs. Because all data mining functions are highly sophisticated from an implementation point of view, data mining experts are demanded who are well trained with the selected data mining toolkit. Namely, these persons must overview how much effort has to be undertaken to solve each step of the mining process and how to solve each task either with the toolkit, the database system, or additional statistical functions.

Understand the business needs.   This skill is specifically tied to the subject matter experts brought forward by the user community and the ability of the mining team to interpret those requirements into mining solutions.

Benefits of Data Mining

Beyond decision support systems, several aspects of a data warehouse can benefit from a mining tool, both in improved data quality and warehouse design. The following sections explore unique ways to apply mining that are often never considered by architects or project planners, including:

- Ensuring data quality
- Identifying relevant dimensions/attributes for a subject area
- Improving analytical value of stars/cubes with mining results
- Enhancing BI access

Data Quality

Data mining can help improve the data quality by checking simple statistical indicators of the data that is loaded into the warehouse. When the warehouse data is regularly updated with current data—for example, with new transactions from the previous day—we can assume that the new data has about the same range of values as the accumulated data in the warehouse. Of course, there may be continuous trends, such as growing sales figures. So we cannot simply check fixed minimal or maximal value. Nevertheless, it is still straightforward to check whether the new average value in certain columns is close to the average value in the corresponding columns in the warehouse data. A typical statistical measure for the closeness of values is to build intervals based on the "standard deviation" of a collection of values. DB2 directly provides statistical functions for computing standard deviation, correlation, and linear regression.

Let's say the average value of new data lies outside the average range currently in the warehouse, plus or minus the standard deviation. Given this scenario, it is likely that the new values are invalid or, at the very least, suspect. There may be several reasons for this disparity—for instance, an error during the transmission of data might have cut off a significant digit or all values may be missing or equal to 0. Equally of concern is if the new average value is too close to the average value of the previous load; in this case it is likely the input data wasn't updated. The implementation of simple prediction models from data mining tools for checking values is an optimum means for data quality checks, ensuring the data being propagated into the warehouse is of the quality user communities assume.

Relevant Dimensions

Another aspect of mining that can be exploited by data architects has to do with identifying the relevant dimensions/attributes that dictate the design of a star schema or cube and, therefore, the ultimate analytical value. To start, let's talk about a pitfall of dimensional tools called the "curse of dimensionality." We will use data mining (a variation of a dimensional tool) as an example. It is not unusual to blend third-party data with company data and use it in mining efforts. The added data is supposed to provide greater insight; however, adding more data does not necessarily improve the models. It can also have a negative effect. Data mining algorithms try to use every input field. If there are too many fields that are not relevant to the business question, then it might be difficult for the mining algorithm to find a relationship, because the input data is too complex. The curse of dimensionality is an increasing problem for a more popular BI tool as well: OLAP.

Mining tools and techniques can be applied to the design of OLAP cubes. When designing an OLAP cube a typical problem is identifying the important dimensions and their related attributes that should be included in the cube or star schema. Data mining can help you define the most relevant contributors to any subsequent dimensional analysis from either of these data structures. The use of common data mining tools such as correlation and sensitivity analysis help you identify the most appropriate dimensions/attributes.

Using Mining Results in OLAP

Many applications of data mining concentrate on the specific feature of mining, but they fail to describe mining in the context of a dimensional data mart where the star schema is the basic data model. That's very similar to organizations that build independent data marts that result in stovepipe applications. Data mining usually works with flat relations as input, but there is also an important connection to the star schema. It turns out that OLAP and data mining represent two different techniques to analyze the same business data. In most cases, we can use the general star schema/cube as a starting point. Whereas OLAP focuses on data in the fact table and the dimensions are used to navigate the cube, data mining usually focuses on one dimension of the star schema and the fact table is used to enrich information about that dimension.

Not unlike OLAP efforts, a mining project always starts with a specific business problem, such as how to find cross-selling opportunities for customers. In this case, we need data that provides a picture of the customer behavior. So, it's not only the plain dimension table that is used in mining. Related hierarchy definitions, such as product groups, are utilized in data mining for association analysis. Moreover, various aggregation operations are used during preprocessing to add derived values to the selected dimension. For example, in a banking application we could select the customer dimension and enhance the customer information via aggregations on the transactions, such as the average amount of transactions done at ATMs during the previous 3 months. These aggregations could also use attributes from other dimensions, for example, the type of transactions done at kiosks, on the Web, and by phone.

While dimensional data can be used as input for data mining, the reverse is also true. We can enrich the dimensional data with results from data mining. A typical instance is to create a clustering model that groups customers into segments. Once this segmentation is defined, the label of the segment can be added as an attribute to the customer dimension. Later we can use that segment label as a dimension in OLAP or we can build an OLAP cube that filters customers in a specific segment—for example, for further analysis of a high-profit group of customers.

Finally, mining can enhance the data access layer for end users. For instance, IM Scoring is used to embed mining results into end-user applications. Mining is transparent to the user. Examples include online ranking of insurance risk or personalization in a Web application where a mining model is used to make specific product recommendations. Other examples of mining at the access layer are CRM systems for mailing campaigns. Mining is used to find the target customers who are most likely to respond or have a high propensity to buy a certain product. Managing the campaign is done in the CRM system, which internally calls mining.

Benefits of Mining DB2 OLAP Server

IBM's Intelligent Miner is an exceptional mining tool that complements more common analytical methods used in warehousing, specifically OLAP. The difference between mining and OLAP is that data mining is discovery-driven while OLAP techniques are defined as hypothesis-driven. Therefore, mining will dig for insights within the data, whereas OLAP requires the analyst to navigate through the data to find insight. And even when OLAP is implemented with a sophisticated tool such as IBM's DB2 OLAP Server, the vast amounts of data make it difficult for even a seasoned analyst to locate all insight. That's where data mining comes in.

Referred to as OLAP Miner, this technology merges the discovery-driven value of Intelligent Miner with the hypothesis-driven strength of DB2 OLAP Server. This offers BI environments and their user communities a broader analytical landscape, for instance:

- OLAP Miner can support a fast path to actionable information and detect new business opportunities within large cube data sets.

- The technology affords ad hoc data exploration of OLAP cubes.

- OLAP Miner allows exhaustive, machine-driven, algorithm-based mining for uncovering unexpected values in OLAP cubes.

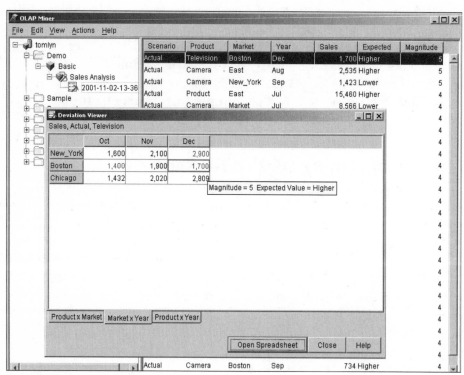

Figure 14.5 OLAP Miner deviations.

Users must first define the subset of the cube that OLAP Miner will be running against, as well as the number of deviations to report back to the users. OLAP Miner considers a cell of a cube to be deviant if it is significantly different from the expected value, which is calculated by the mining algorithm. Once a mining run is completed, users can utilized the Deviation Viewer (see Figure 14.5) to examine each deviation found in the OLAP cube subset of data.

Summary

When some data architects and project planners hear the term *data mining*, there is immediate resistence. The technology is not for the faint of heart. Even now, mining requires a skilled individual to create effective mining models that produce relevant and important information content. But that doesn't mean we all need to be mining experts to exploit the technology. We do, however, have to understand the technology so that we know when data mining makes the most sense for a BI application and what the data warehouse environment can do to support that mining effort.

However, don't become distracted by technical details often included in textbooks on data mining. The technology is becoming more and more mature. The key to a successful application of data mining lies in understanding its value for your business. The two pillars of data mining are discovery and prediction. They provide you with a better understanding of your business and with the ability to quickly anticipate the behavior of your customers, suppliers, or even of internal production processes. Your business decisions will become more precise and you will be able to act faster.

Too often our mining models are taken off-site, created and supported by third parties. These consulting services use our business rules, our data, and our money to produce information that we need to run our companies. This is critical information and it seems reasonable that the BI team should be an active participant. Think about it. If the information is essential to our organization and the process to acquire that information is based on everything being supplied from our organization, then why don't we demand to play an active role in its creation and maintenance? The answer is simple: We should.

CHAPTER 15

DB2-Enhanced BI Features and Functions

Key Issues:

- Database-resident functions provide a means for the database to actively participate in BI solutions for more than just data storage for other BI tools.

- Data architects can use DB2 V8 BI-centric functions in combination with DB2 V8 OLAP functions to implement complex solutions at the database level.

- Database-resident functions allow architects to create more meaningful BI information content at the engine level and store that information as derived data to be propagated and exploited by subsequent BI applications.

- DB2 V8 BI functions allow DBAs to actively participate in BI solutions.

- DB2 V8 BI functions afford a means to centrally control meta data for derived information content.

DB2 V8 provides a wide array of BI-centric functions that enhance your ability to perform robust analytics at the database level. This has several benefits to your efforts. One benefit is that you can implement various BI functions using SQL anywhere in your BI environment where you can execute an SQL statement. Another benefit is that you can implement these various BI solutions to gain derived values that will be stored for all subsequent BI applications—a single source of the truth, if you will.

Think of it. Such common BI functions as random sample aggregations or providing total sales revenue per quarter and cumulative sales over multiple years can be executed with SQL. We not only create an effective means of control for derived data, but we make a more efficient environment, since the raw data required for these types of functions does not have to be collected and shipped off to another technology for calculation.

In this chapter, we define the functions available in DB2 V8, as well as provide sample applications of their use in a typical warehouse setting.

DB2 Analytic Functions

There are 20 functions specific to advanced analytics in DB2 V8. Table 15.1 summarizes the functions themselves, and this section covers each in more detail.

Table 15.1   DB2 Analytic Functions

ANALYTIC FUNCTIONS	DESCRIPTION
AVG	Returns the average of a set of numbers.
CORRELATION or CORR	Returns the coefficient of correlation of a set of number pairs.
COUNT	Returns the count of the number of rows in a set of rows or values.
COUNT_BIG	Returns the number of rows or values in a set of rows or values. Result can be greater than the maximum value of the integer.
COVARIANCE or COVAR	Returns the covariance of a set of number pairs.
MAX	Returns the maximum value in a set of values.
MIN	Returns the minimum value in a set of values.

Table 15.1 *(Continued)*

ANALYTIC FUNCTIONS	DESCRIPTION
RAND	Returns a random floating-point number between 0 and 1.
STDDEV	Returns the standard deviation of a set of numbers.
SUM	Returns the sum of a set of numbers.
VARIANCE or VAR	Returns the variance of a set of numbers.
Regression Features	
REGR_AVGX	Returns quantities used to compute regression diagnostic statistics.
REGR_AVGY	Returns quantities used to compute regression diagnostic statistics.
REGR_COUNT	Returns the number of non-null number pairs used to fit the regression line.
REGR_INTERCEPT or REGR_ICPT	Returns the y-intercept of the regression line.
REGR_R2	Returns the coefficient of determination for the regression.
REGR_SLOPE	Returns the slope of the regression line.
REGR_SXX	Returns quantities used to compute regression diagnostic statistics.
REGR_SXY	Returns quantities used to compute regression diagnostic statistics.
REGR_SYY	Returns quantities used to compute regression diagnostic statistics.

Following are descriptions of each function listed in the table, as well as its syntax and use.

AVG

The AVG function returns the average of a set of numbers. ALL indicates duplicate rows are to be included, and this is the default. The average function is applied to a set of values after eliminating all null values. If DISTINCT is specified, duplicate values are eliminated as well. (See Figure 15.1.)

```
       .-ALL---------.
>>-AVG--(----+---------------+---expression--)----------------------------><
            '-DISTINCT-'
```

Figure 15.1 AVG syntax.

CORRELATION

The CORRELATION function returns the coefficient of correlation of a set of number pairs. The coefficient indicates the strength of the linear relationship between the set of variables. The input values must be numeric, and the data type of the result is double-precision floating-point.

As shown in Figure 15.2, the function is applied to the set of numeric pairs derived from the argument values (*expression1,expression2*) by the elimination of all pairs for which either *expression1* or *expression2* is null:

- A null result implies the input set is empty.
- When the result is not null, it will be between -1 and 1.
- A zero value means the two expressions are not linearly related.
- A -1 or a +1 means they are linearly perfectly related.

COUNT

The COUNT function counts the number of rows or values in a set of rows or values. A row that includes only null values is included in the count, thus the result cannot be null. The result is a large integer that is the number of rows in the set. The syntax is found in Figure 15.3.

```
>>-+-CORRELATION-+--(----expression1--,--expression2--)--------------------><
   '-CORR-------------'
```

Figure 15.2 CORRELATION syntax.

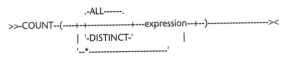

Figure 15.3 COUNT syntax.

COUNT_BIG

The COUNT_BIG function counts the number of rows or values in a set of rows or values. It functions the same as COUNT except that the result can be greater than the maximum value of integer. The result data type of COUNT_BIG is a decimal with precision 31 and scale 0. Nulls are treated like they are in COUNT. (See Figure 15.4.)

COVARIANCE

The COVARIANCE function, shown in Figure 15.5, is used to determine if a relationship exists between two variables. This function calculates the population covariance of a set of number pairs. (A *population* is a collection of all data points for a given subject of interest.) If both variables tend to be above or below the average simultaneously, then the covariance is positive. On the other hand, if one variable tends to have above average values when the other variable has below average values, then the covariance is negative.

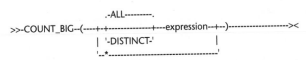

Figure 15.4 COUNT BIG syntax.

```
>>-+-COVARIANCE-+--(----expression1--,--expression2--)--------------------><
   '-COVAR-----------'
```

Figure 15.5   COVARIANCE.

Input for a covariance test is a set of numeric pairs, and the output is double-precision floating-point. (See Figure 15.5.) The function is applied to the set of numeric pairs derived from the argument values (expression1,expression2) by the elimination of all pairs for which either expression1 or expression2 is null. A null result indicates an empty input set.

MAX

The MAX function, shown in Figure 15.6, returns the maximum value in a set of values. The result is considered to be a derived value and can be null. The function is applied to the set of values derived from the argument values by the elimination of null values.

If the function is applied to an empty set, the result is a null value. The specification of DISTINCT has no effect on the result and therefore is not recommended. It is included for compatibility with other relational systems.

MIN

The MIN function (syntax shown in Figure 15.7) returns the minimum value in a set of values. The result is considered to be a derived value and can be null. The function is applied to the set of values derived from the argument values by the elimination of null values.

If the function is applied to an empty set, the result is a null value. The specification of DISTINCT has no effect on the result and therefore is not recommended. It is included for compatibility with other relational systems.

```
            .-ALL------.
>>-MAX--(----+--------------+--expression--)--------------------><
            '-DISTINCT-'
```

Figure 15.6   MAX syntax.

Figure 15.7 MIN syntax.

RAND

The RAND function returns a random floating-point value between 0 and 1 using the argument as the optional seed value. The function is defined as nondeterministic. An argument is not required, but if it is specified, it can be either an INTEGER or SMALLINT. Providing a seed value guarantees the repeatability of the result and is generally used for debugging purposes. The result can be null if the argument is null. (See Figure 15.8.)

The following SQL results in a 10 percent sample (corresponding to 0.1) of all the rows in the CUSTOMERS table:

```
SELECT * FROM CUSTOMERS
WHERE RAND() < 0.1
```

In the preceding SQL, if there were 100,000 rows in the CUSTOMERS table, the actual number of rows in the sample is random, but is equal on average to (100,000/10) = 10,000. Since this technique involves a complete scan of the CUSTOMERS table, it is appropriate in situations where a sample is created once and then used repeatedly in multiple queries. In other words, the cost of creating the sample is amortized over multiple queries.

This is a "Bernoulli sample," where each row is selected for inclusion in the sample with probability $q=(n/N)$ where n is the desired sample size, and N is the total number of rows and rejected with probability $(1-q)$, independently of the other rows. The final sample size is random but is equal to n on average.

Figure 15.8 RAND syntax.

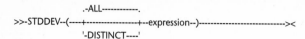

```
            .-ALL------------.
>>-STDDEV--(----+-----------------+--expression--)----------------------------><
                '-DISTINCT----'
```

Figure 15.9 STDDEV syntax.

STDDEV

The STDDEV function returns the standard deviation of a set of numbers. The input must be numeric and the output is double-precision floating-point. The STDDEV function is applied to the set of values derived from the argument values by the elimination of null values. If the input data set is empty, the result is null. Otherwise, the result is the standard deviation of the values in the set. (See Figure 15.9.)

SUM

The SUM function returns the sum of a set of numbers. The function is applied to the set of values derived from the argument values by the elimination of null values. The syntax of SUM is shown in Figure 15.10. If the function is applied to an empty set, the result is a null value. Otherwise, the result is the sum of the values in the set.

VARIANCE

The VARIANCE function returns the variance of a set of numbers. The argument values must be numeric. The function is applied to the set of values derived from the argument values by the elimination of null values. If the function is applied to an empty set, the result is a null value. (See Figure 15.11.)

```
            .-ALL-------------.
>>-SUM--(----+-----------------+--expression--)----------------------------><
                '-DISTINCT----'
```

Figure 15.10 SUM syntax.

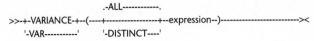

```
                .-ALL------------.
>>-+-VARIANCE-+--(----+-----------------+--expression--)-------------------------><
   '-VAR-----------'      '-DISTINCT----'
```

Figure 15.11   VARIANCE syntax.

Regression Functions

The regression functions (see Figure 15.2) support the fitting of an ordinary-least-squares regression line of the form: $Y = aX + b$, where:

- Y is the dependent variable.
- X is the independent variable.
- a is the slope of the regression line.
- b is the intercept.

Both a and b are called coefficients.

There are nine distinct regression functions:

REGR_SLOPE.   Calculates the slope of the line (the parameter a in the preceding equation).

REGR_INTERCEPT (REGR_ICPT).   Calculates the y-intercept of the regression line (b in the preceding equation).

REGR_COUNT.   Determines the number of non-null pairs used to determine the regression.

REGR_R2.   Expresses the quality of the best-fit regression. R2 (R-squared) is referred to as the *coefficient of determination* or the "goodness-of-fit" for the regression.

REGR_AVGX.   Returns quantities that can be used to compute various diagnostic statistics needed for the evaluation of the quality and statistical validity of the regression model.

REGR_AVGY, REGR_SXX, REGR_SYY and REGR_SXY.   Defined similarly to REGR_AVGX.

```
>>-+-REGR_AVGX-------------+--(----expression1--,--expression2--)--><
   +-REGR_AVGY------------- +
   +-REGR_COUNT---------- +
   +-+-REGR_INTERCEPT-+-+
   | '--REGR_ICPT-----------' |
   +-REGR_R2----------------- +
   +-REGR_SLOPE------------ +
   +-REGR_SXX--------------- +
   +-REGR_SXY---------------+
   '-REGR_SYY----------------'
```

Figure 15.12   Regression function syntax.

Each function is applied to the set of values derived from the input numeric pairs (*expression1,expression2*) by the elimination of all pairs for which either *expression1* or *expression2* is null. In other words, both values must be non-null to be considered for the function. As defined, *expression1* corresponds to the Y variable and *expression2* corresponds to the X variable.

When using regression functions, you need to keep a few considerations in mind. The first consideration is whether the input for all of the regression functions must be numeric; the output of REGR_COUNT is integer and all the remaining functions output is done in double-precision floating point. Second, the regression functions are all computed simultaneously during a single pass through the data set. Another consideration you must examine has to do with the input set. If the input set is not empty and VARIANCE(*expression2*) is positive, then REGR_COUNT returns the number of non-null pairs in the set, and the remaining functions return results that are defined in Table 15.2. Furthermore, if the input set is not empty and VARIANCE(*expression2*) is equal to zero, then the regression line either has infinite slope or is undefined. In this case, the functions REGR_SLOPE, REGR_INTERCEPT, and REGR_R2 each return a null value, and the remaining functions return values that are defined in Table 15.2.

On the other hand, if the input set is empty, REGR_COUNT returns zero, and the remaining functions return a null value.

A final consideration is when the result is not null. In this case:

- REGR_R2 is between 0 and 1.

- REGR_SXX and REGR_SYY is non-negative. This non-negative value is used to describe the spread of the values for either X or Y from their average values.

Refer to Table 15.2 for more information regarding the regression computations.

Table 15.2   Function Computation

FUNCTION	COMPUTATION
REGR_SLOPE (expr1, expr2)	COVAR (expr1, expr2) / VAR (expr2)
REGR_ICPT (expr1, expr2)	AVG (expr1) – REGR_SLOPE (expr1, expr2) * AVG (expr2)
REGR_R2 (expr1, expr2)	POWER (CORR (expr1, expr2), 2) if VAR (expr1) > 0
REGR_R2 (expr1, expr2)	1 if VAR (expr1) = 0
REGR_AVGX (expr1, expr2)	AVG (expr2)
REGR_AVGY (expr1, expr2)	AVG (expr1)
REGR_SXX (expr1, expr2)	REGR_COUNT (expr1, expr2) * VAR (expr2)
REGR_SYY (expr1, expr2)	REGR_COUNT (expr1, expr2) * VAR (expr1)
REGR_SXY (expr1, expr2)	REGR_COUNT (expr1, expr2) * COVAR (expr1, expr2)

NOTE The difference between REGR_AVG and AVG is that all nulls are excluded in the REGR_AVG computations, while they are included in the AVG(expression) computation.

The order in which the values are aggregated is undefined, but every intermediate result must be within the range of the result data type. In general, it is more efficient to use the regression functions to compute the statistics needed for a regression analysis than to perform the equivalent computations using ordinary column functions such as AVG, VARIANCE, and COVARIANCE.

The usual diagnostic statistics that accompany a linear-regression analysis can be computed in terms of the preceding functions as follows and are offered with minimal explanation:

Adjusted r2:

```
1 - ((1-REGR_R2)*((REGR_COUNT - 1) / (REGR_COUNT - 2)))
```

The preceding expression applies to a simple linear regression, meaning that a model includes only one independent variable.

Standard error is the standard deviation of the sample mean:

```
SQRT((REGR_SYY-(POWER(REGR_SXY,2)/REGR_SXX)) / (REGR_COUNT-2))
```

Total sum of squares:

```
REGR_SYY
```

Regression sum of squares:

```
POWER(REGR_SXY,2) / REGR_SXX
```

Residual sum of squares:

```
(Total sum of squares) - (regression sum of squares)
```

t statistic:

For each coefficient (slope and intercept in the simple linear regression model), there is a concern as to whether the coefficient's value is meaningful or if the coefficient is really zero. That is, the independent variable (x) does not contribute to the value of the dependent variable (y). The t statistic can help make this determination for slope:

```
REGR_SLOPE * SQRT(REGR_SXX) / (Standard error)
```

t statistic for intercept:

```
REGR_INTERCEPT/((Standard error) *
```

```
SQRT((1/REGR_COUNT)+(POWER(REGR_AVGX,2)/REGR_SXX))
```

COVAR, CORR, VAR, STDDEV, and Regression Examples

The following examples give a flavor of the use of these functions in a number of scenarios.

COVARIANCE Example

We suspect there is a relationship between employee salary and the bonus that they receive, and we use the data shown in Table 15.3.

Table 15.3   D11 Employee Salary and Bonus

FIRST NAME	SALARY	BONUS
IRVING	32,250.00	500.00
BRUCE	25,280.00	500.00
ELIZABETH	22,250.00	400.00

Table 15.3   *(Continued)*

FIRST NAME	SALARY	BONUS
MASATOSHI	24,680.00	500.00
MARILYN	21,340.00	500.00
JAMES	20,450.00	400.00
DAVID	27,740.00	600.00
WILLIAM	18,270.00	400.00
JENNIFER	29,840.00	600.00

The DB2 SQL for covariance could be as follows:

```
SELECT COVARIANCE (salary,bonus)
FROM employee
WHERE workdept = 'D11'
```

The result of this query is 23650.86.

This large positive result indicates there is a direct relationship between salary and bonus. In other words, as an employee's salary increases so does the bonus. While this conclusion appears intuitive with only a few data points, it is less obvious when there are a large number of data points involved—say, 1,000 or 10,000 employees. The covariance test thus enables you to identify possible relationships between variables.

Correlation helps quantify the strength of the relationship. It does not indicate how strong the relationship is. It merely indicates one exists and whether it is a direct or indirect relation. To determine the strength of a relationship, the correlation must be calculated.

CORRELATION Examples

Using the same salary bonus example in Table 15.3, we can quantify the strength of the relationship with the following SQL:

```
SELECT CORRELATION (salary,bonus) AS cor
FROM employee
WHERE workdept = 'D11'
```

The result of the query is 0.739.

This quantitatively confirms the reasonably strong relationship between salary and bonus for the employees in department D11.

Let's consider another example of correlation involving the retail industry. Assume we have the transactions of purchases from all the customers of a retail organization selling a variety of products and we would like to identify customers with similar buying habits. For example, when Customer A bought a particular product, Customer X also tended to buy the same product. Such information can be put to effective use in target marketing.

A view called transhist is created that contains the customer ID, product ID, and the dollar amount purchased over all transactions:

```
SELECT a.custid as custid1, b.custid as custid2,
CORR(a.amount, b.amount) AS cor
FROM transhist a, transhist b
WHERE a.prodid = b.prodid AND a.custid < b.custid
GROUP BY a.custid, b.custid
HAVING CORR(a.amount, b.amount) >= 0.5 AND COUNT(*) > 100
ORDER BY a.custid, cor DESC
```

This query joins the view with itself and uses the HAVING clause to restrict the output to cases of high correlation (>= 0.5) and to cases where there are at least a 100 products involved—that is, there are at least 100 data points used to compute the correlation.

The results of the preceding query are shown in Table 15.4

The result shows a high correlation between the buying habits of Customer 1071 and Customer 2014; that is, whenever customer 1071 bought a large amount of a given product, then customer 2014 also tended to buy a large amount of the same product.

Table 15.4 CORRELATION Results

CUSTID1	CUSTID2	CORR
1026	8271	0.51
1071	2014	0.74 <<===
1071	7219	0.63
2014	7219	0.58
8271	9604	0.56

VARIANCE Example

DB2 has a built-in function to calculate variance. Using the same salary and bonus data shown in Table 15.3, our SQL is as follows:

```
SELECT AVG(salary), VARIANCE(salary) AS Variance
FROM employee
WHERE workdept = 'D11'
```

The average salary is \$24,677.78, while the variance in our case is $1.885506172839506E7$. However, this is not very intuitive, and standard deviation provides a more intuitive answer.

STDDEV Examples

Using the same data as shown in Table 15.3, the standard deviation of salary of employees in department D11 can be computed as follows.

```
SELECT AVG(salary), STDDEV(salary) AS StandDev
FROM employee
WHERE workdept = 'D11'
```

The result of this query is an average of \$2,477.78 and a standard deviation of \$4,342.24. It represents the average distance of any given salary from the average salary for the set, which is a lot more intuitive than the variance function discussed earlier.

Another example of standard deviation involves computing the various statistics of an organization's sales worldwide over multiple years. The data is contained in three tables—trans, transitem, and loc:

```
SELECT loc.country AS country, YEAR(t.pdate) AS year,
COUNT(*) AS count, SUM(ti.amount) AS sum,
AVG(ti.amount) AS avg, MAX(ti.amount) AS max,
STDDEV(ti.amount) AS std
FROM trans t, transitem ti, loc loc
WHERE t.transid = ti.transid AND loc.locid = t.locid
GROUP BY loc.country, year(t.pdate)
```

The results of the query are in Table 15.5.

Table 15.5 STDDEV Results

COUNTRY	YEAR	COUNT	SUM	AVG	MAX	STDDEV
USA	1998	235	127505	542.57	899.99	80.32
USA	1999	349	236744	678.35	768.61	170.45
GERMANY	1998	180	86278	479.32	771.65	77.41
GERMANY	1999	239	126737	530.28	781.99	72.22

The result shows commonly gathered statistics related to sales such as COUNT, SUM, AVG, and MAX. The STDDEV function shows that U.S. sales in 1999 are much more variable (STDDEV of $170.45) than sales in other years and other locations. In other words, the amounts in the individual sales transactions vary more widely from their average value of $678.35.

Linear Regression Examples

Using the same data shown in Table 15.3, we will derive a regression model where salary is the independent variable and bonus is the dependent variable using the following DB2 SQL:

```
SELECT REGR_SLOPE (bonus , salary) AS slope,
REGR_ICPT (bonus , salary) AS intercept
FROM employee
WHERE workdept = 'D11'
```

The result of this query is a slope of 0.0125 and an intercept is $179.313.

The columns referenced in the regression functions are reversed from those in the variance and covariance examples. Since we wish to determine BONUS as a function of SALARY, it is listed first before SALARY.

DB2 has a R^2 function, REGR_R2. The properties of R^2 are as follows:

- R^2 bound is between 0 and 1.
- If R^2 equals 1, then all the points fit on the regression line exactly.
- If R^2 equals zero, then the two attributes are independent.

The closer R^2 is to 1, the better the computed linear regression model. In general, an R^2 greater than 0.90 is considered a good fit for most applications. However, it varies by application, and it is eventually up to the user to decide what value constitutes a good model.

The DB2 SQL could look like this:

```
SELECT REGR_R2 (bonus , salary) AS R2
FROM employee
WHERE workdept = 'D11'
```

The result of this query is 0.54624.

Since R^2 is not very close to 1, we conclude that the computed linear regression model does not appear to be a very good fit. Another example of using regression involves the assumption of a linear relationship between the advertising budget and sales figures of a particular organization that conforms to the equation $y = ax + b$, where:

- y is the sales dependent variable.
- x is the advertising budget independent variable.
- a is the slope.
- b is the y-axis intercept corresponding to budget cost even with zero sales.

The following queries determine the values for a and b given a set of non-null values of budget and sales data points in a table t.

```
SELECT
REGR_COUNT(t.sales, t.ad_budget) AS num_cities,
REGR_SLOPE(t.sales, t.ad_budget) AS a,
REGR_ICPT(t.sales, t.ad_budget) AS b
FROM t;
```

The result of the query is as follows, with REGR_COUNT returning the number of (x,y) non-null pairs used to fit the regression line: Num_cities = 126, a = 1.9533 and b = 13.381.

The input data and the derived linear model is shown in Figure 15.13.

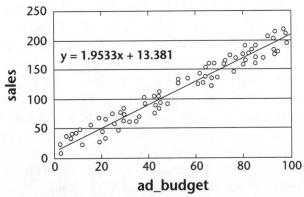

Figure 15.13   Linear regression.

While the preceding SQL models the equation, it does not tell you the quality of the fit—that is, the accuracy of the regression line. Another diagnostic statistic called R^2 must be computed to determine this. R^2 is the square of the correlation coefficient (CORR) as follows. R^2 can also be interpreted as the proportion of variation in the y values that is explained by the variation in the x values, as opposed to variation due to randomness or to other variables not included in the model.

```
SELECT
REGR_COUNT(t.sales, t.ad_budget) AS num_cities,
REGR_SLOPE(t.sales, t.ad_budget) AS a,
REGR_ICPT(t.sales, t.ad_budget) AS b,
REGR_R2(t.sales, t.ad_budget) as r-squared
FROM t;
```

The result shows R^2 to be 0.95917, which is a very high quality of fit of the regression line.

There is one limitation in DB2 V8: It does not support nonlinear regression models.

BI-Centric Function Examples

To provide you with a perspective of what can be done with these BI functions, we have included the following three examples. Each demonstrates a practical application of the function or functions, as well as the required syntax.

Using Sample Data

In many cases the volume of data available may be very large, and it may not be cost-effective or timely enough to analyze the entire data. In such cases, it would be appropriate to take a representative sample of the data and perform analyses on it instead. An efficient and cost-effective sampling function can have a significant impact on the scalability of a system involving large volumes of data that typify the e-business environment.

DB2 provides support for a RAND function that uses a Bernoulli sampling technique. The quality of the sample and the size of the sample play a significant role in the accuracy of the result obtained. A discussion of these considerations is beyond the scope of this book. Suffice it to say that these factors are unique to each domain and possibly to each organization.

Anyone implementing these functions is strongly urged to have a thorough understanding of sampling theory and its application to their business environment prior to using the DB2 V8 RAND function.

When sampling from a single table, care should be taken to ensure that the extracted sample is sufficiently representative to provide an acceptable degree of accurate results. Trial and error is probably the best approach to hone in on an acceptable sample size.

Another factor to be considered is that, in general, a join of sampled tables is not statistically equivalent to a sample from the join of the original tables. An acceptable approach for a join involving referentially constrained tables may be to sample the foreign key table and then extract the rows in the referenced table using the foreign key values in the sample. You should evaluate the efficacy of this approach in your particular environment.

One possible technique (without using the RAND function) to obtain a sample of a fixed size—say, m rows—is to:

1. Append a column of random numbers to the target table.

2. Order the rows of the table by this column.

3. Fetch the first m rows.

While this technique is not efficient, its cost can be reduced by amortizing it over multiple queries.

Another possibility is to store the rows of the target table in random order by either loading the data in random order initially or appending a column of random numbers to the table and using DB2's reorganization utility to cluster the rows according to this column. A random sample can then be quickly obtained by simply scanning the table. There are obvious issues of maintaining random order as data is added, as well as performance issues relating to non-sampling queries, which must be evaluated on a case-by-case basis.

Sampling may be used for auditing and data mining, as well as getting approximate answers to aggregation-type questions. Assume we have a very large table containing sales data by country. We would like to obtain the sales summary by year and country using sampling and assess the "standard error" of the estimate. We use the familiar trans, transitem, and loc tables for this query:

```
SELECT loc.country AS country, YEAR(t.pdate) AS year,
SUM(ti.sales) / :samp_rate AS est_sales,
SQRT((1e0/:samp_rate)*(1e0-(1e0/:samp_rate))*SUM(sales*sales)) AS
std_err
FROM trans t, transitem ti, loc loc
WHERE t.transid = ti.transid AND loc.locid = t.locid
AND RAND(1) < :samp_rate
GROUP BY loc.country, YEAR(t.pdate)
```

The preceding query takes a Bernoulli sample from a join of the three tables, using a sampling rate of 0.01 resulting in approximately 1 percent of the rows being selected. To estimate the sum for the entire table, we need to scale the answer up by a factor of (1/:samp_rate), which is 100 percent. The standard error is computed as shown.

The result of the query is shown in Table 15.6.

Typically, there is a high probability that the true sum will lie within +/- 2 standard errors of the estimate. Therefore, in the preceding query, given the low standard error computation, there is a high probability that the estimated sums are accurate to within about a 2 percent error.

When the original table is very large and the sampling rate is not extremely small, we can typically be more specific about the precision of our estimator. For example, the true value of the sum is within +/- 1.96 standard errors with probability approximately 95 percent, and within +/- 2.576 standard errors with probability approximately 99 percent.

The optimizer can treat the sampling predicate like any other predicate for optimization purposes. The main drawback to this approach is that a scan of the entire table is required, so there are no I/O savings. In practice, it may be desirable to amortize the sampling cost over multiple queries by saving the sample as a table. The sample should be refreshed periodically, however, so that sampling anomalies do not systematically influence the results.

In the following queries, we obtain a better estimate of total sales for each group by scaling up using the true sampling rate; that is, the group size in the entire table is divided by the group size in the sampled table. This scaleup, though more expensive to compute, leads to more stable and precise estimators.

The following SQL creates the sample table:

```
CREATE TABLE samp_table(country, year, sales) AS
SELECT loc.country, YEAR(t.pdate), ti.sales
FROM trans t, transitem ti, loc loc
WHERE t.transid = ti.transid AND loc.locid = t.locid
AND RAND(1) < :samp_rate
```

Table 15.6 Sample.

COUNTRY	YEAR	EST_SALES	STD_ERR
USA	1998	127505	1326.09
USA	1999	236744	2133.17
GERMANY	1998	86278	961.45
GERMANY	1999	126737	1488.66
...			

The following SQL creates a view that computes the group size `g_size`:

```
CREATE TABLE big_group_sizes(country, year, g_size) AS
SELECT loc.country, YEAR(t.pdate), COUNT(*)
FROM trans t, transitem ti, loc loc
WHERE t.transid = ti.transid AND loc.locid = t.locid
GROUP BY loc.country, YEAR(t.pdate)
```

You need to make sure that the appropriate indexes are created and statistics collected before running the following query. The SQL scales up the estimate by the true sampling rate as highlighted.

```
SELECT s.country, s.year, b.g_size * AVG(s.sales) AS est_sales,
SQRT(b.g_size * b.g_size * ((1e0 - :samp_rate)/COUNT(s.sales))
* (1e0 - (1e0/COUNT(s.sales))) * (COUNT(s.sales)/(COUNT(s.sales)-1e0))
* VAR(s.sales)) AS std_err
FROM samp_table s, big_group_sizes b
WHERE s.country = b.country AND s.year = b.year
GROUP BY s.country, s.year, b.g_size
```

We do the scaleup by computing the average sales for a group in the sampled table (i.e., total sales for the group divided by the group size) and then multiplying by `g_size` the size of the group in the original table.

Listing the Top Five Salespersons by Region This Year

This query requires that the salespersons have completed at least 10 sales transactions. The query would typically be used for recognition purposes.

Data Description

The main source of input to this query is sales information with the key attributes of date of sale, salesperson, region, and count of sales transactions. All our data resides in the SALES table.

BI Functions Showcased

The example features the following functions:

- RANK
- OVER
- PARTITION BY
- ORDER BY

Steps

We executed the following SQL via the DB2 Control Center:

```
WITH temp(region,sales_person,total_sale,sales_rank) AS
(
SELECT region, sales_person, COUNT(sales) AS total_sale,
RANK() OVER (PARTITION BY region ORDER BY COUNT(sales) DESC) AS
sales_rank
FROM rmres7.sales
GROUP BY region, sales_person
)
SELECT * FROM temp WHERE sales_rank <=5 AND total_sale >10;
```

TOTAL_SALE counts the number of sales transactions.

Table 15.7 shows the results of the query. A temporary table, temp, is first created with results from number of sales (TOTAL_SALE) with partitioning over a region. The temp table is then ranked to show the top five salesmen whose TOTAL_SALE is >=10.

Table 15.7 Top Five Salespersons by Region

REGION	SALES_PERSON	TOTAL_SALE	SALES_RANK
Manitoba	LEE	16	1
Manitoba	CHANG	14	2
Manitoba	GOUNOT	14	2
Manitoba	LUCCHESSI	12	4
Manitoba	ADAMS	11	5
Ontario-North	LUCCHESSI	16	1
Ontario-North	CHANG	15	2
Ontario-North	ADAMS	14	3
Ontario-North	LEE	14	3
Ontario-North	GOUNOT	12	5

Determining Relationships between Product Purchases

The purpose of this query is to try and establish whether there is a relationship between products purchased by customers. This allows a salesperson to cross-sell complementary products.

It is well known that there is a strong relationship between certain product purchases, such as hammers and nails, and paint and paintbrushes. However, other relationships may not be so readily apparent. For example, suppose a supermarket chain discovered a relationship between beer and candies (sweets), while another retailer discovered a relationship between late-night gasoline purchases and flowers.

Data mining is often used to discover unexpected or complex relationships; however, it is possible to use DB2 UDB's CORRELATION function to identify the nature of a relationship between two sets of data.

Many retailers now offer "loyalty" cards with the intention of being able to collect data based on people's purchase pattern and thereby create targeted sales campaigns. Often these campaigns are based on very simple analysis of large volumes of data.

Data Description

The main source of data is the transactions obtained from purchases from a loyalty card scheme database. The key attributes of interest in our example are card number and the purchases of six items (coffee, beer, snack foods, bread, ready meals, and milk).

BI Functions Showcased

The example features the following functions:

CORRELATION

Steps

We executed the following SQL:

```
SELECT DEC(CORRELATION(beer,snacks),15,2) AS "Beer_Snacks",
DEC(CORRELATION(beer,milk),15,2) as "Beer_Milk"
FROM lc_purchases
```

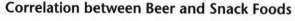

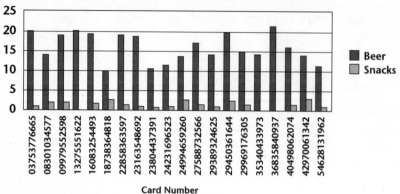

Figure 15.14 Beer and snacks correlation.

The SQL does two simple correlation calculations between purchases of beer and snack foods and beer and milk. The result of this query based on our sample data is Beer_Snacks = 0.83 and Beer_Milk = 0.01.

The sample data shows a very high correlation between purchases of beer and snack foods, but almost no correlation between beer and milk. The sample data used in this example was charted using BRIO. Figures 15.14 and 15.15 show that in our given sample, almost everyone who bought beer also bought some snack foods. However, only one person bought beer and milk together.

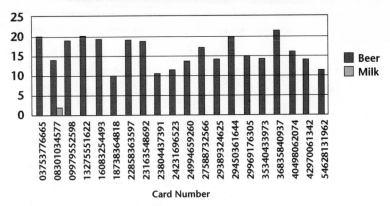

Figure 15.15   Beer and milk.

Summary

Data architects will find DB2 residence BI functions to be extremely useful. They provide significant control over the implementation of complex and often time-consuming applications. You no longer have to store and forward data to other BI tools. You can apply the same functionality using the database functions, implemented with standard SQL. Moreover, because these functions are merely extensions of SQL, your existing team of DBAs can readily gain the skill necessary to successfully carry out complex BI-centric solutions.

For more information regarding DB2-enhanced BI features and functionality, refer to DB2 UDB's *High Function Business Intelligence in e-business* from IBM.

CHAPTER 16

Blending Spatial Data into the Warehouse

Key Issues:

- *Who*, *what*, and *when* get plenty of analytical attention, but the *where* aspect is completely underexploited. Spatial data will enhance the *who* by binding substantial third-party data—from companies like Dunn & Bradstreet—to your existing data, thus creating new informational content. And spatial data will directly enable analysis for the *where*.

- Spatial analysis should be considered mandatory for the forward-thinking BI organization. It represents a critical BI pylon, enhancing the informational content of warehoused data and broadening the analytical landscape capability of the organization.

- Most architects don't even realize it, but the foundation of spatial analysis—addresses—is jealously protected and groomed in many organizations today. But what do organizations do with all these addresses? A common analytical use for addresses is householding; yet even this application is often outsourced to companies like Axiom.

- It is hard for many companies to justify the dollar investment put toward the gathering, verifying, and cleansing of addresses. We must go the extra step and use that address as the basis for creating spatial information content and enable spatial analysis.

- The technology exists for the natural integration of spatial data into our warehouse repositories. DB2 UDB is optimized and aware of the nuances of spatial objects. Its spatial extension is based on the most powerful spatial technology on the market from ESRI.

No one questions the value that time brings to the analytical table. Without it we have no definition to our analysis, only amorphous results. But time is only one pylon supporting the entire spectrum of analysis available. Space is another. It is imperative that architects and project planners understand the value spatial data brings to user communities and plan for its natural inclusion.

Your data warehouse, data mart, operational data store, OLAP cubes, and just about every other database in your organization—from personal contact databases to those underpinning your corporate ERP, CRM, and supply chain management (SCM) are full of spatial data. Blending it in, exploiting the analytical fodder it brings about, is really not an option, because the basis of spatial data is already in your databases. The challenge for most data architects and project sponsors is to appreciate what spatial data is, where it comes from, and how it can be used to enhance and extend the decision-making capabilities of your BI environment.

The basis of spatial data is an inherent, almost assumed part of most databases; nevertheless, most individuals, including IT, do not recognize the effort as having spatial relevance. Companies around the world spend enormous resources collecting and cleansing addresses for customers, stores, offices, warehouses, and virtually anything else that might have an address associated with it. Utilization of this hard-won address data is often trivial and includes events such as mass mailings and stovepipe market analysis. This is due, in large part, to a lack of understanding within the business community of what spatial data/analysis is and the types of business problems it can tackle. The situation is exacerbated because IT professionals, data architects, and others are equally naïve regarding spatial technology.

This chapter begins by examining where spatial data and related analysis impacts our BI organization. Once we have a sense of where it fits in BI, the chapter defines what spatial data is, how we obtain it, and how it influences decision support. We end the chapter with a review of how best to serve up spatial data in our warehouse.

Spatial Analysis and the BI Organization

Figure 16.1 illustrates the areas within the information organization that are influenced or impacted by spatial data, related analysis, and technologies. Each area is described in the following numbered list, which corresponds with the diagram:

1. **Operational databases.** Generally, the start of spatial data is in the operational systems of our organizations. This is where addresses are collected for any number of targets, including customers, stores, warehouses, and so on.

2. **Third-party data.** Having a good address of a customer is the critical point of spatial analysis. However, that is all a company needs; all other demographic data can be purchased from a number of vendors, including Dunn & Bradstreet, Urban Data Systems, ESRI, and the Census Bureau. This is a very important aspect of spatial analysis. Your organization can focus on securing accurate, cleansed addresses while purchasing valuable demographics for a thorough analytical landscape. This means you can invest in demographic data per business requirement and minimize, if not eliminate, the investments necessary to collect your own demographics.

3. **Staging area.** A large portion of your company's investment in spatial data will be securing a clean, accurate address. This most likely will involve the purchase and implementation of technology specifically designed to address this issue, including Trillium and Firstlogic's Postalsoft, among others.

4. **Atomic level.** Spatial data should first be introduced to the BI environment at the atomic layer of the warehouse in the form of a process discussed in this chapter called geocoding. If this is done at the atomic level of your warehouse, all subsequent use of spatial data and related analysis is consistent throughout the organization. This ensures that warehouse managers have a single point of entry and, therefore, control. Also, for database engines such as DB2 Universal Database with Spatial Extender, spatial analysis can be conducted within advanced SQL reports typical of atomic-level data. This is available because of an extended SQL that is discussed in this chapter.

5. **Data marts.** Spatial data and analysis is not uncommon for star schemas where geography dimensions are established. As for cube technology, you can still exploit spatial data by preprocessing spatial analysis that lends value to the subsequent OLAP analysis. For

example, the calculation of drive time or distance can be done as part of the ETL process for loading a star schema or cube, where the net value of the calculation is physically stored as an attribute to the data mart. OLAP analysis can then exploit these spatially derived attributes as part of their typical constraints, where the analysis itself can be conducted with sophisticated OLAP technologies or even a simple Excel PivotTable. No special map-rendering software is required.

6. **Analyst.** The analyst should have available spatial visualization technologies and analysis. This means that investments in products capable of rendering maps would be valuable. Existing warehouse-centric technology already makes map rendering available, including Crystal Writer and Business Objects, to name a few. Or you can implement high-end analysis tools such as ESRI's Business Analyst or simple map-rendering software like MapPoint. Also, all of this analysis should be available via a Web browser and the corporate BI portal.

7. **Customer touch points.** The spatial value of your BI effort should extend to the customers themselves. This can be done via your company Web site, where customers could log in and identify themselves (with a company discount or membership ID), and a map would be rendered showing the closest distributor/store that sells your products in relation to where the customer lives.

8. **Back-feed loop.** As with everything else in our BI environment, we must consciously design a means to feed back into our business environment as a whole the net value of our analysis. In the case of spatial data, one common back-feed would be a cleansed, accurate, and geocoded address for each customer that can be used by events such as mass mailing campaigns or CRM support.

This chapter introduces the use of spatial data and analysis in decision making and gets you started on the road to a planned and thoughtful blending of spatial data into your warehouse efforts. We answer questions such as the following:

- What is spatial data?
- What does spatial data do for your analysis?
- Where do you find spatial data in your organization?
- How do you manage spatial data?
- What tools are used for spatial analysis?
- How is this analysis shared with the rest of the organization?

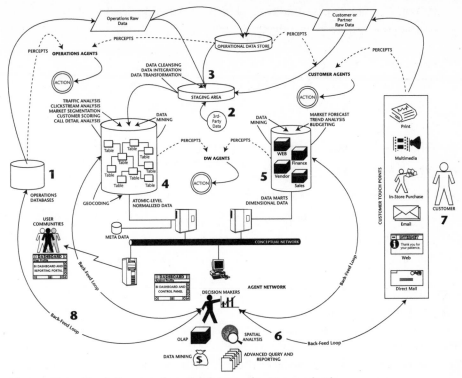

Figure 16.1   The influence of spatial data on the BI organization.

In the process, we hope to remove the fear, uncertainty, and doubt (FUD factor) that is often associated with the use of spatial data and technologies. This chapter demonstrates that incorporating spatial data into the warehouse is not only possible but practical, using common, off-the-shelf software and industry-leading databases such as DB2 Universal Database with DB2 Spatial Extender.

The Impact of Space

Many business problems explicitly or implicitly require that geography be taken into account. Consider the following everyday business questions:

- Where are my customers located?
- How big is my market area?
- What is my share of the market area?

- Which market areas offer the greatest potential for growth?
- What is the spending potential for my product in this market?
- How many stores can this market support?
- What's the best mix of products to carry in each store?
- Where should I target my direct mailing to get the most from my marketing dollars?
- What media channel will reach the audience I'm targeting?
- Where should I open new sites?
- Can I consolidate sites without hurting customer service?

These questions illustrate how spatial considerations are part of many common business problems. A complete list would cover several pages and be outdated as soon as it was published. Nevertheless, such is the growing use of spatial analysis in all types of decisions for all kinds of industries from utilities to retail store chains to banks and insurance companies to public agencies.

Common BI tools do a good job of analyzing the basic who, what, when, and how questions. Data needed to discover *who* is buying *what* product on *what day* through *what channel* is captured with virtually every transaction. And the tools for conducting the analysis have become mature and accepted by decision support system (DSS) professionals. From these modest data elements, data mining tools can identify cross-sell and up-sell opportunities, determine market-basket relationships, profile customers, and evaluate distribution channels.

But these traditional analysis tools fall short in answering the tougher questions of *why* people buy and *where* customers live in relation to their purchases. Although many organizations actively try to determine why customers buy, these reasons are rarely captured at the time of the transaction and stored as a natural part of the OLTP database. They are more often captured as a separate process, such as warranty registration cards or surveys, from all or a portion of the customer base. Well-known statistical methods are then applied to help determine what causes people to buy. Though plagued by the problem that these statistical cause-and-effect associations often don't pan out at the register, the methods nevertheless provide additional insights to a complex and evolving customer base.

Although the *why* of a transaction is rarely captured with it, the *where* of the transaction, its geographic location, is almost always captured. In fact, multiple locations are often captured. Ship-to, bill-to, and customer contacts are all often captured at companies everywhere. But unlike the dimensions of who, what, and when (customer, product, time), the where, or geographic dimension, gets little attention. Although a part of many star schemas, the geographic dimension has been underexploited analytically, if not overlooked altogether. This lack of attention is mainly because analysts are not familiar with spatial analysis applications and techniques, because planners think the technology is too expensive or complex, or because user communities and IT are unaware of the analytic packages available.

The impact of space is as natural to our thinking process as time. Just as a date explodes data into a wealth of analytical power, so, too, does an address. From addresses, you can build one or more elaborate space-related dimensions and data-access-layer applications. Attributes of the dimension could include longitude and latitude, street address, street block, city quadrant, zip code, street, city, county, state, and country. And these spatial-centric attributes can be combined with a variety of demographic information such as household income, education, family size, and home value, or numeric characteristics such as drive time between the customer and his or her favorite store.[1]

Space is an information windfall for the analyst and is as critical to the process of interrogating our data as time. There are even aspects of space that go beyond the value of time. For example, where time has a single, constant perspective, space can represent information about the people who live at a location, as well as information about where that location physically is in relation to the rest of the world.

We naturally think spatially. However, most of our decision support systems are spatially handicapped. This situation has never stopped us from thinking spatially; it has only stifled our ability to fully exploit the data heaped into our warehouses.

Putting your data in the context of space, like time, greatly adds to your understanding of it. Given the availability and affordability of spatial application products and spatial data management extensions like DB2 Spatial Extender that provide this spatial context is a real and compelling option. Spatial data is such a boon to analysis that the definition of a modern warehouse must include characteristics such as integrated, nonvolatile, time-variant, and space-centric.

---

[1] Gonzales, 1999.

What Is Spatial Data?

When we think of spatial data, we naturally think of a map and elements we see on it, such as roads, lakes, and points of interest. The map does not contain all of the possible real-world objects that could be displayed. It would be impossible to represent everything on the map. Similarly, since it is impossible to capture reality inside a computer, geographic information systems (GIS) users must abstract real-world phenomena, or entities, into a geometric representation of reality. Three basic geometric shapes are used to represent reality: points, lines, and polygons (areas). These shapes are often called geometric objects, geometric features, or feature types.

The Onion Analogy

Think of the world as a large onion. When you peel an onion, you see that it is composed of many layers. Real-world entities can be seen the same way: The earth can be "peeled" into many layers, each representing a different theme. You could put all the streets in one layer and all zip code boundaries in another layer. As you can imagine, the complexity of the earth allows you to create as many layers as you want.

Spatial data stores the locations of tangible geographic features such as roads, stores, customer locations, or other real-world entities, as well as the locations of nontangible features such as territory, zip code, or census tract boundaries. It also stores attribute information describing those features, such as street address, store or customer name, territory sales volume, census demography, or other tabular information. The question then becomes how to best organize these real-world entities into manageable geometric shapes (point, line, or area) linked to their associated attributes and to store them digitally.

Spatial Data Structures

With a GIS, you can model data in three basic ways: as a collection of discrete features in vector format, as a grid of cells in raster format, or as a set of triangulated points modeling a surface.

Vector Data

Vector data represents geographic features as points, lines, and polygons and is very well suited to recording the location of discrete geographic features with precise locations like territory boundaries, customer locations, trade areas, on so forth. (See Figure 16.2.) Vector data records spatial information as x-y coordinates in a rectangular (planar) coordinate system. Point features are recorded as single x-y locations. Line features, such as streets, or the outlines of polygons, such as zip code boundaries, are recorded as an ordered series of x-y coordinates. Additional information about the feature, such as territory sales volume, customer score, or disposable income, can be stored in an associated attribute table.

Raster Data

Raster data represents imaged or continuous data. The most common source for a raster data set is a satellite image or aerial photograph. Figure 16.3 shows both a raster data set and an aerial photograph. A raster data set can also be a photograph of a feature, such as a building. Raster data sets excel in storing and working with continuous data, such as elevation, water table, pollution concentration, and ambient noise level. A *raster* is a rectangular array of equally spaced cells. A *cell* is a uniform unit that represents a defined area of the earth, such as a square meter or square mile. Each cell within this array contains a number representing an attribute of the geographic feature, such as soil type, elevation, census tract, or slope. Additional information about the cell, such as population, age, or sales volume, can be stored in an associated attribute table.

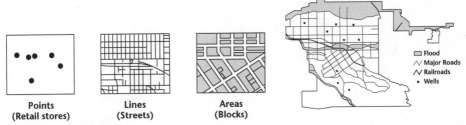

| Points
(Retail stores) | Lines
(Streets) | Areas
(Blocks) | ☐ Flood
／\ Major Roads
／\ Railroads
• Wells |

Figure 16.2   Vector data.

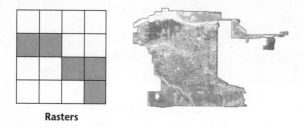

Rasters

Figure 16.3   Raster data.

Triangulated Data

Triangulated data, also known as triangulated irregular networks (TINs), is a useful and efficient way to capture the surface of a piece of land. TINs support perspective views like that shown in Figure 16.4. You can drape a photographic image on top of a TIN for a photorealistic terrain display. TINs are particularly useful for modeling watersheds, visibility, line-of-sight, slope, aspect, ridges and rivers, and volumetrics. They can also be used to summarize statistics for a surface, such as customer density against a reference layer.

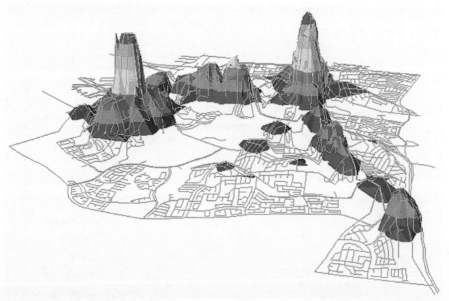

Figure 16.4   Triangulated data.

Spatial Data vs. Other Graphic Data

There are four main differences between spatial data and data created in computer-aided drafting (CAD) or graphic applications or scanned from paper sources, such as reports and photographs as follows:

■ In spatial data there is an explicit relationship between the real-world geometric feature and its associated attribute information, so that both are always available when you work with the data. If you select particular features displayed on a map, you can automatically select the records containing the attributes of these features whether they reside in separate tabular files or in a database. So when you click on a customer, for example, you have access to all the tabular information associated with that customer, such as address, sales, products purchased, and whatever else your operational data store (ODS) or data warehouse may capture on the customer.

■ Spatial data is georeferenced to known locations on the Earth's surface. To ensure that location is accurately recorded, spatial data always employs a specific coordinate system, unit of measurement, and map projection. When spatial data is displayed, it has a particular scale, just like any paper map. Graphic files used in CAD programs or other commercial graphics packages are typically stored in units such as inches rather than geographic coordinate systems required for spatial data.

■ Spatial data is designed to enable specific geographic features and phenomena to be managed, manipulated, and analyzed easily and flexibly to meet a wide range of needs. Other types of graphic data may be oriented solely toward presentation and display, and may store features such that they can only be analyzed in a limited number of ways. For example, drive time analysis is not possible with linear data created by a CAD or graphics application because there is no explicit network connectivity and direction maintained. Similarly, none of the graphics objects created in these packages have any idea of where they are in relation to all the other graphics, which prohibits any kind of proximity or adjacency analysis. They are just "dumb" graphic objects.

■ Spatial data is organized thematically into different layers, like the layers of an onion. There is one layer for each set of geographic features or phenomena for which information will be recorded. For example, census tracts, streets, sales territories, and customer locations will each be stored as a separate spatial layers, rather than stored all together in one as CAD or other graphic applications do.

This makes it easier to manage and manipulate the data, especially because much of the power of working geographically comes from being able to analyze the spatial relationships between different geographic layers.

There is no other data like spatial data. It provides a unique perspective and an enhancement to traditional forms of data found in warehouses.

Obtaining Spatial Data

There are two main ways to obtain spatial data for your application: creating it yourself or acquiring it. Let's look at each of these.

Creating Your Own Spatial Data

Most spatial application venders provide tools for creating and maintaining spatial data, and a discussion of them goes beyond the scope of this book. Suffice it to say, however, that some tools are better than others, and their selection may have a significant impact on the quality of the spatial data that goes into the warehouse. With these tools, spatial data can be created from many different sources, including digitizing paper maps by hand, directly reading satellite or aerial imagery, scanning and converting paper maps or photographs, converting CAD data, reading of raw x-y coordinates from files or GPS devices, and more.

Creating your own data internally allows you to create exactly the spatial data you need. It can be expensive, however. Major creators of their own spatial data are private and public utilities, government agencies such as counties and municipalities, defense departments, and other organizations whose affairs require the management of widely dispersed assets. Often they have invested millions of dollars in spatial data creation and ongoing maintenance. Equally as often these data assets have been created for specific stovepipe applications used by a single department within the overall organization and are neither well-known throughout the organization nor integrated with other IT assets.

Acquiring Spatial Data

Your own organization may have spatial data somewhere already. You should start there first. Some of the data created by government agencies is available free or for sale, such as data from the Census Bureau or U.S. Geological Service. Other data is not available at all to anyone outside of the group it was created for because of privacy, security, or other concerns. GIS vendors often bundle data with their products. Finally, there are pure spatial data vendors who specialize in creating data and selling it to a broad base of users.

Companies who specialize in providing spatial data are numerous and cover a broad range of data, from street data to image data to business locations to trade areas to demographic data. They often include or enhance government data, such as census data, through specialized forecasts and surveys, or they aggregate data by custom boundaries such as postal code or media boundaries.

Finding spatial data has always been a bit like finding your way around a new town. You go down a few dead ends and talk to a lot of people who may or may not understand just where you are trying to go. Fortunately, this task is getting easier through the appearance of spatial data clearinghouses and gateways, better spatial meta data and search engines, and the delivery of spatial data via Web-based data services. For now, however, talk to your spatial application vendor, spatial data providers, or their competitors to find sources of spatial data. It will often be the best alternative to creating the data yourself or simply doing without. Since many of the companies building data warehouses are global in reach, this inconsistency of data availability can be a major problem for some types of applications.

Government Data

Much of the data created by government agencies is available for free or for a small fee. The U.S. Geological Service has a geospatial data clearinghouse that provides direct access to spatial data and links to other spatial data providers, both government and commercial. Likewise, the U.S Census Bureau provides maps and boundary files for census demography. Outside of the United States, data availability and cost is widely variable. Some countries restrict access to geographic data in the same ways they restrict media. Other countries may not have the resources to build and maintain base-level spatial data such as street centerlines, and there may not be enough business opportunity for a commercial data provider to do it alone.

Vendor Data

General-purpose GIS applications typically include ready-to-use map and tabular data, such as all of the county boundaries in the United States, and associated tabular data, such as county name, population, and other summary demographics. For many applications, you'll find this is the only data you need. You can use this data by itself to create maps for a wide variety of map display and analysis purposes. You can also use this data as a base to which to add your own data, such as sales by store or territory, so you can render and query maps based on data from your own organization, as well as the included demographic and other data.

Specialized GIS applications often include data specific to the purpose of the application. Some include detailed boundary files down to the block group and associated census data, business locations, lifestyle demographics, and more. These applications are used for general business purposes such as customer profiling, competitive analysis, and market segmentation. Some come with detailed street files with associated attributes for navigation, such as street speed, direction, and turn restrictions that are used in routing applications. In addition to providing all of the data needed, these specific-purpose applications may come packaged with standard analysis tools hidden behind wizard-based interfaces that reduce the complexity of data extraction and analysis, making it easier for end users to understand and use the spatial tool.

Spatial Data in DSS

Although spatial data has been used to support decisions for millennia in the form of static maps, we'll start with the more recent use of spatial data in electronic form. Among the first users of spatial data were government agencies and private companies, such as the Census Bureau and forestry companies, interested in better understanding and managing human or natural resources. The technology was new and required specialized software, databases, and skill sets. Strategic decision support was the main emphasis of these early systems, since they were too expensive for management or operational decision support.

By the late 1980s, advances in computer technology made desktop systems affordable to a broader range of organizations, both public and private. Business unit managers and operational managers could acquire and use spatial technology to help make better decisions. And that's just what they did, most often as project or departmental systems that were outside the IT department's realm of influence. A great deal of effort was put into creating the spatial data needed to support their decision-making needs, and it was rarely shared outside the project or department that created it.

By the late 1990s, huge and varied spatial data sets had been created by traditional government and private users of spatial technology. Every kind of spatial data imaginable was becoming available at affordable prices: street databases with address ranges, direction, and speed attributes for algorithmically locating customers on maps and routing vehicles; point databases containing all businesses in the United States, together with information on sales, number of employees, and so on for competitive analysis; polygon databases containing demographic information by state, county, zip code, census tract, and block group for customer profiling; and a wide variety of other data created by commercial spatial data providers for a myriad of decision support functions.

The continued technological advancement of computing platforms, availability of relatively cheap spatial data, and the incorporation of traditional decision support tools into the products offered by the spatial application vendors has put spatial analysis well within the reach of strategic, management, and operational decision makers. Today, spatial data is inexpensive and readily available in standard formats, and spatial analysis tools are comprehensive and affordable.

Spatial Analysis and Data Mining

Automatic discovery of patterns and trends, the great expectation from data mining, is more of an aspiration than an achievement. Broader definitions of data mining recognize that the application of algorithms to data is only a part of data mining. As important, if not more important, is natural human pattern recognition combined with appropriate knowledge of the subject area and accurate interpretation of the results.

Under this broader definition, spatial analysis tools and data mining tools have a common purpose: to automate the process of trend analysis and data discovery. Spatial analysis combines the mathematics of both statistics and topology with query and visualization tools to help decision makers see and explore patterns and trends not possible with pure data mining tools alone. In addition, since mainstream data mining tools are simply not aware of spatial relationships, they provide little algorithmic aid in the discovery of geographic patterns and trends based on factors such as proximity, adjacency, coincidence, containment, or connectivity.

Spatial analysis tools augment and extend the capabilities of data mining tools. Neither are single tools, but a suite of tools that include visualization, statistical analysis, and modeling, as well as specialized tools such as neural networks, fuzzy logic, and multidimensional analysis. Both are designed to assist managers in semistructured or unstructured tasks. Both support, rather than replace, management judgment.

Since spatial analysis and data mining share a common purpose, it is only natural that they follow a common approach, as described in Table 16.1.

Table 16.1 Data Mining and Spatial Analysis Comparison

PROBLEM-SOLVING APPROACHES	DATA MINING	SPATIAL ANALYSIS
Association	Things done together	Things located together
Sequences	Events over time	Events over time and space
Classifications	Pattern recognition	Spatial pattern recognition
Clusters	Define new groups	Locate new groups
Forecasting	Prediction from time series	Prediction from time and space

How data mining and spatial analysis complement each other can be illustrated by considering a common data mining function: clustering. Clustering is a well-known mining method that groups data sharing similar characteristics. Consider a cluster study that has grouped your customers into a number of groups based on profitability, age, and income. One group, your most profitable customers, is predominately in the grouping of 40- to 50-year-olds with over $100,000 in annual income. This type of clustering, or segmentation, is quite common in data mining. Unfortunately, a spatial analyst would find much lacking:

- Can we expect this cluster, or segment, to behave the same if they are located in New York or Nebraska? Probably not. The issue of geographic extrapolation is just one of the problems associated with clustering. The goal is to find clusters that behave the same, and regional differences in behavior can vary greatly.

- Can we locate this cluster? If so, we may be able to use the combined underlying demographic, economic, and psycho-graphic attributes of the cluster's area to help us further profile the customer and identify other areas with similar characteristics and, quite likely, behavior. Spatial analysis tools are perfect for profiling clusters of customers and prospecting for new ones.

- Can we determine the size and shape of this cluster? This is critical to determining market potential or penetration, which in turn is critical to deciding what to do with the cluster. Spatial analysis tools can reveal the size and shape of the cluster in relation to existing or proposed stores using simple rings or drive-time polygons, can be used to compute penetration polygons or cannibalization potential, and can locate potential competitors who will compete for the same cluster's business.

Similar examples could be given for each of the other approaches to data mining, but the point should be clear: Spatial analysis not only serves a common purpose with data mining but also follows a common technical approach to solving data mining problems.

Spatial analysis also shares the same basic process steps as data mining. The data mining steps as described in Chapter 14 are identical to those of spatial analysis and are repeated here intact, with minor editing to reflect spatial terminology:

1. Develop an understanding of the application, relevant prior knowledge, and the end user's goal.

2. Create a target spatial and associated attribute data set to be used for discovery.

3. Clean and process the data (fix and standardize address data, account for differences in spatial coordinate systems, etc.).

4. Reduce the number of variables, both spatial and nonspatial, and find invariant representations of the data, if possible.

5. Choose the data mining task (trade area analysis, segmentation).

6. Choose the data mining algorithm (Euclidian distance, actual drive time).

7. Search for patterns of interest (the actual data mining).

8. Interpret the pattern mined, using spatial visualization tools. If necessary, iterate through any of Steps 1 through 7.

9. Consolidate the knowledge discovered and communicate it, usually via maps.

Now that we've seen how spatial analysis can augment and extend data mining studies, let's get into the specifics of how to do it.

Serving Up Spatial Analysis

Perhaps the most commonly recognized form of spatial analysis is the investigation and understanding that goes on intuitively when we look at a map. We naturally draw conclusions from the things we see: Stores are conveniently located near freeways or are too far away; most of our customers live in the north side of town; the customer base (population) is increasing or decreasing. When we see a map, most of us don't need a calculator to perform this level of spatial analysis; we inherently think spatially.

For example, Figure 16.5 shows store sales in relation to customer density. Customer density is represented by the 3D contours and store sales by each of three cylinders. Clearly we have a problem with one of our stores that seems to be related to its poor proximity to any customer base. No math needed here. The map is interpreted based on a combination of innate knowledge and past experience. Although creating the map involved some fairly sophisticated calculations, such as surface generation, its interpretation was purely intuitive. But absent the map, without a visual representation, it is doubtful that one would see the pattern so quickly, or perhaps at all.

Broadly defined, spatial analysis includes the transformations, manipulations, and methods that apply to geographic data to add value to them, to support decisions, and to reveal patterns and anomalies that are not immediately obvious. This includes such things as visualization, linear analysis, coincidence analysis, and adjacency modeling. Like data mining, the techniques used in spatial analysis could easily fill an entire book. Indeed, a whole new set of analytical tools becomes available.

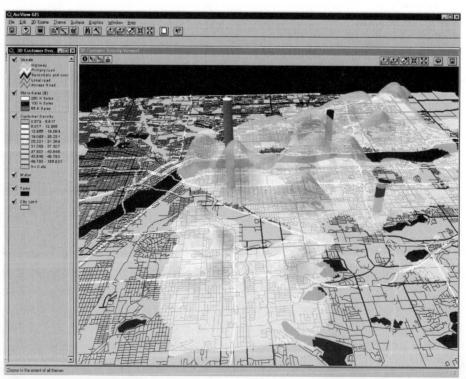

Figure 16.5 Spatial 3D.

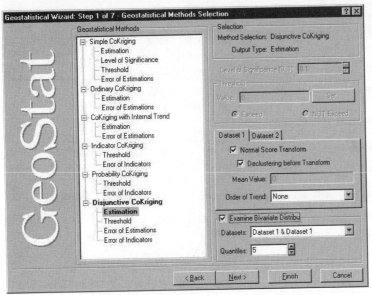

Figure 16.6 GeoStatistical Analyst.

Like all good data analysis tools, good geo-analytic tools have good user interfaces with easy-to-use wizards for performing their analytic functions. Figure 16.6 shows one such tool from ESRI, GeoStatistical Analyst. The results of the analysis are visually displayed in Figure 16.7, where higher concentrations of air pollution are shown toward the orange end of the spectrum.

Although the technique illustrated here could easily be applied to determining the density of customers who might buy based on a sample survey, a fairly good grasp of the underlying mathematics is necessary to formulate the problem and select the best model to evaluate the data. This is a common problem with data mining tools. For our purpose, we'll stick to some easy-to-understand techniques used to answer some of the fundamental business questions directed at the data warehouse. While they are by no means exhaustive, they are representative of the types of spatial analysis beginning to be used to augment and extend traditional data analysis for business analytics.

Typical Business Questions Directed at the Data Warehouse

Spatial data is a catalyst for numerous business question opportunities. Attempting to identify all the possible business questions is not practical. It would be similar to defining all the OLAP questions you could ask. However, there are typical questions that are asked of spatially enabled data.

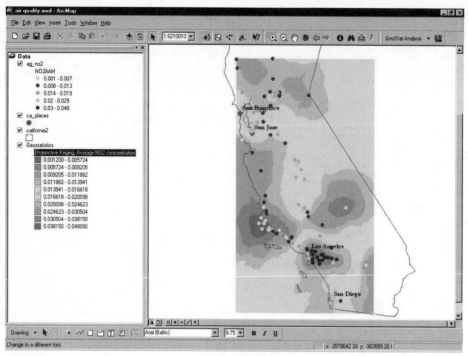

Figure 16.7 Air pollution.

Where Are My Customers Coming From?

This is by far the most common business question asked of the data warehouse. Although the warehouse holds this information in almost every case, the distribution of customers is difficult to see from transactional queries or lists. Putting customers on the map is one of the great benefits of spatial analysis tools.

Figure 16.8 shows customers of a shopping mall. Notice the linear distribution of customers along major roads. It might be safe to assume that many customers live close to bus lines. That bit of insight might, in turn, lead marketers to spend more of their advertising dollars on billboards, on buses, or at bus stops as opposed to a shotgun mailing to several zip codes.

The technology to do this bit of magic is quite mature within the spatial industry. Most spatial vendors have products that include the ability to *geocode* customers, vendors, or any other address information. Address cleansing software vendors generally have more sophisticated address cleansing algorithms and geocoders than those tools provided by spatial vendors; however, the visualization and analysis tools necessary to extract real value from clean, accurate addresses is still the domain of spatial vendors. Consequently, products from both types of vendors are often used together with the warehouse, providing a robust capability to ensure that address data going into the warehouse is clean and that it can be accessed and utilized by advanced spatial analysis tools to extract meaningful and actionable information.

I Don't Have Customer Address Information— Can I Still Use Spatial Analysis Tools?

One of the most common tools is simple ring analysis. The analysis begins with no knowledge of what a store or other facility's market area may be, so simple rings of 1-, 3-, and 5-mile radii (or other user-defined radii) are created around the facility by the spatial analysis tool. Once created, the underlying demographics within the rings can be extracted and compared to the demographics of similar rings around successful facilities. Many other questions can be answered as well, such as these: How many households are within 1, 3, and 5 miles of the facility? What is the average income of households within 3 miles of the facility? Simple ring studies are a typical first cut at visualizing the market area around a facility and are a useful tool for helping to decide whether to expand into new markets or leave existing ones. Figure 16.9 is an example of a simple ring analysis.

Figure 16.8 Shopping mall.

Simple ring analysis requires no data from the warehouse. A variation of the analysis uses an attribute of the facility, such as sales or square footage, to vary the size of the ring proportionally when compared to all other facilities. The ring becomes larger the greater the sales or the larger the size of the store. These data-driven rings give an idea of the drawing radius of a facility and can be used to extract demographic data to determine if the underlying population can support the business needed to sustain the store. They are also useful to get a rough idea of competitors' trade areas in the absence of detailed information on the competitor's operations other than their locations and approximate size in term of sales, facilities, or other comparable factors. Figure 16.10 is an example of a data-driven ring analysis.

Simple and data-driven rings are easy to create, but they do not consider potentially important factors such as the drive time to get to a facility. To consider drive time, specialized spatial network analysis tools and navigable street data are required. Fortunately, both are available at a reasonable cost from most spatial tool vendors. Drive time rings add a higher level of realism to ring analysis, and depending on the business, may be well worth the added investment. Pizza chains, for example, are very concerned about the time it takes to deliver a pizza to ensure a fresh and hot product is delivered every time. Figure 16.11 is an example of a drive-time analysis.

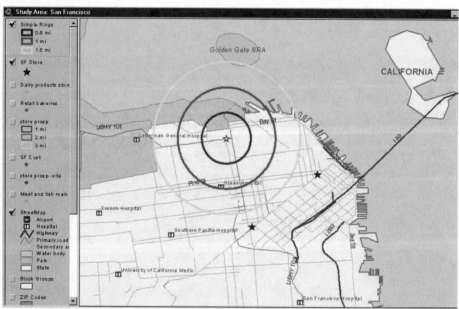

Figure 16.9   Ring analysis.

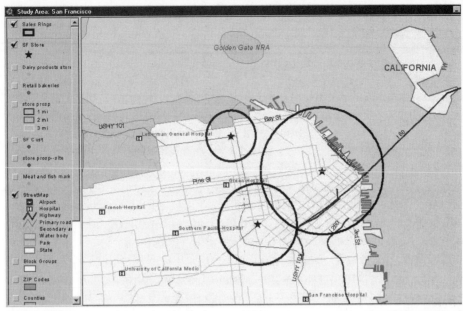

Figure 16.10   Data-driven ring analysis.

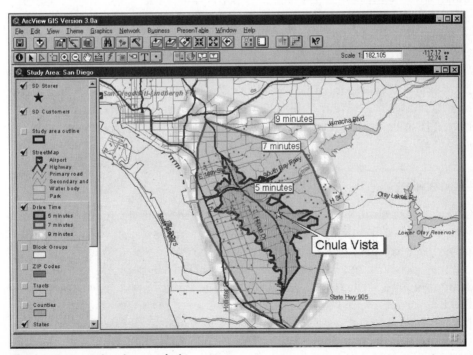

Figure 16.11   Drive-time analysis.

Understanding a Spatially Enabled Data Warehouse

Introducing spatial data across your source systems can be very disruptive. Of course, most GIS vendors try to sell spatial techniques and technologies by focusing on their graphical appeal and front-end applicability (logistics departments, utility companies, and government agencies are favorite targets). This strategy ultimately fed the negative impact of stovepipe data and analysis within organizations. There are many reasons and business requirements that drive the need for spatial analysis, but you don't have to limit the value of spatial data and related analysis to the enterprise. To that end, we recommend that if you have tactical requirements for spatial data, then the data gathered and used toward that requirement should be propagated into the warehouse to the benefit of all potential strategic analysis that might benefit from such data. And, if there are no tactical requirements driving spatial techniques or technologies on the operational side of your business, you should consider, at the very least, geocoding your production data. For example, most companies go through great pains and often make significant resource investments to collect and scrub their customer addresses. Why? Well, if you do not exploit the spatial aspect of the address, then the only value of this effort is to mail material to your customers or provide fodder for householding processes.

Since you have gone through all the trouble of maintaining clean addresses for your organization, it seems a waste not to exploit its real value: spatial analysis. The foundation of spatial analysis is your clean address. We discuss how to bind the address to spatial data in the following section.

Geocoding

The data warehouse is often responsible for the transformation of simple address-based data, in the form of customer addresses, store locations, and so forth, into legitimate spatial data that represents the explicit geographical relationships between these addresses. This is typically achieved by assigning a geocode (longitude and latitude value) to each address during the ETL process. This unique value serves as the cornerstone to all subsequent analysis, such as understanding the distance between a store location and its best customers or the drive time from a freeway exit and a store location. Moreover, once a geocode has been assigned, you can enhance your informational content by binding demographic data from third parties, such as Dunn & Bradstreet, to your existing data, which increases your analytical landscape.

Essentially, spatial data is any location-based data, including addresses, zip codes, zones, roads, census blocks, and so on. And geocoding is the process used to transform this location-based data into other spatial data that can be recognized and exploited by visualization tools, analysis tools, and RDBMS environments. Geocoding commonly represents spatial data as a latitude/longitude coordinate. Spatial data represents locations in terms of points (e.g., a specific address), lines (e.g., a road or river) and polygons (e.g., a county or state boundary, lakes, tax entities).

Geocoding is the single most important key to blending spatial data into your warehouse. The process of geocoding should be considered a natural part of your ETL transformation steps and can support either batch processing or be assigned as rows that are inserted into the atomic layer of the warehouse.

If you are geocoding addresses in a large table of existing customer data, you will probably need to perform the following tasks:

1. Add a spatial column to the customer table to contain the spatial data.

2. Register the spatial column for geocoding, indicating which columns (e.g., number, street, city, state) are to be input to the geocoder.

3. Run the geocoder in batch mode to update the location columns with the geocoded data.

After the initial geocoding, you can then indicate that you want geocoding to occur only on insert or update. This process is controlled by insert and update triggers on the data.

Think about how and when you want geocoding to take place. For example, if you are planning on launching a new CRM application that lets your service personnel track a location on a map while on the phone with the customer, you very well might want to geocode on the operational side in real time and carry the geocoded data forward into the data warehouse. This may require some conversion to the OGC well-known text or binary format.

Otherwise, you probably want to do batch geocoding as a separate transformation step, either in a staging area or after the data is loaded into the warehouse. You may also need to build iterative steps into the geocoding process to allow for the possibility of investigating any problems in generating points, which might be caused by invalid addresses or a mismatch between the base map and the set of addresses being geocoded.

Technology Requirements for Spatial Warehouses

While it is true that some GIS applications are extremely complex and require specialized skills and technologies, this is usually the domain of government and utilities industries. For general business applications, GIS is a straightforward effort that affords huge upside dividends for end users. There are two reasons that business GIS is painless:

- Leading RDBMS technology provides integration for GIS at the database engine level.

- Most business applications require less specific granularity. For example, customer addresses might be categorized by block groups or zip codes as opposed to being individually geocoded.

That is not to say that GIS for business applications cannot require exacting detail and specificity, such as logistics planning. The point is that general business GIS is much simpler to implement than in the past, without compromising the analytical value.

In the case of business applications, maximum functionality and technical transparency are achieved when integrating spatial data as a natural part of the atomic level and implementing it at the database engine level.

DB2 Spatial Extender provides optimum integration between spatial objects and DB2 Universal Database for several reasons, including:

- Central management of spatial objects is treated as any other object to the database. Database administration tools include spatial utilities, including the ability to import and export spatial data files,[2] optimization for spatial indexes, and replication support.

- Spatial-centric functions are run at the engine level. Traditional spatial functions include DISTANCE, OVERLAP, INTERSECT, and WITHIN.

- Standard SQL with spatial extensions is available to all applications. For example:

  The engine is optimized to address querying and indexing spatial objects. For example, the standard indexing used for textual data cannot deal with the multidimensional nature of spatial objects. IBM has developed a grid index technique to ensure DB2 Universal Database Spatial Extender can provide the performance and functionality expected.

---

[2] "Shapefile" is a de facto industry standard from ESRI for such an interchange file form, but others exist as well.

DB2 Spatial Extender also provides support for all the established spatial data types, including point, line, and polygon objects established by the Open GIS Consortium (OGC)[3] and in the SQL standard (SQLMM, 1999). Additionally, DB2 Spatial Extender ensures that processes fundamental to handling spatial data are included, specifically geocoding.

Additionally, you can merge SQL with spatial functions as outlined in the following three examples:

Finding zones. The following query finds the average customer distance from each department store. The spatial functions used in this example are ST_Distance and ST_Within (the SQL spatial standard names for these functions):

```
SELECT s.id, AVG(ST_Distance(c.location,s.location))
FROM customers c, stores s
WHERE ST_Within(c.location,s.zone)=1
GROUP BY s.id
```

Converting spatial data to text format. The following query finds the customer locations for those who live in the San Francisco Bay Area and converts it to the OGC well-known text representation. The spatial functions used in this example are ST_AsText and ST_Within:

```
SELECT ST_AsText(c.location,cordref(1))
FROM customers c
WHERE ST_Within(c.location,:BayArea)=1
```

Creating searchable zones. This query finds the customers who live within the flood zone or within 2 miles from the boundary of the flood zone. The spatial functions used in this example are ST_Buffer and ST_Within:

```
SELECT c.name,c.phoneNo,c.address
FROM customers c
WHERE ST_Within(c.location,ST_Buffer(:floodzone,2))=1
```

Adding Spatial Data to the Warehouse

The first step for data architects is to understand which of the two possible types of spatially biased warehouse iterations you are focused on. At the risk of oversimplification, spatial warehouse implementations are defined by two general categories with regard to the enterprise data warehouse:

[3] See www.opengis.org.

Entities.   This type of warehouse iteration is defined by requiring spatial entities to be added. This is essentially the addition of spatial layers to your spatial data, such as streets, lots, forests, sections of pipes, oil wells, and flood zones.

Attributes.   In this type of iteration you bind descriptive characteristics about existing entities, such as income level for a neighborhood, population densities, SIC codes and represented businesses for a particular study area, and amount of oil being pumped for specific wells.

The difference between spatial entities and attributes isn't trivial. One very distinguishing characteristic is how the information will appear to users; spatial entities usually require software that understands the objects, for instance, map rendering applications. A spatial entity iteration of your warehouse will undoubtedly dictate that you add a geographic tool to access the data being stored or that your existing tool can handle the new spatial entities. Conversely, implementation of spatial attributes can be used virtually everywhere in the warehouse—as constraints to existing filters for spatial analysis using spatial tools or for use with common warehouse access tools such as SQL reports and OLAP.

There are at least five issues that the data architect must keep in mind when adding spatial data into the warehouse:

Determine if the iteration evolves spatial entities or spatial attributes or both.   If you are implementing spatial entities, you must examine if there is any additional impact on the data storage resources and if existing data access tools will suffice.

Determine if you need to purchase third-party demographic data. This is particular to a spatial attribute iteration of your warehouse. It is common for companies to have the address information but little else. Consequently, the purchase of third-party demographics is a natural part of dealing with a business requirement. But that doesn't mean that you purchase all of your demographic data all at once. The purchase of third-party data will be driven by business requirements.

Focus on ensuring accurate address information.   This means that address cleansing should be inherent in the ETL processing done for the atomic layer of the warehouse. But this is only half of the quality equation. It is critical that operational systems update their processes to ensure that addresses are being entered consistently.

Add a geocoding process.   A geocoding process should become a natural part of ETL efforts to load data into the atomic layer of your warehouse. If you cannot provide a consistent address, then consider geocoding at the zip code level.

Consider disk space and indexing strategies.   A spatial implementation will affect disk space and related issues, such as portioning. Moreover, DBAs will need to understand special indexing requirements of spatial objects, as well as become intimate with how the database engine optimizes such objects.

Summary

The single most important question organizations need to ask themselves is not *if* they should evolve their data with spatial content but *when* this effort starts. The technological road map has existed for years, evolving considerably in the past few years in terms of features and functionality. Leading database systems like DB2 V8 have consciously embedded leading spatial technology at the engine level. Moreover, ETL and data access tools have equally met the trend by enabling their application with spatial features.

Organizations can acquire data from any number of established vendors such as Dunn & Bradstreet, Urban Data System, ESRI, and even the Census Bureau. But the availability of spatial data and analysis goes much further than vendors promoting their goods. The new trend is spatial Web services. Companies like ESRI provide Internet services that include all the core features, functionality, and benefits of spatial data, technology, and analysis. Consequently, companies who want to blend spatial content and benefits into their BI organization but do not want to tackle the technology can simply integrate their BI environment to include spatial content via the Web.

The technology is mature and widely supported, the data is readily available, and even for the spatially inept company, spatial analysis can be conducted over the Internet. Why, then, would an organization not make spatial content a natural part of their BI landscape? Good question.

Bibliography

Berry, Michael J.A. and Gordon S. Linoff. *Mastering Data Mining*. New York: John Wiley & Sons, 2000.

Boehm, Barry W. "A Spiral Model of Software Development and Enhancement." *IEEE*. May 1988.

Boon, Simon. "COBIT: Control Objectives for Information and Related Technologies." *Journal of Data Warehousing*. IT Governance Institute. Volume 2, Number 4, Winter 1997.

Cockburn, Alistair. "Using 'V-W' Staging to Clarify Spiral Development." www.methodjournal.com. 2001.

Gonzales, Michael L. "Spatial OLAP: Conquering Geography." *DB2 Magazine*. Spring 1999.

Gonzales, Michael L. "Seeking Spatial Intelligence." *Intelligent Enterprise*. January 20, 2000.

Gonzales, Michael L., Rafael Coss, and Kathryn Zeidenstein. "Picture This! A Spatially Aware Data Warehouse." *Journal of Data Warehousing*. Volume 6, Number 3, Summer 2001.

Gonzales, Michael L. "Fear and Loathing in Project Management." *Intelligent Enterprise*. June 13, 2002.

Gonzales, Michael L. "Bird's Eye BI." *DB2 Magazine*. Winter 2002.

Harris, K. "Changing the View of ROI to VOI." *Gartner*. November 14, 2001.

IBM. "IBM DB2 OLAP Miner: An Opportunity-Discovery Feature of DB2 OLAP Server." November 2001.

Inmon, William H. *Building the Data Warehouse*. New York: John Wiley & Sons, 1996.

Inmon, William H. *Building the Operational Data Store*. New York: John Wiley & Sons, 1999.

Kimball, Ralph. *The Data Warehouse Toolkit*. New York: John Wiley & Sons, 1996.

Kimball, Ralph. *The Data Warehouse Lifecycle Toolkit*. New York: John Wiley & Sons, August 1998.

Kimball, Ralph. "Is your Data Correct?" *Intelligent Enterprise*, December 5, 2000.

McKnight, William. "Data Warehouse Justification and ROI." *DM Review*. November 1999.

Raskino, M. "ROI Comes from Strategic Capabilities, Not Applications." *Gartner*. February 5, 2002.

Tillman, George. *A Practical Guide to Logical Data Modeling*. New York: McGraw-Hill, 1993.

Voelker, Michael P. "Data Warehousing: What Works?" *Technology Decisions for Insurance*. July 2001.

Index